THE GREAT WESTERN PICTURES

by
JAMES ROBERT PARISH
and
MICHAEL R. PITTS

Editor:
T. Allan Taylor

Research Associates:
John Robert Cocchi, Edward Connor, Richard Picchiarini,
Florence Solomon, Vincent Terrace

The Scarecrow Press, Inc.
Metuchen, N.J.   1976

Library of Congress Cataloging in Publication Data

Parish, James Robert.
The great western pictures.

Bibliography: p.
1. Western films--History and criticism.
I. Pitts, Michael R., joint author. II. Title.
PN1995.9.W4P27   791.43'0909'32   76-28224
ISBN 0-8108-0980-X

Dedicated to
BOB STEELE
One of the Western Film Greats

"Life ain't such a sweet proposition anyway; just three squares a day, forty winks, and a lot of powdersmoke."

--Tom Tyler as Sundown Saunders in Powdersmoke Range (1935).

CONTENTS

PREFACE

More so than with the preceding volumes in this genre series, we have had a very difficult time in narrowing down the selections to be included for full text discussion. Western film enthusiasts take their genre seriously--and rightly so--and to find even the lightest-weight grade C oater omitted is a disappointment to someone. Our apology to anyone who feels that his or her favorite Western picture has been overlooked.

It is our intention here to offer the reader and researcher a broad spectrum of the Western motion picture as produced in the United States. We have included a few select entries from the European film market, which seem to us to be Westerns produced in Europe which reflect the American cowboy film tradition.

The authors would be grateful for any suggestions, amplifications, and corrections regarding the text that readers care to supply.

Acknowledgment must be made to the following for their helpfulness: Benny Baker; Richard Braff; David Bucove and the staff of the Anderson (Ind.) Public Library; Morris Everett, Jr.; Filmfacts (Ernest Parmentier); Film Fan Monthly; Film Favorites (Charles Smith); Films and Filming; Films in Review; Focus on Film; Pierre Guinle; Ken D. Jones; Gary Kramer; William T. Leonard; Doug McClelland; John Malone; Gregory Mank; Albert B. Manski; Jim Meyer; Peter Miglierini; Norman Miller; Monthly Film Bulletin; Movie Poster Service (Bob Smith); Movie Star News (Paula Klaw); Carolyn Mudd; Maureen O'Sullivan; Dale Robertson; Screen Facts (Alan G. Barbour); Anthony Slide; Mrs. Peter Smith; Vincent Terrace; Teresa Wright; and Don Willis.

And special thanks to Paul Myers, curator of the Theatre Collection at the Lincoln Center Library for the Performing Arts, and his staff: Monty Arnold, David Bartholomew, Rod Bladel, Donald Fowle, Maxwell Silverman, Dorothy Swerdlove, Betty Wharton, and Don Madison of Photo Reproductions.

James Robert Parish
Michael R. Pitts

WESTERNS: AN INTRODUCTION

by Edward Connor

One could write a history of western films simply by correcting misconceptions that have grown up about them.

First of all there's the old "wheeze" that The Great Train Robbery (1903) was the first film to tell a story. It had been preceded by three Passion Plays in 1897 and 1898, plus the Méliès Cinderella (1900) and Trip to the Moon (1902). Certainly they told stories.

It might be more correct to say that The Great Train Robbery was the first American-made film to tell a story based on an original screen idea. This short film, running a bare ten minutes, does contain many basic ingredients later found in countless westerns: a scene in a saloon, the hold-up of a train, a lot of gunfire, a telegrapher trying to summon help, the fight on a moving train (a jump cut allowing time for a dummy to be substituted for a man's body about to be hurled from the train-tender), the posse of good guys chasing after the bad guys, and a climactic shoot-out. The final scene of a gunman firing at the audience not only had great shock value but also anticipated the close-up, sound, and the revolutionary 3-D process.

Then there's the old adage that no western has ever lost money. Of course, some B and C oaters were cuffed off in such a short space of time (two to three days) and for so little money (five to ten thousand dollars) that they couldn't have lost money if they tried--especially since they always played the lower half of a double bill.

The 1943 Ox-Bow Incident, one of the finest, most realistic westerns ever made, just about broke even, according to Fox boss, Darryl F. Zanuck. The speed with which some expensive westerns of recent years have turned up on TV also gives cause for speculation as to how well they did at the box-office.

Then there's the high-budgeted 1930 Fox picture, The Big Trail, which is down in all the cinema reference and historical books as a box office disaster and the film that set back (or held back) John Wayne's career for ten years. It was actually a first-class western of epic proportions, done in semi-documentary style, and it holds up very well today. Its failure at the box office is generally attributed to its having been made in the Grandeur widescreen process for which very few theatres--even first-run ones in the large cities--were at the time equipped. Actually the film was also shot in ordinary 35 mm, and why this widely shown version was not widely attended is one of filmdom's mysteries.

Certainly it's a much better film than the 1923 Covered Wagon or the 1931 Cimarron which have been praised far above their merits (according to the advertising campaign for the 1948 Red River, they were the two best westerns ever made prior to Red River, which was now being modestly offered as the third). The Covered Wagon may have been the first really big western but it is not particularly well put together. Its leading man, J. Warren Kerrigan, had little acting ability and less personality, and some of its incidents (the wagonmaster leading the wagon train into a box-canyon deep in Indian territory and making them sitting ducks for the attack that follows) left old-timers aghast and snickering. John Ford's The Iron Horse (1924) is a far superior epic and holds up much better today.

Cimarron has its best sequence--the land rush--at the very beginning, and what follows is inept and spotty, sometimes using as many titles as Greed to fill in the gaps in its story. The later Sutter's Gold (1936) also used many titles in an attempt to hold together its many disparate elements. It, too, incidentally, was a box office failure and nearly bankrupted Universal.

A third misconception is that Tom Mix was the screen's first western star. Certainly in the twenties he was the number one western box office attraction. However, he had been preceded by "Broncho Billy" Anderson, who made hundreds of successful one- and two-reel oaters beginning with the 1908 Broncho Billy and the Baby, and by William S. Hart of the granite face, who began his screen career in 1914 at the age of 44, and made many popular features culminating with the 1925 Tumbleweeds (with a land rush climax bigger, more thrilling and better integrated into the plot than Cimarron's). The film was re-issued in 1939 with a deeply moving prologue spoken by Hart--his only spoken words from the screen.

Hart's feature films are the answer to another popular misconception: that adult westerns began only with the 1943 Ox-Bow Incident and The Gunfighter (1946). Not only were the Hart westerns adult in the extreme but some had plots--e.g., the 1916 Hell's Hinges, centering on a minister corrupted by drink and loose women --that might be considered a little touchy even today.

But the realism of the Hart films did give way to the romanticism of Mix's products, which set out to offer the movie public one thing: pure escapist entertainment--and that, it turned out, was just what the public wanted. Mix's career began and ended with indifferent films (the Selig shorts from 1914 to 1917, the 1935 Mascot serial, The Miracle Rider) but in between he made some fabulously successful features such as the 1921 Sky High, the 1922 Just Tony, the 1926 Great K. and A. Robbery, and the 1932 My Pal the King (with Mickey Rooney as the title character).

The idealized west of these films became standard for westerns--with only rare exceptions--for nearly thirty years.

Following Mix in popularity were Ken Maynard, Hoot Gibson, Tim McCoy and George O'Brien, who, for the most part, made A silents and B talkies. Also appearing briefly on the scene was Fred Thomson who had studied for the ministry and who presented the ultimate in a clean-cut western hero. No one who saw his 1927 Jesse James (an early whitewash of that notorious character) ever forgot it. Unfortunately Thomson died of blood-poisoning at the peak of his career and before the talkies arrived. Johnny Mack Brown made a great personal hit as the 1930 Billy the Kid and thereafter appeared mainly in western features (A's and B's) and serials.

Starring in B, C and D westerns, silents and talkies, were a host of actors, the heroes of all small fry of the twenties and thirties: Buck Jones, Tom Tyler, Buddy Roosevelt, Edmund Cobb, Jack and Al Hoxie, Bob Steele, Bob Custer, Buffalo Bill, Jr., Leo Maloney, Wally Wales (who later reverted to his real name, Hal Taliaferro), Jack Perrin, Rex Bell, Guinn "Big Boy" Williams, George Duryea (later known as Tom Keene, and then as Richard Powers). Kermit Maynard, a better actor and more sturdy personality than his brother Ken, never quite achieved the fame of the latter. Stunt man and later second-unit director Yakima Canutt starred in a few inexpensive silent westerns, the 1926 Devil Horse being the first to present the fight between a black horse and a painted stallion, later re-used as stock in countless films.

Singing stars Gene Autry and Roy Rogers appeared at Republic in the mid-thirties, though Ken Maynard swore to his dying day that he was the first western singing star (he did burst into song fairly frequently in early talkies but these musical intervals were short and casual).

In the 1940 Republic serial, Adventures of Red Ryder, the title role was played by Don "Red" Barry, while later features in the series starred Alan "Rocky" Lane and "Wild Bill" Elliott (the latter amazingly like William S. Hart in looks, personality and acting style). Little Beaver--Red Ryder's little Indian companion--was played in all features by Bobby Blake, who was later formally "introduced" to the movie-going public as Robert Blake, one of the two killers in the 1968 In Cold Blood.

Republic also fostered the western careers of Sunset Carson, Rex Allen and Monte Hale.

For Paramount and United Artists William Boyd starred in no less than 60 Hopalong Cassidy features, and fit the role so per-

fectly that to this day many believe the books and films were written
with him in mind.   Actually the Hopalong Cassidy of the Clarence E.
Mulford novels is a middle-aged cowboy suffering from a bad limp
which gave rise to his nickname.   Jimmy Gleason was the first actor Paramount had in mind for the role but, happily, second thoughts
resulted in the choice of Bill Boyd who, playing the role without the
limp, made a great personal success, and played little else on the
screen for thirteen years.   It's not well known that he came to the
role so poorly "equipped" that a double had to be used for all the
riding scenes in the earliest films.

Almost paralleling the Hopalong Cassidy series in numbers
was that of the Three Mesquiteers, from the books of William Colt
MacDonald.   The first film based on these three characters (Stony
Brooke, Tucson Smith and Lullaby Joslyn), the 1935 RKO Powdersmoke Range had the biggest western cast ever assembled.   Harry
Carey (another popular western star of silents and talkies, who had
appeared in John Ford's first feature/first western, the 1917
Straight Shooting), Hoot Gibson (who also played in Straight Shooting)
and Guinn "Big Boy" Williams played the Mesquiteers and were
backed up by Tom Tyler and Bob Steele (both of whom would later
play Mesquiteers at Republic), Sam Hardy, Buzz Barton (a popular
young cowboy star congenitally unable to deliver a line without em-
phasizing it with a fervent nod of his head), William Farnum and
Franklyn Farnum, William Desmond (star of four silent western
serials), Wally Wales, Art Mix, Buffalo Bill, Jr. , Buddy Roosevelt,
Ray Mayer, Eddie Dunn, Ethan Laidlaw, Barney Furey, Bob Mac-
Kenzie, James Mason (the American actor, not the English thespian),
Irving Bacon and Frank Rice.   Boots Mallory played the heroine.
Unfortunately the script was not up to the cast.

The situation improved when Republic took over the series
the following year.   The fifty-one Three Mesquiteers films they
made from 1936 to 1943 include some of the fastest, most action-
packed B westerns ever made, each accompanied by a rousing musical score.   Bob Livingston, Ray Corrigan and Max Terhune played
the Mesquiteers in sixteen of the earliest and best of the series.
John Wayne played Stony in eight of the features during 1938 and 1939,
just around the time of his great personal triumph and comeback in
the 1939 Ford Stagecoach.   One of these, the 1939 Night Riders,
had the same plot as the later 1950 Baron of Arizona (with Vincent
Price), telling the true life story of the American who established
himself as Spanish owner of millions of acres in Arizona, through
the use of clever forgeries.

Others who played Mesquiteers were Sid Saylor (who was
Lullaby in the initial film), Ralph Byrd ("Dick Tracy" himself),
Raymond Hatton, Duncan Renaldo, Tom Tyler, Bob Steele, Rufe
Davis and Jimmy Dodd (of the later TV Mousketeers).   Among the
many surprises in the series was the appearance of Rita Hayworth
(Rita Cansino) in the 1937 Hit the Saddle, Louise Brooks (her last
screen appearance) in the 1938 Overland Stage Raiders, Carole
Landis in the 1939 Three Texas Steers and Cowboys from Texas

(whose cast also included famous old-time actress Betty Compson),
Jennifer Jones (Phylis Isley) in the 1939 New Frontier, Julie Bishop
(Jacqueline Wells) in the 1939 Kansas Terrors, and Gale Storm in
the 1941 Saddlemates.

The Durango Kid (Charles Starrett) series at Columbia, and
the Rough Riders, Trail Blazers and Range Busters groupings at
Monogram, couldn't begin to hold a candle to the Hopalong Cassidy,
Three Mesquiteers or even the Red Ryder series.

Of the series of Billy the Kid and Billy Carson westerns,
first starring Bob Steele and then Buster Crabbe, at PRC let us be
merciful and say nothing.

The cheapness of these series precludes their being accurate
in content, but what of the 1930 Billy the Kid which ends with Sheriff
Pat Garrett (Wallace Beery) helping Billy (Johnny Mack Brown) escape across the border with his sweetheart (Kay Johnson)!

Studios frequently give out stories of the meticulous research
expended on their western epics but the screenplays still come up
with massive inaccuracies. Deadwood Dick, hero of many a movie,
and of the 1940 Columbia serial (with Don Doublas), was actually a
black man in real life but has never been played as such on the
screen. Walter Brennan made a believable Judge Roy Bean in the
static, overpraised The Westerner (1940), but in the final reel he is
shown meeting and dying in the presence of his beloved Lily Langtry.
Actually, as was made clear in the 1972 Life and Times of Judge
Roy Bean (a very inaccurate historical film), he never met her.

Mistakes seem to be most prevalent in films dealing with
George Custer. Researchers seemingly could not even agree on
whether he ever graduated from West Point. In the 1940 Warner's
Santa Fe Trail (a never fully appreciated, thrilling action epic on
the rise and fall of John Brown), Custer (Ronald Reagan) is shown
graduating from West Point with "Jeb" Stuart (Errol Flynn). In the
1941 Warner's They Died With Their Boots On, Custer (now played
by Flynn) is taken out of senior class before graduation and sent on
duty out west. In real life both Stuart and Custer did graduate from
the Point, but seven years apart.

In the earliest films Custer was always presented in the
heroic mold, done in by conniving, treacherous Indians who didn't
fight fair at the Little Big Horn. Gradually, screenplay writers
grew bolder with their theme--and "facts"--until in They Died With
Their Boots On Custer is shown as knowingly sacrificing the 7th
Cavalry at the Little Big Horn to save his brother officers and their
men who would otherwise have been trapped by the Sioux! After this
turnabout script-writers began to take an ever dimmer view of Custer, until the 1968 Custer of the West presented him (played by
Robert Shaw) as a vain, self-seeking psychoneurotic.

If the films treated our traditional heroes like this, the mind

boggles at what they did with the villains of western folk-lore: Billy
the Kid, Jesse and Frank James, the Daltons and Youngers, Belle
Starr, et al. , to say nothing of the infamous Mexican bandit, Muri-
eta. According to Hollywood, it seems such desperadoes were all
kindly, peaceable, family- and home-loving folks driven to an un-
wanted life of crime because of villainies perpetrated on them and
their families by the government and its agencies. Only in later
films, beginning perhaps with the 1953 Jack Slade (with Mark Stevens),
was there some attempt at getting at the truth.

     In the mid-forties Universal, having assembled all of their
famous monsters in the successful 1945 House of Frankenstein and
House of Dracula decided to do the same with their western villains.
In such films as the 1946 Badman's Territory the script managed to
get Billy the Kid, the James, Dalton and Younger brothers, Sam
Bass and Belle Starr all in one place at one time, generally opposed
by a stalwart Randolph Scott.

     In these film fantasies the villains were really villains, the
white-washing having ceased momentarily. However, before the return to the unglamorized west and its unromantic heroes and bad
guys, there was a series of expensive non-historical westerns at
Warner's--made over a period of fifteen years--in which Errol
Flynn played a very unconvincing cowboy-hero who had a British accent, tailor-fitted "dude" clothes, and was never in need of a bath,
shave or haircut no matter how long he was out on the trail, on a
cattle drive, chasing villains or what have you. The Errol Flynn of
Virginia City or Dodge City would, with luck, have lasted just about
five minutes in the old west.

     Until the appearance of such non-heroes as The Gunfighter and
the anti-heroes (like Hud and those in Point Blank), the western hero
possessed all of the manly virtues and was truly a paragon of perfec-
tion. He didn't smoke, drink or play around with loose women. He
was kind to old ladies and children, treated the heroine with the ut-
most of respect, and in all things was motivated by the highest and
noblest of ideals. But every once in a while, one came along who
didn't quite fit the pattern.

     Movie fans have come to think that westerns use the same
half-dozen standard plots over and over again with only the mildest
of variations. Actually some strange anomalies have shown up along
the way.

     In the first place, there are westerns which aren't really
westerns, at least by my definition, because they take place east of
the Mississippi. Such features would include the many film versions
of Last of the Mohicans and other films based on James Fenimore
Cooper's "Leatherstocking" tales; plus the 1939 Allegheny Uprising
and Drums Along the Mohawk. The 1939 Three Mesquiteers' Kansas
Terrors takes place entirely on an island in the Caribbean where the
cowboys have come to buy horses.

Then there are oaters in which the wild plots defy description.
Two notable examples are the 1932 Smoking Guns and the 1945
Salome, Where She Danced. In the former, after the weirdest credit music imaginable and an establishing opening scene in which star
Ken Maynard is accused of a murder he didn't commit, he is seen
months, or years, later heavily bearded and almost unrecognizable
in a dismal, desolate swamp liberally inhabited by alligators. Lawman Walter Miller shows up to arrest him, falls into the river and
loses a leg to a 'gator. Ken nurses the lawman back to health and
says he's thinking of amputating the latter's leg (according to the
preceding scene there was nothing left to amputate). Walter commits suicide and Ken decides to impersonate him. Using hair-
blackening and nothing else in the way of disguise, he does make his
return and is immediately accepted by everyone, nobody seeming to
notice his change in height, weight, voice or facial characteristics.
Ken takes time out from a Halloween party to go to a haunted house,
and there establishes his innocence of the crime of which he was accused at the beginning. If you think the foregoing is incredible and
confusing, be assured that the picture plays much worse than it
reads.

Smoking Guns, nevertheless, is a symphony of clichés compared to Salome, Where She Danced, the most bizarre western ever
filmed. Its plot seems born of a hashish nightmare. Audiences
must have thought they were watching the wrong film when the opening scenes set them down in the middle of the Franco-Prussian war
and the court of Bismarck. By degrees--if not altogether by logic
--the film does make its way to the American west, and a kind of
rhythm pervades the rest of the film: in every scene one plot com-
plication is resolved while another is set up. At one point, several
boatloads of westerners travel out to a Chinese junk to resolve one
of these plot complications, but forget their purpose when they wit-
ness Yvonne De Carlo (who must have seen them coming) perform an
exotic dance before a shrine in the ship's hold. The picture reaches
its zenith of nuttiness when introducing a Chinese doctor (Abner
Biberman) who speaks English with a Scottish accent.

Sometimes westerns have standard plots but non-standard
casts. Such would include the 1938 Harlem on the Prairie and the
1939 Harlem Rides the Range, with all-black casts, and the 1938
Terror of Tiny Town, with a cast of midgets (the hero, Billy Curtis,
later appeared in such films as the 1942 Hitchcock Saboteur, the
1950 Pygmy Island, and the 1974 Little Cigars; while the villain,
Little Billy, was a friend of John Wayne's in the 1932 Mascot serial,
Shadow of the Eagle).

One gross misconception is that Indians were not treated
sympathetically in films until the 1950 Broken Arrow. Nothing could
be further from the truth. White men have always been shown having faithful, trustworthy Indian companions in films, the best example being the strong friendship between Hawkeye and Chingachgook
in the many film versions of Last of the Mohicans, to say nothing of
the companionship between the Lone Ranger and Tonto in two serials
and two features.

But in regard to Indians generally, the 1932 End of the Trail, with Tim McCoy, was a strong indictment of the white man's encroachment on Indian lands and mistreatment of Indians.

Many films attempted to show these injustices through the eyes of the Indian, especially the 1910, 1916, 1928 and 1936 versions of Ramona. An even stronger indictment was the 1925 The Vanishing American, which begins with a magnificent prologue showing the pre-history of the American Indian, then goes on to a modern story in which Richard Dix gives a solid portrayal of an Indian fighting for the rights of his people at home, and for those of his country overseas in World War I.

Later, in 1929, Dix also starred in Redskin, which had a similar theme somewhat less effectively done but photographed mainly in brilliant two-color Technicolor.

Then, the 1934 Massacre, with Richard Barthelmess (another film which never received its just due), proved strongest of all in portraying the plight of the Indian today: still suffering injustice, indifference and outright villainy from a government that has ceased to care.

Films dealing entirely with Indians range from the many versions of Hiawatha (1909 to 1952) to the 1930 Silent Enemy, one of the last of the silents, a stark semi-documentary detailing the life of the American Indian before the coming of the white man. Acted by non-professionals, it told of the tribes' constant fight against hunger ("the silent enemy"), and included scenes of a big caribou hunt, human sacrifice (an Indian being burned at the stake to "appease" the Great Spirit), and an allegorical sequence of death (a ghostly canoe coming to carry away the soul of the deceased).

It has also been erroneously stated that Broken Arrow was the first film in which a white man was allowed (by the Hays office) to marry an Indian maid. How about Cimarron, in which Irene Dunne's son marries an Indian; or the 1935 Behold My Wife, in which Gene Raymond marries Indian Sylvia Sidney; to say nothing of the 1913, 1918 and 1931 versions of The Squaw Man, in which a British officer marries an Indian girl?

What was the first western serial? Oddly enough it was one that did not star Pearl White, Ruth Roland, Allene Ray or any other serial luminary, and one that does not have an instantly recognizable title. It was the 1916 Universal Liberty, in twenty episodes, with Jack Holt, Marie Walcamp, Eddie Polo and Neal Hart, co-directed by Jacques Jaccard (who wrote the screenplay) and Henry MacRae.

However, the first of the historical western serials was the 1921 Universal Winners of the West, in eighteen chapters, with Art Acord, Myrtle Lind and Burton C. Law (as Captain John Fremont), directed by Edward Laemmle. Universal followed it with other vigorous western serials such as the 1922 In the Days of Buffalo Bill,

with Art Acord, Dorothy Woods and Duke Lee (as "Buffalo Bill"),
and the 1923 In the Days of Daniel Boone, with Jack Mower, Eileen
Sedgwick and Charles Brinle (as "Boone").

Then, in 1924, Universal produced The Riddle Rider in which
the hero (William Desmond) went around in a cloak and various dis-
guises to avenge the wrongs being perpetrated on the townspeople by
the villain and his outlaw gang. The year 1927 saw the release of
Return of the Riddle Rider (also with Desmond), and he was to have
many successors in future serials.

Buck Jones donned white hat, mask and cassock-like cape
(which seemed to hamper rather than help his movements) in Universal's 1935 Phantom Rider to oppose villain Harry Woods and
gang. Republic's The Vigilantes Are Coming (1936) had Robert
Livingston as the masked "Eagle" (posing as a witless organist),
seeking to save California from the dictatorship of Jason Burr (Fred
Kohler) who was aided by an army from Czarist Russia. Then,
John Carroll played the masked great grandson of Zorro in the 1937
Republic Zorro Rides Again.

Even women got into the act. Republic's The Painted Stallion
(1937) had a Comanche Indian maid, known as "the Rider," appear
at crucial moments and aid the good guys with well-aimed whistling
arrows.

The following year the most famous of all masked riders,
The Lone Ranger, appeared in a Republic serial. The film proved
to be the best western talking serial ever made, its fifteen chapters
super-charged with fast action, thrills, and high production values.
Alberto Colombo arranged the rousing musical score, made up of
the well-known last portion of Rossini's "William Tell Overture" and
other classics such as Liszt's "Les Preludes," plus music written
to order for silent films and action series on radio. According to
the screenplay the Lone Ranger was one of five men--Lee Powell,
Herman Brix (later Bruce Bennett), Lane Chandler, Hal Taliaferro
(the former Wally Wales), or George Letz (later George Montgomery), with his identity not given away until the last minutes of the
last chapter. The serial had a sequel: the less inspired 1939 Lone
Ranger Rides Again, with Robert Livingston known to be the masked
man right from chapter one. Meanwhile, the first serial was re-
edited into an excellent 69-minute feature, released in 1940 as Hi-Yo
Silver.

In the 1939 Zorro's Fighting Legion the masked hero opposed
a masked villain (Don Del Oro), and the same situation prevailed in
the 1940 Columbia Deadwood Dick when the hero fought the machinations of a mysterious villain called "The Skull."

Neither heroes nor villains were masked in the 1941 Universal
Riders of Death Valley, which assembled the biggest cast ever for a
western serial: Dick Foran, Buck Jones, Leo Carrillo, Charles Bickford, Lon Chaney, Jr., Guinn "Big Boy" Williams and Noah Berry,

Jr. However, just as with Powdersmoke Range, the script wasn't
up to the cast and the results were only average.

Republic's 1943 Daredevils of the West (Allan Lane, Kay
Aldridge and Robert Frazer) was far better. After The Lone Ranger
it is really the finest western talkie serial ever made. Wartime
restrictions were not apparent in this brilliant serial, but after the
war the market slumped and serials, especially Westerns, became
progressively poorer, being built around stock shots from features
or earlier chapter-plays. In the last serial ever made, Columbia's
1956 Blazing the Overland Trail, hero Lee Roberts was dressed
like Buck Jones in the 1940 White Eagle--for obvious reasons.

In all, there were 118 western serials: 55 silent, 62 talkie,
and one--Universal's The Indians Are Coming (1930), with Tim Mc-
Coy and Allene Ray--released in both silent and talkie versions.

Of course, it was not western serials alone that used stock
shots. Many A and B western features followed this practice and
did so in a way to break the viewer's heart. A prime example is
the 1939 Geronimo from Paramount which, though sold as an A
product, used reels of stock shots from the 1937 Wells Fargo and
from other films going all the way back to silents, and which builds
its climax around the filmed climax of the 1936 DeMille The Plainsman. As if determined to give the moviegoer nothing original for
his money, the film also used the plot-line of the 1935 Lives of a
Bengal Lancer.

Mention has already been made of westerns like End of the
Trail, Massacre, and Santa Fe Trail, which never received their
just due from critics or film historians. There are many others.

The 1932 Law and Order, with Harry Carey and Walter Huston, tells the Wyatt Earp/Doc Holliday story (using fictitious names)
with characterizations, dialogue and action that have the ring of
truth throughout, and the reenactment of the gun battle at the O.K.
Corral is unexcelled in films. However, the most haunting sequence
is one with overtones of Billy Budd. Strict justice calls for the hanging of Andy Devine, a hulking, lovable oaf who has accidentally
killed a man. The day set for the execution is celebrated as a holiday and the doomed Andy sits on the gallows, happily munching pop-
corn. He makes a little speech exonerating his judges, then submits
meekly to the ghastly business of being hanged.

Perhaps the best B western ever made was the 1935 When a
Man's a Man, with George O'Brien. The stereotyped characterizations are all there--hero, heroine, chief villain, good buys and bad
guys--but never did they act less in stock fashion. These are flesh
and blood people, talking and acting in the most natural and believable way possible. Even villain Harry Woods is only partly villainous, and shows in a forthright manner that even a bad guy can have
good thoughts and aspirations. No love story on the screen has been
presented more simply and heart-warmingly than that between George

O'Brien and Dorothy Wilson.   A beautiful musical score completes
the picture.

The 1936 The Last Outlaw presents the same basic idea as
the later and far more famous Ride the High Country (1962):   the
reaction of an old-timer to the new west.   In the earlier film Harry
Carey (again) plays the cowboy emerging from a long prison term,
trying to adapt himself to a world and a west that have completely
changed.

But if some westerns have been underrated, others, such as
The Covered Wagon, Cimarron, The Westerner, and, in the estima-
tion of this writer, the Cagney/Bogart Oklahoma Kid, have been
grossly overrated.   And what can be said of the 1947 Selznick Duel
in the Sun (perhaps the most expensive western ever made)?   Its
stellar cast--Gregory Peck, Jennifer Jones, Joseph Cotten, Lionel
Barrymore, Lillian Gish, Walter Huston, Herbert Marshall, Harry
Carey, Sidney Blackmer, Otto Kruger, Charles Bickford--is thrown
away on a worthless story.   Its most colorful and memorable sequence, Tilly Losch dancing the "Orizaba" to Dimitri Tiomkin's
stunning score, occurs in the first reel.   The only real action--the
gathering of the ranchers to oppose the railroad construction crew--
comes to nothing when the former, under Lionel Barrymore, decide
against firing on the government troops defending the railroad crew.
Walter Huston plays a minister called "The Sin-Killer" so broadly
that he comes across as both ridiculous and comic.   In the trailer,
indeed, his performance is billed as such, although it was probably
conceived, directed and acted with other intentions.   Life magazine
said that audiences everywhere were laughing hysterically at the
film's tragic climax.   It ended up on the New York Times' list of
the Ten Worst Films of 1947.   It also ended up on lists of the greatest money-makers of all time!

Was the 1966 Fistful of Dollars the first European western?
Hardly, since the Germans had filmed Last of the Mohicans, with
Bela Lugosi as "Uncas," as far back as 1920.   Later in the early
forties, the Germans made a series of westerns starring Hans
Albers, such as the 1942 Water for Canitoga.   The British made
The Great Barrier in 1936, with Richard Arlen and other such Holly-
wood western worthies as J. Farrell MacDonald, Tom London, Jack
Rockwell and Slim Whittaker, and then Sheriff of Fractured Jaw with
Kenneth More in 1958.   Many other countries, including Australia,
made westerns long before Serge Leone got into the act.

Was the 1953 Charge at Feather River the first western feature in 3-D?   Actually it came 21 years too late for that distinction.
The first western in 3-D was also the first feature in 3-D: the 1922
Power of Love, its plot set in the California of the early 19th century, with plenty of colorful action and swordplay.   It was made in
the anaglyph process and had to be viewed through red and blue
glasses to achieve the stereoscopic effect.

The 1974 Blazing Saddles and My Name Is Nobody may have

struck some fans as the first western satires but actually such satires go as far back as Mack Sennett's His Bitter Pill (1916), which
made fun of all oater-ingredients up to that time.   Both Ben Turpin
and Will Rogers made devastating satires of westerns in the silents,
and the triply-filmed Merton of the Movies even had to do with the
making of a western satire.

   Finally, fans are sometimes surprised to find out how many
film classics have been remade with western settings.   Thus the
1933 Lost Patrol became the 1939 Badlands; the 1947 Kiss of Death
turned into the 1958 Fiend Who Walked the West; and the 1952
Rashomon was remodeled as the 1964 The Outrage.   Jack London's
The Sea Wolf (filmed many times) acquired a western setting in
Warner's Barricade (1950), with Raymond Massey in the equivalent
of the "Wolf Larsen" role.

   And in 1945 Warner's released one of the most unique alle-
gories ever seen on the screen: the two-reel Star in the Night,
telling the Nativity story in a modern western setting.   Mary and
Joseph are Mexican peasants unable to find shelter until J. Carrol
Naish, owner of a motel, puts them up in a barn.   Three cowboys
laden with gifts from a spending spree see a glimmering light in the
distance (a malfunctioning electric sign at the motel) and arrive in
time to present their gifts to Mary, who has just given birth.

THE GREAT WESTERN PICTURES

ADVENTURES OF RED RYDER   (Republic, 1940)   twelve chapters

Associate producer, Hiram S. Brown, Jr.; directors, William Witney, John English; based on the newspaper comic strip by Fred Harman; screenplay, Ronald Davidson, Franklyn Adreon, Sol Shor, Barney Sarecky, Norman S. Hall; music, Cy Feuer; camera, William Nobles.

Don "Red" Barry (Red Ryder); Noah Beery (Ace Hanlon); Tommy Cook (Little Beaver); Bob Kortman (One Eye); William Farnum (Colonel Tom Ryder); Maude Pierce Allen (Duchess); Vivian Coe [Austin] (Beth); Hal Taliaferro (Cherokee); Harry Worth (Calvin Drake); Carleton Young (Sheriff Dade); Ray Teal (Shark); Gene Alsace (Deputy Lawson); Gayne Whitman (Harrison); Hooper Atchley (Treadway); John Dilson (Hale); Lloyd Ingraham (Sheriff Andrews); Charles Hutchinson (Rancher Brown); Gardner James (Barnett); Wheaton Chambers (Boswell); Lynton Brent (Clark).

Chapters: 1) Murder on the Santa Fe Trail; 2) Horsemen of Death; 3) Trail's End; 4) Water Rustlers; 5) Avalanche; 6) Hangman's Noose; 7) Framed; 8) Blazing Walls; 9) Records of Doom; 10) One Second to Live; 11) The Devil's Marksman; 12) Frontier Justice.

A feud over land to be utilized for railroad expansion results in the murder of a rancher and a sheriff (Ingraham) by a crooked banker (Worth). Not knowing the identity of the murderer, Red Ryder (Barry) and his father (Farnum) set out to find him, but Red's father is killed. When Red and his boy pal, Little Beaver (Cook), capture a henchman (Teal) of Calvin Drake (Worth) and the crooked sheriff (Young), they are set up for ambush but escape. The henchman is later killed by Drake's men. When the ranchers expect a shipment of money to aid their cause, Drake has it hijacked. Red then enters a stage race. He is captured by Drake's forces but Little Beaver helps him escape, and he re-enters the race and wins the $5,000 prize. Still later a bystander is killed in a brawl and the sheriff arrests Red, but Ryder manages to escape. Meanwhile, one of Drake's henchman tells the truth, leading to the capture of the sheriff who is found trying to destroy incriminating evidence. In the final showdown with Red, Drake is killed by falling on his own sword.

Based on the Fred Harman newspaper comic strip, this Republic serial was the first portrayal of the Red Ryder character by Donald Barry, who later continued the characterization in a series for the same studio. Barry became so closely identified with the

1

character that he was frequently billed on screen as Don "Red" Barry, despite the fact he did not have red hair. In this serial, David Sharpe did most of the acrobatic stunting for Barry.

Unfortunately The Adventures of Red Ryder is not available for viewing today because of a contractual agreement Republic made with the copyright owners of the character. One can only wistfully read accounts of this chapterplay in which Noah Beery played a scenery-chewing henchman named Ace Hanlon.

AFTER THE STORM   see   DESERT GOLD   (1914)

THE ALAMO   (United Artists, 1960)   C 192 min.

Producer-director, John Wayne; screenplay, James Edward Grant; art director, Alfred Ybarra; set decorator, Victor A. Gangelin; technical supervisors, Frank Beetson, Jack Pennick; assistant directors, Robert E. Relyea, Robert Saunders; costumes, Beetson, Ann Peck; music, music director, Dimitri Tiomkin; song, Tiomkin and Paul Francis Webster; sound, Jack Solomon, Gordon Sawyer, Fred Hynes, Don Hall, Jr.; special effects, Lee Zavitz; camera, William Clothier; editor, Stuart Gilmore.

Chill Wills, John Wayne, Richard Widmark, Laurence Harvey, et al., in The Alamo (1960).

John Wayne (Colonel David Crockett); Richard Widmark (Colo-
nel James Bowie); Laurence Harvey (Colonel William Travis); Rich-
ard Boone (General Sam Houston); Frankie Avalon (Smitty); Linda
Cristal (Flaca); Patrick Wayne (Captain James Bonham); Joan O'Brien
(Mrs. Dickinson); Chill Wills (Beekeeper); Joseph Calleia (Juan Se-
guin); Ken Curtis (Captain Dickinson); Carlos Arruza (Lieutenant
Reyes); Jester Hairston (Jethro); Veda Ann Borg (Blind Nell); John
Dierkes (Jocko Robertson); Denver Pyle (Gambler); Aissa Wayne
(Lisa Dickinson); Bill Henry (Dr. Sutherland); Hank Worden (Parson);
Bill Daniel (Colonel Neill); Wesley Lau (Emil); Chuck Roberson (A
Tennessean); Guinn "Big Boy" Williams (Lieutenant Finn); Olive
Carey (Mrs. Dennison); Ruben Padilla (General Santa Anna).

When John Wayne made The Alamo for his Batjac Productions
in 1960 it was the fulfillment of a dream that had been with him
since the forties. He believed the project would be the apex of his
career and he spent $12 million in recreating the battle that spawned
freedom for Texas from the yoke of Mexico and has since served as
a stimulus for freedom-loving people the world over. Unfortunately
the film lacks the popular appeal for which Wayne had hoped and in
its first release it earned only $8 million toward recouping its ex-
penses. Later re-issues and television sales, however, have salvaged the star's investment.
    Filmed in Technicolor and Todd-AO (wide screen) on a ninety-
one-day shooting schedule (mostly on location in Texas), this 192-
minute epic* tells of the valiant stand made by 180 men against the
7,000-man army of General Santa Anna (Padilla) in 1836 at a crum-
bling mission in San Antonio called the Alamo. The men are led by
Colonel Travis (Harvey) and Jim Bowie (Widmark) and are joined by
Colonel Davy Crockett (Wayne) and a small band of volunteers. For
audience diversion, there is the sub-plot of Crockett's romance with
a widow (Cristal) whom he sends away before the fatal battle begins.
The Alamo is under siege for thirteen days and a courier (Patrick
Wayne) brings word that no reinforcements are coming. The men
agree to fight a doomed battle in order to give Sam Houston (Boone)
enough time to corral an army. As a result the fort defenders are
massacred. Six weeks later Houston and his small army put Santa
Anna to rout at San Jacinto with the cry, "Remember the Alamo!"
Texas gains its freedom.
    Wayne not only produced and starred in this loosely-accurate
epic, but he also directed the bulk of the footage. Second unit work
was accomplished by others and Wayne's good friend John Ford was
on hand to direct several scenery shots (most of which were deleted
from the release print).
    "It is too bad that one's enthusiasm tends to wilt somewhat
during the several hours of incidental exposition that precedes the
climax.... There is a feeling not so much of disintegration as of

---

*When put into general release, some thirty minutes were shorn
from The Alamo, including the birthday party for Lisa Dickinson
(Aissa Wayne) and a sequence in which Davy Crockett offers a prayer
for one of his fallen men, the Parson (Worden).

a too rich mixture not stirred and melted together into one blend"
(New York Herald-Tribune). Variety observed, "In general, Wayne's
direction bogs down in the more intimate areas. With the rousing
battle sequences at the climax (for which a goodly share of credit
must go to second unit director Cliff Lyons) the picture really com-
mands the spectator's rapt, undivided attention.... Most gratifying
is the absence of any corny strokes when the heroes perish." Perhaps the best summation of The Alamo comes from Michael Parkinson and Clyde Jeavons in A Pictorial History of Westerns (1972);
they rate it as "a big, noisy, spectacular fireworks display, but
rather vacuous in its reconstruction of the Americans' historical
equivalent of Dunkirk. "

ALLEGHENY UPRISING (RKO, 1939) 81 min.

        Producer, P. J. Wolfson; director, William A. Seiter; based
on the novel The First Rebel by Neil H. Swanson; screenplay, Wolf-
son; art director, Van Nest Polglase; choreography, David Robel;
music director, Anthony Collins; camera, Nicholas Musuraca; editor,
George Crone.
        Claire Trevor (Janie MacDougle); John Wayne (Jim Smith);
George Sanders (Captain Swanson); Brian Donlevy (Callendar); Wilfred
Lawson (MacDougle); Robert Barrat (Professor); Moroni Olsen (Cal-
hoon); Eddie Quillan (Anderson); Chill Wills (M'Cammon); Ian Wolfe
(Poole); Wallis Clark (McGlashan); Monte Montague (Morris); Olaf
Hytten (General Gage); John F. Hamilton (Professor); Eddy Waller
(Jailer); Charles Middleton (Doctor); Stanley Blystone, Tom London
(Frontiersmen); Clay Clement (Bit).
        British release title: The First Rebel.

        Six days after Drums Along the Mohawk [q.v.] debuted at a
Broadway theatre, Allegheny Uprising premiered at the Palace in
New York City. It was unusual that the infrequently-treated Revolu-
tionary War period should be the basis for these two historical
Westerns. The former was directed by John Ford for Twentieth
Century-Fox in color and boasted Claudette Colbert and Henry Fonda
as co-stars. Less prestigious and more cautiously budgeted was
RKO's production re-teaming John Wayne and Claire Trevor, the
stars of the popular Stagecoach (1939), q.v.
        The New York Times was too righteous and demanding when
it carped, "Given the Pennsylvania frontier a few decades before the
Revolution, a dash of Indian fighting and the story of one James
Smith [Wayne], who led his rebellious 'Black Boys' against the dis-
ciplinary forces of the crown, you would think that P. J. Wolfson
and his collaborators at RKO could have come along with something
better than a screen translation of a research worker's notes. Yet
that is what Allegheny Frontier [sic] gives the disquieting impression
of being. "
        When frontiersman Jim Smith (Wayne) learns that Trader
Callendar (Donlevy) is selling liquor and guns to the Indians of the
Pennsylvania area, he attempts to stop the dangerous practice. Jim

J. Frank Hamilton, John Wayne, Claire Trevor, in Allegheny Uprising (1939).

is loved by Janie McDougle (Trevor), a rugged, beautiful pioneer
woman, but he abandons her to chase a band of rampaging Indians.
When he gets to Philadelphia he reports Callendar's activities to the
authorities. Under the supervision of Captain Swanson (Sanders),
British soldiers come to Fort Loudon to protect the vulnerable settlers from the Indians. When Swanson refuses to track down the
rumors concerning Callendar's activities, Jim and his men disguise
themselves as Indians and burn Callendar's wagon convoy. Swanson
tries to have his forces arrest Jim, but the wiley frontiersman eludes
them. However, Janie, who has participated in the raiding party, is
captured. Jim and his men surround the soldiers and force them to
release the girl. Later Callendar's men try to frame Jim for the
murder of a settler. In the court hearing Jim's innocence is proven.
The culpable Swanson is thereafter sent back to England. Jim and
Janie, together at last, set out for Tennessee.
      Besides the buoyant presences of Wayne, Trevor, Sanders
and Donlevy, this film does recapture an almost forgotten chapter of
American history. The colorful fabric of the story plus the array
of recreated details of a bygone era make this film very worthwhile
viewing.

ALONG THE MOHAWK TRAIL   see   LAST OF THE MOHICANS

AMERICAN EMPIRE   (United Artists, 1942)   82 min.

    Producer, Harry Sherman; director, William McGann; screen-
play, J. Robert Bren, J. Gladys Atwater, Ben Grauman Kohn; art
director, Ralph Berger; camera, Russell Harlan; editor, Sherman
A. Rose.
    Richard Dix (Dan Taylor); Leo Carrillo (Dominique Beau-
chard); Preston Foster (Paxton Bryce); Frances Gifford (Abby
Taylor); Robert Barrat (Crowder); Jack La Rue (Pierre); Guinn
"Big Boy" Williams (Sailaway); Cliff Edwards (Runty); Merrill Guy
Rodin (Paxton Bryce, Jr.); Chris-Pin Martin (Augustin); Richard
Webb (Crane); William Farnum (Louisiana Judge); Etta McDaniel
(Willa May); Hal Taliaferro (Malone).

Preston Foster, Frances Gifford, Richard Dix, in American Empire (1942).

    For the bulk of his lengthy screen career, Richard Dix was
overshadowed by his work in Cimarron (1931), q.v. As a further
example of this fact, this World War II vintage release, produced
by Harry "Pop" Sherman, was a later attempt to cash in on Dix's
self-sustaining image. It was an elaborate production, by United
Artists standards, and the New York Times noted that Sherman
"has climaxed an otherwise well-behaved drama with a reel that ex-
plodes in all directions."
    In the accepted parlance of Western screenlore, American

Empire offered a vivid panorama of frontier country, grazing cattle, and stern men battling it out with dastardly rustlers. Within
this format, Dix is Dan Taylor who, after the Civil War, goes to
Texas where he settles down and raises cattle, developing an empire there during the Reconstruction period. Vermin such as
Preston Foster's Paxton Bryce make it difficult for the likes of
staunch Dix. Frances Gifford, who would later move to MGM but
never receive her due there, makes a fetching diversion from the
horses and gunplay.
    Certainly producer Sherman was more intent on capturing a
flavor of the Old West (as movie fans expected it to be) than on
depicting the frontier times as they actually were. There are
plenty of flaws in the presentation, but with square-jawed Dix at
the helm it hardly seems to matter.
    After appearing as the Indian hero of The Vanishing American
(1925), q.v., Dix had quite a career in the film genre. He was
Joaquim Murietta in The Gay Defender (1928) and an Indian again in
Redskin (1929), q.v. After the epic Cimarron, resolute Richard
performed similar chores in The Conquerors (1932), q.v., RKO's
attempt to follow-up the success of its Edna Ferber story. RKO
would employ Dix as Pecos Smith in Zane Grey's West of the Pecos
(1934), as a marshal in The Arizonian, and as a miner in Yellow
Dust (1936). Dix turned to comedy as a faded cowboy star in
Columbia's It Happened in Hollywood (1936), but returned to his established form in Republic's expansive Man of Conquest (1939),
playing the great Texan, Sam Houston. Moving on into the Forties,
Dix was an Oklahoma Territory marshal in Cherokee Strip (Para-
mount, 1940), a rancher in The Roundup (Paramount, 1941), and
received special billing as Wild Bill Hickok in Badlands of Dakota
(Universal, 1941). Next he was Wyatt Earp in Tombstone, the Town
Too Tough to Die (Paramount, 1942), a gunfighter in Buckskin
Frontier (United Artists), and a marshal in The Kansan (United
Artists, 1943), his final oater.

ANGEL AND THE BADMAN (Republic, 1947) 100 min.

    Producer, John Wayne; director-screenplay, James Edward
Grant; second unit director, Yakima Canutt; music, Richard Hage-
man; music director, Cy Feuer; songs, Kim Gannon and Walter
Kent; assistant director, Harvey Dwight; production designer, Ernest
Fegte; set decorator, Charles Thompson; sound, Victor Appel; special
camera effects, Howard and Theodore Lydecker; camera. Archie J.
Stout; editor, Harry Keller.
    John Wayne (Quirt Evans); Gail Russell (Penny Worth); Harry
Carey (Wistful McClintock); Bruce Cabot (Laredo Stevens); Irene
Rich (Mrs. Worth); John Halloran (Thomas Worth); Lee Dixon (Randy
McCall); Tom Powers (Dr. Mangrum); Stephen Grant (Johnny Worth);
Paul Hurst (Carson); Olin Howlin (Bradley); Joan Barton (Lila); Craig
Woods (Ward Withers); Marshall Reed (Nelson).

    This entry from Republic pictures marked the first feature

Harry Carey, John Wayne, Gail Russell, in Angel and the Badman (1947).

film which actor John Wayne produced. It was written and directed by James Edward Grant (who later wrote the script for Wayne's The Alamo, 1960, q.v.), and the second unit direction was handled by the star's long-time buddy and stunt man, Yakima Canutt. Gail Russell, then at her peak of physical loveliness, was also an integral part of Wayne's professional "family." In later years when she suffered career and personal misfortunes, he would befriend her, casting her in the female lead of the Wayne-produced Seven Men from Now, 1956, starring Randolph Scott.

Made very much in the John Ford tradition, Angel and the Badman has Wayne as outlaw Quirt Evans, being chased by a posse. He is given refuge by a Quaker family and soon comes under the romantic spell of the daughter (Russell). Though he loves her, he still vows to kill Laredo Stevens (Cabot), the man who murdered his foster father. Eventually she converts Evans to more peaceful ways and they marry. However, Stevens and his men arrive on the scene and try to kill the couple, leaving the pair to drown in a river. Quirt rescues his bride and goes after Stevens, but the girl follows. In town, Quirt puts down his gun to fight Stevens with his fists. The latter attempts to shoot Evans in the back, but marshal Wistful McClintock (Carey) kills the outlaw.

Alan G. Barbour in John Wayne (1974) wrote, "The film had many moments of tenderness and compassion, that underscored the surrounding mayhem." The New York Times noted, "the adventure ... is as much concerned with romance and the pacifist policies of the Friends as it is with such standbys as six shooters and rustlers. In short, Mr. Wayne and company have sacrificed the usual roaring action to fashion a leisurely Western, which is different from and a notch or two superior to the normal sagebrush saga."

Two points about this film should be made: the presence of silent screen heroine Irene Rich as Miss Russell's mother, and the pedestrian film score largely borrowed from Republic's library of nondescript chase music.

ANNIE GET YOUR GUN (MGM, 1950) C 107 min.

Producer, Arthur Freed; director, George Sidney; based on the musical by Dorothy Fields, Herbert Fields, and Irving Berlin; screenplay, Sidney Sheldon; music director, Adolph Deutsch; songs, Berlin; art directors, Cedric Gibbons, Paul Groesse; set decorators, Edwin B. Willis, Richard A. Pefferle; montage, Peter Ballbusch; women's costumes, Helen Rose, Walter Plunkett; men's costumes, Plunkett; makeup, Jack Dawn; choreography, Robert Alton; color consultants, Henri Jaffa, James Gooch; sound, Douglas Shearer; special effects, A. Arnold Gillespie, Warren Newcombe; camera, Charles Rosher; editor, James E. Newcom.

Betty Hutton (Annie Oakley); Howard Keel (Frank Butler); Louis Calhern (Buffalo Bill); J. Carrol Naish (Sitting Bull); Edward Arnold (Pawnee Bill); Keenan Wynn (Charlie Davenport); Benay Venuta (Dolly Tate); Clinton Sundberg (Foster Wilson); James H. Harrison (Mac); Bradley Mora (Little Jake); Diana Dick (Nellie); Susan Odin (Jessie); Eleanor Brown (Minnie); Chief Yowlachie (Little Horse); Robert Malcolm (Conductor); Lee Tung Foo (Waiter); William Tannen (Barker); Anne O'Neal (Miss Willoughby); Evelyn Beresford (Queen Victoria); John Hamilton (Ship Captain); William Bill Hall (Tall Man); Edward Earle (Footman); Marjorie Wood (Constance); Elizabeth Flournoy (Helen); Mae Clarke Langdon (Mrs. Adams); Frank Wilcox (Mr. Clay); Andre Charlot (President Loubet of France); Nino Pipitone (King Victor Emmanuel); John Mylong (Kaiser Wilhelm II); Carl Sepulveda, Fred Gilman, Carol Henry (Riders).

Full-scale Western musicals have traditionally been big productions and most of them have been successful, although their number remains relatively small.

The production history of Annie Get Your Gun is intricate. Richard Rodgers and Oscar Hammerstein II, functioning as producers, had sought Jerome Kern to write a musical score for a musical on Annie Oakley. When Kern died, Irving Berlin was contracted to work with Dorothy and Herbert Fields on the projected Broadway show. The collaboration resulted in Annie Get Your Gun which opened at the Imperial Theatre (New York) on May 16, 1946

Louis Calhern, J. Carrol Naish, Benay Venuta, Howard Keel, Edward Arnold, Keenan Wynn, and Betty Hutton in Annie Get Your Gun (1950).

for a 1,147-performance run.   Ethel Merman starred as Annie Oakley with Ray Middleton as Frank Butler.   MGM producer Arthur Freed acquired the screen rights for Metro at a fee of $650,000, the heftiest price paid to that date for a musical property.   It was agreed that Judy Garland would star as the screen's latest Annie Oakley.*

Sidney Sheldon adapted the stage work for the screen in late 1948 and early 1949, and the search started to find a proper Frank Butler for the project.   John Raitt was considered and tested, but the part went to Howard Keel who was then starring in the London edition of Oklahoma!   Busby Berkeley was selected to direct the venture.   In late March 1949 Miss Garland recorded her songs for the film.   Then chaos set in!

Unsure of herself and of the role, Judy was the major

*The character of Phoebe Anne Oakley Mozee has been played on camera by such actresses as Barbara Stanwyck (Annie Oakley, 1935), Nancy Kovack (The Outlaws Is Coming, 1965), and Angela Douglas (Carry on Cowboy, 1966).

unstable element of the project which began shooting on April 4, 1949. On the second day of filming Howard Keel broke his ankle and he was put on the sidelines for at least three months. On May 3, 1949, Berkeley was fired and Charles Walters was hired in his place. Due to Judy's continued absences, delays, and "illnesses," the production was suspended on May 10, 1949, and a few days later she was taken to Peter Brigham Hospital in Boston for a rest cure. To salvage the money already expended, MGM borrowed Betty Hutton from Paramount to take over Garland's role.

When filming recommenced on September 26, 1949, director Walters had been removed from the picture and George Sidney put in his stead. Frank Morgan had died in the interim and he was replaced by Louis Calhern as Buffalo Bill, and Benay Venuta replaced Geraldine Wall as Dolly Tate. Finally in mid-December, 1949, filming was completed at a cost of $3,768,785.

Was it worth all the aggravation entailed? MGM eventually grossed over eight million dollars on the production. Bosley Crowther (New York Times) confirmed the audience endorsement when he termed the film "a whale of a musical picture."

Most of the songs from the Broadway score were used in the film, although some of the lyrics to "Doin' What Comes Natur'lly" were altered to appease the industry code office. In addition, Berlin's "Let's Go West Again" was deleted from the film. While Betty Hutton proved to be quite acrobatic in the part, she lacked the sense of timing that Miss Merman* had given the part of this raw Western sharpshooter who sets her sites on handsome Frank Butler (Keel) and eventually wins him after a lot of tries and lots of good music.

By today's standards, Annie Get Your Gun seems too stagey and coy for its own good. But taken in its proper perspective the film is hale and hearty entertainment. Especially effective is the set designed by Paul Groesse for Buffalo Bill's Wild West Show. The finale of the show incorporated the rousing "There's No Business Like Show Business."

The success of Annie Get Your Gun would inspire Warner Bros. to trot out their own variation of this format, using Doris Day and borrowing Howard Keel for Calamity Jane (1953). Beyond the enduring song "Secret Love," this imitation, as directed by David Butler, was a stagnant affair.

---

*MGM had considered Miss Merman too "old" to play the role on camera. Other contenders for the choice screen role had been Republic's Judy Canova, and later (after Miss Garland dropped out of the project), Martha Raye and MGM's own Betty Garrett. Ironically, as late as 1967 Miss Merman was playing Annie Oakley on TV. For the 1966 Lincoln Center Revival of AGYG, with Miss Merman, Berlin wrote a new song, "An Old Fashioned Wedding."

ANNIE OAKLEY (RKO, 1935) 90 min.

        Associate producer, Cliff Reid; director, George Stevens;
based on the story of Joseph A. Fields, Ewart Adamson; screen-
play, Joel Sayre, John Twist; art directors, Van Nest Polglase,
Perry Ferguson; music director, Alberto Colombo; camera, J. Roy
Hunt; editor, Jack Hively.
        Barbara Stanwyck (Annie Oakley); Preston Foster (Toby
Walker); Melvyn Douglas (Jeff Hogarth); Pert Kelton (Vera Delmar);
Moroni Olsen (Buffalo Bill); Andy Clyde (MacIvor); Chief Thunder-
cloud (Sitting Bull); Margaret Armstrong (Mrs. Oakley); Delmar
Watson (Wesley Oakley).

        Long eclipsed because of the stage and screen musical,
Annie Get Your Gun (1950), q. v. , this superior Barbara Stanwyck
vehicle was helmed by George Stevens with few concessions for the
low brows. Not that this feature was any masterpiece. Variety
penned, "If the picture misses as outstanding it's because the script
and director are not up to the star and title combination." However, it captured a flavor of the times and through Stanwyck's interpretation it showed Miss Annie Oakley as a mixture of frontier
toughness and feminine softness.
        Miss Stanwyck offered a well-modulated interpretation as the
tomboy young woman who falls in love with Toby Walker (Foster),
the world's top sharpshooter. Annie could easily beat Toby in a
competition of marksmanship, but she loves him too much to do so.
Later, she and Toby join Buffalo Bill's (Olson) Wild West Show and
there she is romanced by the show's dapper manager (Douglas).
But it is Toby she loves, and it is he who claims her affections at
the finale.
        Although highly inaccurate as far as American history is
concerned, the picture was vastly entertaining and presented an
exciting recreation of Buffalo Bill's show, including Chief Thundercloud as the famed Sitting Bull. Not to be overlooked in terms of
appeal to action audiences were the several displays of sharpshooting.
        Annie Oakley served as a pick-up for Miss Stanwyck's career
and the New York Sun wrote, "A western with Miss Stanwyck playing
the shy girlish young queen of the shooting range becomes a superwestern indeed." In later years the superstar would frequently return to the sagebrush genre, which she always admitted was her
first cinema love.

ANY GUN CAN PLAY see VADO, L'AMMAZZO E TORNO

APACHE (United Artists, 1954) C 91 min.

        Producer, Harold Hecht; director, Robert Aldrich; based on
the novel by Paul J. Wellman; screenplay, James R. Webb; music,
David Raksin; assistant director, Sid Sidman; camera, Ernest
Laslo; editor, Alan Crosland, Jr.

Burt Lancaster (Massai); Jean Peters (Nalinle); John Mc-
Intire (Al Sieber); Charles Bronson (Hondo); John Dehner (Weddle);
Paul Guilfoyle (Santos); Ian MacDonald (Glagg); Walter Sande
(Lieutenant Colonel Beck); Morris Ankrum (Dawson); Monte Blue
(Geronimo).

For the initial feature film under their Hecht-Lancaster
Productions, producers Harold Hecht and Burt Lancaster chose
Apache, a story which attempted to turn around the Hollywood
stereotype of the Indian. Its aim was to present a sympathetic
portrayal of the Indian people as seen through the point of view of
a brave (Lancaster), one of Geronimo's (Blue) men who escapes
while being transported to prison at St. Augustine. Having sworn
vengeance on the white race, he wages a near one-man battle.
Later he becomes enamored of Nalinle (Peters) and through her
love he widens his scope in trying to help improve the fate of his
people. His sworn enemy, though, still remains the U.S. Army.
Robert Aldrich, who directed Vera Cruz, q.v., the same
year for Hecht-Lancaster, helmed the production and created a good
action film which offered a compelling portrayal of the redskin.
Wrote Philip French in Westerns (1973), "Particularly memorable are the opening sequences ... where a garish white civilization is seen through the eyes of a fugitive Indian [Lancaster] making
his way back West after escaping from a deportation train taking
him to exile in Florida. A tragic ending was planned for this picture, but the front office insisted on optimism and this is what the
makers delivered in a hopelessly unconvincing manner."
In his final screen portrayal, one-time matinee idol Monte
Blue gave a most credible performance as the dying Geronimo at
the movie's beginning. Lancaster, in his turn, having ably flexed
his muscles through a series of early fifties' swashbucklers, demonstrated here that he was capable of conveying a serious theme in the
midst of an action drama.

BAD BASCOMB (MGM, 1946) 112 min.

Producer, Orville O. Dull; director, S. Sylvan Simon; story,
D. A. Loxley; screenplay, William Lipman, Grant Garrett; music,
David Snell; orchestrator, Wally Heglin; art directors, Cedric Gib-
bons, Paul Youngblood; set decorator, Edwin B. Willis; assistant
director, Early McAvoy; sound, Howard Fellows; special effects,
Warren Newcombe; camera, Charles Schoenbaum; editor, Ben Lewis.
Wallace Beery (Zeb Bascomb); Margaret O'Brien (Emmy);
Marjorie Main (Abbey Hanks); J. Carrol Naish (Bart Yancy); Fran-
ces Rafferty (Dora); Marshall Thompson (Jimmy Holden); Russell
Simpson (Elijah Walker); Warner Anderson (Luther Mason); Donald
Curtis (John Felton); Connie Gilchrist (Annie Freemont); Sara Haden
(Tillie Lovejoy); Renie Riano (Lucy Lovejoy); Wally Cassell (Curley);
Jane Green (Hanna); Henry O'Neill (Governor Winter); Frank Darien
(Elder McCabe); Joseph Crehan (Governor Ames); Clyde Fillmore
(Governor Clark); Arthur Space (Sheriff); Eddie Acuff (Corporal);
Stanley Andrews (Colonel Cartright).

Although the frequent re-teaming of Marjorie Main with
Wallace Beery never equaled that of Marie Dressler and Beery in
the early thirties, it was still a very lucrative combination in
various MGM products. To spice this marquee lure, Metro added
moppet star Margaret O'Brien to the mixture. The little actress
added a new twist to the Hollywood presentation of the white man
battling the redskins. In Bad Bascomb she fends off an Indian attack with a pea shooter.

The unsubtle plot has outlaw Zeb Bascomb (Beery) joining
a Mormon wagon train which is heading to Utah. Zeb's hope is to
keep the federal troops from capturing him. On the trek the rough
outlaw comes under the charms of Emmy (O'Brien) who is in the
charge of her hard-talking grandmother (Main). Bascomb's partner
(Naish) joins the train and tries to persuade him to steal the
Mormons' gold, which is to be used to build a hospital. Zeb refuses, however, and he helps the Mormons fight Indians. During
the attack he saves Emmy's life when her wagon overturns and she
is swept into a swollen river. Later, Bascomb rides for the
troops to save the wagon train. Redeemed by his new associates,
he is now prepared to face justice.

It is interesting to note how many films, including the
famous Friendly Persuasion (1956), use a pacifist religious group
as a counterpoint to the usual rough-and-tumble life style of the
Old West.

BAD DAY AT BLACK ROCK (MGM, 1955) C 81 min.

Producer, Dore Schary; associate producer, Herman Hoffman; director, John Sturges; story, Howard Breslin; screenplay,
Millard Kaufman; color consultant, Alvord Eiseman; music, Andre
Previn; art directors, Cedric Gibbons, Malcolm Brown; set decorators, Edwin B. Willis, Fred MacLean; assistant director, Joel
Freeman; sound, Wesley C. Miller; camera, William C. Mellor;
editor, Newell P. Kimlin.

Spencer Tracy (John J. Macreedy); Robert Ryan (Reno
Smith); Anne Francis (Liz Wirth); Dean Jagger (Tim Horn); Walter
Brennan (Doc Velie); John Ericson (Pete Wirth); Ernest Borgnine
(Coley Trimble); Lee Marvin (Hector David); Russell Collins (Mr.
Hastings); Walter Sande (Sam).

By now the camp expression "Bad Day at Black Rock" is an
almost accepted part of Americanese. More importantly it is the
title of a sound, solid Western, produced under the Dore Schary
("relevant philosophy") regime at MGM. It also proved to be
Spencer Tracy's final feature at his Metro home lot. Times were
certainly changing.

The Southwestern town of Black Rock is a drab stretch of
arid land. One day in 1945, the Santa Fe train stops and the one-
armed John Macreedy (Tracy) disembarks. His mission is to find
a Japanese farmer who resides in the town, to present him with
his son's posthumous war medal. The local people are antagonistic

Spencer Tracy and Ernest Borgnine in <u>Bad Day at Black Rock</u> (1954).

to Macreedy's search, and he later learns that the citizens of Black
Rock were responsible for burning the Oriental's farm and killing
the innocent victim.   Having learned the truth, the righteous, robust Macreedy wreaks his own revenge on the wrongdoers.

John O'Hara (Collier's magazine) enthused, "You are not
going to see many pictures as good as Bad Day at Black Rock.
There just haven't been many pictures as good as Bad Day at
Black Rock. ...   This is one of the finest motion pictures ever
made."

Among the excellent performances in this remarkably adroit
undertaking are, of course, Tracy as the one-arm fighter, Dean
Jagger as a weak sheriff, Ernest Borgnine as the dastardly soul
whom Tracy eventually vanquishes, Lee Marvin as the loud-mouth
lout, and John Ericson as the sniveling hotel worker.

Another champion of this production was Robert Hatch (The
Nation).   "The obvious picture of comparison is High Noon [1952,
q.v.].   Both are suspense thrillers with an evident moral, both
center upon the behavior of a man isolated by mortal danger; both
work toward a blazing climax through an atmosphere of hair-trigger
calm.   The new picture is the better by a variety of measurements. ...
The conflict in Bad Day at Black Rock is less explicit, and the
weight and determination of the opposing forces are less arbitrarily
stated than the rather pat duel of High Noon.   The suspense is
therefore much tighter; it increases with the shifting and hardening
resolution of the performers and is not a mechanical excitement
keyed to the ticking of a clock."

MGM would remake the film as the rather tawdry Platinum
High School (1960).

BAD LANDS   (RKO, 1939)   70 min.

Producer, Robert Sisk; director, Lew Landers; story-screenplay, Clarence Upson Young; camera, Frank Redman; editor, George
Hively.

Robert Barrat (Sheriff); Noah Beery, Jr. (Chic Lyman);
Guinn "Big Boy" Williams (Billy Sweet); Douglas Walton (Mulford);
Andy Clyde (Cluff); Addison Richards (Rayburn); Robert Coote
(Eaton); Paul Hurst (Curley Tom); Francis Ford (Garth); Francis
McDonald (Manuel Lopez).

If the plotline of this modest feature seems familiar to
seasoned film viewers, it is because it is a Western rendition of
RKO's earlier hit, The Lost Patrol (1934).   Lew Landers directed
this tough little film about a sheriff (Barrat) leading a posse into
the desert after renegade Apaches.   One by one the members of
his troop are picked off.   Eventually only the law enforcer is left
at the water hole.   At this point, the Army arrives to "rescue"
the group.   Although it was a star-less feature, the film was much
above the average B picture of the period.

May women's liberation supporters forgive the film and its
studio, as Bad Lands has no females in its compact cast.

Ann Richards and Randolph Scott in Badman's Territory (1946).

BADMAN'S TERRITORY   (RKO, 1946)   97 min.

Producer, Nat Holt; director, Tim Whelan; screenplay, Jack
Natteford, Luci Ward; additional sequences, Clarence Upson Young,
Bess Taffel; art directors, Albert S. D'Agostino, Walter E.
Keller; set decorators, Darrell Silvera, James Altwies; assistant director,
Harry Mancke; music, Roy Webb; musical director, C. Bakaleini-
koff; sound, Jean L. Speak, Terry Kellum; montage, Harold Palmer;
camera, Robert de Grasse; editor, Philip Martin.

Randolph Scott (Mark Rowley); Ann Richards (Henryette Al-
cott); George "Gabby" Hayes (Coyote Kid); Ray Collins (Colonel Fare-
well); James Warren (John Rowley); Morgan Conway (Bill Hampton);
Virginia Sale (Meg); John Halloran (Hank McGee); Andrew Tombes
(Doc Grant); Richard Hale (Ben Wade); Harry Holman (Hodge); Chief
Thundercloud (Chief Tahlequah); Lawrence Tierney (Jesse James);
Tom Tyler (Frank James); Steve Brodie (Bob Dalton); Phil Warren
(Grat Dalton); William Moss (Bill Dalton); Nestor Paiva (Sam Bass);
Isabel Jewell (Belle Starr).

After Universal's success in the mid-forties with grouping a
number of monsters in individual horror films, RKO tried the same
approach in order to breathe new life into its Westerns.   This entry
was a virtual who's who of the genre's famous folk and included both
the James and Dalton gangs, plus Sam Bass and Belle Starr.   Still
the New York Times had to admit, "the only thing unusual about
Badman's Territory is the inordinate length [97 minutes].   Westerns
seem to have a lot more life when told rapidly and concisely."
The scenario finds Marshal Mark Rowley (Scott) coming to
the Oklahoma town of Quinto, a place known as no man's land and
lacking both law and order.   Rowley is searching for his brother
who has been wounded in a fight with the James Gang (Lawrence
Tierney as Jesse; Tom Tyler as Frank), and he runs into that
notorious crew as well as the infamous Sam Bass (Paiva), Belle
Starr (Jewell), and the Dalton Brothers (Steve Brodie as Bob, Phil
Warren as Grat, and William Moss as Bill).   Thereafter Mark is
framed on a horse-stealing charge by a corrupt U.S. marshal.
Later, when freed, Rowley stays on to help crusading newspaper
editor Henryette Alcott (Richards) in her campaign to make Quinto
part of the Oklahoma Territory.
One of the more interesting aspects of this film was George
"Gabby" Hayes' performance as the harmonica-playing, crusty old
outlaw, The Coyote Kid, the man who drove getaway wagons for
both the James and Dalton gangs.
The film proved successful enough for RKO to make a sequel
called Return of the Bad Men (1949).

THE BANDIT AND THE PREACHER see ON THE NIGHT STAGE

BANDOLERO! (Twentieth Century-Fox, 1968) C 106 min.

Producer, Robert L. Jacks; director, Andrew V. McLaglen;

story, Stanley L. Hough; screenplay, James Lee Barrett; music,
Jerry Goldsmith; orchestrator, Herbert Spencer; stunt co-ordinator,
Hal Needham; makeup, Dan Striepeke; art directors, Jack Martin
Smith, Alfred Sweeney, Jr.; set decorators, Walter M. Scott,
Chester L. Bayhi; assistant director, Terry Morse, Jr.; sound,
Herman Lewis, David Dockendorf; special camera effects, L. B.
Abbott, Emil Kosa, Jr.; camera, William H. Clothier; editor,
Folmar Blangsted.

 James Stewart (Mace Bishop); Dean Martin (Dee Bishop);
Raquel Welch (Maria Stoner); George Kennedy (Sheriff Johnson);
Andrew Prine (Roscoe Bookbinder); Will Geer (Pop Chaney); Clint
Ritchie (Babe); Denver Pyle (Muncie Carter); Tom Heaton (Joe
Chaney); Rudy Diaz (Angel Munoz); Sean McClory (Rubbie); Harry
Carey, Jr. (Cort Hayjack); Donald "Red" Barry (Jack Hawkins);
Guy Raymond (Ossie Grimes); Jock Mahoney (Stoner); Dub Taylor
(Attendant); Bob Adler (Ross Harper); John Mitchum (Customer);
Roy Barcroft (Bartender).

 When a film grosses $5.5 million in distributors' domestic
rentals, it is certainly worthy of consideration. Strangely, its
director, Andrew V. McLaglen, who has a very good track record
in filmmaking, has never developed a cult. Such feature films as
McLintock (1963) [q.v.] and The Way West (1967) [q.v.] show his
competence in handling big name stars in commercially acceptable
Westerns. Films like Shenandoah (1965) [q.v.] indicate that he has
inherited the boisterous, yet warm, humanity that so typified his
father, Victor McLaglen, as a screen performer.
 There are two points of particular interest in Bandolero!
One is the comely presence of Raquel Welch, who by this point had
consolidated her screen reputation as the sex goddess of the sixties.
The other factor, certainly far less tangible than the busty, curvacious Miss Welch, is the problem of how a viewer is to take the
film. Is it a serious Western or a tongue-in-cheek spoof?
 Time did not want to take it either way: "As westerns go,
this one doesn't. It saddles up a big-name cast, but the giddyap!
gets mired in a lot of giddy yapping. The intent was to lighten
carnage with comedy; the result is heavy-handed Grand Old Horse
Opry." The authors of this book disagree; but filmgoers must see
the film and judge for themselves. And be sure to note the appearance of a wide variety of old Western favorites, including
Donald "Red" Barry, Jock Mahoney, Roy Barcroft, Dub Taylor,
and even Robert Mitchum's brother John.
 Dee Bishop (Martin) kills a rich rancher during an attempted
Texas bank robbery. Sheriff Johnson (Kennedy) arrests his entire
gang and they are sentenced to be hung. Mace Bishop (Stewart),
Dee's older brother, poses as the hangman and rescues the five
men. They escape to Mexico, taking the dead rancher's widow
(Welch) with them as hostage. While everyone is chasing the
gang, Mace calmly robs the bank. At a deserted town, the outlaws
hole up, waiting for the inevitable encounter with Sheriff Johnson and
his posse. In the skirmish, both Mace and Dee (he has fallen in
love with the widow) are killed. After burying the brothers, Maria

(Welch) and her beau, Sheriff Johnson, return to Texas.
Two scenes in particular are quite revealing of the film's
intent: the sequence in which the laconic, gangling Mace casually
scoops up the money from the deserted bank, and the other where
a rather prim, if sensuous, Maria confesses, "I was a whore at
thirteen and my family of twelve never went hungry...."

THE BATTLE AT ELDERBRUSH GULCH (Biograph, 1913) two
reels

Director-screenplay, D. W. Griffith; camera, Billy Bitzer.
With: Lillian Gish, Mae Marsh, Dell Henderson, Blanche
Sweet, Kate Bruce, W. Christie Miller, Alfred Paget, Henry B.
Walthall.

This film was shot in July, 1913 in the San Fernando Valley
by D. W. Griffith for Biograph, with the cinematography of trusty
Billy Bitzer. A Western town was especially constructed for the
feature which was issued as a two-reeler by Biograph after Griffith
had left the studio for independent production. The film demonstrates an advanced use of intercutting from one action sequence to
another, a process which the director refined by the time of
Intolerance (1916).
Starring Lillian Gish and Mae Marsh, the story relates the
fate of a small infant who is the sole survivor of an Indian attack.
The baby is rescued by Dell Henderson, the leader of a group of
pioneers seeking a water supply. After traveling for a long time,
the entire party, except for the baby, dies of thirst. However, a
second traveling party, noting the child's waving hand, rescues her
and she grows up to be the character played by Blanche Sweet. It
is Miss Sweet who, in the storyline, becomes involved in the title
battle.
In A Pictorial History of the Western (1969), William K.
Everson terms the short subject, "a superb action film, with
savage massacre scenes, and brilliantly constructed edited battle
scenes." Thus, although America was not very distant from its
pioneer days, the subject of the "old" west had already become
viable in the 1910s.
Interestingly enough, the baby used in the opening sequences
of this movie was a black child Griffith often borrowed from a
nearby foundling home because of the photogenic value of its dark
eyes.

BEHIND THE MASK OF ZORRO see MASK OF ZORRO

THE BIG COUNTRY (United Artists, 1958) C 166 min.

Producers, William Wyler, Gregory Peck; director, Wyler;
based on the novel Ambush at Blanco Canyon by Donald Hamilton;

screenplay, James R. Webb, Sy Bartlett, Robert Wilder; adaptors,
Jessamyn West, Robert Wyler; music, Jerome Moross; art director,
Frank Hotaling; set decorator, Edward G. Boyle; costumes, Emile
Santiago, Yvonne Wood; makeup, Dan Greenway, Jarry Maret, Jr.;
assistant director, Ivan Volkman; second unit directors, John
Waters, Robert Swink; sound, John Kean, Roger Heman; camera,
Franz F. Planer; editor, Robert Swink.

Gregory Peck (James McKay); Jean Simmons (Julie Maragon);
Carroll Baker (Patricia Terrill); Charlton Heston (Steve Leech);
Burl Ives (Rufus Hannassey); Charles Bickford (Major Henry Terrill);
Alfonso Bedoya (Ramon); Chuck Connors (Buck Hannassey); Chuck
Hayward (Rafe); Buff Brady (Dude); Jim Burk (Cracker); Dorothy
Adams (Hannassey Woman); Chuck Roberson, Bob Morgan, John
Morgan, Jay Slim Talbot (Terrill Cowboys).

Gregory Peck, Jean Simmons, Burl Ives, Chuck Connors in The
Big Country (1958).

In A Pictorial History of Westerns (1972) Michael Parkinson
and Clyde Jeavons assess this film as "one of the most successful
Westerns of the late fifties ... [a] massive epic ... a film dis-
liked by critics but nevertheless hugely enjoyable ... it is one of
the few large-scale Westerns to convey successfully the two dimensions of the West."

They were correct about the film being a big grosser--it
earned over $4 million in distributors' domestic rentals--but it was

approved by most of the established Fourth Estate: "A starkly
beautiful, carefully written, classic western that demands comparison with Shane" (Time); "Massive in its pictorial splendor....
Camera has captured a vast section of the southwest with such
fidelity that it leaves an awe-inspiring effect on the viewer"
(Variety); "Magnificently, overwhelming photographed.... Acting
is good throughout, and the story never flags" (New York Herald-
Tribune); "A large-scale, meticulously produced, obviously expensive Western" (Saturday Review). One of the few major dissenters
was Films in Review, which reported, "The story is a mass of in-
consistencies. So is Wyler's direction.... We never understand
anybody.... The motivations do not spring from the characterizations, and the characterizations did not spring from the thoughtful
minds of skillful authors."

Most viewers did agree that the performances did not match
up to the visual splendor or to Wyler's massive concepts. On the
set of the $3.1 million widescreen film, the director told reporters,
"I have never seen any great virtue in the American tradition of
punching a guy in the nose if he said something you didn't like. It
only proves who can punch the quickest or the hardest--nothing else.
The problem that intrigues me is whether people can have faith in
a man who doesn't punch." When the film was released, Bosley
Crowther (New York Times) would harp on this aspect of the picture,
"It skims across standard complications and ends on a platitude.
Peace is a pious precept but fightin' is more excitin.' That's what
it proves." (It should be noted that Wyler utilized the writing
services of Jessamyn West, author of Friendly Persuasion, the
Quaker-Civil War story that Wyler had filmed in 1956.)

In the southwest of the 1870s, wealthy cattle ranchers (Burl
Ives and Charles Bickford) feud over water rights on neutral land
owned by schoolmarm Julie Maragon (Simmons). Former sea
captain James McKay (Peck, also co-producer of this film) arrives
on the scene to wed Major Henry Terrill's (Bickford) daughter
(Baker). He soon finds himself enlisted as the unhappy mediator
of the dispute, which goes against his pacifist grain. He is promptly
at odds with rugged ranch foreman Steve Leech (Heston) and cruel
Huck Hannassey (Connors) the cowardly son of Rufus Hannassey
(Ives). At the finale, it is teacher Julie who wins McKay's hand in
marriage.

Summing up this expansive, expressive feature, Newsweek
magazine said, it "strongly suggests that there is absolutely nothing
wrong with westerns that plenty of money and an offbeat hero can't
cure, or at the very least ameliorate." Films such as The Big
Country offered sterling evidence that the movie industry could combat the competition of small screen Westerns on TV.

THE BIG GUNDOWN   see   LA RESA DEI CONTI

THE BIG SKY   (RKO, 1952)   140 min.

Producer-director, Howard Hawks; based on the novel by

A. B. Guthrie, Jr.; screenplay, Dudley Nichols; music, Dimitri
Tiomkin; art directors, Albert S. D'Agostino, Perry Ferguson;
set decorators, Darrell Silvera, William Stevens; camera, Russell
Harlan; editor, Christian Nyby.
        Kirk Douglas (Jim Deakins); Dewey Martin (Boone); Elizabeth
Threatt (Teal Eye); Arthur Hunnicutt (Zeb); Buddy Baer (Romaine);
Steven Geray (Jourdonnais); Hank Worden (Poordevil); Jim Davis
(Streak); Henri Letondal (Labadie); Robert Hunter (Chouquette);
Booth Colman (Pascal); Paul Frees (McMasters); Frank de Kova
(Moleface); Guy Wilkerson (Longface).

        "The Big Sky is the least of Hawks' Westerns, as surely as
Rio Bravo [1959, q.v.] is the best.   One only intermittently senses
the depth and intensity of personal involvement that give Red River
[1948, q.v.] and Rio Bravo their concentrated significance.   Hawks
failed to achieve the right creative relationship with Kirk Douglas,
and failed to realize the character of Teal Eye, the Indian girl; she
is meant to be remote and mysterious, but one must feel that her
creator understands her.   However, the film is unmistakably Hawks's,
especially in its treatment of the male relationship" (Robin Wood in
Howard Hawks, 1968).
        Shot at Grand Teton National Park, the film is set in 1830
with Jim Deakins (Douglas) and Boone (Martin) as backwoodsmen
who leave Kentucky and head for St. Louis and points West.   They
team up with Zeb (Hunnicutt) a grizzly trapper-scout and a river
boat patron (Geray) and his French crew.   Via boat the group travel
over 2,000 miles up the Missouri, Platte and Cheyenne Rivers to
trade for beaver pelts with the Blackfood Indians.   Once there Boone
falls in love with a Blackfoot princess (Threatt).   Their journey is
also filled with battles with the French and Indians.
        While the New York Times would compliment the feature on
presenting "a facet of history rarely touched on by the movie makers
and a part of our past rich in courage and adventure," it also felt
that the film lacked sufficient drive or inner conflict.   Kirk Douglas,
one of the post-World War II breed of rugged screen toughs, had already played in two Westerns: Along the Great Divide (1951) and
The Big Trees (1952).   In this, his third Western, his over-earnest
style failed to inject the proper spirit and verve into the production.
Oddly enough, he was at his best in a sequence in which a finger
amputation is played for laughs.
        In the seventies, the male camaraderie films were an ac-
cepted part of the film scene; but in the fifties the friendship between the Douglas and Martin characters caused some viewers to
insist that the alliance smacked of homosexuality.   However, it was
nothing more than another illustration of the friendship of males,
long a dominant element in Hawks' features.   The two characters,
who enjoy a saloon scene singing "Whiskey Leave Me Alone," are
just two individuals who maintain an abiding respect for each other.
        While The Big Sky leaves much to be desired as typical
Western entertainment, its presentation of Americana is commend-
able.

THE BIG TRAIL   (Fox, 1930)   125 min.

Director, Raoul Walsh; story, Hal G. Evarts; screenplay, Jack Peabody, Marie Boyle, Florence Postal, Fred Sersen; art director, Harold Miles; incidental music, Arthur Kay; song, Joseph McCarthy and James F. Hanley; sound, Donald Scott, George Leverett; assistant directors, Ewing Scott, Sid Bowen, Clay Crapnell, George Walsh, Virgil Hart, Earl Rettig; wardrobe, Earl Moser; makeup, Jack Dawn, Louise Sloane; camera, Lucien Andriot, Don Anderson, Bill McDonald, Roger Sherman, Bobby Mack, Henry Pollack; Grandeur camera, Arthur Edeson, David Ragin, Sol Halprin, Curt Fetters, Max Cohn, Harry Smith, L. Kunkel, Harry Dawe; editor, Jack Dennis.

John Wayne (Breck Coleman); Marguerite Churchill (Ruth Cameron); El Brendel (Gussie); Tully Marshall (Zeke); Tyrone Power, Sr. (Red Flack); David Rollins (Dave Cameron); Ian Keith (Bill Thorpe); Frederick Burton (Pa Bascom); Russ Powell (Windy Bill); Charles Stevens (Lopez); Louise Carver (Gussie's Mother-in-Law); William V. Mong (Wellmore); Dodo Newton (Abigail); Ward Bond (Sid Bascom); Marcia Harris (Mrs. Riggs); Marjorie Leet (Mary Riggs); Emslie Emerson (Sairey); Frank Rainboth (Ohio Man); Andy Shuford (Ohio Man's Son); Helen Parrish (Honey Girl); Jack Peabody (Bill Gillis); Gertrude Van Lent, Lucile Van Lent (Sisters from Missouri); De Witt Jennings (Boat Captain); Alphonz Ethier (Marshal).

For over a quarter of a century, this and many other Fox features were unavailable for showing. But thanks to the resurrection work accomplished at Twentieth Century-Fox by Alex Gordon, these motion pictures are currently available for private /public /TV screenings. One of the first films to be made in the Grandeur (widescreen) Process was The Big Trail. (Many of the smaller theatres which were not equipped for this 70mm. picture showed it in the standard 35mm version). The picture was a financial disappointment.

Photographed by Lucien Andriot and Arthur Edeson (the chief cinematographers), the 125-minute epic was basically a successor to The Covered Wagon (1923) [q.v.]. It told of the opening of the famed Oregon Trail with a wagon convoy forging the trail from the midwest to the Northwest. "The plot itself is sparse, but the movie moves with much breathless sweep and with such smashing climaxes that the story is relatively unimportant" (Mark Ricci, Boris Zmijewsky, Steve Zmijewsky, The Films of John Wayne, 1970). The picture contained the customary, expected scenes of battles with Indians, a buffalo hunt, the fording of a river, and the dismantling of the wagons to get them over a mountain. However, these ordinary episodes were accomplished with much dispatch and scope (thanks to the widescreen process), and the film remains one of the most visually satisfying features ever produced in Hollywood.

Raoul Walsh had originally intended to play the lead role in this production, but an accident (in which he lost an eye) kept him from assuming the part. (For the same reason, he did not play the

John Wayne and Marguerite Churchill in The Big Trail (1930).

lead in his first talking Western, In Old Arizona, 1929 [q. v.].)
Upon John Ford's recommendation, he tested young John Wayne and
gave him the pivotal assignment.   Unfortunately the picture's failure
was a great step backwards in Wayne's budding movie career.
Thereafter he was thrust into minor releases for nearly a decade
until Ford salvaged his career by casting him in Stagecoach (1939)
[q. v.].
          In recent decades, before The Big Trail again became avail-
able, it was considered chic to mock Wayne's performance in this
film.   The re-emergence of The Big Trail, though, has disproved
these new historians, who apparently paid little heed to contemporary critics.   No less than Mordaunt Hall of the New York Times
approved of Wayne's performance and the Exhibitor Herald-World
called the film an "epic" and added, "John Wayne carries on very
well. "
          Originally running 158 (!) minutes in its 70mm roadshow
version, the feature was chopped to 125 minutes for its 35mm release.
          Fox also filmed German and Spanish-language versions of
The Big Trail.   The Spanish version, entitled Horizontes Huevos,
produced in 1931, was directed by David Howard with George Lewis
and Carmen Guerrero in the leads.
          Action footage from The Big Trail would constantly crop up
in later Fox features.

BILLY THE KID   (MGM, 1930)   90 min.

          Director, King Vidor; based on the book The Saga of Billy
the Kid by Walter Noble Burns; screenplay, Wanda Tuchock,
Laurence Stallings; additional dialogue, Charles MacArthur; art
director, Cedric Gibbons; wardrobe, David Cox; technical advisor,
William S. Hart; sound, Paul Nean, Douglas Shearer; camera,
Gordon Avil; editor, Hugh Wynn.
          John Mack Brown (Billy the Kid); Wallace Beery (Pat Gar-
rett); Kay Johnson (Claire); Wyndham Standing (Tunston); Karl Dane
(Swenson); Russell Simpson (McSween); Blanche Frederici (Mrs.
McSween); Roscoe Ates (Old Stuff); Warner P. Richmond (Ballinger);
James Marcus (Donovan); Nelson McDowell (Hatfield); Jack Carlyle
(Brewer); John Beck (Butterworth); Christopher Martin (Santiago);
Marguerita Padula (Nicky Whoosiz); Aggie Herring (Mrs. Hatfield).
          TV Title: The Highwayman Rides.

---

*Opposite: Two versions of Billy the Kid.   Top (1930), Kay John-
son, John Mack Brown, Roscoe Ates, Blanche Frederici, Russell
Simpson, Jack Carlyle.   Bottom (1941), Cy Kendall, Lon Chaney,
Jr., Brian Donlevy, Mary Howard, Henry O'Neill, Robert Taylor,
Kermit Maynard and Ray Teal.

BILLY THE KID   (MGM, 1941) C 95 min.

    Producer, Irving Asher; director, David Miller; based on the
book The Saga of Billy the Kid by Walter Noble Burns; screenplay,
Gene Fowler; songs, Ormond B. Ruthven and Albert Mannheimer;
camera, Leonard Smith, William V. Skall; editor, Robert J. Kern.
    Robert Taylor (Billy Bonney); Brian Donlevy (Jim Sherwood);
Ian Hunter (Eric Keating); Mary Howard (Edith Keating); Gene Lock-
hart (Dan Hickey); Lon Chaney, Jr. (Spike Hudson); Henry O'Neill
(Tim Ward); Guinn "Big Boy" Williams (Ed Bronson); Cy Kendall
(Cass McAndrews); Ted Adams ("Buz" Cobb); Frank Conlan (Judge
Blake); Frank Puglia (Pedro Gonzales); Mitchell Lewis (Bart Hodges);
Dick Curtis (Kirby Claxton); Grant Withers (Ed Shanahan); Joe Yule
(Milton).

    Walter Noble Burns' 1926 novel on William Bonney, alias
Billy the Kid, * was filmed by Metro in 1930 in its Realife (widescreen) process. It contained exceptionally fine photography and
very naturalistic scenes of the old West--no doubt due to King
Vidor's direction as well as the use of William S. Hart as the picture's technical advisor. Unfortunately, as seen today, the film is
overlong and slow-moving, with the widescreen process (which caused
the failure of Fox's The Big Trail the same year) preventing the use
of close-ups. The lack of a musical score only emphasizes the

---

Interestingly enough, the John Mack Brown version of Billy the Kid
was the first time the outlaw was portrayed on the screen, despite
a number of screen biographies of Western heroes and enemies made
in the twenties. In 1938 Roy Rogers portrayed the character in
Billy the Kid Returns, for Republic, and in 1940 Bob Steele made
six features as the Kid for Producers Releasing Corporation, followed by Larry "Buster" Crabbe who played the character in a
number of PRC films before they changed his character's name to
Billy Carson. In 1949, however, Screen Guild resurrected the Billy
the Kid personage for Lash La Rue in Son of Billy the Kid.   Jack
Beutel played the Billy part in Howard Hughes' The Outlaw which
was finally issued that year. Others who played Billy onscreen
are: Audie Murphy in The Kid from Texas (Universal, 1950),
Donald Barry in I Shot Billy the Kid (Lippert, 1950), Tyler Mac-
Duff in The Boy from Oklahoma (Warner Bros., 1950), Scott Brady
in The Law Vs. Billy the Kid (Columbia, 1954), Nick Adams in
Strange Lady in Town (Warner Bros., 1955), James Craig in Last
of the Desperadoes (Associated, 1956), Anthony Dexter in The
Parson and the Outlaw (Columbia, 1957), Paul Newman in The Left-
Handed Gun (Warner Bros., 1958), Chuck Courtney in Billy the Kid
vs. Dracula (Embassy, 1966), Geoffrey Duel in Chisum (Warner
Bros., 1970), and Kris Kristofferson in Pat Garrett and Billy the
Kid (MGM, 1973). Clu Gulager played Billy the Kid in the tele-
series "The Tall Men" (1960-61) with Barry Sullivan as Pat Garrett.

sluggishness of the scenario.   Coming only a few years after the
general acceptance of all-talking films, this picture used titles to
bridge the action gaps.
    John Mack Brown was at the peak of his physical form when
tackling this role and Wallace Beery (as Sheriff Pat Garrett) managed
to restrain himself and offer a dignified performance.   The plot has
Billy marrying Claire (Kay Johnson--Lucile Brown had been cast
originally in the role, but was replaced by Miss Johnson) in New
Mexico but vowing revenge on the land baron (James Marcus) whose
gang has killed his best friend.   Billy and his men are held at bay
by Garrett and his posse, although eventually the sheriff allows the
outlaw to escape, presumably to find a life of happiness.
    This Metro production was shot mostly on location in the
Lincoln County area of New Mexico where Billy had lived.   John
Mack Brown actually used one of the outlaw's own guns in the film.
The movie industry was in the midst of a cycle of Westerns, pictures that would span the genre from Paramount's The Virginian
(1929) [q.v.], Fox's The Big Trail (with John Wayne), and RKO's
Cimarron (1931) [q.v.] to Universal's Law and Order (1932) [q.v.]
and Destry Rides Again (1932) [q.v.].   Billy the Kid could be rated
only fair when compared to these other epics.

    Eleven years after the John Mack Brown version of the Billy
the Kid story was issued, MGM remade the Walter Noble Burns
book into a breezy retelling of the William Bonney saga.   Just as
Twentieth Century-Fox had cast their "pretty boy" matinee idol
Tyrone Power in Jesse James (1939) [q.v.], so Metro used its ultra-
handsome lead, Robert Taylor, to play the famed outlaw.   To boost
the box-office potential of the project, MGM allotted a big budget
which allowed for the use of color filming.
    This rendition has the Kid at odds with Jim Sherwood, alias
Pat Garrett (Donlevy).   The latter had been Billy's childhood pal
but now is the sheriff who must hunt the lawbreaker.   The unsatis-
fying ending has the Kid allowing the sheriff to beat him to the
draw.
    Besides the use of Technicolor, the best assets of this entry
are the supporting players: Donlevy offers his usual good performance as the sheriff, while Gene Lockhart shines as a dishonest
rancher with Frank Puglia quite effective as Pedro Gonzales, the
Kid's Mexican friend.   Robert Taylor, nearing age thirty, was too
mature for the part of the youthful Kid, and if reality were to be
served, he was too tall for the part.
    The New York Herald-Tribune reported, "in spite of its
elaborate closing and its highly reputed star, Billy the Kid is just
another routine horse opera--another glorified fable about one of
the West's more notorious outlaws and not a very good one at that."
Writing in retrospect, William K. Everson, in A Pictorial History
of the Westerns (1969), said, "except for a well-done climactic
chase, [the 1941 feature] was a weak and totally re-written [by
Gene Fowler] 'adaptation' of the same book by Walter Noble Burns
that had formed the basis of King Vidor's film a decade earlier."
In contrast, Everson found that the 1930 version "is quite certainly the best and most convincing of all the Billy the Kid sagas."

As would be proven time and time again, it is not the expense of a production that makes a successful Western, but the
snap and agility of the lead players, who set the tone of the story
and guarantee interest in the film.

BITE THE BULLET (Columbia, 1975) C   131 min.

Producer-director-screenplay, Richard Brooks; music, Alex
North; art director, Robert Boyle; set decorator, Robert Signorelli;
assistant director, Tom Shaw; sound, Arthur Piantadosi, Les Fres-
holtz, Richard Tyler, Al Overton, Jr.; camera, Harry Stradling,
Jr.; editor, George Granville.
Gene Hackman (Sam Clayton); Candice Bergen (Miss Jones);
James Coburn (Luke Matthews); Ben Johnson ("Mister"); Ian Bannen
(Norfolk); Jan-Michael Vincent (Carbo); Mario Arteaga (Mexican);
Robert Donner (Reporter); Robert Hoy (Lee Christie); Paul Stewart
(J. B. Parker); Jean Willes (Rosie); Dabney Coleman (Gebhardt);
Jerry Gatlin (Woodchopper); Sally Kirkland (Honey); Walter Scott,
Jr. (Steve).

"No point in beating about the bush, Bite the Bullet is just
about as perfect a screen entertainment as anyone could ask for.
It sustains its pulse-pounding pace for well over two hours ... the
attention doesn't falter for a moment" (The Hollywood Reporter).
On the other hand, Vincent Canby (New York Times) pouted, it "is
a big, expensive Western that doesn't contain one moment that might
be called genuine ... the movie looks prefabricated."
Despite these polar views of the film, nearly everyone has
agreed that Bite the Bullet marked the beginning of a resurgence in
the period Western film.
Set in the Old West of 1906, the story focuses on an endurance horse race, a 700-mile stretch. Among the contestants
are Sam Clayton (Hackman) and Luke Mathews (Coburn), who are
friendly rivals; Carbo (Vincent), a novice cowhand; a game Britisher
(Bannen), a veteran cowpoke (Johnson) and, of all things, a prostitute (Bergen). The race occupies the largest time frame of the
story. As Daily Variety observes of the scenario, "His script and
his players know the difference between manliness and macho, between maturity and self-indulgence, between motivated, controlled
violence and undisciplined excess, and between casual, implicit
sexual release and coloring book sado-masochism."
Not to be overlooked in this rousing action tale is Sally Kirkland's Honey, an overly-vivacious frontier woman, played with bite
and humor. Not to be overlooked either is Ben Johnson's very
touching speech about the glory of winning the race.

BLAZING SADDLES (Warner Bros., 1974) C 93 min.

Producer, Michael Hertzberg; director, Mel Brooks; story,
Andrew Bergman; screenplay, Brooks, Norman Steinberg, Bergman,
Richard Pryor; production designer, Peter Wooley; set decorator,

Morey Hoffman; music/music director, John Morris; orchestrators,
Jonathan Tunick, John Morris; songs, Morris and Brooks; title song
sung by Frankie Laine; costumes, Nino Novarese; choreography,
Alan Johnson; titles, Anthony Goldschmidt; sound, Gene S. Canta-
messa; special effects, Douglas Pettibone; camera, Joseph Biroc;
editors, John C. Howard, Danford Greene.

Cleavon Little (Bart); Gene Wilder (Jim); Slim Pickens
(Taggart); Harvey Korman (Hedley Lamarr); Madeline Kahn (Lili
Von Shtupp); Mel Brooks (Governor William J. Lepetomane/Indian
Chief); Burton Gilliam (Lyle); Alex Karras (Mongo); David Huddle-
ston (Olson Johnson); Liam Dunn (Reverend Johnson); John Hillerman
(Howard Johnson); George Furth (Van Johnson); Claude Ennis Star-
rett, Jr. (Gabby Johnson); Carol Arthur (Harriett Johnson); Richard
Collier (Dr. Sam Johnson); Charles McGregor (Charlie); Robyn
Hilton (Miss Stein); Don Megowan (Gum Chewer); Dom DeLuise
(Buddy Bizarre); Count Basie (Himself); Karl Lukas (Tough).

"He rode a blazing saddle, he wore a shining star," Frankie
Laine wails as he sings the title song for this Mel Brooks Western.
This colorful film soon dissolves into an all-out burlesque of the
Western format, leaving no realm of the genre alone before it slips
into a disappointing finale.

As co-scripted and directed by Brooks (who played two roles
in the picture), a black prisoner named Bart is used by a stooge
governor (Brooks) and his conniving underling (Korman) to clean up
the town of Rock Ridge in the year 1874. Despite much racial hatred
among the citizens ("drop dead nigger," a kindly old lady tells the
new marshal on the street), and an attempted seduction of the hero
by a Marlene Dietrich-like saloon singer (Kahn), which backfires, the
marshal accomplishes his job. The cowboy plot is soon sabotaged
for a modern setting in the Warner Bros. studio, with the unmanly
director Buddy Bizarre (DeLuise) handling a dance sequence in an
extravaganza musical. It all ends with Bart (Little) riding his horse
into Grauman's Chinese Theatre to view the finale of Blazing Saddles;
which has Bart and ex-prisoner Jim (Wilder) exchanging their horse
for a chauffeur-driven limousine and riding out of Rock Ridge.

On first viewing, Blazing Saddles is a very adept satire; it
loses much upon a repeat showing. It contains a goodly number of
sidesplitting scenes, as when a group of Ku Klux Klan members are
seen with "have a nice day" emblazoned on their robes. Cleavon
Little as the black sheriff/hero, Madeline Kahn as Lili Von Shtupp
(who sings the suggestive "I'm So Tired"), and Brooks as the in-
competent governor ("work, work, work") and as a Yiddish-speaking
Indian chief lend buoyancy to the production. And then, of course,
there is Wilder as the prissy alcoholic "Waco Kid," and Alex Karras
as Mongo, a dimwitted strongman. Slim Pickens offered a very
convincing send-up of his frequent Western role as a conscienceless
henchman.

It is interesting to note how the British reacted to this very
American spoof. British Monthly Film Bulletin's reaction was
moderately favorable: "There are more than enough details in
Blazing Saddles to provide the material for a sustained comedy

feature, and one suspects that the film's gradual disintegration
derives not--as has been suggested--from its makers' inability to
end it, so much as from their inability to stop laughing at their
own jokes."

Every fan seems to have his or her favorite moment of bad
taste in this campy exercise. Among the best are Miss Kahn's
take-off of Marlene Dietrich (à la Destry Rides Again), and the
church meeting at Rock Ridge where the various members of the
Johnson family are present: Van, Howard, and Olson. Some of
the jokes verge on smut (Kahn asking a cowboy, "Is that a ten-
gallon hat or are you just enjoying the show?") and vulgarity (the
congregation singing "Our town is turning to shit").

Fans of the Western genre, of course, can derive a good
deal of pleasure from Wilder's characterization of the gunfighter,
which borrows heavily from such cowboy classics as The Magnificent Seven (1960) [q. v.] or Rio Bravo (1959) [q. v.].

As Monthly Film Bulletin summed it up, "Perhaps it is
pedantic to complain that the whole is not up to the sum of its
parts when, for the curate's egg that it is, Blazing Saddles contains so many good parts and memorable performances."

The single 45 rpm recording of the title tune (by Frankie
Laine) and "I'm So Tired" (by Madeline Kahn) made spashy sales
in the pop record field for some time after the picture's release.

BLOOD ON THE MOON   (RKO, 1948)   88 min.

Executive producer, Sid Rogell; producer, Theron Warth;
director, Robert Wise; based on the novel by Luke Short; adaptor,
Harold Shumate, Short; screenplay, Lillie Hayward; art directors,
Albert S. D'Agostino, Walter E. Keller; set decorator, Darrell
Silvera, James Altwies; music, Roy Webb; music director, C.
Bakaleinikoff; assistant director, Maxwell Henry; makeup, Gordon
Bau; sound, John C. Cass, Terry Kellum; special effects, Russell
A. Cully; camera, Nicholas Musuraca; editor, Samuel E. Beetley.

Robert Mitchum (Jimmy Garry); Barbara Bel Geddes (Amy
Lufton); Robert Preston (Tate Riling); Walter Brennan (Kris Barden);
Phyllis Thaxter (Carol Lufton); Frank Faylen (Jake Pindalest); Tom
Tully (John Tufton); Charles McGraw (Milo Sweet); Clifton Young
(Joe Shotten); Tom Tyler (Frank Reardan); George Cooper (Fred
Barden); Richard Powers (Ted Elser); Bud Osborne (Cap Willis);
Don Murray (Nels Titterton); Robert Bray (Bart Daniels).

"Lusty, violent, savage tale of the deadliest range war ever
to EXPLODE on the screen!" is how RKO advertised this well-turned-
out Western which, like Mitchum's Pursued (1947) [q. v.], had a
definite psychological bent. This type of introspective story would
gain momentum in the Western genre as the fifties wore on.

Gunslinger Jimmy Garry (Mitchum) is hired by a cattle
rustler-friend Tate Riling (Preston) to persuade a local woman
ranch owner (Bel Geddes) either to sell her cattle cheaply or to
face the consequence of having them stolen. After a time, however,

Garry falls in love with the girl and sides with her in the matter.
His decision leads to a brawl with Riling which the latter loses.
Finally Garry and Amy Lufton are free of their problems and marry.
    Although this feature lacked sufficient outdoor location
shooting to give it the feel of a spacious, adventure yarn, it did
have a most realistic fight sequence between the two male leads,
one that found each combatant completely exhausted by the time the
bout was over.
    The New York Times approved of this motion picture, rea-
soning, "[it] has a sound, sensible story to tell and, besides, it is
well acted. Robert Mitchum carries the burden of the film and his
acting is superior all the way.... Just about everything that can
and should happen in a Western has been crowded into Blood on the
Moon, including a small scale stampede which kicks up a lot of
dust and excitement. Guns go off all over the place and there is a
bruising fist fight...."

BLUE (Paramount, 1967) C 113 min.

    Producers, Judd Bernard, Irwin Winkler; associate producer,
Patricia Casey; director, Silvio Narizzano; story, Ronald M. Cohen;
screenplay, Meade Roberts, Cohen; second unit director, Yakima
Canutt; music, Manos Hadjidakis; orchestrator, Leo Arnaud; art
directors, Hal Pereira, Albert Brenner, Al Roelofs; set decorator,
Claude Carpenter; costumes, Pat Kelley, Ann Landers; visual con-
sultant, Tony Pratt; makeup, Wally Westmore; assistant directors,
Joseph Lenzi, Jack Corrick; sound, John Carter, John Wilkinson;
process camera, Farciot Edouart; camera, Stanley Cortez; editor,
Stewart Linder.
    Terence Stamp (Blue [Azul]); Joanna Pettet (Joanne Morton);
Karl Malden (Doc Morton); Ricardo Montalban (Ortega); Anthony
Costello (Jess Parker); Joe De Santis (Carlos); James Westerfield
(Abe Parker); Stathis Giallelis (Manuel); Carlos East (Xavier); Sara
Vardi (Inez); Robert Lipton (Antonio); Kevin Corcoran (Rory Calvin);
Ivalou Redd (Helen Buchanan); Dorothy Konrad (Alma Wishoff);
Helen Kleeb (Elizabeth Parker); Michael Bell (Jim Benton); Wes
Bishop (Settler); Jerry Gatlin (Wes Lambert); Michael Nader (Mexi-
can Assassin); Sally Kirkland (Sara Lambert); William Shannon
(Police Chief).

    "Blue is a chicken Western [which] has neither the courage
nor the conviction of its own cliches" (New York Times).
    So why include it in this book? Visually the film is a stun-
ning example of Stanley Cortez's cinematography. More importantly,
it had an interesting production. Back-to-back with the shooting of
this film in Utah, Italian director Silvio Narizzano shot Fade In
with Burt Reynolds, which dealt with Hollywood stunt men and used
the making of Blue as interpolated background material. Fade-In
was considered such a potential commercial disaster that, unlike the
equally poor Blue, it was never officially released by Paramount.
    The script of Blue has a youth (Stamp) adopted by a Mexican

bandit after his parents are massacred.   This bandit teaches him a
life of crime.   During a raid in Texas, Blue shoots one of his
foster brothers who is about to molest a girl.   Blue is injured in
the shooting and the girl and her father nurse him back to health.
From this point onwards he is torn between his wild, unlawful life
and the possibility of a more civilized existence.

In dismissing this effort, Time informed its readers, "The
tired bloodshed of the plot about gringos and greasers--as the
script tastefully refers to Texans and Mexicans--is a vehicle for
England's Terence Stamp, Cheapside accent and all.   Would you believe that he plays a gunman raised from childhood by a band of
Mexican brigands?"

THE BOLD CABALLERO (Republic, 1936) C 69 min.

Producer, Nat Levine; director, Wells Root; based on Johnston McCulley's character; screenplay, Root; music, Harry Grey;
costumes, Eloise; camera, Alvin Wyckoff, Jack Marta; editor,
Lester Orlebeck.

Robert Livingston (Zorro/Don Diego Vega); Heather Angel
(Lady Isabella Palma); Sig Rumann (Commandante); Robert Warwick
(Governor Palma); Ian Wolfe (Priest); Emily Fitzroy (Duenna);
Charles Stevens (Captain Vargas); Walter Long (Chato); Ferdinand
Munier (Landlord); Carlos de Valdez (Alcalde); Chris-Pin Martin
(Pedro); John Merton (Sergeant); Chief Thundercloud (Servant).
See MARK OF ZORRO for commentary.

THE BORDER LEGION (Goldwyn, 1918) six reels

Director, T. Hayes Hunter; based on the novel by Zane
Grey; screenplay, Victor de Viliers, Laurence Marston.
With: Hobart Bosworth, Blanche Bates, Horace Morgan,
Eugene Strong, Russell Simpson, Art Morrison, Bull Montana,
Richard Souzade, Kate Elmore.

THE BORDER LEGION (Paramount, 1924) 7,048'

Presenters, Adolph Zukor, Jesse L. Lasky; director,
William K. Howard; based on the novel by Zane Grey; screenplay,
George Hull; camera, Alvin Wyckoff.
Antonio Moreno (Jim Cleve); Helene Chadwick (Joan Randle);
Rockliffe Fellowes (Kells); Gibson Gowland (Gulden); Charles Ogle
(Harvey Roberts); James Corey (Pearch); Edward Gribbon (Blicky);
Luke Cosgrave (Bill Randle).

THE BORDER LEGION (Paramount, 1930) 6,088'

Directors, Otto Brower, Edwin H. Knopf; based on the novel
by Zane Grey; screenplay, Percy Heath, Edward E. Paramore, Jr.;
sound, Earl Hayman; camera, Mack Stengler; editor, Doris Drought.

Richard Arlen and Fay Wray in <u>Border Legion</u> (1930).

Richard Arlen (Jim Cleve); Jack Holt (Jack Kells); Fay Wray (Joan Randall); Eugene Pallette (Bunco Davis); Stanley Fields (Hack Gulden); E. H. Calvert (Judge Savin); Ethan Allen (George Randall); Syd Saylor (Shrimp).

THE BORDER LEGION (Republic, 1940) 58 min.

Associate producer, director, Joseph Kane; based on the novel by Zane Grey; screenplay, Olive Cooper, Louis Stevens; camera, Jack Marta; editor, Edward Mann.
Roy Rogers (Steve Kells); George "Gabby" Hayes (Honest John Whittaker); Carol Hughes (Alice); Joe Sawyer (Gulden); Maude Eburne (Hurricane Hattie); Jay Novello (Santos); Hal Taliaferro (Sheriff); Dick Wessel (Red); Paul Porcasi (Tony); Robert Emmett Keane (Willets).
TV title: <u>West of the Badlands</u>.

Zane Grey, that prolific writer of the Old West, has provided

a tremendous amount of raw material for screenplays. His The
Border Legion, published in 1916, was no exception.
        The first of five screen versions of this work appeared in
1918 and starred Hobart Bosworth, who had attained screen promi-
nence with The Count of Monte Cristo (Paramount, 1913).
        William K. Howard directed the first of three Paramount
versions. This 1924 film, reported Photoplay, "will not stand
minute inspection, but is a mighty good entertainment." The story
has the heroine (Chadwick) telling Jim Cleve (Moreno) that he is
too lazy to be bad. To prove her wrong, he goes West and joins a
notorious gang, the Border Legion. Joan Randle (Chadwick) regrets
her actions and follows him out West. She is captured by the gang's
leader (Fellows) and in self-defense shoots him. She then nurses
him back to health and the impressed man succumbs to her charms.
Later she escapes with Cleve, but they are retaken during a stagecoach holdup. Jim is shot. In a scene paralleling the famous
episode in David Belasco's The Girl of the Golden West [q.v.],
Gulden and Kells play cards; the former wins the girl and the latter
the gold. Jim tries to fight for Joan's honor, but it is Kells who
sacrifices his life to save her, and Joan and Jim escape.
        Paramount, as part of the craze in the early talkie period
to rehash silent photoplays, remade The Border Legion in 1930.
Contract players Richard Arlen and Fay Wray play the leads, with
very popular Jack Holt--usually at Columbia in these years--as
good-natured outlaw Jack Kells. There were some new twists to
the plot. In Alder Creek, Idaho, Kells saves Jim Cleve from being
hanged for a crime committed by one of his own men. In gratitude,
Jim joins Kells' gang. Later, gang member Hack Gulden kidnaps
Joan Randall (Wray). Jim guards her and prevents Gulden from
making advances to the girl. Fearing that an armed posse will attack his stronghold, Kells orders an attack on the town of Alder
Creek. Jim cannot convince the townfolk of the impending peril
and he is imprisoned. Still later, Fells aids Jim in escaping.
Just as Gulden is about to confront Cleve in a final showdown, Kells
appears on the scene and shoots Gulden before he himself is killed.
        Ever anxious to hit paydirt from already owned properties,
Paramount remade The Border Legion yet again, this time under
the aegis of Henry Hathaway. Hathaway had worked as assistant
director to Victor Fleming on Paramount's The Virginian (1929)
[q.v.], and in the early thirties he was promoted to helming his
own batch of sagebrush ventures for the studio. In 1971 Hathaway
would recall for Focus on Film, "I mostly learned from them [i.e.,
those Zane Grey remakes] how to handle people. I would take a
script home and think. Now what would I tell those people to do
to make the scene, how would I start it, where would be the climax,
how would I get out of it, how do I get rid of the people, where
would I do it--in front of the fire or on the couch, what would I do?
And I'd make up my mind, and I'd make a lot of notes and then I'd
see what they did."

        The 1934 edition, entitled The Last Round-Up,* closely fol-
lowed the other versions, with a gang leader of rustlers sacrificing

his life to save the lovers, one of them being Randolph Scott as Jim Cleve. With stock footage from the earlier versions, the film boasted fine photography by Archie Stout.

The most recent version of the novel, again called The Border Legion, was made by Republic Pictures in 1940. Joseph Kane directed this streamlined version as a part of the Roy Rogers series. Carol Hughes and George "Gabby" Hayes were co-starred.

THE BRAZEN BELL   see   THE VIRGINIAN

THE BRIDE WASN'T WILLING   see   FRONTIER GAL

BROKEN ARROW   (Twentieth Century-Fox, 1950)   C   93 min.

Producer, Julian Blaustein; director, Delmer Daves; based on the novel Blood Brother by Elliott Arnold; screenplay, Michael Blankfort; music director, Alfred Newman; art directors, Lyle Wheeler, Arthur Hogsett; camera, Ernest Palmer; editor, J. Watson Webb, Jr.

James Stewart (Tom Jeffords); Jeff Chandler (Cochise); Debra Paget (Sonseeahray); Basil Ruysdael (General Howard); Will Geer (Ben Slade); Joyce MacKenzie (Terry); Arthur Hunnicutt (Duffield); Raymond Bramley (Colonel Bernall); Jay Silverheels (Goklia); Argentina Brunetti (Nalikadeya); Jack Lee (Boucher); Robert Adler (Lonergan); Harry Carter (Miner); Robert Griffin (Lowrie); Billy Wilkerson (Juan); Mickey Kuhn (Chip Slade); Chris Willow Bird (Nochalo); J. W. Cody (Pionsenay); John War Eagle (Nahilzay); Charles Soldani (Skinyea); Iron Eyes Cody (Teese); Robert Foster Dover (Machogee); John Marston (Maury); Edward Rand (Sergeant); John Doucette (Mule Driver); Trevor Bardette (Stage Passenger).

(This was one of Hollywood's first large-scale attempts to present a sympthetic picture of the American Indian and how he has been mistreated by his white conquerors.) The film was quite popular and spawned a TV special as well as a TV series.

James Stewart starred as Tom Jeffords, a Civil War veteran and now a scout in the 1870s who becomes upset at the mistreatment of the Indians. In his efforts to make peace with the Chiricahua Apaches he learns the dialect and the ways of the tribe. He searches for the tribe's chief, Cochise (Chandler), whom no white man has seen in a decade. When he locates Cochise, whose family was murdered in the last white man's "peace," they agree to abandon the warfare. Cochise even permits the mail to go through

---

*In 1947 Republic released a film entitled The Last Round-Up which was not related to any Zane Grey work. It was a Gene Autry Production starring the cowboy actor-singer.

James Stewart in Broken Arrow (1950).

his territory.   While living with the tribe Jeffords falls in love with
Sonseeahray (Paget), the attractive Indian maiden.   Later they are
wed according to the tribe's customs.   During a three-month interim
period before the announced peace goes into effect, renegade Apaches
attack the mail stagecoach but are driven away by Cochise and his
warriors.   Later, renegade whites attack Cochise and his people,
and Sonseeahray is killed.   Despite the ensuing troubles, the peace
is maintained and warfare, for the time being, is ended.
        Newsweek termed this film "undoubtedly one of the most
emotionally satisfying Westerns since Stagecoach [1939, q.v.] and
The Virginian [1929, q.v.]."   Jack Spears, in his book, Hollywood:
The Golden Era (1971), states, ["Broken Arrow further stimulated
the flood of pro-Indian films and the oppressed but valiant redmen,
usually personified by a dignified chief, became as much of a stereotype as the villainous savage had been.   All the injustices to his race
were charged to greedy, brutal and insensitive whites--and to an impersonal government that ignored its responsibilities to the Indians."
        One of the most sterling directors of Westerns is none other
than Delmer Daves, who would leave more of a commercial mark
as the director of four highly successful Troy Donahue vehicles in
the late fifties and early sixties.   Daves would go on to direct such
superior Westerns as 3:10 to Yuma (1957) [q.v.], and Cowboy (1958)
[q.v.].   Jeff Chandler's career was really launched by this film and

he would play several other Indian roles in the fifties, including a
repeat (guest) appearance as Cochise in Rock Hudson's Taza, Son
of Cochise (1954). Obviously, a good deal of the financial success
of Broken Arrow was due to superstar James Stewart, who represented such an idealized all-American that his characterization took
on special meaning for many viewers: he was basically a representative of the better nature of Americans.

BROKEN LANCE (Twentieth Century-Fox, 1954) C 96 min.

        Producer, Sol C. Siegel; director, Edward Dmytryk; based
on the material supplied by Philip Yordan, et al.; screenplay,
Richard Murphy; music, Leigh Harline; music director, Lionel
Newman; art directors, Lyle Wheeler, Maurice Ransford; set
decorators, Walter Scott, Stuart Reiss; costumes, Travilla; sound,
W. D. Flick, Roger Heman; special effects, Ray Kellogg; camera,
Joseph McDonald, Anthony Newman; editor, Dorothy Spencer.
        Spencer Tracy (Matt Devereaux); Robert Wagner (Joe Deve-
reaux); Jean Peters (Barbara); Richard Widmark (Ben); Katy Jurado
(Senora Devereaux); Hugh O'Brian (Mike Devereaux); Eduard Franz
(Two Moons); Earl Holliman (Danny Devereaux); E. G. Marshall
(The Governor); Carl Benton Reid (Clem Lawton); Harry Carter,
Edmund Cobb, King Donovan, Arthur Bryan, Russell Simpson (Bits).

        If one has seen Twentieth Century-Fox's House of Strangers
(1949) with Edward G. Robinson and Susan Hayward, or The Big
Show (1961) with Esther Williams and Cliff Robertson, the plot of
Broken Lance should seem familiar. They are all the same; only
the settings are different.
        Cattle baron Matt Devereaux (Tracy) is a tough, stern old
codger who brooks no obstacle and refuses to owe anyone a favor.
He bullies his sons into submission and treats them as common
ranch hands. When a local copper works pollutes the water on the
Devereaux spread, Matt arranges a raid on the works. When he
realizes he will have to face up to the consequences of this illegal
activity, he subdivides his ranch among his sons. Son Joe (Wagner)
who, despite everything, admires his dad, accepts responsibility for
the misdeed and as a result is sent to jail for three years. Thereafter, the remaining three sons (Widmark, O'Brian, Holliman) revolt against Matt, and he buckles under the strain and dies of a
stroke. When Joe is released from jail he seeks revenge on his
brothers, but his mother (Jurado) convinces him otherwise. But
Ben (Widmark) eggs Joe into a fight in which Ben is killed. Joe
then gains control of the ranch.
        Newsweek reported of this big-budgeted feature, "Despite
a quantity of horse-opera cliche and distractingly handsome scenery,
the focus is made clear and sometimes intense by a couple of
eminently competent craftsmen, Spencer Tracy and Richard Widmark."

BRONCO BILLY AND THE BABY   (1908)   one reel

Based on the story by Peter B. Kyne; with: G. M. ("Bronco
Billy") Anderson.

There has been a great deal of controversy as to which film
was actually the first in G. M. Anderson's Bronco Billy series,
and thus the first series Western.   The late star always said Bronco
Billy and the Baby was the first, although his initial Western movies,
like The Bandit Makes Good (1908) were not Bronco Billy films.
Bronco Billy and the Baby is very representative of the early
films in that series, which amounted to some 376 short films in a
seven-year period, making G. M. Anderson the screen's first continually successful Western player, despite competition from Harry
Carey, and later, William S. Hart.   For in these early one- and
later two-reelers Anderson exemplified all the traits of an oater
hero, the good-bad man, an individual to be both respected and
somewhat feared.   Although the individual films had no continuing
theme, except the character of Bronco Billy, they were exceedingly
popular and made producer-actor Anderson of the cinema's first
big names.
Bronco Billy and the Baby was adapted from a Peter B. Kyne
story and the author later requested that he be paid for such adaptations, especially since he liked the way Anderson treated his work.
Filmed at Golden, Colorado, the simple plot had Bronco Billy
(Anderson) an outlaw, giving up his freedom to help a lost child and
ultimately being reformed by love.   Anderson took the lead in the
series because he could find no one else to do so.   The film cost
less than $1,000 to produce and grossed over $50,000 on its states
rights market release.   The film was re-issued and copyrighted by
Essanay (in which Anderson was part owner) in 1915.
The Peter Kyne story would later be revamped and expanded,
serving as the basis for several productions of The Three Outlaws
[q.v.].

BUFFALO BILL   (Twentieth Century-Fox, 1944)   C   90 min.

Producer, Harry Sherman; director, William A. Wellman;
based on the story by Frank Winch; screenplay, Aeneas MacKenzie,
Clements Ripley, Cecile Kramer; music, David Buttolph; art di-
rectors, James Basevi, Lewis Creber; special effects, Fred Sersen;
camera, Leon Shamroy; editor, James B. Clark.
Joel McCrea (Buffalo Bill); Maureen O'Hara (Louise Cody);
Linda Darnell (Dawn Starlight); Thomas Mitchell (Ned Buntline);
Edgar Buchanan (Sergeant Chips); Anthony Quinn (Yellow Hand)
Moroni Olsen (Senator Frederici); Frank Fenton (Murdo Carvell);
Matt Briggs (General Blazier); George Lessey (Mr. Vandevere);
Frank Orth (Sherman); George Chandler (Trooper Clancy); Chief
Many Treaties (Tall Bull); Chief Thundercloud (Crazy Horse); Sidney
Blackmer (President Theodore Roosevelt); Evelyn Beresford (Queen
Victoria); Cecil Weston (Maid); Vincent Graeff (Crippled Boy); Fred

Maureen O'Hara, Edwin Stanley, Joel McCrea, Cecil Weston and
George Lessey in Buffalo Bill (1944).

Graham (Editor); Harry Tyler, Arthur Loft, Syd Saylor (Barkers);
Robert Homans (Muldoon, the Policeman); Cordell Hickman, Gerald
Mackey, Eddie Nichols. Fred Chapman, George Nokes (Boys); John
Reese (Tough Guy); John Dilson (President Hayes); Edwin Stanley
(Doctor); Tatzumbia Dupea (Old Indian Woman); Margaret Martin
(Indian Servant); George Bronson (Strong Man).

     Astute director William A. Wellman was so eager to direct
the film version of The Ox-Bow Incident (1943) [q. v.] that he agreed
to direct two other film projects at Twentieth Century-Fox sight un-
seen. The first such movie was Thunder Birds (1942), the second,
Buffalo Bill. Even years later, when he composed his autobiography,
A Short Time for Insanity (1974), he was still embarrassed by the
feature and refused to mention it per se in his narrative.
     Actually, Buffalo Bill is one of the lesser Westerns to be
helmed by Wellman, a sentimental biography of William F. "Buffalo
Bill" Cody (1846-1917). What emerged was a stereotyped portrait
of the man with long hair who wore buckskins. Joel McCrea was
more than competent as Cody, as the movie traced his career from
cavalry scout to his meetings with Cheyenne warriors, his courtship with an Eastern girl (O'Hara) who later becomes Mrs. Cody,
his battle to the death with Yellow Hand (Quinn), his dislike of
Washington politicians and his most famous role, that of an arena

showman and the owner of the exciting and authentic wild west show at the turn-of-the-century.

Not to be overlooked in this somewhat conventional drama (at least by Wellman standards) is the fine supporting cast which included Linda Darnell as the attractive Indian maiden Dawn Starlight, Thomas Mitchell as Ned Buntline, Sidney Blacker as rough-and-ready President Theodore Roosevelt, and Chief Thundercloud as the Indian leader Crazy Horse. The big highlight of this relatively slow-moving entry was a finely-accomplished river battle between cavalrymen and Indians.

In succeeding years, there would be other screen biographies of Buffalo Bill. For example, in 1964 Gordon Scott played Cody in Buffalo Bill, Hero of the Far West (Das War Buffalo Bill) a European co-production which is often presented on TV as Buffalo Bill, causing confusion with the Wellman film. In mid-1976, Paul Newman would star in the movie Buffalo Bill and the Indians or Sitting Bull's History Lesson, directed and produced by Robert Altman and suggested by the Arthur Kopit play, Indians.

BUFFALO BILL, HERO OF THE FAR WEST   see   BUFFALO BILL

BUFFALO STAMPEDE   see   THE THUNDERING HERD

BULLET AND THE FLESH   see   DIE LETZEN ZWEI VOM RIO BRAVO

BULLETS DON'T ARGUE   see   DIE LETZEN ZWEI VOM RIO BRAVO

IL BUONO, IL BRUTTO, IL CATTIVO (THE GOOD, THE BAD AND THE UGLY) (United Artists, 1968) C 161 min.

Producer, Alberto Grimaldi; director, Sergio Leone; story, Age Scarpelli, Luciano Vincenzoni, Leone; screenplay, Vincenzoni, Leone; music, Ennio Morricone; music director, Bruno Nicolai; costumes, Carlo Sini; special effects, Eros Bacciucchi; camera, Tonio Delli Colli; editors, Nino Baragli, Eugenio Alabiso.

Clint Eastwood (Joe); Eli Wallach (Tuco); Lee Van Cleef (Setenza); and: Aldo Giuffre, Mario Brega, Rada Rassimov, Claudio Scarchilli, Livio Lorenzon, Sandro Scarchelli, Benito Stefanelli, Chelo Alonso, Luigi Pistilli, Enzo Petito, Al Mulloch, Antonio Casale, Angelo Novi, Silvana Bacci.

The New York Times blasted this moneymaker (it grossed over $10 million in its U.S. and Italian releases alone): "Zane Grey meets the Marquis de Sade.... [It] must be the most expensive, pious and repellent movie in the history of its peculiar genre."

Eli Wallach in Il Buono, Il Brutto, Il Cattivo (1966).

In the southwest of the Civil War era, $200,000 is stolen
and hidden in an unmarked grave. Joe (Eastwood), a questionable
character, joins forces with Mexican bandit Tuco (Wallach). Their
scheme is to have Joe turn Tuco over to one sheriff after another,
collect the reward money, and then arrange for Tuco's escape.
(This gimmick would be used in James Garner's The Skin Game,
1971.) When this plan almost fails on one occasion, Tuco determines to be disloyal to Joe. Tuco hires three men to kill Joe, but
the latter kills his adversaries. Tuco then proceeds to recapture
Joe and torture him. When Joe tells his captor of the $200,000
cache, Tuco has a change of heart, or so it seems. Meanwhile
the cruel Setenza (Van Cleef) is also seeking the loot. Tuco's and
Joe's paths cross with Setenza's, and the latter almost brings about
their downfall. Eventually each of the three opportunists heads on
his own to the graveyard treasure trove. In the climactic showdown,
Joe kills Setenza but leaves Tuco alive (he mockingly pretends to
hang the man). He leaves a share of gold for his one-time companion and then rides away.

Esoteric critics such as Arthur Knight (Saturday Review) refused to judge the film for what it was--grand commercialism for
its own sake, saturated with an overabundance of audience-grabbing
gambits. Instead, he carped, "Crammed with sadism and a dis-
taste for human values that would make the ordinary misanthrope
seem like Pollyanna, their only possible excuse for existence is that
[movies such as this] make money. Somehow, that isn't enough."

With this entry, Sergio Leone and Clint Eastwood completed
their trio of European-lensed "American" Westerns (the other two
were Per Un Pugno Di Dollari, 1964 [q.v.] and Per Qualche Dollaro
in Pie, 1966 [q.v.]). The Good, the Bad and the Ugly, with its
thumping music score by the prolific Ennio Morricone, was the
apogee of the Leone-Eastwood partnership. Thereafter each went
his own way. Leone would return to his beloved genre, as in
Once Upon a Time in the West, 1969 [q.v.] but the same violent
spirit and coolness of manner were missing.

If the syrupy, sterile singing cowboy entries of the thirties
represented one side of Westerns, certainly the Leone-Eastwood association of the sixties was at the opposite pole. The seventies has
yet to produce its distinct format for the ever-popular Western
species.

BUTCH CASSIDY AND THE SUNDANCE KID   (Twentieth Century-Fox,
1969) C   110 min.

Executive producer, Paul Monash; producer, John Foreman;
director, George Roy Hill; screenplay, William Goldman; second
unit director, Michael Moore; music-music conductor, Burt Bacharach; song, Bacharach and Hal David; art directors, Jack Martin
Smith, Philip Jefferies; set decorators, Walter M. Scott and Chester
L. Bayhi; orchestrators, Leo Shuken, Jack Hayes; main titles, Glenn
Advertising; costumes, Edith Head; makeup, Dan Striepeke; assistant
director, Steven Bernhardt; sound, William Edmondson, David E.

Dockendorf; special camera effects, L. B. Abbott, Art Cruickshank; camera, Conrad Hall; second unit camera, Harold E. Wellman; editors, John C. Howard, Richard C. Meyer.

Paul Newman (Butch Cassidy); Robert Redford (The Sundance Kid); Katharine Ross (Etta Place); Strother Martin (Percy Garris); Henry Jones (Bike Salesman); Jeff Corey (Sheriff Bledsoe); George Furth (Woodcock); Cloris Leachman (Agnes); Ted Cassidy (Harvey Logan); Kenneth Mars (Marshal); Donnelly Rhodes (Macon); Jody Gilbert (Large Woman); Timothy Scott (News Carver); Don Keefer (Fireman); Charles Dierkop (Flat Nose Curry); Francisco Cordova (Bank Manager); Nelson Olmstead (Photographer); Paul Bryar (Card Player); Charles Akins (Bank Teller); Eric Sinclair (Tiffany's Salesman); Percy Helton (Sweet Face).

Toward the end of the sixties, especially after the success of Bonnie and Clyde (1966) in the gangster film field, there was a rush of features glorifying outlaws. While most of these romantic fictions tended to be gangster yarns, there were several movies which white-washed Western bad guys and gals, the most popular being Butch Cassidy and the Sundance Kid. This entry grossed nearly $30 million in its U.S. and Canadian release alone.

Highlighted by crisp photography, racy dialogue and tongue-in-cheek performances, the film traces the lives of actual bandits Butch Cassidy (Newman) and The Sundance Kid (Redford) who rob a

Paul Newman, Katharine Ross and Robert Redford in Butch Cassidy and the Sundance Kid (1969).

train and escape from a pursuing posse in 1905. The two take
refuge with Sundance's girl, schoolmarm Etta Place (Ross). The
trio head for New York to enjoy the night life and then to Bolivia,
hoping to avoid the law enforcers put on their trail by the Union
Pacific Railroad. Having been tutored in the patois of the Spaniards
by Etta, the outlaws pull off several successful railroad heists.

Their idyll draws to a close when U.S. law enforcers arrive
in the South American country to track down the wanted men. Etta
has tired of the wild life and returns to the States. The duo decide
to go straight but on their first assignment--as honest-to-goodness
payroll guards--they become involved in a hold-up attempt and have
to kill the would-be robbers. Deciding that fate has determined
their future, they abscond with the payroll funds. At a building
hideout, they are surrounded by Bolivian Army troops. As the two
men seek to break out from their retreat, they are hit by a barrage
of gunfire and....

"In the case of Butch Cassidy and the Sundance Kid, the word
'slick' is applicable in the purely professional sense, on the basis
of its writing, its direction and its performance, and these make it,
in its aftertaste, more than the first-rate 'entertainment' it is in the
watching.... For beyond the literacy and the wit that make the
script sparkle, Mr. Goldman makes the stuff of legend human,
telling the tale of two men who run their crooked route with gusto
and guts and wouldn't take the straight road if they could" (Judith
Crist, New York magazine).

An intriguing analysis of the film was offered by Paul D.
Zimmerman in Newsweek: "The Western, that Hollywood archetype,
has outlived its usefulness as a straight dramatic device in which
good, dressed in white, guns down evil, dressed in black. Instead,
screen-writer William Goldman and director George Roy Hill have
turned out an anti-Western in much the way Arthur Penn treated
Bonnie and Clyde as an anti-gangster movie.... In Butch Cassidy
and the Sundance Kid, the railroads [are] the villainous symbols of
an increasingly impersonal, industralized and mercantile society.
It is 1898; the century and frontier life are both ending, but Butch
Cassidy and the Sundance Kid refuse to surrender to this changing
America, holding up trains and banks as though the sheriff and the
local posse were their only adversaries. Paul Newman as Butch, a
man chasing a vision of total freedom, and Robert Redford as the
Sundance Kid, a professional triggerman as out-of-date as a samurai
warrior, play their doomed roles with all the charm of children
dancing in a setting sun."

Another interesting diversion provided by the film was its
theme song, "Raindrops Keep Falling on My Head," which won an
Academy Award and made the composers a small fortune.

A further legacy of Butch Cassidy was the commercial resurgence of motion pictures about male camaraderie, taking off
from where the trio-of-pals in the thirties and forties' Westerns
had left off. Newman and Redford, as the closest of friends who
enjoy their joint adventures more than associating with others, would
continue onward in the mold with the even more commercial The
Sting (1973), a shaggy dog tale of twenties' gangsterism.

In 1974, ABC-TV would produce a telefeature entitled Mrs. Sundance [q.v.], with Elizabeth Montgomery as the wife of you-know-who.

CANYON PASSAGE   (Universal, 1946)   C   99 min.

Producer, Walter Wanger; associate producer, Alexander Golitzen; director, Jacques Tourneur; based on the story by Ernest Haycox; screenplay, Ernest Pascal; Technicolor consultants, Natalie Kalmus, William Ritzche; art directors, John Goodman, Richard H. Riedel; set decorators, Russell A. Gausman, Leigh Smith; music director, Frank Skinner; song, Hoagy Carmichael and Jack Brooks; dialog director, Anthony Jowitt; assistant director, Fred Frank; sound, Bernard Brown; special camera, D. S. Horsley; camera, Edward Cronjager; editor, Milton Carruth.

Dana Andrews (Logan Stuart); Brian Donlevy (George Camrose); Susan Hayward (Lucy Overmire); Patricia Roc (Caroline Dance Marsh); Hoagy Carmichael (Hi Linnet); Ward Bond (Honey Bragg); Andy Devine (Ben Dance); Stanley Ridges (Jonas Overmire); Lloyd Bridges (Johnny Steele); Fay Holden (Mrs. Overmire); Victor Cutler (Vane Blazier); Tad Devine (Asa Dance); Denny Devine (Bushrod Dance); Onslow Stevens (Lestrade); Rose Hobart (Marta Lestrade);

Dana Andrews and Susan Hayward in Canyon Passage (1946).

Dorothy Peterson (Mrs. Dance); Halliwell Hobbes (Clenchfield);
James Cardwell (Gray Bartlett); Ray Teal (Neil Howison); Virginia
Patton (Liza Stone); Francis McDonald (Cobb); Erville Alderson
(Judge); Ralph Peters (Stutchell); Jack Rockwell (Teamster); Joseph
P. Mack, Gene Stutenroth, Karl Hackett, Jack Clifford, Daral
Hudson, Dick Alexander (Miners); Wallace Scott (MacIvar); Chief
Yowlachie (Indian Spokesman); Peter Whitney (Van Houten); Harry
Shannon (McLane); Chester Clute (Proprietor); Frank Ferguson
(Minister); Eddie Dunn (Mormon); John Berkes (Man in Hallway);
Harlan Briggs (Dr. Balance); Will Kaufman, Rex Lease (Players);
Casey McGregor, Frank Arnold (Poker Players); Sherry Hall
(Clerk); Jack Ingram (Pack Train Leader); David Blair (Boy).

Producer Walter Wanger and Universal threw budgetary
caution to the wind for this horse opera which was expertly directed by Jacques Tourneur and heightened by the use of Technicolor. The end result was a "whopping Western show" with "a
lot of good old-fashioned thrills" (New York Times).
Set in 1856, the plot relates the lives of a number of people
in the wild Oregon country. Logan Stuart (Andrews) is the owner
of a general store and a mule freight service; George Camrose
(Donlevy) is a banker who gets into hot water by losing his deposi-
tors' gold in poker games. Lucy Overmire (Hayward) and Caroline
Dance Marsh (Roc) provide the requisite balance of female pulchri-
tude. Also there is Honey Bragg (Bond), a tough and mean outlaw;
wandering minstrel Hi Linnet (Carmichael), and gravel-voiced, ro-
tund Ben Dance (Devine) for comic relief. (Actor Devine's two sons,
Tad and Dennis also had comedy relief roles in this film.) Among
the numerous sub-plots are the love rivalry between pals Stuart
and Camrose over Lucy, Stuart's bloody brawl with Honey, an
Indian attack, and a well-staged cabin-raising ceremony for newlyweds. The Hoagy Carmichael-Jack Brooks song, "Ole Buttermilk
Sky," which was featured in the movie, was Oscar-nominated.
It was no coincidence that this film bore a striking resemblance to Stagecoach (United Artists, 1939) [q.v.]. The latter was
also based on a Haycox story, was also produced by Wanger, and
also featured Andy Devine (there as a stagecoach driver).
As Doug McClelland wrote of this underrated feature in The
Complete Life Story of Susan Hayward (1975), "It has aged well.
Today when seen on television and compared, especially to that
medium's studio-bound, claustrophobic, "Gunsmoke"-type Westerns
telling their tales mostly via close-ups, the scope and wide open
spaces of this unpolluted Passage look even more inviting than on
initial release."

THE CASTAWAY COWBOY (Buena Vista, 1974) C 97 min.

Producers, Ron Miller, Winston Hibler; associate producer,
Christopher Hibler; director, Vincent McEveety; story, Don Tait,
Richard Bluel, Hugh Benson; screenplay, Tait; art director, John
B. Mansbridge; production designer, Robert Chatworthy; assistant

director, Dick Caffey; music, Robert F. Brunner; sound, Herb
Taylor, Frank Regula; camera, Andrew Jackson; editor, Cotton
Warburton.

James Garner (Lincoln Costain); Vera Miles (Henrietta Mac-
Avoy); Robert Culp (Bryson); Eric Shea (Booton MacAvoy); Elizabeth
Smith (Liliha); Manu Tupou (Kimo); Gregory Sierra (Marrujo); Shug
Fisher (Captain Cary); Nephi Hannemann (Malakoma); and: Lito
Capina, Ralph Hanalei, Kahana, Lee Woodd, Luis Delgado, Buddy
Joe Hooker, Patrick Sullivan Burke.

The power and effect of Walt Disney Productions should never
be underestimated, even in the seemingly alien field of Westerns.
That studio always organizes its live-action products in such a way
that they will be of general interest to the widest possible family-
oriented audience.   And film audiences can rest assured that, like
the other products of Buena Vista, the film will be reissued over
and over again in years to come.   Amazingly, no matter how
childish or prefabricated some of the Disney products of recent
vintage may appear to jaded moviegoers, they always manage to
earn tremendous rentals at the box-office.

The Castaway Cowboy is no exception.   The wild plotline
finds Texas cowpoke Lincoln Costain (Garner) escaping from the
ship on which he had been shanghaied and landing on Kauai in the
Hawaiian Islands.   There he is "adopted" by a twelve-year old
(Shen) and his widowed mother (Miles).   It is not long before Lincoln is hired by Mrs. MacAvoy (Miles) to turn her wasting potato
spread--the workers would rather play on the beach--into a thriving
cattle ranch.   Having the time frame placed in the 1850s gives this
fantasy story more of a credible story book approach.

To add some punch to the proceedings there is Robert Culp
as the hissable Banker Bryson who holds a mortgage on Mrs.
MacAvoy's ranch.   He is willing to forget the deed if she will become his wife, a situation Lincoln Costain will not allow to happen.

A pacified New York Times reported, "The picture has genuine
charm and sturdiness in the scenes of the natives becoming cowboys,
learning to lasso and punch wild steers.   For stand-bys, there are
several good old cattle stampedes ... it's hard to resist the sight
of Tex Garner, Master Shea and those happy island buckaroos singing
'Come-a-Ki-Yi-Yippy" as they hit the Hawaii trail."

CAT BALLOU (Columbia, 1965) C 96 min.

Producer, Harold Hecht; associate producer, Mitch Lindemann; director, Elliott Silverstein; based on the novel by Roy
Chanslor; screenplay, Walter Newman, Frank R. Pierson; art director, Malcolm Brown; music, De Vol; songs, Mac David and
Jerry Livingston; camera, Jack Marta; editor, Charles Nelson.

Jane Fonda (Cat Ballou); Lee Marvin (Kid Shelleen/Tim
Strawn); Michael Callan (Clay Boone); Dwayne Hickman (Jed); Nat
King Cole (Shouter); Stubby Kaye (Another Shouter); Tom Nardini
(Jackson Two-Bears); John Marley (Frankie Ballou); Reginald Denny

Lee Marvin in his dual role for Cat Ballou (1965).

(Sir Harry Percival); Jay C. Flippen (Sheriff Cardigan); Arthur Hun-
nicutt (Butch Cassidy); Bruce Cabot (Sheriff Maledon); Burt Mustin
(Accuser); Charles Wagenheim (James); Robert Phillips (Klem); Duke
Hobbie (Homer); Gail Bonney (Mabel Bentley); Harry Harvey, Sr.
(Train Conductor); Dorothy Claire (Singing Tart); Charles Horvath
(Hardcase); Chuck Roberson (Armed Guard); Ivan Middleton (Train
Fireman); Carol Veazie (Mrs. Parker); Nick Cravat (Ad Libber);
Hallene Hill (Honey Girl).

    Originally made as a straightforward Western, Cat Ballou
proved to be a dull effort. In desperation, the producers instilled
a tongue-in-cheek tone into the production. By accident the result
was a mild spoof of the genre, which emerged more popular than
funny, mainly due to Lee Marvin's dual role performance which
garnered him an Academy Award. Directed by Elliott Silverstein
with excellent second unit work by Yakima Canutt, the motion picture
grossed nearly $7 million in U.S. and Canadian rentals alone.
    Told almost entirely in flashback, the picture opens with
pretty young schoolmarm Cat Ballou (Fonda) about to be hung. She
recounts the story--with the aid of Nat "King" Cole and Stubby Kaye
as troubadours who sing along the song of "Cat Ballou," which
loosely holds together the slapstick episodes within the feature.
    The flashback tells of Cat coming West from finishing school

and helping Jed (Hickman) aid Clay Boone (Callan) in escaping from
Sheriff Maledon (Cabot). At home she finds that crooked investors
are anxious to control her father's (Marley) water rights and to accomplish their evil deed have hired a gunfighter, Tim Strawn
(Marvin). Jed and Clay join Cat in aiding her father and to further
their cause she writes a note of plea to pulp hero Kid Shellen
(Marvin) who turns out to be a useless drunk. Later on, Strawn
kills Frankie Ballou (Marley). In revenge, Cat and her pals plan
a train robbery. At a still later point, the angered Cat confronts
the chief of the swindlers, one Sir Harry Percival (Denny) and she
accidentally shoots him in his bath. Meanwhile a sobered Shelleen
kills Strawn. On the way to meet her destiny, Cat is rescued by
her friends.

     Time magazine said: "As honest-to-gosh Westerns go, Cat
Ballou is disgraceful. As a shibboleth-shattering spoof, it dumps
all the heroic traditions of horse opera into a gag bag, shakes
thoroughly and pulls out one of the year's jolliest surprises. What's
good about the comedy is nigh irresistible." Films in Review, on
the other hand, offered a more sober appraisal: "Had Cat Ballou
been written and directed by lighter hands it could have been quite
amusing."

     One of the legacies of this slap-dash feature was the
emergence of Lee Marvin as a mugging leading man instead of a
cinema heavy. It took nearly a decade for his star to set yet
again.

     Even more so than the superior Blazing Saddles (1974), this
lampoon of the Western seems destined for obscurity. Already, by
1970s' standards, it seems an outmoded vehicle when it shows up
on TV. (A project pilot for a video series based on the property
never sold. Starring Forrest Tucker and Jack Elam, it was tele-
cast over ABC-TV on September 5, 1971.)

C'ERA UNA VOLTA IL WEST (ONCE UPON A TIME IN THE WEST)
(Paramount, 1969) C 166 min.

     Executive producer, Bino Cicogna; producer, Fulvio Mor-
sella; director, Sergio Leone; story, Dario Argento, Bernardo Ber-
tolucci, Leone; screenplay, Leone, Sergio Donati; music-music director, Ennio Morricone; art director-costumes, Carlo Simi; set
decorator, Carlo Leva; makeup, Alberto De Rossi; assistant director,
Giancarlo Santi; sound, Claudio Maielli; camera, Tonino Delli Colli;
editor, Nino Baragli.

     Henry Fonda (Frank); Claudia Cardinale (Jill McBain); Jason
Robards (Cheyenne); Charles Bronson (Harmonica--the Man); Frank
Wolff (Brett McBain); Gabriele Ferzetti (Morton); Keenan Wynn
(Sheriff); Paolo Stoppa (Sam); Marco Zuanelli (Wobbles); Lionel
Stander (Barman); Jack Elam (Knuckles); John Frederick (Member
of Frank's Gang); Woody Strode (Stony); Enzio Santianello (Timmy);
Dino Mele (Harmonica--as a Boy); and: Benito Stefanelli, Salvo
Basile, Aldo Berti, Luigi Ciavarro, Marco Zuanelli, Marilu Cart-
ney, Spartaco Conversi, Livio Andronico.

Following the immensely popular trio of Westerns that director Sergio Leone made in Italy with Clint Eastwood (A Fistful of
Dollars, For a Few Dollars More, and The Good, the Bad and the
Ugly [all q.v.]), Paramount agreed to finance Leone's ultimate
genre entry: C'era Una Volta Il West. He co-wrote and directed
this vehicle on location in Spain and in Monument Valley Utah, with
interiors shot at the Cinecitta Studios in Rome. Leone constructed
an entire Western set at Guadix, Spain, at a cost of $250,000, and
an authentic 1870s locomotive was used in the action.

A tribute to the Western format and to various genre directors, the picture relates the story of Brett McBain (Wolff) who
lives on a ranch with his three motherless children, and of how the
railroad wants to buy his land, promising him enough money to make
him rich. He also awaits the arrival of his new bride Jill (Cardinale), whom he married in New Orleans. A railroad executive
(Ferzetti) and a vengeful gunslinger named Frank (Fonda) plan to
take McBain's land for themselves. Jill arrives on a train which
brings a harmonica-playing stranger (Bronson) who is searching for
Frank. Meanwhile Frank and his men murder McBain and his
family and put the blame on half-breed Cheyenne (Robards). Jill
arrives in time for the funeral and then searches the ranch, in
vain, for the alleged hidden gold. Frank plans to take over the
ranch and therefore decides to kill Jill. But Cheyenne and Harmonica stop him, taking a horrible revenge on the gunman. Before
Frank dies, Harmonica relates how, as a boy, he had been forced
to play the harmonica while Frank and his men tortured the boy's
brother and hung him. Left alone at the ranch, Jill offers water to
the work crew who are now helping to construct a new railroad.

It is interesting to note that Sergio Leone cast both Fonda
and Bronson against the grain of their usual celluloid portrayals.
Each actor enjoyed the change of pace, but apparently the U.S. public did not. The expansive, meticulously-conceived Western grossed
only a bare $1 million in the U.S. (It did far better in Europe.)

Some critics tried very hard to find positive factors in this
slow-moving, lengthy production. "The irresistible thing about
Leone is that his affection for both Westerns and moviemaking is
unbounded. He goes for large pictorial compositions and operatic
effects at a time when most films are modestly or forlornly shrinking
to a size suitable television.... The story itself is rather spare
and predictable; what turns it into an epic is Leone's peculiar talent
for embellishment. This movie has the longest prelude with a brilliant piece of business between Jack Elam and a fly and the longest
coda I've seen; in between it's full of grand ominous entrances and
exits, buildups and showdowns" (Washington Post).

On the other hand Time tersely summed up the vehicle as
"Tedium in the tumbleweed." New Republic was more intellectually
analytical, "The Hollywood Western, as a genre, is a realm of
fantasy. Once Upon a Time in the West is, in its pseudo-realistic
way, a fantasy superimposed on that general fantasy."

No matter how much one may approve of its detailed reconstruction of the old West, this film is not the ultimate Western and
one hopes it will not be the final entry in this genre by the brilliant
Leone.

CHEYENNE AUTUMN (Warner Bros., 1964) C 159 min.

Producer, Bernard Smith; director, John Ford; based on the book by Mari Sandoz; screenplay, James R. Webb; music, Alex North; art director, Richard Day; set decorator, Darrell Silvera; associate director, Ray Kellogg; assistant directors, Wingate Smith, Russ Saunders; second unit director, Kellogg; camera, William Clothier; editor, Otho Lovering.

Richard Widmark (Captain Thomas Archer); Carroll Baker (Deborah Wright); James Stewart (Wyatt Earp); Edward G. Robinson (Secretary of the Interior Carl Schurz); Karl Malden (Captain Wessels); Sal Mineo (Red Shirt); Dolores Del Rio (Spanish Woman); Ricardo Montalban (Little Wolf); Gilbert Roland (Dull Knife); Arthur Kennedy (Doc Holliday); Patrick Wayne (Second Lieutenant Scott); Elizabeth Allen (Guinevere Plantagenet); John Carradine (Major Jeff Blair); Victor Jory (Tall Tree); Mike Mazurki (Top Sergeant Stanislas Wichowsky); George O'Brien (Major Branden); Sean McClory (Dr. O'Carberry); Judson Pratt (Mayor "Dog" Kelly); Carmen D'Antonio (Pawnee Woman); Ken Curtis (Joe); Walter Baldwin (Jeremy Wright); Shug Fisher (Skinny); Nancy Hsueh (Little Bird); Chuck Roberson (Platoon Sergeant); Harry Carey, Jr. (Trooper Smith); Ben Johnson (Trooper Plumtree); Jimmy O'Hara, Dan Borzage, Bing Russell, Chuck Hayward (Troopers); Lee Bradley, Frank Bradley (Cheyennes); Walter Reed (Lieutenant Peterson); Denver Pyle (Senator Henry); John Qualen (Svenson); Nanomba "Moonbeam" Morton (Running Deer);

John Carradine, Judson Pratt, James Stewart and Arthur Kennedy in Cheyenne Autumn (1964).

This very long (159 minutes) and diverting film, John Ford's last epic Western, is a harsh condemnation of the American genocide of the Indian nations. A motion picture with such a mighty theme should have been far more striking and entertaining; only occasionally here does the brilliance of the typical Ford style show through the elongated proceedings.

Badly cut before its release, the film told the touching and true account of the 1,800-mile flight of 286 Cheyenne Indians from an Oklahoma reservation to their native Yellowstone land. Along the way they are dogged by the Army, white civilians, death, and superstitions.

Filmed at Monument Valley, Utah, and at Garrison, Colorado, the project was quite empty from the point of view of its plot, but did benefit from vivid performances. Even so, there were some players, such as Karl Malden (as Captain Wessels), who badly overacted. In addition such extraneous sequences as the one in Dodge City--played for comedy--were totally out of context. It did not take a seasoned filmgoer to realize that Carroll Baker as Deborah Wright was hardly the missionary type. On the plus side, there were respectable characterizations by such veterans as Dolores Del Rio (as the Spanish woman) and a memorable cameo by Mike Mazurki as a cavalry officer. Ex-wrestler Mazurki gave a poignant performance as the aging soldier, a part that would have been handled by Victor McLaglen if the Ford film had been made two decades before.

J. A. Place in The Western Films of John Ford (1973) suggests, "In the book from which the story and title of the film were taken, the Indians' point of view is taken throughout, and the few white characters do not stand out as individuals. Ford makes no attempt to bring this point of view to the screen, seemingly acknowledging that, as a white man, he should not presume to work from an Indian sensibility. The Indians in Cheyenne Autumn are much like the Indians of his earlier films in that they stand for something rather than being people in their own right. None, not even Spanish Woman and her son Red Shirt [Sal Mineo], are really explored on the screen to the extent that we know what makes them different from any other members of the tribe."

Summing up the critical and public appraisal of the film, Arthur B. Clarke wrote in Films in Review, "... except for two scenes [Monument Valley scenery and the Dodge City sequence] ... I don't think anyone would recognize the directorial hand of John Ford in Cheyenne Autumn." This film, as Clarke notes, is a sad testimony to the passing talent of Ford, one of the bastions of the Western film genre. Films in the late sixties and thereafter would follow a different course in portraying the old West, seeking new gimmicks to induce people away from their homes and out to the movies. Heroics as depicted in "Fordian" studies of the frontier would be considered passé by the new breed of filmmakers. Instead, heavy violence, ultra realism, and very adult themes would be the new keystones of cowboy films.

THE CHEYENNE SOCIAL CLUB see STRANGER ON THE RUN

CHIEF CRAZY HORSE (Universal, 1955) C 86 min.

Producer, William Alland; co-producer, Leonard Goldstein; director, George Sherman; story, Gerald Drayson Adams; screenplay, Adams, Franklin Coen; art directors, Alexander Golitzen, Robert Boyle; music director, Joseph Gershenson; music, Frank Skinner; costumes, Rosemary Odell; assistant directors, Marsh Green, Phil Bowles, Dick Evans; camera, Harold Lipstein; editor, Al Clark.

Victor Mature (Crazy Horse); Suzan Ball (Black Shawl); John Lund (Major Twist); Ray Danton (Little Big Man); Keith Larsen (Flying Hawk); James Millican (General Crook); David Janssen (Lieutenant Cartwright); Robert Warwick (Spotted Tail); Paul Guilfoyle (Worm); Morris Ankrum (Conquering Bear/Red Cloud); Stuart Randall (Old Man Afraid); James Westerfield (Caleb Mantz); Donald Randolph (Aaron Cartwright); Dennis Weaver (Major Carlisle); Robert Simon (Jeff Mantz); John Peters (Sergeant Guthrie);

Filmed in color, this was part of the fifties' continuing series of specious biographies of Indian chiefs. Like most of the others, it was historically inaccurate and relied heavily on widely-held American myths about Indian life for its focal points.

According to a seer, a warrior would come among the Indian tribes and inflict a terrible defeat on the white man. Crazy Horse (Mature) believes he is that leader. He weds Black Shawl (Ball) but they lose their child. There are many skirmishes between the whites and Indians, leading up to the Battle of the Little Big Horn (which gets a rather tame treatment here). At the finish, renegade half-breed Little Big Man (Danton) kills Crazy Horse by stabbing him in the back. As the New York Times viewed it, "A sense of his [Crazy Horse] being a noble redman, which is what this film was meant to convey, depends wholly upon how susceptible one is to the wooden cliche."

The life and times of Chief Crazy Horse had been adapted to the screen on several occasions, with this Indian leader being portrayed by such actors as: Anthony Quinn (They Died with Their Boots On, 1941 [q.v.]) and Iron Eyes Cody (Sitting Bull, 1954 [q.v.]) and The Great Sioux Massacre, 1965). A forthcoming film, Crazy Horse, is being scripted at Twentieth Century-Fox by Oris Carney for producers Frank Yablans and Marty Ransohoff.

CHIP OF THE FLYING U (Selig, 1914) 2 reels

Director, Colin Campbell; story-screenplay, B. M. Bower.
With: Tom Mix (Chip); Wheeler Oakman, Bessie Eyton, Frank Clark, Kathlyn Williams, Fred Huntley.

CHIP OF THE FLYING U (Universal, 1926) 6,596'

Director, Lynn Reynolds; story, B. M. Bower; screenplay, Reynolds, Harry Dittmar; camera, Harry Neumann.

Hoot Gibson (Chip Bennett); Virginia Browne Faire (Dr. Della
Whitmore); Philo McCullough (Duncan Whittaker); Nora Cecil (Dr.
Cecil Grantham); DeWitt Jennings (J. G. Whitmore); Harry Todd
(Weary); Pee Wee Holmes (Shorty); Mark Hamilton (Slim); Willie
Fung (Chinese Cook); Steve Clements (Indian).

CHIP OF THE FLYING U   (Universal, 1939)   55 min.

Director, Ralph Staub; based on the story by B. M. Bower;
screenplay, Larry Rhine, Andrew Bennison; camera, William Sickner.
Johnny Mack Brown (Chip Bennett); Bob Baker (Dusty); Fuzzy
Knight (Weary); Doris Weston (Margaret Whitmore); Forrest Taylor
(J. C. Whitmore); Anthony Warde (Duncan); Karl Hackett (Hennessey);
Henry Hall (Wilson); Claire Whitney (Miss Robinson); Ferris Taylor
(Sheriff); Cecil Kellogg (Red).

Based on B. M. Bower's original story, this plot went
through several reworkings over the years.
It was first utilized in 1914 by Selig as an entry for Tom
Mix.   Colin Campbell, who directed The Spoilers (1914) [q. v.],
one of Tom's best early Westerns helmed this production.   In 1920
the independent company, Canyon Pictures, released its version of
Chip of the Flying U, entitled The Galloping Devil.   (It would be
reissued in 1925 as The Galloping Dude.)
Then in 1926 Lynn Reynolds, who had directed many of Tom
Mix's Fox features, co-wrote and helmed the third version at Universal.   Hoot Gibson now played Chip Bennett, a ranch hand who
falls for a woman doctor (Faire) who is also the owner of the Flying
U ranch.   Chip fakes an accident so that he will come under her
care.   Soon they are in love with one another, and eventually they
wed.   This Western was notable for its lack of violence and its
utilization of intended comedy sequences.
The 1939 version, also produced by Universal, had nothing
to do with the original premise, save for the use of its title.   In
it Johnny Mack Brown played Chip Bennett, the foreman of the
Flying U ranch who is accused of shooting a bank president (Hall)
and robbing his bank.   His new boss (Weston) believes him to be
guilty, but Chip, of course proves otherwise.   He discovers that the
culprits are foreign agents dealing in munitions.

CHISUM   (Warner Bros., 1970)   C   110 min.

Executive producer, Michael A. Wayne; producer, Andrew J.
Fenady; director, Andrew V. McLaglen; screenplay, Fenady; assistant director, Fred R. Simpson; art director, Carl Anderson; set
decorator, Ray Moyer; music Dominic Frontiere; music supervisor,
Sonny Burke; songs, Frontiere and Norman Gimbel, Frontiere and
Fenady; paintings, Russ Vickers; special effects, Howard Jensen;
camera, William H. Clothier; editor, Robert Simpson.

Opposite: John Wayne and Geoffrey Deuel in Chisum (1970).

John Wayne (John Chisum); Forrest Tucker (Lawrence
Murphy); Christopher George (Dan Nodeen); Ben Johnson (James
Pepper); Glenn Corbett (Pat Garrett); Bruce Cabot (Sheriff Brady);
Andrew Prine (Alex McSween); Patric Knowles (J. H. Tunstall);
Richard Jaeckel (Jess Evans); Geoffrey Deuel (Billy "The Kid"
Bonney); Pamela McMyler (Sally Chisum); Lynda Day (Sue McSween);
John Agar (Patton); Lloyd Battista (Neemo); Robert Donner (Morton);
Ray Teal (Justice Wilson); Edward Faulkner (Dolan); Ron Soble
(Bowdre); John Mitchum (Baker); Glenn Langan (Dudley); Alan Bax-
ter (Governor Axtell); Pedro Armendariz, Jr. (Ben); Christopher
Mitchum (O'Folliard); Abraham Sofaer (White Buffalo); Gregg Palmer
(Riker).

Based on historical fact, Chisum offered John Wayne in
another big, colorful Western vehicle. Here he is John Chisum,
the largest ranch owner in the area of Lincoln County, New Mexico
in the late 1870s. He is opposed by newcomer-landgrabber Lawrence
Murphy (Tucker) and his corrupt sheriff-henchman (Cabot). Billy the
Kid (Deuel) joins forces with Chisum to oppose the dishonest Murphy
and the result is the famous Lincoln County cattle wars, with a
final confrontation between Chisum and Murphy that established
Chisum as the victor. Pat Garrett (Corbett) is appointed the new
sheriff. Chisum is again free to control his cattle empire.
    "After the self-assertive aggressiveness of True Grit [1969,
q.v.] John Wayne has clearly decided to take it easy in Chisum.
In a large cast he plays a comparatively subsidiary role; apart from
the final burst of action spends most of the time mouthing somewhat
risible homilies which include oblique references to God. The film,
in fact, is a curious mixture of styles and myths, taking in a portrait of Billy the Kid as a bible-packing, steely killer which makes
an interesting comparison with earlier portrayals like Paul Newman's
in The Left-Handed Gun [1958, q.v.]" (British Monthly Film Bulletin).
    Made on a $4.8 million budget, the picture grossed $6 mil-
lion in distributors' domestic rentals.

CIMARRON   (RKO, 1931)   131 min.

    Producer, William Le Baron; associate producer, Barney
Sarecky; director, Wesley Ruggles; based on the novel by Edna
Ferber; screenplay, Howard Estabrook; assistant directors, Doran
Cox, Dewey Starkey; art director-costumes, Max Ree; sound, Clem
Portman; camera, Edward Cronjager; editor, William Hamilton.
    Richard Dix (Yancey Cravat); Irene Dunne (Sabra Cravat);
Estelle Taylor (Dixie Lee); Nance O'Neil (Felice Venable); William
Collier Jr. (The Kid); Rosco Ates (Jess Rickey); George E. Stone
(Sol Levy); Stanley Fields (Lon Yountis); Robert McWade (Louie
Heffner); Edna May Oliver (Mrs. Tracy Watt); Frank Darien (Mr.
Bixley); Eugene Jackson (Isaiah); Dolores Brown (Ruby Big Elk--
elder); Gloria Vonic (Ruby Big Elk--younger); Otto Hoffman (Murch
Rankin); William Orlamond (Grat Gotch); Frank Beal (Louis Venable);
Nancy Dover (Donna Cravat--younger); Helen Parish (Donna--

youngest); Donald Dillaway (Cim--elder); Junior Johnson (Cim--younger); Douglas Scott (Cim--youngest); Reginald Street (Yancy, Jr.); Lois Jane Campbell (Felice, Jr.); Ann Lee (Aunt Cassandra); Tyrone Bereton (Sabney Venable); Lillian Lane (Cousin Bella); Henry Roquemore (Jonett Goforth); Nell Craig (Arminta Greenwood); Robert McKenzie (Pat Leary); Clara Hunt (Indian Girl); Bob Kortman (Killer); Dennis O'Keefe (Extra); William Janney (Worker).

CIMARRON (MGM, 1961) C 147 min.

Producer, Edmund Grainger; director, Anthony Mann; based on the novel by Edna Ferber; screenplay, Arnold Schulman; music, Franz Waxman; song, Waxman and Paul Francis Webster; art directors, George W. Davis, Addison Hehr; set decorators, Henry Grace, Hugh Hunt, Otto Siegel; assistant director, Ridgeway Callow; makeup, William Tuttle; color consultant, Charles K. Hagedon; costumes, Walter Plunkett; recording supervisor, Franklin Milton; special effects, A. Arnold Gillespie, Lee LeBlanc, Robert R. Hoag; camera, Robert L. Surtees; editor, John Dunning.

Glenn Ford (Yancey Cravat); Maria Schell (Sabra Cravat); Anne Baxter (Dixie Lee); Arthur O'Connell (Tom Wyatt); Russ Tamblyn (The Cherokee Kid); Mercedes McCambridge (Sarah Wyatt); Vic Morrow (Wes); Robert Keith (Sam Pegler); Charles McGraw (Bob Yountis); Henry "Harry" Morgan (Jesse Rickey); David Opatoshu (Sol Levy);

Richard Dix, Douglas Scott and Irene Dunne in Cimarron (1931).

Aline MacMahon (Mrs. Pegler); Lili Darvas (Felicia Venable); Edgar
Buchanan (Neal Hefner); Mary Wickes (Mrs. Hefner); Royal Dano
(Ike Howes); L. Q. Jones (Millis); George Brenlin (Hoss); Vladimir
Sokoloff (Jacob Krubeckoff); Helen Westcott (Schoolteacher); Ivan
Triesault (Lewis Venable); Eddie Little Sky (Ben Red Feathers);
Dawn Little Sky (Arita Red Feather).

Perhaps the most famous western epic of the early sound
era was Cimarron. Adapted from Edna Ferber's novel of 1930, it
was the sweeping story of a young Kansas girl (Dunne) who weds a
wanderer (Dix), he being a poet and a gunfighter. They move to
the Oklahoma Territory and take part in the great land rush of
1889. They settle in Osage where he establishes the local newspaper. However, the spirit of wanderlust reclaims him and he
departs, leaving Sabra (Dunne) to manage the office. In 1911 they
meet again, she being by then a distinguished Congresswoman and
he a dying oil worker.

This sprawling epic earned over $2 million and won three
Academy Awards. Both Dix and Dunne were nominated for their
acting. The film contains a striking Cherokee land strip sequence
that has often been imitated. Popular acceptance of this feature
led other producers to try and duplicate its success, but few succeeded. Of this outdoor epic, the New York Daily News reported,
"Magnificent in scope, powerful in treatment, admirable in action....
It is one of the few talking picture productions which inspires rather
than awes."

On December 1, 1941, Miss Dunne repeated her role for
radio's "The Cavalcade of America."

In the worst of Hollywood's traditions (i.e., reworking a
once commercial property), the remake of Cimarron boasted Cinemascope and color but in no other way was superior to the original.
According to Films in Review, director Anthony Mann and scripter
Arnold Schulman were at fault for "overemphasizing action ... [they]
threw away the chance to dramatize emotion." Paul V. Beckley
(New York Herald-Tribune) analyzed this overblown remake: "Basically, the fault seems to arise from a conflict of viewpoint between
what I can only call the masculine and feminine, for whereas Mann
and the screenwriter dig into the earlier, more violent sequences
with an admirable lustiness, they do not seem to be as sympathetic
with Miss Schell's attitude, and the picture loses its force."

Ironically, in this remake Anne Baxter, as the lusty dancehall girl, Dixie Lee, was the most dynamic personality on camera,
but her scenes were chopped down for the final release print. Evi-
dently MGM felt she was too strong competition for the film's
nominal stars: Glenn Ford (Yancy Cravat) and Maria Schell (Sabra
Cravat).

THE CISCO KID (Fox, 1931) 60 min.

Director, Irving Cummings; based on the story The Caballero's
Way by O. Henry; screenplay, Alfred A. Cohn; sound, George P.

Warner Baxter in The Return of the Cisco Kid (1939).

Costello; camera, Barney McGill; editor, Alex Troffe.

Warner Baxter (The Cisco Kid); Edmund Lowe (Sergeant
Mickey Dunn); Conchita Montenegro (Carmenetta); Nora Lane (Sally
Benton); Frederick Burt (Sheriff Tex Ransom); Willard Robertson
(Enos Hankins); James Bradbury, Jr. (Dixon); Jack Dillon (Bouse);
Charles Stevens (Lopez); Chris-Pin Martin (Gordito); Douglas Haig
(Billy); Marilyn Knowlden (Annie).

Following his winning of an Academy Award for his acting
in Fox's In Old Arizona (1929) [q. v.], Warner Baxter again portrayed The Cisco Kid. Irving Cummings, who co-directed the first
entry, helmed this work and Edmund Lowe repeated his part as
Cisco's enemy.

Set in the West of the 1880s, the feature has The Cisco Kid
(Baxter) coming to the aid of a girl (Lane) who once saved his life.
For her he steals $5,000 from a bank to pay an impending fore-
closure on her ranch. The same amount is placed as a reward for
his arrest. His perennial nemesis (Lowe) vows to win the reward
by capturing The Kid. However, in a happy ending format, when
Sergeant Dunn (Lowe) does corral Cisco he is sympathetic to his
tale of woe and allows The Kid to ride into the sunset across the
border.

The theme song, "My Tonia," of the first film was used again.
Of this follow-up, Mordaunt Hall (New York Times) offered, "It is a
pleasing entertainment with well selected sites, artistic photography
and an efficient cast."

Baxter would play The Cisco Kid yet a third time in The
Return of the Cisco Kid (1939).

CODE OF THE WEST see HOME ON THE RANGE

COLORADO TERRITORY (Warner Bros., 1949) 94 min.

Producer, Anthony Veiller; director, Raoul Walsh; screen-
play, John Twist, Edmund H. North; art director, Ted Smith; dia-
logue director, Eugene Busch; makeup, Perc Westmore; music,
David Buttolph; orchestrator, Maurice de Packh; assistant director,
Russell Saunders; sound, Leslie G. Hewitt; special effects, H. F.
Koenekamp; camera, Sid Hickox; editor, Owen Marks.

Joel McCrea (Wes McQueen); Virginia Mayo (Colorado Car-
son); Dorothy Malone (Julie Ann); Henry Hull (Winslow); John Archer
(Reno Blake); James Mitchell (Duke Harris); Morris Ankrum (U.S.
Marshal); Basi Ruysdael (Dave Rickard); Frank Puglia (Brother
Thomas); Ian Wolfe (Wallace); Harry Woods (Pluthner); Houseley
Stevenson (Prospector); Victor Kilian (Sheriff); Oliver Blake (Station
Agent).

In the same year that director Raoul Walsh made the classic
White Heat (1949) at Warner Bros., he turned out Colorado Territory. It was a reworking of his earlier success, High Sierra (1941),
that had starred Humphrey Bogart and Ida Lupino.

Henry Hull, Virginia Mayo and Joel McCrea in Colorado Territory
(1949).

Bandit Wes McQueen (McCrea) is sprung from jail by his
gang. He soon meets a nice girl (Malone) and decides to plan one
last job, a train robbery, in order to insure their future. He discovers, however, that the girl has betrayed him and the train is
full of lawmen. He and his faithful half-breed companion (Mayo)
head to the hills where he dies on a high ledge of a canyon wall.
The posse had all too successfully stalked its victim.

The New York Times labeled it "a hard-riding, ya-hoo
Western" while William K. Everson evaluated it in A Pictorial

History of the Western Film (1969) as "an excellent and underrated
western ... its tragic ending dovetailing neatly into the fashionable
defeatism that marked so many psychological melodramas of the
late forties."

Ever-practical Warner Bros. would reuse the plot a third
time in 1955 for I Died a Thousand Times, this time as a reshooting of the gangster version, High Sierra.

THE COMANCHEROS (Twentieth Century-Fox, 1961) C 107 min.

Producer, George Sherman; director, Michael Curtiz; based
on the novel by Paul I. Wellman; screenplay, James Edward Grant,
Clair Huffaker; action sequences director, Cliff Lyons; art directors,
Jack Martin Smith, Alfred Ybarra; set decorators, Walter M. Scott,
Robert Priestly; costumes, Marjorie Best; music, Elmer Bern-
stein; orchestrators, Leo Shuken, Jack Hayes; assistant director,
Jack R. Berne; sound, Alfred Bruzlin, Sarren DeLaplain; camera,
William H. Clothier; editor, Louis Loeffler.

John Wayne (Jake Cutter); Stuart Whitman (Paul Regret); Ina
Balin (Pilar); Nehemiah Persoff (Graile); Lee Marvin (Crow); Michael
Ansara (Amelung); Pat Wayne (Tobe); Bruce Cabot (Major Henry);

Ina Balin and Stuart Whitman in The Comancheros (1961).

Joan O'Brien (Melinda); Edgar Buchanan (Judge Bean); Guinn "Big
Boy" Williams (Ed McBain); Jack Elam (Horseface); Henry Daniell
(Gireaux); Richard Devon (Estevan); Steve Baylor (Comanchero);
John Dierkes (Bill); Roger Mobley (Bub Schofield); Bob Steele (Pa
Schofield); Aissa Wayne (Bessie); Tom Hennessy (Graile's Body-
guard); Jackie Cubat, Leigh Snowden (Hotel Girls); Luisa Triana
(Spanish Dancer); Iphigenie Castiglioni (Josefina); George Lewis
(Iron Shirt).

     For this film John Wayne was in his tongue-in-cheek period
and played the role for "horse laughs." The results were both
professionally pleasing and great fun for the legion of Wayne fans.
     Texas Ranger Cutter (Wayne) in 1843 arrests gambler Paul
Regret (Whitman) in Galveston and rides with him for Louisiana
where the prisoner is wanted for killing another gambler in a gun
duel. Along the way, Regret makes his escape. Jake heads for
the Rangers' office, where he is told to impersonate a gun smug-
gler to find out where the Comancheros have their stronghold.
The outlaws are a gang of white renegades. Soon thereafter Jake
re-encounters Regret and takes him into custody. The duo reach
the Comancheros' headquarters where Paul renews his acquaintance
with Pilar (Balin), a girl of questionalbe reputation from Galveston.
It develops that Pilar's dad, Graile (Persoff), is the head of the
Comancheros. She decides to team up with Paul and Jake against
him. Just as it seems that the Comancheros will overwhelm Cutter
and the others, the Texas Rangers ride into view. Having con-
quered their prey, the Rangers ride off. Cutter says goodbye to
Regret and Pilar, and he trails off into the distance.
     Wayne and Whitman were especially strong in the leads in
this vivid shoot-'em-up and Bob Steele and Guinn "Big Boy" Williams
added delightful cameos (Steele as the harried rancher about to become a father again, and Williams as a rather dim-witted gun runner
who is jailed and does not know why).
     Time took this occasion to offer an essay on living legend
John Wayne: "In 35 years Wayne's 155 movies have grossed $300
million and his broad, dull, pleasant, Hereford face has become as
much a part of the western scene as the Petrified Forest. But at
54, Big John is getting a bit long in the tooth and short in the wind
for all this biffbang and muscling around. In Comancheros the
camera discreetly looks the other way whenever he tries to haul
himself up the side of a horse. The day is plainly not far off when
Wayne will have to trade that palomino for a sensible buckboard...."
(Not untypically for both parties, Time has been proven wrong in the
case of Wayne.)

THE CONQUERORS (RKO, 1932) 88 min.

     Executive producer, David O. Selznick; director, William A.
Wellman; based on the story by Howard Estabrook; screenplay,
Robert Lord; music director, Max Steiner; makeup, Ern Westmore;
assistant directors, D. M. Zimmer, James Anderson; art director,

Carroll Clark; sound, John Tribby; camera, Edward Cronjager;
editor, William Hamilton.
    Richard Dix (Roger Standish/Roger Lennox); Ann Harding
(Caroline Ogden Standish); Edna May Oliver (Matilda Blake); Guy
Kibbee (Dr. Daniel Blake); Donald Cook (Warren Lennon); Walter
Walker (Mr. Ogden); Wally Albright, Jr., Marilyn Knowlden
(Twins); Julie Haydon (Frances Standish); Harry Holman (Stubby);
Jason Robards (Lane); Jed Prouty (Auctioneer); Robert Greig (Bit);
E. H. Calvert (Doctor).

    For some people imitation is the sincerest form of flattery.
RKO had fared so well with its Cimarron (1931) [q.v.] that it
hastily sought to repeat the formula, even to using the same stalwart star, Richard Dix. The photography was accomplished by
Edward Cronjager who had also filmed Cimarron. Everything possible was done to insure that this film would be a major picture,
and would be regarded as such by the press and the public. RKO's
"First Lady of the Cinema," Miss Ann Harding, was given the demanding heroine's role, that of Caroline Ogden who, in the course
of the film's eighty-eight minutes, must endure several decades of
turmoil.
    Robert Lord's scenario finds Roger Standish (Dix) and Caro-
line Ogden as newlyweds who move to Fort Allen, Nebraska during
the tumultuous days of the post-Civil War age. Among the calami-
ties facing them is the death of their little son. Later, after defeating a group of bandits, Standish opens the town's first bank, but
in the financial panic of 1892 the enterprise fails. The empire,
however, is built again and the story closes with the family's grandson (also played by Dix) becoming a World War I hero as a member
of the Lafayette Escadrille and of the American Flying Forces. On
hand is the aging Caroline, who by the film's end is exceedingly
elderly but still filled with the conquering spirit that made her such
a forceful settler years back.
    In A Pictorial History of the Western Film (1969), William K.
Everson notes of this film, "it contains some unusually powerful
sequences, including the death of the family's son in an accident as
the crowds are lined up to welcome the first locomotive and a grim
mass of lynching episodes so starkly designed and lit and so casually
underplayed, that it quite outshines the more carefully and lengthy
constructed lynching scenes in Wellman's much later The Ox-Bow
Incident [1943, q.v.]."
    What separated films like The Conquerors and Cimarron from
the B Westerns turned out by series stars was more than just the
quality of the mounting. These major pictures were geared to appeal to all segments of audiences, carefully balancing the rugged outdoor action with focal romantic and domestic sequences, with an all-
too-obvious comedy relief (here provided by Edna May Oliver and
Guy Kibbee).

THE COVERED WAGON (Paramount, 1923) 9,407'

    Presenters, Jesse L. Lasky, Adolph Zukor; producer-director,

Lois Wilson in The Covered Wagon (1923).

James Cruze; based on the novel by Emerson Hough; screenplay,
Jack Cunningham; music, Hugo Riesenfeld; technical advisor,
Colonel Tim McCoy; camera, Karl Brown; editor, Dorothy Arzner.
    Lois Wilson (Molly Wingate); J. Warren Kerrigan (Will
Banion); Ernest Torrence (Jackson); Charles Ogle (Mr. Wingate);
Ethel Wales (Mrs. Wingate); Alan Hale (Sam Woodhull); Tully
Marshall (Bridger); Guy Oliver (Kit Carson); Johnny Fox (Jed Win-
gate); Tim McCoy (Rider).

    "Perhaps the value of The Covered Wagon as a film tends to
be exaggerated a little today, but its importance as one of the major
milestones in the history of the 'western' movie can never be emphasized too much.   The first real epic western, and the first
American epic not directed by [D. W.] Griffith, it gave an enormous
boost to the popularity of the western, which had begun to show
signs of falling into a slump" (Joe Franklin, Classics of the Silent
Screen, 1959).
    Told in a semi-documentary fashion, this Western is con-
sidered to be the first major sagebrush blockbuster to be produced
in Hollywood.   The film did much to establish the career of director
Cruze, and it provides a brilliant example of Karl Brown's excellent
cinematography.
    In 1848 two wagon convoys, one led by Wingate (Ogle) and
the other by Will Banion (Kerrigan), start out from Kansas City over

the Oregon Trail with their final destination being California and
Oregon. Along the way they must cross the dangerous Platte River,
combat an Indian attack, and resist a prairie fire. The film focuses on Will Banion and Molly Wingate (Wilson), as well as Sam
Woodhull (Hale), the latter a rascal who hopes to discredit Banion
in order to protect his romance with Molly. As a result of Woodhull's skullduggery, Banion and his wagons are cut out from the
main convoy and head to California to follow the gold rush. When
Molly realizes what a skunk Woodhull is, she sends reliable Jackson
(Torrence) to find Will. Eventually, after Woodhull is subdued,
Molly and Will wed.

The impact of The Covered Wagon was immediate, and the
film's popularity continues onward to the present day. It is one of
the few silent Westerns to still get prime time exposure on TV.
Even now, a half-century after its distribution, Western films are
still being judged by the standards of The Covered Wagon as to
authenticity in depicting the Old West. The many sagebrush epics
that followed this landmark film were often superior to it, but none
yet has gained the popularity or artistic acclaim of this film.

In 1923 Will Rogers made a short subject parody of The
Covered Wagon, entitled Two Wagons--Both Covered which finds
the settlers reaching the West Coast only to discover that real estate leeches have beaten them there.

COWBOY (Columbia, 1958) C 92 min.

Producer, Julian Blaustein; director, Delmer Daves; based
on the book My Reminiscences as a Cowboy by Frank Harris; screenplay, Edmund H. North; assistant director, Sam Nelson; music,
George Duning; music director, Morris Stoloff; orchestrator, Arthur
Morton; color consultant, Henri Jaffa; art director, Cary Odell; set
decorator, William Kiernan, James M. Crowe; sound, Josh Westmoreland; camera, Charles Lawton, Jr.; second unit camera, Ray
Corey; editor, Al Clark.

Glenn Ford (Tom Reece); Jack Lemmon (Frank Harris); Anna
Kashfi (Maria Vidal); Brian Donlevy (Doc Bender); Dick York
(Charlie); Victor Manuel Mendoza (Mendoza); Richard Jaeckel (Paul
Curtis); King Donovan (Joe Capper); Vaughn Taylor (Mr. Fowler);
Donald Randolph (Senor Vidal); James Westerfield (Mike Adams);
Eugene Iglesias (Manuel Arriega); Frank de Kova (Alcaide); Buzz
Henry (Slim Barrett); Amapola Del Vando (Aunt); Bek Nelson
(Charlie's Girl); William Leslie (Tucker); Guy Wilkerson (Peggy).

Jack Lemmon in a serious film, and a Western yet? Yes,
and he and the film were both very sombre and good. Time lauded
the production as "an engaging mixture of saddlesore truth and
reach-for-leather fiction." The New York Herald-Tribune corrobo-
rated this opinion: "Unusual film.... An honest portrait of the
man who opened the cattle trails and of the way they lived."

This delightful feature detailed the progress into manhood of
a hotel clerk (Lemmon) in the 1870s as he goes on a 2,000-mile

cattle drive from Chicago to the Rio Grande. Along the way the
tenderfoot is toughened into rugged self-sufficiency as he outdoes
the more seasoned members of the drive in the art of survival.
Glenn Ford was Tom Reece, the hard boss of the cattle drive.
En route, the men encounter an Indian attack, a Mexican fiesta,
and a cattle stampede.
        Films in Review, no easy bastion to conquer, approved of
this feature: "... it's one of the most interesting, and important
Westerns ever made, and one not likely to be exceeded for authenticity."

THE COWBOYS (Warner Bros., 1972) C 128 min.

        Producer, Mark Rydell; associate producer, Tom Zinnemann;
director, Rydell; based on the novel by William Dale Jennings;
screenplay, Irving Ravetch, Harriet Frank, Jr., William Dale Jennings; assistant director, Zinnemann; second unit director, Robert
"Buzz" Henry; production designer, Philip Jefferies; set decorator,
William Kiernan; music, John Williams; titles, Phill Norman;
makeup, Emile La Vigne, Dave Grayson; costumes, Anthea Sylbert;
sound, Kay Rose, Jack Solomon, Richard Portman; camera, Robert
Surtees; editors, Robert Swink, Neil Travis.
        John Wayne (Wil Anderson); Roscoe Lee Browne (Jebediah
Nightlinger); Bruce Dern (Long Hair); Colleen Dewhurst (Kate);
Slim Pickens (Anse); Lonny Chapman (Preacher); Charles Tyner
(Mr. Jenkins); A. Martinez (Cimarron); Alfred Barker, Jr. (Singing
Fats); Nicolas Beauvy (Four Eyes); Steve Benedict (Steve); Robert
Carradine (Slim Honneycutt); Norman Howell, Jr. (Weedy); Stephen
Hudis (Charlie Schwartz); Clay O'Brien (Hardy Fimps); Sam O'Brien
(Jimmy Phillips); Sarah Cunningham (Annie Anderson); Allyn Ann
McLerie (Ellen Price); Matt Clark (Smiley); Larry Finley (Jake);
Jerry Gatlin (Howdy); Charise Cullin (Elizabeth); Larry Randles
(Ben); Fred Brookfield, Tap Canutt, Chuck Courtney, Gary Epper,
Henry Wills, Kent Hays, J. R. Randall, Joe Yrigoyen (Rustlers).

        A blend of comedy, tragedy, and the ambience of the Old
West, this feature opened at Radio City Music Hall and went on to
gross over $4 million domestically. One of its major plot twists
was to have the hero killed (!) before the finale.
        In the 1870s, aging rancher Wil Anderson (Wayne) is
organizing a cattle drive to market, when his ranch hands desert
him to follow a gold rush. Saloon keeper Anse (Pickens) suggests
he hire the local school boys to substitute, and Wil agrees.
Eleven youngsters, ranging in age from nine to fifteen, are hired.
Anderson refuses to sign on half-breed Cimarron (Martinez) because the youth is so antagonistic, and Long Hair (Dern) is rejected
because he lied about his prison past.
        After a tough training period, Wil hires Jebediah Nightlinger
(Browne) as cook. The group set out on the 400-mile journey with
their 1200 head of cattle. On the trail, the youths soon mature.
Cimarron, who has been following along on his own, manages to

John Wayne and the boys in The Cowboys (1972).

rescue one of the youngsters from drowning and is then allowed to
sign on with the regular crew. Along the way the boys try a night
of drinking and are tempted by (but do not experience) the pleasures
provided by a bordello wagon. Long Hair has been following the
herd convoy and in a fight with Wil is badly whipped. Angered,
Long Hair shoots Anderson in both legs and in the back, and then
rides off with the cattle. Wil dies the next morning and the youths
he has helped make adults determine to get revenge on the rustlers
and they do. The cattle are brought to market and the youthful
cowpokes buy a tombstone for Wil. Although the grave site has
been lost in the rain and wind, the boys set up the marker. The
"seasoned" cowboys now ride home.

     Highlighted by a variety of good performances--Wayne of-
fered a quite poignant characterization--tight direction, and appealing
photography, the film offered good diversion.

     A good many critics were amazed and aghast at the violence
within The Cowboys, especially when the film, which had a P(arental)
G(uidance) rating, was being touted as a family entertainment offering.
Gary Arnold (Washington Post) argued, "If The Cowboys becomes a
huge, generally accepted family favorite, it would tend to indicate
that most Americans are insensitive to the moral implications of this
material, and substantiate the thesis that violence doesn't upset us as
much as sex. "

On the other hand, a more restrained, thoughtful review was offered by Arthur Knight in Saturday Review: "... while the sight of a dozen or so kids wiping out a band of rustlers has its sanguinary aspects, it is a model of restraint compared to the wholesale slaughter in Kurosawa's The Seven Samurai, long considered a classic.... Although I suspect he [director Rydell] was being just a bit disingenuous when, on several occasions, he referred to it as a 'fairy tale, ' the main thrust of his narrative is entirely within the tradition of the American Western.   The forces of good and evil are clearly and broadly oversimplified, with virtue inevitably triumphant." And Arthur B. Clarke wrote in Films in Review, "The Cowboys is the kind of folkstory you want to believe; hence indictments of it for not being realistic are irrelevant and/or tendentious."

A teleseries based upon the film had a brief run on ABC-TV in the fall of 1974.

THE CULPEPPER CATTLE CO.   (Twentieth Century-Fox, 1972) C   92 min.

Producer, Paul A. Helmick; associate producer, Jerry Bruckheimer; director-story, Dick Richards; screenplay, Eric Bercovici, Gregory Prentiss; music, Tom Scott, Jerry Goldsmith; art directors, Jack Martin Smith, Carl Anderson; set decorator, Walter M. Scott; stunt co-ordinator, Hal Needham; makeup, Del Armstrong; assistant director, Terry Morse, Jr.; costumes, Ted Parvin; special mechanical effects, Cliff Wenger; sound, Richard Overton, Jesus Gancy, Don Bassman; camera, Lawrence Edward Williams, Ralph Woolsey; editor, John F. Burnett.

Gary Grimes (Ben Mockridge); Billy "Green" Bush (Frank Culpepper); Luke Askew (Luke); Bo Hopkins (Dixie Brick); Geoffrey Lewis (Russ Caldwell); Wayne Sutherlin (Missoula); John McLiam (Thornton Pierce); Matt Clark (Pete); Raymond Guth (Cook); Anthony James (Nathaniel); Charlie Martin Smith (Tim Slater); Bob Morgan (Old John); Jerry Gatlin (Wallop); Walter Scott (Print); Royal Dano (Cattle Rustler); John Pearce (Spectator); Dennis Fimple (Wounded Man in Bar); Patrick Campbell (Brother Ephraim), and Hal Needham.

"... [It is] a considerably better-than-average western with a real feeling for time, place and the life" (Charles Champlin, Los Angeles Times).   This film marked the directorial debut of still photographer and TV commercial director Dick Richards, and was the result of more than three years of research concerning the post-Civil War West.   Because it was so low-keyed and only had Gary (Summer of '42) Grimes for box-office draw, it failed to make a mark in today's competitive marketplace.   But it is a film worth viewing.

Ben Mockridge (Grimes) desperately wants to become a cowboy.   It is post-Civil War Texas and times are tough.   He persuades Frank Culpepper (Bush) to hire him for a cattle drive to Colorado; his post is to be assistant to the group cook.   No sooner has the drive actually begun than Ben learns how unromantic and grim a way of life he has chosen.   Rustlers stampede the herd and insist upon a

ransom payment. Ben is aghast when Culpepper's crew slaughter
the outlaws (three of the Culpepper team are killed in the melee).
More horror piles up as Ben goes to town to find replacement for
the killed men. The new crew calmly mow down the thieving
trappers who had stolen Ben's horse. Later, when rustlers steal
the camp's horses while Ben is on duty, Culpepper seeks to send
the boy back to Texas. Before he can board the stage, he and
Luke head to the local saloon where they spot the rustlers. In the
fight, Ben has to shoot the bartender to protect Luke. Culpepper
now allows Ben to return to his job on the drive.

      Further on, the cowboys encounter a religious sect who, like
the Culpepper contingent, are having problems with landowner
Thornton Pierce who is exhorting huge sums of money for any
grazing or farming use of his lands. When the homesteads refuse
to leave, Ben decides to help their fight. Others from Culpepper's
crew join him in the stand. In the fight with Pierce and his henchmen, most of Ben's cohorts are killed and thereafter the religious
sect moves on. Ben forces them to first bury his fallen friends.
After the burial, Ben throws away his gun and rides off alone.

      While Time thought the film to be "episodic and rather punchy,
and the visual style is too pretty," the movie offers an unpretentious
re-creation of the West as it probably was, seen through the eyes
of an idealistic youth. It is as far removed from the Sergio Leone-
Clint Eastwood Westerns of the sixties as it is from the old saddle-
and-guitar musical Westerns of the thirties. It offers a worthwhile
direction for the oater to follow in the seventies, but the format is
probably too uncommercial to be feasible on any major scale.

CUSTER OF THE WEST (Cinerama, 1967) C 146 min.

      Producers, Philip Jordan, Louis Dolivet; director, Robert
Siodmak; associate producer-director of Civil War sequences, Irving
Lerner; screenplay. Bernard Gordon, Julian Halevy; music-music
director, Bernardo Segall; songs, Segall and Will Holt; Segall and
Robert Shaw; art directors, Jean-Pierre D'Eaubonne, Eugene Lourie,
Julio Molina; set decorator, Antonio Mateos; costumes, Laure De
Zarate; assistant director, Jose Maria Ochoa; sound, Kurt Herrn-
feld, Alban Streeter; camera, Cecilio Paniagua; editor, Maurice
Rootes.
      Robert Shaw (General George Armstrong Custer); Mary Ure
(Elizabeth Custer); Jeffrey Hunter (Lieutenant Benteen); Ty Hardin
(Major Marcus Reno); Charles Stalnaker (Lieutenant Howells); Robert
Hall (Sergeant Buckley); Lawrence Tierney (General Philip Sheridan);
Kieron Moore (Chief Dull Knife); Marc Lawrence (The Goldminer);
and Robert Ryan (Sergeant Mulligan).

      Robert Siodmak took over the direction of this latter-day
screen biography of General George Armstrong Custer after both
Akira Kurasowa and Fred Zinnemann withdrew from the project.
It was lensed in Spain in the (super) Cinerama process. Originally
shown in wide-screen Cinerama it was later released in conventional
screen projection size by MGM. In the United States it proved to be

a financial and critical bust, although in Europe it made an acceptable commercial showing.

Once again the flamboyant George Armstrong Custer (Shaw), a Civil War veteran, heads Westward to take command of the 7th Cavalry and to deal with the warring Indians. At the fort he must contend with the heavy-drinking Major Reno (Hardin) and Lieutenant Benteen (Hunter), the latter sympathetic to the Indians' plight. Later, under orders from General Sheridan (Tierney), Custer and his men attack an Indian village, creating a needless massacre for the sake of Washington politicians. Later Custer becomes an advocate of good treatment of the Indians, but his crusades against top-level politicians prove almost fruitless. When he learns his regiment is to proceed against the Indians, his wife (Ure) intercedes to have Washington officials allow Custer to lead his men into battle. At the battle of Little Big Horn he and his troops are overwhelmed by Chief Dull Knife (Moore) and his braves. All that remains alive of the troop's forces is Custer's horse, allowed to live as a tribute to its fallen master.

The slaughter of American troops at the June 25, 1876 battle of Little Big Horn has been the subject of more than a score of films over the decades, including Errol Flynn's They Died With Their Boots On (1941) [q.v.] and Little Big Man (1970) [q.v.]. Most of these features have focused on the so-called bravery of the flashy Custer without detailing the foolhardiness of this army officer who so often caused needless deaths among both the enemy and his men. Custer of the West was no exception to the general glamorization of Custer, and obviously was hoping to gain its audience through its widescreen spectacle.

Some critics did note and appreciate the meticulous performances provided by the leading players, and that the script--considering it was so revised and butchered along the way to the final release--was extremely sound. Judith Crist, writing in New York magazine, reported, "... [The] script is oddly topical as well as literate, and made more so by Robert Shaw's complex portrait of Custer, Mary Ure's subtlety as his wife, Lawrence Tierney's interesting Sheridan. Shaw's interpretation of Custer gives substance to both story and history and elevates the inevitable cavalry vs. Indians cliches. The result is an engrossing adventure film that puts the emphasis on character and, perhaps wisely, avoids putting the final word on an historical controversy. The winning point is performance --and for a lagniappe there's a slightly more than cameo-sized bit by Robert Ryan [as the deserting officer] that shows in miniature, as Shaw does throughout, just how the pros perform."

Variety, ever aware of alerting exhibitors to films' potential selling points, noted, "But the main bait will be the Cinerama tricks of eye involvement, well carried out by director Robert Siodmak and cameraman Cecilio Paniagua. Sequences with an out-of-control train, a similarly undirected wagon, a soldier escaping down rapids--all these have the queasy-stomach appeal of those early Cinerama travelogues. The fighting, too, makes great play with arrows going through necks and other assorted mayhem, and the action sequences are appropriately noisy and lethal."

When the film opened in the U.S.--sometimes under the title,

A Good Day for Fighting--a lawsuit was filed in a New York City
court by a relative of Major M. A. Reno, stating that the film
maligned his deceased ancestor whose rank had been restored by
the U.S. government, after the film was made.

DAKOTA   (Republic, 1945)   82 min.

     Associate producer-director, Joseph Kane; story, Carl Fore-
man; adaptor, Howard Estabrook; screenplay, Lawrence Hazard; art
directors, Russell Kimball, Gano Chittenden; set decorators, John
McCarthy, Jr., James Redd; music director, Walter Scharf; choreog-
raphy, Larry Ceballos; song, Andrew Sterling and Harry Von Tilzer;
assistant director, Al Wood; sound, Fred Stahl; special effects,
Howard and Theodore Lydecker; camera, Jack Marta; editor, Fred
Allen.
     John Wayne (John Devlin); Vera Hruba Ralston (Sandra
"Sandy" Poli Devlin); Ward Bond (Jim Bender); Walter Brennan
(Captain Bounce); Mike Mazurki (Bigtree Collins); Hugo Haas (Marko
Poli); Ona Munson (Jersey Thomas); Paul Fix (Carp); Nicodemus
Stewart (Mose); Olive Blakeney (Mrs. Stowe); Robert Livingston
(Lieutenant); Robert H. Baratt (Mr. Stowe); Pierre Watkin (Wexton
Geary); Olin Howland (Devlin's Driver); Grant Withers (Slagin);
Selmer Jackson (Dr. Judson); Claire Du Brey (Wahtonka); Jack
LaRue (Slade); Jonathan Hale (Colonel Wordin); Roy Barcroft (Poli's
Driver); Larry Thompson (Poli's Footman); Sarah Padden (Mrs.
Plummer); George Cleveland (Mr. Plummer); Houseley Stevenson
(Railroad Clerk); Bobby Blake (Boy); Paul Hurst (Captain Spotts);
Dorothy Christy (Nora); Michael Visaroff (Russian); Victor Varconi
(Frenchman); Paul E. Burns (Swede); Linda Stirling (Girl).

     This Republic Western should have been on the same high
level as Dark Command (1940) [q.v.] and other epic "specials"
Republic was releasing during the forties.   But production problems,
including John Wayne's dissatisfaction with his co-star, director,
and script, led to a heavy-handed end result.   It proved rather
sluggish going for even its relatively short eighty-two minutes of
running time.   Despite a fine, large cast, the feature failed to live
up fully to its promise; only the opening riverboat sequences with
Walter Brennan and the later plains fire were of any major interest.
     Sandra Poli (Ralston) is the daughter of a railroad executive
(Haas) and has eloped with John Devlin (Wayne).   He wants her to
move to the Dakotas in order to buy land so he can make a profit
when the railroad comes through that area.   On the way West, the
couple encounter two men, Jim Bender (Bond) and Bigtree Collins
(Mazurki) who own the town of Fargo and are burning out homesteaders and blaming the Indians.   When the Devlins do arrive in
Fargo, John sides with the wheat farmers against Bender.   The
latter agrees finally to stop the war if Devlin will leave town.
Devlin agrees on condition that the money stolen from the local folk
is returned.   Devlin later becomes involved in a fight with Bender
and beats him.   However, Bigtree is more direct: he kills Bender

and absconds with the funds. Devlin eventually overtakes Bigtree
and defeats him. He returns the money to its rightful owners,
while the cavalry arrives to restore law and order to Fargo.

THE DALTONS RIDE AGAIN (Universal, 1945) 72 min.

        Producer, Howard Welsch; director, Ray Taylor; story-
screenplay, Roy Chanslor, Paul Gangelin; assistant director, William
Tummel; additional dialogue, Henry Blankfort; art directors, John B.
Goodman, Harold H. MacArthur; set decorators, Russell A. Gaus-
man, Arthur D. Leddy; music director, Frank Skinner; dialogue di-
rector, Willard Holland; sound, Jess Moulin; camera, Charles Van
Enger; editor, Paul Landres.
        Alan Curtis (Emmett Dalton); Kent Taylor (Bob Dalton); Lon
Chaney (Grat Dalton); Noah Beery, Jr. (Ben Dalton); Martha
O'Driscoll (Mary); Jess Barker (Jeff); Thomas Gomez (McKenna);
Milburn Stone (Graham); John Litel (Bohannon); Walter Sande (Wil-
kins); Douglass Dumbrille (Sheriff); Virginia Brissac (Mrs. Walters);
Stanley Andrews (Walters); Fern Emmett (Miss Crain); Charles
Miller (Haines); Cyril Delevanti (Jennings); Frank Dae (Judge); Ruth
Lee (Mrs. Bohannon); Ed Cassidy (Sproules); Ethan Laidlaw (Trailer);
Henry Hall (Marshal).

        This Universal rehash of the Dalton Brothers' story was
originally assigned to director Ford Beebe but he turned down the
project when its shooting schedule was reduced from 32 to 16 days.
It was then handed to Ray Taylor as a quickie project. To Taylor's

Thomas Gomez, Kent Taylor, Alan Curtis, Walter Sand and Lon
Chaney, Jr. in The Daltons Ride Again (1945).

credit, the film emerged as a handsome little oater with good performances and a fine, violent shootout as its climax.

"Not for a single sequence does the picture take its content
too seriously.... [It] is lively, lusty and full of surprises" (Irene
Thirer, New York Post). Set in the 1890s, the four outlaw brothers
(Curtis, Taylor, Chaney, Jr. and Noah Beery, Jr.) embark on a
robbing spree in the Old West. Eventually three of the brothers are
gunned down in Coffeyville, Kansas during a bank robbery. Emmett
Dalton (Curtis) survives to be tried and sentenced to life in prison.
Perky Martha O'Driscoll provides the love interest.

Even for a public jaded by the traumas of World War II, The
Daltons Ride Again had sufficient killings, posse chases, and bank
and stagecoach holdups to maintain audience interest. More serious-
minded critics did ponder, along with the New York Times, "whether
the cast is acting tough in the stony-faced manner, or is just generally apathetic."

Among the films to deal with the (in)famous Dalton Gang are:
When the Daltons Rode (1940), Badman's Territory (1946) [q.v.],
Return of the Badmen (1948), The Dalton Gang (1949, directed by
Ford Beebe), The Cimarron Kid (1952), Montana Belle (1952), Jesse
James Versus the Daltons (1954), as well as The Daltons' Women
(1951) and The Dalton Girls (1957).

DANIEL BOONE (RKO, 1936) 77 min.

Producer, George A. Hirliman; director, David Howard;
story, Edgecomb Pinchon; screenplay, Daniel Jarrett; camera,
Frank Good; editor, Ralph Dixon.

George O'Brien (Daniel Boone); Heather Angel (Virginia);
John Carradine (Simon Girty); Ralph Forbes (Stephen Marlowe);
Clarence Muse (Pompey); George Regas (Black Eagle); Dickie Jones
(Jerry); Huntley Gordon (Sir John Randolph); Harry Cording (Joe
Burch); Aggie Herring (Mrs. Burch); Craufurd Kent (Attorney
General); Keith Kenneth (Commissioner).

Because a film is not heavily-budgeted or elaborately staged
does NOT mean it cannot be a superior product. Such was the
case with Daniel Boone, made as part of a George O'Brien Western
series for RKO. It emerged from production as a solid, if historically exaggerated, entry, recounting the trail blazing done by Daniel
Boone as he led American pioneer settlers into "Kain-tuck-ee" in
1775. Along the way he and his followers must battle hostile Indians,
the latter being led into battle by the infamous Simon Girty (Carradine) who is selling rifles to the Wyandotte tribe. The picture
climaxes with the famous attack on the white settlement in which the
Indians are defeated after rain causes their underground diggings to
collapse. At the finale Girty meets his demise.

Daniel Boone effectively recaptured the ambience of that bygone era and had some good, thrilling action en route as well as
bright characterizations by O'Brien and Carradine (warming up for
a similar role three years later in John Ford's Drums Along the
Mohawk [q.v.]).

Don Miller wrote in B Movies (1973): "[It] had superior production values and an action setting befitting the muscular star [O'Brien]." The New York Times, obviously miffed at having to review such a B production, wrote, "For all his physical prowess, George O'Brien manages to project Daniel Boone as a shy, unassuming adventurer, which is presumably what the man was."

DARK COMMAND (Republic, 1940) 94 min.

Associate producer, Sol. C. Siegel; director, Raoul Walsh; based on the novel by W. R. Burnett; screenplay, Grover Jones, Lionel Houser, F. Hugh Herbert; camera, Jack Marta; editor, Murray Selden.
Claire Trevor (Mary McCloud); John Wayne (Bob Seton); Walter Pidgeon (William Cantrell); Roy Rogers (Fletch McCloud); George Hayes (Doc Grunch); Porter Hall (Angus McCloud); Marjorie

John Wayne, Claire Trevor and Roy Rogers in Dark Command (1940).

Main (Mrs. Cantrell); Raymond Walburn (Buckner); Joseph Sawyer
(Bushropp); Helen MacKellar (Mrs. Hale); J. Farrell MacDonald
(Dave); Trevor Bardette (Hale); Harry Woods (Dental Patient); Jack
Rockwell (Assassin); Alan Bridge (Slave Trader); Edward Hearn,
Edmund Cobb (Jurymen); Hal Taliaferro (Vigilante); Yakima Canutt
(Townsman/Stunts); Tom London (Messenger); Cliff Lyons (Stunts);
Ben Alexander (Sentry); Ernie Adams (Another Townsman).

By 1940 Republic Pictures was occasionally producing class
A features. This entry, costing a mammoth $700,000, was the
studio's most expensive project to that point. Adapted from W. R.
Burnett's novel, the film was directed by Raoul Walsh and emerged
as a flavorful, if historically inaccurate, retelling of the Quantrill
Raiders episode during the Civil War.
The story opens prior to the Civil War with Cantrell [sic]
(Pidgeon) running for the office of marshal but losing to Bob Seton
(Wayne). The later also likes Cantrell's girl, Mary McCloud
(Trevor). When Seton insists that Mary's brother Fletch (Rogers)
be tried for a murder he has committed, Cantrell uses collusion to
pressure the jury into an acquittal. Later, Cantrell organizes a
guerrilla band with Fletch as part of it. They proceed to raid the
countryside, supposedly acting on the part of the Confederacy, but
really to fatten their own pockets. By this point Cantrell has wed
Mary who is faithful to him but begins to suspect his activities.
Finally the gang loots and burns Lawrence, Kansas, killing many
innocent people. Subsequently Seton kills Cantrell in a fight. Now
Mary is free to express her love for Bob.
Dark Command was a well-made motion picture with a number of solidly-constructed scenes, including the burning of Lawrence.
Yakima Canutt contributed some excellent stunt work, especially a
scene in which a wagon plunges down a cliff. The leads were good
(Pidgeon was borrowed especially from MGM), although Roy Rogers
was a bit stiff in his dramatic assignment. George "Gabby" Hayes
provided his usual cantankerous, lovable performance. In A Pictorial History of the Western Film (1969), William K. Everson rates
this as "the best of all the deluxe Republic Westerns."

DAS WAR BUFFALO BILL   see   BUFFALO BILL

DAVY CROCKETT, KING OF THE WILD FRONTIER   (Buena Vista,
1955)   C   93 min.

Producer, Bill Walsh; director, Norman Foster; screenplay,
Tom Blackburn; art director, Marvin Aubrey Davis; music director,
George Bruns; orchestrator, Edward Plumb; songs, Blackburn and
Bruns; assistant director, James J. Cox; costumes, Norman Martien;
camera, Charles Boyle; editor, Chester Schaeffer.
Fess Parker (Davy Crockett); Buddy Ebsen (George Russel);
Basil Ruysdael (Andrew Jackson); Hans Conried (Thimblerig); William
Bakewell (Tobias Norton); Kenneth Tobey (Colonel Jim Bowie); Pat
Hogan (Chief Red Stick); Helene Stanley (Polly Crockett); Nick Cravat

(Bustedluck); Don Megowan (Colonel Billy Travis); Mike Mazurki
(Bigfoot Mason); Jeff Thompson (Charlie Two Shirts); Henry Joyner
(Swaney); Benjamin Hornbuckle (Henderson); Hal Youngblood (Oppo-
nent Political Speaker); Jim Maddux, Robert Booth (Congressmen);
Eugene Brindel (Billy); Ray Whitetree (Johnny); Colonel Campbell
Brown (Bruno).

Originally shown as three parts on the Frontierland segment
of the "Disneyland" TV series, this film was issued theatrically to
make additional money from the Davy Crockett craze. The Crockett
bonanza made a fortune for those merchandizing tie-in items (ranging
from coonskin caps to toy guns, records, etc.), and it made a national hero of Fess Parker who played the title character.
The film opens with Crockett winning the respect of an
Indian leader (Hogan) and later defeating badman Bigfood Mason
(Mazurki) to become a local hero in frontier Tennessee. Sent to
Congress, Davy becomes a friend of his former General, Andrew
Jackson (Ruysdael), and a U.S. hero for speaking truths and as a
result of the articles written about him by his pal George Russell
(played by Buddy Ebsen--the first choice for the role of Crockett).
When Davy and Andy Jackson later disagree over an Indian bill,
Crockett and Russell head for Texas where they die valiantly at the
Alamo.
Although filmed economically by director Norman Foster,
this color production made ideal movie fodder after its TV exposure. Several of the scenes were well staged (such as those
dealing with the early Indian wars and the fall of the Alamo). In
the midst of the idealism and fantasy of this romantic interpretation
of the old West, Davy Crockett managed to evoke something of the
hardships suffered by the pioneers, as when Davy's wife Polly
(Stanley) dies of fever.
Despite the fact that their initial Davy Crockett mini-series
ended with the death of the hero, the Disney organization was not to
be stymied. Obviously, it was too valuable a property to let disappear. Thus Disney Enterprises filmed a sequel, Davy Crockett and
the River Pirates, issued in 1956, first on TV and then to theatres.
Again directed by Foster, the emphasis here was on the character
of river man Mike Fink (Jeff York), who was first Crockett's enemy
and then his friend. The film sported an especially well-staged boat
race, including some scenes of Davy guiding a longboat down the
dangerous river rapids.

THE DEERSLAYER see LAST OF THE MOHICANS

DESERT GOLD (Kay Bee, 1914) five reels

Director, Scott Sidney; based on the novel by Zane Grey;
screenplay, Thomas H. Ince, Richard Spencer.
Charles Ray (Jim Hardy); Frank Borsage (John Carson); Clara
Williams (Mary); and: Robert Korman.
Reissue title: After the Storm.

80 Desert Gold

DESERT GOLD   (W. W. Hodkinson, 1919)   seven reels

Presenters, Benjamin B. Hampton, Eltinge F. Warner; di-
rector, T. Hayes Hunter; based on the novel by Zane Grey; screen-
play, Fred Myton; camera, Abraham Scholtz, A. L. Todd.
E. K. Lincoln (Dick Gale); Edward Coxen (Captain George
Thorn); Eileen Percy (Nell); Margery Wilson (Mercedes); William H.
Bainbridge (Jim Belding); Laura Winston (Mrs. Belding); Walter
Long (Rojas); Russell Simpson (Lad/James Warren); Arthur Morri-
son (Lash); Mrs. Dark Cloud (Papago Indian Mother); Frank Lanning
(Papago Indian Son); Mary Jane Irving (The Child).

DESERT GOLD   (Paramount, 1926)   6,900'

Presenters, Adolph Zukor, Jesse L. Lasky; supervisors,
Hector Turnbull, B. P. Schulberg; director, George B. Seitz; based
on the novel by Zane Grey; screenplay, Lucien Hubbard; camera,
Charles Edgar Schoenbaum.
Neil Hamilton (George Thorne); Shirley Mason (Mercedes
Castanada); Robert Frazer (Dick Gale); William Powell (Landree);
Josef Swickard (Sebastian Castanada); George Irving (Richard Stanton
Gale); Eddie Gribbon (One Round Kelley); Frank Lackteen (Yaqui);
Richard Howard (Sergeant); Bernard Siegel (Goat Herder); George
Regas (Verd); Ralph Yearsley (Half Wit); Aline Goodwin (Alarcon's
Wife).

DESERT GOLD   (Paramount, 1936)   58 min.

Producer, Harold Hurley; director, James Logan; based on the
novel by Zane Grey; screenplay, Stuart Anthony, Robert Yost; art
directors, Hans Dreier, Dave Garber; camera, George Clemens; edi-
tor, Chandler House.
Larry "Buster" Crabbe (Moya); Robert Cummings (Fordyce
Mortimer); Marsha Hunt (Jane Belding); Tom Keene (Dick Gale);
Glenn (Leif) Erickson (Glenn Kasedon); Monte Blue (Chetley Kasedon);
Raymond Hatton (Doc Belding); Walter Miller (Ladd); Frank Mayo
(Lash); Phillip Morris (Sentry).

The year after Zane Grey's Desert Gold was published in
1913 Thomas H. Ince turned out the first of a quartet of screen
versions of the novel. This first try at Grey's bestselling tale
starred Clara Williams, Frank Borsage, Robert Kortman, and
Charles Ray, the latter to become famous for his interpretation of
the ideal wholesome all-American. In 1919 the W. W. Hodkinson
Company did another version, starring E. K. Lincoln and directed
by T. Hayes Hunter.
In the height of the silent picture era, Paramount produced
the first of its two versions of the Grey book. This 1926, George
B. Seitz-directed feature, Photoplay called only "fair." It concerned an Easterner (Frazer) disowned by his family who travels

Leif Erickson, Robert Cummings and Tom Keene in <u>Desert Gold</u>
(1936).

west to aid his pal (Hamilton).   An outlaw-killer (Powell) plunders
a bordertown and tries to kidnap George Thorne's (Hamilton) girl,
Mercedes Castenada (Mason).   She manages to escape disguised as
a boy.   An Indian (Lackteen) leads her and Dick Gale (Frazer) into
the desert.   A raging sandstorm causes the outlaws to give up their
pursuit, but in the storm the trio's horses are lost and the Indian
guide is injured.   Meanwhile Thorne, who has been hurt in a battle,
learns of Mercedes' plight and rides to the rescue.   With such a
sterling cast, one can only wish this film was more readily available for modern viewing.

       A decade after the Seitz version, James Hogan directed the
only talking film derived from this book.   Using stock footage from
the 1926 edition, this cheapie used its young, ambitious stock
players (Crabbe, Cummings, Hunt) and Tom Keene to flesh out the
story.

DESPERATE SIEGE   see   RAWHIDE

DESTRY   (Universal, 1954)   C   95 min.

       Producer, Stanley Rubin; director, George Marshall; based
on the novel Destry Rides Again by Max Brand; screen story, Felix
Jackson; screenplay, Edmund H. Smith; art directors, Alexander
Golitzen, Alfred Sweeney; assistant directors, Frank Shaw, Phil
Bowles; music, Arnold Hughes, Frederick Herbett; choreography,
Kenny Williams; costumes, Rosemary Odell; camera, George Robin-
son; editor, Ted J. Kent.

Advertisement for the 1932 version of Destry Rides Again.

Audie Murphy (Tom Destry); Mari Blanchard (Brandy); Lyle
Bettger (Decker); Lori Nelson (Martha Phillips); Thomas Mitchell
(Rags Barnaby); Edgar Buchanan (Mayor Hiram Sellers); Wallace
Ford (Doc Curtis); Mary Wickes (Bessie Mae Curtis); Alan Hale,
Jr. (Jack Larson); Lee Aaker (Eli Skinner); Trevor Bardette (Sheriff
Joe Bailey); Walter Baldwin (Henry Skinner); George Wallace (Curley);
Dick Reeves (Mac); Frank Richards (Dummy); Mitch Lawrence
(Dealer); Ralph Peters (Bartender).

DESTRY RIDES AGAIN (Universal, 1932) 55 min.

Producer, Stanley Bergerman; director, Ben Stoloff; based
on the novel by Max Brand; screenplay, Isadore Bernstein, Robert
Keith; art director, Thomas F. O'Neil; sound, C. Roy Hunter;
camera, Daniel B. Clark; editors, Maurice Pivar, Arthur Hilton.
Tom Mix (Tom Destry); Claudia Dell (Sally Dangerfield);
ZaSu Pitts (Temperance Worker); Stanley Fields (Sheriff Wendell);
Earle Foxe (Brent); Edward Piel, Sr. (Warren); Francis Ford (Judd
Ogden); George Ernest (Willie); John Ince (The Judge); Edward Le-
Saint (Mr. Dangerfield); Charles K. French (Jury Foreman); Tony
the Wonder Horse (Himself).

DESTRY RIDES AGAIN (Universal, 1939) 94 min.

Producer, Joe Pasternak; director, George Marshall; based
on the novel by Max Brand; screenplay, Felix Jackson, Henry
Meyers, Gertrude Purcell; art director, Jack Otterson; assistant
director, Vernon Keays; music, Frank Skinner; music director,
Charles Previn; Miss Dietrich's costumes, Vera West; sound,
Bernard B. Brown; camera, Hal Mohr; editor, Milton Carruth.
Marlene Dietrich (Frenchy); James Stewart (Tom Destry);
Charles Winninger (Wash Dimsdale); Mischa Auer (Boris Callahan);
Brian Donlevy (Kent); Irene Hervey (Janice Tyndall); Una Merkel
(Lilybelle Callahan); Allen Jenkins (Gyp Watson); Warren Hymer
(Bugs Watson); Samuel S. Hinds (Hiram J. Slade); Jack Carson
(Jack Tyndall); Lillian Yarbo (Clara); Tom Fadden (Lem Claggett);
Dickie Jones (Eli Whitney Claggett); Virginia Brissac (Ma Claggett);
Joe King (Sheriff Keogh); Lloyd Ingraham (Express Agent); Billy
Gilbert (Bartender); Ann Todd (Claggett Girl); Harry Cording (Rowdy);
Harry Tenbrook (Stage Rider); Chief Big Tree (Indian); Bud McClure
(Stage Driver); Billy Bletcher (Pianist); Dick Alexander (Cowboy).

None of the three screen versions of the 1930 novel by Max
Brand (Frederick Faust) has ever followed the book very closely but
two of the versions--in 1932 and 1939--are considered genre classics.
The initial screen version of the novel came two years after
its publication and starred the most popular cowboy star of all time,
Tom Mix, along with his wonder horse Tony. The feature was made
as part of a deal Mix had with Universal which required the studio
to pay him $10,000 per week during the production of six films.

Marlene Dietrich in <u>Destry Rides Again</u> (1939).

He also had story and casting control, and was allowed the use of
his favorite Fox cameraman, Daniel B. Clark.   The result of this
association was the production of several fine Westerns, with Destry
Rides Again the best remembered.

Mix plays Tom Destry, who owns a stagecoach line with
Brent (Foxe).   He catches thieves who hold up the stage and forces
them to pull the coach back into town where Destry is now cam-
paigning to become sheriff.   In actuality Brent is working with dishonest Sheriff Wendell (Fields).   The two of them conspire to re-
move Tom from the scene.   To accomplish this they frame him on
a murder charge.   Destry is sentenced to prison and vows revenge.
He is pardoned later and, once back in town, he feigns illness.
When the sheriff's gang attacks him, he quickly dispatches them.
Two of the outlaws are killed as Tom pursues them.   Later, Tom
captures Sheriff Wendell and the latter confesses to having framed
him.   In the finale Tom rescues his girl (Dell) from the clutches
of Brent.

Despite the change in plot from the book, the film was
smooth and did very well at the box-office.   The opening sequences
had the bulk of the film's comedy, what with a conversation between temperance worker Zasu Pitts and a bartender as well as
the dialogue among passengers when the villains hold up a stagecoach.   The film also had the diverting romantic interlude between
Mix and heroine Claudia Dell.   Mix did most of his own stunts except for the vigorous fights, while Tony the horse was only used in
close-up (the champion steed had a double for the rest of the hard-
riding!).

This Mix feature would be later reissued as Justice Rides
Again in order not to conflict with the 1939 remake.

When Universal remade Destry Rides Again, it did not follow
the novel any more closely than did the Mix film.   But this remake
is far better remembered today, even though it is not of the same
calibre as the Mix venture.   The new edition's chief claim to fame
is a bevy of fine performances, topped by Marlene Dietrich's appearance as Frenchy the raucuous saloon girl who sings "See What
the Boys in the Backroom Will Have."

The 1939 adaptation is set in the town of Bottle Neck which
is controlled by a ruthless gambler (Donlevy) who cheats suckers
out of their land.   He owns the saloon where Frenchy (Dietrich)
sings and is a hostess.   When the sheriff is murdered, the crooked
town officials appoint drunk Wash Dimsdale (Winninger) in his place.
He takes the job seriously and sends for the son (Stewart) of his
old pal.   Tom Destry (Stewart) arrives in town--without guns!--and
is mocked by the evil elements of Bottle Neck.   Meanwhile, Frenchy
has a slam-bang fight with the wife (Merkel) of a customer, a man
who has lost his pants to Frenchy in a card game.   Destry stops
the fight by pouring water over the two battling females.   Later he
locates the body of the dead sheriff but is stymied when Kent (Donlevy) has Wash killed.   The death of the beloved Wash does unite
the good elements of the town against the corrupt forces.   Because
Frenchy has succumbed to the laconic charms of gangling Destry,
she persuades the women of the town to join the newcomer in

battling Kent. When Kent attempts to shoot Destry at the saloon,
Frenchy blocks the bullets and dies. Destry then shoots Kent and
the town is made safe. At the finale, Destry wins Janice Tyndall
(Hervey), the girl with whom he rode into town on the stage.

A rowdy, comical Western with serious undertones, the film
was a big moneymaker and re-established Miss Dietrich's ailing
movie career; it also gave a big boost to the futures of Stewart and
Donlevy in the cinema.

The 1954 re-re-make was a pale successor to the earlier
versions. Wholesome, baby-faced Audie Murphy inherited the lead
role, while Mari Blanchard was the saloon girl, now called Brandy.
Director George Marshall, who handled the 1939 version and was no
newcomer to Westerns, seemingly could do little with the vapid cast
or watered-down script.

THE DEVIL'S CHILDREN see THE VIRGINIAN

THE DEVIL'S DOORWAY (MGM, 1950) 84 min.

Producer, Nicholas Nayfack; director, Anthony Mann; story-
screenplay, Guy Trosper; art directors, Cedric Gibbons, Leonid
Vasian; music, Daniele Amfitheatrof; camera, John Alton; editor,
Conrad A. Nervig.

Robert Taylor and Paula Raymond in Devil's Doorway (1950).

Robert Taylor (Broken Lance Poole); Louis Calhern (Verne Coolan); Paula Raymond (Orrie Masters); Marshall Thompson (Rod MacDougall); James Mitchell (Red Rock); Rhys Williams (Scotty MacDougall); Spring Byington (Mrs. Masters); James Millican (Ike Stapleton); Bruce Cowling (Lieutenant Grimes); Fritz Leiber (Mr. Poole); Harry Antrim (Dr. C. O. MacQuillan); Chief John Big Tree (Thundercloud).

This was Anthony Mann's premier Western film. Its downbeat finale and its blatant sympathy for the American Indian (very unfashionable at the time) caused Dore Schary, new head of MGM, to hold back its release. After Twentieth Century-Fox led the way with Broken Arrow (1950) [q. v.], The Devil's Doorway made its delayed, spotty release. Despite the presence of box-office figure Robert Taylor in a very offbeat assignment, the film was a financial disappointment.

Robert Taylor starred as "Broken Lance" Poole, an educated Shoshone Indian who becomes a decorated hero in the Civil War. After the surrender of Lee he turns West to his homeland. There he begins a ranch which soon grows into a large and fertile spread. A crook (Calhern), however, manipulates the terms of the Homestead Act to acquire Poole's land, claiming that the Indian was really "a ward of the American government." Broken Lance hires lawyer Orrie Masters (Raymond) to defend his case, telling the woman attorney that "a hundred years from now it [their romance] might have worked." Soon thereafter the Army converges on the ranch and, in the slaughter of the tribe, Broken Lance is killed defending his rights and his land. The plotline of The Devil's Doorway is said to be drawn from the real-life account of Chief Joseph of the Nez Perce tribe.

DODGE CITY (Warner Bros., 1939) C 104 min.

Executive producer, Hal B. Wallis; associate producer, Robert Lord; director, Michael Curtiz; screenplay, Robert Buckner; music, Max Steiner; orchestrator, Hugo Friedhofer; dialogue director, Jo Graham; art director, Ted Smith; costumes, Milo Anderson; makeup, Perc Westmore; assistant director, Sherry Shourds; color consultant, Morgan Padelford; sound, Oliver S. Garretson; special effects, Byron Haskin, Rex Wimpy; camera, Sol Polito, Ray Rennahan; editor, George Amy.

Errol Flynn (Wade Hatton); Olivia de Havilland (Abbie Irving); Ann Sheridan (Ruby Gilman); Bruce Cabot (Jeff Surrett); Frank McHugh (Joe Clemens); Alan Hale (Rusty Hart); John Litel (Matt Cole); Henry Travers (Dr. Irving); Victor Jory (Yancey); William Lundigan (Lee Irving); Guinn [Big Boy] Williams (Tex Baird); Bobs Watson (Harry Cole); Gloria Holden (Mrs. Cole); Douglas Fowley (Munger); Georgia Caine (Mrs. Irving); Charles Halton (Surrett's Lawyer); Ward Bond (Bud Taylor); Cora Witherspoon (Mrs. McCoy); Russell Simpson (Orth); Monte Blue (Barlow); Nat Carr (Crocker); Clem Bevans (Barber); Joseph Crehan (Hammond); Thurston Hall (Twitchell); Chester Clute (Coggins).

Frank McHugh, Henry Travers, Nat Carr, Bruce Cabot, Errol
Flynn and Alan Hale in Dodge City (1939).

      Dodge City was Warner Brothers' Technicolor extravaganza
answer to the year's revival of the "A" western with such films as
Stagecoach, Destry Rides Again, Jesse James, Union Pacific and
Man of Conquest [all q. v.].   The studio poured lots of money into
this big, lush production with its huge cast and bountiful action.
Unfortunately, the film's script did not live up to its other ingredients and resulted in "... merely an exciting thriller for the kiddies,
or for grown folk with an appetite for the wild and woolly" (New
York Times).
      Headlining Dodge City was Errol Flynn, cast as Irish soldier-
of-fortune Wade Hutton who had fought in India and Cuba before
coming to the U.S. and joining Jeb Stuart's Grey-Coats before
drifting westward.   Out West he finds Dodge City is a wide-open
cattle town, the most northern shipping point to St. Louis and Chicago for long-horn cattle being brought up the Old Chisholm Trail
from Texas.   Graft, corruption and lawlessness are rampant and
mainly controlled by Jeff Surrett (Cabot).   For romance, saloon
girl Ruby (Ann Sheridan) and good girl Abbie (Olivia de Havilland)
both become involved with Wade, who finally wins Abbie's heart
after thwarting the evil forces of Surrett and thus cleans up the
cattle town, making it safe for further westward migration.
      Dodge City is a vastly entertaining Western and one that has

stood the test of time very well.   Director Curtiz used action in
deference to plot and as a result the film moves very quickly and
easily holds audience attention.   Its magnificently staged saloon
brawl has since been used in countless films and TV shows as stock
footage and the use of Technicolor in the film proved that the Western
was the ideal genre for the developing process.

For Errol Flynn, Dodge City was the first of eight oaters he
would do for Warner Brothers and it was the best of them.   Despite
his British manners, however, the actor made an ideal Western film
hero and more often than not it was his personality that popularized
some of his later, and mediocre, efforts like Silver City and Rocky
Mountain.

In 1951 Dodge City was reissued in a black and white version,
along with Virginia City, and the double-bill proved to be a popular
item.

UN DOLLARO A TESTA (Navajo Joe)   (United Artists, 1966)   C
89 min.

Producers, Ermanno Donati, Luigi Carpentieri; director,
Sergio Corbucci; story, Ugo Pirro; screenplay, Dean Craig, Fernando Di Leo; art director, Aurelio Curgnola; music, Ennio Morricone; wardrobe, Marcella Machis; assistant director, Deodato Rug-
gero; sound, Fernando Terol; camera, Silvano Ippoliti.

Burt Reynolds (Navajo Joe); Aldo Sanbrell (Marvin "Vee"
Duncan); Nicoletta Machiavelli (Estella); Tanya Lopert (Maria);
Fernando Rey (Rattigan); Franca Polesello (Barbana); Lucia Modugno
(Geraldine); Pierre Cressoy (Lynne); Nino Imparato (Chuck); Alvaro
De Luna (Sancho); Valeria Sabel (Honor); Mario Lanfranchi (Clay);
Lucio Rosato (Jeffrey); Simon Arriaga (Monkey); Angel Ortiz (El
Cojo); Fianni Di Stolfo (Reagan); Angel Alvarez (Blackwood); Rafael
Albaicin, Lorenzo Robledo (Bandits).

The combination of Burt Reynolds and the theme of the triumphant underdog gives this Italian-Spanish Western some intrinsic
worth.

Navajo Joe (Reynolds) is the only survivor of an Indian village
massacred by Marvin Duncan (Sanbrell) and his gang of outlaws.
Navajo Joe vows revenge on the attackers.   He hunts down the villains who are themselves seeking a half million dollars in gold.   In
a film already overstocked with murder, mayhem, and bloodshed,
Navajo Joe, at the bloody climax, singlehandedly kills the entire gang.

Beyond the gore and the usual "macho" performance by Reynolds, the film boasts an excellent Ennio Morricone music score.
His theme to the film is considered one of his finest compositions.

DON Q, SON OF ZORRO   see   MARK OF ZORRO

DRIFT FENCE   (Paramount, 1936)   56 min.

Producer, Harold Hurley; director, Otho Lovering; based on
the novel by Zane Grey; screenplay, Robert Yost, Stuart Anthony;
camera, Virgil Miller; editor, C. A. Hisserich.

Larry "Buster" Crabbe (Slinger Dunn); Katherine DeMille
(Molly Dunn); Tom Keene (Jim Travis); Benny Baker (Jim Traft);
Glenn (Leif) Erickson (Curley Prentiss); Stanley Andrews (Clay
Jackson); Richard Carle (Sheriff); Irving Bacon (Windy Watkins);
Effie Ellsler (Granny Dunn); Jan Duggan (Carrie Bingham); Walter
Long (Bev Wilson); Chester Gan (Clarence); Richard Alexander (Seth
Haverly); Bud Fine (Sam Haverly); Jack Pennick (Weary).
Reissue title: Texas Desperadoes.

Most Zane Grey works have been filmed more than once, but
Drift Fence was filmed only once.   It was in 1936 that, as part of
its series on Grey's novels, Paramount turned out this economy
feature.   The production was highlighted by better-than-ordinary location work, a good combination of action and humor, and a brevity
of stock footage.

Young dude Jim Traft (Baker) comes West to take control of
a ranch he has inherited.   He does not welcome the stiff challenge.
A veteran wrangler, Travis (Keene), comes onto the scene, having
assumed Traft's identity.   Travis helps string a drift fence at the
ranch, which is anathema to the cattle ranchers who demand an open
range.   Crook Clay Jackson (Andrews) is behind the effort to force
small ranchers in the district out of business.   He instigates a com-
mittee of the neighboring landowners to oppose--by force--this fence-
building.   Slinger Dunn (Crabbe), a young rancher under Clay's influence, finds that his sister (DeMille) is coveted by boss Jackson.
Travis meets Molly (DeMille) and soon they are in love.   Eventually
Slinger realizes how corrupt Jackson's machinations are and he helps
Travis and the ranchers combat the villains.   At the finale a jubilant Jim Traft takes over control of the ranch.

Drift Fence enjoyed the benefits of Grey's plotline and the
actionful pacing typical of many B oaters of this period.   In his
performance as the hero Keene was restrained, reminding his viewers
and fans of how good he had been in his prior RKO Western series.
Baker's presence provided the comedy relief.   Ironically, Buster
Crabbe, who that same year would enjoy enormous popularity in Universal's chapterplay Flash Gordon, was sadly wasted in a small role.

DRUMS ALONG THE MOHAWK   (Twentieth Century-Fox, 1939)   C
103 min.

Executive producer, Darryl F. Zanuck; producer, Raymond
Griffith; director, John Ford; based on the novel by Walter D. Edmonds; screenplay, Lamar Trotti, Sonya Levien; Technicolor consultants, Natalie Kalmus, Henry Jaffa; music, Alfred Newman; art
directors, Richard Day, Mark Lee Kirk; set decorator, Thomas
Little; costumes, Gwen Wakeling; camera, Bert Glennon, Ray Rennahan; editor, Robert Simpson.

Claudette Colbert (Lana Borst Martin); Henry Fonda (Gilbert Martin); Edna May Oliver (Mrs. McKlennan); Eddie Collins (Christian Reall); John Carradine (Caldwell); Doris Bowdon (Mary Reall); Jessie Ralph (Mrs. Weaver); Arthur Shields (Father Rosenkranz); Robert Lowery (John Weaver); Roger Imhof (General Nicholas Herkimer); Francis Ford (Joe Boleo); Ward Bond (Adam Hartmann); Kay Linaker (Mrs. Demooth); Russell Simpson (Dr. Petry); Chief Big Tree (Blue Back); Spencer Charters (Fisk the Innkeeper); Arthur Aylesworth (George); Si Jenks (Jacobs); Jack Pennick (Amos); Charles Tannen (Robert Johnson); Paul McVey (Captain Mark Demooth); Elizabeth Jones (Mrs. Reall); Lionel Paper (General); Clarence Wilson (Paymaster); Edwin Maxwell (Pastor); Clara Blandick (Mrs. Borst); Beulah Hall Jones (Daisy); Robert Greig (Mr. Borst).

For some strange reason, few Hollywood films have dealt with the period surrounding the American Revolution. Drums Along the Mohawk was one of the few; it was also director John Ford's first color feature and it remains one of his most commercial entries.

At the start of the Revolutionary War, a young couple (Colbert and Fonda) move to the Mohawk Valley. When their farm is burned by Indians, the Martins are hired by Mrs. McKlennan (Oliver) to help work her farm. Later Gil Martin (Fonda) goes to war and it is up to Lana (Colbert), now pregnant again (she lost her first baby), to be the emotional strength of the pioneer couple. She gives birth to a healthy child, but the family's joy is shortlived; the Indians attack again. The villagers go to the fort where the redskins almost overrun the stockade. However, Gil returns in the nick of time with reinforcements. Having won the skirmish, the settlers are confident of their future.

In the New York Times, Frank S. Nugent termed this epic "a first-rate historical film, as rich atmospherically as it is in action." The New York Herald-Tribune gave a more conservative endorsement: "Drums Along the Mohawk lacks unity but, thanks to its direction and its playing, it is a genuinely distinguished historical film."

J. A. Place, analyzing this feature in The Western Films of John Ford, writes, "In many of the traditional respects [it] ... is not a Western at all; it does not use horses except as farm animals, and it is set in the Mohawk Valley. The time period--that of the Revolutionary War--predates considerably the post-Civil War period we associate with the Western. In more basic, important ways, however, Drums Along the Mohawk is definitely a Western and even more definitely a John Ford Western. Many of his ideas about white civilization and its mission in the West have their purest expression in this film."

Greatly aiding the verisimilitude of this production was the casting. Miss Colbert might have been a bit too mature to properly portray the heroine, but she brought conviction to her characterization of the Eastern girl who struggles to adapt to pioneer life style (paralleling her later performance in the contemporary The Egg and I, (1946). Henry Fonda as the sleek-footed farmer was the ideal hero, as he would prove again in Ford's The Grapes of Wrath

(1940), and Edna May Oliver was impressive as the widowed farm
owner. For contrast there was Chief Big Tree as the religious
brave, Blue Back, and John Carradine as the Tory, Caldwell, the
man who leads the Indians against the settlers.

Although much of Walter D. Edmonds' book was excised for
the screenplay, what remained was still a sound historical study
and faithful to the author's concept. Footage from this feature
would later be used in Buffalo Bill (1944) [q.v.] and Mohawk (1956).

DUEL IN THE SUN   (Selznick Releasing Organization, 1946)   C
138 min.

    Producer, David O. Selznick; directors, King Vidor, (un-
credited: Otto Brower, William Dieterle, Sidney Franklin, William
Cameron Menzies, Selznick, Josef von Sternberg); based on the
novel by Niven Busch; adaptor, Oliver H. P. Garrett; screenplay,
Selznick; second unit directors, Brower, B. Reeves Eason; art di-
rectors, James Basevi, John Ewing; production designer, J. Mc-
Millan Johnson; set decorator, Emil Kuri; music-music director,
Dimitri Tiomkin; song, Allie Wrubel; assistant directors, Lowell
Farrell, Harvey Dwight; solo dances, Tilly Losch; group dances,
Lloyd Shaw; sound, James Stewart, Richard DeWeese; special
camera effects, Clarence Slifer, Jack Cosgrove; camera, Lee
Garmes, Hal Rosson, Ray Rennahan; additional camera, Charles P.
Boyle, Allen Davey; editors, Hal C. Kern, William Ziegler, John
D. Faure, Charles Freeman.

    Jennifer Jones (Pearl Chavez); Joseph Cotten (Jesse McCanles);
Gregory Peck (Lewt McCanles); Lionel Barrymore (Senator McCanles);
Lillian Gish (Laura Belle McCanles); Walter Huston (The Sin Killer);
Herbert Marshall (Scott Chavez); Charles Bickford (Sam Pierce); Joan
Tetzel (Helen Langford); Harry Carey (Lem Smoot); Otto Kruger (Mr.
Langford); Sidney Blackmer (The Lover); Tilly Losch (Mrs. Chavez);
Scott McKay (Sid); Butterfly McQueen (Vashti); Francis McDonald,
Victor Kilian (Gamblers); Griff Barnett (The Jailer); Frank Cordell
(Frank); Dan White (Ed); Steve Dunhill (Jake); Lane Chandler (Captain,
U.S. Cavalry); Lloyd Shaw (Barbecue Caller); Bert Roach (Eater); Si
Jenks, Hank Worden, Rose Plummer (Dancers); Guy Wilkerson (Bar-
fly); Lee Phelps (Engineer); Al Taylor (Man at Barbecue); Orson
Welles (Narrator).

    Hell-bent on creating a screen production to top his Gone
With the Wind (1939), producer David O. Selznick invested over $5
million and some twenty months of actual filming to make this mammoth (138 minutes) feature which, when it was finally released in
1946, was jocularly dubbed "lust in the dust." Both fanatic on
details and insistent that his actress-wife, Jennifer Jones, be show-
cased in every way, Selznick indulged himself with numerous retakes of almost every scene. Several directors came and went in
the course of this elaborate undertaking.

    Reduced to a simple plotline, Duel in the Sun seems even
more childish and absurd than present-day filmgoers may find it.

Gregory Peck and Jennifer Jones in Duel in the Sun (1946).

The picture chronicles the life and times of crusty, crippled Senator
McCanles (Barrymore) who owns a million-acre ranch and who
fights the oncoming railroad which wants to build tracks across his
spread. McCanles' two sons, Harvard-educated lawyer Jesse (Cotten) and no-good Lewt (Peck) constantly bicker in the best Cain and
Abel tradition. Their uneasy relationship boils over into mutual
anger when they both become involved with the tempestuous reckless
half-breed, Pearl Chavez (Jennifer "Song of Bernadette" Jones as a
vixen-siren?--Selznick thought she could outdo Jane Russell in a
sultry part). In the course of events, Lewt kills Pearl's husband,
wrecks a train, and attempts to murder Jesse. At the climax, in
a sequence now regarded as high camp, Pearl and Lewt engage in
a shoot-out on a mountainous expanse. They die in each other's
arms.

Duel in the Sun received one of the biggest selling campaigns
in American film history. As a result it grossed over $17 million
in its initial release. Because of its "stormy" love scenes, the
Legion of Decency demanded several retakes of certain romantic
scenes. Local censor boards had a field day in banning the picture.
Memphis, Tennessee and Hartford, Connecticut were among those to
forbid the film from being shown in their cities--at least, at first.
Duel in the Sun was roundly denounced by both Catholic and Protes-
tant public interest groups. The Pennsylvania Board of Motion Picture Censors ruled the film had to be toned down before it could be
shown in Philadelphia.

Producer-writer Charles Brackett called Duel in the Sun "The
Outlaw in bad taste," while Newsweek decided that "... a lot of this
makes for flamboyant action and a sweeping panorama of the great
Southwest--and a lot more makes for sexy pulp writing that should
have stayed on the wrong side of the railroad tracks."

However, no critic could deny that the excellent cinematography gave the viewer a sweeping panorama, in color, of the great
American west. And Dimitri Tiomkin's score is a fine accompani-
ment to the turgid action oncamera. Lillian Gish, as Barrymore's
patient, brave wife who dies, and Miss Jones were both Oscar-
nominated for their roles. Jennifer lost to Olivia de Havilland (To
Each His Own) while Miss Gish was beaten in the Academy Award
sweepstakes for best supporting actress by Anne Baxter (The Razor's
Edge).

Selznick had the practical sense to pepper the film with many
good supporting players, including Herbert Marshall as Pearl's
father, Walter Huston as a Bible-thumping preacher, Charles Bickford as the man who truly loves Pearl, and other stalwart performers
such as Harry Carey, Otto Kruger, and Sidney Blackmer. Having
used Butterfly McQueen in Gone with the Wind, Selznick could not
resist utilizing her services once more--here as the bizarre domestic,
Vashti. The epic's narration was provided by sonorous Orson Welles.

Perhaps the most concise summation of Duel in the Sun was
provided by Walter Clapham in The Movie Treasury of Western
Movies (1974) when he labeled it "a top-heavy piece of deep purple,
laughable at times, which quite overpowered some likely action
aspects."

EHI, AMICO ... C'E SABATA, HAI CHIUSO! (SABATA) United Artists, 1970) C 106 min.

Producer, Alberto Grimaldi; director, Frank Kramer [Gianfranco Parolini]; screenplay, Renato Izzo, Parolini; assistant director, Ignazio Dolce; art director, Carlo Simi; music, Marcello Giombini; sound, Tonino Palombi, Pietro Stadoni; special effects, Stacchini; camera, Sandro Mancori; editor, Edmondo Lozzi.

Lee Van Cleef (Sabata); William Berger (Banjo); Franco Ressel (Stengel); Linda Veras (Jane); Pedro Sanchez [Ignazio Spalla] (Carrincha); Gianni Rizzo (Judge O'Hara); Anthony Gradwell [Antonio Gradoli] (Fergusson); Nick Jordan (Alley Cat); Robert Hundar [Claudio Undari] (Oswald); Spanny Convery [Spartaco Conversi] (Slim); Marco Zuanelli (Sharky); Gino Marturano (McCallum); Joseph Mathews [Pino Mattei] (Frankie); Franco Ukmar (Cutty); Bruno Ukmar (Jumping Kid); R. Lodi (Father Brown); Allan Collins [Luciano Pigozzi] (False Father Brown); Vittorio Andre (Logan); Romano Puppo (Rocky Bendato); Andrew Ray [Andrew Aureli] (Daniel); Franco Marletta (Captain); Mimmo Poli (Hotel Workman).

Taking place in Texas in the post-Civil War period, this Italian production starred Lee Van Cleef as the title character, a man of steel nerves who prevents the robbery of $100,000 from a bank by killing all seven bandits and then blackmailing their employers for a similar sum of money before also killing them. Assisted by a Mexican drifter (Sanchez) and an acrobatic Indian (Jordan), Sabata (Van Cleef) then outfoxes a rich man's private army of

Lee Van Cleef in Sabata (1970).

hired assassins, killing off the mercenaries before eventually elimi-
nating their leader as well.

A violent, bloody feature, this film was immensely popular
in Europe. Of the dubbed version shown in the United States, Roger
Greenspun (New York Times) wrote, it "is a very long, hugely event-
ful, moderately bloody, immoderately inventive, generally good-
humored Italian western...." Across the Atlantic Ocean, the British
Monthly Film Bulletin judged, "A certain cold-blooded ingenuity provides a substitute for inspiration in this colourful but extended anthology of Italian Western cliches. Its baroque details prove most
effective when borrowed most directly...."

In 1972 Van Cleef reteamed with director Frank Dramer
[Gianfranco Parolini] for the sequel, Return of Sabata. This time
around, the one-time Confederate major (Van Cleef) is a circus
sharpshooter who comes to a small town and puts a violent stop to
a dishonest public improvements program while making money for
himself (naturally). This sequel was not up to the original, being
almost two solid hours of violence and mayhem.

THE EMIGRANTS   see   THE NEW LAND

THE EROTIC ADVENTURES OF ZORRO   see   MARK OF ZORRO

ESCAPE FROM FORT BRAVO   (MGM, 1953)   C   98 min.

Producer, Nicholas Nayfack; director, John Sturges; story,
Philip Rock, Michael Pate; screenplay, Frank Fenton; music, Jeff
Alexander; art directors, Cedric Gibbons, Malcolm Brown; set
decorators, Edwin B. Willis, Ralph Hurst; women's costumes,
Helen Rose; makeup, William Tuttle; color consultant, Alvard Eiseman; special effects, Warren Newcombe; camera, Robert Surtees;
editor, George Boemler.

William Holden (Captain Roper); Eleanor Parker (Carla For-
rester); John Forsythe (Captain John Marsh); William Demarest
(Campbell); William Campbell (Cabot Young); John Lupton (Bailey);
Richard Anderson (Lieutenant Beecher); Polly Bergen (Alice Owens);
Carl Benton Reid (Colonel Owens).

Filmed in Ansco color, this John Sturges Western was set in
the Arizona Territory during the Civil War. The Union troops at
Fort Bravo are at odds with rampaging Mescalero Apaches and
restless Confederate prisoners. Captain John Marsh (Forsythe) and
three other Southern pals, confined to the Fort, plan to escape.
Marsh's fiancée, Carla Forrester (Parker) arrives at the stockade,
allegedly to attend a wedding. Actually she is on hand to provide
help for the jailbreak. The quartet escapes with Captain "Bring'em-
back" Roper (Holden) pursuing them. Soon both factions find themselves surrounded by combative Indians.

Considering the facilities and technical resources at MGM's

beck and call, there is little that is remarkable about Escape from Fort Bravo beyond its multi-hued cinematography and the luscious presence of a radiant Miss Parker. In his first Western since Streets of Laredo (1949), Holden was appropriately brusque as the army officer. Calling on the tried and true ploy of the inevitable redskin attack, the picture "perks up for some random, tingling Indian skirmishes" (New York Times).

FADE-IN   see   BLUE

THE FIGHTING PHANTOM   see   THE MYSTERIOUS RIDER (1933)

THE FINAL HOUR   see   THE VIRGINIAN

FIRECREEK   see   STRANGER ON THE RUN

THE FIRST REBEL   see   ALLEGHENY UPRISING

A FISTFUL OF DOLLARS   see   PER UN PUGNO DI DOLLARI

UN FIUME DI DOLLARI (THE HILLS RUN RED/A RIVER OF DOLLARS) (United Artists, 1967)   C   89 min.

Executive producer, Dino De Laurentiis; producers, Ermanno Donati, Luigi Carpentieri; director, Lee W. Beaver [Carlo Lizzani]; screenplay, Dean Craig; music, Ennio Morricone; song, Nichols Nohra; art director, Aurelio Crugnola; costumes, Elio Micheli; camera, Antonio Secchi; editor, Ornella Michell.

Thomas Hunter (Jerry Brewster); Henry Silva (Mendez); Dan Duryea (Getz); Nando Gazzolo (Ken Seagall); Nicoletta Machiavelli (Mary Ann); Gianna Serra (Hattie); Loris Loddi (Tim); Geoffrey Copleston (Homer); Paolo Magalotti (Stayne); Tiberio Mitri (Federal Sergeant); Vittorio Bonos (Gambler); Mirko Valentin (Sancho); Guglielmo Spoletini (Pedro); Guido Celano (Burger); Mauro Mannatrizio (Soldier Mitch); Gian Luigi Crescenzi (Carson).

This Italian-made oater was issued in its homeland as Un Fiume di Dollari (A River of Dollars) and was directed by Carlo Lizzani, known in the U.S. as Lee W. Beaver. Although popular in Europe, it was just one of a string of spaghetti Westerns which were flooding the U.S. at this time. In America it played on the drive-in circuit to mediocre business, as The Hills Run Red.

Actually the film is better than the average Western, if compensation is made for the asinine dubbing and the incongruity of the Italians portraying American settlers of the Old West. The plot

concerns an ex-Confederate soldier Jerry Brewster (Hunter) who is
put in jail for stealing an Army payroll. Actually the heist was
accomplished by his pal Ken Seagall (Gazzolo). After five years in
prison Jerry is released and seeks revenge against Seagall, only to
find the man is now a ruthless range dictator. To add to the suspense there is Getz (Duryea), a mysterious stranger who continually
rescues Jerry from danger.

Variety wrote of the picture, that it had "enough action ...
to fill three pix, but film carries on the European tradition of
shooting up everyone in sight." The American advertising campaign
for the film read: "They meet--and The Hills Run Red."

FLAME OF SACRAMENTO   see   IN OLD SACRAMENTO

FLAMING FRONTIER   (Universal, 1926)   8,828'

Director-story, Edward Sedgwick; screenplay, Edward J.
Montagne, Charles Kenyon; adaptor, Raymond I. Schrock; camera,
Virgil Millet.

Hoot Gibson (Bob Langdon); Anne Cornwall (Betty Stanwood);
Dustin Farnum (General Custer); Ward Crane (Sam Belden); Kathleen
Key (Lucretia); Eddie Gribbon (Jonesy); Harry Todd (California Joe);
Harold Goodwin (Lawrence Stanwood); George Fawcett (Senator Stan-
wood); Noble Johnson (Sitting Bull); Charles K. French (Senator
Hargess); William Steele (Penfield); Walter Rodgers (President U.S.
Grant); Ed Wilson (Grant's Secretary); Joe Bonomo (Rain in the
Face).

FLAMING FRONTIER (a.k.a. FLAME OF THE WEST)   (Monogram
1945)   70 min.

Producer, Scott R. Dunlap; director, Lambert Hillyer; story,
Bennett Foster; screenplay, Adele Buffington; art director, E. R.
Hickson; music director, Frank Sanucci; camera, Harry Neumann;
editor, Dan Milner.

Johnny Mack Brown (John Poore); Raymond Hatton (Add); Joan
Woodbury (Poppy); Douglass Dumbrille (Nightlander); Harry Woods
(Wisdon); John Merton (Compton); Riley Hill (Midland); Steve Clark
(Hendricks); Bud Osborne (Pircell); Jack Rockwell (Knott); Raphael
Bennett (Rocky); Tom Quinn (Ed); Jack Ingram (Slick); Pee Wee King
and His Golden West Cowboys (Themselves).

Prior to the sound era Hoot Gibson was Universal's most
popular Western star, earning as much as $14,000 per week in the
late twenties. Flaming Frontier was one of his most enthusiastically-
received efforts, typical of the light but actionful films with which he
delighted action-bent audiences.

Directed and written by Edward Sedgwick, the film offered
Hoot as Pony Express rider Bob Langdon whom a senator (Fawcett)

helps to win an appointment to West Point. It is not long before Bob
succumbs to the charms of the senator's daughter, Betty Stanwood
(Cornwall). Good-natured Bob even protects her brother (Goodwin)
from scandal involving another woman. He accepts the guilt for the
latter's misdeeds and for his efforts is expelled from the Academy.
Bob returns to the West to serve with General Custer (Farnum).
At the Battle of the Little Big Horn he rides for help but arrives
too late to save the troops. Later Bob brings a crooked Indian
agent to justice. His reputation restored, Bob can now return to
West Point.

This Gibson feature encompassed spectacle but could not be
termed an epic drama. However, it did include a number of fine
battle scenes (used later in Universal's first all-talking serial, The
Indians Are Coming, 1930 [q.v.]). One of the more memorable
sequences within the film was when Indians were seen attacking buffalo hunters in order to protect their herds from being further
slaughtered.

In 1945, Monogram issued another film entitled Flaming
Frontier, a.k.a. Flame of the West. It was directed by Lambert
Hillyer who once worked with William S. Hart. This Johnny Mack
Brown series Western was an interesting departure from the run-
of-the-reel oater of the time. Brown played a mild-mannered and
pacifist doctor who rouses the ire of his girlfriend (Carver), who
thinks he is a coward because he will not oppose the local outlaws.
When the sheriff (Dumbrille) is killed by a dishonest gambler our
hero is goaded into stopping the gang. This seventy-minute feature
also spotlighted Pee Wee King (co-composer of "Tennessee Waltz"
and "Slow Poke") and his Golden West Cowboys. They provided the
musical interludes which by then were so firmly established in series
Westerns.

FLAMING STAR   (Twentieth Century-Fox, 1960) C 101 min.

Producer, David Weisbart; director, Don Siegel; based on the
novel by Clair Huffaker; screenplay, Huffaker, Nunnally Johnson;
music, Cyril J. Mockridge; music director, Lionel Newman; orchestrator, Edward B. Powell; songs, Sherman Edwards and Sid Wayne;
Sid Tepper and Roy Bennett; art directors, Duncan Cramer, Walter
M. Simonds; set decorators, Walter M. Scott, Gustav Berntsen; assistant director, Joseph E. Rickards; costumes, Adele Balkan; makeup, Ben Nye; choreography, Josephine Earl; sound, E. Clayton Ward,
Warren B. Delaplain; camera, Charles G. Clarke; editor, Hugh S.
Fowler.

Elvis Presley (Pacer Burton); Barbara Eden (Roslyn Pierce);
Steve Forrest (Clint Burton); Dolores Del Rio (Neddy Burton); John
McIntire (Pa Burton); Rudolph Acosta (Buffalo Horn); Karl Swenson
(Dred Pierce); Ford Rainey (Doc Phillips); Richard Jaeckel (Angus
Pierce); Anne Benton (Dorothy Howard); L. Q. Jones (Tom Howard);
Douglas Dick (Will Howard); Tom Reese (Jute); Marian Goldina (Ph'-
Sha Kney); Monte Burkhardt (Ben Ford); Ted Jacques (Hornsby); Rodd
Redwing (Indian Brave); Perry Lopez (Two Moons); Sharon Bercutt
(Bird's Wing); The Jordanaires (Themselves).

This vehicle had been written originally for Marlon Brando
but was revised by director Donald Siegel and Clair Huffaker for
Elvis Presley. With the rock 'n roll idol singing only the title
tune and another song ("A Cane and a High Starched Collar"), it
was the best feature to that date for Presley. It proved that he
could emote as well as undulate.

The narrative concerned a family, in 1870s Texas, which is
caught between loyalty to whites and Indians. Rancher Pa Burton
(McIntire) has one son Clint (Forrest) by a white woman, and the
other, Pacer (Presley), by his present wife, an Indian woman (Del
Rio). When the Kiowa Indians massacre a white family in the
vicinity, the settlers demand that the Burtons prove their loyalty to
the white folk. Meanwhile, Neddy (Del Rio) and Pacer go to the
Kiowa camp hoping to arrange a truce. They fail in their task and
on the way back to the spread, Neddy is fatally wounded by a crazed
settler. Later, Neddy "sees" the "flaming star" of death and leaves
her death bed to wander onto the windswept fields where she dies.
Not long afterward, Pa is killed by rampaging redskins. Thereafter Clint is wounded by the Kiowas, and Pacer, realizing his half-
brother needs him, leaves the tribe to help Clint. He manages to
stave off the marauding Indians and after the skirmish he goes to
town to bid goodbye to Clint. Then he too follows the "flaming
star" of death.

The British Films and Filming called this production a "minor
western classic," while Arthur Knight wrote in Saturday Review that
Presley's performance was "a singularly effective one.... It is the
depth of feeling he reveals that comes as such a surprise." On the
other hand, the New York Herald-Tribune compared it to the similar
but better The Unforgiven (1960) [q.v.] and added, "subtlety has been
sacrificed to melodrama in Flaming Star.... Violence abounds.
The death toll is appalling, and a truce would be welcome after the
first eighty minutes of carnage. Oddly enough, and despite its best
intentions, Flaming Star indulges in some foolish racism while
preaching a sermon of tolerance."

Thanks to the artistry of director Don Siegel, now very much
a cult figure, both Presley and the film emerged as far more realistic and sound than anyone had a right to hope. Originally Barbara
Steele (one of the queens of the horror genre) was scheduled to play
the role done by Barbara Eden.

FOR A FEW DOLLARS MORE   see   PER QUALCHE DOLLARO
IN PIU

FORT APACHE   (RKO, 1948)   127 min.

Producers, John Ford, Merian C. Cooper; director, Ford;
based on the story "Massacre" by James Warner Bellah; screenplay,
Frank S. Nugent; music, Richard Hageman; music director, Lucien
Cailliet; art director, James Basevi; set decorator, Joe Kish; costumes: Michael Meyers (men), Ann Peck (women); assistant

directors, Lowell Farrell, Jack Pennick; second unit director, Cliff
Lyons; makeup, Emile La Vigne; choreography, Kenny Williams;
technical advisors, Major Philip Keiffer, Katherine Spaatz; costume
researcher, D. R. O. Hatswell; sound, Frank Webster, Joseph
Kane; special effects, Dave Koehler; camera, Archie Stout; editor,
Jack Murray.

John Wayne (Captain Kirby York); Henry Fonda (Lieutenant
Colonel Owen Thursday); Shirley Temple (Philadelphia Thursday);
John Agar (Lieutenant Michael O'Rourke); Ward Bond (Sergeant
Major O'Rourke); George O'Brien (Captain Sam Collingwood); Victor
McLaglen (Sergeant Mulcahy); Pedro Armendariz (Sergeant Beaufort);
Anna Lee (Mrs. Collingwood); Irene Rich (Mrs. O'Rourke); Guy
Kibbee (Dr. Wilkens); Grant Withers (Silas Meacham); Miguel Inclan
(Cochise); Jack Pennick (Sergeant Schattuck); Mae Marsh (Mrs.
Gates); Dick Foran (Sergeant Quincannon); Frank Ferguson (News-
paperman); Francis Ford (Bartender); Ray Hyke, Movita Castenada,
Mary Gordon (Bits).

Thank heaven for John Ford and Westerns such as Fort
Apache! The film's visual and verbatim definition of the Old West
smacks of complete reality, even when truth is being stretched for
the sake of the plotline and Hollywood standards.

This lengthy cavalry film was Ford's initial entry into a trio
on the U.S. cavalry, the others being She Wore a Yellow Ribbon
(1949) [q.v.] and Rio Grande (1950) [q.v.]. As J. A. Place observes
in The Western Films of John Ford (1975), "... it is the simplest
and most uncomplicated expression of the [cavalry] theme. The ideal
of the cavalry is never brought into question, only individuals within
it. Methodology is questioned, not the mythology behind it ... the
firm belief expressed virtually that there is a oneness about the
cavalry, a wholeness that makes the sacrifice of individuality worthwhile. The men are not even remembered by their names except
for Thursday, who is remembered as something he was not. Never
again is Ford so sure about the sacrifice of the individual."

Told in a leisurely, assured fashion, Fort Apache copes with
the plight of a Civil War general, Owen Thursday (Fonda), demoted to
lieutenant colonel and shipped West to take command of a desert outpost, Fort Apache. At the stockade the veteran soldiers resent his
being sent as commanding officer, for the newcomer knows nothing
about fighting Indians. They soon realize he is only after fame,
glory and a restoration of his former rank.

Thursday insists on stern discipline, much to the chagrin of
his men. When his comely daughter Philadelphia (Temple) falls in
love with a non-commissioned man, Lieutenant O'Rourke (Agar), her
father is dismayed; her actions are not according to rules and regu-
lations. Later, Thursday seizes a chance for recognition and decides
to follow Cochise (Inclan) who has led braves into Mexico after grow-
ing tired of government corruption at the reservation. Stern, Thursday
dispatches leathery Captain Kirby York (Wayne), whom Cochise trusts,
and a sergeant (Armendariz) to arrange a meeting with the Indian
chief. However, Thursday double-crosses them by arriving with his
Army and ordering Cochise and his braves to return to the appointed

lands. Instead, the Indian leader attacks the soldiers and wipes out
Thursday's unit, leaving only York's small band unharmed. Returning to the fort, gallant Kirby covers over his superior's blunder,
making the late commander appear a hero.

Critical reaction to this important film was mixed. The New
York Times thought it a "rootin', tootin' Wild West show," while
the New York Herald-Tribune weighed it as "a visually absorbing
celebration of violent deeds." Newsweek reported: it succeeds "in
bringing back the time-honored business of making redskins bite the
dust as first-rate entertainment," while Time called it "an unabashed
potboiler" and added that it contained "some of the bleakest Irish
comedy and sentimentality since the death of vaudeville."

Shamrock-drenched blarney does permeate many of the non-
action scenes, particularly when Ward Bond and Victor McLaglen
stretch the human interest aspects of the film to the limit. But
such a minor transgression is allowable when compared to Ford's
broad theme as he delineates the life styles and individual personalities that make up the storyline. Through Miss Temple and the likes
of Mae Marsh, Irene Rich, and Anna Lee viewers of the film can
obtain a concept of domestic life on a frontier army post and a sense
of how the wives and families of these prairie fighters felt, reacted,
and survived.

Obviously in Henry Fonda and John Wayne, two long-standing
members of Ford's stock company, the director had extremely competent acting tools to express the polar views of nineteenth century
army life: of living by the rules, or of bending them, as the case
need be. If anything, Fort Apache stands as a belated recruiting
picture for the Army, demonstrating its camaraderie and that a man
never need be alone there.

It is noteworthy that the Indian massacre of the soldiers in
this film is one of Ford's finest excursions onto the cinematic battle-
field. One can only wonder what Marlon Brando and other Wounded
Knee supporters would have to say about this aspect of the film.

FOUR FACES WEST (United Artists, 1948) 90 min.

Producer, Harry Sherman; associate producer, Vernon E.
Clark; director, Alfred E. Green; based on the novel Paso Por Aqui
by Eugene Manlove Rhodes; adaptors, William and Milarde Brent;
screenplay, Graham Baker, Teddi Sherman; art director, Duncan
Cramer; set decorator, Ray Robinson; music-music director, Paul
Sawtell; assistant director, Nate Barrager; makeup, Gus Norin;
sound, Frank Webster; camera, Russell Harlan; editor, Edward
Mann.

Joel McCrea (Ross McEwen); Frances Dee (Fay Hollister);
Charles Bickford (Pat Garrett); Joseph Calleia (Monte Marquez);
William Conrad (Sheriff Egan); Martin Garralaga (Florencio); Ray-
mond Largay (Dr. Eldredge); John Parrish (Flenger); Dan White
(Clint Waters); Davison Clark (Burnett); Eve Novak (Mrs. Winston);
George McDonald (Winston Boy); Houseley Stevenson (Anderson); Sam
Flint (Storekeeper); Forrest Taylor (Conductor).

British release title: They Passed This Way.

Charles Bickford in <u>Four Faces West</u> (1948).

A surprisingly non-violent Western, this diverting low-keyed
feature was done in an upbeat style that caused Newsweek to say
that it was "the same old wine in the same old bottle [with] a
pleasantly new flavor."

This Harry "Pop" Sherman production's basic premise had
Ross McEwen (McCrea) stealing $2,000 from a New Mexico bank
in order to save his father's ranch. Ross is thereafter chased by
an honest lawman (Bickford). Along the way McEwen is aided by a
pretty railroad nurse (Dee), who wants him to return and face
justice, and a saloon keeper (Calleia). The ending finds Sheriff
Pat Garrett (Bickford) capturing Ross because he stayed behind to
save a Mexican family plagued with illness.

Truly this gentle film is "easy on the eyes and ears" (New
York Times). The interaction between McCrea and Dee, real life
husband-and-wife, was smooth and effective.

FROM HELL TO TEXAS (Twentieth Century-Fox, 1958) C 100 min.

Producer, Robert Buckner; director, Henry Hathaway; based
on the book The Hell-Bent Kid by Charles O. Locke; screenplay,
Robert Buckner, Wendell Mayes; music, Daniele Amfitheatrof; or-
chestrator, Edward B. Powell; art directors, Lyle R. Wheeler,
Walter Simonds; set decorators, Walter M. Scott, Chester Bayhi;
costumes, Adele Balkan; makeup, Ben Nye; assistant director,
Stanley Hough; sound, Eugene Irving; special camera effects, L. B.
Abbott; camera, Wilfred M. Cline; editor, Johnny Ehrin.

Don Murray (Tod Lehman); Diane Varsi (Juanita Bradley);
Chill Wills (Amos Bradley); Dennis Hopper (Tom Boyd); R. G. Arm-
strong (Hunter Boyd); Jay C. Flippen (Jake Leffertfinger); Margo
(Mrs. Bradley); John Larch (Hal Carmody); Ken Scott (Otis Boyd);
Rodolfo Acosta (Bayliss); Salvador Baquez (Cardito); Harry Carey,
Jr. (Trueblood); Jerry Oddo (Morgan); Jose Torvay (Miguel); Mal-
colm Atterbury (Hotel Clerk).

British release title: Manhunt.

In this film, which combined the rawness of the Old West
with vast and epic themes, yet was accomplished in a modern day
style, Henry Hathaway fused successfully the old and new method
of Western filmmaking. "If flames and movie gunplay don't distress
you, you'll find this Western big enough, lively enough and suffi-
cently pictorial to give you extraordinary enjoyment" (New York
Herald-Tribune).

Wrongly accused of killing one of the three sons of Hunter
Boyd (Armstrong), Tod Lohman (Murray) heads across the New
Mexico wastelands. Tod is aided by a sympathetic rancher (Wills)
and falls in love with the man's tomboy daughter Juanita (Varsi).
Eventually this leads to Bradley's demise at the hands of a vengeful
helper of Boyd. Tom realizes that he can no longer keep running
and must make a stand. In the scuffle that ensues, Boyd's last
remaining son, Tom (Hopper), is caught in a blaze. Tod drops
his firearms to help put out the flame. Appreciating this gesture,

Don Murray, Chill Wills and Diane Varsi in From Hell to Texas
(1958).

Boyd calls off the vendetta.   Tod and Juanita are now able to re-
sume their romance.
        This big colorful, CinemaScope film was especially enhanced
by a memorable performance by Wills as the affluent rancher, who
is married to a Mexican woman and has a parcel of small daughters.

FRONTIER BADMEN (Universal, 1943) 80 min.

        Producer-director, Ford Beebe; screenplay, Gerald Geraghty,
Morgan B. Cox; art directors, John B. Goodman, Ralph DeLacy;
set decorators, Russell Gausman, Leigh Smith; assistant director,
Seward Webb; music director, H. J. Salter; sound, Bernard B.
Brown, Charles Carroll; camera, William Sickner; editor, Fred
Feitshans, Jr.
        Diana Barrymore (Claire); Robert Paige (Steve); Anne Gwynne
(Chris); Leo Carrillo (Chinto); Andy Devine (Slim); Noah Beery, Jr.
(Jim); Lon Chaney, Jr. (Chango); Tex Ritter (Kimball); William
Farnum (Courtwright); Thomas Gomez (Ballard); Robert Homans
(Sheriff); Tom Fadden (Thompson); Arthur Loft (Lindsay); Frank
Lackteen (Cherokee); Norman Willis (Randall); Jack Rockwell (Mack);
Stanley Price (Blackie); George Eldredge (Cattle Buyer); Earle

Hodgins (Desk Clerk); Eddy Waller (Auctioneer); Charles Waggen-
heim (Melvin); Fern Emmett (Milliner); Kermit Maynard (Townsman); Beverly Mitchell (Waitress).

Although made on a medium budget, this Western had a
great deal of authenticity plus a fine cast. It received some critical praise, but not from sources such as the New York Times
("Strictly according to formula"). Even old-time Western lead Hoot
Gibson told producer-director Ford Beebe that Frontier Badmen was
the finest Western he had ever seen!
        Set in 1869, the story details how two cattlemen (Paige and
Beery, Jr.) drive their herd on the Old Chisholm Trail to Abilene.
Once there, they find that a syndicate has been set up to halt direct
dealings between cattle owners and buyers. Steve (Paige) then
organizes a cattlemen's exchange and fights the leader of the syndicate (Gomez) after the latter's hired gunman (Chaney, Jr.) has
killed the father of heroine Chris (Gwynne).
        Besides the sensible direction of veteran Beebe, the feature
boasted a well handled cattle stampede, organized by Lewis D.
Collins. The obvious selling point of the production, though, was
its cast, which included Universal's monster star, Lon Chaney, Jr.,
as well as romantic lead Robert Paige, cowboy star Tex Ritter,
silent film lead William Farnum, and the ill-fated daughter (Diana)
of celebrated John Barrymore. With his special billing as Chango
the Mad Killer, Chaney turned in a well-modulated performance as
the sadistic murderer.

FRONTIER GAL (Universal, 1945) C 84 min.

        Executive producer, Howard Benedict; producers, Michael
Fessier, Ernest Pagano; director, Charles Lamont; screenplay,
Fessier, Pagano; art directors, John S. Goodman, Richard H.
Riedel; set decorators, Russell A. Gausman, Oliver Emert; songs,
Jack Brooks and Edgar Fairchild; music-music director, Frank
Skinner; vocal director, H. J. Salter; assistant director, William
Tummel; sound, William Hedgcock; special camera, John P. Fulton;
camera, George Robinson, Charles P. Boyle; editor, Ray Snyder.
        Yvonne De Carlo (Lorena Dumont); Rod Cameron (Johnny
Hart); Andy Devine (Big Ben); Fuzzy Knight (Fuzzy); Sheldon Leonard
(Blackie); Andrew Tombes (Judge Prescott); Beverly Sue Simmons
(Mary Ann Hart); Clara Blandick (Abigail); Frank Lackteen (Chero-
kee); Claire Carleton (Gracie); Eddie Dun, Harold Goodwin (Bailiffs);
Jack Overman (Buffalo); Jan Wiley (Sheila Winthrop); Rex Lease,
George Eldredge, Jack Ingram, Joseph Haworth (Henchmen); Lloyd
Ingraham, Joseph E. Bernard, Douglas Carter, Lou Wood, Paul
Bratti (Dealers); Edward M. Howard (Henchman at Bar); Jean Trent,
Joan Shawlee, Kerry Vaughn, Karen Randle (Hostesses); Eddie Lee
(Wing Lee the Candy-Shop Proprietor); Jack O'Shea, Billy Engle
(Barflies); Cliff Lyons (Brawler in Candy Shop/Double for Sheldon
Leonard); Jack Rutherford (Bit at Table); Eddie Borden (Man at
Table); William Desmond, Kit Guard (Extras in Saloon).
        Release title in England: The Bride Wasn't Willing.

This color project was originally slated for the popular team
of Maria Montez and Jon Hall, but that exotic duo already had lost
much of their box-office lure. Instead Yvonne De Carlo and Rod
Cameron, both relative newcomers on the lot, were given the assignment and it helped to develop these two stars into two of the
Westerns' top box-office names.
        Johnny Hart (Cameron) rides into the rough town of Red
Gulch in the early 1900s with a posse fast on his trail. He is
sought for the killing of his partner. At the local saloon he takes
a shine to fiery singer Lorena Dumont (De Carlo) and forces the
rambunctious lass to wed him--with a pistol as his ace card. After
one night together, Lorena turns her spouse over to the sheriff.
Six years later Hart is released from jail and returns to Red Gulch,
surprised to learn that he is the father of a five-year old girl
(Simmons). The fact that Johnny is a father seems to annoy
Johnny's new flame, Sheila Winthrop (Wiley). The remainder of
the film has Lorena and Johnny squaring off in angry passion.
Eventually it is their daughter who brings about a reconciliation.
        Although made on a $1.4 million budget (a hefty production
by Universal standards), Frontier Gal was rather vapid artistically.
The comely presence of Miss De Carlo and the ingratiating personality of Cameron helped somewhat to smooth over the rough, dull
stretches.

FRONTIER MARSHAL (Fox, 1934) 66 min.

        Director, Lew Seiler; based on the novel Wyatt Earp, Fron-
tier Marshal by Stuart N. Lake; screenplay, William Conselman,
Stuart Anthony; sound, Bernard Fredericks; camera, Robert Planck.
        George O'Brien (Michael Wyatt); Irene Bentley (Mary Reid);
George E. Stone (Abe Ruskin); Alan Edwards (Doc Warren); Ruth
Gillette (Queenie LaVerne); Berton Churchill (Hiram Melton); Frank
Conroy (Oscar Reid); Ward Bond (Ben Murchison); Edward LeSaint
(Judge Walters); Russell Simpson (Editor Pickett); Jerry Foster
(Jerome).

FRONTIER MARSHAL (20th Century-Fox, 1939) 71 min.

        Producer, Sol M. Wurtzel; director, Allan Dwan; based on
the novel Wyatt Earp, Frontier Marshal by Stuart N. Lake; screen-
play, Sam Hellman; art directors, Richard Day, Lewis Creber; set
decorator, Thomas Little; costumes, Herschel; camera, Charles G.
Clarke; editor, Fred Allen.
        Randolph Scott (Wyatt Earp); Nancy Kelly (Sarah Allen);
Cesar Romero (Doc Holliday); Binnie Barnes (Jerry); John Carra-
dine (Ben Carter); Edward Norris (Dan Blackmore); Eddie Foy, Jr.
(Eddie Foy); Ward Bond (Town Marshal); Lon Chaney, Jr. (Pringle);
Tom Tyler (Buck Newton); Chris-Pin Martin (Pete); Joe Sawyer
(Curly Bill); Del Henderson (Proprietor of Bella Union Cafe); Harry
Hayden (Mayor Henderson); Ventura Ybarra (Pablo); Si Jenks

(Prospector); Gloria Roy (Dance Hall Girl); Margaret Brayton
(Mother); Pat O'Malley (Customer); Charles Stevens (Indian Joe);
Harry Woods, Dick Alexander (Curly Bill's Men); Tom Tyler (Buck
Newton); Harry Woods, Dick Alexander (Henchmen); John Bleifer,
Hank Mann, Edward Le Saint, Heinie Conklin, George Melford
(Men); Fern Emmett (Hotel Maid); Kathryn Sheldon (Mrs. Garvey);
Ferris Taylor (Doctor); John Butler (Harrassed Man); Pat O'Malley
(Customer); Arthur Aylesworth, Eddie Dunn (Card Players); Philo
McCullough, Ethan Laidlaw (Toughs).

This was the first talking version of Stuart N. Lake's novel
which was later used for Allan Dwan's 1939 version of the same
title and for John Ford's My Darling Clementine (1946) [q.v.].   In
the first version, Wyatt Earp was called Michael Wyatt and was portrayed by Fox's contract star George O'Brien.
       In Tombstone, Arizona, a crooked mayor (Churchill) is
responsible for stage holdups as well as the gambling and dance
hall activities in town.   Not long after the mayor kills his banking
cohort (Conroy), law enforcer Earp arrives in town.   He is attracted to Mary Reid (Bentley), the daughter of the murdered man,
and rejects Queenie LaVerne (played à la Mae West by Ruth Gillette).
Also involved in the good-versus-evil conflict are Doc Warren (Edwards), who has robbed from the rich, and Editor Pickett (Simpson),
the crusading newspaper man.   Also in the sterling cast are Ward
Bond and Edward LeSaint, no strangers to Sagebrush ventures.
       Mordaunt Hall wrote in the New York Times, "Frontier
Marshal, being a frank melodrama, does not bother about plausi-
bility and one gathers that it was produced with the adapter and the
director having their tongue in their cheeks."

The 1939 version of Stuart Lake's novel was a glossy retelling of the legend of Wyatt Earp (Scott), who brings law and order
to Tombstone with the support of Doc Holliday (Romero).   A popular
film, it was director Allan Dwan's first sound Western.   Because
studio head Darryl F. Zanuck insisted that the lead character be
called Wyatt Earp, although the film could have just as well been
about any frontier marshal, the studio had to pay $5,000 to a rela-
tive of Earp's then residing in San Francisco.   (After the picture
was made she sued the studio, claiming that the romance between
Earp and Sarah Allen [Kelly] was fictitious--which it was--and a
misrepresentation of truth.)
       Lanky Scott played the lawmaker in his usual laconic style
while Holliday, as interpreted by slick Romero, became a more
glamorous creature, pictured here as a gambler with a bad heart
who loses the girl (Kelly) to Earp.   Of far more interest in the
story are saloon owner Ben Carter (Carradine) and his prime singer,
Jerry (Barnes).   Eddie Foy, Jr. was hired to impersonate his
famous vaudevillian dad.
       Peter Bogdanovich stated in Allan Dwan: The Last Pioneer
(1971) that the film "is tough and to-the-point."   And that it is!
This feature was later used by John Ford as a basis for his interpretation of the Earp-Holliday saga, My Darling Clementine (1947)
[q.v.], with Henry Fonda and Victor Mature playing the lead parts.

THE FURIES (Paramount, 1950) 109 min.

   Producer, Hal B. Wallis; director, Anthony Mann; based on
the novel by Niven Busch; screenplay, Charles Schnee; art directors,
Hans Dreier, Henry Bumstead; set decorators, Sam Comer, Ber-
tram Granger; music, Franz Waxman; costumes, Edith Head; special
effects, Gordon Jennings; process camera, Farciot Edouart; camera,
Victor Milner; editor, Archie Marshek.
   Barbara Stanwyck (Vance Jeffords); Walter Huston (T. C.
Jeffords); Wendell Corey (Rip Darrow); Judith Anderson (Flo Burnett);
Gilbert Roland (Juan); Thomas Gomez (El Tigre); Beulah Bondi (Mrs.
Anaheim); Wallace Ford (Hyslip); Albert Dekker (Mr. Reynolds);
Blanche Yurka (Herrera Mother); Louis Jean Heydt (Bailey); Frank
Ferguson (Dr. Grieve); Charles Evans (Old Anaheim); Movita Cas-
tenada (Chicquita); Craig Kelly (Young Anaheim); Myrna Dell (Dallas
Hart).

   Writer Niven Busch, married to actress Teresa Wright in
the forties, seemed to favor deep, psychological Westerns. After
the successful filming of his novel Duel in the Sun (1946) [q. v.],
much of his best work was in cinema, including this effort. The
Furies was an incest-bent genre picture, best remembered today
as Walter Huston's last film.
   It was directed by Anthony Mann who, that same year,
helmed James Stewart's Winchester '73 [q. v.]. Location work was
accomplished at Tucson, Arizona, and the cast was an assemblage
of familiar names and faces (including Movita, who had been in

Walter Huston, Barbara Stanwyck and Wendell Corey in The Furies
(1950).

Clark Gable's Mutiny on the Bounty, 1935). Pitting no-nonsense
Walter Huston against Miss Stanwyck gave the picture its inner drive.
    The rather bleak and rambling storyline is set in the 1870s,
with T. C. Jeffords (Huston), a self-made cattle baron, riding herd
for a huge ranch with his iron-willed daughter Vance (Stanwyck).
When Jeffords weds Washington society matron Flo Burnett (Anderson) the jealous Vance throws scissors in her face. As a punishment, Jeffords banishes Vance from his spread. She plots revenge
and tries to overthrow the old man with the aid of a gambler
(Corey), who once refused her love and is a man her father des-
pises.
    With an over-emphasis on dialogue, this feature, although
blessed with subdued photography by Victor Milner, emerged too
arty for its own good. The critical reaction to the film was decidedly mixed. The New York Mirror termed it a "taut and stirring
drama ... [a] superior film." However, Newsweek judged it "a
pretentious exercise in Freudian dramatics ... notable only as a
sample of what Zane Grey might have done if he had tried to write
like Eugene O'Neill." Audiences were apathetic to this adult drama;
they still craved good, old-fashioned visual action with plenty of
hard-riding and fast gunplay.
    It certainly was an ill omen for the feature when Walter
Huston died of a heart attack on April 7, 1950. At the film's
premiere in Tucson, later that year, Miss Stanwyck offered a
speech of tribute to the late star.

THE GALLOPING DEVIL   (Canyon Pictures, 1920)   4,900'

        Producer, William N. Selig; director, Nate Watt; from the
novel by B. M. Bowers.
        Franklyn Farnum (Andy Green); Genevieve Berte (Elsie Gray);
Bud Osborne (Chip); Joseph Chatterton (The Kid); Veser Pegg (Pink).
        See CHIP OF THE FLYING U

THE GALLOPING DUDE   see CHIP OF THE FLYING U

GERONIMO   (Paramount, 1939)   89 min.

        Director-screenplay, Paul H. Sloane; art directors, Hans
Dreier, Earl Hendrick; music, Gerald Carbonara, John Leopold;
special effects, Farciot Edouart; camera, Henry Sharpp; editor,
John Link.
        Preston Foster (Captain Starrett); Ellen Drew (Alice Hamilton);
Andy Devine (Sneezer); William Henry (Lieutenant Steele); Ralph
Morgan (General Steele); Gene Lockhart (Gillespie); Marjorie Gateson
(Mrs. Steele); Kitty Kelly (Daisy Devine); Monte Blue (Interpreter);
Addison Richards (Frederick Allison); Pierre Watkin (Colonel White);
Joseph Crehan (President U. S. Grant); Chief Thundercloud (Geroni-
mo); Joe Dominguez (Pedro); William Haade (Cherrycow); Ivan Miller

(Hamilton Fish); Frank M. Thomas (Politician); Syd Saylor (Sergeant); Richard Denning (Lieutenant Larned); Steve Gaylord Pendleton (Private Young); Pat West (Soldier); Francis Ford, Billy Edmunds, Russell Simpson (Scouts); Cecil Kellogg (Soldier Kells); Harry Templeton (Soldier Burns); Archie Twitchell (General's Orderly).

GERONIMO   (United Artists, 1962)   C   101 min.

Executive producers, Jules Levy, Arthur Gardner, producer-director, Arnold Laven; story, Pat Fielder, Laven; screenplay, Fielder; music, Hugo Friedhofer; music director, Herschel Burke Gilbert; art director, Robert Silva; set decorator, Carlos Granjean; assistant director, Mario Cisneros; sound, Rafael Esparza, Buddy Meyers; camera, Alex Phillips; editor, Marsh Hendry.

Chuck Connors (Geronimo); Kamala Devi (Teela); Ross Martin (Mangus); Pat Conway (Maynard); Adam West (Delahay); Enid Jaynes (Huera); Larry Dobkin (General Crook); Denver Pyle (Senator Conrad); Armando Silvestre (Natchez); John Anderson (Burns); Amanda Ames (Mrs. Burns); Joe Higgins (Kincaide); Robert Hughes (Corporal); James Burk (Cavalryman); Bill Hughes (Indian Scout); Mario Navarro (Giantah).

This fearless Apache Indian warrior has always intrigued the public, ever anxious to know more details of his background and his

Preston Foster and William Henry in Geronimo (1939).

years as a major adversary to the westward expansion of white settlers.

In 1939 Paramount turned out its Geronimo, which proved to be a reworking of the earlier adventure epic, Lives of a Bengal Lancer (1935). To economize still further, the feature utilized stock footage from several earlier Paramount releases, including The Plainsman (1936) [q. v.], The Texas Rangers (1936) [q. v.], Wells Fargo (1937) [q. v.] and even some silent pictures.

Sadly, Chief Thundercloud as Geronimo had a very small part to play in the 89 minutes of storyline. The bulk of the picture concerned the hero, Captain Starrett (Foster), trying to stop the Indian war, with Geronimo pictured as one-dimensionally bloodthirsty and evil. Perhaps the most impressive performance was offered by Gene Lockhart as Gillespie, the gun runner who is eventually undone by his duplicity (and suffers a gory death). Even second-billed Ellen Drew as Alice Hamilton had only a few scenes in the film. Once the scenario has her involved in a stagecoach wreck (borrowed from Wells Fargo) she remains in a coma for the balance of the storyline.

Obviously this entry was made to cash in on the renewed cycle of Western pictures and was the forerunner of a series of epic Westerns to be turned out by Paramount in the early Forties.

In 1962 Arnold H. Laven directed a new movie version of the Geronimo legend. Chuck Connors was badly miscast as the Indian leader who, in 1883, has his remaining Apache warriors surrender to the U. S. Cavalry in return for the promise of land, food, and proper shelter. When corrupt white men plot to steal part of the Indian lands, Geronimo and his followers rebel and flee to Mexico where they begin again to attack the Cavalry. Senator Conrad (Pyle) is sent West to study the situation and arrives in time to prevent the massacre of Geronimo and his surviving warriors. A new peace treaty is signed.

"They sure don't make Injun pictures the way they used to.... Time was when Indians on the warpath were known to claim a few scalps in their pursuits. Although Geronimo's band of idealistic warriors are acknowledged to be scalpers, there is no evidence of such menacing behavior in this film. In fact, the Indians are unbelievably henpecked, domesticated and generally wishy-washy-proud and arrogant in their war-making, but meek enough to be bossed about by a frail, lone white woman in more intimate business.... Geronimo and his braves are probably the most literate and certainly the most fluent Indians ever to grace the screen, able to communicate with several nationalities simply by employing English in the most articulate, up-to-date American fashion. Gone are the days of the 'how' and the 'white man speak with forked tongue'" (Variety).

GHOST OF ZORRO   (Republic, 1949)   twelve chapters

Associate producer, Franklyn Adreon; director, Fred C.

Brannon; screenplay, Roy Cole, William Lively, Sol Shor; music
director, Stanley Wilson; special effects, Howard and Theodore
Lydecker; camera, John MacBurnie.
        Clayton Moore (Zorro/Ken Mason); Pamela Blake (Rita);
Roy Barcroft (Kilgore); George J. Lewis (Moccasin); Eugene Roth
(Crane); John Crawford (Mulvaney); I. Stanford Jolley (Green);
Steve Clark (White); Steve Darrell (Marshal Simpson); Dale Van
Sickel (Hodge); Tom Steele (Brace); Alex Montoya (Yellow Hawk);
Marshall Reed (Fowler); Frank O'Connor (Doctor); Jack O'Shea
(Freight Agent); Holly Bane (Larkin).
        Chapters: 1) Bandit Territory; 2) Forged Orders; 3) Rob-
ber's Agent; 4) Victims of Vengeance; 5) Gun Trap; 6) Deadline at
Midnight; 7) Tower of Disaster; 8) Mob Justice; 9) Money Lure;
10) Message of Death; 11) Runaway Stagecoach; 12) Trail of Blood.
        See MARK OF ZORRO.

THE GIRL OF THE GOLDEN WEST (Paramount, 1915) five reels

        Producer-director, Cecil B. DeMille; based on the play by
David Belasco; screenplay, DeMille; camera, Alvin Wyckoff; editor,
DeMille.
        Mabel van Buren (The Girl); Theodore Roberts (Rance);
House Peters (Ramerez); Anita King (Wowkle); Sydney Deane (Sid
Duck); Billy Elmer (Ashby); Jeanie Macpherson (Nina); Ed Harley
(Old Minstrel); Raymond Hatton (Castro); Dick L'Estrange (Senor
Slim); Tex Driscoll (Nick the bartender); Art Ortego (Antonio); John
Ortego (Stagecoach Driver); James Griswold (Guard).

THE GIRL OF THE GOLDEN WEST (Associated First National,
1923) 6,800 ft.

        Presenter, Edwin Carewe; producer, Robert North; director,
Carewe; based on the play by David Belasco; adaptor, Adelaide
Heilbron; art director, Milton Menasco; assistant director, Wallace
Fox; camera, Sol Polito, Thomas Storey; editor, Robert De Lacy.
        Sylvia Breamer (The Girl); J. Warren Kerrigan (Ramarez);
Russell Simpson (Jack Rance); Rosemary Theby (Nina Micheltorena);
Wilfred Lucas (Ashby); Nelson McDowell (Sonora Slim); Charles
McHugh (Trinidad Joe); Hector V. Sarno (Castro); Jed Prouty (Nick);
Cecil Holland (Antonio); Thomas Delmar (Handsome Harry); Fred
Warren (Old Jed Hawkins); Sam Appel (Pedro Micheltorena); Minnie
Prevost (The Squaw).

THE GIRL OF THE GOLDEN WEST (First National, 1930) 81 min.

        Associate producer, Robert North; director, John Francis
Dillon; based on the play by David Belasco; screenplay, Waldemar
Young; camera, Sol Polito.
        Ann Harding (Minnie); James Rennie (Dick Johnson); Harry

Bannister (Jack Rance); Ben Hendricks, Jr. (Handsome Charlie); J.
Farrell MacDonald (Sonora Slim); George Cooper (Trinidad Joe);
Johnny Walker (Nick); Richard Carlyle (Jim Larkins); Arthur Stone
(Joe Castro); Arthur Housman (Sidney Dick); Norman McNeil (Happy
Holiday); Fred Warren (Jack Wallace); Joe Girard (Ashby); Newton
House (Pony Express Rider); Princess Noola (Wowkle); Chief Yow-
lachie (Billy Jackrabbit).

THE GIRL OF THE GOLDEN WEST   (MGM, 1938)   120 min.*

Producer, William Anthony McGuire; director, Robert Z.
Leonard; based on the play by David Belasco; screenplay, Isabel
Dawn; Boyce DeGraw; music director, Herbert Stothart; choreog-
raphy, Albertina Rasch; songs, Sigmund Romberg and Gus Kahn;
art director, Cedric Gibbons; sound, Douglas Shearer; montages,
Slavko Vorkapich; camera, Oliver Marsh; editor, W. Donn Hayes.
Jeanette MacDonald (Mary Robbins); Nelson Eddy [Ramerez
(Lieutenant Johnson)]; Walter Pidgeon (Sheriff Jack Rance); Leo
Carrillo (Mosquito); Buddy Ebsen (Alabama); Leonard Penn (Pedro);
Priscilla Lawson (Nina Martinez); Bob Murphy (Sonora Slim); Olin
Howland (Trinidad Joe); Cliff Edwards (Minstrel Joe); Billy Bevan
(Nick); Brandon Tynan (The Professor); H. B. Warner (Father
Sienna); Monty Woolley (Governor); Charley Grapewin (Uncle Davy);
Noah Beery, Sr. (The General); Bill Cody, Jr. (Gringo); Jeanne
Ellis (The Girl Mary); Ynez Seabury (Wowkle); Victor Potel (Stage
Driver); Nick Thompson (Billy Jack Rabbit); Tom Mahoney (Hand-
some Charlie); Phillip Armenta (Long Face); Chief Big Tree (Indian
Chief); Russell Simpson (Pioneer); Armand "Curley" Wright, Pedro
Regas (Renegades); Gene Coogan (Manuel); Sergei Arabeloff (Jose);
Alberto Morin (Juan); Joe Dominguez (Felipe); Frank McGlynn (Pete,
a Gambler); Cy Kendall (Hank, a Gambler); E. Alyn Warren, Francis
Ford (Miners); Hank Bell (Deputy); Walter Bonn (Lieutenant Johnson);
Richard Tucker (Colonel); Virginia Howell (Governor's Wife).
*Filmed in Sepia.

David Belasco's 1905 play was first a drama and then an
opera by Puccini (1910); then Cecil B. DeMille produced and directed its first screen treatment in 1915. In this five-reeler, a
girl (van Buren) loves a road agent named Ramerez (Peters) and
hides him in her store/saloon. When Sheriff Rance (Roberts) finds
him, the girl agrees to play a card game to decide his fate. Luckily
she wins. Later Rance nearly hangs Ramerez, but the girl saves
him again. Eventually they find happiness together. The film was
filled with good scenery and photography, and Motion Picture News
reported that it included "wonderful examples of what can be done by
competent cameramen and directors." The New York Dramatic-
Mirror thought it a "dramatic force ... [it] is fresh as though it
were written yesterday."
If this warhorse was good enough for constant stage revivals,
Hollywood deemed it worthy of several remakes. First National offered two versions of the play--in 1923 and in 1930. The first was

Jeanette MacDonald and Nelson Eddy in <u>The Girl of the Golden West</u>
(1938).

supervised by Edwin Carewe who also directed remakes of Ramona
(1928) [q.v.] and The Spoilers (1923) [q.v.]. This expanded silent
version of the Belasco original had a girl saloon owner (Breamer)
succumbing to the charms of bandit Ramarez (Kerrigan). When he
spends the night with her in a snowstorm another girl (Theby),
jealous of his attentions to the saloon owner, reveals his identity
to sheriff Jack Rance (Simpson). The latter also loves Miss
Breamer. Once more, the climactic game card occurs with the
girl saving Ramarez from the sheriff's clutches. Photoplay warned
its readers, "another return engagement, but the fine old story is
marred by difficulties of casting."

The talkie craze saw a rash of remakes of silent properties,
and Girl of the Golden West was no exception. To give its sound
version added prestige, First National borrowed the services of
lovely ash blonde Ann Harding from Pathé Pictures. As part of the
package, her then husband, actor Harry Bannister, was hired to
play the role of Jack Rance, the sheriff. James Rennie was cast
as outlaw Dick Johnson. Variety's review said, "The dialog version
is practically the stage piece in unchanged transcription even to the
arrangement of scenes.... Such an arrangement only emphasizes
the mechanical limitations of the stage and calls attention to the
artificiality of the whole affair."

The 1930 version contained no songs, but in 1938 MGM used
Belasco's play as a vehicle for the love and singing team of Jeanette
MacDonald and Nelson Eddy. In this sepia-tinged version, Gus Kahn
and Sigmund Romberg provided a music score, but it resulted in no
hit tunes. If the Ann Harding adaptation had seemed a bit tattered,
this rehash proved once and for all that Belasco's primitive drama
should be laid to rest. The film, however, did have an interesting
supporting cast, including Buddy Ebsen and Cliff Edwards. (Scenes
including Ray Bolger were deleted from an already over-long picture
by worried MGM executives.) The movie's best-liked musical interlude was Jeanette's and Nelson's rendering of "Who Are We to Say?"
Critics and fans alike admitted that Eddy was a bit too genteel (and
stiff) to be the forceful romantic rogue Ramerez. As usual, however, there were few complaints about the ever-lovely Miss Mac-
Donald.

GO WEST (MGM, 1925) 6,293'

       Presenter, Joseph M. Schenck; director-story, Buster
Keaton; screenplay, Raymond Cannon; technical director, Fred
Gabourie; camera, Elgin Lessley, Bert Haines.
       Buster Keaton (Homer Holiday, "Friendless"); Kathleen
Myers (Gloria Thompson); Howard Truesdale (Thompson); Ray
Thompson (Foreman); Brown Eyes (The Cow).

       Even stern Western star William S. Hart had permitted
Douglas Fairbanks, Sr. to kid the cowboy genre, while he, in turn,
occasionally poked fun at Fairbanks' swashbuckling epics. Among
screen comics, Roscoe "Fatty" Arbuckle had successfully satirized

the Western and in 1925 Buster Keaton developed his own ideas into
this film which he and director producer Joseph M. Schenck did for
Metro Pictures. By anyone's standards the results were amusing,
but compared to the level of earlier Keaton masterpieces (such as
Sherlock, Jr., 1924) it was a bit of a disappointment.

Homer Holiday (Keaton), a friendless drifter heads Westward
and endures a number of misfortunes until he lands a job at the
Thompson ranch run by a stern reancher-owner (Truesdale). There
Homer befriends a cow, Brown Eyes, who saves his life. Later he
goes along with her when she is included in a shipment for market.
A rival rancher attacks the train but Friendless takes control and
gets the shipment safely to market. Thompson gives Friendless
his choice of rewards and he chooses Brown Eyes. The film con-
cludes with Friendless, Thompson, and the man's daughter Gloria
(Myers) and Brown Eyes driving away in a car.

"... Go West is one of Keaton's most endearing films [des-
pite its "thinly spread" gags and the diminished "heart for acrobatic
miracles"]. It is unique as the only picture in which the comedian
deliberately aimed at pathos; and though it is totally unexpected in
him and he never tried it again to the same degree, he brings it off
without the least embarrassment or mawkishness. What led him to
this temporary deviation we shall now never know. Go West was a
film about which he seems to have talked little in his old age, except to recall his relations with the nice little cow who was his
leading lady.... The gags one recalls from the film are not the
feats and marvels and extravagant inventions of Our Hospitality
[1923] or Sherlock Junior, but quiet and charming little gestures:
the politeness with which he raises his hat to Brown Eyes; the absurd little gun which he finds on a railroad siding early on in the
film and which keeps reappearing through his cowboy career (it is
always mislaying itself in the depths of a man-size holster until he
has the inspiration of putting string on like a baby's gloves); the
step-ladder he fixes so that he can mount his horse; the minute calf
which he cautiously selects as his contribution to the round-up, but
which nevertheless foils all his attempts to lasso it" (David Robinson
in Buster Keaton, 1969).

Quite rightly, Keaton saved the best laughs for the end, when
the herd reaches the Los Angeles destination and he becomes em-
broiled in a stampede through the city streets with the expected results to the baffled inhabitants. (It was a far more joyous barb at
the standard cowboy stampede than the miniature, one-cow episode
in Barbra Streisand's For Pete's Sake, 1974).

GO WEST (MGM, 1940) 80 min.

Producer, Jack Cummings; director, Edward Buzzell; screenplay, Irving Brecher; art directors, Cedric Gibbons, Stan Rogers;
set decorators, Edwin B. Willis; music, Georgie Stoll; song, Roger
Edens and Gus Kahn; Charles Wakefield Cadman; camera, Leonard
Smith; editor, Blanche Sewell.

Groucho Marx (S. Quentin Quale); Harpo Marx (Rusty Panello);

Chico Marx (Joseph Panello); John Carroll (Terry Turner); Diana
Lewis (Eve Wilson); Robert Barrat (Red Baxter); Walter Woolf King
(Mr. Beecher); June MacCloy (Lulubelle); George Lessey (Railroad
President); Mitchell Lewis (Halfbreed); Tully Marshall (Dan Wilson);
Clem Bevans (Official); Joe Yule (Bartender); Arthur Houseman
(Drunk).

    It was almost inevitable that at one time or another every
screen comedy team would spoof the Western genre. However, one
of filmdom's most famous funster groups went astray when they
tackled the old West. With the Marx Brothers it was less a case of
the three comedians transferring their comic talents to the sagebrush
milieu than of the cactus and desert locale just happening to be in
their merry path. It is a shame that this film did not live up to
their earlier excursions at the opera, the racetrack, or even at the
circus. But ever since their MGM mentor, Irving Thalberg, had
died (1936), the group seemed to be only half-heartedly fulfilling its
studio obligations.
    The film does open with a splash as S. Quentin Quale
(Groucho) arrives at the railroad station with a line of porters
carrying his baggage. When they do not have change for a dime,
he grandly insists, "Well--keep the baggage." Quale soon meets
up with the Panello brothers (Harpo and Chico) and tries to fleece
them of the price of a train ticket to go west. Joseph (Chico) says
Rusty (Harpo) intends to shovel the gold right up off the streets in
the legendary Gold Strikes in California.
    After the above scene, in which the Panello brothers outwit
the usually crafty Quale, the film goes downhill. As Allen Eyles
explained in The Marx Brothers (1966), "For, once the Marx
Brothers actually move out to the West, they prove to be no match
at all for the inhabitants until the climax. One doesn't expect to
find Chico confiding nervously to Harpo, 'Rusty, I no like-a the
West,' the moment they get out there. Groucho goes out with no
kind of status and there is no Margaret Dumont or Siegfried Rumann
for him to take a firm hand with."
    Once the trio is in the wild West their efforts are concen-
trated on getting back a land deed presently in the clutches of villain Red Baxter (Barrat). Things move along sluggishly--at least
by Marx Brothers' standards--until the finale aboard the train where
the three Easterners are racing after the villains. With the zany
trio in control the train is destined for a bumpy ride. "Brake ...
the brake!" screams Joe Panello. The good-natured, silent Rusty
obliges by smashing the brake and throwing it away. Thereafter
the train smashes through a house which it pulls along to the break-
neck finale.
    To reassure Marx Brothers enthusiasts, the authors of this
volume do not think that this film should be ignored. We would
much rather see it over again than a good many other Westerns--
either lampoons or straight boots and saddle drama.

THE GODCHILD   (ABC-TV, 1974)   C   90 min.

Executive producer, Charles Robert McLain; producer,
Richard Collins; director, John Badham; based on the story by
Peter B. Kyne; teleplay, Ron Bishop; music, David Shire; art director, Robert E. Smith; sound, George Maly, Harry W. Tetrick;
special effects, Harold P. Elmendorf; camera, Stevan Larner; editor, Frank Morriss.

Jack Palance (Rourke); Jack Warden (Dobbs); Keith Carradine
(Lieutenant Louis); Ed Lauter (Crees); Jose Perez (Sanchez); Bill
McKinney (Crawley); Jesse Vint (Loftus); John Quade (Denton); Simon
Deckard (William); Ed Bakey (Shaw); Kermit Murdock (Mony); Fion-
nuala Flanagan (Virginia).

See   The Three Godfathers.

GODDESS OF SAGEBRUSH GULCH   (Biograph, 1912)   one reel

Director-screenplay, D. W. Griffith; camera, G. W. "Billy"
Bitzer.

Blanche Sweet (The Girl); Dorothy Bernard (The Sister);
Charles West (Blue-grass Pete).

Subtitled A Story of the Golden West, this early D. W. Griffith film for Biograph was filmed in California in January, 1912,
and was issued some two months later.

Griffith often used the West for his one-reelers and this
melodrama concerned a young girl (Sweet) who is beloved by all in
a mining camp and whose sister (Bernard) attracts the one man
(West) she loves. West is a charming outlaw, Blue-grass Pete,
who later leads a party of miners to rescue the sister after the
girl has been kidnapped by West's renegade pal and left to die in a
burning cabin.

This entertaining entry showed a great improvement in Griffith's filming technique, especially in his camera set-ups and the
utilization of lighting for close-ups.

A GOOD DAY FOR FIGHTING   see   CUSTER OF THE WEST

THE GOOD, THE BAD AND THE UGLY   see   IL BUONO, IL
BRUTTO, IL CATTIVO

GORDON OF GHOST CITY   see   THE RED RIDER

THE GREAT K & A TRAIN ROBBERY   (Fox, 1926)   4,800'

Presenter, William Fox; director, Lewis Seiler; based on

the book by Paul Leicester Ford; screenplay, John Stone; assistant
director, Wynn Mace; camera, Dan Clark.
    Tom Mix (Tom Gordon); Dorothy Dwan (Madge Cullen);
William Walling (Eugene Cullen); Harry Grippe (DeLuxe Harry);
Carl Miller (Burton); Edward Piel (Bandit Leader); Curtis McHenry
(Cullen's Butler); Tony the Horse (Himself).

    Taken from Paul Leicester Ford's 1897 novel, this Tom Mix
vehicle used the Denver and Rio Grande Railroad for background and
contained some of the star's best and most elaborate stunt work.
It was shot on location at Royal Gorge, Colorado.
    The narrative finds the K & A Railroad undergoing a series
of robberies, with Tom Gordon (Mix) being hired to solve the case.
In the guise of a bandit, Tom boards the train owned by Eugene
Cullen (Walling) and is discovered by the man's daughter (Dwan)
who promptly falls in love with him. It develops that Cullen's
secretary (Miller) works with the bandits. Tom learns of the gang's
operations and, with the help of his wonder horse, Tony, captures
the outlaws and wins the affection of the heroine.

THE GREAT NORTHFIELD, MINNESOTA RAID (Universal, 1972)
C   91 min.

    Associate producer, Bruce Graham; director-screenplay,
Philip Kaufman; art directors, Alexander Golitzen, George Webb;
set decorator, Hal Gausman; matte supervisor, Albert Whitlock;
music, Dave Grusin; costumes, Helen Colvig; assistant director,
Ralph Sariego; sound, Waldon O. Watson, Melvin M. Metcalf, Sr.,
Robert Hoyt; camera, Bruce Surtees; editor, Douglas Stewart.
    Cliff Robertson (Cole Younger); Robert Duvall (Jesse James);
Luke Askew (Jim Younger); R. G. Armstrong (Clell Miller); Dana
Elcar (Allen); Donald Moffat (Manning); John Pearce (Frank James);
Matt Clark (Bob Younger); Wayne Sutherlin (Charley Pitts); Robert
H. Harris (Wilcox); Jack Manning (Heywood); Elisha Cook, Jr.
(Bunker); Royal Dano (Gustavson); Mary Robin Redd (Kate); Barry
Brown (Henry Wheeler); Madeline Taylor Holmes (Granny Woman);
Erik Holland (Sheriff); Marjorie Durant (Maybelle); Valda J. Nansen
(Nude Girl).

    In 1876 the state of Missouri decides to grant amnesty to
both Cole Younger (Robertson) and Jesse James (Duvall), as well as
their gang. The state officials feel that perhaps these men were
driven to becoming outlaws by the misdeeds of others. Cole wants
to accept the offer but Jesse counters that the railroad companies
will continue to misappropriate their land even if freedom from
arrest is offered to the wanted outlaws. But the railroad executives
pay off the legislative leaders to drop the amnesty bill and Cole and
Jesse decide to rob the Northfield, Minnesota bank, supposedly the
biggest one west of the Mississippi.
    With an ingenious plan, Cole gets the folk of Northfield to
deposit their savings in the bank (telling them there are outlaws in

the area), and later, with Jesse and the men, he robs the stronghold. Everything goes well until an accidental mishap occurs,
leading to bloodshed. The wounded Cole is surrounded by a mob
which hails him as the greatest outlaw ever. Acknowledged a folk
hero, he is content to meet his fate.

'[It is] a lovely, odd sort of middle Western. That is, it's
neither conventional Western fiction nor completely documented fact,
although it makes full use of history and is crammed with the arti-
facts of 19th-century America--everything from dolls to a working
calliope.... The film is funny and cruel and, in a couple of in-
stances, technically awkward. Kaufman is not the world's greatest
stager of crowd scenes and gun fights. But the places and people
look right and the talk is not the slave of melodrama. It is full of
quiet surprises, like the moment in a whorehouse when one of the
bandits, feeling very guilty and low, says, 'I'd rather gone frog-gig-
ging'" (New York Times).

Making few concessions to glamour, this low-key entry was
appreciated by those who learned about it by word-of-mouth, but it
failed to draw any mass support. Robert Duvall's Jesse James was
a far cry from the romantic image created by Tyrone Power in the
1939 movie [q.v.], and the film itself was a factual recreation of
true events--more than can be said for that Twentieth Century-Fox
feature or many other accounts of the legendary Jesse and his cohorts. In many respects this entry is similar to the popular heist
film of the gangster genre, detailing the plotting and execution of the
robbery, and the snowballing set of miscalculations that lead to
disaster and defeat.

A GUNFIGHT (Paramount, 1971) C 90 min.

Producers, A. Roland Lubin, Harold Jack Bloom; director,
Lamont Johnson; screenplay, Bloom; music, Laurence Rosenthal;
song, Johnny Cash; production designer, Tambi Larsen; set decorator, Darrell Silvera; costumes, Mickey Sherard; makeup, Otis Malcolm, Jack Young; assistant directors, William Green, William
Sheehan; sound, Jack Solomon; camera, David Walsh; editor, Bill
Mosher.

Kirk Douglas (Will Tenneray); Johnny Cash (Abe Cross);
Jane Alexander (Nora Tenneray); Raf Vallone (Francisco Alvarez);
Karen Black (Jenny Simms); Eric Douglas (Bud Tenneray); Phillip
L. Mead (Kyle); Dana Elcar (Marv Green); John Wallwork (Toby);
Robert J. Wilke (Cater); George Le Bow (Dekker); James D. Cavasos
(Newt Hale); Keith Carradine (Cowboy); Paul Lambert (Ed Fleury);
Neil Davis (Canberry); David Burleson, Dick O'Shea (Poker Players);
Douglas Doran (Teller); John Gill (Foreman); Timothy Tuinstra (Joey);
R. C. Bishop (MacIntyre); Donna and Paula Dillenschneider (Saloon
Hostesses).

The primary distinction of this feature film is that it was
produced by American Indians, the Jicarilla Apaches of New Mexico,
who raised the $2 million necessary for the project.

What might have been a decent premise for a film--a planned gun duel for money between two aged gunfighters, with winner take all--degenerated into the inane, with a tacked-on and hopelessly corny ending.

In a southwestern town, ex-gunslinger Will Tenneray (Douglas) lives with his wife Nora (Alexander) and their son Bud (Eric Douglas). Will works as bouncer at the local bar. Abe Cross (Cash), a retired gunfighter, comes into town and decides to stay. Will and Abe become friends and enjoy the bevy of rumors of their impending shootout. But then it dawns on them that there could be a lot of money to be made by staging an arena gunfight. Bullfighter promoter Alvarez (Vallone) arranges the presentation, which makes Will suspicious, as his wife once had an affair with Alvarez. In the arena Cross kills Will with a single shot. But victory is bittersweet, for Cross realizes that sooner or later he will have to face a deadly contest with a younger and better gunman.

Ironically this Indian-produced Western has no Indians in it. That wasn't the only problem facing the filmmakers in trying to entice some audience interest in the story. "If ever a Western needed low-key treatment to succeed, this morality tale about guns, guts, and greed is one. Director Lamont Johnson obviously sensed the challenge and tried to keep things cool. But how do you cool it with an acting line-up like Kirk Douglas, Johnny Cash, Jane Alexander, and Karen Black ... they approach every scene as if this were their big moment. Even though their playing style is low-key, it is still so obviously a style that the story seems too contrived to be taken as seriously as it should" (Cue).

With his low-energy performance in A Gunfight, Johnny Cash revealed why he had never before pursued a film career.

GUNFIGHT AT THE O.K. CORRAL (Paramount, 1957) C 122 min.

Producer, Hal B. Wallis; associate producer, Paul Nathan; director, John Sturges; based on the magazine article "The Killer" by George Scullin; screenplay, Leon Uris; art directors, Hal Pereira, Walter Tyler; music-music conductor, Dimitri Tiomkin; song, Tiomkin and Ned Washington; song sung by Frankie Laine; assistant director, Michael D. Moore; costumes, Edith Head; special camera effects, John P. Fulton; camera, Charles Lang, Jr.; editor, Warren Low.

Burt Lancaster (Wyatt Earp); Kirk Douglas (Doc Holliday); Rhonda Fleming (Laura Denbow); Jo Van Fleet (Kate Fisher); John Ireland (Ringo); Lyle Bettger (Ike Clanton); Frank Faylen (Cotton Wilson); Earl Holliman (Charles Bassett); Ted De Corsia (Shanghai Pierce); Dennis Hopper (Billy Clanton); Whit Bissell (John P. Clum); George Mathews (John Shanssey); John Hudson (Virgil Earp); DeForest Kelley (Morgan Earp); Martin Milner (James Earp); Kenneth Tobey (Bat Masterson); Lee Van Cleef (Ed Bailey); Joan Camden (Betty Earp); Olive Carey (Mrs. Clanton); Brian Hutton (Rick); Nelson Leigh (Mayor Kelley); Jack Elam (Tom McLowery); Don Castle (Drunken Cowboy).

Burt Lancaster and Rhonda Fleming in <u>Gunfight at the O.K. Corral</u>
(1957).

In Fort Griffith, outlaw Ed Bailey (Van Cleef) rides into town to kill Doc Holliday (Douglas), the latter an ex-dentist turned gunfighter who killed Bailey's brother in a card game. Holliday is warned by his former girlfriend Kate Fisher (Van Fleet), who is now a saloon keeper. Dodge City sheriff Wyatt Earp (Lancaster) also warns Holliday of Bailey's fighting tactics. When the two men confront one another in the saloon it is Holliday who kills Bailey. The local sheriff (Faylen) then wants to hang Holliday but Doc, Kate, and Wyatt leave for Dodge City.

In Dodge City, Wyatt's brother Virgil, sheriff of Tombstone, Arizona, arrives to ask help in cleaning out the marauding Clanton Brothers. But Wyatt is sidetracked by the arrival of lady gambler Laura Denbow (Fleming) and although he arrests the lawbreaking girl, he falls in love with her. Wyatt then rides with Holliday to Tombstone. Along the way Doc saves Wyatt's life on two occasions, once when they are ambushed by Johnny Ringo (Ireland), the Clantons' hired gun. In Tombstone, one of the Clantons kills James Earp (Milner) thinking he is Wyatt. Thereafter the Earps join together with Holliday to fight the oncoming Clantons at the O.K. Corral. The law wipes out the outlaw brood.

From the opening credits with Frankie Laine wailing out the title tune, this color, VistaVision Western, with much location shooting (in Tucson, Phoenix, Fort Griffith and Tombstone), was a sound but inaccurate reconstruction of the famous gunfight and the myriad events leading up to it. The showdown, lensed at Old Tucson, lasted five minutes on the big screen, but took forty-four hours to film. The motion picture proved commercially viable and grossed $4.7 million in distributors rentals in the U.S. and Canada alone.

In 1967, director John Sturges made the error of filming Hour of the Gun, a sequel which took up where this film left off. James Garner was Wyatt Earp, with Jason Robards (Doc Holliday); Robert Ryan (Ike Clanton); Sam Melville (Morgan Earp); Walter Gregg (Billy Clanton). The result was a dismal production in all respects.

THE GUNFIGHTER (Twentieth Century-Fox, 1950) 84 min.

Producer, Nunnally Johnson; director, Henry King; story, William Bowers, Andre de Toth; screenplay, Bowers, William Sellers; art directors, Lyle Wheeler, Richard Irvine; music, Alfred Newman; camera, Arthur Miller; editor, Barbara McLean.

Gregory Peck (Jimmie Ringo); Helen Westcott (Peggy Walsh); Millard Mitchell (Sheriff Mark Strett); Jean Parker (Molly); Karl Malden (Mac); Skip Homeier (Hunt Bromley); Anthony Ross (Charlie); Verna Felton (Mrs. Pennyfeather); Ellen Corby (Mrs. Devlin); Richard Jaeckel (Eddie); Alan Hale, Jr., David Clarke, John Pickard (Brothers); B. G. Norman (Jimmie); Angela Clarke (Man's Wife); Houseley Stevenson, James Millican, Mae Marsh, Kenneth Tobey, Michael Branden (Bits).

A tough but worn-out gunfighter, Jimmie Ringo (Peck) comes

to a small Western town hoping to escape his past.   But he is
trailed by a troublemaker seeking to supplant Ringo's reputation as
"the top gun in the West."   Ringo is also haunted by memories of
his bloody past.   Eventually the younger gun kills the older man,
only to discover that he is now the hunted man.
     This was one of the first "adult" Westerns and one of the
early Hollywood examples of the anti-hero.   Although Gregory Peck
was a big box-office attraction (he was now supplanting Tyrone
Power as the top star of Twentieth Century-Fox) the downbeat nature
of The Gunfighter did not make it attractive entertainment for moviegoers seeking escapism.   Nevertheless, artistically the picture is
quite important and is a connecting link between past cowboy tales
and the next Western genre milestone, High Noon (1952) [q.v.].
     In A Pictorial History of the Western Film (1969), William
K. Everson observes, "[It] creates such a mood of inexorable Greek
tragedy that no matter how many times one sees it, one is always
hoping subconsciously for that accidental change of circumstances or
timing that will bring about a happy ending.... [It] is a major
classic among Western movies."
     Besides top direction by King the film also contained a fine
performance by Richard Jaeckel as a young gunfighter itching to
challenge the famed Jimmie Ringo.
     Over the succeeding decades, the theme of the gunfighter
loner trying to live down his reputation would be refilmed in numerous guises, but never as effectively or starkly as The Gunfighter.

GUNS DON'T ARGUE   see   DIE LETZEN ZWEI VOM RIO BRAVO

GUNS IN THE AFTERNOON   see   RIDE THE HIGH COUNTRY

THE GUNS OF FORT PETTICOAT   see   WESTWARD THE WOMEN

GUNS OF THE MAGNIFICENT SEVEN   see   THE MAGNIFICENT
SEVEN

HANG 'EM HIGH   (United Artists, 1968)   C   114 min.

     Producer, Leonard Freeman; associate producer, Irving
Leonard; director, Ted Post; screenplay, Freeman, Mel Goldberg;
music, Dominic Frontiere; music supervisor, John Capter, Jr.;
orchestrator, Edward Powell; art director, John B. Goodman; set
decorator, Arthur Krams; wardrobe, Gene Murray, Glen Wright,
Elva Martiens; makeup, Keester Sweeney, Irving Pringle; assistant
directors, Richard Bennett, Don Klune; sound, Franklin Milton, Al
Strasser, Jr.; special effects, George Swartz; camera, Leonard
South, Richard Kline; editor, Gene Fowler, Jr.
     Clint Eastwood (Jed Cooper); Inger Stevens (Rachel); Ed
Begley (Cap'n Wilson); Pat Hingle (Judge Adam Fenton); Charles

McGraw (Sheriff Ray Calhoun); Ruth White (Madame Sophie); Arlene Golonka (Jennifer); James MacArthur (Preacher); Bruce Dern (Miller); Alan Hale, Jr. (Stone); James Westerfield (Prisoner); Dennis Hopper (The Prophet); Ben Johnson (Sheriff Dave Bliss); Bob Steele (Jenkins); Jack Ging (Marshal Hayes); L. Q. Jones (Loomis); Bert Freed (Schmidt the Hangman); Michael O'Sullivan (Francis Duffy); Herb Ellis (Swede); Russell Thorson (Mr. Maddow); Todd Andrews (Defense Attorney); Rick Gates (Ben); Bruce Scott (Billy Joe); Rick Gates (Ben); Paul Sorenson (Reno); Roy Glenn (Guard); and: Jonathan Lippe, Barry Cahill, Tony Di Milo.

      After years as the co-star of the teleseries "Rawhide" and the subsequent international success in a trio of Sergio Leone Italian Westerns, Clint Eastwood finally attained stardom in his homeland with the great success of the Hollywood-made Hang 'em High. The film was directed by his old pal, Ted Post, who had helmed many "Rawhide" segments.
      Attempting to duplicate the successful formula of the Leone Westerns, this colorful, violent picture opens with rangler Jed Cooper being overtaken by a posse of ranchers. Law is swift in 1889 Oklahoma and the nine-man lynch mob hangs Jed. Fortunately a sheriff (Johnson) passes by. He shoots down the still-alive Jed and takes him to town. There Judge Fenton (Hingle) exonerates Cooper and makes him a federal marshal to bring in the men who attempted to kill him. One of the men (Steele), who was opposed

Clint Eastwood in Hang 'em High (1968).

to the hanging at the time, voluntarily turns himself in to the law.
Jed then captures or kills most of the others, and along the way
has an affair with widow Rachel (Stevens) who has been haunting the
federal prison seeking the killer of her husband.   At the finale Jed
corners powerful rancher Cap'n Wilson (Begley), the man who instigated the hanging.   Rather than allow Jed to capture him Cap'n
commits suicide.   In order to let the voluntary prisoner (Steele) go
free, Jed agrees to continue his work as a law enforcer although he
detests the odious job.
      "A rambling tale which glorifies personal justice, mocks and
derogates orderly justice" (Variety).   Hang 'em High nevertheless
pleased an action-hungry public who enjoyed the vicarious thrills of
violence pulsating throughout this picture.   The film cost $1.7
million to produce, yet made a gross of $17 million worldwide.
      At the time of its release, Time posed this query: "'Are
the seeds of violence nurtured through the screens of neighborhood
theaters?' So asked President Johnson in his statement to the
National Commission on the Causes and Prevention of Violence.
Good question.   In Hang 'em High, the year's grisliest movie so
far, those seeds are tended until they burst into bloody bloom....
With some evocative photography and a touch of gallows humor,
Director Ted Post tries to make Hang 'em High stylish and spirited
enough to swing.   It swings all right--like a body at the end of a
rope."

HARD ON THE TRAIL   (Brentwood International, 1971) C 92 min.

      Producer, Maurice Smith; director-screenplay, Greg Corarito.
      With: Al "Lash" LaRue, Donna Bradley, Bruce Kemp, Bob
Romero.

      Billed as "a very unusual western!" this triple-X-rated
melodrama is one of the first* hard-core pornographic features to
offer a complete Western theme and background.   To add to the
authenticity the producers even obtained the services of forties'
cowboy hero, Al "Lash" LaRue for a leading role.   (LaRue worked
only two days on the project and claimed he did not know it was to
be an X-rated film.   The spicy footage was interpolated around him
and he does not appear in any of the sex scenes.)   LaRue portrayed
a grizzled gang leader on the trail of a lost gold mine, and along
the way there is plenty of action--all of it of the lustful variety.

---

*Although it is cheaper to shoot pornographic film in modern bed-
room settings, a surprising number of blue movies do have cowboy
themes and there are even a few which have good budgets.   Among
the X-rated films dealing with the old West are: Lonesome Cowboys
(1968); The Scavengers (1970), a Civil War setting; Six Guns for Six
Women (1971); Two Rode with Death (1971); The Marauders! (1972);
The Erotic Adventures of Zorro (1972); Rawhide (1974); and Wanted:
Billy the Kid (1975), a homosexual treatment of this Western legendary figure.

Writing in Contemporary Erotic Cinema (1973), William
Rotsler calls the picture a "fast cowboy drama that would have been
better shot three years later, with easier eroticism." Not long
after the completion of this X-rater, which was given brief exposure by Clover Films in 1971 as Hard Trail, LaRue left show
business completely and devoted himself to religious mission work.

HAUNTED GOLD   (Warner Bros., 1932)   58 min.

Producer, Leon Schlesinger; director, Mack V. Wright;
story-screenplay, Adele Buffington; camera, Nick Musuraca; editor,
William Clemens.
John Wayne (John Mason); Sheila Terry (Janet Carter);
Erville Alderson (Benedict); Harry Woods (Joe Ryan); Otto Hoffman
(Simon); Martha Mattox (Mrs. Herman); Edgar "Blue" Washington
(Clarence).

After his starring debut in the unpopular The Big Trail (1930)
[q.v.], John Wayne worked briefly at Columbia and then switched
during 1932-33 to Warner Bros. where he appeared in a number of
films, including his first series Westerns, six oaters which greatly
aided in establishing him as a young and most likable sagebrush
hero.   Given fairly decent production values and good casts and directors, these modest Westerns proved to be quite acceptable to the
public.   When Wayne later left to join Lone Star productions, Dick
Foran succeeded him as Warner Bros.' B-Western star.
Haunted Gold was the first and best of the Warner Bros.
series.   This quickie had Wayne and Sheila Terry (later Sheila
Bromley) at odds with an outlaw gang over an abandoned gold mine.
To complicate matters, a mysterious figure, "The Phantom," who
wears a mask and black cape, supposedly haunts the mine.   At the
finale, Big John defeats the outlaws and unmasks the Phantom who
turns out to be ... (Why spoil the fun?--see the film for yourself).
Haunted Gold was reissued to theatres as late as 1962 and,
like most of the series, it was filmed in about a week's time, com-
bining new footage with action shots from 1920s' Ken Maynard
features.   This entry was helmed by Mack V. Wright who would
direct Wayne in one of his best small Westerns of the decade, Winds
of the Wasteland (Republic, 1936) [q.v.].

HAWK OF THE HILLS   (Pathé, 1927)   ten chapters

Director, Spencer Gordon Bennet; story-screenplay, George
Arthur Gray; camera, Edward Snyder, Frank Redman.
Allene Ray (Mary Selby); Walter Miller (Laramie); Robert
Chandler (Clyde Selby); Jack Ganzhorn (Henry Selby); Frank Lack-
teen (The Hawk); Paul Panzer (Manson); Wally Oettel (Shorty); Harry
Semels (Sheckard); Jack Pratt (Colonel Jennings); J. Parks Jones
(Lieutenant MacCready); Frederick Dana (Larry); John T. Prince
(The Hermit); Chief Whitehorse, George Magrill, Evangeline Rus-
sell (Bits); Chief Yowlache (Chief Long Hand).

Frank Lackteen in <u>Hawk of the Hills</u> (1927).

Chapters: 1) The Outlaws; 2) In the Talons of the Hawk;
3) Heroes in Blue; 4) The Attack; 5) The Danger Trail; 6) The
Death Menace of Lost Canyon; 7) Demons of the Darkness; 8)
Doomed to the Arrows; 9) The House of Horror; 10) The Triumph
of Law and Love.

Shot in Newhall, California, this strong ten-chapter Pathé
serial cast Allene Ray as the attractive heroine who heads West to
join her miner father who, it develops, is being held by a gang led
by the evil "Hawk" (Lackteen) and his assistant (Panzer). The
latter hope to make the old man reveal the location of his hidden
mine. Also kidnapped is the miner's brother, a local Indian agent.
Both captives refuse to talk and The Hawk orders Mary Selby (Ray)
killed. However, gang member Laramie (Miller), who is really a
government agent, manages to save Mary and together they defeat
the gang and rescue the two prisoners.

This serial was full of good action and was well-handled by
Spencer Gordon Bennet. In addition to its Western background the
chapter-play expertly interpolated an element of mystery. It .was
one of ten serials made by the team of Allene Ray and Walter
Miller. As an added gimmick to induce patrons to come back week
after week for the serial chapters, "Movie Land Puzzles" were
given free to customers by theatres showing the serial. In 1929
the cliffhanger was issued as a 4,840' feature.

HEARTS OF THE WEST (MGM/United Artists, 1975) C   102 min.

Producer, Tony Bill; director, Howard Zieff; screenplay, Rob
Thompson; music, Ken Louber; art director, Robert Luthardt; set
decorator, Charles R. Pierce; assistant director, Jack B. Bernstein;
sound, Jerry Jost, Harry W. Tetrick; camera, Mario Tosi; editor,
Edward Warschiko.
Jeff Bridges (Lewis Tater); Andy Griffith (Howard Pike);
Donald Pleasence (A. J. Nietz); Blythe Danner (Miss Trout); Alan
Arkin (Kessler); Richard B. Shull (Stout Crook); Herb Edelman
(Polo); Alex Rocco (Assistant Director); Frank Cady (Pa Tater);
Anthony James (Leon Crook); Burtan Gilliam (Lester); Matt Clark
(Jackson); Candy Azzara (Waitress); Thayer David (Bank Manager);
Wayne Storm (Film Star); Marie Windsor (Woman in Nevada); Dub
Taylor (Nevada Ticket Agent).

With the failure of Bite the Bullet (1975) [q.v.] to live up to
box-office expectations, there was great hope that Hearts of the West
would turn the tide and help to start a new Western cycle of movie-
making. As fine as the reviews are, it is not drawing in the hoped-
for audiences.
Jeff Bridges stars as gullible fledgling writer Lewis Tater
who subscribes to a correspondence school. He soon learns that it
is merely a con game run by a trio (Shull, James, Windsor) of
Nevada crooks. Later he becomes involved with the production crew
of a quickie Western movie unit on location. There is Kessler

(Arkin) the director, the ineffectual film star (Storm), the assistant
director (Rocco), and a bunch of stuntmen including the veteran
Howard Pike (Griffith).   While the crooks pursue Tater to Hollywood, the youth becomes involved with Miss Trout (Danner), the
curvacious secretary to filmmaker Pike.   Along the way there is
a peculiar book publisher named A. J. Nietz (Pleasence) who has
the "truth" on the great D. W. Griffith and becomes involved in
Tater's way of life.
        The trade papers were quite enthused about this parody/
spoof, a more gentle lampoon than Mel Brooks' Blazing Saddles
(1974) [q.v.].   '[It] is a film made con amore by a lot of people.
In its unconventional way, it works 100%--an entertainment that
tickles the funnybone without insulting the mind" (Hollywood Reporter).
        The New York critics were impressed by this study of Holly-
wood in 1933; "... [it] is full of surprises, even as it lovingly recalls cliches drawn not only from the Westerns its hero adores but
from almost every Hollywood movie genre of the early sound era....
Among the film's abundant virtues, the most crucial one, perhaps,
is the casting of Jeff Bridges as the hero....   Bridges' naive comic
style and unaffected warmth keep Lewis from being the butt of the
film's jokes and turn him into its vital center instead" (New York
Daily News).
        Truly, for anyone who has viewed and cared about Westerns,
Hearts of the West is a must-see film.

HELL'S HEROES (Universal, 1930) 6,148'

        Presenter, Carl Laemmle; director, William Wyler; based on
the novel The Three Godfathers by Peter Bernard Kyne; adaptor-
screenplay, Tom Reed; sound, C. Roy Hunter; camera, George
Robinson; editor, Harry Marker.
        Charles Bickford (Bob Sangster); Raymond Hatton (Barbwire
Gibbons); Fred Kohler (Wild Bill Kearney); Fritzi Ridgeway (Mother);
Maria Alba (Carmelita); Jose de la Cruz (Jose); Buck Connors
(Parson Jones); Walter James (Sheriff).

        This early talking version of Peter B. Kyne's expanded
story, The Three Godfathers, had been filmed on several occasions,
including under its original title [q.v.] and most recently as an
ABC-TV "Movie of the Week" entitled The Godchild (1975) [q.v.].
Despite the title change this William Wyler-directed adaptation followed the book closely and was a commercial success.   In covering
Wyler's career in Films in Review Ken Doeckel judged the film "a
grim, realistically raw Western which nevertheless has a lot of
sentimentality."   This concise judgment sums up the essence of the
endurance of the original story: a combination of both action and
gentle human emotion, sure-fire winners at the box-office in any
decade.
        Awaiting the arrival of his three outlaw pals, Bob Sangster
(Bickford) flirts with dance hall girl Carmelita (Alba) and annoys a

sheriff (James) in the small frontier town of Wickenburg. When his
cohorts (Hatton, Kohler, de la Cruz) arrive, they join with Bob to
rob a man. During the hold-up Jose (de la Cruz) and another man
are killed. The surviving three bandits escape, fleeing into a
desert during a fierce sandstorm. Nevertheless, the posse continues
to pursue them. In the desert the fugitives discover a woman about
to give birth and she talks them into becoming the baby's godfathers
and taking it back to its father. The woman dies in childbirth and
the trio decide to keep their promise to the mother who has named
her child after each of them. En route to town, Wild Bill Kearney
(Kohler) and Barbwire Gibbons (Hatton) die, leaving Sangster to
care for the baby. Bob accidentally drinks poisoned water, but before expiring he manages to get the infant to its destination.
        Shot on location in the Mojave Desert and the Panamint
Valley, this was both the studio's and director Wyler's first all-
sound outdoor film. It proved an enormous popular and critical
success. Variety praised it as "gripping, real and convincingly
out of the ordinary." It made several best-of-the-month lists and
overseas was highly regarded.

HELL'S HINGES   (Triangle, 1919)   five reels

        Producer, Thomas H. Ince; director, William S. Hart;
story-screenplay, C. G. Sullivan; assistant director, Cliff Smith;
camera, Joseph August.
        William S. Hart (Blaze Tracey); Clara Williams (Faith
Henly); Jack Standing (Reverend Robert Henly); Alfred Hollingsworth
(Silk Miller); Robert McKim (Clergyman); J. Frank Burke (Zeb
Taylor); Louise Glaum (Dolly); Robert Kortman (Henchman); Jean
Hersholt, John Gilbert (Townsmen).

        Many film historians consider this William S. Hart produc-
tion to be the grimmest and perhaps the most "adult" Western
ever filmed in America. Directed by and starring Hart, the picture
reflected Hart's love of depicting the West as it really was: bleak
and hard. In Hell's Hinges he weaved a melodrama that was both
austere and realistic; it predated the mature Western craze by
nearly four decades.
        Wonderfully photographed by Joseph August, the film show-
cased Hart in his portrayal of Blaze Tracey, a respected outlaw
who falls in love with the sister (Williams) of a new minister
(Standing) who has come to the raw frontier town of Hell's Hinges
to build a church. Tracey tells Faith (Williams), via a title card,
"I reckon God ain't wantin' me much, Ma'am, but when I look at
you I feel I've been ridin' the wrong trail."
        The town's leading saloon keeper (Hollingsworth) has the
local tart (Glaum) seduce the weak-willed preacher and send him
on a drunken binge in which he leads the outlaws in burning the
newly-constructed church. Tracey returns to town to find the
minister has been killed in the melee. Angered, he proceeds to
the saloon where he shoots Silk Miller (Hollingsworth) and then sets

the place on fire, a conflagration which spreads throughout Hell's
Hinges. At the finale, Tracey and Faith leave the area, hoping to
find a better life elsewhere.

Surprisingly short on actual action, the picture is a sturdy
melodrama that is well-acted (considering the acting style of the
day) and is still entertaining. This Sodom and Gomorrah oater
stands as one of the most strongly made and enduring of sagebrush
films. Like all of Hart's Westerns, the picture also contains a
good deal of footage of the star with his beloved horse, Fritz.

HIGH NOON (United Artists, 1952) 85 min.

Producer, Stanley Kramer; director, Fred Zinnemann; based
on the story "The Tin Star" by John W. Cunningham; screenplay,
Carl Foreman; art director, Rudolph Sternad; set decorator, Emmett
Emerson; music, Dimitri Tiomkin; song, Tiomkin and Ned Washington; sung by Tex Ritter; sound, Jean Speak; camera, Floyd Crosby;
editors, Elmo Williams, Harry Gerstad.

Gary Cooper (Will Kane); Thomas Mitchell (Jonas Henderson);
Lloyd Bridges (Harvey Pell); Katy Jurado (Helen Ramirez); Grace
Kelly (Amy Kane); Otto Kruger (Percy Mettrick); Lon Chaney (Martin
Howe); Henry "Harry" Morgan (William Fuller); Ian MacDonald
(Frank Miller); Eve McVeagh (Mildred Fuller); Harry Shannon
(Cooper); Lee Van Cleef (Jack Colby); Bob Wilke (James Pierce);
Sheb Woolley (Ben Miller); Tom London (Sam); Ted Stanhope (Station
Master); Larry Blake (Gillis); William Phillips (Barber); Jeanne
Blackford (Mrs. Henderson); James Millican (Baker); Cliff Clark
(Weaver); Ralph Reed (Johnny); William Newell (Drunk); Lucien
Prival (Bartender); Guy Beach (Fred); Howland Chamberlin (Hotel
Clerk); Morgan Farley (Minister); Virginia Christine (Mrs. Simpson);
Virginia Farmer (Mrs. Fletcher); Jack Elam (Charlie); Paul Dubov
(Scott); Harry Harvey (Coy); Tim Graham (Sawyer); Nolan Leary
(Lewis); Tom Greenway (Ezra); John Doucette (Trumbull); Dick
Elliott (Kibbee).

Some will consider it heresy, but High Noon is a somewhat
overrated Western. It does have many assets, particularly in its
variety of performances and in the economical direction by Fred
Zinnemann. There is scarcely a wasted frame in the final print,
as all the oncamera action is made to correspond exactly to the
time spent viewing the film. But, in retrospect, some of the pre-
tentiousness of the storyline and the conventions used in the character relationships do not hold up.

Ironically, this project had great difficulty reaching the
screen. Gregory Peck had been offered the lead role, but he felt it
was too similar in concept to his performance in The Gunfighter [q.v.]
(1950), and he rejected the part. When Cooper accepted the assignment and the film was completed, United Artists executives realized
that it was not a very commercial venture. The film was re-edited
and, to spice up the proceedings, Tex Ritter's singing of the title
tune was interjected at storyline lulls to carry the viewer's interest

Gary Cooper in <u>High Noon</u> (1952).

until the action picked up again.   Thanks to the vast popularity of
the song ("Do not forsake me oh my darling, on this our wedding
day") the movie went on to become a hit in national release.   It
revived Cooper's waning career (he won his second Academy Award
and was re-established as a box-office figure of importance).   It
won the New York Film Critics Prize as best film of the year, and
the Manhattan critics, as did the Screen Directors Guild, voted
Zinnemann the director of the year.

     In the small town of Hadleyville, Sheriff Will Kane (Cooper)
is marrying a young Quaker girl (Kelly).   After the 10:30 A.M.
wedding the couple is planning to leave town.   Then word comes
that Frank Miller (MacDonald) has been released from jail and is
returning to seek revenge against Kane and the town for putting him
in jail.   Miller's brother Ben (Woolley) and two vicious pals (Van
Cleef, Wilke) are waiting at the train station for Frank's imminent
arrival.   Meanwhile Kane is torn between devotion to his bride and
loyalty to the town.   If he leaves, only the incapable deputy sheriff
(Bridges) will be left in charge.   Kane decides to stay and fight the
gunmen, even though Amy (Kelly) says she will not wait for him.

     At the hotel where Amy is waiting for the next stagecoach,
she is met by Helen Ramirez (Jurado), the woman love of Harvey

Pell (Bridges).   Helen tells Amy she should stand by her husband.
By now word has spread through town of the approaching showdown
and no one is willing to come to Kane's aid.   The doctor (Kruger),
the judge (Mitchell), and the town's leading citizen (Morgan) desert
Kane; and although the retired sheriff (Chaney), Kane's mentor and
idol, would like to aid his successor, he is too crippled by arthritis
to do so.   The church contingent refuse to help Kane and tell him
he should leave town.   Kane refuses and fights the outlaws alone in
the ghostly deserted streets of Hadleyville.   He kills two of the culprits and Amy shoots another; and the hero finally shoots Miller.
At the finale, Kane rides out of town with Amy, having thrown his
tin star into the street dust.
    Life magazine summed up viewers' reactions, deciding that
"although High Noon has some defects, few recent Westerns have
gotten so much tension and excitement into the classic struggle between good and evil. "
    This film was the launching point for several players, in-
cluding Miss Kelly and Lee Van Cleef, who each went on to stardom.

HIGH PLAINS DRIFTER   (Universal, 1972) C   105 min.

    Executive producer, Jennings Lang; producer, Robert Daley;
director, Clint Eastwood; screenplay, Ernest Tidyman; art director,
Henry Burnstead; set decorator, George Milo; music, Dee Barton;
stunt co-ordinator, Buddy Van Horn; sound, James R. Alexander;
camera, Bruce Surtees; editor, Ferris Webster.
    Clint Eastwood (The Stranger); Verna Bloom (Sarah Belding);
Mariana Hill (Callie Travers); Mitchell Ryan (Dave Drake); Jack
Ging (Morgan Allen); Stefan Gierasch (Mayor Jason Hobart); Ted
Hartley (Lewis Belding); Billy Curtis (Mordecai Fortusse); Geoffrey
Lewis (Stacy Bridges); Scott Walker (Bill Borders); Walter Barnes
(Sheriff Sam Shaw); Paul Brinegar (Lutie Naylor); Richard Bull
(Asa Goodwin); Robert Donner (Preacher); John Hillerman (Boot-
maker); Anthony James (Cole Carlin); William O'Connell (Barber);
John Quade (Jake Ross); Jane Aull (Townswoman); Dan Vadis (Dan
Carlin); Reid Cruickshanks (Gunsmith); James Gosa (Tommy Morris);
Jack Kosslyn (Saddlemaker); Russ McCubbin (Fred Short); Belle
Mitchell (Mrs. Lake); John Mitchum (Warden); Carl C. Pitti (Team-
ster); Chuck Waters (Stableman); Buddy Van Horn (Marshal Jim
Duncan).

    Clint Eastwood, who directed this venture as well as acted
in it, returned to the screen in the guise of "the man with no
name, " the character he played so effectively in his three Italian
Westerns with Sergio Leone.   Shot at Mono Lake in the Sierras,
the feature was not a true Western in the traditional sense because
it developed more into a symbolic horror story than a genre film.
The ambience of the picture is reminiscent of the writings of such
American authors as Ambrose Bierce and Stephen Crane.   Above
all, the influence of such sagebrush classics as Hell's Hinges (1916)
[q.v.] and High Noon (1952) [q.v.] is obvious.   The former, a

Marianna Hill and Clint Eastwood in High Plains Drifter (1972).

William S. Hart classic, is represented by a town-burning scene
while the latter's influence is demonstrated in High Plains Drifter's
slow pacing and its loner hero.
    The citizens of Largo, an old frontier town of the southwest,
become very aware of the arrival of a stranger in their midst. At
the saloon three men start a fight with him and are shot dead. The
townfolk quickly ask the loner if he will help defend them against a
trio of men who are to be released from the nearby jail and who
have sworn revenge on the people of Largo for "framing them."
The stranger, so we learn, has a dream in which these same three
men beat and whipped Largo's sheriff to death, with the man cursing
them to damnation. The Stranger agrees to take the job. He

appoints the dwarf Mordecai (Curtis) as his deputy and commandeers the hotel and all the available ammunition for the showdown. He also demands that all the houses be painted red and that a banquet feast be placed in the main street. His final demand is that the town sign on the outskirts of Largo be changed to read "Hell." Meanwhile some of the town's leaders, fearing the Stranger's power, try to kill him, but they are subdued. The convicts do ride into town, but the ambush scheme fails and Largo is soon in their control. However, during the night the stranger sets the town on fire, and before long one convict is shot, another hanged, and a third whipped to death. As the stranger, whose identity is still not known, leaves town the next day, he notes the dwarf writing a special inscription on Jim Duncan's tombstone.

An entire Western town was built for this austere production. Unlike most features, it was shot in continuity. Old Testament-like in its theme and symbols, the film was labelled by the Los Angeles Times "a stylized, allegorical Western of much chilling paranoid atmosphere and considerable sardonic humor...." (Perhaps the biggest laugh came from Eastwood himself, for this ambiguous, confusing drama grossed over $7 million in distributors' domestic rentals.)

While many viewers pondered whether Eastwood's stranger was really the sheriff who had been beaten to death or a relative of his; whether the town of Largo was a real place or a ritualistic hell; or whether any of these events really happen, some critics spent their time finding faults within the picture's structure. "The long, brooding pauses, the dramatic low-angle shots, the percussive score and the satirical treatment of the town's corrupt hierarchy, however well copied [from Leone's pictures], are not welded into a convincing whole, and the film never recovers from an opening sequence which crudely burlesques the classic stranger-rides-into-town scene, endlessly intercutting tracking shots of Eastwood on horseback with reaction close-ups of the gaping townspeople, accompanied by the amplified clump and shuffle of the horse's hooves on the soundtrack" (British Monthly Film Bulletin).

This film left no question, however, that Eastwood was and is still one of the major influences in the Western genre in the seventies, as he had been during the sixties.

HIGH SIERRA   see   COLORADO TERRITORY

THE HIGHWAYMAN RIDES   see   BILLY THE KID (1930)

EL HIJO DEL ZORRO   see   MARK OF ZORRO

THE HILLS RUN RED   see   UN FIUME DI DOLLARI

HIT THE SADDLE   (Republic, 1937)   57 min.

    Producer, Nat Levine; associate producer, Sol C. Siegel;
director, Mack V. Wright; based on the characters created by
William Colt MacDonald; adaptors, Oliver Drake, Maurice Geraghty;
screenplay, Drake; music supervisor, Alberto Colombo; songs,
Drake and Sam H. Stept; art director, John Victor Mackay; sound,
Dan Bloomburg; camera, Jack Martz; editor, Lester Orlebeck.
    Robert Livingston (Stony Brooke); Ray Corrigan (Tucson
Smith); Max Terhune (Lullaby Joslin); Rita Cansino [Hayworth]
(Rita); Yakima Canutt (Buck); J. P. McGowan (MacGowan); Edward
Cassidy (Miller); Sammy McKim (Tim); Harry Tenbrooke (Harvey);
Robert Smith (Hank); Ed Boland (Pete); George Plues (Henchman);
Jack Kirk, Russ Powell, Bob Burns (Ranchers); Volcano (Stallion);
Allan Cavan (Judge); Wally West, George Morrell (Patrons); Budd
Buster (Drunk); Kernan Cripps (Bartender).

    The fifth in Republic's long-running The Three Mesquiteers
series evolved as one of the best of the Western series, thanks to
the tight direction by Mack V. Wright and the location photography
in Red Rock Canyon in the Mojave Desert.   For a bonus attraction
today, there is the young Rita Cansino, known later as Rita Hayworth.
    The Three Mesquiteers (Livingston, Corrigan and Terhune)
and a sheriff (Cassidy) round up five rustlers stealing wild horses
from their sanctuary.   They let them go, however, when their boss
(McGowan), who runs a real estate office as a front for rustling
the horses, insists that the men were merely hunting strays.   Because he has an order to sell 1,000 head of horses, MacGowan
tells his men to get rid of the sheriff and the Mesquiteers.   Later

Max Terhune, Bob Livingston, Rita Hayworth and Ray Corrigan in
Hit the Saddle (1937).

a killer horse accomplishes the death of the sheriff.
        Meanwhile Stony (Livingston) meets a saloon girl Rita
(Cansino) with whom he falls in love. Tucson (Corrigan) and Lullaby (Terhune) try unsuccessfully to dissuade their pal from this
ill-fated romance. Stony and Rita actually set a wedding date, but
Lullaby informs the would-be bride that she will have to cook for
sixteen cowhands once she is wed to Stony. Stony's pals offer her
$1,500 and a one-way ticket to New York, which she readily accepts.
        Later, McGowan captures Stony and turns the killer horse
loose on him, but another wild pinto, loyal to Stony, fights the
horse. Tucson and Lullaby arrive and when McGowan tries to escape the killer horse tramples him to death.
        Not only was Hit the Saddle good Saturday matinee fare but
a fine exposé of the rustling of wild horses which was plaguing the
West at that time.

HI-YO SILVER   see   THE LONE RANGER (1938)

HOMBRE   (Twentieth Century-Fox, 1967) C   111 min.

        Producers, Martin Ritt, Irving Ravetch; director, Ritt; based
on the novel by Elmore Leonard; screenplay, Ravetch, Harriet
Frank, Jr.; second unit director, Ray Kellogg; assistant director,
William McGarry; music-music director, David Rose; orchestrators,
Leo Shuken, Jack Hayes; costumes, Don Feld; makeup, Ben Nye;
art directors, Jack Martin Smith, Robert I. Smith; set decorators,
Walter M. Scott, Raphael Bretton; sound, John R. Carter, David
Dockendorf; camera, James Wong Howe; editor, Frank Bracht.
        Paul Newman (John Russell); Fredric March (Alexander
Favor); Richard Boone (Cicero Grimes); Diane Cilento (Jessie Brown);
Cameron Mitchell (Sheriff Frank Braden); Barbara Rush (Audra
Favor); Peter Lazer (Billy Lee Blake); Margaret Blye (Doris);
Martin Balsam (Henry Mendez); Skip Ward (Steve Early); Frank
Silvera (Mexican Bandit); David Canary (Lamar Dean); Val Avery
(Delgado); Larry Ward (Soldier); Linda Cordova (Mrs. Delgado);
Pete Hernandez, Merrill C. Isbell (Apaches).

        In what Variety termed a "handsome production about greed
and survival in the old West," the Hud [q.v.] team (Ritt, Ravetch,
Frank, Newman) created Hombre, a film which grossed $6.5 million
in domestic rentals.
        Filmed on location in Arizona, the story dealt with John
Russell, better known as Hombre (Newman). He is one of the
Apaches of the 1880s who lives by himself in the deserted desert
hills. Actually, as a child he had lost his white parents in an
Indian raid, and was carried off by the Apaches and raised by them
as an Indian. When he learns he has inherited a boarding house,
he decides to trade it for a pack of horses, and following the advice of friend Mendez (Balsam) he has shorn his long hair and dis-
carded his Indian garb for the more traditional white man's dress.

Paul Newman in <u>Hombre</u> (1967).

Having completed his business he leaves town on the stage. The
other passengers include Indian agent Favor (March)--who hates
Hombre--and his young wife Audra (Rush), a young married couple
(Lazer and Blye), the sensuous Jessie Brown (Cilento), and a rambunctious stranger named Cicero Grimes (Boone). The driver is
played by Balsam. It develops that Grimes' men are waiting for
the stage to hold up Favor who has embezzled some $12,000 in
Indian funds. Hombre shoots and kills two of the bandits, including
the one with the money, and takes the passengers (except Audra,
who is taken by Grimes as a hostage) to an abandoned mine.
Eventually Grimes and his men return and in the ensuing combat,
Hombre gives up his life to save the others.

     In the Christian Science Monitor, Frederick H. Guidey calls
the film "An engrossing exploration of mankind's obligations and
frailities. Unfortunately, the film's emphasis turns negative, and
the conclusion seems to be that sacrifice on behalf of another is
useless." Newsweek observed, "Like most good Westerns, Hombre
really isn't about the West at all. High Noon is about responsibility, Shane about courage, and Hombre about color, about the
ambiguous role of the nonwhite American in a white country."

     If there is any major fault with this production it is the
viewer's continual consciousness that the characters are all star
actors seeking their moments stage front and center. By this point
in his career Newman's posturing and mannered behavior had become fixed and it gave a sameness to all his performances, while
March, as the corrupt official with the much younger spouse, looked
all too wide-eyed and shifty (as he pushed his false teeth from side
to side). Not surprisingly, the best performances in the project
came from Martin Balsam and Barbara Rush (who had co-starred
with Newman in The Young Philadelphians, 1959).

HOME ON THE RANGE (Paramount, 1935) 55 min.

     Producer, Harold Hurley; director, Arthur Jacobson; based
on the novel by Zane Grey; screenplay, Ethel Doherty, Grant Gar-
rett, Charles Logue; camera, William Mellor; editor, Jack Dennis.
     Jackie Coogan (Jack); Randolph Scott (Tom Hatfield); Evelyn
Brent (Georgie); Dean Jagger (Thurman); Addison Richards (Beady);
Fuzzy Knight (Cracker); and: Ann Sheridan, Howard Wilson, Phillip
Morris, Albert Hart, Francis Sayles, Richard Carle, Joe Morrison,
C. L. Sherwood, Jack Clark.

     Taken from Zane Grey's novel, Code of the West, this Para-
mount programmer starred Randolph Scott and ex-child star Jackie
Coogan as brothers (!) who own a stable of racing ponies. One of
their horses is scheduled to appear in a big race, with the likeli-
hood of winning the event. A gang of sharpshooters, however,
hopes to fix the race and tries to victimize the brothers. Relative
newcomer Ann Sheridan provided the love interest.
     The story had been filmed as a silent in 1925 by Paramount
as Code of the West and it then starred Owen Moore and Constance

Bennett. (A 1929 film titled Code of the West, issued by FBO, with
Bob Custer and Vivian Bay, was not based on Grey's work.) RKO
did a remake in 1947 using the novel's original title and featuring
James Warren, Debra Alden, and Harry Woods.

HONDO (Warner Bros., 1953) C 93 min.

    Producer, Robert Fellows; director, John Farrow; based on
the story by Louis L'Amour; screenplay, James Edward Grant;
music, Emil Newman, Hugh Friedhofer; art director, Al Yverra;
camera, Robert Burks, Archie Stout; editor, Ralph Dawson.
    John Wayne (Hondo Lane); Geraldine Page (Angie Lowe);
Ward Bond (Buffalo); Michael Pate (Vittorio); James Arness (Len-
nie); Rodolfo Acosta (Silva); Leo Gordon (El Lowe); Tom Irish
(Lieutenant McKay); Lee Aaker (Johnny); Paul Fix (Major Sherry);
Rayford Barnes (Pete).

    Shot in 3-D and color by Wayne-Fellows Productions, this
feature marked the screen debut of New York stage actress Geraldine Page. It was shot on location at Caramango, Mexico, and
Yakima Canutt did some doubling for star John Wayne, just as he
had done some two decades earlier.
    Taken from a Collier's magazine story by Louis L'Amour,
the narrative concerns Hondo Lane (Wayne) who, in 1874, works
as a dispatch rider for the U.S. Cavalry. He comes upon a ranch
where Angie Lowe (Page) and her small son (Aaker) have been
deserted by her husband (Gordon) as the result of an Apache uprising. She refuses to leave her homestead when Hondo advises
her to depart with him. Later the Lowe spread is attacked by a
raiding party and the boy shoots at a brave (Acosta) who is impressed by the lad's bravery. He makes the white boy a blood
brother and immune from further attacks.
    Back at the fort Hondo has words with Lowe (Gordon), not
knowing who he is. Hondo rides to rescue Angie and her boy, and,
later, has to shoot an angered Lowe in self-defense. Only then
does he learn who the man really is. Thereafter the Apaches capture Hondo and decide to torture him. The chief (Pate) is impressed
by the man's courage and orders him to fight Silva (Acosta); he defeats the Indian but spares his life. When Hondo does meet up with
Angie he confesses he has killed her husband. She understands why
and together they plan a new life together in California. When
Vittorio (Pate) is later murdered, Silva begins a murdering rampage
but he is killed while attacking the wagon train Hondo is leading
westward with Angie and her son. Finally the war is over.
    In 1967 this superior entry, which in many ways parallels
Shane (1953) [q.v.], was remade by MGM under the direction of
Lee H. Katzin with Ralph Taeger in the title role. It was contracted with the studio by ABC-TV as a telefeature but was shown
in the fall of that year as the opening segment of the teleseries
"Hondo," which only had a brief network run. The feature itself,
which co-featured Robert Taylor, was issued in Europe in 1967 under
the title Hondo and the Apaches.

HONKY TONK   (MGM, 1941)   105 min.

     Producer, Pandro S. Berman; director, Jack Conway; screen-
play, Marguerite Roberts, John Sanford; music, Franz Waxman;
songs, Jack Yellen and Milton Ager; art director, Cedric Gibbons;
sound, Douglas Shearer; camera, Harold Rosson; editor, Blanche
Sewell.
     Clark Gable (Candy Johnson); Lana Turner (Elizabeth Cotton);
Frank Morgan (Judge Cotton); Claire Trevor (Gold Dust Nelson);
Marjorie Main (Reverend Mrs. Varner); Albert Dekker (Brazos
Hearn); Chill Wills (The Sniper); Henry O'Neill (Daniel Wells); John
Maxwell (Kendall); Morgan Wallace (Adams); Douglas Wood (Governor
Wilson); Betty Blythe (Mrs. Wilson); Hooper Atchley (Senator Ford);
Harry Worth (Harry Gates); Veda Ann Borg (Pearl); Dorothy Granger
(Saloon Girl); Cy Kendall (Man with Tar); Ray Teal (Poker Player);
Esther Muir (Blonde on Train); Francis X. Bushman, Jr., Art
Miles (Dealers); Syd Saylor, Harry Semels, Frank Mills, Art
Belasco, Eddie Gribbon, Ralph Peters (Pallbearers); Eddy C. Waller
(Train Conductor); Will Wright, Alan Bridge, Lee Phelps (Men in
Meeting House); Horace Murphy (Butler).

     If any studio could turn out a glossy Western it was MGM in
the forties. Honky Tonk, which was the first starring vehicle of
the new love team of Clark Gable and Lana Turner, proved to be a
big winner in all departments.
     From the point of view of its plot there was nothing unique
about this film. "It is distinctly in the tradition of Gable pictures--
you know, the sort in which he slugs it out, toe to toe, with equally

Clark Gable, Claire Trevor and Albert Dekker in Honky Tonk (1941).

impetuous women. In the present instance, Lana Turner acts as
his sparring partner, which helps matters no end because Miss
Turner is not only beautiful but ruggedly constructed" (New York
Times).

Gable plays a slick con artist who arrives in the town of
Yellow Creek, Nevada. After giving up his gutsy dancehall-girl
mistress (Trevor), he weds former Bostonian Lucy Cotton (Turner).
Lucy's dad, a drunken judge (Morgan) is later shot by gambling
house owner Hearn (Dekker). The shock of this event causes Lucy
to suffer a miscarriage and forces Candy (Gable) to turn honest.
He pursues Hearn and his gang and shoots the leader. Later the
recovered Lucy follows her man.

Honky Tonk is really a soap opera set in a Western locale,
but with the expansive MGM technical staff to mount the film it
proved an entertaining sagebrush affair. Then, too, the cast was
electric, ranging from Gable and Turner to heart-of-gold Trevor,
the gruff Marjorie Main as the preacher's widow, Frank Morgan as
the befuddled old cheat, and Albert Dekker as the arch villain.

Hoping to recreate the box-office magic of the feature, in
1974 MGM produced a video pilot of "Honky Tonk" with Richard
Crenna. It pleased few viewers and died a quick death.

HOPALONG CASSIDY (HOPALONG CASSIDY ENTERS) (Paramount,
1935) 62 min.

Producer, Harry Sherman; director, Howard Bretherton;
story, Clarence E. Mulford; screenplay-adaptor, Doris Schroeder;
camera, Archie Stout; editor, Edward Schroeder.

William Boyd (Bill Cassidy); Jimmy Ellison (Johnny Nelson);
Paula Stone (Mary Meeker); Robert Warwick (Jim Meeker); Charles
Middleton (Buck Peters); Frank McGlynn, Jr. (Red Connors); Ken-
neth Thomson (Pecos Jack Anthony); George Hayes (Uncle Ben);
James Mason (Tom Shaw); Frank Campeau (Frisco); Ted Adams
(Hall); Willie Fung (Salem the Cook); Franklyn Farnum (Doc Riley);
John Merton (Party Guest).

William Boyd's screen career had sunk into the B field by
the mid-thirties. In 1935, producer Harry "Pop" Sherman offered
him the role of ranch foreman Buck Peters in an adaptation of
Hopalong Cassidy based on the character created by Clarence E.
Mulford in 26 novels. Boyd rejected that part, but agreed to play
the lead if the character was made into a clean-living person. (In
the Mulford books, Hopalong was a hard-drinking, heavy-smoking,
cussing, none-too-clean varmint.) In this role, Boyd created such
a definitive character that he would remain among the highest paid
actors in Hollywood (around $100,000 per year). In later years
he would buy the TV rights to the features and become the center
of the "Hopalong Cassidy" craze of the early fifties.

The initial film, later re-issued as Hopalong Cassidy Enters,
is a very good Western, directed in sprightly fashion by Howard
Bretherton, and providing fine outdoor locales with a minimum of

William Boyd and Jimmy Ellison in <u>Hopalong Cassidy</u> (1935).

stock footage. The strong plot has Bill Cassidy (Boyd) returning to
his old ranch to find ex-boss Buck Peters (Middleton), old pal Uncle
Ben (Hayes) and hotheaded younger Johnny Nelson (Ellison) at odds
with fellow rancher Jim Meeker (Warwick) and his attractive daughter (Stone), she being attracted to Nelson. Meeker's foreman
(Thomson) is actually the culprit, as he creates the cattle war by
hijacking Peters' cattle and blaming it on Meeker. Eventually
Cassidy proves his buddy (Middleton) is innocent. In the meanwhile, Uncle Ben has been murdered by Pecos Jack (Thomson).
"You didn't have a chance, did you old timer?" Cassidy asks the
prostrate body of his friend, after finding him bushwacked on the
range.
   During the course of the storyline, Cassidy is slightly injured in a gun battle, giving him the limp of the title. This malady
is temporary, however, and this entry ends with the range war
terminated and Cassidy, Johnny Nelson, and Red Connors (McGlynn,
Jr.) riding off into the sunset to homestead a new ranch.
   The popularity of the first Hoppy film would lead to sixty-
five other Cassidy screen adventures over the next thirty years.

HOPALONG CASSIDY RETURNS (Paramount, 1936) 71 min.

   Producer, Harry Sherman; associate producer, Eugene
Strong; director, Nate Watt; story, Clarence E. Mulford; screenplay,
Harrison Jacobs; camera, Archie Stout; editor, Robert Warwick.

William Boyd (Hopalong Cassidy); George "Gabby" Hayes
(Windy Halliday); Gail Sheridan (Mary Saunders); Evelyn Brent
(Lilli Marsh); Morris Ankrum (Blackie); William Janney (Buddy
Cassidy); Irving Bacon (Peg Leg Holden); Grant Richards (Bob Clai-
borne); John Beck (Robert Saunders); Ernie Adams (Benson); Al St.
John (Luke); Joe Rickson (Buck); Ray Whitley (Davis); Claude Smith
(Dugan).

The seventh of the sixty-six-feature Hopalong Cassidy series
was one of the very best.

Saloon hostess Lilli Marsh (Brent) heads a gang which steals
from miners and ranchers alike.   She and her henchmen (Richards
and Norris) appoint a newspaper editor as sheriff and then later have
him killed.   Before his death, however, the man sends for Cassidy
(Boyd) and his brother (Janney).   Lilli falls in love with Hoppy, but
he fights her gang and brings peace to the town.   Lilli is killed in
the mayhem by one of her men and dies in Hoppy's arms.

Archie Stout provided handsome camerawork for this entry.
Series regular George "Gabby" Hayes turned in his usual deft comic
performance in the proceedings.

THE HORSE SOLDIERS (United Artists, 1959)   C   119 min.

Producers, John Lee Mahin, Martin Rackin; director, John
Ford; based on the novel by Harold Sinclair; screenplay, Mahin; art
director, Frank Hotaling; makeup, Webb Overlander; wardrobe,
Frank Beetson, Ann Peck; assistant directors, Wingate Smith, Ray
Gosnell, Jr.; music, David Buttolph; song, Stan Jones; sound, Jack
Solomon; special effects, Augie Lohman; camera, William Clothier;
editor, Jack Murray.

John Wayne (Colonel Marlowe); William Holden (Major Ken-
dall); Constance Towers (Hannah); Althea Gibson (Lukey); Hoot
Gibson (Brown); Anna Lee (Mrs. Buford); Russell Simpson (Sheriff);
Stan Jones (General U. S. Grant); Carleton Young (Colonel Miles);
Basil Ruysdael (Boys' School Commandant); Willis Bouchey (Colonel
Phil Secord); Ken Curtis (Wilkie); O. Z. Whitehead (Hoppy Hopkins);
Judson Pratt (Sergeant Major Kirby); Denver Pyle (Jagger Jo);
Strother Martin (Virgil); Hank Worden (Deacon); Walter Reed (Union
Officer); Jack Pennick (Sergeant Major Mitchell); Fred Graham
(Union Soldier); Chuck Hayward (Union Captain); Charles Seel (Newton
Station Bartender); Major Sam Harris, Stuart Holmes (Passengers to
Newton Station); Richard Cutting (General Sherman); and Bing Russell,
William Forrest, William Leslie, Bill Henry, Dan Borzage, Fred
Kennedy, Ron Hagerthy.

In 1863 General Grant (Jones) is having great difficulty laying
siege to Vicksburg.   His only hope of gaining control of the city is
to cut off their supplies.   He sends Colonel Marlowe (Wayne) and
three regiments some 300 miles into Confederate territory to destroy
the railroad lines and depot at Newton Station, Mississippi.   Grant
also assigns to the raiding party Surgeon Major Kendall (Holden), a

William Holden in <u>The Horse Soldiers</u> (1959).

man with whom Marlowe constantly argues. Along the way, Hannah
(Towers), a plantation mistress, and her black maid Lukey (Gibson)
join the party because they have learned of Marlowe's plan. After
his successful attack on Newton Station, Marlowe and his group head
for the safety of Union-held Baton Rouge. During this jaunt, Lukey
is killed, while Marlowe and Hannah fall in love, and Marlowe learns
to accept Kendall. (Marlowe hated all doctors because his wife died
from an unnecessary operation.) The Reb forces are close behind
Marlowe as he puts Kendall, Hannah, and the wounded men on one
side of the Amite River. He then blows up the bridge.

Based on an actual Civil War mission, the film was long and
exciting, but certainly not exceptional. Thanks to the marquee value
of Wayne, Holden and Ford, the film grossed $4 million domestically.

Saturday Review's Arthur Knight was quick to point out that
"The film ... although drawn from the book and following the main
thread of its narrative, is replete with the kind of diversionary actions that turn up with far greater frequency in movies than in war."
On the other hand, Knight did acknowledge, "Best of all, the script
makes no effort to blunt the issues over which the war was fought,
nor does it pretend that war is a glorious pastime.... There remains the question, however, of whether the same effect might not
have been achieved by adhering more closely to the original novel,
or to fact. Certainly, once Wayne and Holden were cast in the
principal roles (at a reported $750,000 each), so in effect was the
die. It had to be a big, popular picture--and almost of necessity
this meant a love interest as well, and a certain amount of further
compromise. Thus, although the script emphasizes that the Raiders
traveled light, Constance Towers seems to have an inexhaustible
supply of lipstick and cosmetics; a romantic lead must look romantic."

Outside of a short segment in How the West Was Won (1963),
this was John Ford's only film to deal with the Civil War period.

HOUR OF THE GUN   see   GUNFIGHT AT THE O.K. CORRAL

HOW THE WEST WAS WON (MGM, 1963) C 165 min.

Producer, Bernard Smith; directors, Henry Hathaway, (The
Rivers, The Plains, The Outlaws), John Ford (The Civil War),
George Marshall (The Railroad); based on a magazine series; screen-
play, James R. Webb; art directors, George W. Davis, William
Ferrari, Addison Hehr; set decorators, Henry Grace, Don Green-
wood, Jr., Jack Mills; music, Alfred Newman; songs, Newman and
Ken Darby; Newman and Sammy Cahn; Newman and Johnny Mercer;
music associate, Ken Darby; assistant directors, George Marshall,
Jr., William McGarry, Robert Saunders, William Shanks, Wingate
Smith; costumes, Walter Plunkett; color consultant, Charles K.
Hagedon; sound, Franklin Milton; special camera effects, A. Arnold
Gillespie, Robert R. Hoag; camera, William H. Daniels, Milton
Krasner, Charles Lang, Jr., Joseph La Shelle; second unit camera,
Harold E. Wellman; editor, Harold F. Kress.

Spencer Tracy (Narrator); Carroll Baker (Eve Prescott); Lee J. Cobb (Marshal); Henry Fonda (Jethro Stuart); Carolyn Jones (Julie Rawlings); Karl Malden (Zebulon Prescott); Gregory Peck (Cleve Van Valen); George Peppard (Zeb Rawlings); Robert Preston (Roger Morgan); Debbie Reynolds (Lilith Prescott); James Stewart (Linus Rawlings); Eli Wallach (Charlie Gant); John Wayne (General Sherman); Richard Widmark (Mike King); Brigid Bazlen (Dora); Walter Brennan (Colonel Hawkins); David Brian (Attorney); Andy Devine (Peterson); Raymond Massey (Abraham Lincoln); Agnes Moorehead (Rebecca Prescott); Henry "Harry" Morgan (General Grant); Thelma Ritter (Agatha Clegg); Mickey Shaughnessy (Deputy); Russ Tamblyn (Reb Soldier); Tudor Owen (Scotsman); Barry Harvey (Angus); Jamie Ross (Bruce); Kim Charney (Sam Prescott); Brian Russell (Zeke Prescott); Claude Johnson (Zeb's Brother); Jerry Holmes (Railroad Clerk); Rudolph Acosta (Desperado) Lee Van Cleef (Marty); Mark Allen (Colin); Charles Briggs (Barber); Jay C. Flippen (Higgins); Clinton Sundberg (Hylan Seabury); James J. Griffith, Walter Burke (Gamblers); Joseph Sawyer (Ship's Officer); John

Carolyn Jones, Wendy Muldoon, Stanley Livingston, Joey Scott, George Peppard and Debbie Reynolds in How the West Was Won (1963).

Larch (Grimes); Jack Pennick (Corporal Murphy); Craig Duncan
(James Marshall).

After years of colorful travelogues, Cinerama, the innovative
three-film widescreen process, turned out an epic story of the
development of America. How the West Was Won proved to be a
broad and colorful panorama, chock-full of name stars.   However,
it was also often a dramatically empty film.   Narrated by Spencer
Tracy, the feature had picturesque location shooting at Battery Rock
along the Ohio River in Illinois, at Courthouse Mountain in the
Pinnacle and Chimmez Rock area in the Colorado Rockies, at Monument Valley, and throughout the Paducah, Kentucky countryside.
Taken from the Life magazine series, the feature grossed $24 mil-
lion-plus in U.S. and Canadian distributor rentals.
       The marathon-length picture was divided into five sequences
supervised by three different directors, with various characters continuing through the narrative.   The opening section was set along the
Erie Canal in 1803 with the Prescott family heading westward.   On
the Ohio River, they encounter river pirates and later, Mr. and
Mrs. Prescott (Malden and Moorehead) drown in the rapids.   The
two daughters (Reynolds and Baker) survive.   Walter Brennan gave
the film's best performance in this segment as a crafty, but deadly,
old river pirate.   Henry Hathaway also directed the second segment, The Plains, which told of a wagon train trip from St. Louis
to California and the gold fields, with an Indian attack en route.
John Ford was in charge of the short The Civil War section which
covered the Battle of Shiloh and had John Wayne as General William
Tecumsah Sherman.   The fourth part, The Railroads, was helmed
by George Marshall and related how the railroad companies broke
treaties with the Indians in order to build their railways.   The
movie's most spectacular sequence, a buffalo stampede (utilizing the
wide screen Cinerama to the fullest extent) was included in this
section.   The last portion, The Outlaws, taking place in 1889, was
also directed by Hathaway and concerned a gunfight on a train.   As
the film ends, one learns that "Law and order has been brought to
the West....   The West has been won."
       George J. Mitchell said, in Films in Review, "Although How
the West Was Won makes it apparent that actors, directors and
technicians have much to learn before Cinerama is fully effective,*
it is an important and significant step forward and an engrossing
and entertaining film."   Paul V. Beckley lauded in the New York
Herald-Tribune: "Cinerama has always been big, but now it's
bigger, not that it is any broader or any higher, but that the movie
How the West Was Won is for everybody, not only a tribute to the
American past, but to American movie-making."
       One can only have wished that more concern had been given
to the storyline and the credibility of performances (the make-up

---

*When one of this book's co-authors saw the film on first run in
Philadelphia, the middle film strip broke half way into the narrative.
The projection continued on the two outer strips for another twenty
minutes before the three projectors could be synchronized again.

used for Miss Baker and Miss Reynolds as they age is laughable).
But the success of this production did prove that a splashy Western
could still draw big box-office, without the necessity for violence
and gore, which seemed to be the latest gimmick in drawing moviegoers back to theatres.

HUD   (Paramount, 1963)   112 min.

     Producers, Martin Ritt, Irving Ravetch; director, Martin
Ritt; based on the novel Horseman, Pass By by Larry McMurtry;
screenplay, Ravetch, Harriet Frank, Jr.; art directors, Hal
Pereira, Tambi Larsen; set decorators, Sam Comer, Robert Benton;
makeup, Wally Westmore; music, Elmer Bernstein; assistant direc-
tor, C. C. Coleman, Jr.; sound, John Carter, John Wilkinson;
special camera effects, Paul K. Lerpae; process camera, Farciot
Edouart; camera, James Wong Howe; second unit camera, Rex
Wimpy; editor, Frank Bracht.
     Paul Newman (Hud Bannon); Melvyn Douglas (Homer Bannon);
Patricia Neal (Alma); Brandon De Wilde (Lon Bannon); John Ashley
(Hermy); Whit Bissell (Burris); Crahan Denton (Jesse); Val Avery
(Jose); Sheldon Allman (Thompson); Pitt Herbert (Larker); Peter
Brooks (George); Curt Conway (Truman Peters); Yvette Vickers
(Lily Peters); George Petrie (Joe Scanlon); David Kent (Donald);
Frank Killmond (Dumb Billy).

     "Hud is a provocative picture with a shock for audiences who
have been conditioned like laboratory mice to expect the customary
bad-guy-is-really-good-guy reward in the last reel of a western....
The point of the picture is as dry and nihilistic as a Panhandle dust
storm.   Once, when Douglas is berating his son, De Wilde asks:
'Why pick on Hud, Grandpa?   Nearly everybody around town is like
him'" (Time).
     Hud Bannon (Newman) is the no-good hellion son of an aged
cattle rancher (Douglas) in contemporary Texas.   Rancher Homer
Bannon detests his selfish son, but young nephew Lee Bannon (De
Wilde) looks up to the Texas stud.   Lee also admires his grandfather but cannot communicate with him.   Adding to the tension is
housekeeper Alma (Neal), who yearns for Hud but refuses to give in
to his sexual advances.   Meanwhile, when some of the cattle contract
hoof-and-mouth disease, Hud suggests selling the entire herd before
the disease spreads.   Homer refuses, insisting that the cattle be
slaughtered.   Hud is now convinced that his grandfather is senile
and hopes to have him committed.   In a drunken rage Hud tries to
assault Alma.   She leaves the next day and Homer, while riding
about his vacant spread, suffers a fatal heart attack.   After the
funeral Lon, having appraised Hud for what he really is, leaves
the ranch.   Hud shrugs his shoulders, sits back, and opens a can
of beer.   Life goes on for him.
     Both Newman and Miss Neal were Oscar-nominated in the
best-acting departments, while Douglas, billed ahead of Neal, won
the award for Best Supporting Actor.

Patricia Neal and Paul Newman in <u>Hud</u> (1963).

Man's alienation from society is a frequent theme with novelist Larry McMurtry, who also wrote The Last Picture Show, among other books. In many ways Hud is an uncompromising study, from director Ritt's decision to film the picture in black-and-white (stunningly accomplished by James Wong Howe), to the unflamboyant performances of the principals. Clearly the real-life cowboys of the sixties had come a long way from the guitar-strumming heroes of thirties' and forties' features.

Summing up the film, Bosley Crowther (New York Times) professed, "While it looks like a modern western and is an outdoor drama indeed, Hud is as wide and profound a contemplation of the human condition as one of the New England Plays of Eugene O'Neill.... The striking, important thing about it is the clarity with which it un-reels. The sureness and integrity of it are as crystal clear as the plot is spare...."

I DIED A THOUSAND TIMES   see   COLORADO TERRITORY

I SHOT JESSE JAMES (Lippert, 1949)   81 min.

Executive producer, Robert L. Lippert; producer, Carl K. Hittleman; director, Samuel Fuller; based on an article by Homer Croy; screenplay, Fuller; assistant director, Johnny Grubbs; art director, Frank Hotaling; set decorators, John McCarthy, James Redd; music, Albert Glasser; song, Katherine Glasser; camera, Ernest Miller; editor, Paul Landres.

Preston Foster (John Kelley); Barbara Britton (Cynthy Waters); John Ireland (Bob Ford); Reed Hadley (Jesse James); J. Edward Bromberg (Harry Lane); Victor Kilian (Soapy); Barbara Woodell (Mrs. Zee James); Tom Tyler (Frank James); Tom Noonan (Charles Ford); Byron Foulger (Room Clerk); Eddie Dunn (Bartender); Jeni Le Gon (Maid); Phil Pine (Man in Saloon); Robin Short (Troubadour); Margia Dean (Singer in Bar); Gene Collins (Young Man Who Wants to Kill Bob Ford); Chuck Roberson (Double for Reed Hadley).

This film was the directorial debut for highly-regarded Samuel Fuller. In recent years the film has come under much scrutiny due to the director's cult following.

This "different" Western centered around Bob Ford (Ireland), "the dirty little coward," as had Fritz Lang's earlier The Return of Frank James (1940) [q.v.]. In order to obtain a pardon for his past crimes and be free to wed his girl (Britton), Ford ingratiates himself into the James gang in order to kill Jesse (Hadley). However the outlaw ends up saving Ford's life. Cynthy Waters (Britton) refuses to wed Ford, however, until he obtains the reward money for James. When he does kill the outlaw he discovers she is in love with another man (Foster). In order to win back the lady's affections, he wants enough money to purchase her a home. Therefore, he takes to the stage, recreating the James shooting for audiences. However, his conscience so bothers him that he manipulates

Reed Hadley and John Ireland in I Shot Jesse James (1949).

the situation so that John Kelley (Foster) kills him in order for the
latter to keep Cynthy.

Unlike John Carradine's evil portrayals of Bob Ford in Jesse
James (1939) [q.v.] and in The Return of Frank James (1940), Ireland's characterization is very humanly conceived, showing a man
driven to a dastardly crime by love and greed.

Some of the interesting casting includes old-time cowboy
star Tom Tyler as Frank James, and Ireland's real-life brother,
Tom Noonan as his oncamera sibling, Charles Ford.

IN OLD ARIZONA (Fox, 1929) 95 min.

Directors, Raoul Walsh, Irving Cummings; based on stories
by O. Henry; story-screenplay, Tom Barry; song, Lew Brown,

B. G. De Sylva, and Ray Henderson; assistant directors, Archibald
Buchanan, Charles Woolstenhulme; sound, Edmund H. Hansen;
camera, Arthur Edeson; editor, Louis Loeffler.
      Edmund Lowe (Sergeant Mickey Dunn); Dorothy Burgess
(Tonia Maria); Warner Baxter (The Cisco Kid); J. Farrell Mac-
Donald (Tad); Fred Warren (Piano Player); Henry Armetta (Barber);
Frank Campeau, Tom Santschi, Pat Hartigan (Cowpunchers); Roy
Stewart (Commandant); James Bradbury, Jr. (Soldier); John Dillon
(Soldier); Frank Nelson, Duke Martin (Cowboys); James Marcus
(Blacksmith); Joe Brown (Bartender); Alphonse Ethier (Sheriff); Soli-
dad Jiminez (Cool; Helen Lynch (Woman); Ivan Linow (Russian Immi-
grant).

      One of the most neglected early sound Westerns--and ironi-
cally, one of the most important entries--is In Old Arizona, which
Raoul Walsh and Irving Cummings co-directed. Walsh had originally
planned to star and direct the project but the accidental loss of an
eye precluded the twin assignments. Still, Walsh proved to be the
first director to bring outdoor action to sound, and he also demonstrated that the Western could adapt extremely well to the newly
viable sound medium.
      Briefly, the film was derived from O. Henry's stories of
"The Cisco Kid, " a dashing caballero-bandit (Baxter) who is for-
ever being chased by a sergeant (Lowe). Cisco's reputation is so
well known that, in order to obtain a Wells Fargo strongbox from a
stagecoach, all he has to do to scare the drivers into compliance is
to fire two warning shots. Eventually Cisco becomes attracted to
the beautiful Tonia Maria (Burgess) who secretly betrays him to
Sergeant Dunn (Lowe). As a result the dashing Cisco is nearly
captured. However, the Kid is too smart for his adversaries. In
a turnabout, he frames Tonia, causing the sergeant to accidentally
shoot the girl. "Justice" having been served, the Cisco Kid rides
away.
      To enhance the audio effects of In Old Arizona, Walsh had
his sound men take their microphones outdoors to capture the natural
noises of hoof beats, gunshots, and such other effects as the sound
of frying bacon. The film, with its superior sound (for its time),
single-handedly revitalized the sagebrush genre. Moreover, this
feature greatly aided Warner Baxter's cinema career. He won an
Academy Award for his performance in the film and by 1936 he was
Fox's and Hollywood's top-paid male star. He would again portray
the Cisco Kid oncamera in The Cisco Kid (1931) and The Return of
the Cisco Kid (1939) [both q. v.].
      Another important aspect of this motion picture was that it
introduced music to the Western. The song "My Tonia" by Lew
Brown, B. G. De Sylva and Ray Henderson was sung in the picture.
(Nick Lucas' recording of the song was a best-seller on Brunswick
Records in 1929.) After seeing this film, cowboy actor Ken Maynard was so impressed that he began to include music in his series
Westerns at Universal. Thus, Walsh's film was the beginning of a
vogue that would reach its greatest popularity in the thirties and
early forties.

IN OLD SACRAMENTO   (Republic, 1946)

Associate producer-director, Joseph Kane; based on the
story "Diamond Carlisle" by Kane; story, Jerome Odlum; screenplay, Frances Hyland; adaptor, Frank Gruber; art director, James
Sullivan; set decorators, John McCarthy, Jr., Earl Wooden; music
director, Morton Scott; orchestrator, Dale Butts; music numbers
staged by Fanchon; assistant director, Rollie Asher; sound, Bill
Clark; special effects, Howard and Theodore Lydecker; camera,
Jack Marta; editor, Fred Allen.

William Elliott (Johnny Barrett); Constance Moore (Belle
Malone); Hank Daniels (Sam Chase); Ruth Donnelly (Zebby Booker);
Eugene Pallette (Jim Wales); Lionel Stander (Eddie Dodge); Jack La
Rue (Laramie); Grant Withers (Captain Marc Slayter); Bobby Blake
(Newsboy); Charles Judels (Marchetti); Paul Hurst (Stage Driver);
Victoria Horne (Ma Dodge); Dick Wessel (Oscar).

Re-issue title: Flame of Sacramento.

Gordon "Wild Bill" Elliott had been in films since the
twenties. His career seemed on the upswing when the talkies suddenly demoted him to bit player once again. For nearly a decade
he had mere walk-ons in numerous films. Then in 1938 he starred
in Columbia's The Great Adventures of Wild Bill Hickok, which established him as a major Western player. He became a series cowboy star for that studio and later, at Universal (where he co-starred
with Tex Ritter in films), he consolidated his popularity. Thereafter he moved to Republic where he replaced Don "Red" Barry in
the ever-popular Red Ryder movie series.

Despite popular belief at the time and thereafter, Elliott had
no real desire to become a class A Western star. He was content
with his programmer boots-and-saddle films. However, when Randolph Scott proved unavailable for In Old Sacramento, studio boss
Herbert J. Yates decided to give Elliott the starring role. For the
next five years "Wild Bill" starred in a number of well-made and
entertaining "major" Westerns for Republic. In these outings, his
screen character was a constant reminder of the good-badman
image projected so nobly by William S. Hart some three decades
earlier.

In Old Sacramento set the stage for Elliott's new image.
The film was made by director Joseph Kane from his own story,
"Diamond Carlisle." (It had been filmed twice before, first in
1920 with George Chesebro and again by Kane in 1940 as Republic's
The Carson City Kid, a Roy Rogers' series Western in which Bob
Steele was the villain.)

Kane's 1946 rendition of the tale has Elliott as Spanish Jack,
a masked road agent, man who enjoys numerous exciting adventures
with the law and the ladies before dying at the finale in the arms
of his love (Moore). As Belle Malone, the attractive Miss Moore
was given the chance to sing several songs. While hardly children's
matinee fare, the film proved quite popular with most action fans,
thus launching Elliott into genuine stardom within the genre.

The New York Times commented, appropriately, "It must be

immediately noted that there is nothing new or sensational in the story itself. But this is hardly a condemnation, since all Western plots must have been exhausted some decades ago." Deserving special commendation were character performers Ruth Donnelly, Eugene Pallette, and Lionel Stander, all of whom added substance and zest to the proceedings.

IN THE DAYS OF BUFFALO BILL   (Universal, 1922)   eighteen chapters

Director, Edward Laemmle; screenplay, Robert Dillon.
George A. Williams (Calvert Carter); Dorothy Woods (Alice Carter); Art Acord (Art Taylor); Duke R. Lee (Buffalo Bill Cody); J. Morley (Lambert Ashley); Otto Nelson (Alden Carter); Pat Harmon (Gaspard); Jim Corey (Quantral); Burton C. Law (Allan Pinkerton); William P. Devauel (Edward M. Stanton); Charles Colby (William H. Seward); Joe Hazelton (Gideon Wells); G. B. Philips (Montgomery Balis); Joel Day (Abraham Lincoln); Clark Comstock (Thomas C. Durant); Burt Frank (General Hancock).
Chapters: 1) Bonds of Steel; 2) In the Enemies' Hands; 3) The Spy; 4) The Sword of Grant and Lee; 5) The Man of the Ages; 6) Prisoners of the Sioux; 7) Shackles of Fate; 8) The Last Shot; 9) From Tailor to President; 10) Empire Builders; 11) Perils of the Plains; 12) The Hand of Justice; 13) Trails of Peril; 14) The Scarlet Doom; 15) Men of Steel; 16) The Brink of Eternity; 17) A Race to the Finish; 18) Driving the Golden Spike.

During the silent era Universal produced a number of exciting serials with kiddie matinee hero Art Acord. In this lengthy entry--eighteen chapters--the studio retained a historical background, gaining marquee lure from the popularity of both the title and star.
Although this lengthy cliffhanger contained some historical fact, it was mostly pulp fiction with a great deal of action. The episodic entry covered William F. "Buffalo Bill" Cody's (Acord) career as a scout and Indian fighter, from the construction of the Union Pacific Railroad and the days of the Civil War to his Wild West show period.
The next year, 1923, Universal produced a similar historical chapterplay, In the Days of Daniel Boone, with Jack Mower and Eileen Sedgwick.

IN THE DAYS OF DANIEL BOONE   see   IN THE DAYS OF BUF-FALO BILL

IN THE MONEY   see   WAY OUT WEST

INDIAN LOVE CALL   see   ROSE MARIE

THE INDIAN MASSACRE   (Ince, 1912)   one reel

>   Director, Thomas H. Ince.
>   With: Francis Ford, Anne Little, Art Acord.

While D. W. Griffith was working at Biograph and turning out several short subjects with Western themes, Thomas H. Ince was also doing similar films, some of which were quite sympathetic to the American Indian. This particular one-reeler starred Francis Ford and Anne Little and had future genre star Art Acord playing two small parts.

While a simple little item, the film showed the quest of the white settlers for land in their westward movement, as well as the plight of the Indian as a result of this migration. Its touching finale was a scene showing the silhouette of an Indian woman praying by her dead child's grave.

THE INDIANS ARE COMING   (Universal, 1930)   twelve chapters

>   Associate producer/director, Henry McRaoe; based on the life of William F. Cody; screenplay, George H. Plympton, Ford Beebe.
>   Allene Ray (Mary Woods); Tim McCoy (Jack Manning); Francis Ford (Tom Woods/George Woods); Charles Royal (Uncle Amos); Edmund Cobb (Bill Williams); Don Francis (Bit); Wilbur McGaugh (Rance Carter); Bud Osborne (Bull McGee); Pal (The Dog).
>   Chapters: 1) Pals in Buckskin; 2) A Call to Arms; 3) A Furnace of Fear; 4) The Red Terror; 5) The Circle of Death; 6) Hate's Harvest; 7) Hostages of Fear; 8) The Dagger Duel; 9) The Blast of Death; 10) Redskins of Vengeance; 11) Frontiers Aflame; 12) The Trail's End.

Talkies put a dent in motion picture serial production because the pioneer sound machinery, by necessity, slowed down the possible action to be put onscreen. At Universal, however, director Henry McRae worked closely with sound technicians to make this twelve-chapter serial work effectively. The project was produced for $160,000 and grossed over $1 million. It became the first chapter-play to have a Broadway opening.

Issued in both silent and sound versions, the serial was the bittersweet story of Jack Manning (McCoy), who returns to the Midwest with news that a friend (Cobb) has struck gold and wants his brother and his niece (Ray) to come West by wagon train. Jack and Mary Woods (Ray) fall in love but Rance Carter (Ford) also wants the girl. Along the trek, the wagon convoy is besieged by warring Indians who attack them (as well as a town) and set a prairie fire. Mary's dad is later murdered by Carter and Jack's friend Bill Williams (Francis) is killed by the rampaging Indians. Eventually Jack and Mary settle down, realizing nevertheless the expense in heartbreak and lost lives that had occurred en route to their happiness.

Most of the serial's battle scenes were lifted from the
studio's The Flaming Frontier (1926) [q.v.]. Sadly, the project
also marked the destruction of serial queen Allene Ray's career,
for she possessed a high, squeaky voice that displeased moviegoers.

After its release, film czar Will Hays wrote to Universal
Pictures' president Carl Laemmle regarding the venture: "The entire motion picture industry owes you a debt of gratitude for The
Indians Are Coming. It brought 20 million children back to the
theatres." (It also helped to convince other movie producers that
talkies and Westerns could be profitable partners.)

THE IRON HORSE (Fox, 1924) 11, 335'

Presenter, William Fox; director, John Ford; story, Charles
Kenyon, John Russell; screenplay, Kenyon; titles, Charles Darnton;
music, Erno Rapee; assistant director, Edward O'Fearn; camera,
George Schneiderman; additional camera, Burnett Guffey.

George O'Brien (Davy Brandon); Madge Bellamy (Miriam
Marsh); Cyril Chadwick (Jesson); Fred Kohler (Deroux); Gladys
Hulette (Ruby); James Marcus (Judge Haller); J. Farrell MacDonald
(Corporal Casey); James Welch (Private Schultz); Walter Rogers
(General Dodge); George Waggoner (Colonel "Buffalo Bill" Cody);
Jack Padjan (Wild Bill Hickok); Charles O'Malley (Major North);
Charles Newton (Collins P. Huntington); Charles Edward Bull (Abra-
ham Lincoln); Colin Chase (Tony); Delbert Mann (Charles Crocker);
Chief Big Tree (Cheyenne Chief); Chief White Spear (Sioux Chief);
Edward Piel (Old Chinaman); James Gordon (David Brandon, Sr.);
Winston Miller (Davy as a Child); Peggy Cartwright (Miriam as a
Child); Jack Ganzhorn (Thomas Durant); Stanhope Wheatcroft (John
Hay); Frances Teague (Polka Dot); Will Walling (Thomas Marsh).

If there was one particular genre to which the silent cinema
was especially suited it was the Western picture. With a focus on
the visuals a film could create the sweep and majesty of the Old
West where action spoke far louder than (title card) words.

Released with tinted sequences, this twelve-reel epic was
director John Ford's first huge success. (Closeups of heroine
Madge Bellamy were added after Ford's completion of the movie.)
Shot on location in the Nevada desert, the production's cost soon
rose to epic proportions and forced the studio to promote it as a
competitor to Paramount's earlier The Covered Wagon (1923) [q.v.].
Two towns were especially built for the film and the project utilized
some 5000 extras, as well as a regiment of U.S. cavalry (if publicity releases are to be believed), 3000 railroad workers, some
1000 Chinese laborers, 800 Indians, buffalo, cattle herds, and 2000
horses.

The film closely follows history, opening with President
Lincoln's (Bull) desire for the construction of the first transcontinental railroad to aid the Civil War effort. There follows the race between the Union Pacific and the Central Pacific railway lines. On a

more personal basis there is the story of a young man (O'Brien)
who is searching for his dad's killer and who has a romance with
a childhood sweetheart (Bellamy) whose father is a railroad builder.
Eventually Davy Brandon (O'Brien) joins in the gigantic effort to
build the railroad. The epic completion of this effort forms the
film's mighty finale.

It is perhaps an understatement when Joe Franklin, in his
Classics of the Silent Screen (1959), weighs The Iron Horse "as one
of the biggest and best of all the superwestern films."

THE JACKALS see YELLOW SKY

JEREMIAH JOHNSON (Warner Bros., 1972) C 108 min.

Producer, Joe Wizan; associate producers, John R. Coonan,
Mike Moder; director, Sydney Pollack; based on the novel Mountain
Man by Vardis Fisher and the story "Crow Killer" by Raymond W.
Thorp and Robert Bunker; screenplay, John Milius, Edward Anhalt;
music, John Rubenstein, Tim McIntire; art director, Ted Haworth;
set decorator, Raymond Molyneaux; animal supervisor, Kenneth Lee;
makeup, Gary Liddiard, Ken Chase; sound, Charles Wilborn, J. Von
Stroheim, Mike Colgan; camera, Andrew Callaghan; editor, Thomas
Stanford.

Robert Redford (Jeremiah Johnson); Will Geer (Bear Claw);
Stefan Gierasch (Del Gue); Allyn Ann McLerie (Caleb's Mother);
Charles Tyner (Robidoux); Delle Bolton (Swan); Josh Albee (Caleb);
Joaquin Martinez (Paints His Shirt Red); Paul Benedict (Reverend);
Matt Clark (Qualen); Richard Angarola (Lebeaux); Jack Colvin
(Lieutenant Mulvey).

For Robert Redford this film was a labor of love. It took
him far afield from his more typical romantic picture lead to the
unenviable task of portraying a rugged individualist of the 1830s.

He is an ex-soldier who tires of civilization and becomes a
fur trapper in the wilderness of the Rocky Mountains. An inexperi-
enced outdoorsman, he is saved from near starvation by Bear Claw
(Geer) who teaches him the basics of survival, including how to skin
the treacherous grizzly bear. Later, Jeremiah is able to establish
a rapport with the Indians, learning to trade with them. When he
comes across a widow and her son, the sole white survivors of an
Indian raid, he is persuaded by the crazy woman to take the child
with him while she tends the graves of her family. A chance
meeting with a bald trapper, Del Gue (Gierasch), leads to Jeremiah's contact with the friendly Flathead Indians (arch enemies of
the Blackfeet) and they regard Johnson as a hero (he has the scalps
of thieving Blackfeet in his possession--actually scalped by Del Gue).
The Flatheads offer the chief's virgin daughter (Bolton) to Jeremiah
as his squaw. Johnson builds a cabin for Swan (Bolton), the boy,
and himself. Later the cavalry arrives and asks Jeremiah to guide
them. When they desecrate a Crow burial ground--against Jeremiah's

Robert Redford and director Sydney Pollack on the set of Jeremiah Johnson (1972).

advice--the Crows retaliate by murdering Johnson's "family." Enraged, the woodsman responds by killing each and every Crow he meets. Eventually, the hardened Jeremiah heads for Canada to make a new life for himself. En route he encounters his old enemy, the Crow chief. The two salute each other silently and each goes his own way.

The Village Voice labeled this a "graceful little movie" while the Washington Post relegated it to being a "rather ponderous reverie on the making of a mountain man." Actually the film is somewhere in between, at times too self-consciously arty and at other moments a genuine tribute to an American Robinson Crusoe.

This entry bears comparison to Richard Harris' A Man Called Horse (1970) [q.v.], a more commercial venture that showed how another white man coped with an alien society (the Indians) by becoming not only one of them, but a superior individual respected by them for his endurance. (Such cinematic exercises on man's endurance among strange forces would continually crop up in the seventies, as in The White Dawn, 1973, a study of fishermen-- Timothy Bottoms, Warren Oates, Lou Gosset--stranded among Eskimos.) Unlike A Man Called Horse, most of Redford's heroic struggles are internalized as he seeks intellectually to cope with savages and finds that he has turned into a more deviant anti-social creature than any redskin. If Will Geer's cameo performance seems a bit too theatrical, it is compensated for by the other performers' restrained and sincere interpretations.

Jeremiah Johnson was reissued after Redford's great box-office hit, The Way We Were (1973) with Barbra Streisand. Like The Candidate (1972), another initial misfire, it did much better the second time around.

JESSE JAMES (Paramount, 1927) 8, 656'

Presenters, Adolph Zukor, Jesse L. Lasky; supervisor, Alfred L. Werker; director, Lloyd Ingraham; story-screenplay, Frank M. Clifton; technical advisor, Jesse James, Jr.; camera, Allen Siegler.
Fred Thomson (Jesse James); Nora Lane (Zerelda Mimms); Montagu Love (Frederick Mimms); Mary Carr (Mrs. Zerelda Samuels); James Pierce (Frank James); Harry Woods (Bob Ford); William Courtright (Parson Bill); Silver (King of the Wild Horse).

JESSE JAMES (Twentieth Century-Fox, 1939) C 105 min.

Producer, Darryl F. Zanuck; associate producer, Nunnally Johnson; director, Henry King; screenplay, Johnson; Technicolor consultant, Natalie Kalmus; art directors, William Darling, George Dudley; music director, Louis Silvers; camera, George Barnes, W. H. Greene; editor, Barbara McLean.
Tyrone Power (Jesse James); Henry Fonda (Frank James); Nancy Kelly (Zee); Randolph Scott (Will Wright); Henry Hull (Major); Slim Summerville (Jailer); J. Edward Bromberg (Runyon the Pinkerton Man); Brian Donlevy (Barshee); John Carradine (Bob Ford); Donald Meek (Mr. Coy); John Russell (Jesse James, Jr.); Jane Darwell (Mrs. Samuels); Charles Tannen (Charles Ford); Claire Du Brey (Mrs. Ford); Willard Robertson (Clark); Paul Sutton (Lynch); Ernest Whitman (Pinky); Paul Burns (Bill); Spencer Charters (Preacher); Arthur Aylesworth (Tom); Charles Halton (Heywood); George Chandler (Roy); Erville Alderson (Old Marshal); Harry Tyler (Farmer); George Breakston (Farmer Boy); John Elliott (Judge Matthews); Virginia Brissac (Boy's Mother); Don Douglas (Infantry Captain); Edward J. LeSaint (Judge Rankin); Wylie Grant, Harry Holman, Ethan Laidlaw (Barshee's Henchmen); Charles Middleton (Doctor); James Flavin (Cavalry Captain); George O'Hara (Teller); Lon Chaney (One of Jesse's Gang).

Fred Thomson became Paramount's successor to William S. Hart in the 1920s and before his sudden death later in the decade made a series of well-executed features for the studio. Many of them, like this entry, were semi-historical oaters.
Jesse James opens with a well-staged Civil War sequence and later provides a well-done train hold-up scene. Like so many of the feature films concerning the legendary William Bonney, better known as Billy the Kid, this rendition of the life of that other famous American outlaw-folkhero, Jesse James, was a glossy re-creation of James' troubled life.

Arthur Aylesworth, Lon Chaney, Jr., Tyrone Power, Paul E.
Burns, Henry Fonda and Harold Goodwin in <u>Jesse James</u> (1939).

     For this film the chronicle begins with James (Thomson) as
a member of Quantrill's Raiders during the Civil War. He later
meets a Northern girl (Lane) who saves him from being captured
as a spy. After the War, Jesse's mother (Carr) is hurt by returning Union soldiers, and still later Frederick Mimms (Love) attempts to throw James out of his Missouri home. As a result of
these abuses, Jesse becomes an outlaw, a man with a price on his
head. Bob Ford, who happens to love Zerelda Mimms (Lane) too,
joins James' gang hoping to capture the leader. The story ends on
an upbeat note, with Jesse and Zerelda escaping on his horse,
Silver King. He then forces a minister (Courtright) to marry him
and his sweetheart.
     Interestingly enough, six years before the release of this
film, Mesco Pictures starred the outlaw's son, Jesse James, Jr.
(who provided the technical advice on this Paramount entry), in two
features: <u>Jesse James as the Outlaw</u> and <u>Jesse James under the
Black Flag</u>. James, Jr. played both himself and his famous father
in these pictures.
     Filmed in Technicolor and with an expensive mounting, the
1939 version was a highly-fictional and glamorized account of the
life of Jesse James (Power). It recounts how the young man drifts

to the wrong side of the law when his mother (Darwell) is murdered
by land grabbers who want her Missouri property for a railroad.
With his tobacco-chewing farmer brother Frank (Fonda), Jesse forms
an outlaw gang which is portrayed as belonging to the Robin Hood
tradition.   Zee (Kelly) is the girl with whom Jesse intends to settle
down to a peaceable life.   However, he is shot by traitorous gang
member Bob Ford (Carradine) while he is hanging a picture for his
wife.   Also in the sterling cast is Henry Hull as a newspaper editor
who remains loyal to Jesse, and lanky Randolph Scott as a lawman
friend of the hunted outlaw.

        With a great deal of location work in Missouri, this colorful
action picture is considered one of the better Westerns made by di-
rector Henry King.   It was a big hit with the public and convinced
Twentieth Century-Fox that it should return to the making of
Westerns on a larger scale, especially biography pictures such as
The Return of Frank James (1940) [q.v.].

        When Jesse James debuted, the New York Herald-Tribune
termed the proceedings a "glittering and generally exciting cops and
robbers show," while the New York Times lauded it as "authentic
American panorama, enriched by dialogue, characterizations and
incidents imported directly from the Missouri Hills."

        Clive Denton, in Hollywood Professionals, Vol. II (1974), in
discussing the career of Henry King, said: "Whatever distortions
of history it contains, Jesse James manages to be both a stirring
adventure (in its earlier stages), and, finally, a moving study of
notoriety unable to turn peaceable and live unmolested.   The closing
scenes look forward to Gregory Peck's similar troubled last days
as The Gunfighter [1950, q.v.].   Peck there is still an idealised
figure, not much corrupted by violence, although the latter film has
an 'adult' reputation which Jesse James does not.   Perhaps the body
of the 1939 film is too exciting, too energetic for that sort of
critical attention.   It is worth remarking that never can horses have
been so thoroughly used as (literally) carriers of action (symboli-
cally), agents of movement.   They crash through plate-glass windows,
ride tumultuously over the terrain and even plunge over a cliff into
the river, as Frank and Jesse make a particularly daring escape...."

JOHNNY CONCHO (United Artists, 1956) 84 min.

        Associate producer, Henry Sanicola; director, Don McGuire;
based on the story "The Man Who Owned the Town" by David P.
Harmon; screenplay, Harmon, McGuire; music-music conductor,
Nelson Riddle; orchestrator, Arthur Morton; art director, Nicolai
Remisoff; set decorator, Gustav Bernsten; costumes, Gwen Wake-
ling; makeup, Bernard Ponedel, Ernest J. Park; assistant director,
Emmett Emerson; sound, Dean Thomas, Robert Roderick; camera,
William Mellor; editor, Eda Warren.

        Frank Sinatra (Johnny Concho); Keenan Wynn (Barney Clark);
William Conrad (Tallman); Phyllis Kirk (Mary Dark); Wallace Ford
(Albert Dark); Christopher Dark (Walker); Howard Petrie (Helgeson);
Dan Russ (Judge Tyler); Harry Bartell (Sam Green); Robert Osterloh

(Duke Lang); Leo Gordon (Mason); Dorothy Adams (Sarah Dark); Jean Byron (Pearl Lang); Claude Akins (Lem); John Qualen (Jake); Wilfred Knapp (Pearson); Ben Wright (Benson); Joe Bassett (Bartender).

Frank Sinatra has made occasional forays into the Western genre, usually without much success. He produced and starred in this low-keyed affair which according to Bosley Crowther (New York Times), "falls into a standard western style."

Johnny Concho (Sinatra) is a bully and a coward living in the town of Criple Creek, Arizona in 1875. He exists in the reflected glory of his gunfighter-brother until the latter is killed. When another gunslinger (Conrad) shows up, Concho initially runs away from the confrontation. Then he develops enough courage to return and engage the man in a showdown. Keenan Wynn added some life to the proceedings as a gun-toting preacher, as did Phyllis Kirk, the pert love interest.

JOHNNY GUITAR (Republic, 1954) C 110 min.

Producer, Herbert J. Yates; director, Nicholas Ray; based on the novel by Roy Chanslor; screenplay, Philip Yordan; music, Victor Young; song, Peggy Lee and Young; wardrobe, Sheila O'Brien; art director, James Sullivan; assistant director, Herb Mendelson; camera, Harry Stradling; editor, Richard L. Van Enger.

Joan Crawford (Vienna); Sterling Hayden (Johnny Guitar); Mercedes McCambridge (Emma Small); Scott Brady (Dancin' Kid); Ward Bond (John McIvers); Ben Cooper (Turkey Ralston); Ernest Borgnine (Bart Lanergan); John Carradine (Old Tom); Royal Dano (Carey); Frank Ferguson (Marshal Williams); Paul Fix (Eddie); Rhys Williams (Mr. Andrews); Ian MacDonald (Pete); Will Wright (Ned); John Maxwell (Jake); Robert Osterloh (Sam); Frank Marlowe (Frank); Trevor Bardette (Jenks); Sumner Williams, Sheb Wooley, Denver Pyle, Clem Harvey (Possemen).

In her first Western after appearing with Colonel Tim McCoy at MGM in the twenties and with John Mack Brown in 1930, Joan Crawford starred in Johnny Guitar. A flamboyantly psychological Western, it was directed by Nicholas Ray from Roy Chanslor's novel. The picture seemed to be Miss Crawford's response to Marlene Dietrich's Rancho Notorious (1952), an equally bizarre but not so entertaining a venture.

There is much entertainment to be gained from this vehicle, which was highly regarded in Europe almost from its initial release. The garish hues of TruColor give individual scenes in the movie an intensity and color contrast that remain as vivid memories. The highly-mannered performance of Miss Crawford is put into perspective by the more artificial interpretation of Mercedes McCambridge in her Lady Macbeth-type role. Not the least of the film's virtues is the theme song especially written by Peggy Lee and Victor Young. Today, even Miss Crawford realizes what a landmark in

the Western film this venture was, for director Nicholas Ray, in
very overstated terms, showed how women's liberation could and
did come to the West long before contemporary society took up the
hue and cry. During this mid-fifties period, another cinema legend,
Barbara Stanwyck, was also turning out Westerns (her favorite
genre), but none of them could match the intensity or enduring
values of Johnny Guitar. The determinedly sophisticated may see
this intense melodrama as high camp, but the average viewer can
enjoy it on its own terms. Part of the pleasure in this film is for
the moviegoer to supply his own imagery associations to the multi-
hued sequence compositions and to decide how much director Ray
was intentionally spoofing the genre or whether he was enhancing
the drama with his own special, high-powered theatrics.

In the midst of untamed Arizona in the post-Civil War
period, attractive, ambitious Vienna (Crawford), an ex-dancehall
girl, constructs a gaming saloon which she turns into a successful
venture. Her property is coveted by the railroad which is expanding
into the territory. But her prosperity enrages boss McIvers (Bond)
of a nearby town. McIvers is in cahoots with Emma Small (Mc-
Cambridge), a soured soul who is anxious to keep the territory
open for cattle grazing. Meanwhile Vienna and the Dancin' Kid
(Brady) are engaged in a love affair. He is actually the leader
of a gang of outlaws.

Thrown into this brewing holocaust is Johnny Guitar (Hayden),
a gunless loner who hates bloodshed. Soon Vienna and Johnny are
in love again (they had a romance some years earlier), and he finds
it necessary to carry a six-shooter to protect Vienna from her assorted enemies. Later, Emma arouses the town people and they
burn down Vienna's saloon. Vienna escapes and in the showdown
Johnny saves her from the would-be executors. Finally she and
Johnny can plan their future.

Probably the Variety reviewer (Brog) would be chagrined to
read his review of Johnny Guitar today. At the time he stated,
"It proves [she] should leave saddles and Levis to someone else
and stick to city lights for a background.... [It] becomes so involved with character nuances and neuroses, all wrapped up in dialogue, that [the film] never has a chance to rear up in the saddle."

In a perceptive study of the film, Michael Wilmington,
writing in Velvet Light Trap (#12, 1974), observes, "It is its combination of emotional sensitivity and gutsy straightforwardness
which makes Johnny Guitar such a marvelous film.... Johnny
Guitar did not gain its world-wide audience by accident. It is a
film both consummately fashioned and passionately alive. "Never
trust appearances, ' [François] Truffaut warned at the beginning of
his review [of the film], and that might be Johnny Guitar's official
caveat. It survives to remind us that beauty and profundity are
not always found in the 'obvious' traditional places--that a Trucolor Western from humble Republic can throb with the passion of
l'amour fou or whisper with an evening delicacy."

Joan Crawford in <u>Johnny Guitar</u> (1954).

JUBILEE TRAIL   (Republic, 1954)   C   103 min.

    Producer, Herbert J. Yates; associate producer-director,
Joseph Kane; based on the novel by Gwen Bristow; screenplay,
Bruce Manning; music-music conductor, Victor Young; songs,
Young and Sidney Clare; choreography, Bob Mark; technical ad-
visor, D. R. O. Hatswell; assistant director, A. J. Vitarelli;
costumes, Adele Palmer; art director, Frank Arrigo; set decora-
tors, John McCarthy, Jr., George Milo; sound, Earl Crain, Sr.,
Howard Wilson; camera, Jack Marta; editor, Richard L. Van Enger.
    Vera Ralston (Florinda Grove [Julie Latour]); Joan Leslie
(Garnet Hale); Forrest Tucker (John Ives); John Russell (Oliver
Hale); Ray Middleton (Charles Hale); Pat O'Brien (Ernest "Texas"
Conway); Buddy Baer (Nicholai Gregorovitch Karakozeff); Jim Davis
(Silky); Barton MacLane (Deacon Bartlett); Richard Webb (Captain
Brown); James Millican (Rinardi); Nina Varela (Doña Manuela);
Martin Garralaga (Don Rafael Velasco); Charles Stevens (Pablo, a
Peon); Nacho Galindo (Rico, a Bartender); Don Beddoe (Mr. Maury,
the Hotel Manager); John Holland (Mr. Drake); William Haade
(Jake the Sailor); Alan Bridge (Mr. Turner); John Halloran, Sayre
Dearing (Turner's Men); Stephen Chase (Mr. Forbes, an Admirer);
Daniel M. White (Henry); Eugene Borden (Kimball, a Detective);

Vera Ralston, John Russell, Barton MacLane and Jim Davis in
Jubilee Trail (1954).

Morris Buchanan (Waiter); Rodolfo Hoyos, Jr., Rico Alansiz
(Spaniards); Bud Wolfe (Blandy); Paul Stader (Barbour); Marshall
Reed (Detective); Frank Puglia (Don Orosco); Clenn Strange (Tom
Branders); Emmett Lynn (Drunk Man with Little Hat); Jack Elam
(Sergeant); Robert "Buzz" Henry, Ted Smile (Velasco's Sons).

Screen rights to Gwen Bristow's Literary Guild prize-winning
novel were purchased by Republic Pictures for $100,000 and the film
was allotted a big production budget by the studio. Van Heflin and
Gloria Grahame were originally sought for the leads, but Vera Ralston, wife of studio head Herbert J. Yates, and Forrest Tucker
eventually were the stars of this TruColor Western.
Set in California, prior to the time the territory became a
state, the lengthy (103-minute) story concerns Easterner Garnet
Hale (Leslie) who comes West with her infant after the death of her
husband (Middleton). She lives under the thumb of her tyrannical
brother-in-law (Russell). On her trek Garnet encounters New Orleans
saloon queen Florinda Grove (Ralston) who shows the mild city girl
how to cope with her new life style. It is not long before Florinda
has found love in the person of a trader named John Ives (Tucker).
This sweeping historical film proved quite successful for Republic, which in a few years would withdraw from the theatrical film
market.
For those ungallant souls who shudder at the mere mention of
Vera Ralston's name, the much-maligned film personality only has the
nominal lead in this feature.

JUNIOR BONNER (Paramount, 1972) C 100 min.

Producer, Joe Wizan; associate producer, Mickey Borofsky;
director, Sam Peckinpah; screenplay, Jeb Rosebrook; second unit
director, Frank Kowalski; music, Jerry Fielding; songs, Rod Hart;
set designer, Angelo Graham; art director, Edward S. Haworth; set
decorator, Jerry Wunderlich; technical advisor, Casey Tibbs; cos-
tumes, Eddie Armand; makeup, Donald Roberson; assistant directors,
Frank Baur, Michael Messinger, William Sheehan; sound, Charles
Wilborn, Richard Portman, Larry Hooberry; camera, Lucien Ballard;
editor, Robert Wolf.
Steve McQueen (Junior Bonner); Robert Preston (Ace Bonner);
Ida Lupino (Elvira Bonner); Ben Johnson (Buck Roan); Joe Don Baker
(Curly Bonner); Barbara Leigh (Charmagne); Mary Murphy (Ruth
Bonner); Bill McKinney (Red Terwiliger); Sandra Deel (Nurse Arlis);
Don "Red" Barry (Homer Rutledge); Dub Taylor (Bartender); Charles
Gray (Burt); Matthew Peckinpah (Tim Bonner); Sundown Spencer (Nick
Bonner); Rita Garrison (Flashie); Casey Tibbs, Rod Hart (Guest Ap-
pearances).

Several Westerns of the seventies (such as J. W. Coop
(1972) with Cliff Robertson, When the Legends Die (1972) with
Richard Widmark, and Monte Walsh (1970) with Lee Marvin) have
attempted to depict how the cowboy of today is an outmoded

convention, a man out of time with no future in his profession.
Obviously this downbeat theme is not going to appeal to any mass
market, but filmmakers have persisted in turning out such artis-
tically-motivated ventures.   One of the best of these is Junior
Bonner.   Sadly it was badly neglected by the public and had only
spotty distribution; a strange fate for two such box-office magnets
as Peckinpah and McQueen.

Junior Bonner (McQueen), an over-aged rodeo rider, returns
to his home town of Prescott, Arizona.   If Junior thought his July
homecoming would be fruitful he was sadly mistaken.   His parents
Ace (Preston) and Elvira (Lupino) are living apart, his younger
brother Curly (Baker) has purchased the old man's spread and sub-
divided it into small lots for senior citizens, and Ace is now in
the hospital recovering from an accident while he was drunk.

In a lyrical section Ace and Junior meet for a drink and
Ace retells his dream of going to Australia to prospect for gold.
Father and son enter the rodeo contests, but neither achieves a
victory.   Later Junior and Curly, as well as Ace and Elvira, attempt to patch up their differences.   To prove to everyone that he
is not washed up, Junior arranges to ride the wild bull that previously threw him.   He wins the contest and the prize money. With
the proceeds Junior buys his dad a one-way, first-class ticket to
Australia.   Junior explains he must go his own way, to the next
rodeo wherever it may be.

Some critics were generous in their praise of this film.
"Like The Ballad of Cable Hogue [1970], it is a lament for the
passing of the Old West and its rugged individualists, expressed
with a deeply felt poignance that is set off with much rambunctious
humor....   [It] has a remarkable sense of completeness and fulfillment to it.   Visually, it is an extraordinarily graceful yet unflinching
rendering of a slice of Americana" (Kevin Thomas, Los Angeles
Times).

Would that Peckinpah and others would make more films like
this; perhaps public taste might turn in more interesting and headier
directions.

JUST TONY   (Fox, 1922) 5,233'

Presenter, William Fox; director, Lynn F. Reynolds; based
on the novel Alcatraz by Max Brand; screenplay, Reynolds; camera,
Dan Clark.

Tony the Horse (Himself); Tom Mix (Red Ferris); Claire
Adams (Marianne Jordan); J. P. Lockney (Oliver Jordan); Duke Lee
(Manuel Cordova); Frank Campeau (Lew Hervey); Walt Robbins
(Shorty).

Although William S. Hart's horse Fritz was the first horse
star of American films, it was Tom Mix's white steed Tony that
became the best known and most popular in cowboy films.   This
film actually stars the animal and the picture's title bears his name.
Mix made the feature as a tribute to his loyal mount and to please

the large number of fans who endorsed the display of camaraderie between the star and his animal.

Tony appears as a wild mustang who leads a desert herd of horses and who tries to take revenge against the men who have mistreated him. A cowboy named Red Ferris (Mix) saves the horse from being beaten. In appreciation Tony demonstrates his gratitude by saving Red and the rancher's daughter Marianne (Adams) when they are captured by the villains.

In the silent era Tom Mix and Tony were Fox Films' top assets, with the cowboy star earning as much as $17,500 per week. Today a soundstage at Twentieth Century-Fox is named in their honor.

JUSTICE RIDES AGAIN   see   DESTRY RIDES AGAIN (1932)

KING COWBOY   (FBO, 1928)   6,269'

Director, Robert De Lacy; story, S. E. V. Taylor; screenplay, Frank Howard Clark; titles, Helen Gregg, Randolph Bartlett; assistant director, James Dugan; camera, Norman Devol; editor, Henry Weher.

Tom Mix (Tex Rogers); Sally Blane (Polly Randall); Lew Meehan (Ralph Bennett); Barney Furey (Shorty Sims); Frank Leigh (Abdul El Hassan); Wynn Mace (Ben Suliman Ali); Robert Fleming (Jim Randall).

Moviemakers were always seeking new locales to spruce up the tried-and-true storylines of their Western films. Over the years the North African terrain provided just such a diversion in several films.

The somewhat exotic plot of this film finds ranch foreman Tex Rogers (Mix) and his crew of cowpokes coming to a small North African town to find their boss (Fleming), who has been kidnapped by the Riffs. The man's daughter (Blane) is later kidnapped by the Emir (Leigh). Tex manages to save her, but he is captured in the process. In the see-saw of the storyline she is found, later, back in the Emir's control. However, the hero makes good his escape and he again rescues Polly (Blaine). In the final showdown, the Emir is killed and Tex is named in his stead to rule the area. Needless to say, Tex wins the love and devotion of Polly.

After a decade with Fox Films, Tom Mix had joined FBO for a series of Westerns which would prove to be his last silent films. Although the FBO batch was below the quality of the Fox series, they found a ready market. After completing his FBO films, the aging cowboy star did not attempt a talking film series until he was coaxed back into moviemaking by Universal in the early thirties.

THE KISSING BANDIT   (MGM, 1948)   C   102 min.

Producer, Joe Pasternak; director, Laslo Benedek; screen-play, Isobel Lennart, John Briard Harding; music supervisor-director, George Stoll; arranger, Leo Arnaud; incidental music, George Stoll, Albert Sendry, Scott Bradley, Andre Previn; additional orchestrations, Sendry, Calvin Jackson, Conrad Salinger, Robert Van Eps, Paul Marquardt, Earl Brent; songs, Nacio Herb Brown and Edward Heyman, Brown and Brent; choreography, Stanley Donen; art directors, Cedric Gibbons, Randall Duell; set decorators, Edwin B. Willis, Jack D. Moore; costumes, Walter Plunkett; make-up, Jack Dawn; assistant director, Marvin Stuart; color consultant, Henri Jaffa; sound, Wilhelm W. Brockway; special effects, A. Arnold Gillespie; camera, Robert Surtees; editor, Adrienne Fazan.

Frank Sinatra (Ricardo); Kathryn Grayson (Teresa); J. Carrol Naish (Chico); Mildred Natwick (Isabella); Mikhail Rasumny (Don Jose); Billy Gilbert (General Torro); Sono Osato (Bianca); Clinton Sundberg (Colonel Gomez); Carleton Young (Count Belmonte); Edna Skinner (Juanita); Vicente Gomez (Guitarist); Henry Mirelez (Pepito); Nick Thompson (Pablo); Jose Dominguez (Francisco); Alberto Morin (Lotso); Pedro Regas (Esteban); Julian Rivero (Postman); Mitchell Lewis (Fernando); Byron Foulger (Grandee); and: Ricardo Montalban, Ann Miller, Cyd Charisse (Dance of Fury Number).

Cyd Charisse, Ricardo Montalban and Ann Miller in The Kissing Bandit (1948).

If Frank Sinatra were a far lesser personality with fewer talent resources, this movie might well have finished his film career. As it stands, the dismal The Kissing Bandit is a celluloid testimony to how a major studio with every conceivable facility at its fingertips can (and did) go astray--and badly!

Set in old California--in the same era that had nearly vanquished Jeanette MacDonald and Nelson Eddy in MGM's The Girl of the Golden West (1938) [q.v.]--the film "showcases" Sinatra as Ricardo, a shy young man who inherits his father's mantle as the leader of a group of masked highwaymen. When not embarked on some caper, he is busily romancing a series of fair ladies. However, one woman in particular, Teresa (Grayson), captures his heart and by the fadeout she is leading him hopefully into a better way of life.

Despite the promise of the title, there is only one tired kiss in the entire dull 102 minutes of the film and only the song "If I Steal a Kiss" has any substance. As an afterthought, Metro added a production number, "Dance of Fury," which starred Ricardo Montalban, Ann Miller, and Cyd Charisse. While diverting in itself, it could not salvage the rest of the stagnant proceedings.

KIT CARSON (Paramount, 1928) 7,464'

Directors, Alfred L. Werker, Lloyd Ingraham; story, Frank M. Clifton; screenplay, Paul Powell; titles, Frederick Hatton; camera, Mack Stengler; editor, Duncan Mansfield.

Fred Thomson (Kit Carson); Nora Lane (Josefa); Dorothy Janis (Sings-in-the-Clouds); Raoul Paoli (Shuman); William Courtright (Old Bill Williams); Nelson McDowell (Jim Bridger); Raymond Turner (Smokey).

KIT CARSON (United Artists, 1940) 97 min.

Producer, Edward Small; director, George B. Seitz; screenplay, George Bruce; music director, Edward Ward; art director, John Ducasse Schulze; special effects, Jack Cosgrove, Howard A. Anderson; camera, John Mescall, Robert Pittack; editors, Fred Feitshans, Jr., William Claxton.

Jon Hall (Kit Carson); Lynn Bari (Dolores Murphy); Dana Andrews (Captain John C. Fremont); Harold Huber (Lopez); Ward Bond (Abe); Renie Riano (Miss Pilchard); Clayton Moore (Paul Terry); Rowena Cook (Alice Terry); Raymond Hatton (Jim Bridger); Harry Strang (Sergeant Clanahan); C. Henry Gordon (General Castro); Lew Merrill (General Vallejo); Stanley Andrews (Larkin); Edwin Maxwell (John Sutter); Peter Lynn (James King); Charles Stevens (Rulz); William Farnum (Don Miguel Murphy).

Along with Buffalo Bill Cody, Billy the Kid, Daniel Boone, et al., one of the most frequently selected legendary characters of the Old American West to be depicted oncamera was (and still is)

Kit Carson.   Christopher "Kit" Carson (1809-1868), the famed
trapper and frontiersman, has inspired many filmmakers to weave
fictional accounts around his amazing exploits.
    The year after he played Jesse James (1927) [q.v.], Fred
Thomson was cast in the title role of Kit Carson, a good oater co-
directed by Lloyd Ingraham and Alfred L. Werker.
    Kit Carson (Thomson) and his pal Shuman (Paoli) arrive in
the town of Taos as part of a government peace-keeping mission
ordered into the troubled Blackfoot country.   The two men fight
over a girl (Lane) in a saloon and then ride north where Kit meets
Sings-in-the-Clouds (Janis), the daughter of an Indian chief.   Carson
saves her from a ferocious bear and this action establishes peace
between the redskins and white man.   The truce is almost destroyed
when Shuman is angered against the Indian maiden and attacks her
with a knife.   Kit shoots him in the hand.   Later Shuman attacks
Sings-in-the-Clouds in the desert, causing her death.   Kit vows
revenge against his former friend and follows Shuman, eventually
killing him.   The peace between the Indians and the white men remains intact.
    In the thirties there would be several films that featured the
character of Kit Carson, especially serials.   There was Johnny Mack
Brown in Fighting with Kit Carson (1933), Sammy McKim in The
Painted Stallion (1938), and William Elliott in Overland with Kit
Carson (1939).   Then, in 1940, producer Edward Small, who managed the film epic stories on minimal budgets, turned out Kit Carson
The resultant film may have been "sheer nonsense," as the New York
Times insisted, but even that paper's scribe had to admit it was "a
straight old-fashioned action picture with more violent mayhem per
linear foot of celluloid than we've seen in recent weeks."
    The flimsy but actionful story tells of Captain John C. Fre-
mont's (Andrews) expedition to California with Kit Carson (Hall) as
his chief scout.   On the arduous trek they not only fight the hostile
Indians but the two leaders compete for lovely Dolores Murphy (Bari)
The film was filled with Indian battles and gunplay, enough to stir
the heart of any true action fan.   One memorable sequence finds the
marauding savages surrounding an enclosed circle of covered wagons,
with the settlers forced to fight for their lives.
    The same year, 1940, Twentieth Century-Fox came out with
its period expedition film, Brigham Young-Frontiersman, an elaborate retelling of the Mormons' attempt to reach Utah after being
forced out of Missouri.   In plot structure there are many similarities between these two outdoor features from United Artists and Fox
(and, for that matter, with many other similar ventures in the
Western genre).

THE LAST DROP OF WATER   (Biograph, 1911)   one reel

        Director-screenplay, D. W. Griffith; camera, G. W. "Billy"
Bitzer.
        With: Blanche Sweet, Joseph Graybill, Charles West, W.
Christie Miller, William J. Butler, Jeannie MacPherson, Robert
Harron, Dell Henderson.

Predating The Covered Wagon (1923) [q.v.] by more than a
decade, this realistic one-reeler tells of the trials and tribulations
of settlers heading Westward. Shot May 14-20, 1911 and issued in
July of that year, the film was made on location at San Fernando,
Topango Canyon and Lookout Mountain, California, in a desert area
by D. W. Griffith. Eight prairie schooners and livestock were used
for authenticity.

The story opens before the wagon train heads westward.
Charles West is rejected by Blanche Sweet for a second suitor who
turns into a shiftless drunkard. Later the trio join the wagon
caravan heading to the frontier. In the desert, the settlers are attacked by Indians who surround them and cut off their supply of
water. Both West and Sweet's husband go for water. In their
wandering, West collapses from thirst. His companion offers him
his last drop of water, thus saving his life. Later West finds
water which he carries back to the settlers. At this point the
cavalry arrives to save the pioneers from the Indians. A search
of the desert reveals that Miss Sweet's spouse has expired. Later
the settlers continue their Westward journey.

Subtitled "A Story of the Great American Desert," the short
film was an interesting item with its recreation of the Old West.
The Indian attack sequence was especially well-staged.

THE LAST FRONTIER (Metropolitan, 1926) 7,800'

Presenter, John C. Flinn; director, George B. Seitz; based
on the book by Courtney Ryley Cooper; adaptor, William M. Ritchey;
camera, C. Edgar Schoenbaum.

J. Farrell MacDonald, Jack Hoxie and William Boyd in The Last
Frontier (1926).

William Boyd (Tom Kirby); Marguerite De La Motte (Beth);
Jack Hoxie (Buffalo Bill Cody); Junior Coghlan (Buddy); Mitchell
Lewis (Lige); Gladys Brockwell (Cynthia Jaggers); Frank Lackteen
(Pawnee Killer).

Nearly a decade before he starred as Hopalong Cassidy,
William Boyd appeared in his first Western, The Last Frontier.
The project was first conceived by Thomas H. Ince but was sold
to producer Hunt Stromberg, who in turn sold it to Metropolitan
Pictures. The latter company made this adaptation from Courtney
Ryley Cooper's 1923 novel.
On the way to Salina, Kansas, a wagon train is attacked by
Indians and a family is killed. The surviving daughter Beth (De La
Motte) blames her fiancé, scout Tom Kirby (Boyd), who suggested
the trip. Beth joins the household of Lige (Lewis), a Salina trader,
and at the suggestion of his friend, Wild Bill Hickok (MacDonald),
Tom joins General George Custer's scouting expedition. Lige in-
forms Beth that Tom supposedly aided Pawnee Killer (Lackteen), the
Indian chief who led the attack on her family. Later she learns
this is false and that Tom really adores her. She seeks him out
just as Indians stampede cattle through the town. The lovers find
refuge in a sanctuary and survive. Custer then defeats the warring
Indians, and Pawnee Killer murders his one-time comrade, Lige.
Within its eight reels, director George B. Seitz incorporated
a good deal of action.

THE LAST HUNT (MGM, 1956) C 108 min.

Producer, Dore Schary; director, Richard Brooks; based on
the novel by Milton Lott; screenplay, Brooks; music, Daniele Am-
fitheatrof; assistant director, Robert Sanders; camera, Russell
Harlan; editor, Ben Lewis.
Robert Taylor (Charles Gilson); Stewart Granger (Sandy Mc-
Kenzie); Lloyd Nolan (Woodfoot); Debra Paget (Indian Girl); Russ
Tamblyn (Jimmy); Constance Ford (Peg); Joe DeSantis (Ed Black);
Ainslie Pryor (Buffalo Hunter); Ralph Moody (Indian Agent); Fred
Graham (Bartender); Ed Lonehill (Spotted Hand).

The wasteful slaughter of the buffalo has occasionally been
touched upon in films, usually as an excuse for assorted screen
wars between whites and Indians. This film, however, attempts to
delve into the psychological aspects of the decimation of the mammal.
Although it was a box-office failure at the time of release, it remains both a different and a quite interesting study.
Frederic Remington's paintings of the old West were utilized
for illustrations behind the title credits of The Last Hunt and these
same drawings were incorporated into the actual episodes of the
killing of buffalo. Location work was accomplished at Custer State
Park in South Dakota.
Robert Taylor had one of his sturdiest screen roles as the
vicious buffalo hunter Charles Gilson who hates both the buffalo and

the Indian. He intends to destroy the bison herds because "one less buffalo means one less Indian." He is joined on the hunt by Sandy McKenzie (Granger), who is pro-Indian and who falls in love with an Indian maiden (Paget) they encounter along the way. The party is also joined by buffalo skinner Woodfoot (Nolan), a man with one leg, and by half-breed Jimmy (Tamblyn), whom Gilson beats. Finally, learning to respect the buffalo and loving the Indian girl, Sandy turns on his partner and kills him in a shootout.

Shot in CinemaScope and color, The Last Hunt is exceptionally well-photographed and deserves restudy as an offbeat picture of a special facet of Americana.

LAST OF THE DUANES (Fox, 1919) six reels

Director, J. Gordon Edwards; based on the story by Zane Grey; screenplay, Charles Kenyon.

William Farnum (Buck Duane); Miss Frankie Raymond (His Mother); Harry De Vere (His Uncle); Charles Clary (Cheseldine); G. Raymond Nye (Poggin); Clarence Burton (Bland); Lamar Johnston (Captain Neil); Henry J. Herbert (Cal Bain); Edward Hatton (Stevens); Louise Lovely (Jenny Lee); Genevieve Blinn (Mrs. Lee); Frederic Herzog (Euchre).

THE LAST OF THE DUANES (Fox, 1924) 6,942'

Presenter, William Fox; director, Lynn Reynolds; based on the story by Zane Grey; screenplay, Edward J. Montagne; camera, Dan Clark.

Tom Mix (Buck Duane); Marian Nixon (Jenny); Brinsley Shaw (Cal Bain); Frank Nelson (Euchre); Lucy Beaumont (Mother); Harry Lonsdale (Father).

LAST OF THE DUANES (Fox, 1930) 5,500'

Presenter, William Fox; associate producers, Edward Butcher, Harold B. Lipsitz; director, Alfred L. Werker; based on the story by Zane Grey; screenplay, Ernest Pascal; art director, William Darling; assistant director, William J. Scully; costumes, Sophie Wachner; songs, Cliff Friend; sound, Barney Fredericks; camera, Daniel Clark.

George O'Brien (Buck Duane); Lucille Brown (Ruth Garrett); Myrna Loy (Lola); Walter McGrail (Bland); James Bradbury, Jr. (Euchre); Nat Pendleton (Bossamer); Blanche Frederici (Mrs. Duane); Frank Campeau (Luke Stevens); James Mason (Morgan); Lloyd Ingraham (Mr. Garrett); Willard Robertson (Captain of the Rangers).

LAST OF THE DUANES (Twentiety Century-Fox, 1941) 57 min.

Producer, Sol M. Wurtzel; director, James Tinling; based on

Marian Nixon and Tom Mix in The Last of the Duanes (1924).

the story by Zane Grey; screenplay, Irving Cummings, Jr., William Conselman, Jr.; art directors, Richard Day, Chester Gore; music director, Cyril J. Mockridge; camera, Charles Clark; editor, Nick De Maggio.

George Montgomery (Buck Duane); Lynne Roberts (Nancy); Eve Arden (Kate); Francis Ford (Luke Stevens); George E. Stone (Euchre); William Farnum (Major McNeil); Joe Sawyer (Bull Lossomer); Truman Bradley (Captain Laramie); Russell Simpson (Tom Duane); Don Costello (Jim Bland); Harry Woods (Morgan); Andrew Tombes (Sheriff); Tom London (Deputy); Tim Ryan (Bartender); Lane Chandler, LeRoy Mason (Henchmen); Arthur Aylesworth (Old Man); Ann Carter (Cannon's Daughter); Harry Hayden (Banker); Tom London (Deputy); Tim Ryan (Bartender); Walter McGrail, Russ Clark (Ranger Guards); Lew Kelly (Old Timer); Jack Stoney, Tom Moray, Syd Saylor (Men).

One of the most intriguing exercises in cinema history is to examine the similarities and differences between various screen versions of the same basic property. Not only does it reveal the varying tastes of different decades, in which emphasis is placed on particular aspects of a story in order to please the filmgoer, but it also demonstrates just how filmmaking has progressed (or regressed as the case may be) over the years.

One can only wonder where Hollywood would have been without the works of Zane Grey, that most prolific writer about the American West, whose works, when filmed, seemed to guarantee some degree of box-office success. Grey's Last of the Duanes is a fine illustration of the changing scope of picture-making, Hollywood style.

Eve Arden and George Montgomery in Last of the Duanes (1941).

The 1914 novel was first filmed in 1919 with William Farnum
in the lead. He was one of the most popular stars of the silent era,
a forthright and stalwart performer whom the younger generation
could respect as an exemplary man.

In 1924, Fox Films remade the Grey story for its new cowboy hero, Tom Mix. The plotline remained as before: after being
continually insulted by Cal Bain (Shaw), Buck Duane (Mix) is forced
to fight and shoot him. Buck escapes and later aids a dying cattle
rustler and saves a girl named Jenny (Nixon) from an outlaw band.
Buck eventually captures the gang members and turns them over to
the Texas Rangers.

Six years later Fox used the story yet again, this time as a
property for George O'Brien. This edition has Buck Duane (O'Brien)
rescuing Ruth Garrett (Brown) from Bland (McGrail). The latter's
wife Lola (Loy) is entranced with the hero, which leads to assorted
complications. Songs were added to the plotline for this first talkie
version of Last of the Duanes. David Howard, who usually directed
O'Brien's Fox Westerns, helmed a Spanish-language version of the
film, made simultaneously with the Werker version. Entitled El
Ultimo de Los Vargas, the picture starred George Lewis and
Luana Alcaniz.

In 1941 Twentieth Century-Fox re-used the Grey work for its
latest star, George Montgomery, who had just proved a hit in another Zane Grey remake, Riders of the Purple Sage (1940) [q.v.].
As directed by James Tinling, this programmer was more than acceptable, but Montgomery was soon promoted to being a studio
leading man and withdrew from the Western field for several years.

THE LAST OF THE MOHICANS   (Associated Producers, 1920)
six reels

Directors, Maurice Tourneur, Clarence Brown; based on the
novel by James Fenimore Cooper; screenplay, Robert Dillon.
Wallace Beery (Magua); Albert Roscoe (Uncas); Barbara Bed-
ford (Cora Munro); Lillian Hall (Alice Munro); Henry Woodward
(Major Duncan Hayward); Boris Karloff (Indian Chief); and: Harry
Lorraine, Nelson McDowell, George Hackathorne, Jack McDonald.

THE LAST OF THE MOHICANS   (United Artists, 1936)   91 min.

Producer, Edward Small; director, George B. Seitz; based
on the novel by James Fenimore Cooper; screenplay, Philip Dunne,
John Balderston, Paul Perez, Daniel Moore; camera, Robert Planck;
editor, Jack Dennis.
Randolph Scott (Hawkeye); Binnie Barnes (Alice Munro);
Heather Angel (Cora Munro); Hugh Buckler (Colonel Munro); Henry
Wilcoxon (Major Duncan Heyward); Bruce Cabot (Magua); Robert
Barrat (Chingachgook); Phillip Reed (Uncas); Willard Robertson
(Captain Winthrop); Frank McGlynn, Sr. (David Gamut).

James Fenimore Cooper's rather long and vapid novels of

Barbara Bedford, Albert Roscoe, Harry Lorraine and Lillian Hall
in The Last of the Mohicans (1920).

early pioneer life in upper New York state with their vast tales of
Indian lore have been collectively called The Leatherstocking Tales.
Of these yarns, The Last of the Mohicans and The Deerslayer have
been the most enduring, with the former filmed on a number of occasions.

In 1909 one of D. W. Griffith's first films for Biograph was
Leatherstocking, based freely on Cooper's fictional works. It was
filmed at Cuddebackville, New York, in the summer of that year
with camerawork by Billy Bitzer and Arthur Marine. Biograph
billed the short feature as an Indian scout melodrama. In 1911
there were two films of The Last of the Mohicans, each one reel
long (Powers and Thanhouser were the releasing companies, the
latter filming its story at Lake George, New York).

The Cooper novels have always been popular in Germany and
in 1920 a German film company, Luna-Film, made a lengthy version
of the Cooper work called Lederstrumpf (Leatherstocking). Directed
by Arthur Wellin, the film was issued in two parts: Der Wildtoter
(The Deerslayer) and Der Letzte der Mohikaner (Last of the Mohicans). The film had the authentic look of Upper New York even
though filmed in Germany, where it did big business. The role of
the brave Uncas was played by Bela Lugosi in a very convincing
manner. The film was issued in the United States in 1921 as The
Deerslayer and was trimmed from twelve to five reels.

In 1922 Associated Producers made the best version of Last

of the Mohicans to date, this edition being directed by Maurice
Tourneur and Clarence Brown. The picture was a spirited retelling
of the Cooper fiction with top-notch direction and well-staged scenes,
including the Fort William Henry massacre. A memorable sequence
has the villainous Indian Magua (Wallace Beery) pursuing the heroine
(Bedford), with the girl nearly being saved by Uncas (Roscoe) before
plunging off a cliff to her death.

Pathé produced a serial entitled Leatherstocking in 1924, although the final product was more of a reworking of The Deerslayer. Released in ten chapters, it was directed by George B.
Seitz and starred Edna Murphy, Harold Miller, and Frank Lackteen.

The first talkie version of Last of the Mohicans came in
1932 when Mascot filmed the novel as a twelve-episode cliffhanger
with the starring team of Harry Carey and Edwina Booth (who had
scored a sensation in 1930 in Trader Horn and had the next year
headlined the serial The Vanishing Legion). Carey was paid
$10,000 for his role as Hawkeye, who with Uncas (Junior Coughlin)
and the Sagamore (Hobart Bosworth), the last of the Mohicans, are
at odds with evil Magua (Robert Kortman) and the Hurons in the
French-Indian wars. The three work for the British while Magua is
allied with the French. Most of the serial focuses on the three men
and the two daughters (Miss Booth, Lucille Browne) of a British
colonel, fighting the Hurons. Eventually Magua is killed by the
Sagamore in the final chapter. The chapterplay was lensed in a
month's period and released immediately thereafter. The opening
sequence, in which the Mohican tribe is massacred, remains memorable.

The best-known celluloid version of Last of the Mohicans was
released in 1936 when director George B. Seitz, who had done the
Leatherstocking serial twelve years prior, helmed a version for
United Artists. Randolph Scott made an excellent Hawkeye, the
colonial scout who is loved by Alice Munroe (Barnes), while her
younger sister (Angel) loves the Mohican brave Uncas (Reed). The
flavorful film contains a most touching death scene involving Cora
(Angel) and Uncas.

In 1947 Columbia produced a color version of Last of the
Mohicans but called it Last of the Redmen. It was a mediocre effort, directed by George Sherman and starring expatriate Universal
stars, Jon Hall and Evelyn Ankers, with a solid job by Buster
Crabbe in an Indian role.

That version was the last Hollywood filming of the book to
date, although a German-Italian-Spanish co-production was produced
in 1965 called Der Letzte Mohikaner (The Last Tomahawk) and was
based on Cooper's Leatherstocking tales. Directed by Harold Reinl,
the picture starred Joachim Fuchsberger and Karin Dor. Still on
the production charts is a new version of Last of the Mohicans to
be produced in Europe and starring that box-office champ, Charles
Bronson.

The Deerslayer has not been filmed as often as Last of the
Mohicans although Vitagraph did a version in 1913 with Wallace
Reid and Florence Turner.

In 1943 the irrepressible Republic studio issued an independent-

made version of the 1841 novel, The Deerslayer, which Lew
Landers churned out on a shoestring budget. The New York Daily
News called the film "just like a refugee from a nickelodeon." It
was quite inept; its only saving grace was Yvonne De Carlo as a
most delightful-looking Indian maiden, Wah-Tah.
    In 1957, Twentieth Century-Fox made The Deerslayer in
color with Lex Barker, Rita Moreno, and Forrest Tucker. Kurt
Neufeld directed this programmer. The previous year a syndicated
TV series filmed in Canada by producer Sigmund Neufeld called
"Hawkeye and the Last of the Mohicans" was issued to TV in thirty-
nine episodes. Most of the segments were directed by Sam New-
field and the cheapie series starred John Hart in the title role with
Lon Chaney as Chingachgook. In 1962 four features were culled
from the segments and issued to TV by International Television
Corporation (ITC). They were: Along the Mohawk Trail, The Redmen and the Renegades, The Long Rifle and the Tomahawk (co-
directed by Sidney Salkow), and The Pathfinder and the Mohican.
    And that to date is the account of the filming of the Leather-
stocking works of that prolific author, James Fenimore Cooper.

THE LAST OUTLAW (RKO, 1936) 62 min.

    Producer, Robert Sisk; director, Christy Cabanne; screen
story, John Ford, E. Murray Campbell; screenplay, John Twist,
Jack Townley, E. Murray Campbell; camera, Jack MacKenzie;
editor, George Hively.
    Harry Carey (Dean Payton); Hoot Gibson (Chuck Wilson); Tom
Tyler (Al Goss); Henry B. Walthall (Cal Yates); Margaret Callahan
(Sally); Ray Mayer (Joe); Harry Jans (Jess); Frank M. Thomas (Dr.
Mason); Russell Hopton (Billings); Frank Jenks (Tom); Maxine Jen-
nings (Billings' Secretary); Fred Scott (Larry Dixon).

    Harry Carey was one of the cinema's first Western film
stars, predating even William S. Hart. In the mid-thirties he was
still portraying his familiar stern, earnest, heroic character.
During this period he made a trio of classy Westerns for RKO:
Powdersmoke Range [q.v.], The Law West of Tombstone (1938)
[q.v.] and this entry, which was the best of the lot. The film
was based on a story "The Last Outlaw," co-written by John Ford
who had previously directed it for Universal in 1919. Veteran director Christy Cabanne helmed the new production. Upon Ford's
later request, the rights to the story were conveyed to Carey for a
proposed remake in the post-World War II period, but the project
came to naught.
    Dean Payton (Carey) is an aging outlaw who is freed from
jail, only to find racketeers on the range and his daughter (Callahan) the mistress of a lawbreaker (Tyler). Payton is nearly killed
in saving his daughter from herself, but all ends happily. Co-
starred were Hoot Gibson (who got his start in films in Carey's
early John Ford Westerns) and Henry B. Walthall, the latter a com-
patriot of Carey's in the Biograph days with D. W. Griffith.

Harry Carey in The Last Outlaw (1936).

        The New York Times judged this "a thoroughly enjoyable
Western melodrama, deftly streamlined and softly satiric concerning
a few current disaffections like crooning cowboys and bureaucracy....
In a retrospective article for Film Fan Monthly, Leonard Maltin
called it "a delightful, unpretentious blend of comedy and Western
formulas." Among the more amusing moments in the film were
young outlaws referring to Carey's Payton as "Pop," much to his
chagrin. The new fad of singing cowboys was represented in this
film by Fred Scott.

THE LAST ROUND-UP (Paramount, 1934) 61 min.

        Director, Henry Hathaway; based on the novel The Border
Legion by Zane Grey; screenplay, Jack Cunningham; art director,
Earl Hedrick; camera, Archie Stout.

Randolph Scott (Jim Cleve); Barbara Fritchie (Joan Randall);
Fred Kohler (Sam Gulden); Monte Blue (Jack Kells); Fuzzy Knight
(Bunko McGee); Richard Carle (Judge Savin); Barton MacLane
(Charley Benson); Charles B. Middleton (Sheriff); Frank Rice
(Shrimp); Dick Rush (Rush); and: Jack M. Holmes, James Mason,
Sam Allen, Ben Corbett, Jim Corey.

See THE BORDER LEGION (1919, 1924, 1930, 1940).

THE LAST TOMAHAWK see LAST OF THE MOHICANS

THE LAST TWO FROM RIO BRAVO see DIE LETZTEN ZWEI
VOM RIO BRAVO

THE LAST WAGON (20th Century-Fox, 1956) C 99 min.

Producer, William B. Hawks; director, Delmer Daves;
story, Gwen Bagni Gielgud; screenplay, James Edward Grant,
Daves, Gielgud; art directors, Lyle R. Wheeler, Lewis H. Creber;
music, Lionel Newman; orchestrator, Bernard Mayers; costumes,
Mary Willis; assistant director, Joseph E. Rickards; camera, Wil-
frid Cline; editor, Hugh S. Fowler.

Richard Widmark and Felicia Farr in The Last Wagon (1956).

Richard Widmark (Todd); Felicia Farr (Jenny); Susan Kohner
(Jolie); Tommy Rettig (Billy); Stephanie Griffin (Valinda); Ray
Stricklyn (Clint); Nick Adams (Ridge); Carl Benton Reid (General
Howard); Douglas Kennedy (Colonel Normand); George Mathews
(Bull Harper); James Drury (Lieutenant Kelly); Ken Clark (Sergeant);
Timothy Carey (Sarge); Juney Ellis (Mrs. Clinton); Abel Fernandez
(Apache Medicine Man).

Oppressed by the competition of television as both a more
prolific and cheaper medium, moviemakers hoped the "gimmicks"
of wide screen processes and more adult themes would lure viewers
away from their homes and back into movie theatres. In the rash
of Westerns churned out in the mid-fifties, one still rather un-
heralded director stands at the fore, Delmer Daves. This former
Warner Bros. scripter would turn out, in the late fifties, a series
of highly-profitable Troy Donahue young love stories for Warner
Bros. But in the mid-fifties, Daves directed such sturdy sagebrush
entries as Jubal (1956), 3:10 to Yuma (1957), and Cowboy (1958)
[q. v.]. The Last Wagon, shot in CinemaScope and color, and co-
scripted by Daves, appeared in the 1956 film season. Unfortunately,
jaded reviewers like Bosley Crowther (New York Times) were un-
impressed: "a familiar and unexciting journey across a plateau of
western cliches. "
Having taken revenge on the two men who raped and murdered
his wife and killed his children, Todd (Widmark) joins a wagon train.
Fortunately for the settlers, Todd is a resourceful man. In the
course of the trek he saves six people from an Apache attack and
one of them (Farr) becomes enamored of him. Later, a brutal
sheriff (Mathews) brings in Todd for killing the two men. In the
courtroom, Todd explains why he murdered them. The judge sets
him free, in the custody of Jenny (Farr).
Any seasoned filmgoers knows that the true test of durability
in a Western is not always the highly-exploitable action scenes, but
those interludes between settler-redskin skirmishes, the big showdown, etc. Those moments around the campfire, when romance
usually stirs (to the annoyance of the small fry in the audience) are
indicative of the director's capability of handling atmosphere credibly.
Daves generally captures the flavor of the period without straining,
making his characters act in a manner appropriate to the situation
and to the time frame.

LAW AND ORDER   (Universal, 1932)   70 min.

Director, Edward Cahn; based on the novel Saint Johnson by
W. R. Burnett; screenplay, John Huston, Tom Reed; sound, C. Roy
Hunter; camera, Jackson Rose; editor, Milton Carruth.
Walter Huston (Frame Johnson); Harry Carey (Ed Brandt);
Raymond Hatton (Deadwood); Russell Simpson (Judge Williams);
Russell Hopton (Luther Johnson); Ralph Ince (Poe Northrup); Harry
Woods (Walt Northrup); Richard Alexander (Kurt Northrup); Alphong
Ethier (Fin Elder); Andy Devine (Johnny Kinaman); Dewey Robinson
(Ed Deal); Walter Brennan (Lanky Smith).

Russell Hopton, Harry Carey, Walter Huston and Raymond Hatton
in Law and Order (1932).

LAW AND ORDER (Universal, 1940) 57 min.

 Director, Ray Taylor; based on the novel Saint Johnson by
W. R. Burnett; screenplay, Sherman Lowe, Victor McLeod; music
director, Hans J. Salter; camera, Jerome Ash.
 Johnny Mack Brown (Bill Ralston); Fuzzy Knight (Deadwood);
Nell O'Day (Sally Dixon); James Craig (Brant); Harry Cording (Poe
Daggett); Earle Hodgins (Sheriff Fin Elder); Robert Fiake (Ed Deal);
Jimmy Dodd (Jimmy Dixon); William Worthington (Judge Williams);
Ted Adams (Walt Daggett); Ethan Laidlaw (Kurt Daggett); Bob Kort-
man (Pete); Jim Corey (Ranch Hand); Charles King (Henchman);
The Notables (Singers).

LAW AND ORDER (Universal, 1953) C 80 min.

 Producer, John W. Rogers; director, Nathan Juran; based on
the novel Saint Johnson by W. R. Burnett; screenplay, John and
Owen Bagni, D. D. Beauchamp; art directors, Alexander Golitzen,
Robert Clatworthy; camera, Clifford Stine; editor, Ted J. Kent.
 Ronald Reagan (Frame Johnson); Dorothy Malone (Jeannie
Bristow); Alex Nicol (Luta Johnson); Preston Foster (Kurt Darling);

Ruth Hampton (Maria); Russell Johnson (Jimmy Johnson); Barry
Kelley (Fin Elder); Chubby Johnson (Denver Cahoon); Dennis Weaver
(Frank Darling); Jack Kelly (Jed); Valerie Jackson (Clarissa); Don
Garner (Johnny Benton); Tom Browne Henry (Dixon); Richard Gar-
rick (Judge Williams); Tristram Coffin (Parker); Mike Ragan
(Horseman); James Stone (Martin); John Carpenter, Buddy Roose-
velt, Victor Romito (Bits); Dick Cutting (Card Player); Britt Wood
(Drunk); Martin Garralaga (Mexican Man).

One of the more stark and austere Western classics is Edward Cahn's Law and Order, based on W. R. Burnett's novel. This
was Cahn's directorial debut and proved to one of the few sound
cowboy films to recapture the grim West of William S. Hart pictures.
Largely an overlooked film and one that encompassed little
action, it was a retelling, using fictional names, of the story of
Wild Bill Hickok. Walter Huston was the sheriff and Harry Carey
played Ed Brandt, a character modeled after Doc Holliday. It was
a bleak tale of the cleaning up the West and of how men grew tired
of the endless killing that was an inevitable part of the eviction of
disorder from new frontier towns. A neat subplot had the lawmen
being forced to hang a dimwitted young farmer (Devine) who has
accidentally killed another man. The finale contains the famous
gunfight at the O.K. Corral in Tombstone.
In A Pictorial History of the Western Film (1969), William
K. Everson calls this film "the finest reconstruction yet of the
famous gun duel at the O.K. Corral."
In 1940 Universal released another Western entitled Law and
Order. Although it claimed to be based on W. R. Burnett's telling
novel, there is hardly any resemblance to either it or the fine
feature made eight years prior by Edward Cahn. Instead this
version had a former marshal (Brown) coming to a small town to
settle down. He discovers that a lawless element controls the settlement. Eventually he is forced to clean up the community, aided
by a reformed gambler (Craig) and an inept loudmouth (Knight). In
production and action the film was little more than a notch above the
B oater of that time. Much of the Destry Rides Again (1939) [q.v.]
set was utilized to good effect for this feature. However, senseless
musical and comedy sequences with both Knight and Jimmie Dodd
were included, greatly depreciating the film's overall worth.
Universal resurrected the property yet again for an inexpensive color remake in 1953. Future Governor of California Ronald
Reagan plays the marshal who cannot give up his gunslinging profession until justice triumphs once again. Dorothy Malone's
character was utilized to provide the mundane story with a romantic
sub-plot.

LAW OF THE LAWLESS (Paramount, 1964) C 87 min.

Producer, A. C. Lyles; director, William F. Claxton;
screenplay, Steve Fisher; assistant director, Harry Hogan; art
directors, Hal Pereira, Al Roelofs; set decorators, Sam Comer,

George Chandler (left), Kent Taylor and John Agar in <u>Law of the
Lawless</u> (1964).

Darrell Silvera; makeup, Wally Westmore; dialogue coach, Jerry
Buss; sound, Frank McWhorter, John Wilkinson; special camera
effects, Paul K. Lerpae; camera, Lester Shorr; editor, Otho
Lovering.
    Dale Robertson (Judge Clem Rogers); Yvonne De Carlo
(Ellie Irish); William Bendix (Sheriff Ed Tanner); Bruce Cabot (joe
Rile); Barton MacLane (Big Tom Stone); John Agar (Pete Stone);
Richard Arlen (Bartender); Jody McCrea (George Stapleton); Kent
Taylor (Rand McDonald); Bill Williams (Silas Miller); Rod Lauren
(Deputy Tim Ludlow); George Chandler (Hotel Clerk); Lon Chaney,
(Tiny); Donald "Red" Barry (Tuffy); Roy Jenson, Jerry Summers,
Reg Parton (Johnson Brothers); Alex Sharp (Drifter); Wally Wales
(Rider/Stunts).

    This film was the first of eleven B oaters producer A. C.
Lyles rushed out for Paramount which had quick playoffs and did
sufficiently good business. The opener was one of the best of the
series. Like the others, it sported a covey of veteran faces in its
cast along with average production values (thanks to the Paramount
facilities boosting the film in every department). Its mediocre plot
was peppered with violence.
    Clem Rogers (Robertson) is known as the hanging judge. He
is an ex-gunfighter who rides into a Kansas town in 1889 to preside
over the trial of an ex-friend, Pete Stone (Agar). The man's father
(MacLane) hires a gunslinger (Cabot), the man who killed Rogers'
dad, to shoot the judge. Stone's former girlfriend, saloon singer

Ellie Irish (De Carlo), is used by Big Tom Stone (MacLane) to try
and seduce the judge. Instead she becomes enamored of him, and
is beaten up by Tiny (Chaney) who, in turn, is mauled by Rogers.
        At the trial, it is brought out by the sheriff-prosecutor
(Bendix) that Pete killed his victim because he was having an affair
with the man's wife. Pete is found guilty and is sentenced to hang.
Joe Rile (Cabot) then confronts the judge and tells him he killed his
dad. Rogers still refuses to fight him and Joe lays down his gun
and leaves town. Big Tom tries to kill the judge but is thwarted.
Justice prevails.
        The New York Times noted the obvious: "A cast studded
with familiar faces makes this frontier outpost look like an old
folks home." On the other hand, Variety was more generous and
reported, "The modestly designed production is fortified with a cast
loaded with seasoned veterans, most of them reassuringly familiar
faces to the oater buff." The Times went on to explain, "A funda-
mental advantage enjoyed by the western over most other film
forms is the intrinsic opportunities it affords to tell a simple story
with a maximum of action and visual, outdoor values. And yet the
trend in recent years seems to be away from these very aspects
that built the great appeal of the sagebrush idiom. Law of the
Lawless suffers from this recently-developed affliction of pretension
and stuffiness. It is a verbose, inner-directed western, one that
by and large settles for words where action, though costlier, might
be a more profitable dramatic method."
        Nevertheless, devout moviegoers, such as this book's authors,
cheered the return of one-time name players. In the succeeding
years, Lyles--to his credit--gave similar comeback chances to a
bevy of veteran performers, including Jane Russell, Marilyn Maxwell, Terry Moore, Howard Keel, Brian Donlevy, and that perennial
favorite, Richard Arlen.

THE LAW WEST OF TOMBSTONE (RKO, 1938) 72 min.

        Producer, Cliff Reid; director, Glenn Tryon; story, Clarence
Upson Young; screenplay, John Twist, Young; art director, Van
Nest Polglase; music director, Roy Webb; camera, J. Roy Hunt.
        Harry Carey (Bill Parker); Tim Holt (The Tonto Kid); Evelyn
Brent (Clara Martinez); Jean Rouverol (Nitta Moseby); Clarence
Kolb (Sam Kent); Allan Lane (Danny); Esther Muir (Madame Mus-
tache); Bradley Page (Doc Howard); Paul Guilfoyle (Bud McQuinn);
Robert Moya (Chuy); Ward Bond (Mulligan); George Irving (Mort
Dixon); Monte Montague (Clayt McQuinn).

        Situated in Arizona in the 1880s, this black-and-white feature
incorporated the legends of a number of famous Western desperadoes
into one seventy-two minute story. Harry Carey starred as a tall-
tale telling judge (à la Roy Bean) who settles in Martinez and sets
up his court of law in a bar room. The law of his jurisdiction is
his six-shooter. His daughter, who thinks he is dead, comes to
town to marry a good-for-nothing, but the latter is soon dispatched

Esther Muir, Eddy Waller and George Irving (both seated), and
Harry Carey (center) in Law West of Tombstone (1938).

by the town's young gunslinger, The Tonto Kid (Holt).   Judge Parker
likes The Kid and lets the crime pass unpunished, especially when
The Kid and Parker's daughter fall in love.   At the finale, the
Judge and The Kid join together in ridding the town of the menace
of the evil McQuinn gang.
        Even the uninitiated viewer of Western folklore could spot
the similarities between The Tonto Kid and Billy the Kid, the Mc-
Quinn gang and the Clayton gang, and so forth.   Former actor
Glenn Tryon allowed Carey full rein to embellish his role as the
loquacious judicial rogue.   The Law West of Tombstone may not
have pleased sophisticates like the New York Times (who labeled
the film "just a cut above the ordinary Western") but it was a
crowd-pleaser among the action set.   It was one of a trio of superior Westerns (Powdersmoke Ridge, 1935 [q.v.] and The Last Outlaw, 1936 [q.v.]) that veteran Harry Carey made for RKO in this
period.

THE LEATHERSTOCKING TALES   see   LAST OF THE MOHICANS

LEDERSTRUMPF   see   THE LAST OF THE MOHICANS

THE LEFT-HANDED GUN   (Warner Bros., 1958)   102 min.

Producer, Fred Coe; director, Arthur Penn; based on the
teleplay, The Death of Billy the Kid by Gore Vidal; screenplay,
Leslie Stevens; art director, Art Loel; set decorator, William
Kuehl; music, Alexander Courage; costumes, Marjorie Best; make-
up, Gordon Bau; assistant director, Russ Saunders; ballad, William
Goyen and Courage; sound, Earl Crain, Jr.; camera, J. Peverell
Marley; editor, Folmar Blangsted.

Paul Newman (Billy Bonney); Lita Milan (Celsa); John Dehner
(Pat Garrett); Hurd Hatfield (Moultrie); James Congdon (Charlie
Boudre); James Best (Tom Folliard); Colin Keith-Johnston (Turn-
stall); John Dierkes (McSween); Bob Anderson (Hill); Wally Brown
(Moon); Ainslie Pryor (Joe Grant); Martin Garralaga (Saval); Denver
Pyle (Ollinger); Paul Smith (Bell); Nestor Paiva (Maxwell); Jo
Summers (Mrs. Garrett); Robert Foulk (Brady); Anne Barton (Mrs.
Hill).

In 1955 Paul Newman starred in NBC-TV's "Philco Play-
house" production of The Death of Billy the Kid by Gore Vidal.
Director Arthur Penn transferred the teledrama to films in this
adult treatment which presented Billy as a manic-depressive--which
he probably was in real life. For the record, the famed outlaw
was definitely not left-handed.

The Leslie Stevens scenario finds Billy Bonney (Newman)
being befriended by a mild-manner rancher (Dierkes). After the
man is murdered by four cowpokes Billy seeks revenge on them,
killing not only the slayers but three others to boot. The storyline
focuses on Billy's search for a father figure, which is sublimated
in his relationship with Sheriff Pat Garrett (Dehner), along with a
glory and death wish. In the end Garrett and his posse track down
Billy and he is killed.

Newman, then fast reaching his peak as a Hollywood screen
star, played William Bonney as a homosexually-inclined young man
who had been violent since childhood. Via Newman's characterization, the outlaw is a man to be pitied, a person too illiterate and
not bright enough to cope with his problems.

In Hollywood in the Fifties (1971) Gordon Gow writes of the
film that it "was the best of several attempts to cut the Western
myth down to size." Contemporary reviewer Howard Thompson
(New York Times) felt "very little of it makes sense and the whole
thing is so laboriously arty that it hurts.... The picture moves
self-consciously, at a snail's pace...." On the other hand, Variety
was of the opinion that "The best parts of the film are the moments
of hysterical excitement as the three young desperadoes rough-house
with each other as freckless as any innocent boys and in the next
instant turn to deadly killing without flicking a curly eyelash."

In the fifties, Paul Newman's acting was often regarded as
merely a medley of the more artificial acting mannerisms of
Marlon Brando and the late James Dean. In The Left-Handed Gun
he demonstrates the truth of this opinion all too often, although
today his pivotal performance and the film itself are much more
highly-regarded than when the movie was released.

One could not conceive of Johnny Mack Brown, Robert
Taylor, Buster Crabbe, etc. ever portraying the famed Billy in
such an introspective, sullen manner as that offered by Newman.
Anyone attempting to predict a trend regarding Hollywood
Westerns would have been baffled by the appearance of two such
divergent films as The Left-Handed Gun and The True Story of
Jesse James (1957) within a year of one another. The former was
clearly a psychological study, while the latter effort, directed by
Nicholas Ray for Twentieth Century-Fox and starring Robert Wagner
and Jeffrey Hunter, was a glossy, fictitious account geared to per-
petrate the accepted legends. Clearly, at this point in Hollywood
history, there was no answer as to where the American sagebrush
film was heading.

THE LEGEND OF NIGGER CHARLEY (Paramount, 1972) C
99 min.

Producer, Larry G. Spangler; associate producer, Steve
Bono; director, Martin Goldman; screenplay, Spangler, Goldman;
music-songs, John Bennings; music arrangers, Robert Banks,
George Butcher; art director, Merrill Sindler; costumes, Joseph
Garibaldi Aulisi; makeup, Enrico Cortese; assistant directors, John
E. Quill, Joseph Ellis, James Geallis; stunt, Jerry Gatlin; sound,
Leland M. Haas, Jeffrey Haas; special effects, Joe Day; camera,
Peter Eco; editor, Howard Kuperman.
Fred Williamson (Nigger Charley); D'Urville Martin (Toby);
Don Pedro Cooley (Joshua); Gertrude Jeanette (Theo); Marcia Mc-
Broom (Julia); Alan Gifford (Hill Carter); John Ryan (Houston); Will
Hussung (Dr. Saunders); Mill Moor (Walker); Thomas Anderson
(Shadow); Jerry Gatlin (Sheriff Rhinehart); Tricia O'Neil (Sarah
Lyons); Doug Rowe (Dewey Lyons); Keith Prentice (Nils Fowler);
Tom Pemberton (Willie); Joe Santos (Reverend); Fred Lerner
(Ollokot).

In the late sixties there was an explosion of black exploita-
tion features, usually violent gangster yarns. But the successful
cycle was extended also to Westerns, one of the first being Soul
Soldier (1971) which had been originally released the previous year
as The Red, White and Black. The Legend of Nigger Charley
starred that hard-working ex-athlete Fred Williamson and did so
well at the box-office that a sequel, The Soul of Nigger Charley,
was made the following year.
Twenty-one-year-old blacksmith Charley (Williamson) is
freed on his master's death in 1841 Virginia. But the late owner's
overseer Houston (Ryan) destroys the declaration of freedom and
determines to sell the ex-slave at auction. Later, in a fight,
Charley kills him and runs off with two other slaves, Joshua (Col-
ley) and Toby (Martin). The three fugitives head west, pursued by
slave-catcher Nils Fowler (Prentice) and a posse. At a frontier
town Charley refuses to budge in the face of local prejudice, but
announces that he will make a stand there against Fowler and his

men. At the saloon the showdown occurs, with Fowler and his cohorts killed. Homesteader Dewey Lyons (Rowe) offers the black
men a job, for he needs protection against the "Reverend" (Santos)
who heads a gang of bandits. Charley at first refuses but then decides to help. In the final assault many of Charley's pals are
killed, but the Reverend and his men are either killed or dispersed.
Charley and Toby are now free to ride off to their future.

Judith Crist (New York magazine) labeled this "the blaxploi-
tation flick of the week." Some poked fun at the commercialism of
the project, "Trash, bless its heart, knows no discrimination....
[This is] a hackneyed melodrama whose every plot twist and turn
is as obvious as its name...." (Washington Post). Producer-co-
author Larry Spangler said publicly that he thought the film would
gross "an easy $10 million." In fact, he added that "it could be
the worst picture ever made and still slop in $5 million." [It
actually grossed a little less than $2,000,000--not a bad take at
all, considering the low production costs.]

If its decision was somewhat equivocal, the Chicago Sun-
Times was one of the few voices raised in support of this film,
"The Legend of Nigger Charley is an amiable black western with
sufficient episodes of violence to give it the appearance of heading
somewhere. Actually, though, it mostly just drifts, and gets incredible mileage out of some nice guitar and banjo work on the
sound track while the heroes ride everlastingly into the sagebrush."

DER LETZTE MOHIKANER see LAST OF THE MOHICANS

DIE LETZTEN ZWEI VOM RIO BRAVO (THE LAST TWO FROM
RIO BRAVO) (Jolly/Trio/Constantin, 1964) C 93 min.

Director, Mike Perkins [Manfred Rieger]; screenplay, Manuel
Waller, Donald Mooch [Frank Forester]; music, Dan Sovid [Ennio
Morricone]; camera, Julio Ortas.
Rod Cameron (Pat Garrett); Dick Palmer (Billy Clampett);
Vivi Bach (Agnes); Kai Fisher (George Clampett); and: Angel
Aranda, Horst Frank, Hans Nielson, Ludwig Duran.

On his wedding day, Sheriff Pat Garrett (Cameron) of River-
town is forced to chase the Clampett Brothers (Palmer and Fisher)
south of the border into Mexico after they have robbed the town
bank of $30,000. During the robbery Billy (Palmer) killed by-
standers in the bank. Garrett captures them in Mexico and the
three trek across Devil's Valley, a desert, with Mexican bandits
in hot pursuit. At the edge of the desert they are aided by a girl
(Bach) and her younger brother. Billy escapes into the desert
where he is killed later by bandits. George (Fisher) rides for the
cavalry which saves the survivors from the marauders. Garrett
takes the money and returns to his bride, leaving a free George
with Agnes (Bach).
Produced in Italy at the same time that company made Per

Un Pugno Di Dollari (A Fistful of Dollars) (1964) [q.v.], this production was one of the first of the spaghetti Westerns. It was
quite well-received in Europe, but received only TV playdates in
the U.S. In many respects it is every bit as good as the Clint
Eastwood film and aging Cameron turns in a strong performance
as the lawman. This film contains most of the action that would
become clichés in the later European oaters; it also contains one
of Ennio Morricone's most neglected but better scores for a Western.
    Rod Cameron was first a series Western star in the 1940s at
Universal and then graduated to class A cowboy movies in the late
forties and early fifties. His appearance in this melodrama made
him one of the first U.S. stars to appear in Continental Westerns.
In 1964 he also appeared in the Spanish-German-Italian co-production, Bullet and the Flesh, in which he portrayed a lumber baron
who plans to plunder Cherokee timberlands while his daughter
(Patricia Vitterbo) carries on a love affair with an Indian chief
(Dan Harrison). In 1966 Cameron was Karl May's character, Old
Firehand, in Winnetou und sein Freund Old Firehand [q.v.].
    Die Letzten Zwei Vom Rio Bravo was released to U.S. tele-
vision by Walter Manley Productions as Bullets Don't Argue or
Guns Don't Argue.

THE LIFE AND TIMES OF JUDGE ROY BEAN (National General,
1972) C 124 min.

    Producer, John Foreman; associate producer, Frank Caffey;
director, John Huston; screenplay, John Milius; music-music director, Maurice Jarre; song, Jarre and Marilyn and Alan Bergman;
art director, Tambi Larsen; set decorators, Robert Benton; animal
trainer, Ron Oxley; stunt coordinator, James Arnett; costumes,
Edith Head; makeup, William Tuttle, Monty Westmore; assistant
director, Mickey McCardle; sound, Keith Stafford, Larry Jost,
Richard Portman; camera, Richard Moore; editor, Hugh S. Fowler.
    Paul Newman (Judge Roy Bean); Jacqueline Bisset (Rose
Bean); Ava Gardner (Lily Langtry); Tab Hunter (Sam Dodd); John
Huston (Grizzly Adams); Stacy Keach (Bad Bob); Roddy McDowall
(Frank Gass); Anthony Perkins (Reverend LaSalle); Victoria Princi-
pal (Marie Elena); Ned Beatty (Tector Crites); Anthony Zerbe
(Hustler); Jim Burk (Bart Jackson); Matt Clark (Nick the Grub);
Steve Kanaly (Whorehouse Lucky Jim); Karen Carr (Mrs. Grubb);
Dolores Clark (Mrs. Whorehouse Jim); Lee Meza (Mrs. Parlee);
Neil Summers (Snake River Rufus Krile); Stan Barrett (Killer);
John Hudkins (Man at Stage Door); Roy Jenson, Gary Combs, Fred
Brookfield, Ben Dobbins, Dick Farnsworth, LeRoy Johnson, Fred
Krone, Terry Leonard, Dean Smith (Outlaws).

    The preface to this self-indulgent class production states
that it is not historically accurate but does portray the story of
Judge Roy Bean (Newman) as it should have been. Despite this
feeble apology the film is a heavy travesty of the old West. Bean
is pictured as having no respect for law and order, as in his

murder of the drifter Sam Dodd (Hunter) and his enduring partiality for the legendary stage performer, Lilly Langtry (Gardner).

The storyline in this $4 million production covers two periods. The first is Texas in 1890, when fugitive Bean slaughters all his enemies in the town of Vinegaroon and thereafter proclaims himself to be a god-appointed Judge. Eventually Bean renames the town Langtry in a tribute to the famous entertainer who is his idealized woman figure. When Mexican Maria Elena (Principal) dies in childbirth, the heartbroken Bean rides off. Twenty years later the town of Langtry has expanded due to the discovery of oil. On the day that the grown Rose (Bisset) is to be expelled from her property, the aged, grizzled Bean rides back to town, a place whose streets are now filled with autos. In a fight with Gass (McDowall) and his henchmen, the town is set ablaze. Shouting "for Texas and Miss Lily" Bean dies in a volley of pistol shots. Some years later, the legendary Miss Lily alights from a train to pay respects to the town named in her honor. At the Judge Roy Bean Museum (once the town saloon) Miss Lily examines the memorabilia, learns that Rose has wed an aviator, and as she departs, the actress states of her late champion, "he must have been some man."

Few directors have had so many high and low points in their careers as John Huston. From the man who helmed The Maltese Falcon (1941) and The Treasure of Sierra Madre (1948) came this bit of claptrap, which made a splash on the distribution scene due to its all-star cast. Newsday termed it a "revisionist western that makes fun of its own characters and the heroic legends of manifest destiny ... the film is not only anti-heroic, it's anti-dramatic." The San Francisco Chronicle was even harsher: "It is a string of sequences, some for the sake of a gag which isn't worth the footage, some for a grotesque but hearty laugh, some to bridge the gap between Blood & Guts and Hearts & Flowers."

On the other hand, such journalist sources as the Los Angeles Times were of the opinion that "[the film] plays upon our traditional love of the tall tale to confront us with what the cherished myths of the Old West reveal about ourselves and our heritage. For Judge Roy Bean's appeal is that of rugged individualism--and his sin is his naivete in having attempted to play God. This film ... exerts a tremendous nostalgic pull--for a time when men were men (and therefore larger than life), when spaces really were wide open, when morality was black and white, when just about everything seemed so much simpler--only to snap back on itself. For as endearing a figure as Bean becomes he is nevertheless a willful ignoramus and the precursor to all the evil that befalls him and his people in the decades to come."

The Life and Times of Judge Roy Bean was scripted by John Milius, who was much more adept when he co-wrote Jeremiah Johnson (1972) [q.v.]. Now turned director, Milius would have done well to have studied Samuel Goldwyn's The Westerner (1940), in which Walter Brennan was Judge Roy Bean (and won his third Oscar). Gary Cooper was the star of that far more romantic, glossy film, which while slick and typically Hollywood, was a far more stable, satisfying entry.

THE LIGHT OF WESTERN STARS   (United Picture Theatres of
America, Inc., 1918) 90 min.
   Director, Charles Swickard; based on the novel by Zane
Grey; camera, Homer Scott.
   Dustin Farnum (Gene Stewart); Winifred Kingston (Majesty
Hammond); Burt Apling (Sheriff Hawes); Joseph Swickard (Padre
Marcos); Virginia Eames (Bonita); Charles Rogers (Danny Marns);
Eddie Hearns (Al Hammond); George Fields (Don Carlos); Jeanne
Maddock (Florence Kingsley).

THE LIGHT OF WESTERN STARS   (Paramount, 1925) 6,859'

   Presenters, Adolph Zukor, Jesse L. Lasky; director, Wil-
liam K. Howard; based on the novel by Zane Grey; screenplay,
George C. Hull, Lucien Hubbard; camera, Lucien Andriot.
   Jack Holt (Gene Stewart); Billie Dove (Madeline Hammond);
Noah Beery (Brand); Alma Bennett (Bonita); William Scott (Al Ham-
mond); George Nichols (Billy Stillwell); Mark Hamilton (Monty Price);
Robert Perry (Nelse); Eugene Pallette (Stub).

THE LIGHT OF WESTERN STARS   (Paramount, 1930) 70 min.

   Directors, Otto Brower, Edwin H. Knopf; based on the novel
by Zane Grey; screenplay, Grover Jones, William Slavens McNutt;
sound, Earl Hayman; camera, Charles Lang; editor, Jane Loring.
   Richard Arlen (Dick Bailey); Mary Brian (Ruth Hammond);
Harry Green (Pie Pan); Regis Toomey (Bob Drexell); Fred Kohler
(Stack); William Le Maire (Grif Meeker); George Chandler (Slig
Whelan); Sid Saylor (Square-Toe Boots); Guy Oliver (Sheriff); Gus
Saville (Pop).

THE LIGHT OF WESTERN STARS   (Paramount, 1940) 67 min.

   Producer, Harry Sherman; director, Lesley Selander; based
on the novel by Zane Grey; screenplay, Norman Houston; art di-
rector, Lewis J. Rackmil; music, Victor Young; camera, Russell
Harlan; editor, Sherman A. Rose.
   Victor Jory (Gene Stewart); Jo Ann Sayers (Madeline "Majesty"
Hammond); Noah Beery, Jr. (Poco); Russell Hayden (Alfred Ham-
mond); Morris Ankrum (Not Hayworth); Ruth Rogers (Flo Kingsley);
J. Farrell MacDonald (Bill Stillwell); Esther Estrella (Bonita); Alan
Ladd (Danny); Georgia Hawkins (Helen); Earl Askam (Sneed); Tom
Tyler (Sheriff Hawes); Eddie Dean (Nels); Rad Robinson (Nonty).

   Sherman-United Pictures first brought Zane Grey's novel,
The Light of Western Stars, to the screen in 1918, four years after
its publication. With the promotional value of Zane Grey's name,
the film drew in more than the usual audience for a Western film.
   In 1925 Paramount made the first of its three versions of the

Grey novel, the silent edition directed by William K. Howard. It
begins during a poker game in which Al Hammond (Scott) kills the
henchman of a notorious outlaw (Beery) and then flees to Mexico.
Hammond's sister Madeline (Dove) arrives from the East and soon
thereafter is accosted by a drunken gunfighter, Gene Stewart (Holt),
who claims he wants to marry her. Later a tug of war develops
between Stewart and Brand (Beery) over the girl and the cattle on
her ranch. By the fade-out, Stewart has killed Brand and renewed
his romance with Madeline.

     In the 1930 version it is Richard Arlen who falls in love
with Easterner Ruth Hammond (Brian), must contend with nefarious
Stack (Kohler), compete with the heroine's beau (Toomey) for her
affection, and confront the outlaws. It was all handled with dispatch
and was geared for an action market that was assumed to be filled
with undemanding filmgoers.

     A decade later Harry "Pop" Sherman, who was having such
great success producing the Hopalong Cassidy films for Paramount,
turned out yet another remake of this Zane Grey perennial. The
offbeat casting found Victor Jory as the hero, a departure from his
usual villain's role. Blossoming film player Alan Ladd had a supporting role in this Lesley Selander-directed quickie.

     The production history of The Light of Western Stars shows
how Hollywood could tear through a literary property, milking it for
its obvious effects in a typical film-land assembly-line manner, and
finally discarding the worn-out book premise altogether.

LITTLE BIG MAN   (National General, 1970)   C   147 min.

     Producer, Stuart Millar; associate producer, Gene Lasko;
director, Arthur Penn; based on the novel by Thomas Berger;
screenplay, Calder Willingham; assistant director, Mike Moder;
production designer, Dean Tavoularis; art director, Anglo Graham;
set decorator, George R. Nelson; music, John Hammond; additional
music arranged by John Strauss; costumes, Dorothy Jeakins; sound,
Al Overton, Jr., Bud Alper; camera, Harry Stradling, Jr.; editor,
Dede Allen.
     Dustin Hoffman (Jack Crabb); Faye Dunaway (Mrs. Pendrake);
Martin Balsam (Allardyce T. Merriweather); Richard Mulligan
(General George A. Custer); Chief Dan George (Old Lodge Skins);
Jeff Corey (Wild Bill Hickok); Amy Eccles (Sunshine); Jean Peters
(Olga); Carole Androsky (Caroline); Robert Little Star (Little Horse);
Cal Bellini (Younger Bear); Ruben Moreno (Shadow that Comes in
Sight); Steve Snehmayne (Burns Red in the Sky); William Hickey
(Historian); Thayer David (Reverend Silas Pendrake); James Ander-
son (Sergeant); Jesse Vint (Lieutenant); Philip Kenneally); Jack
Bannon (Captain); Steve Miranda (Younger Bear as a Youth); Linda
Dyer (Corn Woman); Tracy Hotchner (Flirtatious Girl).

     When confronted by a historian, the very aged Jack Crabb
(Hoffman) relates his life during the Indian wars. He recounts how
as a boy he had been captured by the redskins, brought up as a

Cheyenne brave by Chief Old Lodge Skins (George), and how he had
earned the name Little Big Man during a skirmish with the Pawnee.
Later he is recaptured by the Army and given over to Reverend
Pendrake (David) whose wife (Dunaway) has a yearning for the local
drug store owner.   Next Little Big Man joins the sideshow of patent-
medicine spieler Allardyce T. Merriweather (Balsam).   Further
adventures include an encounter with Wild Bill Hickok (Corey) and
then his marriage to Swedish immigrant Olga (Peters).   Olga is
later kidnapped by the Indians and in searching for her, Little Big
Man meets Sunshine (Eccles), a maiden from his old tribe.   They
eventually live together under the aegis of Old Lodge Skins.   General
Custer (Mulligan) attacks the Indian camp; although Little Big Man
rescues Old Lodge Skins, Sunshine and their child are massacred.
Disillusioned by the episode, Little Big Man becomes a drunkard and
later a hermit.   Still later, he encounters Custer again and Jack
Crabb is made a scout.   In the massacre at Little Big Horn, Younger
Bear (Bellini) a Cheyenne boyhood pal, saves Jack's life.   After re-
storing Old Lodge Skins' spirits, the old man and Jack return to the
village, and so ends the story.

    Throughout this lengthy but generally entertaining feature, one
wonders if it is all a shaggy dog story or actually the study of a
very overlooked American hero.   In recounting his wild and expansive adventures, Jack's life provides a focus of the education of a
pioneer spirit in the ways of the old West.   Ironically his status is
one of passivity and most things that happen to enhance his reputation are not of his own doing.

    In analyzing this unusual, hard-to-classify Western, the
British Monthly Film Bulletin reports, "Penn himself has expressed
doubt about the conviction of the Indian way of life he has created;
and in the scenes of Jack's first arrival in the Cheyenne camp there
is little to distinguish this set of Indians from that of an average
Western.   But in more special circumstances, Penn's individuality
flourishes; in the desolate poetry of the snowbound reservation on
the riverbank, where Jack quietly accepts both family and tribal obligations...."

    Perhaps only in this confused age could such an ambiguous
film project be such a commercial success.

THE LONE RANGER   (Republic, 1938)   fifteen chapters

    Associate producer, Sol C. Siegel; directors, William Whit-
ney, John English; based on the radio serial by Frank Striker;
screenplay, Barry Shipman, Franklyn Adreon, Ronald Davidson,
Lois Eby, George Worthington Yates; music, Alberto Colombo;
camera, William Nobles.
    A Man of Mystery (The Lone Ranger); Silver King (Silver the
Horst); Chief Thundercloud (Tonto); Lee Powell (Allen King); Herman
Brix [Bruce Bennett] (Bert Rogers); Lynn Roberts (Joan Blanchard);
Stanley Andrews (Jeffries); William Farnum (Father McKim); George
Cleveland (Blanchard); Hal Taliaferro (Bob Stuart); Lane Chandler
(Dick Forrest); George Letz [Montgomery] (Jim Clark); John Merton

(Kester); Sammy McKim (Sammy); Tom London (Felton); Raphael "Ray" Bennett (Taggart); Maston Williams (Snead); Frank McGlynn, Sr. (Lincoln).

Chapters: 1) Heigh-Yo Silver!; 2) Thundering Earth; 3) The Pitfall; 4) Agents of Treachery; 5) The Steaming Cauldron; 6) Red Man's Courage; 7) Wheels of Disasters; 8) Fatal Treasure; 9) The Missing Spur; 10) Flaming Fury; 11) The Silver Bullet; 12) Escape; 13) The Fatal Plunge; 14) Messengers of Doom; 15) The Last of the Rangers.

The famous masked man with a horse called Silver and an Indian companion named Tonto began his radio career in 1932, as created by George W. Trendle. The Lone Ranger first came to films in 1938 in the format of a fifteen-chapter Republic serial.

Set in the period after the Civil War, the narrative concerns five lawmen (Powell, Brix, Chandler, Taliaferro and Letz) who unite to fight a gang led by Jeffries (Andrews). They are aided by a masked "man of mystery," the Lone Ranger, and his faithful Indian ally Tonto (Chief Thundercloud). One by one, the valiant five are killed off, until only one of their number is left to combat Jeffries' nefarious gang.

The film was issued in a feature version called Hi-Yo Silver (1940).

Sadly, this landmark serial has all but disappeared from sight, the negatives supposedly having been lost. It is a shame that it is not available so that devotees of the Western could enjoy the interacting of Herman Brix (later Bruce Bennett); George Letz (who became George Montgomery at Twentieth Century-Fox), Hal Taliaferro (better known as cowboy star Wally Wales), and popular Western lead Lane Chandler. Lee Powell, who proved to be an enduring serial lead, would die in combat during World War II.

THE LONE RANGER (Warner Bros., 1956) C 86 min.

Producer, Willis Goldbeck; director, Stuart Heisler; based on the Lone Ranger legend; screenplay, Herb Meadow; art director, Stanley Fleischer; music director, David Buttolph; assistant director, Robert Farfan; camera, Edwin DuPar; editor, Clarence Kolster.

Clayton Moore (The Lone Ranger); Jay Silverheels (Tonto); Lyle Bettger (Reece Kilgore); Bonita Granville (Welcome Kilgore); Perry Lopez (Ramirez); Robert Wilke (Cassidy); John Pickard (Sheriff Kimberly); Beverly Washburn (Lila); Michael Ansara (Angry Horse); Frank De Kova (Red Hawk); Charles Meredith (The Governor); Mickey Simpson (Powder); Zon Murray (Goss); Lane Chandler (Whitebeard).

Brace Beemer played The Lone Ranger on radio for many years and he wanted the job when the series came to television but it went to Republic's serial hero Clayton Moore. During one season Moore was replaced by John Hart but Moore was soon back in the

saddle.   In 1956 he starred in the first of two features with his TV
co-star, Jay Silverheels, as Tonto.
  Shot in CinemaScope and color, the feature has the governor
(Meredith) of a territory hiring the Lone Ranger and Tonto to find
out the cause of fresh trouble between the whites and Indians.   They
soon rescue a cowboy (Lopez) from Indians and he tells them that
rancher Reece Kilgore (Bettger) is causing the problem, hoping to
prevent statehood for the territory because it would ruin his chances
to obtain the silver ore from the Indian lands.   Kilgore wires to the
governor to send troops but the request is denied.   Later, Kilgore's
daughter Lila (Washburn) is kidnapped by Indians but is returned to
her mother (Granville).   The Lone Ranger and Tonto stop a settlers'
march on an Indian village by dynamiting the trail and not long
thereafter Kilgore is arrested for the murder of Ramirez (Lopez).
The Masked Rider and his faithful Indian companion then ride off
into the sunset, with The Lone Ranger shouting his cry, "Hi-ho
Silver," to his trusty steed.
  For the record, Bonita Granville, the one-time Warner Bros.
star, was wed to Jack Wrathers, producer of the "Lassie" series
and also the executive supervisor of this project.

THE LONE RANGER AND THE LOST CITY OF GOLD   (United
Artists, 1958)   C   80 min.

  Producer, Sherman A. Harris; director, Lesley Selander;
based on the Lone Ranger legend; screenplay, Robert Schaefer, Eric
Freiwald; music, Les Baxter; song, Lenny Adelson and Baxter; art
director, James D. Vance; set decorator, Charles Thompson; make-
up, Layne Britton; sound, Philip Mitchell; camera, Kenneth Peach;
editor, Robert S. Golden.
  Clayton Moore (The Lone Ranger); Jay Silverheels (Tonto);
Douglas Kennedy (Ross Brady); Charles Watts (Oscar Matthison);
Noreen Nash (Frances Henderson); Lisa Montell (Paviva); Ralph
Moody (Padre Vincente Esteban); Norman Frederic (Dr. James
Rolfe); John Miljan (Tomache); Maurice Jara (Redbird); Bill Henry
(Travers); Lane Bradford (Wilson); Belle Mitchell (Caulama).

  After the success of The Lone Ranger (1956) [q. v.], released by Warner Bros., United Artists issued this follow-up, directed by Western veteran Lesley Selander.
  The narrative centers on the key to the Indians' lost gold
mine, the clue being found in the combination of five medallions,
each of which is now being held by friends of the chief (Miljan).
The leader (Kennedy) of a gang of hooded raiders and his girlfriend
(Nash) kill three of the medallion holders, obtaining three of the
discs.   But the Lone Ranger (Moore) and Tonto (Silverheels) step
in to thwart the plot.   Ross Brady (Kennedy) kills a fourth person,
after which Brady is killed by his angered girl (Nash).   She is then
captured by the Lone Ranger.   Thereafter the Indians retain control
of their Lost City of Gold.
  This is the final feature to date on the Lone Ranger, although

John Hart (who had played the role on TV for one season) and Jay
Silverheels repeated their roles in cameos in the little-seen camp
feature The Phynx (1969). In the seventies, Clayton Moore and
Silverheels were seen in their well-known parts in a series of
personal appearances and TV commercials.

THE LONE RANGER RIDES AGAIN   (Republic, 1939)   fifteen chapters

    Associate producer, Robert Beche; directors, William Witney,
John English; based on the radio serial by Fran Striker; screenplay,
Robert Beche, Barry Shipman, Franklyn Adreon, Ronald Davidson,
Sol Shor; music, William Lava; camera, William Nobles.
    Robert Livingston (The Lone Ranger/Bill Andrews); Chief
Thundercloud (Tonto); Silver Chief (Silver the Horse); Duncan
Renaldo (Juan Vasquez); Jinx Falken[berg] (Sue); Ralph Dunn (Bart
Dolan); J. Farrell MacDonald (Craig Dolan); William Gould (Jed
Scott); Rex Lease (Evans); Ted Mapes (Merritt); Henry Otho (Pa
Daniels); John Beach (Hardin); Glenn Strange (Thorne); Stanley Bly-
stone (Murdock); Edwin Parker (Hank); Al Taylor (Colt); Carleton
Young (Logan); Ernie Adams (Doc Grover).
    Chapters: 1) The Lone Ranger Returns; 2) Masked Victory;
3) The Black Raiders Strike; 4) The Caves of Doom; 5) Agents of
Deceit; 6) The Trap; 7) The Lone Ranger at Bay; 8) Ambush; 9)
Wheels of Doom; 10) The Dangerous Captive; 11) Death Below; 12)
Blazing Peril; 13) Exposed; 14) Besieged; 15) Frontier Justice.

    A year after directing the immensely popular serial The
Lone Ranger [q. v.], the directing team of William Witney and John
English turned out this fifteen-chapter sequel.
    Here the nephew (Dunn) of a cattle baron (MacDonald) de-
clares war on settlers to keep them out of cattle grazing country.
Meanwhile, Jed Scott (Gould), the leader of a wagon train, hires
a scout (Livingston) to fight the cattlemen. He is unaware that
Bill Andrews (Livingston) is actually the Lone Ranger. With the
aid of Tonto (Chief Thundercloud) and a Mexican comrade (Renaldo),
the Lone Ranger thwarts Bart Dolan (Dunn) in his schemes, including the sending of a wagon full of explosives to the fort where
the settlers are housed. When Dolan investigates why the wagon
did not blow up as expected, he is killed in the delayed explosion.
Finally the range war is over.
    In The Thrill of It All (1971) author Alan G. Barbour re-
calls the mysterious disappearance of the negatives to this serial,
as with The Lone Ranger. He then adds, "The Lone Ranger Rides
Again, dealing with the same hot property, should have been even
better than the first, considering how much the quality of production
had increased at Republic in a very short period of time--but it
wasn't. A detailed study of the cutting continuity (a scene-for-
scene breakdown of the entire film) shows it to be merely a routine
Western adventure containing only the usual Republic chases, fights,
etc. (Not that that was bad, by any means, but audiences expected
much more considering the excellent quality of the first serial.)

Robert Livingston played the masked rider of the plains and turned in his usual fine performance. "

LONELY ARE THE BRAVE (Universal, 1962) 107 min.

      Producer, Edward Lewis; director, David Miller; based on the novel Brave Cowboy by Edward Abbey; screenplay, Dalton Trumbo; art directors, Alexander Golitzen, Robert E. Smith; set decorator, George Milo; makeup, Bud Westmore; assistant directors, Tom Shaw, Dave Silver; music, Jerry Goldsmith; sound, Waldon O. Watson, Frank Wilkinson; camera, Phil Lathrop; editor, Leon Barsha.
      Kirk Douglas (Jack Burns); Gena Rowlands (Jerri Bondi); Walter Matthau (Sheriff Johnson); Michael Kane (Paul Bondi); Carroll O'Connor (Hinton); William Schallert (Harry): Karl Swenson (Reverend Hoskins); George Kennedy (Gutierrez); Dan Sheridan (Deputy Glynn); Bill Raisch (One Arm); William Mims (Deputy in Bar); Martin Garralaga (Old Man); Lalo Rios.

      Hollywood, and Kirk Douglas in particular, can point to this film with pride. While it is a self-consciously arty Western, it still remains an effective narrative of the alienation of the cowboy in contemporary society. This film's view of the cowboy is that he is a professional who has outlived his usefulness in today's mechanical set-up.
      "Kirk Douglas has produced, and stars in, that rarity of rarities in films today--an honest tragedy that makes bold comment on the plight of man in an overmechanized world.... Dalton Trumbo has fashioned for him the finest Western script since High Noon [1952, q.v.] and The Gunfighter [1950, q.v.]. As in those earlier films, the West has been stripped of every legend except its legendary beauty; and in their place is the sad realization that the breed of men we once admired have become misfits in a society that only dimly comprehends their values" (Arthur Knight, Saturday Review).
      Wandering cowboy Jack Burns (Douglas) finds it difficult to live in the wide-open spaces in today's mechanized society. When his best and only pal, Paul Bondi (Kane), is jailed for helping Mexicans cross the border illegally into the states, Jack deliberately causes a disorder so that he will be jailed with his friend. When Bondi refuses to be broken out of jail--he is married and wants to serve out his time peaceably--Jack goes it alone. He escapes to the hills with his horse Whisky. The sheriff (Matthau) no longer combats lawbreakers in the old-fashioned way; he drives a jeep and an Air Force helicopter, and walkie talkies provide his posse. Burns manages to shoot down the plane, but later, when trying to cross a highway into Mexico, his horse balks and soon both the animal and Burns are hit by a big truck. The sheriff arrives to put the horse out of its misery, and while Jack is being carted away in an ambulance, the law enforcer speaks a few words of testimony for the lamentable cowboy.

Kirk Douglas in <u>Lonely Are the Brave</u> (1962).

"This is a picture not only stirring to watch but stirring to
think about. There aren't too many around like that" (Paul V.
Beckley, New York Herald-Tribune). But audiences of the sixties
much preferred to watch the antics of John "Duke" Wayne rather
than such sober stuff as Lonely Are the Brave. More the pity as
this film was a well-intentioned and well-wrought feature.

THE LONG RIFLE AND THE TOMAHAWK   see   LAST OF THE
MOHICANS

THE LOST PATROL   see   BAD LANDS

LUST FOR GOLD   (Columbia, 1949)*   90 min.

     Producer-director, S. Sylvan Simon; based on the novel
Thunder God's Gold by Barry Storm; screenplay, Ted Sherdeman,
Richard English; art director, Carl Anderson; music director,
Morris Stoloff; camera, Archie Stout; editor, Gene Havlick.
     Ida Lupino (Julia Thomas); Glenn Ford (Jacob Walz); Gig
Young (Pete Thomas); William Prince (Barry Storm); Edgar Bu-
chanan (Wiser); Will Geer (Deputy Covin); Paul Ford (Sheriff
Early); Jay Silverheels (Coroner); Eddy Waller (Coroner); Will
Wright (Parsons); Virginia Mullen (Matron); Antonio Moreno (Ramon
Peralta); Arthur Hunnicutt (Ludi); Myrna Dell (Lucille); Tom Tyler
(Luke); Elspeth Dudgeon (Mrs. Bannister); Paul E. Burns (Bill
Bates); Hayden Rorke (Floyd Buckley).
     *Filmed in Sepia.

     Director S. Sylvan Simon replaced George Marshall on this
forgotten and unsuccessful film which was issued in Sepia-tone.
Unfortunately the motion picture got off to a bad start due to a
rash of publicity when novelist Barry Storm, from whose book,
Thunder God's Gold, the screenplay was derived, sued Columbia
Pictures, charging plagiarism among other counts. Storm's work
was based on fact, and concerned the fabulous Lost Dutchman gold
mine, still hidden somewhere in Arizona.
     To unfold the narrative, the film has William Prince as
Barry Storm relating the events. There is Jacob Waltz (Ford)
who discovers the mine and who willingly kills to keep it his,
while Julia Thomas (Lupino) is the scheming woman who attempts
to seduce him in order to obtain control of the prized property for
herself and her no-good husband (Young). A modern story was interpolated into this tale of the Old West, with a descendant of
Waltz searching for the mine and being mysteriously thwarted in a
number of ways.
     The plotline was the type favored so much on TV's long-
running series, "Death Valley Days."

McLINTOCK!   (United Artists, 1963) C 127 min.

    Producer, Michael Wayne; director, Andrew V. McLaglen;
screenplay, James Edward Grant; music, Frank De Vol; songs, De
Vol and By Dunham; Dunham; art directors, Hal Pereira, Eddie
Imazu; set decorators, Sam Comer, Darrell Silvera; costumes,
Frank C. Beetson, Jr.; assistant director, Frank Parmenter; sound,
Jack Solomon; camera, William H. Clothier; editor, Otho Lovering.
    John Wayne (George Washington McLintock); Maureen O'Hara
(Katherine McLintock); Yvonne De Carlo (Louise Warren); Patrick
Wayne (Devlin Warren); Stefanie Powers (Becky McLintock); Jack
Kruschen (Birnbaum); Chill Wills (Drago); Jerry Van Dyke (Matt
Douglas, Jr.); Edgar Buchanan (Bunny Dull); Bruce Cabot (Ben
Sage); Perry Lopez (Davey Elk); Michael Pate (Puma); Strother
Martin (Agard); Gordon Jones (Matt Douglas); Robert Lowery
(Governor); Ed Faulkner (Young Ben Sage); H. W. Gim (Ching);
Alissa Wayne (Alice Warren); Chuck Roberson (Sheriff Lord); Hal
Needham (Carter); Pedro Gonzales, Jr. (Carlos); Hank Worden
(Jeth); Leo Gordon (Jones); Mary Patterson (Beth); John Hamilton
(Fauntleroy); Ralph Volkie (Loafer); Kari Noven (Millie); John Stan-
ley (Running Buffalo); Mari Blanchard (Camille); Bob Steele (Train
Conductor); Dan Borgaze (Loafer).

    Andrew V. McLaglen, the son of actor Victor McLaglen, had
worked as assistant director to John Farrow on Hondo (1954) [q.v.],

Stefanie Powers, Pat Wayne, John Wayne and Maureen O'Hara in
McLintock (1963).

a production made successful by star John Wayne. It was Wayne who hired McLaglen to direct this Batjac production, which was shot in Arizona near Nogales, Tombstone, and Tucson. James Earl Grant, who had scripted Hondo, wrote the story, a rough, tough Western with a good deal of action and including an amusing mud fight sequence. The public responded to their decades-old hero, the Duke, to the tune of $4.5 million in domestic distributors rentals.

John Wayne plays George Washington McLintock, a large (in every way) ranch owner, who is asked by the Comanches to speak for them when the government attempts to put them under the thumb of an Indian agent. Land baron McLintock even has a town named after him, but his wife (O'Hara) has left him because of his past romantic entanglements. Now Katherine (O'Hara) is dating the territorial governor (Lowery). She returns, however, to the McLintock spread because their Eastern-schooled daughter (Powers) is being courted by rivals Devlin Warren (Patrick Wayne) and Matt Douglas, Jr. (Van Dyke). Devlin is the son of McLintock's housekeeper, the comely Louise Warren (De Carlo). It is with Louise that McLintock becomes drunk and tumbles down a flight of stairs, much to the chagrin of Katherine. Meanwhile, the train which brought Katherine and Becky (Powers) home also brought back the imprisoned Comanche chiefs whom McLintock had helped to set free. After a Fourth of July celebration, McLintock chases Katherine all over the town and finally catches and spanks her. He informs the spunky woman that she is free to divorce him; but instead she returns to live at the ranch.

McLintock! shovels up songs, slapstick, civic spirit and a drawing room comedy cut to the size of a range war. It is dedicated to the proposition that where there's a will, there's a Wayne, or even several of them. McLintock! is produced by son Michael, 29, casts daughter Aissa, 7, in a minor role, and features heir apparent Patrick Wayne, 24. But, at 56, Big John is still king. "In Wayne's West, a bit of rough-and-tumble is all it takes to keep a girl's mind off divorce" (Time).

What makes Wayne's Westerns so appealing is that they rarely, at least after the mid-fifties, ever take themselves too seriously. There is a jaunty air which allows scripters, directors, and players to kid the genre while showing respect for it. The fact that many regular cast members of Wayne films are offcamera pals of the star shows in the relaxed, warm interplay between the characters. And in the seventies it is refreshing to be able to escape into a make-believe world where a rugged he-man like John Wayne makes right with might in a most friendly but determined way.

THE MAGNIFICENT SEVEN   (United Artists, 1960) C 126 min.

Executive producer, Walter Mirisch; associate producer, Lou Morheim; producer-director, John Sturges; based on the Japanese film Seven Samurai (1954); screenplay, William Roberts; art director,

Yul Brynner in <u>The Magnificent Seven</u> (1960).

Edward Fitzgerald; set decorator, Rafael Suarez; music, Elmer
Bernstein; assistant directors, Robert Relyea, Jaime Contreras;
wardrobe, Bert Henrikson; makeup, Emile LaVigne, Daniel Striepke;
sound, Jack Solomon, Rafael Esparaza; special effects, Milt Rice;
camera, Charles Lang, Jr.; editor, Ferris Webster.

Yul Brynner (Chris); Eli Wallach (Calvera); Steve McQueen
(Vin); Horst Buchholz (Chico); Charles Bronson (O'Reilly); Robert
Vaughn (Lee); Brad Dexter (Harry Luck); James Coburn (Britt);
Vladimir Sokoloff (Old Man); Rosenda Monteros (Petra); Jorge Mar-
tinez De Hoyos (Hilario); Whit Bissell (Chamlee); Val Avery (Henry);
Bing Russell (Robert); Rico Alaniz (Sotero); Robert Wilke (Wallace).

"... A rip-roaring, rootin' tootin' western with lots of bite
and tang and old-fashioned abandon." That was how Variety des-
cribed this Hollywood adaptation of Akira Kurosawa's Japanese
classic, Seven Samurai (1954).

Updated to the old West, the American version of that chronicle now takes place along the Rio Grande River in the post-Civil
War period. A group of beleagured Mexican farmers hire gunman
Chris (Brynner) to protect them from a gang of bandits led by
Calvera (Wallach). Chris takes their money and hires six others
(McQueen, Buchholz, Bronson, Vaughn, Dexter and Coburn) to join
him in the venture. Before long the gunslingers and the townfolk
have developed a strong rapport, which sees them through the
sieges and trickery of Calvera and his supporters. In the final
showdown, Calvera and three of Chris' men are among those killed.
Chris and sidekick Vin (McQueen) leave town as the victors, while
cohort Chico (Buchholz) remains behind to settle down with a local
girl.

While some fourth estate sources carped that the American
rendition of the Japanese masterpiece dissipated the virtues of the
original, there were those like Paul V. Beckley (New York Herald-
Tribune) who reasoned, "An interesting example of international
cross fertilization in film.... Americanizing a familiar and formal
Oriental theme seems to be the first conscious formalizing of the
Western as a classic movie form. This has not numbed or blunted
the action; on the contrary, by discarding the suprise element in the
plot [the moviemakers] have both dignified it and enabled themselves
to give the individual incidents and characterizations more finish."

The Magnificent Seven was a fine showcase for the rugged
talents of Continental film star Yul Brynner, and this crowd-pleasing
action picture did a great deal for the burgeoning careers of many
others in the cast.

So successful was the 1960 film that six years later United
Artists produced a sequel, Return of the Seven (1966), again head-
lining Yul Brynner in the title role. Unlike its predecessor, which
emphasized the psychological aspects of the characters (e.g., Chris
as a drifter who could not be a cowpoke, O'Reilly as a man who
loves children, Chico as a neurotic, etc.), the follow-up stressed
hot and heavy action with the flimsiest of character motivation. This
Burt Kennedy-directed production finds Chico joining with six others
to stop desperadoes from tormenting the peasants of a Mexican

village.   In the mass violence tradition of the sixties, the shootout
at the finale is filled with visual and audio carnage.

Three years later the same producing company released <u>Guns</u>
<u>of the Magnificent Seven</u> (1969), this time filmed in Spain and star-
ring former screen heavy George Kennedy in the lead part.   Many
thought this Paul-Wendkos-directed Western had a good deal to offer
its viewers.   In contrast, the final sequel to date, <u>The Magnificent</u>
<u>Seven Ride</u> (1972), starring Lee Van Cleef, had little to distinguish it
from a myriad of other spaghetti Westerns: the usual pulsating
music score, the angered hombres, the smoking six-shooters, the
rising dust as the outlaws ride through, in, and out of town.   Plans
for a projected teleseries based on the property never materialized.

THE MAGNIFICENT SEVEN RIDE   see   THE MAGNIFICENT SEVEN

MAJOR DUNDEE   (Columbia, 1965)   C   134 min.

Producer, Jerry Bresler; director, Sam Peckinpah; story,
Harry Julian Fink; screenplay, Fink, Oscar Saul, Peckinpah; music,
Daniele Amfitheatrof; song, Amfitheatrof and Ned Washington; art
director, Al Ybarra; costumes, Tom Dawson; assistant directors,
Floyd Joyer, John Veitch; sound, Charles J. Rice, James Z.
Flaster; special effects, August Lohman; camera, Sam Leavitt;
editors, William A. Lyon, Don Starling, Howard Kunin.

Charlton Heston (Major Amos Dundee); Richard Harris (Cap-
tain Ben Tyreen); Jim Hutton (Lieutenant Graham); James Coburn
(Samuel Potts); Michael Anderson, Jr. (Tim Ryan); Senta Berger
(Teresa Santiago); Mario Adorf (Sergeant Gomez); Brock Peters
(Aesop); Warren Oates (O. W. Hadley); Ben Johnson (Sergeant Chil-
lum); R. G. Armstrong (Reverend Dahlstrom); L. Q. Jones (Arthur
Hadley); Slim Pickens (Wiley); Karl Swenson (Captain Wallar);
Michael Pate (Sierra Charriba); John Davis Chandler (Jimmy Lee
Benteen); Dub Taylor (Priam); Jose Carlos Ruiz (Riago); Aurora
Clavell (Melinche).

<u>Major Dundee</u>, in retrospect, would be just a small-scale
prelude to the production problems and controversy that would surround director Peckinpah's <u>The Wild Bunch</u> (1969) [q.v.].   There
were so many conflicts on the Mexican locations that near the end
of filming Heston and Peckinpah agreed to pay personally for reshooting some key scenes that Columbia had ordered done their
way.   When the studio recut the film later, Peckinpah wanted his
name removed from the credits.   Ten minutes or more was cut
from the release print after press screenings.

Near the end of the Civil War, Sierra Charriba (Pate) and
his band of renegade Apaches massacre a cavalry post in New
Mexico.   Nearby, Major Dundee (Heston) is commandant of an outpost with four hundred Confederate prisoners, Union deserters,
desperadoes, and convicted thieves.   Dundee adds volunteers to his
group from the fort and decides to retaliate against the Apaches.

Mario Adorf and Charlton Heston in <u>Major Dundee</u> (1965).

Captain Benjamin Tyreen (Harris), who had killed a prison guard,
agrees to assist Dundee in leading this bizarre expedition. Once in
Mexico the conflicts between the two officers intensify, especially
when they both become attracted to widowed Teresa Santiago (Berger).
Later Dundee is wounded but still leads the attack against Charriba's
redskins. This battle won, the group must now face an attack force
of French troops. Tyreen makes a solo sweep into enemy territory
and is killed. As Dundee crosses the river back into the United
States, he has a contingent of only eleven survivors.
        Many were willing to admit that Peckinpah had a noble
scheme in mind for this film and that it had been sabotaged along
the way. "Rugged action but too many delaying sequences ...
Somewhere in the development of this production the central premise
was sidetracked and a maze of little-meaning action substituted"
(Variety). "Major Dundee, a sprawling Western, gets lost on the
trail and never does find its way, thanks to a confusing continuity
and several meaningless sub-plot sidetracks.... The viewer is
soon forced into a constant guessing game in the effort to bridge
actions, whys and wherefores. (An off-screen narration, ostensibly
drawn from the diary of one of Dundee's troopers, adds beautifully
to the over-all fog.)" (New York Herald-Tribune).

THE MAN TRAILER (Columbia, 1934) 59 min.

        Director-story-screenplay, Lambert Hillyer; camera, Benja-
min Kline; editor, Gene Milford.
        Charles "Buck" Jones (Dan Lee); Cecilia Parker (Sally Ryan);
Arthur Vinton (Burk); Clarence Geldert (Sheriff Ryan); Steve Clark
(Bishop); Charles West (Gorman); Silver the Horse (Himself); and:
Tom Forman, Lew Meshan.

        Many uninformed viewers and critics insist that the B
Western has a type of picture in which almost every film was a
carbon copy of the others. Of course, the assembly line effect on
the genre in the late forties and early fifties added to this opinion.
However, an actual survey of the product prior to this period reveals there was a great deal of freshness and creativity, even when
ideas were re-used. Generally each film adopted a new approach,
making the follow-up film different in many ways from its predecessors. An example of this is The Man Trailer, a picture Buck Jones
made late in his first series for Columbia. It was a plot concept
director-writer Lambert Hillyer borrowed from his old boss William
S. Hart, who had used the same premise in The Return of Draw
Egan (1916) [q.v.].
        In The Man Trailer Dan Lee (Jones) is a fugitive from Texas
law, unjustly accused of having committed murder during a recent
cattle war (in the silent film, Hart was a true outlaw). While on
the lam, Dan prevents a gang from making off with the proceeds of
a stagecoach robbery and also saves the sheriff's daughter (Parker).
As a reward, Lee is made the sheriff of a small nearby town and
soon wins the girl's heart. The outlaw chief, however, has other

plans and warns Dan that he will expose his past if he attempts to prevent the robbery of a Wells Fargo station. A troubled Dan admits his past to Sally (Parker), who stands by him. When Lee and his horse are captured by the outlaws, they make their escape and lead the posse to the outlaws' hideout where a shootout ensues. Having captured the lawbreakers, Dan learns from a Texas marshal that he has been exonerated. As in The Return of Draw Egan the story ends with Dan still marshal and retaining the girl's affections.

Hillyer's sensible script and capacity to locate excellent outdoor setups added greatly to the over-all effect of this motion picture. Combined with its adult plotline--Jones even kisses Miss Parker!--The Man Trailer found a ready audience.

MAN WITHOUT A STAR   (Universal, 1955) C   89 min.

Producer, Aaron Rosenberg; director, King Vidor; based on the novel by Dee Linford; screenplay, Borden Chase, D. D. Beauchamp; art directors, Alexander Golitzen, Richard H. Riedel; music supervisor, Joseph Gershenson; title song sung by Frankie Laine; camera, Russell Metty; editor, Virgil Vogel.

Kirk Douglas (Dempsey Rae); Jeanne Crain (Reed Bowman); Claire Trevor (Idonee); William Campbell (Jeff Jimson); Richard Boone (Steve Miles); Jay C. Flippen (Strap Davis); Myrna Hansen (Tess Cassidy); Mara Corday (Moccasin Mary); Eddy C. Waller (Tom Cassidy); Sheb Wooley (Latigo); George Wallace (Tom Carter); Frank Chase (Little Waco); Paul Birch (Mark Tolliver); Roy Barcroft (Sheriff Olson); William "Bill" Phillips (Cookie).

When Universal remade this entry as A Man Called Gannon (1969), with Michael Sarrazin, Tony Franciosa, and Susan Oliver, one could appreciate all the more the original as directed by King Vidor.

Using the symbolic barbed wire of civilization, this film traces the passing of the free, wide-open Old West. Happy-go-lucky wanderer Dempsey Rae (Douglas) keeps chasing away from civilization, moving further and further Westward. He meets Jeff Jimson (Campbell) who accepts Dempsey as his mentor. The two pair up, with Dempsey jubilant about showing off his skills as a real cowboy. The duo accept jobs working for attractive Reed Bowman (Crain) who proves to be a duplistic lass, belying her innocent looks. When Reed becomes involved in range wars, Dempsey wants no part of it and goes to town where he encounters Idonee (Trevor), the heart-of-gold madam. Later Dempsey is attacked by Miles (Boone), his successor at Reed's ranch. At this point Dempsey drops his smile and joins with the local ranchers to stop Bowman and her men. At the finale, since there is no place to hang his star of hope, Dempsey wanders off into the distance, his future very uncertain.

Thanks to the bouncy performance by Douglas, who never once twirls a six-shooter in this entry, but plucks the strings of a guitar and even sings a song, Man without a Star is well worth the investment of time to view.

MANHUNT   see   FROM HELL TO TEXAS

MARK OF THE AVENGER   see   THE MYSTERIOUS RIDER (1938)

MARK OF ZORRO   (United Artists, 1920)   seven reels

     Producer, Douglas Fairbanks, Sr.; director, Fred Niblo;
based on the novel The Curse of Capistrano by Johnston McCulley;
screenplay by Elton Thomas [Fairbanks]; camera, William C. Mc-
Gann, Harry Thorpe.
     Douglas Fairbanks, Sr. (Senor Zorro/Don Diego Vega);
Marguerite de la Motte (Lolita); Robert McKim (Captain Juan Ramon);
Noah Beery (Sergeant Pedro); Charles H. Mailes (Don Carlos Pulido);
Claire McDowell (Donna Catalina); George Periolat (Governor Alvarado); Walt Whitman (Fra Felipe); Sidney de Grey (Don Pulido Ale-
jandao); Tote Du Crow (Bernardo).

MARK OF ZORRO   (Twentieth Century-Fox, 1940)   93 min.

     Producer, Raymond Griffith; director, Rouben Mamoulian;
based on the novel The Curse of Capistrano by Johnston McCulley;
screenplay, John Tainton Foote; adaptors, Garrett Fort, Bess
Meredyth; assistant director, Sidney Bowen; art directors, Richard
Day, Joseph C. Wright; set decorator, Thomas Little; music, Al-
fred Newman; costumes, Travis Banton; sound, W. D. Flick, Roger
Heman; camera, Arthur Miller; editor, Robert Bischoff.
     Tyrone Power (Diego Vega); Linda Darnell (Lolita Quintero);
Basil Rathbone (Esteban Pasquale); Gale Sondergaard (Inez Quintero);
Eugene Pallette (Fra Felipe); J. Edward Bromberg (Don Luis Quin-
tero); Montagu Love (Don Alejandro Vega); Janet Beecher (Senora
Isabella Vega); Robert Lowery (Rodrigo); Chris-Pin Martin (Turnkey);
George Regas (Sergeant Gonzales); Belle Mitchell (Maria); John
Bleifer (Pedro); Frank Puglia (Proprietor); Pedro de Cordoba (Don
Miguel); Guy D'Ennery (Don Jose); Eugene Borden (Officer of the
Day); Fred Malatesta, Fortunio Bonanova (Sentries); Harry Worth,
Gino Corrado, Lucio Villegas (Caballeros); Paul Sutton (Soldier);
Michael Ted North (Bit Part); Ralph Byrd (Student/Officer); Franco
Corsaro (Orderly); Hector Sarno (Peon at Inn); Stanley Andrews
(Commanding Officer); Victor Kilian (Boatman).

THE MARK OF ZORRO   (ABC-TV)   C   74 min.

     Producers, Robert C. Thompson, Rodrick Paul; director, Don
McDougall; teleplay, Brian Taggert; music, Don Frontiere; music
supervisor, Lionel Newman; assistant director, Joe Ellis; camera,
Jack Wolff; editor, Bill Martin.
     Frank Langella (Don Diego/Zorro); Ricardo Montalban (Captain
Estaban); Gilbert Roland (Alejandro Vega); Yvonne De Carlo (Isabella

Vega); Louise Sorel (Inez); Anne Archer (Teresa); Robert Middleton
(Luis); Tom Lacy (Fra Felipe); George Cervera (Sergeant Gonzales),
and: Jay Hamer, Inez Peres, John Rose, Robert Carricart.

In 1920 movie-stage star Douglas Fairbanks decided to make
a departure from his usual comedy roles. For his vehicle he selected Johnston McCulley's novel The Curse of Capistrano, which
featured the Robin-Hood-like character Zorro who avenged evil and
upheld justice. (The premise had already been turned into a comic
strip by the time Fairbanks decided to utilize it.) The resultant
Fairbanks picture was a combination Western-comedy-swashbuckler
in which acrobatic Doug portrayed a foppish young nobleman, Don
Diego. It started a new trend in filmmaking.
In Mark of Zorro, Fairbanks had a field day with his dual
role as the highbrow snob who is also the masked Robin Hood,
fighting the aggressive military to aid the poor in Old California.
Charles H. Mailes and Claire McDowell played his parents who
were embarrassed and disgusted by their son's passive ways, while
the lovely Marguerite de la Motte was the young maiden who detests
Diego but adores the dashing Zorro. Robert McKim was cast as
the evil Captain Juan Ramon who constantly was engaging in sword
duels with the too agile Zorro. At the finale he throws down his
sword and decides to be friends (!) with the masked man.
The public and the critics alike adored the film with its mixture of comedy and action. This commercial formula Fairbanks
would use successfully throughout the remainder of the decade. The
feature also provided the star with many opportunities to demonstrate
his physical prowess--thus there were many fights, duels, and bal-
cony leapings in the screenplay (by Fairbanks) as well as a long
chase sequence near the film's finale.
Mark of Zorro proved so commercially viable that Fairbanks
made a sequel to the venture, entitled Don Q, Son of Zorro (1925), in
which he used an Australian stock whip as a weapon. The film, unfortunately, was not up to its lively predecessor.
The celluloid character of Zorro lay dormant until 1936 when
Republic revived it in the feature, The Bold Cabellero [q.v.], filmed
in a two-color process. There Robert Livingston played the masked
man who fought against unjust taxation and a false murder charge.
Fencing master Fred Cavens instructed Livingston in the fine art of
dueling for this film.
The following year Republic filmed Zorro Rides Again [q.v.],
a twelve-chapter serial directed by William Witney and John English.
Handsome John Carroll played James Vega, alias Zorro, and Noah
Beery (who appeared in the 1920 Mark of Zorro) was the villain.
In 1939 Republic again used Witney and English to direct another
twelve-chapter serial, Zorro's Fighting Legion [q.v.], with lithe
Reed Hadley as Don Diego Vega (Zorro).
In 1940 Darryl F. Zanuck hired prestigious director Rouben
Mamoulian to direct a remake of Mark of Zorro. It proved an
artistic and financial success, retaining much of the flavor of the
Fairbanks versions, although Tyrone Power was far better in the
foppish role than as the dashing and athletic Zorro. Mamoulian

accented the relationship between Zorro and Lolita Quintero (here
Linda Darnell) with a number of well-composed close-up shots.
The main asset of the feature is the climactic duel between Zorro
and the chief villain, Esteban Pasquale (Rathbone).   It emerged as
one of the finest examples of swordplay on the screen.   Rathbone
did much of his own work in the sequence and technical director
Fred Cavens supervised the proceedings.   Power was doubled in the
important dueling interplay by Fred Cavens' son, Albert.

In 1944 Republic produced Zorro's Black Whip [q. v.], directed
in twelve chapters by Spencer Gordon Bennet and Wallace Grissell.
The character of Zorro, as audiences had come to expect him, was
nowhere to be seen, although Linda Stirling played a female masked
avenger.   Three years later Republic turned out a thirteen-chapter
cliffhanger, Son of Zorro [q. v.], directed by Bennet and Fred C.
Brannon.   Here George Turner played a Westerner who decides to
resurrect the Zorro character to defeat corruption in the post-Civil
War West.   Republic manufactured its last cliffhanger in the series,
the twelve-chapter Ghost of Zorro, in 1949.   Directed by Fred C.
Brannon, it starred Clayton Moore (later to be famous as TV's
"The Lone Ranger") as an engineer and descendant of Zorro who
employs the disguise of the masked man to fight a crime leader
(Roth) in the Old West so that the telegraph line may be completed.
As with past Zorro serials, the entry was re-edited and issued as
a feature.

In 1959 Walt Disney produced an ABC-TV series called
"Zorro" with Guy Williams in the title role and Henry Calvin as
Sergeant Garcia.   It lasted for one season (39 episodes), but was
resurrected later as a popular TV re-run.   In the 1960-1961 video
season, Disney ran four one-hour segments of "Zorro" on his weekly
TV program, again with Williams as the masked hero.   In 1960
Disney's Buena Vista distribution company issued The Sign of Zorro
to theatres.   Directed by Norman Foster and Lewis R. Foster, the
film was a paste-up of aired segments from the ABC-TV series.

In 1961 the Zorro character was revived in Europe in Zorro,
a Spanish production with Frank Latimore in the title role.   Two
years later, Latimore repeated the role in another Spanish-made
film, Zorro the Avenger.   That year also saw the release of two
other European-made Zorro films, Zorro e i Tre Moschettierei
(Zorro and the Three Musketeers) and Zorro contre Maciste (Zorro
vs. Maciste).   The former was produced in Italy and directed by
Luigi Capuano.   In it Gordon Scott played Zorro, who joins the
Three Musketeers (Gianni Rizzo, Livio Lorenzon, Giacomo Rossi
Stuart) and D'Artagnan (Franco Fantasia) to expose a traitor.   It
played on TV as Mark of the Musketeers.   Zorro contre Maciste
was turned out by Italian-Roma Film and was directed by Umberto
Lenzi.   Here Sergio Ciane (a. k. a. Alan Steel) as Maciste (better
known as Samson) fights with and against Zorro (Pierre Brice).
The film appears on TV as Samson and the Slave Queen.

Another Italian film, Three Swords of Zorro, turned up in
1964 and in it Guy Stockwell portrayed a descendant of Zorro who
fights corrupt politicians in California.   That same year Tony Russell donned the mask and black cape of the crusader to fight a

tyrant in the Italian-made Behind the Mask of Zorro. Four years
later George Ardisson took over the role in Zorro le Renard, an
Italian-made quickie directed by Guido Zurli.
      Over the years there have been many other Zorro-derived
swashbucklers churned out in Continental and South American
countries, but the nod for originality must go to the American producers who conceived The Erotic Adventures of Zorro (1972). With
a pornographic slant to the decades-old plot, it retold the famed
exploits of the daring swordsman, with the focus clearly on the bedroom capers. Having an X-rating, it certainly appealed to its
designated market.
      In 1973 El Hijo Del Zorro was made as an Italian-Spanish
co-production. It was directed by Gian Franco Baldanelle and
featured Robert Widenar, Elisa Ramrez, and Fernando Sandro.
      Mark of Zorro, the original property that started the Zorro
craze, was exhumed for television and limped onto the small screen
in the fall of 1974 as an entry on ABC-TV's "Tuesday Movie of the
Week." Filmed late in the summer of that year in Tucson, Arizona,
the film was trimmed to 74 minutes but its creaky plotline showed
through all too clearly. Frank Langella was mediocre as both Diego
and Zorro. Louise Sorel, as the heroine who tumbles for Zorro's
charm, and Yvonne De Carlo, as Diego's mother, were wasted. At
least the presence of Ricardo Montalban and Gilbert Roland gave the
production some class. Montalban was seen as an evil captain who
works with corrupt governor Robert Middleton to rule a portion of
Old California. Roland engaged in a sword duel with the villain and,
despite his advanced middle age, was as dashing and athletic as he
had been as a star in the silent cinema.
      Most recently, France's Alain Delon starred in a new Zorro,
bringing the weatherbeaten property up to the mid-seventies.

MARKED MEN (Universal, 1919) 5 reels

      Producer, P. A. Powers; director, Jack (John) Ford; based
on the story "The Three Godfathers" by Peter B. Kyne; screenplay,
H. Tipton Steel; camera, John W. Brown; editors, Frank Lawrence,
Frank Atkinson.
      Harry Carey (Cheyenne Harry); J. Farrell MacDonald (Tom
"Placer" McGraw); Joe Harris (Tom Gibbons); Winifred Westover
(Ruby Merrill); Ted Brooks (Tony Garcia); Charles Lemoyne (Sheriff
Pete Cushing); David Kirby (Warden "Bruiser" Kelly).

      Peter B. Kyne was the first Western story writer whose works
were regularly purchased for the screen. His story "The Three Godfathers" became one of the most often filmed sagebrush works.
Marked Men was the third film version of the story and the first of
two screen works done by John Ford from the Kyne tale.
      In this, Cheyenne Harry (Carey) and two outlaw pals (Mc-
Donald and Harris) escape from jail and meet up at a mining camp.
Together they execute a bank robbery but are chased out of town
and into the Mojave Desert. There they come across a dying mother

(Westover) and her infant and they decide to give up their freedom
to save the child.   Only Cheyenne Harry survives the trek back to
civilization with the baby.
    This Universal-Special five-reeler was John Ford's (he was
billed as Jack Ford then) favorite of his early films.
    The other versions of the story are Broncho Billy and the
Baby (1909) [q.v.], The Three Godfathers (1916) [q.v.], directed by
Edward Le Saint; Hell's Heroes (1930) [q.v.], Three Godfathers
(1935) [q.v.], and Ford's 1948 version, Three Godfathers [q.v.],
dedicated to the late Harry Carey.
    The working title for Marked Men was The Trail of Shadows.

MELODY RANCH   (Republic, 1940)   84 min.

    Associate producer, Sol C. Siegel; director, Joseph Santley;
screen play, Jack Moffitt, F. Hugh Herbert; art director, Joseph
Victor Mackay; music director, Raoul Kraushaar; songs, Jule Styne
and Eddie Cherkose; camera, Joseph August; editor, Murray Seldeen.
    Gene Autry (Gene); Jimmy Durante (Cornelius J. Courtney);
Ann Miller (Julie); Barton MacLane (Mark Wildhack); Vera Vague
(Veronica Whipple); George "Gabby" Hayes (Pop); Jerome Cowan
(Tommy Summerville); Mary Lee (Penny); Joseph Sawyer (Jasper
Wildhack); Horace McMahon (Bud Wildhack); Clarence Wilson (Judge
Henderson); William Benedict (Slim).

    Despite his enormous and seemingly enduring popularity,
Gene Autry was not, even among the cowpoke stars, a very convincing actor and his singing left a good bit to be desired.   (Ironically he is one of the best selling recording stars of all-time.)
Republic often took great pains to bolster his films with good supporting casts, tight editing, and medium-priced production numbers.
These musical interludes actually saved the studio a good deal of
money, because it was far cheaper to shoot a cowpoke and his band
in front of some cactus doing a reel of songs rather than a reel of
dialogue and/or action.
    For this film the radio motif was added to give the Western
a wide audience interest, and several big names (Jimmy Durante,
Vera Vague and Ann Miller) supplemented the line-up for marquee
lure.
    The simple premise finds Gene, a big-time radio singer, re-
turning home to his small Western town as an honorary sheriff.
He soon discovers there is more to his job than merely fulfilling an
empty title.   The locale is under the control of three brothers
(MacLane, Sawyer and McMahon).   Before the finale Gene has
cleaned-up the racketeers and has won Julie's (Miller) heart.
    Besides the comedy patter of Durante and "your darn tootin"
Hayes, there were assorted musical numbers, including "We Never
Dream the Same Dream Twice" by Autry and Fred Rose.   The
sharp viewer will note that in the trolley car crash stunt, the
double for Autry is none other than John Wayne.
    Nineteen-forty was also the year that Gene, riding high on

the box-office range, was loaned out to Twentieth Century-Fox for
Jane Withers' Shooting High.

THE MIDNIGHT STAGE   see   ON THE NIGHT STAGE

MIRACLE IN THE SAND   see   THE THREE GODFATHERS (1936)

THE MIRACLE RIDER   (Mascot, 1935)   fifteen chapters

Producer, Nat Levine; supervisor, Victor Zobel; directors,
Armand Schaefer, B. Reeves Eason; story, Barney Sarecky, Wellyn
Totman, Gerald Geraghty; screenplay, John Rathmell; sound, Terry
Kellum.

Tom Mix (Tom Morgan); Joan Gale (Ruth); Charles Middleton
(Zaroff); Jason Robards, Sr. (Carlton); Bob Kortman (Longboat);
Edward Earle (Adams); Edward Hearn (Janss); Robert Frazier (Chief
Black Wing); Tom London (Sewell); Niles Welsh (Metzger); Edmund
Cobb (Vining); Ernie S. Adams (Stelter); Max Wagner (Morley);
Charles King (Hatton); Black Hawk (Chief Two Hawks); George
Chesebro (Crossman); Jack Rockwell (Rogers); Chief Standing Bear
(Chief Last Elk); Stanley Price (Chapman); George Burton (Mort).

Chapters: 1) The Vanishing Indian; 2) The Firebird Strikes;
3) The Flying Knife; 4) A Race with Death; 5) Double Barreled
Doom; 6) Thundering Hoofs; 7) The Dragnet; 8) Guerrilla Warfare;
9) The Silver Band; 10) Signal Fires; 11) A Traitor Dies; 12)
Danger Rides with Death; 13) The Secret of X-94; 14) Between Two
Fires; 15) Justice Rides the Plains.

Tom Mix in The Miracle Rider (1935).

By 1935, after ending a successful movie series at Universal, Tom Mix had no real interest in returning to the cinema. The aging cowboy hero was content to tour with his circus. Mascot owner-producer Nat Levine, however, knew a serial top-lining Mix meant big money. He convinced "the Idol of Every Schoolboy in the World" to return to films by playing on his conservative political opinions and creating a film project for him which would be "fit entertainment" for children. The result was the fifteen-chapter The Miracle Rider, Mix's only serial and his final film appearance.

Mix played Tom Morgan, the captain of the Texas Rangers who is also known as The Miracle Rider, a man who is made the blood brother of an Indian tribe because he has so frequently aided them. Meanwhile, a crook named Zaroff (Middleton) tries to occupy the Indians' land because they contain deposits of a powerful explosive. A traitorous Indian (Kortman), who wants to be chief, convinces the present Indian leader (Frazer) that Tom Morgan is their enemy; and the chief is killed in an attack on Morgan. The chief's daughter Ruth (Gale), however, falls in love with Tom and together they expose Zaroff and his gang.

The serial was made in one month at a cost of $80,000, half of which went to pay Mix's salary. The film grossed over $1 million and its feature version was in release in the U.S. throughout the early forties and in some foreign countries as late as 1960.

Compared to the later Republic serials, this entry was a sparse offering and rather primitive in many ways: it lacked a proper music score, the acting styles were jerky, and the suspense plotline was not too convincing.

THE MISFITS (United Artists, 1961) 124 min.

Producer, Frank E. Taylor; director, John Huston; screenplay, Arthur Miller; music, Alex North; assistant director, Carl Beringer; art directors, Stephen Grimes, William Newberry; camera, Russell Metty; editor, George Tomasini.

Clark Gable (Gay Langland); Marilyn Monroe (Roslyn Taber); Montgomery Clift (Perce Howland); Thelma Ritter (Isabelle Steers); Eli Wallach (Guido); James Barton (Old Man in the Bar); Estelle Winwood (Church Lady); Kevin McCarthy (Raymond Taber); Dennis Shaw (Young Boy in Bar); Philip Mitchell (Charles Steers); Walter Ramage (Old Groom); Peggy Barton (Young Bride); J. Lewis Smith (Fresh Cowboy in Bar); Mariette Tree (Susan); Bobby La Salle (Bartender); Ryall Bowker (Man in Bar); Ralph Roberts (Ambulance Driver).

This production was the most expensive film ever made in black-and-white. The feature cost over $4,000,000 and barely grossed that amount in its U.S. and Canadian release. It was long branded a jinx film (Clark Gable died some two weeks after filming was completed in November 1960, and three other stars from the film have since died), and nearly everyone has a rationale for why this intended definitive film went astray. (James Goode wrote The

Montgomery Clift and Clark Gable in The Misfits (1961).

Story of The Misfits, 1963, offering a diary history of the making
of this ill-fated feature.)
        As adapted by Arthur Miller (his first scenario) from his
short story as a tribute to his then wife Miss Monroe, the film
was called by Time, "terrible ... clumsy ... obtuse ... disgusting
... nauseous ... ponderous ... wooly ... glum ... rambling ...
banal ... and fatuously embarrassing." It may be all that, but
there is some poignancy in the performances offered by the cast,
most of whose screen careers were verging on the brink of disaster.
        Aging cowboy Gay Langland (Gable) meets and falls in love
with a recently divorced woman named Roslyn Taber (Monroe) in
Reno, Nevada. The oddly-matched couple moves in with his buddy,
Guido (Wallach) at the latter's ranch house. Guido persuades Gay
and a has-been rodeo performer, Perce Howland (Clift), to join him
in rounding up "misfits," wild horses too small for riding. They
intend to sell them for dog food. Roslyn persuades idealistic Perce
to let the animals go free, but Gay overtakes the four-legged leader
and subdues him after a grueling battle. Then in a moment of compassion, he lets the beast loose. Gay and Roslyn are reunited.
        A pessimistic attitude permeates The Misfits, from the wise-
cracking Isabelle Steers (Ritter) to the glib but down-hearted Guido
who hopes to follow in Gay's big footsteps.
        When first released The Misfits had the box-office gimmick
of being Clark Gable's final film, and reviewers and viewers alike
hastened to read meaning into every gesture and vocal inflection
used by the veteran matinee idol, who endured a grueling production

schedule to complete this athletic cinema exercise. (The physical exertion endured by Gable was not helped by the psychologically-troubled Miss Monroe who found it difficult to show up for shooting sessions on time and seemed incapable of delivering her lines for any given scene.)

Today, viewed in retrospect, it is still difficult to decide whether The Misfits is a very flawed masterpiece or a superior failure. In the same vein as the very downbeat Junior Bonner (1972) [q.v.] and Lonely Are the Brave (1962) [q.v.], The Misfits offers a paean to the past, a rapidly disappearing West unable to compete with today's complex industrial society. Men like Gable's Gay Langland are a lost breed, doomed to extinction.

MRS. SUNDANCE (ABC-TV, 1974) C 90 min.

Producer, Stan Hough; director, Marvin Chomsky; teleplay, Christopher Knopf; music, Pat Williams; art director, Carl Anderson; camera, Michael Hugo; editor, Jack McSweeney.

Elizabeth Montgomery (Etta Place); Robert Foxworth (Jack Maddox); L. Q. Jones (Charlie Siringo); Arthur Hunnicutt (Walt Putney); Lurene Tuttle (Mrs. Lee); Claudette Nevins (Mary Lant); Robert Donner (Ben Lant); Dean Smith (Avery); Tod Shelhorse (David).

It was a catchy gimmick to produce a semi-sequel to Butch Cassidy and the Sundance Kid (1969) [q.v.], with Elizabeth Montgomery, the queen of the telefeatures, as the title figure.

The intriguing premise had Etta Place (a.k.a. Mrs. Sundance) in a ticklish situation when she learns that the Sundance Kid did not die with Butch Cassidy but is waiting for her at their old hideout. What makes the set-up so dangerous is that bounty hunters are aware of the planned reunion of the famed outlaw and the school-teacher of a small Colorado town.

Elizabeth Montgomery, very much Robert's daughter, offered a strong performance in this flashy role, giving an enriched characterization in a genre far removed from her days as the star of the teleseries "Bewitched."

MY DARLING CLEMENTINE (Twentieth Century-Fox, 1946) 97 min.

Producer, Samuel G. Engel; director, John Ford; based on the novel Wyatt Earp, Frontier Marshal by Stuart N. Lake; screen story, Sam Hellman; screenplay, Engel, Winston Miller; art directors, James Basevi, Lyle R. Wheeler; set decorators, Thomas Little, Fred J. Rode; costumes, Rene Hubert; assistant director, William Eckhardt; music, Cyril J. Mockridge; music conductor, Edward B. Powell; sound, Eugene Grossman, Roger Heman; special camera effects, Fred Sersen; camera, Joseph MacDonald; editor, Dorothy Spencer.

Henry Fonda (Wyatt Earp); Linda Darnell (Chihuahua); Victor

Henry Fonda, Fred Libby, Walter Brennan, Grant Withers, John Ireland, Mickey Simpson and Alan Mowbray in My Darling Clementine (1946).

Mature (Dr. John "Doc" Holliday); Walter Brennan (Old Man Clanton); Tim Holt (Virgil Earp); Ward Bond (Morgan Earp); Cathy Downs (Clementine Carter); Alan Mowbray (Granville Thorndyke); John Ireland (Billy Clanton); Grant Withers (Ike Clanton); Roy Roberts (Mayor); Jane Darwell (Kate Nelson); Russell Simpson (John Simpson); Francis Ford (Dad--the Old Soldier); J. Farrell McDonald (Mac the Barman); Don Garner (James Earp); Ben Hall (Barber); Arthur Walsh (Hotel Clerk); Jack Pennick (Coach Driver); Louis Mercier (Francois); Mickey Simpson (Sam Clanton); Fred Libby (Phin Clanton); Harry Woods (Luke); Charles Stevens (Indian Joe); Mae Marsh (Bit).

Returning from his film work in World War II, director John Ford resumed his filming in the Western genre with still another version of Stuart N. Lake's book, which had resulted in two earlier Fox films, both called Frontier Marshal (1934, 1939) [q.v.].
As in the earlier renderings, My Darling Clementine relates the story of the Earp brothers (Fonda, Holt, Bond and Garner) who team with Doc Holliday (Matyre) to rid the town of Tombstone of the evil Clanton family (Brennan, Ireland, Withers, Libby and Simpson). The narrative has the Earps on a cattle drive, with one of the brothers (Garner) being killed and the others remaining behind to rid Tombstone of its corrupt citizens. As expected, the finale is a well-staged version of the famed gunfight at the O.K. Corral

(a far more exuberant rendering of the time-honored showdown than
in the 1957 Kirk Douglas, Burt Lancaster rendering [q.v.]).

It is hard to fault the male performers in this film. Henry
Fonda plays the rather bland but stalwart Wyatt Earp, while Mature,
in an extremely sound characterization, performs the colorful part
of Doc Holliday. Walter Brennan won the acting honors as the
vicious and evil Ike Clanton whose brood includes such toughs as
Ireland and Withers. Far less effective were Fox contract players
Linda Darnell, as the Mexican Chihuahua, and Cathy Downs in the
title role, as an Eastern girl who was once Doc's nurse when he
had practiced medicine.

J. A. Place notes in The Western Films of John Ford (1975),
"In all Ford's films there is an element of legend. This is especially true of the Westerns, in which a whole body of mythology
has been created. My Darling Clementine is unique among Ford's
Westerns, however, in dealing with a specific and personal legend
(Wyatt Earp and Doc Holliday) and expanding it to a larger Western
myth.... The story and characters in My Darling Clementine might
seem limiting and restrictive, but Ford uses the viewer's already
established awareness of the legend to enhance the myth he is
creating."

With such a well-mounted film, it was easy for the critics
to heap hosannahs on the production. "The gentlemen are perfect.
Their humors are earthy. Their activities are taut. The morality
rate is simply terrific. And the picture goes off with several
bangs" (New York Times). "[It is] a smooth and superior motion
picture, wild and wooly Western though it certainly is" (New York
Herald-Tribune). "Having assembled all the elements of a conventional Western in My Darling Clementine, John Ford as director
proceeds to make an excellent film out of his material, using the
formula technique to say something about pioneer days in Arizona.
What he has done bespeaks his artistry, his humor and his under-
standing of human nature" (Christian Science Monitor).

MY LITTLE CHICKADEE (Universal, 1940) 83 min.

Executive producer, Lester Cowan; director, Edward Cline;
screenplay, Mae West and W. C. Fields; music, Frank Skinner;
music director, Charles Previn; song, Milton Drake and Ben Oakland; art director, Jack Otterson; gowns, Vera West; sound,
Bernard B. Brown; camera, Joseph Valentine; editor, Ed Curtiss.

Mae West (Flower Belle Lee); W. C. Fields (Cuthbert J.
Twillie); Joseph Calleia (Jef Badger Masked Bandit); Dick Foran
(Wayne Carter); Margaret Hamilton (Mrs. Gideon); George Moran
(Clarence); Si Jenks (Old Man); James Conlon (Bartender); Gene
Austin (Piano Player); Russell Hall (Candy); Otto Heimel (Coco);
Eddie Butler, Bing Conley (Henchmen); Fuzzy Knight (Cousin Zeb);
Anne Nagel (Miss Foster); Ruth Donnelly (Aunt Lou); Willard
Robertson (Uncle John); Donald Meek (Amos Budget); William B.
Davidson (Sheriff); Addison Richards (Judge); Jackie Searle (Boy);
Fay Adler (Mrs. "Pygmy" Allen); Jan Duggan (Woman); Wade

Mae West and W. C. Fields in <u>My Little Chickadee</u> (1940).

Boteler, Morgan Wallace (Men); Harlan Briggs (Clerk); and Walter McGrail, Delmar Watson, Chester Gan, George Melford, Lloyd Ingraham, Hank Bell, Lane Chandler, Eddit Hearn, Jack Roper, Dick Rush, Billy Benedict, Bill Wolf.

  The teaming of Miss Mae West and W. C. Fields resulted in this bizarre Western satire. It is the most widely shown of the two stars' feature films. Most critics and viewers seem to agree that it is much better in retrospect than actuality. However, it is still a pleasant, and never draggy, effort with occasionally funny lines and situations. Written by Miss West with individual scenes by W. C. Fields (although he is given equal screen billing for the scenario), the film presented this unique duo in their only truly Western foray.
  Flower Belle Lee (West) finds that being romanced by a masked bandit (Calleia) is not as onerous as one might suspect. For her brazen attitude, the good ladies of the community run her out of town. Forced to take the next train out, she embarks for Greasewood City, knowing that her "infamy" will precede her. Aboard, she meets Cuthbert J. Twillie (Fields), a middle-aged con artist. She spots his bag full of money (actually worthless coupons)

and persuades a card sharp (Meek) to marry them. Once in Greasewood City, Miss Flower Belle proves a difficult bride, refusing to
consummate her wedding "vows." "The child's afraid of me--she's
all a'twit," remarks the befuddled Cuthbert. Embarking on a tour
of the town, Flower Belle discovers that Jeff Badger (Calleia) is the
local saloon owner, and a romance promptly blossoms between the
two. Meanwhile Twillie is made the sheriff of the town. Later,
Cuthbert is mistaken for the real masked bandit and is sentenced to
hang, but Flower Belle persuades the real outlaw to make his presence known. Cuthbert is freed and Miss Flower Belle informs Cuthbert that their marriage was a fake. This forces Cuthbert now to
compete with Wayne Carter (Foran) the crusading newspaper editor,
for Flower Belle's affections.

At the finale, as Flower Belle sashays up the stairs to her
hotel room, Cuthbert tells her, "C'mon up and see me sometime."
The sirenish Flower Belle agrees, referring to him as "my little
chickadee."

Possibly the best analysis of this one-of-a-kind film is supplied by Jon Tuska in The Films of Mae West (1973): "There is
something strange about Chickadee. The dialogue and the situations
constantly promise to provide more comedy than they do. As placid
as their relations are on screen, I suspect that the fault in Chickadee
lies in the antipathy between Bill Fields and Mae in terms of tem-
perament and personality. They are essentially unfunny as a team,
however good each is at comedy alone. There is no magic interplay,
and so there is less than everyone had a right to anticipate."

But there is a great deal to be appreciated in individual scenes
of the film, especially for those who are well-acquainted with the
formulas and cliches of the cowboy and Indian film. Advantageous
use is made of the studio's stock Western sets, as well as such
Western picture perennials as Dick Foran, Si Jenks, and especially
Fuzzy Knight. One has only to recall landmark moments in My
Little Chickadee to set one's funny bone into action: Flower Belle's
display of Annie Oakley marksmanship during the Indian attack on the
train, Cuthbert's wooing of the goat in the wedding bed (thinking it to
be Flower Belle), Flower Belle's arithmetic lesson to the school
children ("two and two are four and five will give you ten if you play
your cards right"), and her moaning of the song "Willie of the
Valley."

For a woman nearing the half-century mark, Mae West in this
film still cut a most desirable (hour-glass) figure. And Fields, perhaps because Miss West forbade him to smoke or drink on the set,
appears to be in better physical condition than in any other of his
Universal films of this period.

Had Miss West and Fields been in better harmony Universal
might have teamed them in further vehicles. But their jealousy and
opposing temperaments were too much to handle for another filming
session.

MY NAME IS NOBODY see STRANGER ON THE RUN

MY PAL, THE KING (Universal, 1932) 63 min.

Director, Kurt Neuman; story, Richard Schayer; screenplay, Jack Natteford, Tom Crizer; camera, Dan Clark.
Tom Mix (Tom Reed); Mickey Rooney (King Charles); Paul Hurst (Red); Noel Francis (Princess Elsa); Finis Barton (Gretchen); Stuart Holmes (Kluckstein); James Kirkwood (Schwartz); Jim Thorpe (Cludy); Christian Frank (Etzel); Clarissa Selwynne (The Dowager Queen); Ferdinand Schumann-Heink (General Wiederman); Wallis Clark (Dr. Lorenz); Tony the Horse (Himself).

In the kingdom of Alvonia, the boy king (Rooney) sneaks away from a dreary council meeting about taxes and joins a sidewalk throng watching a circus parade. When he is pushed into the street, Tom Reed (Mix) rescues him. As they both ride Tony, Tom's horse, the crowd recognizes the youth, and King Charles informs his benefactor of his real identity. Then the monarch goes to see Tom's circus show. Later a wicked count (Kirkwood) puts King Charles and his tutor (Clark) in a dungeon and plans to drown them because the ruler will not sign a bill the villainous Schwartz (Kirkwood) wants signed. Tom and Tony arrive on the scene in time to save the boy and put a stop to the evil nobleman's activities.
Made as a part of Tom Mix's final film series at Universal, this picture was breezy and vastly entertaining, especially with its dash of Ruritanian flavor. The aging Mix still proved to be quite agile in the movie's many stunt sequences. An amusing scene has the star teaching young Rooney slang. My Pal, the King has a number of good cameo performances, including Paul Hurst as Tom's assistant and Indian athlete Jim Thorpe as a performer in Mix's troupe.
Mordaunt Hall wrote in the New York Times, "The result is a good entertainment for children, who not only have the opportunity of following a melodramatic story but also of seeing crack riders from the Far West in action in a circus arena."

THE MYSTERIOUS RIDER (W. W. Hodkinson, 1921) 5,500'

Director, Benjamin B. Hampton; based on the novel by Zane Grey; camera, Gus Peterson, F. H. Sturges.
Robert McKim (Hell Bent Wade); Claire Adams (Columbine); Carl Gantvoort (Wilson Moore); James Mason (Jack Bellounds); Walt Whitman (Bellounds); Frederick Starr (Ed Smith); Maude Wayne (Madge Smith); Frank Hayes ("Smokey Joe" Lem Billings); Aggie Herring (Maria the Cook).

THE MYSTERIOUS RIDER (Paramount, 1927) 5,957'

Presenters, Adolph Zukor, Jesse L. Lasky; associate

228   The Mysterious Rider

producer, B. P. Schulberg; director, John Waters; based on the
novel by Zane Grey; screenplay, Fred Myton, Paul Gangelin; titles,
Alfred Hustwick; camera, C. Edgar Schoenbaum.

Jack Holt (Hell Bent Wade); Betty Jewel (Dorothy King);
Charles Sellon (Cliff Harkness); David Torrence (Mark King); Tom
Kennedy (Lem Spooner); Guy Oliver (Jack Wilson); Albert Hart
(Sheriff); Ivan Christie (Tom Saunders); Arthur Hoyt (King's Secre-
tary).

THE MYSTERIOUS RIDER   (Paramount, 1933)   59 min.

Director, Fred Allen; based on the novel by Zane Grey;
screenplay, Harvey Gates, Robert N. Lee; camera, Archie Stout.
Kent Taylor (Wade Benton); Lona Andre (Dorothy); Irving
Pichel (Cliff Harkness); Gail Patrick (Mary Foster); Warren Hymer
(Jitney Smith); Berton Churchill (Mark King); Niles Welch (John
Foster); Cora Sue Collins (Jo-Jo); E. H. Calvert (Sheriff Matt
Arnold); Sherwood Bailey ("Sheriff" Arnold, Jr.); Clarence Wilson
(Gentry).
TV title: The Fighting Phantom.

THE MYSTERIOUS RIDER   (Paramount, 1938)   74 min.

Producer, Harry Sherman; director, Lesley Selander; based
on the novel by Zane Grey; screenplay, Maurice Geraghty; art di-
rector, Lewis Rachmil; music director, Boris Morros; camera,
Russell Harlan; editor, Sherman Rose.
Douglass Dumbrille (Pecos Bill/Ben Wade); Russell Hayden
(Wils Moore); Sidney Toler (Frosty Kilburn); Stanley Andrews (Wil-
liam Bellounds); Weldon Heyburn (Jack Bellounds); Charlotte Fields
(Collie); Monte Blue (Cap Folson); Earl Dwire (Sheriff Burley); Glenn
Strange (Cramer; Jack Rockwell (Lem); Arch Hall (Andrews); Dick
Alexander (Hudson); Mabel Colcord (Woman); Bob Kortman (Morris);
Ed Brady (Jake).
TV title: Mark of the Avenger.

No less than four versions of Zane Grey's 1921 novel The
Mysterious Rider have been produced, the first occurring in the
same year the novel was published.
The W. W. Hodkinson version finds a girl named Columbine
(Adams) loving a ranch foreman (Gantvoort). But to make her
foster father (Whitman) happy she marries his son (Mason). Bellounds (Whitman) later becomes friends with The Mysterious Rider,
Hell Bent Wade (McKim), while his son (Mason) is drawn into a
plot to rustle his father's cattle. The blame for the rustling is
placed on Wilson Moore (Gantvoort). Meanwhile Hell Bent recognizes the scheme's organizer, Ed Smith (Starr), as his wife's murderer and discovers that Columbine is actually his daughter. Wade
is forced to kill Smith in a showdown and Moore is cleared. Bellounds' son goes to jail while Columbine and Moore are united in
marriage. Reviewing this film, Photoplay reported, "Zane Grey

himself can find no new situations lurking amidst cactus and cotton-
woods. Everything that could be done, has been done!"
     In 1927 Paramount re-filmed the novel. Like many of the
Zane Grey stories in the studio's series, it was directed by John
Waters. In the expanded format, homesteaders in the California
desert area learn that a Spanish land grant owned by Cliff Harkness
(Sellon) supersedes their claim. Harkness offers to sell the claim
for $25,000 and Hell Bent Wade (Holt) advises the settlers to buy it.
Accordingly, they give him their collected money. Then a power
company offers Harkness more money. The crafty man accepts the
money from Wade and signs the receipt with disappearing ink, then
sells his land to the energy company. The homesteaders, about to
be relocated, vent their anger on Wade and try to hang him. Instead, he is jailed. When he eventually escapes he rushes to warn
the ranchers to go to court to protect their property. Still later he
forces a confession from Harkness and then marries Dorothy King
(Jewel), the daughter of the power company owner (Torrence).
     Six years later Paramount remade the film as part of its new
budget Zane Grey series. Fred Allen directed, with Kent Taylor
and Gail Patrick in the leads. Five years after that, the same
studio had producer Harry Sherman and director Lesley Selander
turn out the fourth version of The Mysterious Rider. This seventy-
four-minute edition featured Russell Hayden, Monte Blue, and Douglass Dumbrille, the latter cast in a good guy role for a rare change.
     The production history of The Mysterious Rider once again
proved how faithful action movie audiences were. The same plot
could be used over and over again, and as long as there were some
new faces to pepper the script, the viewers indulgently accepted the
rehashed fare.

THE MYSTERY RIDER (Universal, 1928) ten chapters

     Director, Jack Nelson.
     William Desmond (Winthrop Lane); Derelys Perdue (Grace
Wentworth); Tom London (The Claw); and Syd Saylor, Walter Shumway, Bud Osborne, Red Bassett, Ben Corbett.
     Chapters: 1) The Clutching Claw; 2) Trapped; 3) The Stam-
pede; 4) Hands Up; 5) Buried Alive; 6) The Fatal Shot; 7) Hurled
through Space; 8) Unmasked; 9) Doomed; 10) The End of the Trail.

     After success as a mysterious masked horseman in Univer-
sal's serial The Vanishing Rider (1928) with Ethlyn Clair, William
Desmond starred in a similar serial, The Mystery Rider, which
proved to be his last starring thriller chapterplay. This cliffhanger
came at the twilight of the silent era. With the emergence of the
talkies, Desmond would find himself reduced to playing first supporting roles and then later, just bits. In later years, he would be
a tour lecturer for Universal Studios.
     In The Mystery Rider the beefy Desmond plays Winthrop
Lane, the lover of Grace Wentworth (Perdue), whose father has
spent years formulating a way to make rubber from the sap of the
mesquite plant. After confiding the formula to his daughter, he is

230   Navajo Joe

murdered by the mysterious "The Claw" (London), who then sets out
to obtain the formula, after blaming the killing on "The Mystery
Rider." Winthrop has to endure various hazards for several chapters before The Claw is captured. Victorious at last, naturally,
Lane now can claim Grace as his own.

NAVAJO JOE   see   UN DOLLARO A TESTA

NEVADA   (Paramount, 1927)   6,258'

        Presenters, Adolph Zukor, Jesse L. Lasky; director, John
Waters; based on the novel by Zane Grey; screenplay, John Stone,
L. G. Rigby; titles, Jack Conway; camera, C. Edgar Schoenbaum.
        Gary Cooper (Nevada); Thelma Todd (Hettie Ide); William
Powell (Clan Dillon); Philip Strange (Ben Ide); Ernie S. Adams (Cash
Burridge); Christian J. Frank (Sheriff of Winthrop); Ivan Christy
(Crawthorne); Guy Oliver (Sheriff of Lineville).

NEVADA   (Paramount, 1935)   58 min.

        Producer, Harold Hurley; director, Charles Barton; based on
the novel by Zane Grey; screenplay, Garnett Weston, Stuart Anthony;
camera, Archie Stout.
        Larry "Buster" Crabbe (Nevada); Kathleen Burke (Hettie Ide);
Syd Saylor (Cash Burridge); Monte Blue (Clem Dillon); William Duncan (Ben Ide); Richard Carle (Judge Franklidge); Stanley Andrews
(Cawthorne); Frank Sheridan (Tom Blaine); Raymond Hatton (Sheriff);
Glenn (Leif) Erikson (Bill Ide); Jack Kennedy (McTurk); Henry Roquemore (Bartender); and William Desmond, Frank Rice, O. C. Dutch
Hendrian.

NEVADA   (RKO, 1944)   62 min.

        Executive producer, Sid Rogell; producer, Herman Schlom;
director, Edward Killy; based on the novel by Zane Grey; screen-
play, Norman Houston; art directors, Albert S. D'Agostino, Lucius
Croxton; set decorators, Darrell Silvera, William Stevens; music,
Paul Sawtell; music director, C. Bakaleinikoff; sound, Richard Van
Hessen; camera, Harry J. Wild; editor, Roland Gross.
        Robert Mitchum (Jim Lacy-Nevada); Anne Jeffreys (Julie
Dexter); Guinn "Big Boy" Williams (Dusty); Nancy Gates (Hattie Ide);
Richard Martin (Chito Rafferty); Craig Reynolds (Cash Burridge);
Harry Woods (Joe Powell); Edmund Glover (Ed Nelson); Alan Ward
(William Brewer); Harry McKim (Marvie Ide); Larry Wheat (Ben
Ide); Jack Overman (Red Barry); Emmett Lynn (Comstock); Wheaton
Chambers (Dr. Darian); Philip Morris (Ed Nolan); Mary Halsey,
Patti Brill, Margie Stewart, Virginia Belmont, Bryant Washburn,
Bert Moorhouse (Bits); George De Normand, Sammy Blum (Bar-
tenders); Russell Hopton (Henchman).

Zane Grey's novel Nevada has been filmed on three occasions and each time it has been as a programmer employed to launch the starring careers of prospective new stars.

Paramount made the first two versions. The initial film starred a young fledgling actor named Gary Cooper as Nevada, a bad guy who tries to go straight. He protects a girl (Todd) and her brother (Strange) from rustlers and eventually he proves that a supposedly respected rancher (Powell) is the actual gang leader. The film was an average B entry with good action and story value. Only later would the cast, especially Cooper, Todd, and Powell, have tremendous marquee value. Photoplay, rating the film, penned, "Thrills with suspense, dazzles with fine performances, glamorous outdoor photography and a hero with a sense of humor, Gary Cooper."

In 1935 the studio remade the story as a part of its ongoing Zane Grey Western series, which had begun earlier in the decade, with Henry Hathaway directing Randolph Scott in a number of oaters. This version, however, was directed by Charles Barton and starred Larry "Buster" Crabbe as the very wholesome, athletic hero. The supporting cast had the benefit of such stalwarts as Stanley Andrews, Monte Blue, and Raymond Hatton. Buried in the bit roles was former silent leading man William Desmond.

Throughout the thirties RKO had been known as the home of intimate women's stories. Occasionally it broke out of the mold with films like King Kong (1933) or a series of Harry Carey Westerns in the mid-decade. In the early forties it assigned Tim Holt to a series of cowboy stories. When he joined the military service the studio attempted to replace him with another cowboy star by returning contractee Robert Mitchum to the saddle. It was the first of two Zane Grey films (the other was West of the Pecos, 1944) the performer made before he too joined Uncle Sam's service. The plot has Jim Lacy (Mitchum) as a cowpoke who is unjustly accused of murder. He escapes from a lynch mob and proves that claim-jumpers were the real culprits. Guinn "Big Boy" Williams and Richard Martin, the former for comedy and the latter for vocal value, were cast as the hero's partners, and Anne Jeffreys as Julie Dexter provided a very attractive romantic interest.

NEVADA SMITH (Paramount, 1966) C 128 min.

Executive producer, Joseph E. Levine; producer-director, Henry Hathaway; based on a character in The Carpetbaggers by Harold Robbins; screenplay, John Michael Hayes; music, Alfred Newman; art directors, Hal Pereira, Tambi Larsen; set decorator, Bob Benton; wardrobe, Frank Beetson, Jr.; makeup, Del Acevedo; assistant directors, Danny McCauley, Joseph Lenzi; special effects, George C. Thompson; camera, Lucien Ballard; editor, Frank Bracht.

Steve McQueen (Max Sand/Nevada Smith); Karl Malden (Tom Fitch); Brian Keith (Jonas Cord); Arthur Kennedy (Bill Bowdre); Suzanne Pleshette (Pilar); Raf Vallone (Father Zaccardi); Janet Margolin (Neesa); Howard Da Silva (Warden); Pat Hingle (Big Foot);

Steve McQueen and Brian Keith in <u>Nevada Smith</u> (1966).

Martin Landau (Jesse Coe); Paul Fix (Sheriff Bonnell); Gene Evans
(Sam Sand); Josephine Hutchinson (Mrs. Elvira McCanles); John
Doucette (Uncle Ben McCanles); Val Avery (Puck Mason); Sheldon
Allman (Sheriff); Lyle Bettger (Jack Rudsbough); Bert Freed (Quince);
David McLean (Romero); Steve Mitchell (Buckshot); Merritt Bohn
(River Boat Pilot); Sandy Kenyon (Clerk in Bank); George Mitchell
(Paymaster); Stanley Adams (Storekeeper); John Litel (Doctor); Ted
de Corsia (Hudson the Bartender).

In the sprawling, trashy <u>The Carpetbaggers</u> (1964), based on
Harold Robbins' best seller, Alan Ladd made a tremendous impression as Nevada Smith, an aging cowboy star in Hollywood.   Had
Ladd not died soon after this picture was finished, he might have
been considered for <u>Nevada Smith</u>, the follow-up film which was
based on the character's earlier years.   (It is said that the Nevada
Smith character was based on the career of Ken Maynard.)
When a film grosses over $5.5 million in distributors do-
mestic rental, it must be doing something right, and <u>Nevada Smith</u>
has a good deal to offer.   Steve McQueen is at his prime in the
title role, as a man on the trail of the three outlaws (Kennedy,
Malden and Landau) who brutally killed his father and Indian mother.
Along his path of vengeance he meets a gunsmith (Keith) who teaches
him how to shoot expertly and survive danger.   McQueen later

encounters a priest (Vallone) who shows him that vengeance is wrong.
Thus when he meets Fitch (Malden), the lone survivor of the murderous trio, he shoots the man in both legs, but does not kill him.
Filled with remorse at his act, Nevada rides off seeking a new
future.

Film audiences approved the rugged action stuffed into this
mammoth Western, but the critics were not so easily pleased. "A
good story idea is stifled by uneven acting, often lethargic direction,
and awkward sensation-shock values" (Variety). "The principal
problem with Nevada Smith is that it is just too long. It also is too
episodic" (New York Times).

Taking a cue from the very popular spaghetti Westerns,
Nevada Smith is filled with sex and violence, and thankfully, breath-
taking photography.

In mid-1975, MGM-TV prepared a ninety-minute telefeature,
Nevada Smith, starring Lorne Greene and Cliff Potts. It traces the
relationship between Jonas Cord, Sr. and young Nevada Smith in the
late 1880s. It failed to generate a TV series.

THE NEW LAND (NYBYGGARNA) (Warner Bros., 1973) C
161 min.

        Producer, Bengi Forslund; director, Jan Troell; based on the
novel The Emigrants by Vilhelm Moberg; screenplay, Forslund and
Troell; art director, P. A. Lundgren; music, Bengt Ernryd, George
Oddner; costumes, Ulla-Britt Soderlund; camera-editor, Troell.
        Max von Sydow (Karl Oskar); Liv Ullmann (Kristina); Eddie
Axberg (Robert); Hans Alfredson (Jonas Petter); Halvar Bjork (Anders
Mansson); Allan Edwall (Danjel); Peter Lindgren (Samuel Nojd);
Pierre Lindstedt (Arvid); Oscar Ljung (Petrus Olausson); Karin Nord-
strom (Judit); Agneta Prytz (Fina-Kajas); Per Oscarsson (Pastor
Torner); Monica Zetterlund (Ulrika); George Anaya (Mario Vallejos);
Ed Carpenter (The Doctor); Larry Clementson (Mr. Abbott); Tom C.
Fouts (Pastor Jackson).
        A.k.a. The Settlers.

        This well-regarded film was the second part of Vilhelm Mo-
berg's chronicle novel The Emigrants which director-photographer
Jan Troel made as The Emigrants (Utvandrarna) in 1970 (for 1972
release in the U.S.). The first installment told in great detail of
the hardships endured by a Swedish family who decided to migrate
to North America in the 1850s.

        What makes The New Land a rather unique American Western
is that for a change the settlers heading Westward are not seasoned
Americans but freshly-arrived travelers from a North European
country, hardly the type of pioneers one is so used to witnessing in
Hollywood recreations of the American westward movement.

        In The New Land, which many filmgoers found overly-long at
161 minutes, the story focuses on Karl Osker (von Sydow), his wife
(Ullmann) and the brother (Robert) as they settle in Minnesota.
Robert later leaves the family for two years to pan gold in the hopefully rich terrains of California.

Chris Sottolano wrote in Films in Review, "It's an epic saga and we are meant to savor each scene in terms of long passages of time being dramatically highlighted ... there is much to recommend the acting of all concerned, and the strong sense of time, place and history which makes The New Land memorable."

A very fine, but unsuccessful, teleseries called "The New Land," based upon the film, had a brief run on ABC-TV in the fall of 1974.

In 1974 filmmaker Troell completed his meritorious trilogy with Zandy's Bride for Warner Bros. It was the story of a rough Northwest cattleman (Gene Hackman) who orders a Swedish bride (Ullmann) from Minnesota. He eventually softens his disposition towards her as she teaches him the quality of love. Eileen Heckhart and Frank Cady were excellent in supporting roles as Hackman's parents.

NIGHT CRY   (Warner Bros., 1926)   6,100'

Director, Herman C. Raumaker; story, Paul Klein, Edward Meagher; adaptor, Ewart Adamson; assistant directors, William Mc-Gann, Al Zeidman; camera, Ed Du Par, Walter Robinson; editor, Clarence Kolster.

Rin-Tin-Tin (Himself); John Harron (John Martin); June Marlowe (Mrs. John Martin); Gayne Whitman (Miguel Hernandez); Heinie Conklin (Tony); Don Alvarado (Pedro); Mary Louise Miller (The Martin Baby).

The most popular cinematic star of the late twenties was Rin-Tin-Tin and the canine hero starred in a number of big money-makers for Warner Bros. In the talkie era he worked in Mascot serials. The most popular animal star ever in films, Rinty started the popularity of various animal celebrities in film. Throughout the years he has remained the best-liked of all such animals and even as late as the fifties one of his descendants was starring in a teleseries which used the dog's name as its title.

Night Cry is a rather typical Rin-Tin-Tin starring vehicle. It offered him in a variety of situations in which he is the hero, with the male lead (Harron) virtually dependent on the dog for help. This offering finds a giant condor killing a sheep herd, with the blame falling on Rinty. The sheepmen order him killed. His owner (Harron), however, hides him. Later when the bird kidnaps the man's little daughter (Miller) it is Rinty who rescues her after a brutal encounter with the enraged bird.

The ironical success of the canine performer is "celebrated" in a new feature film entitled Won Ton Ton, The Dog Who Saved Hollywood (1976).

THE NIGHT RIDERS   (Republic, 1939)   58 min.

Associate producer, William Berke; director, George Sherman; based on the characters created by William Colt MacDonald;

screenplay, Betty Burbridge, Stanley Roberts; music, William Lava;
camera, Jack Marta; editor, Lester Oriebeck.
     John Wayne (Stony Brooke); Ray Corrigan (Tucson Smith);
Max Terhune (Lullaby Joslin); Ruth Rogers (Susan Randall); Tom
Tyler (Jackson); Kermit Maynard (Sheriff Pratt); Doreen McKay
(Soledad); George Douglas (Pierce Talbot); Sammy McKim (Tim);
Walter Wills (Hazelton); Ethan Laidlaw (Andrews); Ed Piel, Sr.
(Harper); Tom London (Wilson); Jack Ingram (Wilkins); William
Nestell (Allen); Francis Sayles (President Garfield); and Yakima
Canutt, Bud Osborne, David Sharpe, Glenn Strange.

     The Three Mesquiteers (Wayne, Corrigan and Terhune) are
aboard a riverboat when a crooked gambler (Douglas) is stabbed in
the arm and thrown overboard. The gambler makes his way ashore
and to a forger who creates a land grant for him. He later poses
as a Spanish nobleman and the heir to thirteen million acres. The
court upholds his claim and he and his henchmen begin to levy heavy
taxes on the local ranchers. The Mesquiteers' 3M ranch is taken
by the Don, forcing the trio to pose as Los Capqueros (The Night
Raiders) in order to rob the Don's tax collector. They also enlist
clandestinely in his army to encourage anarchy from within. Eventually they are discovered and sentenced to death. Fortunately, the
execution is supervised by the sheriff (Maynard), who fakes the proceedings. Meanwhile, the local people attack the Don's hacienda,
wanting revenge for the trio's alleged death. The Mesquiteers then
force a confession from the Don whom they recognize as the gambler.
They quickly put an end to his reign of tyranny.
     The Three Mesquiteers series had gotten underway in 1935
at RKO with Harry Carey as Stoney Brooke, Hoot Gibson as Tucson
Smith and Guinn "Big Boy" Williams as Lullaby Joslin, in Powdersmoke Range [q.v.]. The next year the series moved over to Republic with a new leading trio. For entry number eighteen, Pals of
the Saddle (1938), John Wayne took over the role of Stony, continuing
on for seven more installments of the fifty-two part series.
     Like most of the films made in the Mesquiteer series by
Republic in the first four years, The Night Riders benefited from
good direction, fine acting, tight editing and a rousing musical score
(by William Lava). Best of all, the picture focuses on clear-cut
action.

NORTH OF '36   see   THE TEXANS

NORTH WEST MOUNTED POLICE   (Paramount, 1940)   C   125 min.

     Executive producer, William LeBaron; producer, Cecil B.
DeMille; associate producer, William H. Pine; director, DeMille;
screenplay, Alan LeMay, Jesse Lasky, Jr., C. Gardner Sullivan;
music, Victor Young; camera, Victor Milner, W. Howard Green;
editor, Anne Bauchens.
     Gary Cooper (Dusty Rivers); Madeleine Carroll (April Logan);
Paulette Goddard (Louvette Corbeau); Preston Foster (Sergeant Jim

Brett); Robert Preston (Ronnie Logan); George Bancroft (Jacques
Corbeau); Lynne Overman (Tod McDuff); Akim Tamiroff (Dan Duroc);
Walter Hampden (Big Bear); Lon Chaney, Jr. (Shorty); Montagu
Love (Inspector Cabot); Francis McDonald (Louis Riel); George E.
Stone (Johnny Pelang); Willard Robertson (Superintendent Harrington);
Regis Toomey (Constable Jerry Moore); Richard Denning (Constable
Thornton); Douglas Kennedy (Constable Carter); Robert Ryan (Con-
stable Dumont); James Seay (Constable Fenton); Lane Chandler (Con-
stable Fyffe); Ralph Byrd (Constable Ackroyd); Eric Alden (Constable
Kent); Wallace Reid, Jr. (Constable Rankin); Bud Geary (Constable
Herrick); Evan Thomas (Captain Gower); Jack Pennick (Sergeant
Field); Rod Cameron (Corporal Underhill); Davison Clark (Surgeon
Roberts); Jack Chapin (A Bugler); Chief Thundercloud (Wandering
Spirit); Harry Burns (The Crow); Lou Merrill (Lesur); Clara Blan-
dick (Mrs. Burns); Ynez Seabury (Mrs. Shorty); Eva Puig (Ekawo);
Julia Faye (Wapiskau); Norma Nelson (Niska); Phillip Terry (Con-
stable Judson); Jack Luden (Constable Douglas); John Hart (Constable
Norman); Kermit Maynard (Constable Adams); Emory Parnell (George
Higgins); James Flavin (Mountie); Anthony Caruso (Half-Breed at
Riel's Headquarters); Nestor Paiva (Half-Breed); Jim Pierce (Cor-
poral); Ray Mala, Monte Blue, Chief Yowlachie, Chief Thunderbird
(Indians).

   If anyone in America, or the world for that matter, was
foolish enough to doubt the supreme knowledge of Cecil B. DeMille

Madeleine Carroll, Robert Preston (prone), Willard Robertson, Preston Foster and Gary Cooper in North West Mounted Police (1940).

in all matters concerning filmmaking and world history, he need
only have asked the austere producer-director to receive the con-
firmation--i. e. , according to DeMille, he was the last word in
everything he touched. This autocratic way of filmmaking had both
virtues and flaws. On the positive side it gave DeMille autonomy
to make his lavish epics of former times, laboring on one film
while other directors were churning out two or three entries in the
same period. Everyone in Hollywood seemed to be in awe of the
great C.B. Most of his features were greeted with praise far in
excess of their intrinsic merits. On the negative side, it was difficult for anyone to brook the master once he had an idea firmly
implanted in mind. Thus, because he favored soundstage shooting,
even his outdoor Westerns were largely shot indoors, giving the
pictures a very closed-in look. Despite the fact that epic was
DeMille's forte, the calibre of performance given by his players
was usually poorer than was typical of any one of them individually.
It seemed that DeMille had a quest for authenticity in everything
except reality of fact or performance.

Set in the Canada of 1885, North West Mounted Police relates the details of the Riel Rebellion, an uprising of half-breed
Indians who formed the Metic Nation. The Mounties are called in
to put down the revolt. On a more personal level Sergeant Jim
Brett (Foster) is in love with nurse April Logan (Carroll), but she
meets and is entranced by Texas Ranger Dusty Rivers (Cooper) who
has come to the North country in pursuit of a murderer. The
killer, Jacques Corbeau (Bancroft), is also wanted for murder in
Canada and is really the instigator of the rebellion. Dusty and
Brett become rivals for April's affections while her weak brother
(Preston) is seduced by Jacques' half-breed daughter (Goddard).
His romantic pursuit causes Ronnie (Preston) to neglect his duties
and results in the massacre of several Mounties. Eventually resolute Dusty kills Jacques and returns to Texas with the body. April
remains with Brett following the death of her brother.

Of this elaborate, Technicolor epic, Time wrote, "North West
Mounted Police is a movie in the grand style--God's own biggest
trees and mountains for props and backdrop; staunch courage and
lofty aims among the good people; cunning and treachery lurking
within the sinister forces, the ominous note of doom finally stifled
by the fortitude of noble men. " The New York Journal-American
confirmed, "bang-up entertainment, a large-scale outdoor melodrama
packed with exciting soldier-and-Injun fights and boasting gorgeous
Technicolored shots of Canada's mountains, lakes and forests as
well as of the Canadian constabulary. "

The film received five Academy Award nominations with Anne
Bauchens winning for her editing.

On comparing this entry to the earlier teaming of Cooper and
DeMille in The Plainsman (1936) [q.v.] the latter is seen to be far
sounder dramatically. This earlier film is conceived on a lesser
scale, with all the facets more closely drawn together, and the focus
is more clearly on the broad-shouldered hero (Cooper).

Whatever her virtues as "The Sweater Girl, " Paramount's
Paulette Goddard was hardly believable as the half-breed Louvette

Corbeau. It was a toss-up which was less convincing: her swarthy make-up or her mock accent.

NYBYGGARNA   see   THE NEW LAND

OKLAHOMA!   (Magna, 1955)   C   145 min.

    Producer, Arthur Hornblow, Jr.; director, Fred Zinnemann;
based on the musical by Richard Rodgers and Oscar Hammerstein II
which is based on the play Green Grow the Lilacs by Lynn Riggs;
screenplay, Sonya Levien, William Ludwing; songs, Rogers and Ham-
merstein II; choreography, Agnes DeMille; costumes, Orry-Kelly,
Motley; assistant director, Arthur Black; production designer, Oliver
Smith; music director-supervisor, Jay Blackton; camera, Robert
Surtees; editor, Gene Ruggiero.
    Gordon MacRae (Curly); Gloria Grahame (Ado Annie); Gene
Nelson (Will Parker); Charlotte Greenwood (Aunt Eller); Shirley
Jones (Laurey); Eddie Albert (Ali Hakim); James Whitmore (Carnes);
Rod Steiger (Jud Fry); Barbara Lawrence (Gertie); J. C. Flippen
(Skidmore); Roy Barcroft (Marshal); James Mitchell (Dream Curley);
Bambi Linn (Dream Laurey); Jennie Workman, Kelly Brown, Marc
Platt, Lizanne Truex, Virginia Bosler, Evelyn Taylor, Jane Fischer
(Dancers).

    Movie musicals with a Western setting have been relatively
few: Annie Get Your Gun (1950) [q.v.]; Calamity Jane (1953), with
Doris Day and Howard Keel; Seven Brides for Seven Brothers (1954),
with Jane Powell, Howard Keel and Russ Tamblyn; and the earlier
song-and-dance treat, The Harvey Girls (1946), with Judy Garland
and Ray Bolger. But if there is one period, frontier musical that
most Americans know by heart (or at least some of the tunes) it is
Oklahoma!. Not only did this property have a tremendous impact
on Broadway* where it set all kinds of box-office records, but movie
makers were quick to take advantage of its popularity by adapting the
titles of their properties (as in the case of Republic's In Old Oklahoma, 1943), or by duplicating the plot structure and flavor (Universal's Deanna Durbin color musical, Can't Help Singing, 1944), or
merely borrowing the format for a theme song (as in Republic's Roy
Rogers venture Song of Nevada, 1944, in which the finale title tune
goes "'V' is for the valley, where all the horses are...").
    Filmed in Eastman color and Todd-AO widescreen process,
Oklahoma! grossed $7.1 million in distributors domestic rentals.
The casting was rather unique. Sultry Gloria Grahame inherited
Celeste Holm's role as Ado Annie, the girl who "Can't Say No";

---

*Oklahoma! opened at the St. James Theatre on Broadway on March
31, 1943 for a run of 2,212 performances. It starred Betty Garde,
Alfred Drake, Howard da Silva, Celeste Holm, Joan Roberts, Joseph
Buloff, Joan McCracken, Lee Dixon, and Bambi Linn (who was also
in the film version).

burly, Method actor Rod Steiger was cast as the evil Jud, wholesome Eddie Albert played salesman Ali Hakin, and rubber-legged
Charlotte Greenwood shone as Aunt Ellen. Co-leads Gordon MacRae
and Shirley Jones would be re-teamed the next year for Rodgers
and Hammerstein II's Carousel, directed by Henry King for Twentieth Century-Fox.

All the familiar songs were repeated in this film version,
including "Oh What a Beautiful Mornin'," "The Surrey with the
Fringe on Top," "Many a New Day," "Everything's Up-to-Date in
Kansas City," and the rousing title tune.

Actually the film was not shot in Oklahoma for the producers
could not find a sufficiently large stretch of land in which modern
communication lines, etc. did not present a lensing problem. Nevertheless, this lilting movie, as handled by director Fred Zinnemann,
is more than satisfactory as a paean to the bygone West and to farm
life as it once was, in a community where law and order had long
ago been obtained and the cowboy as such was already a somewhat
antiquated institution.

THE OKLAHOMA KID   (Warner Bros., 1939)   85 min.

Associate producer, Samuel Bischoff; director, Lloyd Bacon;
story, Edward E. Paramore, Wally Klein; screenplay, Warren Duff,
Robert Buckner, Paramore; art director, Esdras Hartley; music,
Max Steiner; orchestrators, Hugo Friedhofer, Adolph Deutsch,
George Parrish, Murray Cutter; costumes, Orry-Kelly; assistant
director, Dick Mayberry; technical advisor, Al Jennings; makeup,
Perc Westmore; camera, James Wong Howe; editor, Owen Marks.

James Cagney (Jim Kincaid); Humphrey Bogart (Whip Mc-
Cord); Rosemary Lane (Jane Hardwick); Donald Crisp (Judge Hard-
wick); Harvey Stephens (Ned Kincaid); Hugh Sothern (John Kincaid);
Charles Middleton (Alec Martin); Ward Bond (Wes Handley); Edward
Pawley (Doolin); Lew Harvey (Curley); Trevor Bardette (Indian Jack
Pasco); John Miljan (Ringo); Arthur Aylesworth (Judge Morgan);
Irvin Bacon (Hotel Clerk); Wade Boteler (Sheriff Abe Collins); Joe
Devlin (Keely); Whizzer (Kincaid's Mount); Dan Wolheim (Deputy);
Ray Mayer (Professor); Bob Kortman (Juryman); Tex Cooper (Old
Man in Bar); John Harron (Secretary); Stuart Holmes (President
Cleveland); Jack Mower (Mail Clerk); Frank Mayo (Land Agent); Don
Barclay (Drunk); Horace Murphy, Robert Homans, George Lloyd
(Bartenders); Soledad Jiminez (Indian Woman); Ed Brady (Jury Fore-
man); Jeffrey Sayre (Times Reporter); and Spencer Charters, Joe
Rickson, William Worthington.

It has long been a familiar gambit of filmmakers to take established performers out of their element and put them in new sur-
roundings for the sake of novelty. Such was the case with The Oklahoma Kid which transferred both James Cagney and Humphrey Bogart
from the milieu of the city streets to the dusty trails of the old
West. Although compact, electric Cagney was hardly a quick candidate for cowboy stardom, this actionful film did not take itself
seriously. The result was a big-scale but tongue-in-cheek oater.

James Cagney, Rosemary Lane and Donald Crisp in The Oklahoma
Kid (1939).

Cagney even sang two songs within the feature. One jocular scene
had the pistol-packing Cagney blowing smoke from the barrel of his
pistol after firing at the villains.
        As Jim Kincaid, Cagney had the role of a Robin Hood-like
character in the Cherokee Strip of the 1890s. He took from the
rich and gave to the defenseless in order to revenge the hanging of
his father (Sothern), the latter a one-time reform candidate for
mayor whom outlaws framed for murder. Eventually Kincaid re-
stores his dad's good name by killing the leader (Bogart) of the
bandit group.
        If The Oklahoma Kid, loaded with the professionalism of the
Warner Bros. stock company, were produced today, it would be
greeted with relish. But in 1939 there was such a plethora of solid
celluloid products that this entry was considered just another--in
fact an inferior!--addition to the film season. "The Oklahoma Kid
is a straight 'Western' of the old school, not quite old-school enough
though, to be comic and a ten-gallon hat doesn't set so well on Mr.
Cagney's urban head" (New Yorker). "Stuff and nonsense, " say this
book's authors. On any level, The Oklahoma Kid is fun viewing.

ON THE MIDNIGHT STAGE see ON THE NIGHT STAGE

ON THE NIGHT STAGE   (Mutual, 1915)   five reels

     Producer, Thomas A. Ince; director, Reginald Barker; screenplay, C. Gardner Sullivan; camera, Robert Newhard.
     Rhea Mitchell (The Saloon Girl); Robert Edeson (The Sky Pilot); William S. Hart (Texas); Hershal Mayall (Handsome Jack Malone).
     Reissue titles: On the Midnight Stage, The Midnight Stage, The Bandit and the Preacher.

     After making two short Westerns, William S. Hart agreed to take the tertiary role in this Thomas H. Ince production. Its success solidified his stature in the genre and launched him as its greatest and most authentic film star.
     The forty-three year old Hart was cast as Texas, a road agent. He plans to wed saloon girl Rhea Mitchell with the proceeds from his stagecoach robberies in the Cheyenne territory. A parson called the "Sky Pilot" (Edeson) arrives on the night stage and rents a room over the saloon. He encounters the bar girl and later rescues Texas from a saloon brawl. Not long afterwards, the preacher falls in love with the girl. Texas steps aside knowing she is far better with this man of faith than with himself.
     A few years later the girl comes to a neighboring town where she is introduced to Handsome Jack Malone (Mayall). She rebuffs his advances. Aware of the girl's shady past, Handsome Jack vows revenge. He writes her a letter telling her that she must attend a dance with him. Texas learns of the situation and stops the night stage on which Malone is a passenger. He forces Handsome Jack to proceed onward on foot. Texas plans to leave the man in the desert, but he is almost killed when Malone tries to shoot him with a gun he has hidden. In the ensuing scuffle, Malone is killed. The girl can now return to her minister and Texas agrees to try to re-form.
     Filmed in California, On the Night Stage set the pattern for Hart's future screen portrayals. His characterization of Texas was the first of his famous good-bad man portrayals. The picture was scripted by G. Gardner Sullivan, who would write many of Hart's later films, including Hell's Hinges (1916) [q.v.]. Some sources to the contrary, Reginald Barker, not Hart, directed the film.
     This feature was reissued in 1915 by Mutual and in 1923 by Tri-Stone. Alternative release and reissue titles abound for this production.

ONCE UPON A TIME IN THE WEST   see   C'ERA UNA VOLTA IL WEST

ONE-EYED JACKS   (Paramount, 1961)   C   141 min.

     Executive producers, George Glass, Walter Seltzer; producer, Frank P. Rosenberg; director, Marlon Brando; based on the novel

The Authentic Death of Hendry Jones by Charles Neider; screenplay,
Guy Trosper, Calder Willingham; art directors, Hal Pereira, J.
McMillan Johnson; set decorators, Sam Comer, Robert Benton; as-
sistant directors, Francisco Day, Harry Caplan; color consultant,
Richard Mueller; music, Hugo Friedhofer; choreography, Josephine
Earl; makeup, Phil Rhodes, Wally Westmore; technical advisors,
Rodd Redwing, Rosita Morena; sound, Hugo and Charles Grenzbach;
process camera, Farciot Edouart; special camera effects, John P.
Fulton; camera, Charles Lang, Jr.; second unit camera, Wallace
Kelley; editor, Archie Marshek.

Marlon Brando (Rio); Karl Malden (Dad Longworth); Pina
Pellicer (Louisa); Katy Jurado (Maria); Ben Johnson (Bob Amory);
Slim Pickens (Lon); Larry Duran (Modesto); Sam Gilman (Harvey
Johnson); Timothy Carey (Howard Tetley); Miriam Colon (Redhead);
Elisha Cook, Jr. (Bank Teller); Rudolph Acosta (Leader of the
Rurales); Ray Teal (Bartender); John Dierkes (Bearded Townsman);
Margarita Cordova (Flamenco Dancer); Hank Worden (Doc); Nina
Martinez (Margarita); Snub Pollard (Townsman).

The joint experiences of Marlon Brando and Paramount over
this venture should have ended the star's Hollywood career.
Amazingly, however, they did not. Originally, Stanley Kubrick was
to direct the film, which was being produced by its star, Brando.
By the time the cameras rolled, Kubrick had departed and Brando
stepped in as director. The project was slated for a $1.8 million
budget; it ended up costing the studio some $6 million dollars. (In
U.S. and Canadian release, it only grossed $4.3 million in distribu-
tors' grosses.)

Karl Malden and Marlon Brando in One-Eyed Jacks (1961).

In the alleged original version of <u>One-Eyed Jacks</u>, the footage
ran some five hours and had no real hero or villain. Paramount,
however, became determined to salvage some commercial value from
this arty Western.   The studio took the project away from Brando
and re-cut it to a more feasible 141 minutes.   In the re-edited version, Brando's character becomes the hero, with Malden, now, the
bad guy.   Among the shorn footage were sequences of Brando's Rio
romancing a Chinese girl at a California seaside fishing village.
Brando had originally conceived the ending with Louisa (Pellicer)
dying, but the home lot executives demanded a less downbeat finale.
For the record, the title of the film refers to the playing card and
to the dual side of many people's personalities.

In 1880, three bank robbers (Brando, Malden and Worden)
stop at a Mexican border town with gold from their robberies.   Doc
(Worden) is killed by the law; Rio (Brando) and Dad Longworth
(Malden) hightail it into the desert.   Once in the mountains Longworth rides off with the gold, allegedly to obtain fresh horses but
in actuality to desert Rio, and he is captured and sent to prison.

Five years later, Rio and a cellmate (Duran) escape and begin the manhunt for Dad Longworth.   They join with Bob Amory
(Johnson) and Harvey Johnson (Gilman) and come to Monterey where
Dad is now the sheriff and is wed to the Mexican woman Maria
(Jurado).   Rio plans to help his compatriots rob the bank and obtain vengeance on Dad by seducing the man's stepdaughter Louisa
(Pellicer).   When Rio kills a drunken bully (Carey), Dad uses the
episode as an excuse to beat Rio and to crush his gun hand.   After
recuperation Rio plans to overcome Dad.   Eventually, the inevitable
showdown between the two occurs and Longworth is killed.   Before
leaving town, Rio promises Louisa he will return.

To Brando's credit, one must acknowledge the fine location,
(VistaVision) color photography, the stunt work, the hard riding,
and the authentic settings.   (Much location work was accomplished
at Monterey and in Death Valley.)

By using his <u>A Streetcar Named Desire</u> co-star as his adversary, Brando was able to stage an emotional bout between two
Method actors.   The film is at its most effective when each man is
preying on the other's weakness, as for example when an imprisoned
Brando says to Malden, "You're dying to get me hung."   Bulbous-
nosed Malden responds with sinister calmness, "No Kid.   You've
been dying to get yourself hung and I think this time you're going
to make it."

At one point in <u>One-Eyed Jacks</u>, one of the characters says,
"That's about it.   It ain't gonna help to say it.   But I wish to God
I hadn't."   Those words might well apply to the determined Brando,
who saw this ill-fated project through to completion at everyone's
expense.   As almost every scene in the picture was shot and re-
shot to appease perfectionist Brando, one can only wonder at the
hidden meanings/allusions/nuances buried within the photoplay.
What was running through Brando's mind when in the finale he rides
off into the white desert sands, turns to wave to Louisa, and then
cantors off into the distance?

An interesting sidelight is that two such disparate films

should have the same-named lead figure; Jane Russell's half-breed
in The Outlaw (1943) [q. v.] and Brando's outlaw "hero" of One-Eyed
Jacks are both named Rio.

OPEN RANGE   (Paramount, 1927)   5, 599'

Presenters, Adolph Zukor, Jesse L. Lasky; director, Clif-
ford S. Smith; based on the novel by Zane Grey; screenplay, John
Stone, J. Walter Ruben; titles, Roy Briant; camera, Hal Rosson.
Betty Bronson (Lucy Blake); Lane Chandler (Tex Smith);
Fred Kohler (Sam Hardman); Bernard Siegel (Brave Bear); Guy
Oliver (Jim Blake); Jim Corey (Red); George Connors (Sheriff Daley);
Flash the Wonder Horse (Himself).

During the late twenties Paramount had a number of handsome young leading men under contract, including Lane Chandler.
The actor was first chosen to star in Nevada (1927) [q. v.] but was
replaced by Gary Cooper.   Chandler then was placed opposite Betty
Bronson in Open Range, which proved to be his most prestigious
starring vehicle.   Yakima Canutt performed the stunts for Chandler
in most of the action footage.
Tex Smith (Chandler) is a cowpoke who finds Lucy Blake
(Bronson) enchanting.   Meanwhile an Indian chief (Siegel) is in cahoots with Sam Hardman (Kohler) to steal cattle during a rodeo.
Tex is mistaken for one of the rustlers.   However, he impresses
everyone with his honest ways when he daringly rides a bronco and
saves Lucy who is endangered by her runaway buggy.   Now convinced that Smith is innocent, Lucy hides him at her ranch.   Later
he discovers the gang's hideout and forces Sam Hardman to confess.
However, Hardman manages to alert the Indians, who attack the
town.   Tex engineers a cattle stampede to divert the rampaging
Indians.   Still later Tex saves Lucy and her dad (Oliver) from a
fire, while Hardman falls on his own knife and dies.
Like so many other silent photoplays about the Old West,
Open Range is filled with over-coincidence and amazing feats of
courage by the hero.   Nevertheless, it is a pleasant entry and an
indicator that Chandler's starring career should have been longer
than it was.   (With the coming of sound, Paramount found itself
with an over-abundance of leading men and let him go.   For a time
Lane appeared in minor series Westerns and then drifted into supporting and character roles.)

THE OREGON TRAIL   (Universal, 1923)   eighteen chapters

Director, Ed Laemmle; based on the book by Dr. Marcus
Whitman; screen story, Robert Dillon; screenplay, Anthony Colde-
way, Douglas Bronston, Jefferson Moffitt.
With Art Acord, Louise Lorraine, Duke R. Lee, Jim Corey,
Burton C. Law, Sidney DeGray.
Chapters: 1) Westward Ho!; 2) White Treachery; 3) Across
the Continent; 4) Message of Death; 5) Wagon of Doom; 6) Secret

Foes; 7) A Man of God; 8) Seeds of Civilization; 9) Justice; 10) The
New Era; 11) A Game of Nations; 12) To Save an Empire; 13) Trail
of Death; 14) On to Washington; 15) Santa Fe; 16) Fate of a National;
17) For High Stakes; 18) Victory.

THE OREGON TRAIL   (Republic, 1936)   59 min.

Producer, Trem Carr; supervisor, Paul Malvern; director,
Scott Pembroke; story, Lindsley Parsons, Robert Emmett; screen-
play, Jack Natteford, Emmett, Parsons; camera, Gus Peterson;
editor, Carl Pierson.
John Wayne (Captain John Delmont); Ann Rutherford (Anne
Ridgley); Yakima Canutt (Tom); Ben Hendricks, Jr. (Major Harris);
Joseph Girard (Colonel Delmont); Frank Rice (Red); E. H. Calvert
(Jim Ridgley); Harry Harvey (Tim); Jack Rutherford (Benton); Roland
Ray (Markey); Edward J. LeSaint (General); Octavio Giraud (Don
Miguel); Fern Emmett (Old Maid); Gino Corrado (Californians'
Leader).

THE OREGON TRAIL   (Universal, 1939)   fifteen chapters

Directors, Ford Beebe, Saul A. Goodkind; based on the book
by Dr. Marcus Whitman; screenplay, George Plympton, Basil
Dickey, Edmund Kelson, W. W. Watson; dialogue, Dorothy Cormack;
camera, Jerry Ash, William Stickner.
Johnny Mack Brown (Jeff Scott); Louise Stanley (Margaret
Mason); Bill Cody, Jr. (Jimmie Clark); Fuzzy Knight (Deadwood
Hawkins); Ed LeSaint (John Mason); James Blaine (Sam Morgan);
Jack C. Smith (Bull Bragg); Roy Barcroft (Colonel Custer); Colin
Kenny (Slade); Charles King (Dirk).
Chapters: 1) The Renegade's Revenge; 2) The Flaming
Forest; 3) The Brink of Disaster; 4) Thundering Doom; 5) The
Menacing Herd; 6) Indian Vengeance; 7) Trail of Treachery; 8) Red-
skin's Revenge; 9) The Avalanche of Doom; 10) The Plunge of Peril;
11) Trapped in the Flames; 12) The Baited Trap; 13) Crashing
Timbers; 14) Death in the Night; 15) Trail's End.

OREGON TRAIL   (Republic, 1945)   55 min.

Associate producer, Bennett Cohen; director, Thomas Carr;
based on the novel by Frank Gruber; screenplay, Betty Burbridge;
music director, Richard Cherwin; art director, Gano Chittenden;
camera, Bud Thackery; editor, Richard L. Van Enger.
Sunset Carson (Sunset); Peggy Stewart (Jill Layton); Frank
Jaquet (George Layton); Si Jenks (Andy); Mary Carr (Granny Layton); Lee Shumway (Captain Street); Bud Geary (Fletch); Keene Duncan (Johnny Slade); Steve Winston (Pendleton); Tex Terry (Moyer);
Tom London (Marshal); Earle Hodgins (Judge); Monte Hale, Rex
Lease (Cowboys).

THE OREGON TRAIL   (Twentieth Century-Fox, 1959)   C   82 min.

Producer, Richard Einfeld; director, Gene Fowler, Jr.;
story, Louis Vittes; screenplay, Fowler, Vittes; music, Paul Dunlap; songs, Dunlap and Charles Devlan; Will Miller; makeup, Del
Acerdo; technical advisor, Iron Eyes Cody; camera, Kay Norton;
editor, Betty Steinberg.

Fred MacMurray (Neal Harris); William Bishop (Captain
George Wayne); Nina Shipman (Prudence Cooper); Gloria Talbott
(Shona Hastings); Henry Hull (Seton); John Carradine (Zachariah
Garrison); John Dierkes (Gabe Hastings); Elizabeth Patterson (Maria
Cooper); James Bell (Jeremiah Cooper); Ralph Sanford (Mr. Decker);
Tex Terry (Brizzard); Arvo Ojala (Ellis); Roxene Wells (Flossie
Shoemaker); Gene N. Fowler (Richard Cooper); John Slosser (Johnny);
Sherry Spalding (Lucy); Ollie O'Toole (James G. Bennett); Ed Wright
(Jesse); Oscar Beregl (Ralph Clayman); Addison Richards (President
Polk); Lumsden Hare (British Ambassador).

What magical connotations the three words of this film's title
evoke: thoughts of the Westward expansion of the nineteenth century,
the seeking out of new frontiers unspoiled by the Industrial Revolution.   Naturally there was a less intriguing reality confronting the
pioneers who had to endure environmental hardships, paucity of food
and water, and the constant threat of Indians and wild animals who
preyed on the wagon trains.

In 1923 Universal made an eighteen-chapter cliffhanger with
serial stars Art Acord (in his lasting starring serial) and Louise
Lorraine.   The serial was based on Dr. Marcus Whitman's famous
travel book.   In the given format of the episodic drama, it related
the development of Oregon Trail which brought settlers, trappers,
and missionaries into the great Northwest.   This presentation had
trapper Acord and heroine Lorraine opposed to a crooked land syndicate.   The film added flavor with the recreation of George Washington and Thomas Jefferson planning the purchase of the territory in
a deal with Napoleon Bonaparte, the subsequent Lewis and Clark
expedition which brought civilization closer to the West Coast, and
the invention of the cotton gin by Eli Whitney which was a direct
lead-in to the increase of slave importation and the resultant Civil
War.   The blend of history, adventure, and suspense would make
this chapterplay an ideal candidate for showing during America's Bi-
centennial Celebration in 1976.

The title was next used in 1936 for a Paul Malvern-produced
series Western at Republic starring ever-busy John Wayne.   The
youngish star was featured in a rather trite telling of a man trailing
the killer of his dad.   In this case he is after the man who ambushed his father and his troopers and left the survivors to starve
in the mountains.   While on his manhunt the hero falls in love with
a fetching miss (Rutherford), and with the aid of Spanish soldiers he
captures the killers.

Three years later Universal again adopted the title The Oregon Trail for a fifteen-chapter photoplay.   John Mack Brown starred
and was directed by serial expert, Ford Beebe.   Jeff Scott (Brown)
is hired by the government to stop outlaws and Indians attacking a

wagon train heading for the Oregon country. Scott and his pal
Deadwood Hawkins (Knight) join the convoy and save a girl (Stanley)
and a boy (Cody, Jr.) from an Indian massacre. Jeff suspects the
wagonmaster, Bull Bragg (Smith), of being a spy and has him fired.
Later the Indians do attack the train, but they are thwarted by Jeff
and the cavalry. When the train finally reaches its destination, a
fur syndicate manager (Blaine) claims to own the settlers' land.
However, Jeff exposes him as being the culprit and the man responsible for the settlers' problems. At long last the pioneers are free
to begin their new lives.

In 1945, Republic, in the final years of its golden age, used
the title The Oregon Trail for a Sunset Carson western.

Most recently, Gene Fowler, Jr. in 1959 packaged a film at
Twentieth Century-Fox, for their budget use. Shot in CinemaScope
and color it starred Fred MacMurray as Neal Harris, a New York
Herald writer who is sent West via a wagon train. His mission is
to find out if President James Polk (Richards) has sent soldiers
disguised as pioneers to Oregon to aid in the U.S. British dispute
over the territory. While on the frontier he is also to investigate
the Indian attacks on settlers there. Along the way Neal romances
Prudence Cooper (Shipman), but finds himself at odds with Captain
Wayne (Bishop) over her affections. As Variety pointed out, "The
production makes good use of film from other pix, thus keeping its
own budget in hand. But bits of the new footage--particularly a
sequence in front of a hill-and-dale backdrop--are embarrassingly
phony. The musical score is very good."

THE OUTCASTS OF POKER FLAT   (Universal, 1919)   six reels

        Producer, P. A. Powers; director, John Ford; based on the
stories "The Outcasts of Poker Flat" and "The Luck of Roaring
Camp" by Bret Harte; screenplay, H. Tipton Stock; camera, John
W. Brown.
        Harry Carey (Square Shootin' Lanyon/John Oakhurst); Cullen
Landis (Billy Lanyon/Tommy Oakhurst); Gloria Hope (Ruth Watson/
Sophy); and J. Farrell MacDonald, Charles H. Mailes, Victor Potel,
Joe Harris, Duke R. Lee, Vester Pegg.

THE OUTCASTS OF POKER FLAT   (RKO, 1937)   68 min.

        Producer, Robert Sisk; director, Christy Cabanne; based on
the stories "The Outcasts of Poker Flat" and "The Luck of Roaring
Camp" by Bret Harte; screenplay, John Twist, Harry Segall; camera,
Robert De Grasse; editor, Ted Cheseman.
        Preston Foster (John Oakhurst); Jean Muir (Helen); Van Hef-
lin (Reverend Samuel Woods); Virginia Weidler (Luck); Margaret
Irving (The Duchess); Frank M. Thomas (Redford); Si Jenks (Ken-
tuck); Dick Elliott (Stumph); Al St. John (Uncle Billy); Bradley Page
(Socoma); Richard Lane (High-Grade); Monte Blue (Indian Jim);
Billy Gilbert (Charley); Dudley Clements (Wilkes).

Two versions of The Outcasts of Poker Flat. Top, Monte Blue, Richard Lane, Bradley Page and Preston Foster in the 1937 version; below, Cameron Mitchell and Anne Baxter in the 1952 remake.

THE OUTCASTS OF POKER FLAT   (Twentieth Century-Fox, 1952)
81 min.

Producer, Julian Blaustein; director, Joseph M. Newman;
based on the stories "The Outcasts of Poker Flat" and "The Luck
of Roaring Camp" by Bret Harte; screenplay, Edmund H. North;
music, Hugo Friedhofer; music director, Lionel Newman; camera,
Joseph LaShelle; editor, William Reynolds.
Anne Baxter (Cal); Dale Robertson (John Oakhurst); Miriam
Hopkins (Duchess); Cameron Mitchell (Ryker); Craig Hill (Tom
Dakin); Barbara Bates (Piney); Billy Lynn (Jake); Dick Rich (Drunk);
Russ Conway, Bob Adler (Vigilantes); John Ridgely (Bill Akeley);
Harry T. Shannon (Bearded Miner); Lee Phelps (Man); Harry Carter,
Tom Greenway (Townsmen); Harry Harvey, Jr. (George Larabee).

Bret Harte's popular short story was interpolated with another of his yarns, "The Luck of Roaring Camp," for all of its
screen versions. The first of them was done in 1919 as a Universal
Special by director Jack (later John) Ford and it starred screen
regular Harry Carey. It was one of a number of films that Ford
and Carey made together, most of which were character stories and
not the regular shoot 'em up Western fare of the period.
The first version began and ended with Carey reading Harte's
stories to his son. Within the stories Carey is cast as a gambler
who adopts a small boy who grows up to love the same girl that
Carey's John Oakhurst does. So he gives her up to his adopted son
(Landis). Photoplay reported that this six-reeler had "marvelous
river locations and absolutely incomparable photography."
In 1937 energetic RKO re-filmed the work, again interpolating
the two stories with Christy Cabanne as its director. This version
condensed the number of characters from the original but expanded
the storyline with new figures, while still remaining fairly close to
Harte's work. One of the new characters was a reverend (Heflin)
who succeeds in curing gambler John Oakhurst (Foster) of his
gambling and drinking habits (in the Harte stories he was not a
drinker). Here too the group, led by Oakhurst, is snowbound and
seeks refuge in a cabin. Reviewing this effort, the New York Times
noted that it was "a cake with box office frosting to serve to a screen
public."
By the time it occurred to Twentieth Century-Fox to film the
Harte stories, in 1952, the plotline had worn thin and the production
seemed quite threadbare in its construction. Again there is a group
of people cabin-bound during a snowstorm in the mountains. Among
them are gambler Oakhurst (Robertson), a faded saloon entertainer
(Hopkins), a woman of suffering and easy virtue (Baxter), and Ryker
(Mitchell) a killer. Only Miss Hopkins and Robertson gave the film
any viability as a programmer.

THE OUTLAW (RKO, 1943) 126 min. (post-1943 showings, 117
min.)

Producer, Howard Hughes; supervising film director, Otho

Lovering; directors, Howard Hawks, Hughes; screenplay, Jules
Furthman; music director, Victor Young; assistant director, Sam
Nelson; art director, Perry Ferguson; special effects, Roy Davidson; second unit camera, Lucien Ballard; camera, Gregg Toland;
editor, Walter Grissell.

     Jack Beutel (Billy the Kid); Jane Russell (Rio); Thomas Mit-
chell (Pat Garrett); Walter Huston (Doc Holliday); Mimi Aguglia
(Guadalupe); Joe Sawyer (Charley); Gene Rizzi (Stranger); Frank
Darien (Shorty); Pat West (Bartender); Carl Stockdale (Minister);
Nena Quartaro (Chita); Dickie Jones, Frank Ward, Bobby Callahan
(Boys); Ethan Laidlaw, Ed Brady, William Steele (Deputies); Wally
Reid, Jr. (Bystander); Ed Peil, Sr. (Swanson); Lee "Lasses" White
(Coach Driver); Ted Mapes (Guard); William Newell (Drunk Cowboy);
Cecil Kellogg (Officer); Lee Shumway (Dealer); Emory Parnell
(Dolan); Martin Garralaga (Waiter); Julian Rivero (Pablo); Arthur
Loft, Dick Elliott, John Sheehan (Salesmen).

     One of the most over-publicized films in history, this Howard
Hughes production was made in 1940-41 as an intended rival to
MGM's Billy the Kid (1940) [q.v.]. However, Hughes' Western did
not receive national release until the late forties. During the inter-
vening years Hughes used various publicity gimmicks to create a
"super" aura around the film. When it was finally distributed, it
managed to gross some $5 million, on an investment of $3.4 million.
(The movie had originally been budgeted at $440,000.) Director

Thomas Mitchell, Walter Huston, Jane Russell and Jack Beutel in
The Outlaw (1943).

Howard Hawks left the production after being unable to work with
the demanding Hughes, who finished the film himself.

The narrative opens after the supposed death of Billy the Kid
(Beutel). Actually he is in Lincoln, New Mexico where he and Doc
Holliday (Huston) fight over the ownership of a strawberry roan.
Later Billy is shot at by half-breed Rio (Russell), Holliday's mis-
tress, whose brother Billy once killed in a fight. Next Sheriff Pat
Garrett (Mitchell) tries to arrest Billy and wings the fugitive in the
process. The injured outlaw is taken to Holliday's ranch where
Rio nurses him back to health. They fall in love and secretly wed.
Although Doc later finds out the truth he helps Billy escape into the
desert from the pursuing Garrett. But Billy and Doc discover that
spiteful Rio has filled their water canteens with sand. Garrett
eventually captures Holliday and is forced to shoot him. Billy
thereafter captures Rio but then lets her go free. Still later Billy
tricks Garrett by handcuffing him to a porch. He and Rio leave
together.

As any red-blooded moviegoer of the forties can attest, the
primary charm and fascination of The Outlaw was the anatomy of
statuesque Miss Russell. If the storyline, camera, and direction
had focused more on the plot and the acting than on the actress'
bustline, the film might have been a far more intriguing venture.

After the screening of The Outlaw in San Francisco in 1943,
twenty minutes were deleted from the film, all sections which had
been denounced by the Legion of Decency. Among the more erotic
sequences to be clipped out of the picture were Rio's keeping Billy
"warm" while he was ill, and Doc and Billy playing poker with the
winner having to choose Rio or a horse.

After Hughes' death in 1976, The Outlaw was reissued. The
MPAA rated it "G," fir for general audiences of all ages. How
times and mores have changed!

THE OUTRAGE (MGM, 1964) 97 min.

Producer, A. Ronald Lubin; associate producer, Michael
Kanin; director, Martin Ritt; based on the Japanese film Rashomon
by Akira Kurosawa, from stories by Ryunosuke Akutagawa and the
play by Fay and Michael Kanin; screenplay, Michael Kanin; music-
music director, Alex North; art directors, George W. Davis, Tambi
Larsen; set decorators, Henry Grace, Robert R. Benton; assistant
director, Daniel J. McCauley; costumes, Don Feld; makeup, William
Tuttle; special camera effects, J. McMillan Johnson, Robert R.
Hoag; camera, James Wong Howe; editor, Frank Santillo.

Paul Newman (Juan Carrasco); Laurence Harvey (Husband);
Claire Bloom (Wife); Edward G. Robinson (Con Man); William Shat-
ner (Preacher); Howard Da Silva (Prospector); Albert Salmi (Sheriff);
Thomas Chalmers (Judge); Paul Fix (Indian).

This production was the American remake of Rashomon
(1951), the Japanese classic directed by Akira Kurosawa. (There
had been a Broadway stage version of Rashomon in 1959 with Claire
Bloom, Rod Steiger and Noel Willman.)

Paul Newman, Claire Bloom and Laurence Harvey in The Outrage
(1964).

Set at the end of the nineteenth century, this Hollywood rendition tells of three men, a preacher (Shatner), a prospector (Da
Silva), and a con man (Robinson) who meet at a deserted train station in the Old West.   The first two tell the con man about a trial
they have just witnessed.   According to them, it was the murder
case of an outlaw (Newman) in which three different variations of the
facts were told.   The wife (Bloom) claimed that the outlaw raped her
and she killed her husband (Harvey) for encouraging him.   An old
Indian (Fix), who found the dying husband, said the man committed
suicide out of shame; while the outlaw insisted that he raped the wife
and killed the spouse in a duel.

After the stories are related, the three find an abandoned
baby.   Then it is revealed that it is the prospector, who did not
testify, who actually witnessed the crime.   (In fact, he stole a
jeweled dagger from the dying husband.)   He claims that the outlaw
begged the woman to leave with him but she goaded the two men into
a fight and that the husband fell on the dagger.   In repentance for
his apathy, the prospector offers to raise the infant along with his
five children.   At the same time the preacher's faith in mankind is
restored.

Despite its noble aim, the film hardly matched the prior
success of the American transformation of Kurosawa's The Seven

Samurai (1954) into The Magnificent Seven (1960) [q.v.]. Analyzing
the faults of the Paul Newman picture, the New York Herald Tribune's
Judith Crist penned, "What should be a cogent, almost ritualistic ex-
amination and re-examination of the many facets of truth emerges as
little more than a story told and thrice-re-told simply to provide
three performers with exercises in acting."
       On the plus side the film boasts flavorful appearances by
Robinson as the grizzly old con artist and a sensual performance of
the aloof rape victim by Miss Bloom. But neither swarthy makeup,
a beard, nor raggedy clothes could disguise Newman as anything
other than an American movie star on a Sunday school outing.

OVERLAND STAGE RAIDERS (Republic, 1938) 58 min.

       Associate producer, William Berke; director, George Sher-
man; based on characters created by William Colt MacDonald; story,
Bernard McConville, Edmund Kelso; screenplay, Luci Ward; camera,
William Nobles; editor, Tony Martinelli.
       John Wayne (Stony Brooke); Louise Brooks (Beth Hoyt); Ray
Corrigan (Tucson Smith); Max Terhune (Lullaby Joslin); Frank La-
Rue (Milton); Fern Emmett (Ma Hawkins); Anthony Marsh (Ned
Hoyt); Gordon Hart (Mullins); John Archer (Bob Whitney); Roy James
(Harmon); Olin Francis (Jake); Henry Otho (Sheriff); George Sher-
wood (Clanton); Archie Hall (Waddell); Yakima Canut (Bus Driver);
Slim Whittaker (Hawkins).

Olin Francis and John Wayne in Overland Stage Raiders (1938).

This segment of Republic's "The Three Mesquiteers" is best-
remembered today because it marks the last American film of actress
Louise Brooks, who had been a popular star in the twenties but
whose career had faded in the thirties. At the time of this film
she was still quite beautiful and still a good actress. It was a sad
decline for the once leading lady to be merely a featured performer
in a programmer Western.
    The title of this production had little to do with the film. In
it The Three Mesquiteers (Wayne, Corrigan and Terhune) buy up an
airport near an isolated gold town to ship the precious ore via
plane. After the hijackers in the caper have been dispatched, Stony
(Wayne) wins the heroine (Brooks). This was the second of eight
Mesquiteers entries Wayne would make.
    In an issue of Film Fan Monthly (1975), Michael King wrote,
"Overland Stage Raiders (1938) is not my favorite B Western (especially after the Overland Stage turns out to be a Greyhound bus in
the opening shots!), but the film's cast includes a youthful John
Wayne and a most unusual leading lady for a Republic opus: Louise
Brooks. Seeing her make her entrance is as incongruous as anything in Blazing Saddles; clearly she had taken the wrong bus and
was meant to report to work at MGM--not Republic! Here was a
dark-eyed woman of enigmatic beauty and presence, with a distinctly
Park Avenue accent, speaking lines like, 'But Stony, I don't know
anything about gold shipments. '"

THE OX-BOW INCIDENT (Twentieth Century-Fox, 1943) 75 min.

    Producer, Lamar Trotti; director, William A. Wellman;
based on the novel by Walter Van Tilburg Clark; screenplay, Trotti;
art directors, Richard Day, James Basevi; music, Cyril J. Mock-
ridge; camera, Arthur Miller; editor, Allen McNeil.
    Henry Fonda (Gil Carter); Dana Andrews (Martin); Mary Beth
Hughes (Rose Mapen); Anthony Quinn (Mexican); William Eythe
(Gerald); Henry "Harry" Morgan (Art Croft); Jane Darwell (Ma
Grier); Matt Briggs (Judge Tyler); Harry Davenport (Davies); Frank
Conroy (Major Tetley); Marc Lawrence (Farnley); Victor Kilian
(Darby); Paul Hurst (Monty Smith); Chris-Pin Martin (Poncho); Ted
[Michael] North (Joyce); George Meeker (Mr. Swanson); Almira Ses-
sions (Mrs. Swanson); Margaret Hamilton (Mrs. Larch); Dick Rich
(Mapes); Francis Ford (Old Man); Stanley Andrews (Bartlett); Billy
Benedict (Greene); Rondo Hatton (Hart); Paul Burns (Winder); Leigh
Whipper (Sparks); George Lloyd (Moore); George Chandler (Jimmy
Cairnes); Hank Bell (Red); Forrest Dillon (Mark); George Plues
(Alec Small); Willard Robertson (Sheriff); Tom London (Deputy).

    Critic James Agee wrote of this memorable film, '[It] is 'one
of the best and most interesting pictures I have seen for a long time,
and it disappointed me.... It seems to me that in Ox-Bow artifact
and nature got jammed in such a way as to jive a sort of double
focus, like off-printing in a comic strip." At a later date, Agee
added, "I underpraised [the film]; it stands in memory very firm,

respectable and sympathetic.   But I still think it suffers from <u>rigor</u>
<u>artis.</u> "
       Pre-dating the "adult" Western by nearly a decade, <u>The Ox-</u>
<u>Bow Incident</u> was a truly psychological film about two cowpokes
(Fonda and Morgan) who ride into a small Western town and are
swept along with the fervor of a lynch mob as the town seeks a trio
of men who rustled the cattle herd of a rancher after killing him.
The "posse" comes upon three men (Andrews, Quinn and Ford) who
claim to be innocent of the crime, but due to circumstantial evidence
and the fury of the crowd they are hanged.   On the way back to
town the men learn that the real culprits have been captured and
that the rancher in question is actually still alive.   At the finale
Gil Carter (Fonda) reads aloud the poignant letter Martin (Andrews)
wrote to his wife before being executed.
       Obviously shot on the cheap--Darryl F. Zanuck had no faith
in the project--the picture is shackled with unconvincing studio "exteriors" and such settings as Major Tetley's mansion are totally
lacking in realism.   Nevertheless, the picture is full of fine and
colorful performances: Gil Carter (Fonda), through whose eyes the
tale is told; Art Croft (Morgan) as his partner; Major Tetley (Conroy) as the loud-mouthed ex-Confederate officer who leads the mob
and who commits suicide more because his son turns out to be a
pacifist than because of the murders; the Old Man (Ford), who is
too senile to comprehend his plight beyond the fact that he is to be
hanged; Ma Grier (Darwell) as the tough frontier woman who urged
the mob onward; and Monty Smith (Hurst) the outrageously wicked
bartender who is a ringleader of the crowd's fury.
       Manny Farber rightly wrote in <u>The New Republic,</u> "<u>The Ox-</u>
<u>Bow Incident</u> is a significant moment in our culture. "
       In June 1956 <u>The Ox-Bow Incident</u> was reutilized as a property
for "The Twentieth Century-Fox Hour, " a TV anthology show, with
Wallace Ford and Robert Wagner.
       The 1943 film was released in England as <u>Strange Incident</u>.

PAINT YOUR WAGON (Paramount, 1969) C 164 min.

       Producer, Alan Jay Lerner; associate producer, Tom Shaw;
director, Joshua Logan; based on the musical play by Lerner and
Frederick Loewe; screenplay, Paddy Chayefsky; songs, Lerner and
Loewe; Lerner and Andre Previn; music, Lerner; additional music,
Previn; music arranger-music director, Nelson Riddle; choral arranger, Joseph J. Lilley; choral music director, Roger Wagner;
production designer, John Truscott; art director, Carl Braunger;
set decorator, James I. Berkey; costumes, Truscott; choreography,
Jack Baker; titles, David Stone; sound, William Randall; special effects, Maurice Ayers, Larry Hampton; camera, William A. Fraker;
aerial camera, Nelson Tyler; second unit camera, Loyal Griggs;
editor, Robert Jones.
       Lee Marvin (Ben Rumson); Clint Eastwood (Pardner); Jean
Seberg (Elizabeth); Harve Presnell (Rotten Luck Willie); Ray Walston
(Mad Jack Duncan); Tom Ligon (Horton Fenty); Alan Dexter (Parson);

William O'Connell (Horace Tabor); Benny Baker (Haywood Holbrook);
Alan Baxter (Atwell); Geoffrey Norman (Foster); H. B. Haggerty
(Steve Bull); Terry Jenkins (Joe Mooney); Karl Bruck (Schermer-
horn); John Mitchum (Jacob Woodling); Sue Casey (Sarah Woodling);
Eddie Little Sky (Indian); Harvey Parry (Higgins); H. W. Gim (Wong);
William Mims (Frock-Coated Man); Roy Jenson (Hennessey); Pat
Hawley (Clendennon); The Nitty Gritty Dirt Band (Themselves).

     Despite the tremendous effort that went into filming this
Broadway play, the final product is even more leaden than another
such stage-to-screen translation, The Unsinkable Molly Brown
(1964). "... Set piece follows stolidly upon set piece, with the
camera lethargically waiting while the characters assemble in front
of it, do their stuff, and exeunt severally into the wings.   Characteristic of the film's lack of visual invention is the climactic collapse of the town, where the camera simply cuts endlessly from one
house to the next as they fall down, devoid of wit or rhythm and
driving not only the town but the sequence into the ground" (British
Monthly Film Bulletin).   Nevertheless, this intended blockbuster did
draw a mighty $14.5 million in distributors' gross rentals in the
U.S. and Canada alone.   The wonders of media promotion never fail
to amaze!
     Set in the mining town of No Name City, the sprawling story
concerns two prospectors, hard-drinking Ben Rumson (Marvin) and
his somber friend, Partner (Eastwood).   There are no women in the

Clint Eastwood, Lee Marvin and Jean Seberg in Paint Your Wagon
(1969).

town and when a Mormon wagon train passes through, one of the
group sells a wife (Seberg) to Rumson, who is the highest bidder.
The girl, however, demands both Rumson and Pardner as husbands
to conform to Mormon teachings.   The trio exist blissfully for a
while until puritanical newcomers break up the menage, especially
after Rumson takes a younger member of the new arrivals to the
recently-established brothel.
        Left-over from the Broadway score of this gold-rush musical
are such songs as "They Call the Wind Maria," "I Talk to the
Trees," and "Wand'rin Star." Unfortunately the star trio, never
noted as vocalizers, were allowed to perform their own singing,
adding insult to general injury. (Harve Presnell who did all his own
singing, too, had a strong, clear voice, and should have had the
lead.)
        The Broadway show opened at the Shubert Theatre on Novem-
ber 12, 1951 for a run of 289 performances, featuring James Barton,
Olga San Juan, Tony Bavaar, James Mitchell, and Kay Medford.
The book line was revamped for the screen version.

THE PAINTED DESERT (Pathé, 1931) 80 min.

        Director, Howard Higgins; story-screenplay, Higgins, Tom
Buckingham; sound, Earl Wolcott, Ben Winkler; camera, Ed Snyder;
editor, Clarence Kolster.
        William Boyd (Bill Holbrook); Helen Twelvetrees (Mary Ellen
Cameron); William Farnum (Cash Holbrook); J. Farrell MacDonald
(Jeff Cameron); Clark Gable (Brett); and Charles Sellon, Will Walling,
Guy Edward Hearn, Wade Boteler, William LeMaire, Cy Clegg,
James Donlon, Richard Cramer, George Burton, James Mason,
Brady Kline, Jerry Drew, Hugh Allen Adams.

THE PAINTED DESERT (RKO, 1938) 59 min.

        Producer, Bert Gilroy; director, David Howard; screenplay,
John Rathmell, Oliver Drake; camera, Harry Wild; editor, Frederick
Knudston.
        George O'Brien (Bud McVey); Laraine Johnson [Day] (Carol
Banning); Ray Whitley (Steve); Stanley Fields (Placer Bill); Fred
Kohler (Fawcett); Max Wagner (Kincaid); Harry Cording (Burke); Lee
Shumway (Bart); Lloyd Ingraham (Banning); Maude Allen (Yukon Kate);
William V. Mong (Heist); Lew Kelly (Bartender).

        Two film versions of this tale were produced in the thirties.
The 1931 version by Pathé is better known because it was in this
Western that Clark Gable first achieved cinema notice. The film
told of two prospectors, Cash Holbrook (Farnum) and Jeff Cameron
(MacDonald), who rescue an infant from an abandoned wagon train.
Holbrook adopts the boy and a feud begins between the two friends.
Thirty years later Cameron and his daughter (Twelvetrees) keep
Holbrook's cattle from using their waterhole, holding off Holbrook's
men with guns. Meanwhile, Holbrook's adopted son Bill (Boyd) has

become an engineer and he returns home to mine tungsten. He decides to romance Mary Ellen (Twelvetrees) and hopefully stop the feud. In so doing he is opposed by Brett (Gable), who loves the girl. In retaliation, Brett damages Bill's mine. Bill and Brett have a showdown and the former wins. Bill weds Mary Ellen and at the ceremony the old foes mend their ways.

The _Hollywood Reporter_ wrote, "The picture is filled with lovely views of mountains and the grim stretch known as the Painted Desert.... Much of the dialogue is unconvincing and serves chiefly to slow up the action." _Variety_ complimented the "excellent camera views of the fantastic beauty of the bleak California desert," while _Photoplay_ insisted, "You'll like this Western, which makes no pretense other than entertainment. It's far above the average...."

In 1938 RKO re-made the film as a vehicle for George O'Brien, who inherited the Boyd role. Here the hero outwits an entire gang of crooks who are after his tungsten mine. Fred Kohler as Fawcett was the chief villain and Laraine Johnson [Day] was a coquettish heroine. Good comedy relief was provided by Stanley Fields and partner Maude Allen, while Ray Whitley and his group sang the title tune. The mine blast at the climax of the first version was re-used, but a montage sequence showing mining operation was especially shot for this remake directed by David Howard.

THE PAINTED STALLION (Republic, 1937) twelve chapters

Associate producer, J. Laurence Wickland; directors, William Witney, Ray Taylor, Alan James; story, Morgan Cox, Ronald Davidson; screenplay, Barry Shipman, Winston Miller; music director, Raoul Kraushaar; camera, William Nobles, Edgar Lyons.

Ray Corrigan (Clark Stewart); Hoot Gibson (Jamison); Sammy McKim (Kit Carson); LeRoy Mason (Escobedo Dupray); Jack Perrin (Davey Crockett); Hal Taliaferro (JimBowie); Duncan Renaldo (Zomarro); Julia Thayer (The Rider); Oscar and Elmer (Themselves); Yakima Canutt (Tom); Maston Williams (Macklim); Duke Taylor (Joe); Loren Riebe (Pedro); George de Normand (Juan); Gordon de Main (Governor); Charles King (Bull Smith); Vinegar Roan (Oldham).

Chapters: 1) Trail to Empire; 2) The Rider of the Stallion; 3) The Death Leap; 4) Avalanche!; 5) Volley of Death; 6) Thundering Wheels; 7) Trail Treachery; 8) The Whistling Arrow; 9) The Fatal Message; 10) Ambush; 11) Tunnel of Terror; 12) Human Targets.

This twelve-chapter serial was filmed on location at St. George, Utah, where William Witney replaced Ray Taylor as director when the chapterplay got behind schedule due to weather problems. It was the first of two dozen cliffhangers Witney would make for Republic Pictures, many of them with Alan James.

Agent Clark Stewart (Corrigan) is sent to Santa Fe in the early 1820s to negotiate a trade agreement with the new Mexican governor, who has just thrown off Spanish rule. Simultaneously, a wagon train led by Jamison (Gibson) leaves Missouri with trade goods bound for the Southwest. Both Jim Bowie (Taliaferro) and Kit Carson

(McKim) accompany the convoy. The ex-governor (Mason) of the
territory plans to regain power by putting one of his own men in
Stewart's place and his comrade (Renaldo) attempts to destroy the
wagon train by inciting the Indians.
     Attempts to kill Clark, however, are foiled by a mysterious
Indian girl rider (Thayer) on a painted stallion who shoots a whistling
arrow at the villains. Zomarro (Renaldo), though, does steal Clark's
official papers. Clark trails the desperadoes to Santa Fe and there
meets Davey Crockett (Perrin). Together, Clark, Crockett and the
Indian Rider, along with Jamison's wagon train men, trap the villains
in their cave hideout. Dupray and Zomarro are killed and their gang
captured. Clark then signs an agreement with the Mexican government opening up the area for U.S. trade. The Rider, a Goddess of
the Comanche Indians, is left to continue maintaining the peace.
     Although historically inaccurate, The Painted Stallion proved
to be a very popular serial. In fact, Edward Connor, writing of
Republic serials in Screen Facts magazine (1964), suggests, "The
Painted Stallion had such sweep, drive and power, not to mention
great cast and production values, that it was easily the best serial
of 1937."
     Sharp-eyed viewers might have noticed that stock shots were
used from Devil Horse (1926) and Big Trail (1930). Only the more
jaded moviegoer would have carped at the cheating used to disengage
the heroes from their plights of drowning, being crushed by rocks,
trampled by horses, etc. The stunt work of Yakima Canutt, who
also acted in the serial and did doubling work, was superior, and
Maston Williams as the henchman Macklim added spice to the proceedings. However, the so-called comedy elements supplied by
Oscar and Elmer could have been omitted without loss.
     Old time Western stars Hoot Gibson, Jack Perrin, and Hal
Taliaferro (alias Wally Wales) added a nostalgia aspect to the work.
     The serial was issued in a feature version to theatres in the
fifties. At the same time it was being re-run as a chapterplay on
television, proving once again how Republic's Golden Age of serials
was such a boon to movie fans.

PALEFACE (Paramount, 1948) C 91 min.

     Producer, Robert L. Welch; director, Norman Z. McLeod;
screenplay, Edmund Hartman, Frank Tashlin; additional dialogue,
Jack Rose; art directors, Hans Dreier, Earl Hedrick; set decorators,
Sam Comer, Bertram Granger; music, Victor Young; songs, Joseph
J. Lilley, Jay Livingston, and Ray Evans; choreography, Billy
Daniel; costumes, Mary Kay Dodson; assistant director, Alvin Gan-
zer; sound, Gene Merritt, John Cope; special effects, Gordon Jen-
nings; process camera, Farciot Ecouart; camera, Ray Rennahan;
editor, Ellsworth Hoagland.
     Bob Hope ("Painless" Peter Potter); Jane Russell (Calamity
Jane); Robert Armstrong (Terris); Iris Adrian (Pepper); Robert Wat-
son (Toby Preston); Jack Searl (Jasper Martin); Joseph Vitale (Indian
Scout); Charles Trowbridge (Governor Johnson); Clem Bevans (Hank

Billings); Jeff York (Joe); Stanley Andrews (Commissioner Emerson); Wade Crosby (Web); Chief Yowlachie (Chief Yellow Feather); Iron Eyes Cody (Chief Iron Eyes); John Maxwell (Village Gossip); Tom Kennedy (Bartender); Henry Brandon (Wapato the Medicine Man); Francis J. McDonald (Lance); Skelton Knaggs (Pete); Earl Hodgins (Clem); Arthur Space (Zach); Trevor Bardette, Alan Bridge (Horsemen); Paul Burns (Justice of the Peace).

It was a stroke of casting genius to pair Paramount's wisecracking comedian Bob Hope with sultry, busty Jane "The Outlaw" Russell. The resultant Western spoof was a very popular entry in the 1948 season and showed how effectively the sagebrush genre could be joshed.

Curvaceous, sharpshooting Jane, as Calamity Jane, is paroled in order to hunt a notorious gang of outlaws in the West of the 1870s. She picks as her traveling companion the clumsy correspondence school dentist, "Painless" Peter Potter (Hope), and together (they wed) they head to the frontier which is never the same after their arrival. If films like The Outlaw (1943) and Duel in the Sun (1946) [both q.v.] sought to attract wider audiences by making sensuous Westerns, The Paleface took the occasion to lampoon sex in the wild West setting.

The slapstick satire grossed a healthy $4.5 million in distributors' domestic rental and led to a sequel, Son of Paleface (1952), which reunited Hope and Russell and added Roy Rogers and Trigger as bonus attractions. The follow-up, held on the shelf for well over a year, has its enthusiasts, but it is not nearly as humorous and offbeat as the original. In the 1952 film, Jane is the head of an outlaw band and Ski-nose Hope is the man who falls hopelessly in love with the hard-riding bad girl.

In 1968 Universal Pictures would remake The Paleface as a Don Knotts (diluted) comedy, The Shakiest Gun in the West.

PARDNERS see RHYTHM ON THE RANGE

THE PARSON OF PANAMINT (Paramount, 1916) 5,000'

Director, William Desmond Taylor; based on the story by Peter B. Kyne.

Dustin Farnum (Philo Pharo); Winifred Kingston ("Buckskin Liz"); "Doc" Cannon ("Chuckawalla Bill"); Howard Davies (Bud Deming); Colin Chase ("Chappie" Ellerton); Ogden Crane (Absalom Randall); Jane Keckley (Arabella Randall); Tom Bates ("Crabapple" Thompson).

THE PARSON OF PANAMINT (Paramount, 1941) 84 min.

Producer, Harry Sherman; associate producer, Lewis J. Rachmil; director, William McGann; based on the story by Peter B. Kyne; screenplay, Harold Shumate, Adrian Scott; art director, Ralph

Ellen Drew and Charlie Ruggles in The Parson of Panamint (1941).

Berger; music director, Irvin Talbot; camera, Russell Harlan; editor, Sherman Rose.

Charlie Ruggles (Chuckawalla Bill Redfield); Ellen Drew (Mary Mallory); Phillip Terry (Reverend Philip Phare); Joseph Schildkraut (Bud Deming); Porter Hall (Jonathan Randall); Henry Kolker (Judge Arnold Mason); Janet Beecher (Mrs. Tweedy); Clem Bevans (Jake Crabapple); Douglas Fowley (Chappie Ellerton); Paul Hurst (Jake Waldren); Frank Puglia (Joaquin); Minor Watson (Sheriff Nickerson); Harry Hayden (Timothy Hadley); Russell Hicks (Prosecuting Attorney).

Although not in the same prolific category as Zane Grey, Peter B(ernard) Kyne supplied several stories that were the basis for Western movies. Besides his The Three Godfathers [q.v.], he wrote for the Saturday Evening Post "The Parson of Panamint," which was made at least three times by American filmmakers.

The 1916 Paramount version, directed by the ill-fated William Desmond Taylor, starred Dustin Farnum. Variety reported, "The feature is one of the best that has been turned out by the Pallas [producing] people in some time and well worth playing."

In 1922, under the title, While Satan Sleeps [q.v. for credits], Joseph Henabery directed a new version of the Kyne story, with Jack Holt, Wade Boteler, and Mabel Van Buren in the leads.

Then along came the 1941 remake, which received far more attention than the two earlier editions. Producer Harry "Pop" Sherman, who was coasting along so nicely with his Hopalong Cassidy series, produced this version for the studio. Newcomer Phillip Terry was starred in the title role. Told in flashback by the one-time mayor of Panamint, Chuckawalla Bill Redfield (Ruggles), the film takes place in the rough gold-mining community which is full of lusty examples of drinking, gambling, and killing. A young person (Terry) arrives in town and attempts to reform the community. But he becomes involved in a murder, and then the river overflows and terminates the town's prosperity. It turns into a ghost town but, says Chuckawalla, "People are a little better, a little finer, a little closer to God, just for having known the Parson of Panamint." (It was the kind of story twist so favored by Bret Harte.)

The New York Times found the picture "heartwarming and inspiring," not to mention the distracting presence of the attractive Ellen Drew and the slicky effective Joseph Schildkraut.

PAT GARRETT AND BILLY THE KID (MGM, 1973) C 106 min.

Producer, Gordon Carroll; director, Sam Peckinpah; screenplay, Rudolph Wurlitzer; second unit director, Gordon Dawson; assistant directors, Newton Arnold, Lawrence J. Powell, Jesus Mario Bello; art director, Ted Haworth; set decorator, Ray Moyer; music-songs, Bob Dylan; sound, Charles M. Wilborn, Harry W. Tetrick; special camera effects, A. J. Lohman; camera, John Coquillon; second unit camera, Gabriel Torres; editors, Roger Spottiswoode, Garth Craven, Robert L. Woolfe, Richard Halsey, David Berlatsky, Tony de Zarraga.

James Coburn (Pat Garrett); Kris Kristofferson (Billy the
Kid); Richard Jaeckel (Sheriff Kip McKinney); Katy Jurado (Mrs.
Baker); Chill Wills (Lemuel); Jason Robards (Governor Wallace);
Bob Dylan (Alias); R. G. Armstrong (Ollinger); Luke Askew (Eno);
John Beck (Poe); Richard Bright (Holly); Matt Clark (J. W. Bell);
Rita Coolidge (Maria); Jack Dodson (Llewellyn Howland); Jack Elam
(Alamosa Bill); Emilio Fernandez (Paco); Paul Fix (Maxwell); L.
Q. Jones (Black Harris); Slim Pickens (Sheriff Baker); Jorge Russek
(Silva); Charlie Martin Smith (Bowdre); Harry Dean Stanton (Luke);
John Chandler (Norris); Rudy Wurlitzer (O'Folliard); Elisha Cook,
Jr. (Cody); Gene Evans (Horrel); Dub Taylor (Josh); Don Levy (Sac-
kett); Sam Peckinpah (Will); Rutanya Alda (Ruthie Lee); Walter
Kelly (Rupert); Claudia Bryar (Mrs. Horrell).

Despite the advice of his friend Sheriff Pat Garrett (Coburn),
himself a former outlaw, Billy the Kid (Kristofferson) refuses to
leave the New Mexico Territory. He is taken in custody and sentenced to be executed. But he escapes from the jail in Lincoln and
rejoins his gang at Old Fort Sumner (New Mexico), adding the mysterious young Alias (Dylan) to the group. Meanwhile, Garrett appoints aging Alamosa Bill (Elam) as his assistant, at the same time
as Governor Wallace (Robards) appoints Poe (Beck) to rid the area
of The Kid. In subsequent confrontations, Alamosa Bill is killed
and Billy's old friend Paco (Fernandez) is tortured to death. Finally
Garrett and Poe, with the aid of Sheriff Kip McKinney (Jaeckel),
catch up with Billy back in Fort Sumner. During the night they
sneak up to Billy's house and kill the outlaw. The next morning,
Garrett rides away with his conscience.

Just as Peckinpah had problems with Columbia Pictures over
Major Dundee (1965) [q.v.], so he ran afoul of the MGM hierarchy
with this effort. He later protested the way the Metro regime had
re-edited his work (and rightly so, for the surviving episodes are
quite disjointed).

In evaluating this unpopular Western, the British Monthly
Film Bulletin analyzed, "Pat Garrett seems in its very conception
a paralyzed epic, an impenetrable mood piece. Its title characters
are static figures in a landscape of closed possibilities; and the
studio's ditching of the framework depicting Garrett's death at the
hands of his own employers has not so much undermined the film
as simply abbreviated its catalogue of the circles in Hell.... Pat
Garrett is remarkable for its intensity of mood (and for the growl-
ing, damped-down charisma of Coburn and Kristofferson); a singularly black and poetic evocation of a no-exit life style."

At one point in this moody, dark study, Coburn's character
says, "It feels like times have changed." The Western film certainly had come a long way (for the good?) from the days of Bronco
Billy Anderson and even the prefabricated Gene Autry musical
Westerns.

Few people seemed to be impressed by Bob Dylan's oncamera
or soundtrack contributions to this misfire.

When the film showed up on television some of the extracted
footage, including Barry Sullivan's role as Chisum were reworked
into the print, as well as the prologue-epilogue which detailed how

twenty years after he killed Billy the Kid, Pat Garrett was killed at
the instigation of the same Santa Fe business faction that had hired
him to track down Billy.

THE PATHFINDER AND THE MOHICAN   see   LAST OF THE
MOHICANS

PER QUALCHE DOLLARO IN PIU (FOR A FEW DOLLARS MORE)
(United Artists, 1967)   C   130 min.

     Producer, Alberto Grimaldi; director, Sergio Leone; screen-
play, Luciano Vincenzoni, Leone; music, Ennio Morricone; camera,
Massimo Dallamano; editors, Giorgio Ferralonga, Eugenio Alabiso.
     Clint Eastwood (Man with No Name); Lee Van Cleef (Colonel
Mortimer); Gian Maria Volonte (Indio); Jose Egger (Old Man over
Railway); Rosemarie Dexter (Colonel's Sister); Mara Krup (Hotel
Manager's Wife); Klaus Kinski (Hunchback); Mario Brega, Aldo Sam-
brell, Luigi Pistilli, Benito Stefanelli (Indio's Gang); and Robert
Camardiel, Luis Rodriguez, Panos Papadopulos.

     Following the success of Per un Pugno di Dollari (A Fistful
of Dollars (1966) [q.v.] in Europe, Sergio Leone reteamed with Clint
Eastwood to make the follow-up, Per Qualche Dollaro in Piu. Also
cast in this production was veteran supporting player Lee Van Cleef,
who, thanks to his work in European Westerns, became a big Continental star. Made on a budget of $500,000, the film went on to
gross in the neighborhood of $10 million in U.S. and Italian release
alone.
     In the southwest following the Civil War, bounty hunters Man
with No Name (Eastwood) and Colonel Mortimer (Van Cleef) set out
to corral the vicious outlaw Indio (Volonte), who has a $10,000 price
tag on his head. The Man with No Name is reknowned for his
poncho, wide-brimmed hat, the cheroot he smokes, and his deadly
aim with a gun. The other hunter is a Confederate officer whose
sister committed suicide after being raped by Indio. The two men
come across one another in El Paso and, instead of gunning each
other down to reduce the competition, they decide to join forces.
Hoping to draw Indio into a trap, the Stranger arranges a jail bust
to free Indio's good friend. Thereafter the Stranger joins Indio's
gang. Meanwhile Colonel Mortimer wins Indio's favor by helping
him open a safe box taken in a bank robbery. The crafty Indio
decides to get rid of both bounty hunters and his own men by having
them do each other in. But the scheme backfires. The hunters
kill Indio's gang and then murder the frightened Indio. The Colonel
is now satisfied and rides away; the Stranger remains to deliver the
bodies and collect the reward money.
     Time labeled this "Western Grand Guignol." And that's just
what it was, with gore splashing about the screen throughout the
130 minutes.
     As in his past entry, Leone successfully recaptured the flavor
of the Old West in his special stylized form. It mattered little to

American moviegoers that the film had been shot in Spain, that most
of the performers were Italians, and that the soundtrack dialogue had
been post-dubbed. Why were viewers so engrossed? Variety judged
it was "thanks to Leone's bigger-than-life style, which combines up-
front action and closeup details with a hard-hitting pace reminiscent
of the Bond pix, that this acquires its virile and impactful dimensions. Audiences can laugh with it or at it, but they won't be bored.
The thesping is in order.... The physical values are impressive
too."

PER UN PUGNO DI DOLLARI (A FISTFUL OF DOLLARS) (United
Artists, 1964) C 96 min.

    Producers, Harry Colombo, George Papi; director, Bob
Robertson [Sergio Leone]; story, Tonio Alombi; screenplay, Leone,
Duccio Tessari; music, Ennio Moricone; art director-set decorator-
costumes, Charles Simons; assistant director, Frank Prestland;
sound, Edy Simson; special effects, John Speed; camera, Jack
Dalmas; editor, Bob Quintle [Robert Cinquini].
    Clint Eastwood (Man with No Name); Marianne Koch (Marisol);
Gian Maria Volonte (Ramon Rojo); Wolfgang Lukschy (John Baxter);
S. Rupp (Esteban Rojo); Antonio Prieto (Benito Rojo); Pepe Calvo
(Silvanito); Margherita Lozano (Counseulo Baxter); Daniel Martin

Clint Eastwood in Per un Pugno di Dollari (1964).

(Julian); Benny Reeves (Rubio); Richard Stuyvesant (Chico); Carol
Brown (Antonio Baxter).

By 1964, Western features churned out in Europe were a
popular commodity on the Continent. Already American ex-patriate
stars like Lex Barker and Guy Madison were doing well professionally in the genre, while more durable names such as Rod Cameron
made trips abroad for an occasional oater. This year director
Sergio Leone received financing for a German-Italian-Spanish co-
production, an update of the Japanese film Yojimbo (1961) into an
old West setting. At first Leone had wanted actor Richard Harrison
for the lead but he was busy on another project and as a substitute
he suggested American TV star Clint Eastwood, with whom he had
worked on the "Rawhide" teleseries.

Lanky Eastwood was hired for $15,000 and played Joe (better
known as "The Man with No Name"), a cherott-smoking stranger
wearing a poncho and a dirty, wide-brimmed hat, who arrives in a
small Mexican border town and becomes involved with two feuding
families. From the saloon owner (Calvo) he learns that the town
of San Miguel is controlled by two opposing families, the Rojos and
the Baxters--both of which have made their fortunes in black market
whiskey and firearms. Realizing his chance to earn some quick
money, the Stranger heats up the rivalry between the two factions.
At one point the mercurial man helps Marisol (Koch), the prisoner
of Ramon Rojos (Volonte), escape with her child. As a punishment,
Rojos has the Stranger tortured brutally and later, in retaliation for
the Stranger's alleged help to the Baxters, Rojos sets fire to their
home and kills all of them. When the maimed Stranger recovers
from his injuries, he sharpens up his shooting skill again. In a
confrontation, he outshoots all his opponents. The silent victor
leaves San Miguel astride a mule.

Per un Pugno di Dollari was the real start of the "spaghetti"
Western craze which resulted in the mass production of scores of
imitation oaters, all featuring plenty of pistol play and visual gore.
Leone would make two follow-up films with Eastwood, For a Few
Dollars More (1966) and The Good, The Bad and the Ugly (1967)
[both q.v.].

Due to copyright law suits by the makers of Yojimbo, it was
not until 1967 that A Fistful of Dollars had its general release in
the U.S.

How did the U.S. critics react to this trend-setting film?
Variety pegged it "A major candidate to be the sleeper of the year...
This is a hard-hitting item, ably directed, splendidly lensed, neatly
acted, which has all the ingredients wanted by action fans and then
some." Time confirmed this opinion: "Once in a great while a
western comes along that breaks new ground and becomes a classic
of the genre. Stagecoach was one. So was High Noon. This year
A Fistful of Dollars is the feature that dares to be different. It may
well be the first western since The Great Train Robbery without a
subplot." (Actually the Time reviewer was being quite sarcastic
about the film, but he managed to hit upon one of the major reasons
for its popularity--simplicity of theme.)

This violent, bloody Western grossed nearly $10 million mostly in the U.S. and Italy, setting precedents for all the carbon copies to come. Per un Pugno di Dollari is to the Western genre what Dr. No (1963) and the James Bond pictures are to the spy genre.

Seemingly, the American filmgoing public was indifferent to the criticism of this supposedly authentic Western which pointed out that it was 1) shot in Spain, 2) used Continental players mostly for the "real" American pioneers, and 3) was dubbed into English.

THE PHANTOM RIDER   see   THE RED RIDER

THE PLAINSMAN   (Paramount, 1936)   115 min.

Producer, Cecil B. DeMille; associate producer, William H. Pine; director, DeMille; based on information in the stories "Wild Bill Hickok" by Frank J. Wilstach and "The Prince of Pistoleers" by Courtney Ryley Cooper, Grover Jones; adaptor, Jeanie Mac-Pherson; screenplay, Waldemar Young, Harold Lamb, Lynn Riggs; assistant director, Richard Harlan; art directors, Hans Dreier, Roland Anderson; set decorator, A. E. Freudeman; costumes, Natalie Visart, Dwight Franklin, Joe De Young; music director, Boris Morros; second unit director, Arthur Rosson; sound, Harry M. Lindgren; special camera effects, Gordon Jennings, Farciot Edouart, Dewey Wrigley; camera, Victor Milner, George Robinson; editor, Anne Bauchens.

Gary Cooper (Wild Bill Hickok); Jean Arthur (Calamity Jane); James Ellison (Buffalo Bill Cody); Charles Bickford (John Latimer); Porter Hall (Jack McCall); Helen Burgess (Louisa Cody); John Miljan (General George Armstrong Custer); Victor Varconi (Painted Horse); Paul Harvey (Chief Yellow Hand); Frank McGlynn, Sr. (Abraham Lincoln); Granville Bates (Van Ellyn); Purnell Pratt (Captain Wood); Pat Moriarity (Sergeant McGinnis); Charles Judels (Tony the Barber); Anthony Quinn (Cheyenne Warrior); George MacQuarrie (General Merritt); George "Gabby" Hayes (Breezy); Fuzzy Knight (Dave); George Ernest (An Urchin); Fred Kohler (Jack); Frank Albertson (Young Soldier); Harry Woods (Quartermaster Sergeant); Francis McDonald (Gambler on Boat); Francis Ford (Veteran); Irving Bacon (Soldier); Edgar Dearing (Custer's Messenger); Edwin Maxwell (Stanton); John Hyams (Schuyler Colfax); Bruce Warren (Captain of the "Lizzie Gill"); Mark Strong (Wells Fargo Agent); Charlie Stevens (Injun Charlie); Arthur Aylesworth, Douglas Wood, George Cleveland (Van Ellyn's Associates); Lona Andre (Southern Belle); Leila Mc-Intyre (Mary Todd Lincoln); Harry Stubbs (John F. Usher); Davison Clark (James Speed); C. W. Herzinger (William H. Seward); William Humphries (Hugh McCullough); Sidney Jarvis (Giddeon Welles); Wadsworth Harris (William Dennison).

THE PLAINSMAN (Universal, 1966) C 92 min.

Producer, Richard E. Lyons; director, David Lowell Rich; screenplay, Michael Blankfort; art directors, Alexander Golitzen, William De Cinces; set decorators, John McCarthy, Ralph Sylos; makeup, Bud Westmore; music, Johnny Williams; music supervisor, Stanley Wilson; assistant director, Edward K. Dodds; sound, Waldon O. Watson, David Moriarty; camera, Bud Thackery; editor, Danny B. Landres.

Don Murray (Wild Bill Hickok); Guy Stockwell (Buffalo Bill Cody); Abby Dalton (Calamity Jane); Bradford Dillman (Lieutenant Stiles); Henry Silva (Crazy Knife); Simon Oakland (Black Kettle); Leslie Nielsen (Colonel George A. Custer); Edward Binns (Latimer); Michael Evans (Estrick); Percy Rodriguez (Brother John); Terry Wilson (Sergeant Womack); Walter Burke (Abe Ireland); Emily Banks (Louisa Cody).

In 1936 Cecil B. DeMille returned to the Western for this epic. In his typical style, he was far more concerned with visual sweep and dramatic dialogue than with recreating history accurately. It was another colossal production, which used the services of more than 1,200 Montana Cheyenne Indians for its big scenes. To give the story a familiar flavor to moviegoers, such historical figures as General George A. Custer (Miljan) and Abraham Lincoln (Mc-Glynn, Sr.) were worked into the 115-minute narrative. The chronicle finds Wild Bill Hickok (Cooper) hoping to bring law and order to the West. But he is opposed by renegade gun runner John Latimer (Bickford). When Hickok breaks the law in order to capture Latimer, he endangers his friendship with Buffalo Bill (Ellison). Hickok also opposes an Indian uprising instigated by Latimer. In the course of his activities, Bill Hickok saves feisty Calamity Jane (Arthur) from the Indians. Later the two are captured and tortured by the redskins, with Calamity Jane finally revealing information on a wagon train. Later Hickok manages to kill Latimer in a showdown. He refuses Calamity's offer of love and thereafter, in a card game, he is shot in the back by outlaw Jack McCall (Hall). Wild Bill dies in Calamity's arms. Despite the quite inept performance by James Ellison and large doses of hamming by both Cooper and Arthur, the film found a ready market when released. Variety cautioned that it was "a big and good western ... not a Covered Wagon, but realistic enough." If there were any doubts about the qualities of DeMille's The Plainsman--a great favorite of the video circuit--a comparison of it to the abyssmal 1966 telefeature prepared by Universal would silence any questions. Ironically, CBS-TV, which had contracted with Universal to do the remake, was unsatisfied with the finished product and refused to slot it on the network schedule. Instead the film was thrust into theatrical release, and later, of course, made the rounds of the television late, late shows. Following much the same plotline as the earlier version, this accounting used studio contract players to fill out the acting assignments. "Playing Wild Bill Hickok is Don Murray, who looks like a

prep school version of a cowboy. As Bill Cody, we have Guy Stockwell, who looks as though he went to Eton. Bradford Dillman is
insipid as a snobbish army lieutenant.... Abby Dalton plays Calamity Jane like a poor man's Carol Burnett ..." (New York World
Journal Tribune). As far as the scope of the outdoor drama, the
New York Times reported, "A fly-sized remake of the old DeMille
spectacle.... What a comedown!" Judith Crist in TV Guide wrote,
"A prime example of Hollywood's pointless (and perpetual) attempts
to remake its classics.... Even discounting the predecessor, this
oater stands on its own as a prairie dog."

THE PONY EXPRESS (Paramount, 1925) 9,949'

     Presenters, Adolph Zukor, Jesse L. Lasky; director, James
Cruze; screen story, Henry James Forman, Walter Woods; screen-
play, Woods; assistant director, Harold Schwartz; music, Hugo
Risenfeld; camera, Karl Brown.
     Betty Compson (Molly Jones); Ricardo Cortez (Jack Weston);
Ernest Torrence (Ascension Jones); Wallace Beery ("Rhode Island"
Red); George Bancroft (Jack Slade); Frank Lackteen (Charlie Bent);
Ed Peil, Jr. (Billy Cody); William Turner (William Russell); Al
Hart (Senator Glen); Charles Gerson (Sam Clemens); Rose Tapley
(Aunt); Vondell Darr (Baby); Hank Bell (Townsman); Ernie Adams
(Shorty).

     Paramount's big epic of the season was this Western, James
Cruze's follow-up to his earlier classic, The Covered Wagon (1923)
[q.v.]. This action entry made a star of George Bancroft, who was
cast as the evil Jack Slade, while Wallace Beery appeared as "Rhode
Island" Red, the pal of conventional hero Ricardo Cortez. Photoplay
enthused that this picture was "another great story of the West."
     Taken from a story written especially for the film (and pub-
lished as a novel simultaneously), The Pony Express takes place at
the time just prior to the Civil War. It was a period when a secret
organization, The Knights of The Golden Circle, attempted to have
California secede from the union and then annex a part of Mexico to
form a new empire. The ambitious group is headed by Senator Glen
(Hart) who hires men to stop Jack Weston (Cortez), the one man
brave enough to oppose the scheme. Jack escapes the death plots
and joins the Pony Express, becoming a rival of Jack Slade (Bancroft) for the affections of Molly Jones (Compson). It is Jack who
later carries news of Abraham Lincoln's presidential election to the
people of California, which prevents the Senator's secession plan.
Meanwhile, a half-breed, Charlie Bent (Lackteen), leads an attack
on a settlement. Eventually the secessionists are thwarted, the
Indian problem is alleviated, and Jack is able to wed Molly before
joining the Civil War cause.
     Although more actionful than his earlier The Covered Wagon,
Cruze's The Pony Express was hardly a historically accurate feature.
Reviewing this production in Hollywood in the Twenties (1968), David
Robinson suggests that The Pony Express is "a Western of exceptional

charm....   Again there is an element of documentary reconstruction in the account of the riders of the pony express, linking the
two ends of the continent.   In Ricardo Cortez, Cruze discovered a
hero who combined good looks with a cheerful humor.   An oddity
of the film, which seems somehow characteristic of Cruze's ability
while working at high pressure to avoid conventional clichés and
stereotypes, is that the villain, played by George Bancroft, goes
scot free at the end, despite his interference with the mails and
his collusion with hostile Indians."

THE PONY EXPRESS (Paramount, 1953) C 101 min.

     Producer, Nat Holt; director, Jerry Hopper; story, Frank
Gruber; screenplay, Charles Marquis Warren; art directors, Hal
Pereira, Al Nozaki; music, Paul Sawtell; camera, Ray Rennahan;
editor, Eda Warren.
     Charlton Heston (Buffalo Bill Cody); Rhonda Fleming (Evelyn
Hastings); Jan Sterling (Denny); Forrest Tucker (Wild Bill Hickok);
Michael Moore (Rance Hastings); Porter Hall (Bridger); Richard
Shannon (Barrett); Henry Brandon (Cooper); Stuart Randall (Pember-
ton); Lewis Martin (Sergeant Russell); Pat Hogan (Yellow Hand);
James Davies (Cassidy); Eric Alden (Miller); Willard Willingham
(Cavalryman); Frank Wilcox (Walstrom); Len Hendry (Maldin); Charles
Hamilton (Man).

Charlton Heston, Rhonda Fleming, Jan Sterling and Forrest Tucker
in The Pony Express (1953).

Like James Cruze's 1925 film of the same title, supra, this fifties' picture dealt with the opening of the mail route to the West. Also, like its predecessor, it was a tale that meandered in its telling. The addition of sound and color did little to enhance this variation in contrast to its silent photoplay predecessor.

In 101 minutes, the scenario told a highly fictionalized account of how Buffalo Bill Cody (Heston) and Wild Bill Hickok (Tucker) blazed the trail for the overland mail route of the Pony Express. The yarn opens with Cody kidnapping a brother (Moore) and sister (Fleming) from a stagecoach, only to find out they are the leaders of a movement to split California from the Union. Joined by Hickok and such disparate group members as Denny (Sterling) and Pemberton (Randall), the folk head for Sacramento. Along the way there is intergroup feuding as well as an Indian attack. (During the redskin skirmish Cody is captured and is later forced to partake in a tomahawk duel.) All ends well, naturally, with the Union cause being saved and the hoped-for mail route established.

Muscular Heston was fast reaching his cinema prime and added some (stiff) verve to the proceedings. As to Jerry Hopper's direction, the New York Times nodded affirmatively. '[It] projects and sustains a surprising amount of good-natured inventiveness for the old horse circuit...."

POSSE (Paramount, 1975) C 92 min.

Executive producer, Phil Feldman; producer-director, Kirk Douglas; story, Christopher Knopf; screenplay, William Roberts, Knopf; music, Maurice Jarre; production designer, Lyle Wheeler; set decorator, Fred Price; assistant director, Jack Roe; sound, Richard Portman; camera, Fred J. Koenekamp; editor, John W. Wheeler.

Kirk Douglas (Marshal Nightingale); Bruce Dern (Jack Strawhorn); Bo Hopkins (Wesley); James Stacy (Hellman); Luke Askew (Krag); David Canary (Pensteman); Alfonso Arau (Peppe); Katharine Woodville (Mrs. Cooper); Mark Roberts (Mr. Cooper); Beth Brickell (Mrs. Ross); Dick O'Neill (Wiley); Bill Burton (McCanless); Louie Elias (Rains); Gus Greymountain (Reyno); Allan Warnick (Telegrapher); Roger Behrstock (Sheriff).

Over the years actor-director-superstar Kirk Douglas has won, lost, and re-won a following among moviegoers. In recent years, except for his role in Jacqueline Susann's Once Is Not Enough (1975), his assorted spy-pirate-action movies have played generally the double-bill, action/grind movie houses. Posse, produced and directed by star Douglas, deserved a much better fate. As Vincent Canby wrote in the New York Times, "This is Saturday afternoon entertainment that needn't be ignored at night."

The well-scripted feature finds Marshal Nightingale (Douglas) on the chase for outlaw Jack Strawhorn (Dern) while in the midst of a political campaign. In the tale of corruption and irony the Marshal thinks he can maneuver his home town and district into electing him

Kirk Douglas in <u>Posse</u> (1975).

U.S. Senator from Texas, but he learns the hard way that even the simple man has his threshold for self-respect. The finale finds crafty Strawhorn manipulating the situation (i.e., the candidate's disloyalty to his own men) to his advantage and escaping capture.

Perhaps <u>Variety</u> best pinpointed why the film failed to grasp a ready audience. "... [It] has a quiet and ironic intensity bereft of the formula western action highlights...." <u>Posse</u> did gain a great deal of publicity when Douglas magnanimously hired James Stacy (the actor who lost an arm and a leg in a road accident) for a specially-written role in this film, as a small town newsman.

POWDERSMOKE RANGE (RKO, 1935) 71 min.

Associate producer, Cliff Reid; director, Wallace Fox; based on the novel by William Colt MacDonald; screenplay, Adele Buffington; music director, Alberto Colombo; art directors, Van Nest Polglase, Feild Gray; sound, Hal Bumbaugh; camera, Harold Wenstrom; editor, James Morley.

Harry Carey (Tucson Smith); Hoot Gibson (Stony Brook); Guinn "Big Boy" Williams (Lullaby Joslin); Bob Steele [Guadalupe

Guinn "Big Boy" Williams in <u>Powdersmoke Range</u> (1935).

Kid (Jeff Ferguson)]; Tom Tyler (Sundown Saunders); Boots Mallory
(Carolyn Sibley); Ray Mayer (Chap Bell); Sam Hardy (Mayor Big
Steve Ogden); Adrian Morris (Brose Glascow); Wally Wales (Aloysius
"Bud" Taggart); Art Mix (Rube); Buffalo Bill, Jr. (Tex Malcolm);
Buddy Roosevelt (Burnett); Franklyn Farnum (Reese); William Des-
mond (Happy Hopkins); William Farnum (Banker Orchan); Ethan Laid-
law (Fin Sharkey); Irving Bacon (General Store Keeper); Henry
Roquemore (Doctor); Frank Rice (Sourdough Jenkins); James Mason
(Jordan); Eddie Dunn (Elliott); Buzz Barton (Buck).

In 1935 RKO rounded up a galaxy of contemporary and one-
time Western stars for this feature which was promoted as "The
Barnum and Bailey of Westerns." The film was also the first time
that all three characters in William Colt MacDonald's novel about
The Three Mesquiteers appeared onscreen. (Only two of the characters from the book had been used the year before in Normandy's
Law of the 45s.) Along with Paramount's Hopalong Cassidy Rides
(1935), Powdersmoke Range established in Hollywood the idea of
using multiple heroes for Western series.
        As the film opens, The Three Mesquiteers--Tucson Smith
(Carey), Stony Brooke (Gibson), and Lullaby Joslin (Williams)--have
aided an outlaw (Steele). In return he has deposited a thousand
dollars he had "borrowed" from them as down payment on a ranch.
The real estate investment is made out in Tucson's name. Later,
a stagecoach robbery is planned by crooked town officials. The
blame is to be placed on the Mesquiteers, but the trio expose the
plot. Meanwhile Tucson finds out that Steve Ogden (Hardy), the
saloon owner, is keeping The Guadalupe Kid (Steele) prisoner and
is also trying to locate the deed to Tucson's new ranch.
        Tucson confronts Ogden and is captured. He and The Kid
are tried before the saloon mob who are anxious to lynch them,
but Stony and Lullaby arrive in time to stop the proceedings. The
three men now head for their new home where they promptly become involved in a range war. Eventually Tucson kills Ogden, and
the corrupt sheriff, thinking he has been fatally wounded, confesses
to the crimes that had plagued The Mesquiteers.
        An admirable discussion of Powdersmoke Range in Views and
Reviews (Summer 1970) notes that "Powdersmoke Range captures the
game atmosphere of the frontier, the optimism toward life true of
our mythical cowboys, the easy-going and capable manner with which
frustrations are met and solved, the adventure of a life uncomplicated and unencumbered by psychological division or despair; or, in
other words, merely a different aspect of the pioneer ethic itself,
the unbounded faith Americans have always had in their dream of
building a better world, one of justice, morality, and freedom."
        While Powdersmoke Range, when seen today, does tend to
date and is not up to the action and pace of the later Mesquiteer
entries done at Republic, it does have a wonderful collection of
performers. And the gunfight between Carey and Tyler is a worthwhile sight.

THE PRAIRIE PIRATE   (Producers Distributing Corp., 1925)   4,603

Director, Edmund Mortimer; based on the story "The Yellow
Seal" by W. C. Tuttle; screenplay, Anthony Dillon; art director,
Edward Withers; camera, George Benoit; editor, Harry L. Decker.
Harry Carey (Brian Delaney); Jean Dumas (Ruth Delaney);
Lloyd Whitlock (Howard Steele); Trilby Clark (Teresa Esteban);
Robert Edeson (Don Esteban); Tote Du Crow (Jose); Evelyn Selbie
(Madre); Fred Kohler (Agullar).

Perhaps the most continually successful, if not the most
colorful, cowboy star of them all was Harry Carey. His stardom
in the genre began prior to the First World War and he continued
as a Western star until the late thirties, even after he had been reduced to character parts in bigger films. Although his greatest
cinema success was in MGM's Trader Horn (1930), he is still best-
remembered as a Westerner. This PDC release is a good example
of the type of output the star presented in the final decade of the
silent screen.
The plot starts with Ruth Delaney (Dumas) being mysteriously
murdered. Her brother Brian (Carey) becomes a bandit, determined
to find her killer. He becomes the friend of Don Esteban (Edeson)
and his daughter Teresa (Clark), and the enemy of gambler Howard
Steele (Whitlock). Brian and Teresa plan to marry, but Steele kidnaps the girl and rides into the hill with Brian in hot pursuit. Brian
captures the gambler and forces him to exchange clothes with him.
When a posse comes upon the scene, they mistake Steele for Delaney
and shoot him. Still later, evidence turns up that Steele was actually
the person who killed Brian's sister. With these matters settled,
Brian and Teresa wed.
Taken from W. C. Tuttle's story in Liberty magazine, the
film was rather old-fashioned in its plotline. But it had the salva-
tion of plenty of strong action and melodrama to please the intended
audience.

THE PROFESSIONALS   (Columbia, 1966)   C   117 min.

Producer-director, Richrd Brooks; based on the novel A
Mule for the Marquesa by Frank O'Rourke; screenplay, Brooks;
music-music director, Maurice Jarre; art director, Edward S. Ha-
worth; set decorator, Frank Tuttle; makeup, Robert Schiffer; ward-
robe, Jack Martell; assistant director, Tom Shaw; sound, Charles
J. Rice, William Randall, Jr., Jack Haynes; special effects, Willis
Cook; camera, Conrad Hall; editor, Peter Zinner.
Burt Lancaster (Bill Dolworth); Lee Marvin (Henry Rico
Fardan); Robert Ryan (Hans Ehrengard); Jack Palance (Captain Jesus
Raza); Claudia Cardinale (Maria Grant); Ralph Bellamy (J. W. Grant);
Woody Strode (Jacob Sharp); Joe De Santis (Ortega); Rafael Bertrand
(Fierro); Jorge Martinez De Hoyos (Padillia); Marie Gomez (Chi-
quita); Jose Chavez, Carlos Romero (Revolutionaries); Vaughn Taylor
(Banker).

Woody Strode, Lee Marvin, Robert Ryan and Burt Lancaster in The Professionals (1966).

        As with his more recent Bite the Bullet (1975) [q.v.], Richard Brooks has demonstrated that he fully understands the intricacies of turning out a remarkable Western film.   The New York World Journal Tribune stated that "The Professionals is a sleek, slam-bang adventure-suspense film whose very professionalism is enough to make its flaws and its pretensions minor.... We're ready to forgive the five-cent philosophy and heart-of-gold histionics that boggle the ending a bit. "
        Shot along the Mexican border in Panavision and Technicolor, this hearty tale concerns four mercenaries (Lancaster, Marvin, Ryan and Strode) who are hired by a wealthy man (Bellamy) in 1917 to recover his young Mexican wife, Maria (Cardinale).   Maria has been abducted by a Mexican bandit (Palance) and it seems she prefers the latter's company.   With Dolworth (Lancaster), a dynamite expert, Fardan (Marvin), a professional soldier, wrangler Ehrengard (Ryan) and tracker Sharp (Strode) on the mission, there is no fear that their plan of rescue will fail.   However, Maria is very reluctant to leave Raza (Palance) and when she is re-kidnapped by the quartet, Raza follows in hot pursuit.   In a tight rock canyon, Raza catches up to his prey.   Dolworth sends the others onward while he combats the Mexicans.   Eventually the quartet gets Maria to her husband, at which time she points out what a scoundrel he is.   Raza, whom Dolworth had left for dead, reappears to claim Maria.   The Professionals reevaluate the situation and restrain Grant while Maria and Raza ride off together.

With such a powerhouse cast and a storyline that foreshadows the guerrilla tactics of The Dirty Dozen (1967), The Professionals grossed a whopping $8.8 million in distributors' domestic rentals.

As Time cheered, "There hasn't been a livelier Western whoop-up since villain Jack Palance bared fang and claw against Shane. Only once does the action slow down, during a gun battle between Palance and Burt Lancaster, who seem to be firing off philosophical asides about the life of violence mainly because they need a rest."

As Gary Cooper had in the fifties, Lancaster and Ryan, two aging leading men found a new lease of life in the Western genre.

PURSUED (Warner Bros., 1947) 101 min.

Producer, Milton Sperling; director, Raoul Walsh; story-screenplay, Niven Busch; dialogue director, Maurice Murphy; assistant director, Russell Saunders; art director, Ted Smith; set decorator, Jack McConaghy; music, Max Steiner; music director, Leo F. Forbstein; orchestrator, Murray Cutter; sound, Francis J. Scheid; special effects, William McGann, Willard Van Enger; camera, James Wong Howe; editor, Christian Nyby.

Teresa Wright (Thorley Callum); Robert Mitchum (Jeb Rand); Judith Anderson (Mrs. Medora Callum); Dean Jagger (Grant Callum); Alan Hale (Jack Dingle); John Rodney (Adam Callum); Harry Carey, Jr. (Prentice McComber); Clifton Young (Sergeant); Ernest Severn (Jeb as a Child); Charles Bates (Adam as a Child); Peggy Miller (Thorley as a Child).

"One of those films which you might better come in on toward the end and then see over from the beginning.... This is one of those pictures in which some dark and desperate apprehension gnaws at the mind of the strangely badgered hero through a good nine-tenths of it.... And then, toward the end, the recollection comes to him like a bolt. It is not a very startling revelation but, at least, it clears the mystery--somewhat" (New York Times).

This murky drama opens with Jeb Rand (Mitchum) waiting to be hung. Then, via flashback, he relates how a mysterious stranger has always been a part of his life. It is set in the New Mexico Territory at the turn of the century. Jeb reveals how he had been orphaned and raised by Mrs. Medora Callum (Anderson) along with her two children (Wright and Rodney). Jeb recollects how he never trusted either Mrs. Callum or her son, and how in a toss of a coin decision it was the boy and not he who went to the Spanish-American War and returned a wounded hero. In yet another toss of the coin it is Adam Callum (Rodney) and not Jeb who acquires another portion of the Callum ranch spread. Later Jeb wins a large pot of money in a card game. When Adam tries to snatch it from Jeb, the latter kills his rival. He is tried and acquitted of the deed. Thorley Callum (Wright) agrees to marry him, her real purpose being eventually to kill him. But soon she falls in love with him. Jeb's stepfather (Jagger) later brings a lynch mob after him, but, before he can be hung, Medora arrives and confesses that she once had an

affair with Jeb's father and that is why Callum always hated Jeb.
Medora shoots her spouse and Jeb, who has been haunted by a
crime supposedly committed by his father, reveals the actual culprit.
Finally freed of his past, Jeb can attempt to make a new life for
himself with Thorley.

In tracing the history of the films of the World War II era,
Charles Higham and Joel Greenberg in Hollywood in the Forties
(1968) judged that Pursued "had some striking photography, sombre
and eloquent, by James Wong Howe, and excellent playing by Robert
Mitchum, Teresa Wright and Judith Anderson."

This Warners' picture was quite a departure from Mitchum's
earlier Zane Grey Western remakes at RKO such as Nevada (1944)
[q.v.]. Niven Busch, who also authored Duel in the Sun (1946)
[q.v.], was at this time married to actress Teresa Wright.

THE RAINBOW TRAIL (Fox, 1918) six reels

Director, Frank Lloyd; based on the novel by Zane Grey;
screenplay, Lloyd.
William Farnum (Lassiter/Shefford); Ann Forrest (Fay Lar-
kin); Mary Mersch (Jane Withersteen); William Burress (Waggoner);
William Nye (Shap); Genevieve Blinn (Ruth); George Ross (U.S.
Marshall).

THE RAINBOW TRAIL (Fox, 1925) 5,251'

Presenter, William Fox; director, Lynn Reynolds; based on
the novel by Zane Grey; screenplay, Reynolds; camera, Daniel Clark.
Tom Mix (John Shefford/Lassiter); Anne Cornwall (Fay Lar-
kin); George Bancroft (Jake Willets); Lucien Littlefield (Joe Lake);
Mark Hamilton (Beasley Willets); Vivien Oakland (Bessie Erne);
Thomas Delmar (Venters); Fred De Silva (Shadd); Steve Clemento
(Nas To Bega); Carol Halloway (Jane); Diana Miller (Anne).

THE RAINBOW TRAIL (Fox, 1931) 60 min.

Director, David Howard; based on the novel by Zane Grey;
screenplay, Barry Connors, Philip Klein; sound, Albert Protzman;
camera, Daniel Clark.
George O'Brien (Shefford); Cecilia Parker (Fay Larkin);
Minna Gombell (Ruth); Roscoe Ates (Ike Wilkins); J. M. Kerrigan
(Paddy); W. L. Thorne (Dyer); Robert Frazer (Lone Eagle); Ruth
Donnelly (Abigail); Niles Welch (Willets); Laska Winter (Singing
Cloud); Landers Stevens (Presbey); Alice Ward (Jane Withersteen);
Edward Hearn (Jim Lassiter).

Zane Grey's 1915 novel was first adapted to the screen by
Fox in 1918 as part of a series co-written and directed by Frank
Lloyd. Future studio Western star Buck Jones was featured in this
film as well as in other Grey adaptations made by Fox.

In 1925, Fox again made the Grey book into a film, this time
as a sequel to its earlier Grey adaptation, Riders of the Purple Sage
(1925) [q.v.]. Tom Mix starred, as he did in Riders, but in this
presentation he played a dual role. After Lassiter (Mix) is forced
into a valley and barricaded therein by outlaws, his nephew John
Shefford (Mix) learns of the situation. He joins a wagon train in
order to reach Paradise Valley. But once there he is made a captive. In a small town near the canyon, the freed Shefford rescues
Fay Larkin (Cornwall), the adopted daughter of the woman trapped
in the valley with his uncle. It seems Fay was to be forced into
marrying Jake Willets (Bancroft), the head of the gang that has
harassed Shefford. Eventually Shefford rides to the rescue and, in
the final showdown, Willets is subdued.

For the third time Fox filmed The Rainbow Trail in 1931,
once again as a sequel to its (talkie) re-make of Riders of the Purple
Sage (1931) [q.v.]. George O'Brien, like Mix, starred in both talkie
versions. O'Brien here was cast as the nephew, while silent film
actor Edward Hearn was his uncle and Cecilia Parker (later of the
Andy Hardy series) was the heroine. The New York Times noted
that "The villains are as hard a lot as ever came to the screen; in
fact the sinister leader [W. L. Thorne] wears a mask over the right
half of his face because he has been badly disfigured."

RAMONA (American Biograph, 1910) one reel

Director, D. W. Griffith; based on the novel by Helen Jackson
Hunt; screenplay, Griffith; camera, G. W. "Billy" Bitzer.
With: Henry B. Walthall, Mary Pickford, Francis Grandin,
Robert Herron, Kate Bruce.

RAMONA (Clune, 1916) five reels

Director, Donald Crisp; based on the novel by Helen Jackson
Hunt.
With: Ada Gleason, Monroe Salisbury, Mabel Van Buren,
Richard Sterling, Nigel De Brulier, Harry Tavares, Lurline Lyons.

RAMONA (United Artists, 1928) 7,650'

Director, Edwin Carewe; based on the novel by Helen Hunt
Jackson; screenplay-titles, Finis Fox; assistant directors, Leander
De Cordova, Richard Easton; theme song, Mabel Wayne and L. Wolfe
Gilbert; art director, Albert D'Agostino; set decorator, Tec-Art
Studios; camera, Robert B. Kurrle, Al M. Greene; editor, Jeanne
Spencer.
Dolores Del Rio (Ramona); Warner Baxter (Alessandro); Roland
Drew (Felipe); Vera Lewis (Señora Moreno); Michael Visaroff (Juan
Canito); John T. Prince (Father Salvierderra); Mathilde Comont
(Marda); Carlos Amor (Sheepherder); Jess Cavin (Bandit Leader); Jean
the Dog (Himself); Rita Carewe (Baby).

Warner Baxter and Dolores Del Rio in <u>Ramona</u> (1928).

RAMONA   (Twentieth Century-Fox, 1936)   C   90 min.

    Producer, Sol M. Wurtzel; associate producer, John Stone; director, Henry King; based on the novel by Helen Hunt Jackson; screenplay, Lamar Trotti; music, Alfred Newman; songs, William Kernell and Newman; art director, Duncan Cramer; camera, William Skall, Chester Lyons; editor, Alfred De Graetano.
    Loretta Young (Ramona); Don Ameche (Alessandro); Kent Taylor (Felipe Moreno); Pauline Frederick (Señora Moreno); Jane Darwell (Aunt Ri Hyar); Katherine DeMille (Margarita); Victor Kilian (Father Gaspare); John Carradine (Jim Farrar); Pedro de Cordoba (Father Salvierderra); J. Carroll Naish (Juan Can); Charles Waldron (Dr. Weaver); Claire DuBrey (Marda); Russell Simpson (Scroggs); William Benedict (Joe); Chief Thundercloud (Pablo); Charles Middleton, Tom London (American Settlers); Ruth Robinson (Patient in Doctor's Office); Cecil Weston (Pablo's Wife).

    D. W. Griffith borrowed the plot from Helen Hunt Jackson's 1884 novel Ramona for one of his early Biograph one-reelers. The studio paid $100 to use the plot, the top price paid for screen rights up to that time. The film was shot March 30/April 1, 1910 with exteriors in Peru and Camulos, California, and interiors at Biograph's Los Angeles studio. Mary Pickford and Henry B. Walthall were cast as the lovers and the film was photographed by Billy Bitzer.
    The Biograph Bulletin advertised, "It most graphically illustrates the white man's injustice to the Indian." The film made good use of California locales (it was made during Griffith's first trip West) in its panoramic shots, although the plot was quite similar to other Griffith works. Jack Spears later wrote, in his article, "The Indian on the Screen," in Films in Review, that it was "Griffith's most sympathetic portrayal of Indians...."
    In 1916 the W. H. Clune Company issued the first feature-length version of Ramona, directed by sometime-actor Donald Crisp. Adda Gleason and Monroe Salisbury were the ill-fated lovers.
    The most popular of the four screen versions of the novel came in 1928 when Edwin Carewe directed Ramona for United Artists. The feature was issued with synchronized sound effects.* Photoplay called it "pictorially lovely." The story concerned a wealthy Spanish sheep rancher (Lewis) who adopts a half-breed girl (Del Rio) who is reared under strict tutelage, knowing only the friendship of the woman's son (Drew). Later the girl learns of her ancestry and elopes with a young chieftain (Baxter). When their infant daughter is killed by outlaws, the lovers retreat to the hills, where a settler later kills Alessandro (Baxter) who has been accused of stealing a horse. The girl then loses her memory and becomes an outcast. Eventually Felipe (Drew) finds her and helps her to remember through a childhood song who she is.
    In 1936 the newly-formed Twentieth Century-Fox gave the old

---

*The title song, "Ramona" was especially written for the film. Gene Austin's recording of it in 1928 for RCA Victor Records sold in excess of three million copies.

vehicle a Technicolor mounting with direction by Henry King.
Loretta Young played the title character, a half-breed Indian girl
who deserts her finance (Taylor) and her Southern California hacienda to wed an Indian chief's son (Ameche). The bulk of the
footage then presents their ill-treatment by prejudiced white settlers.
The strife culminates with an Indian-hating farmer (Carradine) shooting Alessandro (Ameche) as the brave takes a horse to ride for a
doctor for his sick infant daughter. Among the many colorful scenes
in the film was a fiesta sequence, which featured a brief song by
Allan Jones.
    Those who remembered the earlier Dolores Del Rio rendition
were disappointed by the new version. The New York Herald-Tribune
complained of "the colorless adaptation" and the "uninspired writing."
As Jack Spears points up in his above-mentioned article on "The Indian
on the Screen," the 1936 version "suffered from poor casting--
Loretta Young was too sophisticated for the simple Indian girl, and
Don Ameche too ill at ease in a fright-wig."

RANGERS OF FORTUNE (Paramount, 1940) 80 min.

    Producer, Dale Van Every; director, Sam Wood; screenplay,
Frank Butler; art directors, Hans Dreier, Robert Usher; music,
Frederick Hollander; camera, Theodor Sparkuhl; editor, Eda Warren.
    Fred MacMurray (Gil Farra); Patricia Morison (Sharon Mc-
Cloud); Albert Dekker (George Bean); Gilbert Roland (Sierra);
Joseph Schildkraut (Colonel Rebstock); Betty Brewer (Squib Clayborn);
Arthur Allen (Mr. Prout); Bernard Nedell (Tod Shelby); Dick Foran
(Johnny Cash); Brandon Tynan (Homer Clayborn); Minor Watson
(Clem Bowdry); Rosa Turich (Caressa).

    The offbeat casting in this Paramount entry should not deter
any potential viewer. Sam Wood, who that year directed Our Town
and Kitty Foyle, helmed this vehicle. The film centered on three
drifters: Gil Farra (MacMurray), a renegade U.S. Army officer,
Sierra (Roland), a happy-go-lucky Mexican, and George Bean (Dekker), an ex-prize fighter. The trio wander into a small town and
find that hoodlums have it under their iron grip and are pushing
around an old man, who runs the local newspaper, and his small
granddaughter (Brewer). The trio do clean up the town, but the old
man and the little girl are killed. Interestingly--by Hollywood
standards--Gil's romance with Sharon McCloud (Morison) comes to
naught!
    This Western appeared to be the beginning of a series, but
no sequels followed. MacMurray would not become a staple of sagebrush tales until the mid-fifties.

RAWHIDE (Twentieth-Fox, 1951) 86 min.

    Producer, Samuel G. Engel; director, Henry Hathaway; story-
screenplay, Dudley Nichols; art directors, Lyle Wheeler, George W.

Davis; music, Lionel Newman; camera, Milton Krasner; editor, Robert Simpson.

Tyrone Power (Tom Owens); Susan Hayward (Vinnie Holt); Hugh Marlowe (Zimmerman); Dean Jagger (Yancy); Edgar Buchanan (Sam Todd); Jack Elam (Tevis); George Tobias (Gratz); Jeff Corey (Luke Davis); James Millican (Tex Squires); Louis Jean Heydt (Fickert); William Haade (Gil Scott); Milton Corey, Sr. (Dr. Tucker); Kenneth Tobey (Wingate); Dan White (Gilchrist); Max Terhune (Miner); Robert Adler (Billy Dent); Judy Ann Dunn (Callie); Howard Negley (Chickenring); Vincent Neptune (Mr. Hickman); Edith Evanson (Mrs. Hickman); Walter Sande (Flowers); Dick Curtis (Halway); Si Jenks (Old Timer).

Susan Hayworth was the queen of the Twentieth Century-Fox lot. Seemingly there was no type of film beyond her acting capabilities. In this Henry Hathaway actioner, she joined with studio star Tyrone Power (then being eclipsed by Gregory Peck) for this taut, well-made thriller. The action is set in a twenty-four hour period at a desolate relay station in Arizona called Rawhide, which is along the 2,700-mile stagecoach route between San Francisco and St. Louis.

Vinnie Holt (Hayward) and her young niece stay overnight at the way station. Soon Vinnie and the bumbling Easterner attendant Tom Owens (Power) are being held captive by a group of outlaws

Tyrone Power and Susan Hayward in Rawhide (1951).

waiting for the morning stage with its shipment of gold. The lawbreakers believe Vinnie and Owens are married; later the latter two
try to escape and warn the oncoming stage. The climax has the
outlaws attempting to take vengeance on Vinnie and Owens through
the child. A sub-plot finds the robbers feuding among themselves,
especially leader Zimmerman (Marlowe) and psychotic underling
Tevis (Elam, in an excellent performance).

"Not the biggest Western you've ever seen, not the most
original, but it's very, very good." That was how Louella Parsons,
dean of the gossip columnists, rated this picture. The New York
Times confirmed, "a surprisingly good entertainment.... Rawhide
may not be a prize addition to the screen's vast Western library,
but it is sufficiently different to warrant attention."

The film's alternate TV title is Desperate Siege, given to it
so that it would not conflict with the later CBS-TV series "Rawhide," which has nothing to do with the Fox film.

THE RED RIDER   (Universal, 1934)   fifteen chapters

Producer, Milton Gatzert; director, Louis Friedlander (Lew
Landers); based on the story "Redhead from Sun Dog" by W. C.
Tuttle; screenplay, George Plympton, Vin Moore, Ella O'Neill,
Basil Bickey; camera, Richard Fryer; editors, Saul Goodkind, Ed-
ward Todd.

Buck Jones (Red Davidson); Grant Withers (Silent Slade);
Marion Shilling (Marie Maxwell); Walter Miller (Jim Breen); Richard
Cramer (Joe Portos); Margaret LaMarr (Joan McKee); Charles
French (Roberto Maxwell); Edmund Cobb (Johnny Snow); J. P. Mc-
Gowan (Scotty McKee); William Desmond (Sheriff); Dennis O'Keefe
(Wedding Guest); Bud Osborne (Kelsey); Al Ferguson (Madden); Den-
nis Moore (Cowboy); Artie Ortego (Player); Mert La Varre (Banty);
Frank Rice (Harp); Monte Montague (Al Abel); Jim Thorpe (Bill
Abel).

Chapters: 1) Sentenced to Die!; 2) A leap for Life!; 3) The
Night Attack; 4) A Treacherous Ambush; 5) Trapped; 6) The Brink
of Death!; 7) The Fatal Plunge!; 8) The Stampede!; 9) The Posse
Rides; 10) The Avenging Trail; 11) The Lost Diamonds; 12) Double
Trouble; 13) The Night Raiders!; 14) In the Enemies' Hideout; 15)
Brought to Justice.

While starring in series Westerns for Universal in the
thirties Buck Jones also made four serials for that studio, including
The Red Rider, a fifteen-chapter entry directed by Louis Friedlander (later Lew Landers). Jones' co-star was Grant Withers,
who had been a leading man at the beginning of the sound era but
whose career had slid into supporting roles or bigger parts in minor
pictures.

Buck played Red Davidson, a sheriff who loses his job and
his standing when he allows his buddy, Silent Slade (Withers), who
has been sentenced to jail for murder, to escape. Red also promises Slade he will help him prove his innocence. Later Red wanders

to the Mexican border where he applies for a job at Robert Maxwell's (French) ranch. He arrives in time to save the man's daughter, Marie (Shilling), from sinister Jim Breen (Miller). Red later
learns that Breen's partner is Silent Slade. Red begins to work at
the ranch and he confides to fellow worker Johnny Snow (Cobb) that
he believes Breen is guilty of the murder in question. They learn
that Breen has tricked Maxwell into working with him on a smug-
gling operation. However, Red saves Maxwell and proves Breen is
the wanted killer. Finally Slade's name is cleared.

This well-done, multi-episode effort had a supporting cast of
very familiar serial names: Walter Miller, Richard Cramer, Edmund Cobb, J. P. McGowan (the murdered man), and William Desmond. The other serials Buck Jones made for Universal in the
thirties were: Gordon of Ghost City (1933), Roarin' West (1935),
and The Phantom Rider (1936). In 1941 Jones would return to the
studio for a leading role in the all-star serial, Riders of Death
Valley [q.v.]. The same year he starred in his final chapterplay,
White Eagle [q.v.], for Columbia.

RED RIVER (United Artists, 1948) 125 min.

Executive producer, Charles K. Feldman; producer-director,
Howard Hawks; based on the novel The Chisholm Trail by Borden
Chase; screenplay, Chase, Charles Schnee; art director, John Datu
Arensma; music-music director-song, Dimitri Tiomkin; assistant di-
rector, William McGarry; makeup, Lee Greenway; sound, Richard
DeWeese, Vinton Vernon; special effects, Allan Thompson, Donald
Steward; camera, Russell Harlan; editor, Christian Nyby.

John Wayne (Tom Dunson); Montgomery Clift (Matthew Garth);
Joanne Dru (Tess Millay); Walter Brennan (Groot); Coleen Gray
(Fen); John Ireland (Cherry); Noah Beery, Jr. (Buster); Chief Yow-
lachie (Quo); Harry Carey, Sr. (Melville); Harry Carey, Jr. (Dan
Latimer); Mickey Kuhn (Matthew - as a boy); Paul Fix (Teeler);
Hank Worden (Simms); Ivan Parry (Bunk Kenneally); Hal Taliaferro
(Old Leather); Paul Fiero (Fernandez); William Self (Wounded wran-
gler); Ray Hyke (Walt Jergens); Tom Tyler (A Quitter); Shelley
Winters (Dancehall Girl); Lane Chandler (Colonel); Glenn Strange
(Naylor).

Following World War II, the Western genre was given a big
boost by the huge success of Howard Hawks' Red River, which
grossed $4.35 million in U.S. and Canadian distributors' gross
rentals. The film represented a return to the concept of the epic
sagebrush tale, a spinoff of earlier adventure pictures such as The
Covered Wagon (1923) [q.v.] and Stagecoach (1939) [q.v.]. Its
broad, and sometimes violent, theme encompassed the spirit of the
genre far better than the then popular sexy Westerns such as Duel
in the Sun (1946) [q.v.] and The Outlaw (1943). Not until High Noon
(1952) [q.v.] would there be another pure-breed Western to equal
Red River.

In fictional terms producer-director Hawks retold the story

John Wayne, Ray Hyke, Montgomery Clift, Noah Beery, Jr., Chief
Yowlachie, and Hal Taliaferro in Red River (1948).

of the beginnings of the famous Chisholm cattle trail. The cast included John Wayne as Tom Dunson, a cattle rancher with no market
for his hefty herd at the end of the Civil War. (It was a theme that
would be re-used later in Wayne's The Cowboys, 1972 [q.v.]) Dunson decides to drive the vast herd north from his Texas domain to
market. He takes his foster son, Matthew Garth (Clift), along for
the young man's first cattle drive. Their path leads along part of
the Red River and into the Missouri territory. In the course of the
drive, the men suffer many hardships. In the process Matthew takes
off on his own, and Dunson loses control of the drive and is forced
to change directions from Missouri to Abilene, Kansas, in order to
use the newly-constructed railroad. Eventually Dunson catches up
with Matthew and they fight. But the latter's girl (Dru) mends their
relationship. At the finale Dunson makes Matthew a partner in the
ranch business.
        There was mixed critical reaction at the time of release and
there still is today. In Howard Hawks (1968) Robin Wood determines,
"The ending of Red River has been much criticised. Everything
hinges on why Dunson (John Wayne) doesn't shoot at Matthew Garth
(Montgomery Clift) at the showdown. Our sympathy, unequivocally
with Dunson at the beginning of the film, has been largely transferred to Matthew; the 'traditional' ending would have Wayne, the
tragic hero of formidable moral stature but fatally flawed, killed

(though not by Clift--we are, I think, sure that Matthew won't shoot), but achieving as he dies the clarity that enables him to judge himself and his actions, and leaving Matthew free for life.   One feels that Hawks, in rejecting this ending, broke more than the rules of the traditional Western--he broke the rules of classical tragedy as well. "

On the other hand, the New York Times rated the film as filled "with the genuine tang of the outdoors....   Mr. Hawks has used real Western scenery for its most vivid and picturesque effects. "

When one considers that this was Hawks' first Western, he showed admirable poignancy in his handling of the major themes encompassed within the drama, only going astray when la femme (in this case Joanne Dru's Tess Millay) enters the scene and everything "goes Hollywood" in what was a real Western.   Few fans or critics disagree that, until True Grit (1969) [q. v.], this was among John Wayne's finest screen performances, showing that he could be a real actor.

RED RIVER RANGE   (Republic, 1938)   59 min.

Associate producer, William Berke; director, George Sherman; based on characters created by William Colt MacDonald; story, Luci Ward; screenplay, Stanley Roberts, Betty Burbridge, Luci Ward; music, William Lava; camera, Jack Marta; editor, Tony Martinelli.
John Wayne (Stony Brooke); Ray Corrigan (Tucson Smith); Max Terhune (Lullaby Joslin); Polly Moran (Mrs. Maxwell); Lorna Gray [Adrian Booth] (Jane Mason); Kirby Grant (Tex Reilly); Sammy McKim (Tommy); William Royle (Payne); Perry Ivins (Hartley); Stanley Blystone (Randall); Lenore Bushman (Evelyn Maxwell); Burr Caruth (Pop Mason); Roger Williams (Sheriff); Earl Askam (Morton); Olin Francis (Kenton).

Many cinema historians feel that the eight entries John Wayne made in 1938-1939 in Republic's The Three Mesquiteers series are the best episodes in that long-running string of oaters.   This opinion may very well derive from the fact that these eight features are the most widely-viewed today, since they are often sold to local TV stations as part of a package of Wayne films.

Nevertheless, most of Wayne's Mesquiteer films were a decided cut above the average B Westerns.   In this mini-saga, the governor appoints the Three Mesquiteers (Wayne, Corrigan and TerHune) as special deputies in order to fight cattle rustlers who have been plaguing the Red River vicinity.   Stony Brooke (Wayne) pretends to be an outlaw with a reward on his head, and by this ruse joins the gang in order to obtain evidence on their lawless activities.   The film did contain a delightful comedy performance by veteran Polly Moran.

And, of course, at the finale of this fifty-nine minute feature, the Three Mesquiteers wave into the camera before riding off, in preparation for their next celluloid adventure.

THE REDMEN AND THE RENEGADES   see   LAST OF THE
MOHICANS

REDSKIN   (Paramount, 1929)   7, 643'   (Some scenes in Technicolor)

Director, Victor Schertzinger; story-screenplay, Elizabeth
Pickett; titles, Julian Johnson; music, J. S. Zamecnik; song, Harry
D. Kerr and Zamecnik; camera, Edward Cronjager, Ray Rennahan,
Edward Estabrook; editor, Otho Lovering.

Richard Dix (Wing Foot); Gladys Belmont (Corn Blossom);
Jane Novak (Judy); Larry Steers (John Walton); Tully Marshall
(Navajo Jim); Bernard Siegel (Chahi); George Regas (Chief Notani);
Augustina Lopez (Yina); Noble Johnson (Pueblo Jim); Joseph W.
Girard (Commissioner); Jack Duane (Barrett); Andrew J. Callaghan
(Anderson); Myra Kinch (Laughing Singer); Philip Anderson (Wing
Foot at Age Nine); Lorraine Rivero (Corn Blossom at Age Six);
George Walker (Pueblo Jim at Age Fifteen); and Paul Panzer.

An educated Navajo, Wing Foot (Dix), returns home and rejects his tribe's customs; he becomes an outcast.   After seeing his
girl Corn Blossom (Belmont), an Indian of a rival village who was
also educated in the East, he is forced to flee to the desert.   There
he discovers oil on Indian land.   He files his claim but learns that
the tribes are about to go to war because the maiden has gone to
the Navajos to avoid an unhappy marriage.   Wing Foot thankfully arrives with the news of the oil strike.   The feud is ended and the
lovers are re-united.

Filmed on location in Canyon de Chelley, the final six minutes
of the picture were projected in Magnascope.   Part of the feature
was shot in Technicolor, which led Photoplay to acclaim it "a magnificent color picture. "

The main difficulty with this presentation was that director
Victor Schertzinger--who would later direct some of the Bing Crosby-
Bob Hope Road pictures--did not have the ability to transfer Indian
lore and customs properly to the screen.   Instead, the picture
evolved as a colorful but empty follow-up to Dix's earlier The
Vanishing American (1926) [q.v.].   In short it was, as Jack Spears
wrote in his Films in Review piece on "The Indian on the Screen" "a
glossy conception of the redman's problems. "   One can only hope
that similar subject matter would be treated more appropriately in
the post-Wounded Knee days of the seventies.

LA RESA DEI CONTI (THE BIG GUNDOWN)   (Columbia, 1968)   C
107 min. *

Producer, Alberto Grimaldi; director, Sergio Sollima; story,
Franco Solinas, Fernando Marandi; screenplay, Sergio Donati, Sergio
Donati, Sergio Sollima; music, Ennio Morricone; music director,

---

*Reduced to 90 minutes for the English-dubbed version.

Bruno Nicolal; sets-costumes, Carlo Simi; art directors, Raphael
Perri, Enrique Alarcon; assistant director, Nino Zanchin; makeup,
Rino Carboni; sound, Pietro Spadoni; special effects, Eros Bacciuc-
chi; camera, Carlo Carlini; editor, Adriana Novelli.
    Lee Van Cleef (Jonathan Corbett); Tomas Milian (Cuchillo);
Luisa Rivelli (Lizzie); Fernando Sancho (Captain Segura); Nieves
Navarro (The Widow); Benito Stefanelli (Jess); Walter Barnes (Brok-
ston); Angel Del Pozo (Brokston's Son-in-Law); Maria Granada
(Rosita); Lanfranco Ceccarelli (Jack); Roberto Camardiel (Jellicol);
Nello Pazzafini (Hondo); Spartaco Conversi (Mitchell); Romano Puppo
(Rocky); Tom Felleghi (Chet); Calisto Calisti (Miller); Antonio Casas
(Dance); Jose Torres (Nathan).

    "Mr. Ugly Comes to Town," the posters for The Big Gun-
down proclaimed. Technically the advertisement was a misnomer,
for star Lee Van Cleef had portrayed "the Bad" in Il Buono, Il
Brutto, Il Cattivo (The Good, The Bad and the Ugly) (1967) [q.v.].
("The Ugly" was actually Eli Wallach, while Clint Eastwood was
"the Good.")
    After a decade of playing supporting roles in Hollywood
Westerns, Lee Van Cleef had gone to Europe in 1965 to co-star
with Clint Eastwood in Per Qualche Dollaro in Piu (For a Few
Dollars More) and then had made the above-mentioned feature with
Eastwood. These pictures launched Lee Van Cleef on a solo starring career in La Resa dei Conti. As a result he was soon topping
Eastwood as the most popular player in European Westerns.
    Directed by Sergio Sollima for PEA in Rome and issued by
Columbia in the United States, The Big Gundown was typical of
spaghetti Westerns: long on action and gore, short on characterization, usually post-dubbed for the English-language market, and often
indistinguishable from any other such entries.
    After a girl is raped and murdered in a Mexican border
town, the famed Jonathan Corbett (Van Cleef) is hired by a Texas
rancher (Barnes) to track the alleged killer, a tattered Mexican
named Cuchillo (Milian). Despite his efforts to track down the lawbreaker, Corbett loses his prey on four different occasions. Eventually Corbett discovers that it is the rancher's son-in-law (Del
Pozo) who is the actual rapist-killer and that Cuchillo had seen the
crime committed. Later Cuchillo outmaneuvers the son-in-law and
does him in, and Corbett kills the rancher. The two former adversaries are now friends, but each goes his separate way.
    "There is the usual feeling of uncertainty on the part of the
scripters in how to handle the subject, during which they fall back
on an over-use of violence and gunplay as a means to whet interest"
(Variety). And that the film did, doing very well in U.S. and
European distribution. (It earned over $2 million in domestic
rentals.)
    Van Cleef as Jonathan Corbett in The Big Gundown presents
a far more realistic picture of the Western good/badman than does
Eastwood's "Man with No Name" in the Leone trilogy. While the
former is more in the starkly-realistic tradition of the cowboy genre
(as per William S. Hart), Eastwood's character is more mystical
and does not have the dimensions of Van Cleef's sagebrush portrayals.

An interesting scene in The Big Gundown has Van Cleef's Corbett rescuing a twelve-year-old girl from Cuchillo and returning her to her Mormon "father," only to be informed that she is the man's young wife!

The Big Gundown also boasts a fine music score by Ennio Morricone who scored the trilogy of Eastwood-Leone Westerns. Many connoisseurs regard the soundtrack music to this film as one of prolific Morricone's best.

THE RETURN OF DRAW EGAN   (Triangle, 1918)   five reels

Producer, Thomas H. Ince; director, William S. Hart; story-screenplay, C. Gardner Sullivan.

The standards that William S. Hart set in his five- and six-reel Western features before the twenties have seldom been equalled, let alone surpassed, in their picturization of the true West. His films were raw, violent, and sombre. They lacked the color and gloss that became so popular in twenties' oaters. Historically, Hart is perhaps the most singularly important person in the Western film genre. It is pictures such as The Return of Draw Egan which emphasize this importance.

Opening in New Mexico, the story has Draw Egan (Hart) as a wanted outlaw, in fact "the most sought after man along the border. He is a member of a gang that includes coward Robert McKim. When the gang is surrounded by the law Draw helps the other men escape through a secret tunnel while McKim deserts them, is captured, and sent to jail. Draw then heads for the town of Broken Bow where he confronts the town's ruffian. The local leaders of a nearby town, Yellow Dog, ask Draw to be their marshal. Now calling himself William Blake, Draw accepts the post and in the new community he meets beautiful Margery Wilson, the girl of his dreams.

Draw stands up to the new town's bad element, upholding the law and rebuffing the advances of vamp Louise Glaum. "You're an awful fool, but I like fools," she tells him. He replies coldly, "I don't dance." Meanwhile Draw continues to court Miss Wilson. Later McKim escapes from jail and comes to Yellow Dog where he becomes Glaum's lover. He threatens to reveal Draw's past to the town.

Caught in a bind, Draw now does nothing to control the community's bad element, fearing Wilson will desert him if she learns of his shady past. Finally, however, the saloon trash taunt the town's religious-minded folk and Draw stands up to the scoundrels. True to his evil word, McKim reveals Egan's background. In a later shootout with McKim, Draw kills him. The townfolk ask Draw to remain as their marshal and he regains Wilson's affection.

This feature was re-issued in 1924 by Tri-Stone Pictures, Inc.

THE RETURN OF FRANK JAMES (Twentieth Century-Fox, 1940)
C 92 min.

Producer, Darryl F. Zanuck; associate producer, Kenneth
Macgowan; director, Fritz Lang; screenplay, Sam Hellman; art directors, Richard Day, Wiard B. Ihnen; set decorator, Thomas Little;
costumes, Travis Banton; music, David Buttolph; camera, George
Barnes, William V. Skall; editor, Walter Thompson.

Henry Fonda (Frank James); Gene Tierney (Eleanor Stone);
Jackie Cooper (Clem); Henry Hull (Major Rufus Todd); J. Edward
Bromberg (George Runyan); Donald Meek (McCoy); Eddie Collins
(Station Agent); John Carradine (Bob Ford); George Barbier (Judge);
Ernest Whitman (Pinky); Charles Tannen (Charlie Ford); Lloyd Corri-
gan (Randolph Stone); Russell Hicks (Agent); Victor Kilian (Preacher);
Edward McWade (Colonel Jackson); George Chandler (Roy); Irving
Bacon (Bystander); Frank Shannon (Sheriff); Barbara Pepper (Nellie
Blane); Louis Mason (Watchman); Stymie Beard (Mose); William Paw-
ley, Frank Sully (Actors); Davison Clark (Officer); Nelson McDowell
(Confederate Veteran); Edmund Elton (Foreman); Lee Phelps (Bar-
tender); Lillian Yarbo (Maid); Adrian Morris (Detective); Almeda
Fowler (Mrs. Stone); Lester Dore, Milton Kibbee, Frank Melton
(Reporters).

After the success of Jesse James (1939) [q.v.], Twentieth
Century-Fox assigned director Fritz Lang to helm the follow-up, The
Return of Frank James, in which Henry Fonda, Henry Hull, and John
Carradine repeated their roles from the initial feature. This color
sequel was slow-paced but had good atmosphere and was a solid box-
office draw. Like the first film, it had a lot of location shooting
during its forty-two days of lensing.

How did a German-born director like Fritz Lang respond to
directing a traditional American Western? As he told Peter Bogdanovich in Fritz Lang in America (1969), "And don't forget the Western
is not only the history of this country, it is what the Saga of the
Nibelungen is for the European. I think the development of this
country is unimaginable without the days of the wild West--when a
dance hall girl was placed on a pedestal because she was the only
woman among a hundred gold miners."

With his characteristic touch of genius, Lang turned out a
superior genre piece, and one that is more intriguing than his next
Western, Western Union (1941) [q.v.]. The New York Herald-Tribune applauded "its emphasis on small things like gestures and
shadows and sounds of nature [which] reveal the Western in a new
and interesting light."

The film opens where Jesse James ended, with the outlaw
being shot in the back by Bob Ford (Carradine). Frank James
(Fonda) then decides to let the law take care of Ford who is sen-
tenced to death by a jury. The governor, however, later pardons
Ford and Frank seeks revenge. To back up the venture Frank robs
a train; in the course of the robbery a man is killed. Eventually
Ford's brother (Tannen) falls to his death as he is being chased by
Frank. Bob Ford is later shot by Clem (Cooper), Jesse's son, who

has joined Frank's vendetta. When James' servant is framed for
the railroad man's murder, Frank returns home and is placed on
trial. He is eventually acquitted with the aid of newspaper man
Rufus Todd (Hull). For the romantic interludes--considered a must
for quality Westerns--Gene Tierney appeared as Eleanor Stone, a
newspaper woman who falls in love with Frank and urges him to
follow the due process of law.

     If there is hardly an excess of gunplay and fast riding,
Lang's recreation of nineteenth century America is, nonetheless
satisfying, especially the scenes in the 1880s theatre.

RETURN OF SABATA   see   EHI, AMICO ... C'E SABATA, HAI
CHIUSO!

RETURN OF THE GUNFIGHTER   (ABC-TV, 1967)   C   100 min.

     Producers, Frank King, Maurice King; associate producer,
Herman King; director, James Neilson; story, Burt Kennedy, Robert
Buckner; screenplay, Buckner; assistant director, Carl Beringer;
art directors, George W. Davis, James W. Sullivan; set decorators,
Henry Grace, Joseph J. Stone; music, Hans J. Salter; sound, Frank-
lin Milton; camera, Ellsworth Fredericks; editor, Richard Heer-
mance.
     Robert Taylor (Ben Wyatt); Ana Martin (Anisa); Chad Everett
(Lee Sutton); Mort Mills (Will Parker); Lyle Bettger (Clay Sutton);
John Davis Chandler (Sundance); Michael Pate (Frank Boone); Barry
Atwater (Lomax); John Crawford (Butch Cassidy); Willis Bouchey
(Judge Ellis); Rodolfo Hoyos (Luis Domingo); Read Morgan (Wid
Boone); Henry Willis (Sam Boone); Robert Shelton (Cowboy); Loretta
Miller, Janell Alden (Dance Hall Girls).

     On January 29, 1967, ABC-TV telecast this motion picture
which had been made in conjunction with MGM. The film was the
network's first telefeature and it obtained a rating of 22.3. The
color feature was issued to theatres in other countries two months
after its videocast.
     When cattle baron Clay Sutton (Bettger) threatens the lands of
Luis Domingo (Hoyos), aging gunfighter Ben Wyatt (Taylor) comes
to the aid of his old pal. Ben arrives at his friend's ranch to learn
that Domingo and his wife are dead, and that their daughter Anisa
(Martin) has disappeared. Ben vows to track down the killers,
leading him to Lordsburg and to the chief culprit, Sutton.
     In sizing up this entry, the British Monthly Film Bulletin re-
ported, "In the opening scene of this likeable and unpretentious
Western, Robert Taylor is forced to gun down a man against his
will ('Why won't they leave me alone?'), but any suggestion that it
will be following the Freudian footsteps of Henry King's The Gunfighter [1950] are quickly dispensed with and the film emerges as a
straightforward, vigorous Western in the classical tradition--and
none the worse for that.... Robert Taylor's gunfighter has a quiet

authority which rather overshadows the other performances: in fact,
the film is something of a tribute to him as an archetypal Western
hero. "

THE RETURN OF THE RIDDLE RIDER   see   THE RIDDLE RIDER

RETURN OF THE SEVEN   see   THE MAGNIFICENT SEVEN

RHYTHM ON THE RANGE   (Paramount, 1936)   87 min.

     Producer, Benjamin Glazer; director, Norman Taurog; story,
Mervin J. Houser; screenplay, John C. Moffett, Sidney Salkow,
Walter DeLeon, Francis Martin; music director, Boris Morros;
songs, Leo Robin and Richard Whiting; Johnny Mercer; Robin and
Frederick Hollander; Robin and Ralph Rainger; Walter Bullock;
Richard Whiting, Whiting and Hollander; Bager Clark and Gertrude
Ross; Billy Hill and J. Keirn Brennan; camera, Karl Struss; editor,
Ellsworth Hoagland.
     Bing Crosby (Jeff Larrabee); Frances Farmer (Doris Halli-
day); Bob Burns (Buck Burns); Martha Raye (Emma); Samuel S.
Hinds (Robert Halliday); Lucile Webster Gleason (Penelope Ryland);
Warren Hymer (Big Brain); George E. Stone (Shorty); James Burke
(Wabash); Martha Sleeper (Constance); Clem Bevans (Gila Bend);
Leonid Kinskey (Mischa); Charles Williams (Gopher); Beau Baldwin
(Cuddles); Emmett Vogan (Clerk; Dennis O'Keefe (Hickler); Duke
York (Officer); James Blaine (Conductor); Herbert Ashley (Brake-
man); James "Slim" Thompson (Porter); Jim Toney (Oil Station
Proprietor); Sid Saylor (Gus); Sam McDaniel (Porter); Harry C.
Bradley (Minister); Charles E. Arnt (Steward); Oscar Smith (Waiter);
Bob McKenzie (Farmer); Heinie Conklin (Driver); Frank Dawson
(Butler); Sons of the Pioneers, including Roy Rogers (Singers).

     This amusing bit of fluff cast city-ite Bing Crosby--of all
people--as a cowpoke who works for Penelope Ryland's (Gleason)
dude ranch. Jeff Larrabee (Crosby) is sent East to Madison Square
Garden with his prize bull, Cuddles, and on the way back he discovers a runaway, Doris Halliday (Farmer). Actually she is
Penelope's niece who is trying to avoid marrying a polo player.
Eventually the duo get to the wide open spaces and Doris decides
she would rather homestead with crooning Jeff than go back East.
     The film is basically remembered today for its introduction
of the song "I'm an Old Cowhand, " as well as for the screen debut
of wide-mouthed, golden-voiced Martha Raye who provided fine
comedy relief with hillbilly comic Bob Burns.
     Of this pleasant outing Variety commented, "Despite the title,
the costumes and the characters, this is no western. There's very
little range, but plenty of rhythm, and the latter makes it pleasant
entertainment.... " Graham Greene wrote in the British The Spectator, "...[It] is quite a tolerable picture with a few scenes which

do deserve to be called popular cinema and an excellent new comedian, Mr. Bob Burns."
        Twenty-one years later director Norman Taurog remade the
film for Paramount, this time as a Dean Martin-Jerry Lewis vehicle
called Pardners.

THE RIDDLE RIDER   (Universal, 1924)   fifteen chapters

        Director, William J. Craft; screenplay, William E. Wing,
Arthur H. Gooden, George Pyper.
        With: William Desmond, Eileen Sedgwick, Helen Holmes,
Claude Payton, William N. Gould, Ben Corbett, Hughie Mack, Joe
Bonomo.
        Chapters: 1) The Canyon Torrent; 2) Crashing Doom; 3) In
the Path of Death; 4) Plunged into the Depths; 5) Race for a Fortune;
6) Sinister Shadows; 7) The Swindle; 8) The Frame-Up; 9) False
Faces; 10) At the Brink of Death; 11) Thundering Steeds; 12) Trapped;
13) The Valley of Fate; 14) The Deadline; 15) The Final Reckoning.

        Popular action star William Desmond played the title role in
this chapterplay, as a masked man who aids oil men in the Old
West who are being done wrong by fuel barons and land grabbers.
When not wearing a black cape and mask, Desmond is the crusading
editor of the local newspaper. Eileen Sedgwick plays the female
lead, a girl hoping to maintain her land holdings despite the ploys
of crooks to take the property away from her.
        In 1927 Desmond would star in a ten-chapter sequel, The
Return of the Riddle Rider. In this well-made follow-up, the masked
leader tries to wrest control of a town from outlaws.

RIDE 'EM COWBOY   (Universal, 1942)   86 min.

        Associate producer, Alex Gottlieb; director, Arthur Lubin;
story, Edmund L. Hartmann; screenplay, True Boardman, John
Grant; art director, Jack Otterson; music director, Charles Previn;
music supervisor, Ted Cain; music, Frank Skinner; songs, Don
Raye and Gene DuPaul; choreography, Nick Castle; camera, John
Boyle; editor, Phil Kahn.
        Bud Abbott (Duke); Lou Costello (Willoughby); Dick Foran
(Robert "Bronco Bob" Mitchell); Anne Gwynne (Anne Shaw); Johnny
Mack Brown (Alabam Brewster); Samuel S. Hinds (Sam Shaw); Doug-
lass Dumbrille (Jake Rainwater); Richard Lane (Pete Conway);
Charles Lane (Martin Manning); Jody Gilbert (Moonbeam); Morris
Ankrum (Ace Henderson); Mary Lou Cook (Dotty Davis); Ella Fitz-
gerald (Ruby); Ted, Judd, and Joe McMichael (Merry Macs); The
Congoroos (Specialty Number).

        Two New York hot dog vendors with a rodeo getting roped
into going to a Western dude ranch--a perfect premise for the antics
of the zany Abbott and Costello, then approaching their peak as a

top box-office attraction.   Western stars Johnny Mack Brown and Dick
Foran were also on hand.   Brown was the ranch foreman who loses
the ranch owner's (Hinds) daughter (Gwynne) to Western writer Foran.
In a dream sequence, Brown also plays an Indian.

Besides the usual Abbott and Costello nonsense, the feature
also contained a number of musical interludes, including Ella Fitzgerald doing "A Tisket, a Tasket," and a group called the Congeroos
(including Dorothy Dandridge) performing a specialty jitterbugging
number.   Other songs in the film included "I'll Remember April"
and "Cow Boggie."

RIDE LONESOME   (Columbia, 1959) C   74 min.

Executive producer, Harry Joe Brown; producer-director,
Budd Boetticher; screenplay, Burt Kennedy; assistant director, Jer-
rold Bernstein; color consultant, Henri Jaffa; art director, Robert
Peterson; set decorator, Frank A. Tuttle; music-music conductor,
Heinz Roemheld; sound, John Livadary, Harry Mills; camera,
Charles Lawton, Jr.; editor, Jerome Thoms.

Randolph Scott (Ben Brigade); Karen Steele (Carrie Lane);
Pernell Roberts (Sam Boone); James Best (Billy John); Lee Van
Cleef (Frank); Dyke Johnson (Charlie); James Coburn (Wid); Boyd
Stockman (Indian Chief); Roy Jenson, Boyd Morgan, Bennie Dobbins
(Outlaws).

James Best and Randolph Scott in <u>Ride Lonesome</u> (1959).

Filmed in Eastman color and CinemaScope, this film was one
of a series that Randolph Scott made with producer-director Budd
Boetticher. This batch of films was noted for compact casts, fine
cinematography, and tight editing.

Lawman Ben Brigade (Scott) arrests Billy John (Best) and
slowly returns him to town as he also hopes to corral the man's
brother, Frank (Van Cleef), who had hanged Ben's wife years before. Two outlaws (Roberts and Coburn), who also want Billy John
for the bounty, join Ben on the ride, as does Carrie Lane (Steele),
whose husband has been killed by Indians. In the course of the
journey Frank is killed, Ben and Sam Boone (Roberts) have a showdown, and the fate of Billy John and Carrie hangs in the balance.

In Horizons West (1969), Jim Kitses writes of Ride Lonesome, '[It] moves through three days and nights, the company
pushing on over dangerous open vistas of arid country each morning
and afternoon to cluster in the dappled dark of an evening camp.
If dusk is often a kind, contemplative time for talk of the future,
danger rides in bright and early at sun-up to temper hope and
throttle dreams." As in Scott-Boetticher's Comanche Station (1960),
reasons Kitses, "the construction and pace are tightly controlled,
the action unwinding with spell-binding formal rigour, the films
finally resembling pure ritual. Seizing on the cyclical pattern of
the journey western, the alternation of drama and lyricism, tension
and release, intimacy and space, Boetticher gradually refines it to
arrive at the remarkable balance of an ambiguous world poised between tragedy and pastoral comedy."

RIDE THE HIGH COUNTRY   (MGM, 1962) C 94 min.

Producer, Richard E. Lyons; director, Sam Peckinpah; screen-
play, N. B. Stone, Jr.; art directors, George W. Davis, Leroy
Coleman; set decorators, Henry Grace, Otto Siegel; color consultant,
Charles K. Hagedon; assistant director, Hal Polaire; music, George
Bassman; makeup, William Tuttle; sound, Franklin Milton; camera,
Lucien Ballard; editor, Frank Santillo.

Randolph Scott (Gil Westrum); Joel McCrea (Steve Judd);
Mariette Hartley (Elsa Knudsen); Ron Starr (Heck Longtree); Edgar
Buchanan (Judge Tolliver); R. G. Armstrong (Joshua Knudsen);
Jenie Jackson (Kate); James Drury (Billy Hammond); L. Q. Jones
(Sylvus Hammond); John Anderson (Elder Hammond); John Davis
Chandler (Jimmy Hammond); Warren Oates (Henry Hammond); Car-
men Phillips (Saloon Girl).

Some years before he became professionally controversial
with Major Dundee (1965) and The Wild Bunch (1969) [both q.v.]
director Sam Peckinpah turned out this unpretentious small Western,
which many regard as a genuine genre classic. It proved to be the
movie swansong for Randolph Scott. Joel McCrea also would only
make an occasional film after this. As the New York Herald-Tribune observed, "It is a resourceful young director's attempt to
create something original within a fairly rigid frame work of tradition.... Admittedly, this is no theme of dazzling originality. So

what? A good director and a good cast need never be enslaved by
other people's clichés. Mr. Peckinpah, experienced in directing
television Westerns, has concentrated on vivid details beautifully
photographed--a race between a horse and a camel, a compelling
wedding brawl in a scrubby mining town--on solid supporting performances, and on the ruggedly handsome faces of two stars who
act their age and act it well. More could not be asked of an unpretentious feature film. "

Aging Steve Judd (McCrea) agrees to forget his years as a
famed lawman and to accept a commission to carry gold from a
mining camp to a local bank. His cohorts on this pick-up mission
are Gil Westrum (Scott), another former law enforcer who is lately
a sideshow sharpshooter, and Heck Longtree (Starr), a young drifter.
Actually Gil and Steve plan to steal the gold and don't care whether
Heck helps or not. Along the way they pick up Elsa Knudsen (Hartley), who is to wed Billy Hammond (Drury) at the mining camp.
But once there she finds that Billy and his family are louts and she
will not stay. She leaves with the gold-carrying trio. At one point,
Gil leaves the transport party, but returns to help his conflicting
partners when they are attacked by the Hammond clan. The Ham-
monds are eventually shot down, but Steve is also wounded fatally.
Before Judd dies, Gil swears to him that he will deliver the gold
and help out the beleaguered young couple.

Ride the High Country, much to MGM's surprise, won a prize
at the Venice Film Festival and it was named one of the top films
of 1962 by both Newsweek and Film Quarterly. In England, the picture was released under the title Guns in the Afternoon.

RIDERS OF DEATH VALLEY (Universal, 1941) fifteen chapters

Directors, Ford Beebe, Ray Taylor; screenplay, Sherman
Lowe, George Plympton, Basil Dickey, Jack Connell; song, Milton
Rosen and Everett Carter.

Dick Foran (Jim Benton); Leo Carrillo (Pancho); Buck Jones
(Tombstone); Charles Bickford (Wolf Reade); Lon Chaney, Jr. (Butch);
Noah Beery, Jr. (Smokey); Guinn "Big Boy" Williams (Borax Bill);
Jeanne Kelly [Jean Brooks] (Mary Morgan); James Blaine (Joseph
Kirby); Monte Blue (Rance Davis); Glenn Strange (Tex); Dick Alex-
ander (Pete); Roy Barcroft (Dirk); William Hall (Gordon); William
Pagan (Marshal); Ernie Adams (Cactus Pete); Bud Osborne (Stage
Driver); Frank Austin (Chuckawala Charlie); Frank Brownlee (Slim);
Art Miles (Evergreen); James Farley (Graham); Jay Michael, Ken
Nolan (Cashiers); Ruth Rickaby (Kate); Ed Payson (Buck Hansen);
Alonzo Price (Wilson); Ted Adams (Hank); James Lucas, Dick Rush
(Bartenders).

Chapters: 1) Death Marks the Trail; 2) The Menacing Herd;
3) The Plunge of Peril; 4) Flaming Fury; 5) The Avalanche of Doom;
6) Blood and Gold; 7) Death Rides the Storm; 8) Descending Doom;
9) Death Holds the Reins; 10) Devouring Flames; 11) The Fatal Blast;
12) Thundering Doom; 13) Bridge of Disaster; 14) A Fight to the
Death; 15) The Harvest of Hate.

The title characters, a vigilante group, break up a corrupt miners' protection group in the town of Panamint. A miner (Austin) is killed and his partner Jim Benton (Foran) and the man's niece Mary Morgan (Kelly), along with the Riders (Jones, Carrillo, Beery, Williams and Glenn Strange), set out to locate the murderers. Meanwhile, corrupt Wolf Reade (Bickford) and his gang terrorize the area as they seek to locate the dead man's lost Aztec mine. Eventually they are thwarted by the Riders.

When directors Ford Beebe and Ray Taylor were handed the script to the film it was to be made on a modest budget. It was not until the scenario was revised that Universal executives agreed to make it the first one million dollar serial production (a fact heavily promoted by the company). Despite a great deal of action in the fifteen chapters, the cliffhanger was not tailored to its many big-name stars, nor was it the sensational product expected by serial enthusiasts. The chapterplay interpolated silent stock footage --an economy "cheat" used by many movie producers. On the other hand, some of the original action scenes for this entry would be the source for future films' stock footage (e.g., two men trapped on a suspension bridge with boulders being rolled down on them, a cattle stampede, a stagecoach going off a steep cliff).

Humor was made an intricate part of the proceedings and one running gag would have Buck Jones leaving Dick Foran in a precarious situation (such as dangling over the end of a cliff) while he calmly carried on a conversation with the endangered man. Also a number of Leo Carrillo's dialect lines were exploited for comedy purposes, such as, "Listen I theenk I hear footprints...."

Sharp-sighted moviegoers perhaps noticed that it was Rod Cameron who doubled for Buck Jones in the action scenes, proving yet again that this multi-episode work was too hastily produced.

In England Riders of Death Valley was first issued as an eighty-minute feature; only later were the chapter episodes released in serial form there.

RIDERS OF DESTINY (Monogram, 1933) 58 min.

Producer, Paul Malvern; director-story-screenplay, Robert North Bradbury; camera, Archie Stout; editor, Carl L. Pierson.

John Wayne (Singin' Sandy Saunders); Cecilia Parker (Fay Denton); George "Gabby" Hayes (Sheriff Denton); Forrest Taylor (Kincaid); Al St. John (Bert); Heinie Conklin (Stage Driver); Earl Dwire (Slip Morman); Yakima Canutt (Stunts); Lafe McKee (Sheriff); Fern Emmett (Farm Woman).

Of the hundreds of B westerns produced by Hollywood in the 1930s and 1940s, the group that is most widely seen today via TV is the 16 films that John Wayne made between 1933-35 for Paul Malvern's Lone Star Productions, which were issued theatrically by Monogram. Due to the star's continued popularity, these little oaters are seen throughout the U.S. on television and as a whole they are pretty representative of the series western of the period--they had

lots of action, traditional plots, good supporting casts, fine scenic
photography, sprightly editing and a young, popular and pleasing
hero (Wayne). Budget-wise the series was about average (around
$10-$12,000 per film), below those of major studios but made for
more than poverty row westerns.

One important aspect of the Western grew out of these films,
however. Star John Wayne and stuntman-player Yakima Canutt (once
a very minor genre star late in the silent days) developed the "fight
scene" still used today. Prior to this, cinema fights often appeared
stagey and unconvincing, more brawls than anything else. Wayne
and Canutt, however, developed a type of fight in which they used
certain poses to throw a punch (many times missing the opponent's
jaw by several inches). With certain camera angles and tight editing,
this developed into so convincing a fight routine that major studios
soon latched onto it and even today's TV and movie fight scenes owe
their origin to this series.

Like most series of 16 films, the Lone Star Productions with
Wayne had their ups and downs (Blue Steel (1934), with its mystery
plot, was one of the best, while the same year's The Man from Utah
was burdened with an overabundance of rodeo stock footage) but the
overall result of the series, which established Wayne among the top
ten moneymaking oater stars, was pleasing. The Riders of Destiny,
issued late in 1933, was the initial entry in the series and typical of
what was to come. Here Wayne was Singin' Sandy Saunders,* a
secret service agent sent West to investigate farmers' claims that
a land speculator (Taylor) was trying to steal their farmland by
daming up the area's water supply. To aid in his task, Wayne joined
in with Taylor and proved him to be the culprit. After many a chase
and fight, Wayne blew up a well on the sheriff's (Hayes) land, causing
the dammed water to be released, ending the villain's evil actions.
Wayne also won Hayes' pretty daughter (Parker) at the finale. An
added attraction had comic touches with Al St. John (later to develop
the popular forties' grizzled western character, "Fuzzy Q. Jones")
and Heinie Conklin, both ex-Keystone Kops, as Taylor's bungling
henchmen.

RIDERS OF THE PURPLE SAGE (Fox, 1918) six reels

Director, Frank Lloyd; based on the novel by Zane Grey;
screenplay, Lloyd.
William Farnum (Lassiter); William Scott (Venters); M. R.
Robbins (Dyer); Murdock MacQuarrie (Tull); Mary Mersch (Jane);
Katherine Adams (Masked Rider-Millie); Nancy Carroll (Fay Larkin);
J. Holmes (Jerry Card); Buck Jones (Bit).

---

*This series if often mistaken as the "Singin' Sandy" series although
Wayne played the character in only this entry. Wayne did "sing" in
the series but his voice was dubbed. For years writers claimed
Smith Ballew did the dubbing, but this has been proven false.

RIDERS OF THE PURPLE SAGE   (Fox, 1925)   5,578'

        Director, Lynn Reynolds; based on the novel by Zane Grey;
screenplay, Edfrid Bingham; camera, Dan Clark.
        Tom Mix (Jim Lassiter); Beatrice Burnham (Millie Erne);
Arthur Morrison (Frank Erne); Seesel Ann Johnson (Bess Erne -
as a Child); Warner Oland (Lew Walters/Judge Dyer); Fred Kohler
(Metzger); Charles Newton (Herd); Joe Rickson (Slack); Mabel Ballin
(Jane Withersteen); Charles Le Moyne (Richard Tull); Harold Good-
win (Bern Venters); Marion Nixon (Bess Erne); Dawn O'Day [Anne
Shirley] (Fay Larkin); Wilfred Lucas (Oldring).

RIDERS OF THE PURPLE SAGE   (Fox, 1931)   58 min.

        Director, Hamilton MacFadden; based on the novel by Zane
Grey; screenplay, John F. Goodrich, Philip Klein, Barry Connors;
dialogue, Klein, Connors; sound, Eugene Grossman; camera, George
Schneiderman.
        George O'Brien (Jim Lassiter); Marguerite Churchill (Jane
Withersteen); Noah Beery (Judge Dyer); Yvonne Pelletier (Bess);
James Todd (Venters); Stanley Fields (Oldring); Lester Dorr (Jud-
kins); Frank McGlynn, Jr. (Jeff Tull); Shirley Nails (Fay Larkin).

RIDERS OF THE PURPLE SAGE   (Twentieth Century-Fox, 1941)
56 min.

        Producer, Sol M. Wurtzel; director, James Tinling; based on
the novel by Zane Grey; screenplay, William Bruckner, Robert Metz-
ler; camera, Lucien Andriot; editor, Nick De Maggio.
        George Montgomery (Jim Lassiter); Mary Howard (Jane Wither-
steen); Robert Barrat (Judge Dyer); Lynne Roberts (Bess); Kane
Richmond (Adam Dyer); Patsy Patterson (Fay); Richard Lane (Oldring); Oscar O'Shea (Nash Judkins); James Gillette (Venters); Frank
McGrath (Pete); Leroy Mason (Jerry Card).

        The first filming of this 1911 Zane Grey novel came in 1918
as part of the series of Grey stories Frank Lloyd co-scripted and
directed for Fox Films, all of which starred William Farnum. Future Western star Buck Jones had a featured role in the proceedings.
        In 1925 Fox re-filmed the story as a vehicle for Tom Mix
and the picture was highlighted by Dan Clark's excellent photography.
When a lawyer (Oland) is run out of town he takes Millie Erne
(Burnham) and her daughter with him--by force. The woman's
brother, Texas Ranger Jim Lassiter (Mix), sets out to locate them.
In the process he becomes a ramrod on a ranch and befriends Bern
Venters (Goodwin), who captured the beautiful female leader of an
outlaw gang and falls in love with her. The ranch owner, attractive
Jane Withersteen (Ballin), informs Lassiter that the man he wants is
now a judge and, in a later skirmish, Lassiter kills Judge Dyer in
his courtroom. A posse chases Lassiter, who flees with Jane

Withersteen, and they take refuge on a plateau. To block the posse, Jim rolls down a boulder which blocks the only entrance to the canyon, leaving the two together and in love. Photoplay reported, "Considering the story, it's a disappointment. But good scenery, good photography--and Tom Mix."

The same year star Mix and director Lynn Reynolds reteamed to make the sequel, The Rainbow Trail [q.v.].

Fox lensed the novel for a third time in 1931 as a project for its successor to Mix, George O'Brien. Hamilton MacFadden directed the new version which had O'Brien as Jim Lassiter, an outcast who saves a ranch from outlaws. Like Mix, O'Brien also did the sequel, The Rainbow Trail, the same year.

What is perhaps the best screen adaptation to date of this Grey novel was shot by Twentieth Century-Fox in 1941 with George Montgomery in the lead. James Tinling directed this version which was the first of two Zane Grey features Montgomery made (the other being Last of the Duanes [q.v.]) before being launched to stardom in A pictures.

RIDERS OF THE WHISTLING SKULL   (Republic, 1937) 54 min.

Producer, Nat Levine; director, Mack V. Wright; based on characters created by William Colt MacDonald; story, Bernard McConville, Oliver Drake; screenplay, Drake, John Rathmell; camera, Jack Marta; editor, Tony Martinelli.

Bob Livingston (Stony Brooke); Ray Corrigan (Tucson Smith); Max Terhune (Lullaby Joslin); Mary Russell (Betty Marsh); Roger Williams (Rutledge); Fern Emmett (Henrietta McCoy); C. Montague Shaw (Professor Flaxon); Yakima Canutt (Otah); John Ward (Professor Brewster); George Godfrey (Professor Frone); Frank Ellis (Coggins); Earle Ross (Professor Cleary); Chief Thunder Cloud (High Priest); John Van Pelt (Professor Marsh).

Perhaps the best of the fine Republic series of The Three Mesquiteers films (1936-1943) was Riders of the Whistling Skull. An unusual Western, it had the Mesquiteers, Stony Brooke (Livingston), Tucson Smith (Corrigan) and Lullaby Joslin (Terhune), helping to locate the lost Indian city of Lukachakai, guarded by the Whistling Skull (a huge rock formation which produces a whistling sound with the help of the winds of the area). A combination mystery-Western, the feature also involved the search for a missing archaeologist in a remote section of the Painted Desert.

This entry was one of the most exciting and biggest hits of the long-lasting series. Fern Emmett as Henrietta McCoy, the man-chasing aunt of the heroine (Russell), provided much of the comedy relief, with Terhune's Lullaby Joslin and the wooden dummy Elmer offering their usual jocular support. The well-engineered finale found Tucson bound to a cross with a rock avalanche about to crush him.

Oliver Drake who had co-scripted this film would reuse the premise in 1949 for Monogram's The Feathered Serpent, a Charlie

Yakima Canutt (left), Tom Steele (center) and Robert Livingston (kneeling) in Riders of the Whistling Skull (1937).

Chan picture starring Roland Winters. Oddly enough, that picture also featured Robert Livingston in the cast.

RIO BRAVO (Warner Bros., 1959) C 141 min.

      Producer-director, Howard Hawks; based on a short story by B. H. McCampbell; screenplay, Jules Furthman, Leigh Brackett; music-music conductor, Dimitri Tiomkin; songs, Tiomkin and Paul Francis Webster; art director, Leo K. Kuter; set decorator, Ralph S. Hurst; costumes, Marjorie Best; makeup, Gordon Bau; assistant director, Paul Helmick; sound, Robert B. Lee; camera, Russell Harlan; editor, Folmar Blangsted.
      John Wayne (John T. Chance); Dean Martin (Dude); Ricky

Nelson (Colorado); Angie Dickinson (Feathers); Walter Brennan
(Stumpy); Ward Bond (Pat Wheeler); John Russell (Nathan Burdette);
Pedro Gonzales-Gonzales (Carlos); Estelita Rodriguez (Consuela);
Claude Akins (Joe Burdette); Malcolm Atterbury (Jake); Harry Carey,
Jr. (Harold); Bob Steele (Matt Harris); Bob Terhune (Nesdon Booth);
George Bruggeman (Ted White); Myron Healey (Barfly); Fred Graham
(Gunman); Tom Monroe (Henchman); Riley Hill (Messenger).

     Nearly a dozen years after the success of Red River (1948)
[q.v.] producer-director Howard Hawks and star John Wayne teamed
up again for Rio Bravo, a lengthy and violent yarn which proved to
be immensely successful, grossing $5.75 million in U.S. and Cana-
dian distributors' rentals. Of course, having crooner Dean Martin
and teen idol Rick Nelson, as well as comely Angie Dickinson in the
cast, did not hurt matters.
     John T. Chance (Wayne), the sheriff of the Texas border
town of Rio Bravo, arrests Joe Burdette (Akins) for a brutal murder.
But Burdette's brother Nathan (Russell), a powerful rancher, orders
his riders, including Chance's old high school pal Matt Harris
(Steele), to close off the small town so that the sheriff cannot get
his prisoner into the custody of the U.S. marshal. Chance's only

Ricky Nelson, Angie Dickinson, Bob Terhune and John Wayne in
Rio Bravo (1959).

help comes from a grouchy old man (Brennan) and a drunk (Martin),
the latter an ex-deputy and a has-been gunfighter. Stranded by the
blockade are a girl (Dickinson), a train of fuel and dynamite under
the supervision of Pat Wheeler (Bond), and a young gunfighter
named Colorado (Nelson). Soon Nathan's men have gunned down
Wheeler, and thereafter Chance and a sobered Dude (Martin) corral
eight of Burdette's men, with Dude shooting Wheeler's killer. Later
Dude is captured by the opponents. Chance agrees to trade Joe
Burdette for the safe return of Dude. However, the sheriff inter-
rupts the exchange when Stumpy (Brennan) sets one of the fuel
wagons on fire and runs it into Burdette's lodgings, ending the battle. At the fade-out, Chance admits his romantic fancy for Feathers
(Dickinson).

"Practically guaranteed to gladden the hearts of the men and
boys.... Although the story line is very standard stuff, the effect
is always chipper and zestful" (New York Herald-Tribune). The
New York Times was more conservative in its praise: "Despite its
slickness, virility, occasional humor and authentic professional approach, it is well-made but awfully familiar fare." Time registered
a few complaints: "The trouble is, Producer-Director Howard
Hawks has put too many shooting irons in the fire. The picture has
not one but three heroes; they divide the sympathies and overpopu-
late the screen. For another thing, the film lasts almost as long
as five TV westerns laid end to end--and it makes about as little
consecutive sense...."

While Duke Wayne was the star of the proceedings, and
Walter Brennan performed his usual scene-stealing bits, it was
Dean Martin who offered the surprise of the picture, for he turned
in a well-conceived performance. Martin and Ricky Nelson sang
"My Rifle, My Pony and Me," while Ozzie and Harriet's younger
son soloed "Cindy."

Perhaps Arthur Knight (Saturday Review) best summed up
the virtues of this well-remembered brawling feature: "As standard
Western fare as has ever turned up on a Hollywood menu.... It
has the regulation number of barroom brawls, the misunderstanding
between girl and sheriff, the walk down the empty main street with
guns at the ready. But when brewed by Howard Hawks ... suddenly
everything begins to work. There is excitement, tension, the
pleasure of looking at Western landscapes, and the age-old gratifi-
cation when the good guys beat the bad...."

RIO GRANDE (Republic, 1950) 105 min.

Producers, John Ford, Merian C. Cooper; director, Ford;
based on the story "Mission with No Record" by James Warner
Bellah; screenplay, James Kevin McGuinness; art director, Frank
Hotaling; set decorators, John McCarthy, Jr., Charles Thompson;
music, Victor Young; songs, Stan Jones; Dale Evans; Tex Owens;
second unit director, Cliff Lyons; camera, Bert Glennon; second
unit camera, Archie Stout; editor, Jack Murray; assistant editor,
Barbara Ford.

John Wayne (Lieutenant Colonel Kirby Yorke); Maureen O'Hara (Kathleen Yorke); Ben Johnson (Trooper Tyree); Claude Jarman, Jr. (Trooper Jeff Yorke); Harry Carey, Jr. (Trooper Sandy Boone); Chill Wills (Dr. Wilkins); J. Carrol Naish (General Philip Sheridan); Victor McLaglen (Sergeant Major Tim Quincannon); Grant Withers (Deputy Marshal); Peter Ortiz (Captain St. Jacques); Steve Pendleton (Captain Prescott); Karolyn Grimes (Margaret Mary); Alberto Morin (Lieutenant); Stan Jones, Jack Pennick (Sergeants); Fred Kennedy (Heinz); The Sons of the Pioneers (Regimental Singers); Chuck Roberson (Indian); Patrick Wayne (Boy); Cliff Lyons (Soldier); and Tommy Doss.

During the Civil War a Union soldier, Kirby Yorke (Wayne) is forced by his commanding officer (Naish) to burn his Southern wife's (O'Hara) plantation. Since then they have been estranged and he has not seen his son (Jarman, Jr.) for some sixteen years. Now Lieutenant Colonel York is fighting Indians in the West. He realizes the fight is hopeless because the Apaches can raid and then escape across the Rio Grande into Mexico. At this juncture, Yorke's son Jeff enlists in the army and ends up in his father's unit as a trooper. Kathleen Yorke (O'Hara) arrives soon thereafter, hoping to get her

Claude Jarman, Jr., Steve Pendleton, John Wayne and Peter Ortiz in Rio Grande (1950).

son discharged, but Yorke refuses. She then embarrasses her
husband and son by living with the enlisted men's wives and mothers
on "laundresses' row. " Philip Sheridan (Naish), now in command,
sends Yorke across the border and in the ensuing fight, Jeff becomes
a hero and the Apaches are defeated. As "punishment" for his illegal act, Yorke is made a military attache at the court of St. James
in England. This pleases Kathleen who has been reconciled by now
with her spouse.

"Rio Grande is an almost balletic story of the relationships
among a man and his two loves--his wife and the cavalry. The use
of music, both as background and as an active element in the narrative, and of formally composed, expressionistic images convey the
emotional resonances of the film in a highly stylized manner" (J. A.
Place, The Western Films of John Ford, 1975).

Rio Grande is the last of director Ford's colorful cavalry
trilogy (Fort Apache, 1948, and She Wore a Yellow Ribbon, 1949,
both q. v.). Compared to the other entries, it is a far more sentimental film, and it has long stretches of non-action. It does, however, contain a great many touches of Ford's typical rough (Irish)
comedy. Once again, the teaming of Maureen O'Hara and John
Wayne added poignancy to the storyline, as well as bringing out the
best in each player.

Watching pictures such as Rio Grande one can only silently
cheer the time when patriotism for one's country--no matter how
misguided the cause may have been--ruled, and, above all, dignity
and honor were an accepted part of life. It is themes like these
which give depth and reason to Ford's cavalry trilogy, raising them
above the standard white-man-versus-Indian plots, or the stories of
internal squabbling of American soldiers at the fort.

RIO LOBO   (National General, 1970)   C   114 min.

Producer, Howard Hawks; associate producer, Paul Helmick;
director, Hawks; story, Burton Wohl; screenplay, Leigh Brackett,
Wohl; production designer, Robert Smith; set decorator, William
Kiernan; second unit director, Yakima Canutt; music, Jerry Goldsmith; technical adviser, William Byrne; sound, John Carter; special
effects, A. D. Flowers; camera, William Clothier; editor, John
Woodcock.

John Wayne (Cord McNally); Jorge Rivero (Pierre Cordona);
Jennifer O'Neill (Shasta); Jack Elam (Phillips); Victor French (Ketch-
am); Chris Mitchum (Tuscarora); Susana Dosamantes (Maria Carmen);
Mike Henry (Sheriff Hendricks); David Huddleston (Dr. Jones); Bill
Williams (Sheriff Cronin); Edward Faulkner (Lieutenant Harris);
Sherry Lansing (Amelita); Dean Smith (Bitey); Robert Donner (Whitey);
Jim Davis (Riley); Peter Jason (Lieutenant Forsythe); Robert Roth-
well, Chuck Courtney, George Plimpton (Whitey's Henchmen); Bob
Steele (Henchman); Donald "Red" Barry (Bartender); and: Chuck
Roberson, Red Morgan, Hank Worden.

Just before the end of the Civil War, Colonel Cord McNally

John Wayne, Victor French, Chris Mitchum and Jack Elam in <u>Rio Lobo</u> (1970).

(Wayne) repossesses a Union gold shipment hijacked by the Rebs.
He captures the Confederate leader Captain Cordona (Rivero) and
his sergeant Tuscarora (Mitchum), but treats them fairly.   The
latter two, after the war is over, are glad to help McNally in his
search for a traitor who had been spying for the enemy.   Later
McNally learns that the traitor is Ketcham (French) and that he is
now trying to take over the town of Rio Lobo where Tuscarora's
"dad," Phillips (Elam), owns a ranch spread.   When McNally arrives he finds Rio Lobo and its sheriff (Henry) being terrorized by
Ketcham and his men.   Later McNally and Phillips are forced to
hold off the attackers at the jail.   In the finale gun battle, the
culprits are defeated.
      If the plot of Rio Lobo seems overly-familiar, it was the
vague basis for Rio Bravo (1959) and El Dorado (1967) [both q. v.],
both of which starred John Wayne and were produced-directed by
Howard Hawks.   "If the preamble this time is distinctly circuitous,
the showdown itself works almost as well as ever, with the traditional quartet--Wayne, a garrulous ancient, and two younger aides--
facing impossible odds and winning through by a nice amalgam of
wit, cunning and luck" (British Monthly Film Bulletin).
      Rio Lobo grossed a healthy $4.25 million in U.S. and Cana-
dian rentals and it demonstrated how superstar Wayne could stress
humor in his films instead of just continuous straight action.
Robert Mitchum had originally been sought to co-star with Wayne,
as he had done in El Dorado, but he did not care for the part offered.   Lovely Jennifer O'Neill, who would make a bigger impression in Summer of '42 (1971), was Wayne's very appealing co-star.
One scene had her sleeping with Wayne on the prairie.   The morning after, Wayne informs her "You're a lot better than a hot rock
to keep a man warm."   The girl then informs Wayne she chose him
because he was "comfortable."   (This becomes a standing joke in
the film and is employed again at the finale when Wayne and O'Neill
depart into the sunset).   The real scene-stealer of the film, though,
is Jack Elam, who gives an outrageously comical performance as
Rivero's father.
      With its jaunty atmosphere to compensate for some slow
stretches of non-action, the film pleased its intended market.   It
proved once again that Wayne was not yet a superannuated star
and that equally aging veteran Hawks could still turn out a commercial hit.

A RIVER OF DOLLARS   see   UN FIUME DI DOLLARI

ROARIN' WEST   see   THE RED RIDER

THE ROBIN HOOD OF EL DORADO   (MGM, 1936)   86 min.

      Producer, John W. Considine, Jr.; director, William A.
Wellman; based on the book by Walter Noble Burns; screenplay,

Wellman, Joseph Calleia, Malvin Levy; camera, Chester Lyons;
editor, Robert H. Kern.
     Warner Baxter (Joaquin Murrieta); Ann Lording (Juanita de
la Cuesta); Bruce Cabot (Bill Warren); Margo (Rosita); J. Carrol
Naish (Three Fingered Jack); Soledad Jimenez (Madre Murrieta);
Carlos de Valdez (Jose Murrieta); Eric Linden (Johnny Warren);
Edgar Kennedy (Sheriff Judd); Charles Trowbridge (Ramon de la
Cuesta); Harvey Stephens (Captain Osborne); Ralph Remley (Judge
Perkins); George Regas (Tomas); Francis McDonald (Pedro the Spy);
Kay Hughes (Louise); Paul Hurst (Wilson); Boothe Howard (Tabbard);
Harry Woods (Pete).

     The colorful Mexican bandit, Joaquin Murrieta, has been the
subject of many screen biographies, including D. W. Griffith's
Scarlet Days (1919) [q.v.]. This 1936 MGM version, however, was
derived from Walter Noble Burns' biography of the outlaw and it attempted to present a fairly accurate, if still somewhat romantic
picture of Murrieta. Frank S. Nugent (New York Times) decided it
was "a brutally frank indictment of American injustice, greed and
cowardice in the years of the California gold rush."
     The picture told of the poor peon Joaquin Murrieta (Baxter),
who lives with his wife Rosita (Margo) at Saw Mill Flat. Four men
order them off their land, and when they refuse to leave they are
beaten and the woman dies as a result. Murrieta then hunts the
men and kills them. Thereafter he is an outlaw with a price on
his head. He takes refuge at his brother's farm and again men arrive and accuse them of stealing a mule. In the scuffle, the brother
is murdered. Joaquin later joins an outlaw band and leads them in

Warner Baxter and Francis McDonald in The Robin Hood of El
Dorado (1936).

a reign of terror against the settlers in which there are some three
hundred murders committed over a three-year period in Southern
California. Eventually he is hunted down and killed, dying at his
wife's grave.

In his autobiography, A Short Time for Insanity (1974), Wellman recalls an anecdote on the set of The Robin Hood of El Dorado:
"J. Carrol Naish as Three Finger Jack ... pulling a gun loaded
with blanks in a scene with Warner Baxter and catching the hammer
in his belt, and it goes off just before he gets it out of his holster.
It dug into him in the upper inside of the thigh, bad, and he wouldn't
look down because he wasn't sure of the location, just gazed at me
with a stricken, pleading face, 'Bill, Bill, tell me it isn't so.'"

ROCKY MOUNTAIN (Warner Bros., 1950) 83 min.

     Producer, William Jacobs; director, William Keighley; story,
Alan LeMay; screenplay, Winston Miller, LeMay; music, Max
Steiner; orchestrator, Murray Cutter; art director, Stanley Fleischer;
set decorator, L. S. Edwards; assistant director, Frank Mattison;
costumes, Marjorie Best; sound, Stanley Jones; camera, Ted Mc-
Cord; editor, Rudi Fehr.
     Errol Flynn (Lafe Barstow); Patrice Wymore (Johanna Carter);
Scott Forbes (Lieutenant Rickey); Guinn "Big Boy" Williams (Pap
Dennison); Dick Jones (Jim Wheat); Howard Petrie (Cole Smith);
Slim Pickens (Plank); Chubby Johnson (Gil Craigie); Buzz Henry (Kip
Waterson); Sheb Woolley (Kay Rawlins); Peter Coe (Pierre Duchesne);
Rush Williams (Jonas Weatherby); Steve Dunhill (Ash); Alex Sharp
(Barnes); Yakima Canutt (Ryan); Nakai Snez (Man Dog).

     This feature was based on an actual incident and was shot on
location near Gallup, New Mexico.
     Errol Flynn played Confederate officer Lafe Barstow, who
with his small band, goes West hoping to recruit outlaws in order
to control the area for the South. The group saves a girl, Johanna
Carter (Wymore) from Indians. It turns out that she was heading to
join her Union soldier fiance, Lieutenant Rickey (Forbes), whose
patrol the Confederates later capture. Eventually the Union soldier
escapes, but to protect the girl the Confederates fight attacking
Indians and they are all killed.
     Rocky Mountain, lensed in black-and-white, was Flynn's final
oater and, compared to such earlier Flynn-Warner Bros. entries
as Dodge City (1939) or They Died with Their Boots on (1941) [q.v.],
it was a sad comedown. However, the film did contain a few good
sequences, such as the Indian attack on a stagecoach and a rousing
chase sequence.
     Flynn met his third wife, Patrice Wymore, during the pro-
duction.

ROOSTER COGBURN (... and the Lady) (Universal, 1975) C
107 min.

     Producer, Hal B. Wallis; associate producer, Paul Nathan;

Rooster Cogburn

director, Stuart Millar; suggested by the character created by
Charles Portis; screenplay, Martin Julien; art director, Preston
Ames; set decorator, George Robert Nelson; music, Laurence Rosen-
thal; second unit director, Michael Moore; assistant directors, Pepi
Lenzi, Richard Hashimoto; stunt coordinator, Jerry Gatlin; men's
costumes, Luster Bayless; Miss Hepburn's wardrobe, Edith Head;
sound, John Carter; special effects, Jack McMasters; camera, Harry
Stradling; second unit camera, Rexford Metz; editor, Robert Swink.

John Wayne (Rooster Cogburn); Katharine Hepburn (Eula Good-
night); Anthony Zerbe (Breed); Richard Jordan (Hawk); John McIntire
(Judge Parker); Paul Koslo (Luke); Jack Colvin (Red); Jon Lormer
(Reverend Goodnight); Richard Romancito (Wolf); Lane Smith (Leroy);
Warren Vanders (Bagby); Jerry Gatlin (Nose); and Strother Martin
(McCoy).

With the phenomenal success of True Grit (1969) [q.v.],
which earned him his only Academy Award to date, it was logical
that John Wayne would return to the role of the gruff, one-eyed,
deputy marshal. To make the sequel even more appealing to the
public, Katharine Hepburn was recruited as his co-lead. Producer
Hal B. Wallis figured that audiences could not resist watching these
two very different superstars in tandem on camera.

If Rooster Cogburn is approached as a sensible, mature
drama, disappointment will be the result. Rather, it is a fun but
very tame Western that is very self-indulgent to each star. Perhaps the most successful aspect of the film is the startling cinematography of Harry Stradling, capturing the splendid beauty of the
Deschutes National Forest and the Rogue River area of Oregon.

In Rooster Cogburn Wayne is the heavy-drinking, paunchy
law enforcer who is too quick on the trigger. District Court Judge
Parker (McIntire) removes Rooster's badge when he reports to the
court that he has just shot three outlaws. The Judge is concerned
that Cogburn's trigger-happy penchant might prevent newcomers from
settling in this western district of Arkansas. At a loss as to how
to handle his demotion, Cogburn returns to his hideaway, the back
of Chen Lee's (Lee) grocery store where he downs several beers
while talking to his Chinese friend and the beer-drinking cat General
Price. Later the judge offers Rooster a $2,000 reward plus rein-
statement if he captures (alive) the outlaws who have just ambushed
a cavalry escort and stolen a wagon load of nitro and guns.

Trailing the criminals to Fort Ruby, Rooster arrives to find
that the bandits have preceded him, killing several peaceful Indians
there. He meets Eula Goodnight (Hepburn) whose preacher father
was also killed at the fort. The tough, Bible-quoting spinster insists upon accompanying Rooster in his search for the murderers.
Her escort is Wolf (Romancito), a young Indian boy. Eventually
they cross paths with their prey, steal the nitro and firearms and
chart a dangerous course down a river.

Once back in civilization, Eula, who has fallen in love with
the feisty Cogburn, defends his actions at Judge Parker's court,
trying to explain why he had to kill the bandits instead of returning
them alive as promised. The Judge is impressed by her rationale
and returns Rooster's marshal's badge.

The next day finds Eula and Wolf returning to Fort Ruby while Cogburn is off to chase more outlaws. Before separating, the two elder citizens drink a toast to their "someday" together.

Even the more indulgent moviegoer will find many flaws and embarrassments in Rooster Cogburn, and it is hard to dismiss the ravages of time on both superstars. Of the two, Wayne fares better, more able to take artistic license in his hammy performance. And how can one avoid the deja vu when Rooster and Eula head down the rapids on the raft. It is all too clearly a copy from Hepburn's trek with Humphrey Bogart in The African Queen (1951).

These days, it seems no Western movie would be complete without the appearance of Strother Martin. Here the well-known character player performs as McCoy the irascible ferryboat owner.

ROSE MARIE (MGM, 1936) 113 min.

Producer, Hunt Stromberg; director, W. S. Van Dyke II; based on the operetta by Otto A. Harbach, Oscar Hammerstein II, Rudolf Friml and Herbert Stothart; screenplay, Frances Goodrich, Albert Hackett, Alice Duer Miller; music director, Stothart; songs, Harbach, Hammerstein II, and Friml; Kahn and Stothart; Sam Lewis, Joe Young, and Harry Akst; and Shelton Brooks; totem pole dance staged by Chester Hale; operatic episodes staged by William von Wymetal; art directors, Cedric Gibbons, Joseph Wright, Edwin B. Willis; gowns, Adrian; sound, Douglas Shearer; camera, William Daniels; editor, Blanche Sewell.

Jeanette MacDonald (Marie de Flor); Nelson Eddy (Sergeant Bruce); James Stewart (John Flower); Reginald Owen (Meyerson); Allan Jones (Romeo); Gilda Gray (Bella); George Regas (Boniface); Robert Greig (Cafe Manager); Una O'Connor (Anna); Lucien Little-field (Storekeeper); Alan Mowbray (Premier); David Niven (Teddy); Herman Bing (Mr. Daniels); James Conlin (Joe); Dorothy Gray (Edith); Mary Anita Loos (Corn Queen); Aileen Carlyle (Susan); Halliwell Hobbes (Mr. Gordon); Paul Porcasi (Emil); Edgar Dearing (Mounted Policeman); Pat West (Traveling Salesman); Milton Owen (Stage Manager); David Clyde (Doorman);Russell Hicks (Commandant); Rolfe Sedan, Jack Pennick (Men); David Robel, Rinaldo Alacorn (Dancers); Leonard Carey (Louis); Bert Lindley (Trapper).

After the tremendous response to teaming songbird Jeanette MacDonald with opera baritone Nelson Eddy in Naughty Marietta (1935), MGM re-matched the performers in another Rudolf Friml operetta, Rose Marie. It was perhaps the most popular film made by the enduring singing team, and would certainly be the finest of the three screen versions of the property turned out by MGM (1928, 1936 and 1954). What made this thirties' rendition of the operetta so refreshing was the excellent feeling of the out-of-doors obtained by director Van Dyke. He not only opened up the storyline (with location filming at Lake Tahoe on the California-Nevada border), but injected many elements of the standard Western into the musical.

The plot concerns temperamental opera diva Marie de Flor (MacDonald) who is kind only to her erring brother, John Flower

Nelson Eddy and Jeanette MacDonald in <u>Rose Marie</u> (1936).

(Stewart). The latter has escaped from jail and has killed a Royal Mountie who was pursuing him. Desperate to find her outlaw brother, Marie hires a guide who robs and then deserts her. She is forced to earn money by singing in a honky tonk. While there she meets Mountie Sergeant Bruce (Eddy) and they promptly fall in, then out, and then in love again, despite the fact that he later captures John. Heartbroken, Marie returns to the opera, but collapses during a performance. She returns to the north country and is eventually reconciled with Sergeant Bruce.

The operetta first opened on Broadway on September 2, 1924 with Dennis King and Mary Ellis in the leads and it ran for 557 performances. Its numerous lovely tunes, "Rose-Marie," "Indian Love Call," "Song of the Mounties," "Totem Tom Tom," and "The Door of My Dreams" were transferred to the film along with two new tunes by Gus Kahn. By having MacDonald cast as an opera singer, the studio was able to interweave some opera arias into the production, which gave Allan Jones (as her onstage Romeo) a chance to demonstrate his improving screen technique.

(Miss MacDonald and Eddy had recorded "Indian Love Call" on RCA Victor Records in 1935 and it would be one of the few discs in the thirties to sell over one million copies. In 1958 they re-

recorded it for RCA on a stereo LP album, along with eleven other
songs associated with them.   In 1966 this album was named a "gold
album, " for sales in excess of $1 million.)
        In order not to be confused with the 1954, CinemaScope,
color version of Rose Marie, the MacDonald-Eddy version is retitled Indian Love Call when shown on television.

RUTH OF THE RANGE   (Pathé, 1923)   fifteen chapters

        Director, Ernest C. Warde; screenplay, Gibson Willets,
Frank Leon Smith.
        With: Ruth Roland, Bruce Gordon, Lorimer Johnston, Ernest
C. Warde, Pat Harmon, Andre Peyre, Harry De Vere, V. Omar
Whitehead.
        Chapters: 1) The Last Shot; 2) The Seething Pit; 3) The
Danger Trail; 4) The Terror Trail; 5) The Temple Dungeon; 6) The
Pitfall; 7) The Fatal Count; 8) The Dynamite Plot; 9) The Lava
Crusher; 10) Circumstantial Evidence; 11) The Desert of Death; 12)
The Vital Test; 13) The Molten Menace; 14) The First Freight; 15)
Promises Fulfilled.

        This film production was serial queen Ruth Roland's last
chapterplay, although it was filmed prior to the previously-issued
Pathé serial, Haunted Valley (1923).   Ernest C. Warde directed the
project, with W. S. Van Dyke II employed to stage some action
scenes, including an Indian attack.
        Miss Roland portrayed a girl who attempts to save her father
(director Warde) who is being held prisoner by men anxious to steal
his coal substitute formula.
        During the course of the production, scripter Gibson Willets
died without revealing the finale, and Frank Leon Smith was forced
to dream up one for the project on very short notice.

SABATA   see   EHI, AMICO ... C'E SABATA, HAI CHIUSO!

SAM WHISKEY   see   SUPPORT YOUR LOCAL SHERIFF

SANTA FE TRAIL   (Warner Bros. , 1940)   110 min.

        Executive producer, Hal B. Wallis; associate producer, Robert
Fellows; director, Michael Curtiz; screenplay, Robert Buckner; music,
Max Steiner; orchestrator, Hugo Friedhofer; assistant director, Jack
Sullivan; art director, John Hughes; costumes, Milo Anderson; make-
up, Perc Westmore; dialogue director, Jo Graham; sound, Robert B.
Lee; special effects, Byron Haskin, H. D. Koenekamp; camera, Sol
Polito; editor, Georgy Amy.
        Errol Flynn (Jeb Stuart); Olivia de Havilland (Kit Carson Halli-
day); Raymond Massey (John Brown); Ronald Regan (George Armstrong

Custer); Alan Hale (Barfoot Brody); Guinn "Big Boy" Williams (Tex
Bell); Van Heflin (Rader); Henry O'Neill (Cyrus Halliday); William
Lundigan (Bob Halliday); John Litel (Harlan); Gene Reynolds (Jason
Brown); Alan Baxter (Oliver Brown); Moroni Olsen (Robert E. Lee);
Erville Alderson (Jefferson Davis); Susan Peters (Charlotte Davis);
Charles D. Brown (Major Summer); David Bruce (Phil Sheridan);
Frank Wilcox (James Longstreet); William Marshall (George Pickett);
George Haywood (John Hood); Russell Simpson (Shoubel Morgan);
Joseph Sawyer (Kitzmiller); Hobart Cavanaugh (Barber Doyle); Spencer
Charters (Conductor); Ward Bond (Townley); Wilfred Lucas (Weiner);
Charles Middleton (Gentry); Russell Hicks (J. Boyce Russell); Napo-
leon Simpson (Samson); Cliff Clark (Instructor); Harry Strang (Ser-
geant); Emmett Vogan (Lieutenant); Selmer Jackson, Joseph Crehan,
William Hopper (Officers); Clinton Rosemond, Bernice Pilot, Libby
Taylor, Mildred Gover (Blacks); Roy Barcroft, Frank Mayo (En-
gineers); Grace Stafford (Farmer's Wife); Louis Jean Heydt (Farmer);
Lane Chandler (Adjutant); Trevor Bardette, Nestor Paiva (Agitators);
Georgia Caine (Officer's Wife); Theresa Harris (Black Maid); Victor
Kilian (Dispatch Rider); Reverend Neal Dodd (Minister).

For their third Western together--having done Dodge City
(1939) and Virginia City (1940) [q.v.]--director Michael Curtiz and
star Errol Flynn teamed for Santa Fe Trail.
Contrary to its title, the picture did not deal with the famous
cattle trail. Rather, it was a very inaccurate, flamboyant biography
of Jeb Stuart (Flynn), later to be famous as one of the Confederate's
greatest generals, culminating with John Brown's (Massey) fateful
raid on Harper's Ferry. The narrative follows Stuart and George
Armstrong Custer (Reagan) as they leave West Point and are sent to
Fort Leavenworth, Kansas where they encounter John Brown and his
abolitionist activities. Both soldiers are involved in countering the
antislaver's attack on Harper's Ferry. Along the way both Stuart and
Armstrong romance the same girl, Kit Carson Halliday (de Havilland).
Employing his usual sweep and verve, Curtiz strove for a
panorama view of the pre-Civil War days, using historical characters
and situations at will to further his storyline. As with many Holly-
wood-made features, the picture tried to straddle the fence, avoiding
the taking of sides as to who was responsible for the catastrophic
Civil War.
Called upon to be gallant, Flynn excelled, as did Miss de
Havilland in her tomboyish role. Raymond Massey, who would be
so closely associated with his later screen portrayal of Abraham
Lincoln, had the meatiest, if most inconsistent, role as the god-
fearing freedom fighter. (Massey would also play John Brown in
Seven Angry Men, 1955.) Alan Hale and Guinn "Big Boy" Williams
were on tap as part of the Warner stock company for "comic" relief, while Van Heflin provided a tough performance as Rader, one
of Brown's corrupt henchmen.

SCARLET DAYS (United Artists, 1919)   seven reels

Director, D. W. Griffith; screenplay, S. E. V. Taylor;
camera, G. W. "Billy" Bitzer.

Richard Barthelmess (Alvarez--a Bandit); Carol Dempster (Lady Fair); Claire Seymour (Chiquita); Ralph Graves (Randolph); Eugenie Besserer (Rosie Nell); George Fawcett (The Sheriff); Walter Long (Bagley the Dancehall Proprietor).

This was D. W. Griffith's last Artcraft film (released through United Artists, of which he was part-founder) and his first Western since working at Biograph. Scarlet Days was also his only feature-length Western, although he would touch on frontier themes again in America (1924) and in Abraham Lincoln (1930), a talkie.

Photographed by Billy Bitzer in Toulumore County, California, the film was set in the California gold rush period and was loosely-based on the life of bandit Joaquin Murrieta. Griffith star Richard Barthelmess played Alvarez, a thinly-disguised adaptation of the famed Mexican bandito. At seven reels the feature was overlong, as well as a bit hollow in its plotline, but fortunately it had solid photography and well-staged climactic chase sequences. Favorite Griffith leading ladies Carol Dempster (as an Eastern girl) and Claire Seymour (as a Mexican dancehall girl) supported Barthelmess in this drama.

THE SEARCHERS (Warner Bros., 1956)   C   119 min.

Executive producer, Merian C. Cooper; producer, C. V. Whitney; associate producer, Patrick Ford; director, John Ford; based on the novel by Alan LeMay; screenplay, Frank S. Nugent; color consultant, James Gooch; music, Max Steiner; title song, Stan Jones; art directors, Frank Hotaling, James Basevi; set decorator, Victor Gangelin; costumes, Frank Beetson, Ann Peck; assistant director, Wingate Smith; special effects, George Brown; camera, Winton C. Hoch; second unit camera, Alfred Gilks; editor, Jack Murray.

John Wayne (Ethan Edwards); Jeffrey Hunter (Martin Pawley); Vera Miles (Laurie Jorgensen); Ward Bond (Captain Reverend Samuel Clayton); Natalie Wood (Debbie Edwards); John Qualen (Lars Jorgensen); Olive Carey (Mrs. Jorgensen); Henry Brandon (Chief Scar); Ken Curtis (Charlie McCorry); Harry Carey, Jr. (Brad Jorgensen); Antonio Moreno (Emlio Figueroa); Hank Worden (Mose Harper); Lana Wood (Debbie as a Child); Walter Coy (Aaron Edwards); Dorothy Jordan (Martha Edwards); Pippa Scott (Lucy Edwards); Pat Wayne (Lieutenant Greenhill); Beulah Archuletta (Look); Jack Pennick (Private); Peter Mamakos (Futterman); Cliff Lyons, Billy Cartledge, Chuck Hayward, Slim Hightower, Fred Kennedy, Frank McGrath, Chuck Roberson, Dale van Sickel, Henry Wills, Terry Wilson (Stunt Men); Away Luna, Billy Yellow, Bob Many Mules, Exactly Sonnie Betsuie, Feather Hat, Jr., Harry Black Horse, Jack Tin Horn, Many Mules Son, Percy Shooting Star, Pete Grey Eyes, Pipe Line Begishe, Smile White Sheep (Comanches); Mae Marsh, Dan Borzage (Bits).

"'Masterpiece' isn't a word to be used lightly but few would quarrel about applying it here," Walter C. Clapham wrote in

John Wayne, Beulah Archuletta and Jeffrey Hunter in The Searchers (1956).

Western Movies (1974), describing The Searchers. Directed by John Ford, and containing what well may be John Wayne's finest screen portrayal, the feature grossed $4.9 million in distributors' U.S. and Canadian rentals.

Ethan Edwards (Wayne) returns home two years after the Civil War and the Mexican conflict have ended, to his brother's family ranch in Texas where he is greeted. The next day the Texas Rangers, led by Captain Reverend Samuel Clayton (Bond) arrive looking for rustlers. Edwards believes the Indians are the rustlers. He and Martin Pawley (Hunter), whose family was massacred by Comanches, join the Rangers. Only later do they realize that the search was a gimmick to draw them away from the spread.

They return to find Aaron Edwards' family killed and the two daughters (Scott and Wood) abducted. Edwards, Pawley, and Lucy Edwards' (Scott) finance, Brad Jorgenson (Carey, Jr.), set out to find the missing girls. A few days later they come across Lucy's body. In grief Jorgensen attacks the Comanche village and is killed. Edwards and Pawley continue their search for Debbie Edwards (Wood), but bad weather forces them to stop at a ranch. There Laurie Jorgensen (Miles) falls in love with Martin Pawley and tries to turn him away from the quest. He refuses.

When winter subsides, the two men continue their trek--in fact, they continue onward for five years! Finally they locate the

318   Secrets

Indian band that raided the Edwards' spread in New Mexico, and
they arrive at the camp posing as traders. They find Debbie has
become a member of the group. The chief (Brandon) remembers
the two white men and in a subsequent fight Edwards is injured.
Pawley takes him back home. At Laurie's ranch, Pawley causes
her to abandon her plans to marry Charlie McCorry (Curtis). At
this point the cavalry arrives and asks the men to join them against
the Indian band. Edwards agrees, hoping he can kill Debbie, whom
he now believes has disgraced his family's memory by becoming so
much a part of the redskins' way. Martin later sneaks into the
Indian settlement and kills Chief Scar (Brandon), and the braves are
thereafter defeated. Edwards finds Debbie but discovers he cannot
murder her. Instead he brings her home to be raised by Laurie
Jorgensen's family. Ethan, now the loner, walks off--a man alone.
     "From its opening scene The Searchers is unified on a visual
and structural level.... Ethan Edwards [Wayne] is perhaps Ford's
most ambiguous character. In him are all the qualities that make
a western hero--strength, individualism, self-sufficiency, leadership,
authority" (J. A. Place, The Western Films of John Ford, 1973).
The same author also notes that "without its rich humor The
Searchers would be an unbearable tragedy."
     To be noted is the rich photography of Winton C. Hoch, whose
color VistaVision camera captured all the splendor of the location
scenes filmed at Monument Valley, Mexican Hat, Utah, and in Colorado. The Searchers contains some of the most splendid visual
scenes of the fifties.

SECRETS   (United Artists, 1933)   90 min.

     Director, Frank Borzage; based on the play by Rudolf Besier,
May Edington; screenplay, Frances Marion; dialogue, Salisbury Field,
Leonard Praskins; sound, Frank Maher; camera, Ray June; editor,
Hugh Bennett.
     Mary Pickford (Mary Marlowe); Leslie Howard (John Carlton);
C. Aubrey Smith (Mr. Marlowe); Blanche Frederici (Mrs. Marlowe);
Doris Lloyd (Susan Channing); Herbert Evans (Lord Hurley); Ned
Sparks (Sunshine); Allan Sears (Jake Houser); Mona Maris (Señora
Martinez).

     Never an overly-popular production and somewhat old-fashioned
even in its own day, Secrets is best remembered as the cinema swansong of the phenomenonally successful career of Mary Pickford. The
film was a free translation by Frances Marion of the play by Rudolf
Besier and May Edginton.
     The chronicle opens in New England where Mary Marlowe
(Pickford) loves John Carlton (Howard), but her tyrannical father
(Smith) urges her to marry a boring Lord (Evans). Instead she
elopes with John and they join a wagon train heading west to California. Once there they become cattle ranchers and fight outlaws.
After a time they become prosperous and John is championed for
governor of the state. However, when it is discovered he has had

an affair with Susan Channing (Lloyd) his political ambitions are
smashed.   Later John reaffirms his love for Mary and she forgives
him his past.
Attempting to duplicate the success of Cimarron (1931) [q.v.]
or even The Conquerors (1932) [q.v.], Miss Pickford was so disappointed by the first version of Secrets that she scrapped the finished
product and began reshooting a new production.   Ill-luck beset this
version too, for it opened in theatres around the country on the day
President Roosevelt closed the banks during the Depression.
Although not a particularly moving or believable story, the
film did offer a few good scenes of rough frontier life.   Mordaunt
Hall (New York Times) acknowledged its "intriguing episodes, notably
in the beginning, but the latter sections are somewhat confusing."

SERGEANT RUTLEDGE   (Warner Bros., 1960) C 111 min.

Producers, Willis Goldbeck, Patrick Ford; director, John
Ford; screenplay, James Warner Bellah, Goldbeck; art director,
Eddie Imazu; set decorator, Frank M. Miller; music, Howard Jack-
son; song, Mack David and Jerry Livingston; costumes, Marjorie
Best; makeup, Gordon Bau; assistant directors, Russ Saunders,
Wingate Smith; sound, M. A. Merrick; camera, Bert Glennon; edi-
tor, Jack Murray.
Jeffrey Hunter (Lieutenant Thomas Cantrell); Constance
Towers (Mary Beecher); Billie Burke (Mrs. Fosgate); Woody Strode
(Sergeant Braxton Rutledge); Juano Hernandez (Skidmore); Willis
Bouchey (Major Fosgate); Carleton Young (Captain Shattuck); Judson
Pratt (Lieutenant Mulqueen); Bill Henry (Captain Dwyer); Walter
Reed (Captain MacAfee); Chuck Hayward (Captain Dickinson); Mae
Marsh (Nellie); Fred Libby (Chandler Hubble); Charles Seel (Dr.
Eckner); Toby Richards (Lucy Dabney); Jan Styne (Chris Hubble);
Cliff Lyons (Sam Beecher); Charles Seel (Dr. Eckner); Jack Pen-
nick (Sergeant); Estelle Winwood, Eva Novak (Spectators); Shug
Fisher (Mr. Owens); Chuck Roberson (Juror).

Director John Ford's love of the cavalry and his respect for
the black man were the stimulus for this feature.   It was basically
a courtroom melodrama transmitted to the beauty and the grandeur
of Monument Valley, where the film was shot.   More importantly,
it was the first major Hollywood film with a Negro as its hero and
it was Ford's tribute to the black cavalrymen.
The rather thin and not terribly interesting story had Woody
Strode as the title character, a member of a black Army cavalry
outfit who is charged with rape and murder.   He is defended by a
young lieutenant (Hunter) in a courtmartial hearing in the 1880s.
Besides crisp photography, the well-placed entry had a good
performance by Strode who mouthed some interesting dialogue:
"It's all right for Mr. Lincoln to say we're free, but we're not
free yet," and "The 9th Cavalry was my home, my freedom, the
9th's record is going to speak for us all one day and it's going to
speak clean."

Jack Pennick, Billie Burke and Carleton Young in Sergeant Rutledge
(1960).

        To be noted are the appearances of Billie Burke and Mae
Marsh, offering a softer note in a very masculine-dominated storyline.
        Of this somewhat lesser Ford entry, the New York Herald-
Tribune noted, "... [It] may not be John Ford's masterpiece but it
is a sweet breeze among current films....   What would seem merely
tricky in other hands somehow achieves a quality of inevitability and
rightness in his...." On the other hand, Philip French in Westerns
(1973) offered, "Unfortunately, Ford's film is gravely weakened by
having as its dramatic structure an indifferent Perry Mason-style
courtroom drama.... In handling this courtmartial aspect, Ford is

at his most embarrassingly self-indulgent and one suspects that it held little interest for him."

THE SETTLERS   see   THE NEW LAND

SEVEN ANGRY MEN   see   SANTA FE TRAIL

SEVEN SAMURAI   see   THE MAGNIFICENT SEVEN

THE SHAKIEST GUN IN THE WEST   see   THE PALEFACE

SHALAKO   (Cinerama, 1968)   C   113 min.

Executive producer, Dimitri De Grunwald; associate producer, Hal Mason; producer, Euan Lloyd; director, Edward Dmytryk; based on the novel by Louis L'Amour; screen story, Clarke Reynolds; screenplay, J. J. Griffith, Hal Hopper, Scot Finch; music, Robert Farnon; music director, Muir Mathieson; song, Farnon and Jim Dale; art director, Herbert Smith; costumes, Cynthia Tingey; make-up, Trevor Crole-Rees, Jean Pierre Berroyer; assistant director, Peter Price, Joe Ochoa; sound, Keith Palmer, George Stephenson; special effects, Michael Collins; camera, Ted Moore; second unit camera, John Cabrera; editor, Bill Blunden.

Sean Connery (Shalako); Brigitte Bardot (Countess Irina Lazaar); Stephen Boyd (Bosky Fulton); Jack Hawkins (Sir Charles Daggett); Peter Van Eyck (Frederick Von Hallstatt); Honor Blackman (Lady Daggett); Woody Strode (Chato); Eric Sykes (Mako); Alexander Knox (Henry Clarke); Valerie French (Elena Clarke); Julian Mateos (Rojas); Donald "Red" Barry (Buffalo); Rodd Redwing (Chato's Father); Chief Tug Smith (Loco); Hans De Vries (Hans); Walter Brown (Pete Wells); Charles Stalnaker (Marker); John Clark (Hockett); Bob Hall (Johnson).

This British-made Western was filmed in Spain and it required some four years for the producers to obtain sufficient international backing to finance the filming. With its multinational cast under Edward Dmytryk's direction, the result was a "robust nineteenth century western adventure" (Variety). But even the novelty of Sean "James Bond" Connery teamed with France's nude queen Brigitte Bardot was not sufficient to make it the huge moneywinner that was anticipated.

This offbeat tale was set in the West of the 1880s with a British sheep hunting expedition being led by Shalako (Connery), an ex-Army officer and Indian scout. It is he who tries to save the group when the Indians go on the warpath. For romance, there was Miss Bardot as Countess Irina Lazaar (her character name was the most exotic thing about her under-performed appearance), and Ireland's Stephen Boyd provided the villainy.

Jaunty Time dissected the film in its usual unkind way: "To the Apache, Shalako means Bringer of Rain.   In movie parlance it merely means Stupefier of Audience."   Renata Adler of the New York Times offered more practical advice: "... [It] is a good, old-fashioned, wide screen Western ... the perfect movie to see in a two-theatre town on a Saturday night."

SHANE   (Paramount, 1953)   C   118 min.

Producer, George Stevens; associate producer, Ivan Moffat; director, Stevens; associate director, Fred Guiol; based on the novel by Jack Schaefer; screenplay, A. B. Guthrie, Jr.; additional dialogue, Jack Sher; art directors, Hal Pereira, Walter Tyler; Technicolor consultant, Richard Mueller; music, Victor Young; camera, Loyal Griggs; editor, William Hornbeck.

Alan Ladd (Shane); Jean Arthur (Mrs. Starrett); Van Heflin (Mr. Starrett); Brandon De Wilde (Joey Starrett); Jack Palance (Wilson); Ben Johnson (Chris); Edgar Buchanan (Lewis); Emile Meyer (Ryker); Elisha Cook, Jr. (Torrey); Douglas Spencer (Mr. Shipstead); John Dierkes (Morgan); Ellen Corby (Mrs. Torrey); Paul McVey (Grafton); John Miller (Atkey); Edith Evanson (Mrs. Shipstead); Leonard Strong (Wright); Ray Spiker (Johnson); Janice Carroll (Susan Lewis); Martin Mason (Howells); Helen Brown (Mrs. Lewis); Nancy Kulp (Mrs. Howells); Howard J. Negley (Pete); Beverly Washburn (Ruth Lewis); George Lewis (Ryker Man); Charles Quirk (Clerk); Jack Sterling, Henry Wills, Rex Moore, Ewing Brown (Ryker Men).

Alan Ladd, Van Hefflin and Henry Wills (right) in Shane (1953).

George Stevens' Shane has proved to be an enduring classic over the decades, and is considered a fine representative Western of the fifties, of the same caliber as High Noon (1952) [q. v.]. Ironically, the film never had a great impact on the genre. In theatrical release, Shane has grossed over $9 million in distributors' U.S. and Canadian rentals.

Rancher Starrett (Heflin) hires drifter Shane (Ladd) to help him make a stand against a ruthless cattle baron (Dierkes) who is trying to take over a small town. At first Starrett's family, his wife (Arthur) and small son Joey (De Wilde), are wary of Shane, but once he removes his gun and begins to help with the farm chores the boy begins to idolize him. A former gunfighter, Shane wants to lead a peaceful existence but the range wars always seem to involve him. Here again he is forced to take up arms and must have a showdown with Wilson (Palance), the black-garbed gunslinger for Morgan (Dierkes). Having shot Wilson, Shane confronts Morgan and the latter is killed. Despite his fondness for Joey and his affection for Mrs. Starrett, Shane knows it is time to leave. He rides off, refusing to heed the boy's cries of "Shane, come back."

Because of its realism, Shane stands out as a superior film. Individual sequences and the well-calculated performances increase the picture's viability. Among the most-remembered scenes are the fight in the general store between Ladd and Heflin on one side and Dierkes' villains on the other side, Palance's murder of Cook (the scene would be imitated by director Burt Kennedy for Cook's murder in Welcome to Hard Times, 1967, q. v.), and of course, the final scene where Ladd rides away and young De Wilde runs after his hero calling pleadingly, "Shane, Shane."

Gordon Gow in Hollywood in the Fifties (1971) pinpointed one of the best qualities of Shane, noting that it was "marvelously spacious."

Just as Alan Ladd's sterling performance in Shane was almost taken for granted due to its low-key pacing, so much of the vibrancy and realism of the film story was taken in stride by moviegoers. At the core of the plot is Shane the outsider, a man who has outlived his time and usefulness. In the middle of the film, Shane says to one character, "Your days are over." The listener replies, "Mine? What about yours, gunslinger?" Shane answers, "The difference is, I know it."

Shane was in theatrical release as late as 1967.

SHE WORE A YELLOW RIBBON (RKO, 1949) C 103 min.

Producers, John Ford, Merian C. Cooper; associate producer, Lowell Farrell; director, Ford; based on the story "War Party" by James Warner Bellah; screenplay, Frank S. Nugent, Laurence Stallings; Technicolor consultants, Natalie Kalmus, Morgan Padelford; music, Richard Hageman; music director, Constantine Bakaleinikoff; orchestrator, Lucien Cailliet; art director, James Basevi; set decorator, Joe Kish; costumes, Michael Meyers, Ann Peck; assistant directors, Wingate Smith, Edward O'Fearna; second unit director, Cliff Lyons; sound, Frank Webster, Clem Portman; special effects, Jack Caffee; camera, Winton Hoch; second unit camera, Charles Boule; editor, Jack Murray.

John Wayne (Captain Nathan Brittles); Joanne Dru (Olivia Dandridge); John Agar (Lieutenant Flint Cohill); Ben Johnson (Sergeant Tyree); Harry Carey, Jr. (Lieutenant Pennell); Victor McLaglen (Sergeant Quincannon); Mildred Natwick (Mrs. Allshard); George O'Brien (Major Allshard); Arthur Shields (R. O. Laughlin); Francis Ford (Barman); Harry Woods (Karl Rynders); Chief Big Tree (Pony That Walks); Noble Johnson (Red Shirt); Cliff Lyons (Trooper Cliff); Tom Tyler (Quayle); Michael Dugan (Hochbauer); Mickey Simpson (Wagner); Fred Graham (Hench); Frank McGrath (Trumpeter); Don Summers (Jenkins); Fred Libby (Colonel Krumrein); Jack Pennick (Sergeant Major); Billy Jones (Curier); Bill Gettinger and Post Park (Officers); Fred Kennedy (Badger); Rudy Bowman (Private Smith); Ray Hyke (McCarthy); Lee Bradley (Interpreter); Chief Sky Eagle and Dan White (Bits).

"In this big Technicolored Western Mr. Ford has superbly achieved a vast and composite illustration of all the legends of the frontier cavalryman" (Bosley Crowther, New York Times). This entry was the second of three features Ford made about the cavalry of the Old American West (Fort Apache, 1948 [q.v.] came first and Rio Grande, 1950 [q.v.] followed).

Harry Carey, Jr., Joanne Dru, John Wayne, John Agar and Ben Johnson in She Wore a Yellow Ribbon (1949).

As a standard for his film composition, Ford sought to dupli-
cate the look of Frederick Remington's style. "I tried to get his
[Remington's] color and movement and I think I succeeded partly,"
Ford would later confide to Peter Bogdanovich in John Ford (1968).
Winton C. Hoch received an Academy Award for the Technicolor
cinematography of She Wore a Yellow Ribbon.

Aging Captain Nathan Brittles (Wayne) has one last mission
to accomplish before returning to civilian life. His goal is to stop
a new Indian war. Brittles trails the Indian braves, and is assigned
to escort his commanding officer's (O'Brien) wife (Natwick) and
daughter (Dru) out of the danger area. Two young lieutenants (Agar
and Carey, Jr.) love Olivia Dandridge (Dru) and each wants her to
wear his yellow ribbon as a token of love. Brittles, the ladies,
and the troops, however, are required to return to the fort when
they find that a stage depot has been destroyed by marauding Indians
--it is now obviously too late to take the ladies away to safety from
the fort.

Meanwhile the savages massacre the fort's sutler who was
making a trade deal with them for rifles, and the redskins take the
guns. Back at the Fort Brittles' military time is over and he is
relieved of his command. But the dedicated officer later goes after
Lieutenant Pennell (Carey, Jr.) and leads him and his men against
the large band of Indians. He orders a column of troops to descend
at the enemy's encampment and scatter the Indians' horses. This
maneuver forces the braves to flee to their reservation on foot.
For his bravery, Brittles is made Chief of Civilian Scouts and a
Brevet Lieutenant Colonel. At the finish, the officer visits the
graves of his family.

"She Wore a Yellow Ribbon is a symphony for the ears and
a canvas for the eyes more than a narrative for the mind. The
feelings of longing and loss, of a better past than present, and of
the dignity of the men who are passing are conveyed through the
sounds and scenes of the film, not through the themes of the story"
(J. A. Place, The Western Films of John Ford, 1973).

As in his other cavalry epics, Ford devotes a certain amount
of time to Irish humor, represented among the players by Victor
McLaglen's Sergeant Quincannon, Arthur Shields' Dr. O'Laughlin, et
al. For some, these interludes of fort life are distracting, while
for others (and rightly so) they provide a counterpoint to the more
impersonal action scenes. As Henry Fonda had in Fort Apache, so
John Wayne in this film acts the role of an older man, one who has
given his best (and worst) to the military service, and who is past
the point of change. This pessimistic but warm-hearted aspect of
the film is offset by the young performers (Agar, Johnson, and
Carey, Jr.) in the cast.

THE SHEEPMAN (MGM, 1958) C 85 min.

Producer, Edmund Grainger; director, George Marshall;
story, James Edward Grant; adaptor, William Roberts; screenplay,
William Bowers, Grant; art directors, William A. Horning, Malcolm Brown; set decorators, Henry Grace, Hugh Hunt; color

consultant, Charles K. Hagedon; assistant director, Al Jennings; costumes, Walter Plunkett; makeup, William Tuttle; sound, Dr. Wesley C. Miller; camera, Robert Bronner; editor, Ralph E. Winters.

Glenn Ford (Jason Sweet); Shirley MacLaine (Dell Payton); Leslie Nielsen [Johnny Bledsoe (alias Colonel Stephen Bedford)]; Mickey Shaughnessy (Jumbo McCall); Edgar Buchanan (Milt Masters); Willis Bouchey (Mr. Payton); Pernell Roberts (Choctaw); Slim Pickens (Marshall); Buzz Henry (Red); Pedro Gonzales Gonzales (Angelo).

What made this George Marshall-directed oater different from other similar productions was that it, "treats the standard rivalry (between cattlemen and sheepmen) with humor and a certain amount of spoof" (New York Times).

Occurring in the 1890s, the film tells of Johnny Bledsoe (Nielsen), a big-time cattle rancher who has a firm grip on the land thanks to his gunman (Shaughnessy). Bledsoe is scheduled to wed young Dell Payton (MacLaine) but sheepman Jason Sweet (Ford) arrives on the scene and falls in love with Dell. Then, too, Jason proves that Jumbo McCall (Shaughnessy) is really a coward--he humiliates the lug in public. Later Jason makes an alliance with the local windbag Milt Masters (Buchanan, in a fine comedy performance) and the climax has Jason and Bledsoe in a showdown. At last the range war is finished.

Those who saw this film when it was initially issued were impressed by the relaxed performance of Miss MacLaine, who was then fast rising to her cinema peak. Along with the other cast members, she instilled this unpretentious drama with a carefree, relaxing quality which made the proceedings disarmingly enjoyable. Sadly, the picture never got very wide distribution. It was later re-issued as The Stranger Wore a Gun.

SHENANDOAH (Universal, 1965) C 105 min.

Producer, Robert Arthur; director, Andrew V. McLaglen; screenplay, James Lee Barrett; assistant director, Terence Kelly; art directors, Alexander Golitzen, Alfred Sweeney; set decorators, John McCarthy, Oliver Emert; music, Frank Skinner; music director, Joseph Gershenson; sound, Waldon O. Watson, William Russell; camera, William Clothier; editor, Otho Lovering.

James Stewart (Charlie); Rosemary Forsyth (Jennie); Doug McClure (Sam); Glenn Corbett (Jacob); Phillip Alford (Boy); Charles Robinson (Nathan); Tim McIntire (Henry); James McMullan (John); Katharine Ross (Ann); James Best (Carter); Eugene Jackson, Jr. (Gabriel); Patrick Wayne (James); Paul Fix (Dr. Witherspoon); Harry Carey, Jr. (Jenkins); Dabbs Greer (Abernathy); Strother Martin (Engineer); Warren Oates (Billy Packer); Gregg Palmer (Union Guard); Peter Wayne (Confederate Corporal); Bob Steele (Union Guard with Beard); Lane Bradford (Tinkham); Buzz Henry, Henry Wills, James Carter, Leroy Johnson (Riders); Pae Miller (Black Woman); Eugene Jackson, Jr. (Gabriel).

The traditional Western has often been blended with many
other genres as in the case of this period, domestic study which
uses the Civil War as a background (just as Gary Cooper's Friendly
Persuasion, 1956, did).
Charlie Anderson (Stewart) has six sons, a daughter, and a
daughter-in-law, and does his best to keep them out of involvement
with the Civil War which is raging just a few miles from their
Virginia farm. He believes the conflict is not their concern. But
the war impinges on the family, as when Jennie's (Forsyth) new
husband Sam (McClure) is called into the Confederate Army. Then
the youngest son, Boy (Alford), is captured by Yankees who think
he is a Confederate soldier. Charlie sets out to find his child,
leaving James (Wayne) and his wife Ann (Ross) behind. Their trail
search is fruitless and on the way home Jacob (Corbett) is shot by
accident by a Confederate soldier. When they reach the farm,
Charlie finds that James and Ann have been killed by Union looters,
although Martha is alive and well. Later, Boy makes his way home
and there is a reunion.
In the U.S. and Canada Shenandoah grossed a healthy $7.75
million in distributors' rentals. Abroad it received favorable com-
ment too: "Basically sentimental, the film even includes a scene
where the longstanding but still sorrowing widower philosophizes
about life over his wife's grave, but the treatment often has a freshness and humour which show that McLaglen has learned from his ad-
miration for John Ford.... James Stewart, whose laconic drawl
makes the dialogue sound funnier than it really is, gives one of the
best performances of his career" (British Monthly Film Bulletin).
In 1974 Shenandoah was turned into a Broadway musical,
which, while bland and regressive, was sufficiently wholesome and
family-oriented to survive the New York test.

THE SHERIFF OF FRACTURED JAW   (Twentieth Century-Fox,
1959) C 102 min.

Producer, Daniel M. Angel; director, Raoul Walsh; based on
the short story by Jacob Hay; screenplay, Arthur Dales; art direc-
tor, Bernard Robinson; music, Robert Farnon; music director, Muir
Mathieson; songs, Harry Harris; makeup, George Partleton; cos-
tumes, Julie Harris; choreography, George Carden; sound, Dudley
Messenger, Winston Ryder; camera, Otto Heller; editor, John
Shirley.
Kenneth More (Jonathan Tibbs); Jayne Mansfield (Kate); Henry
Jull (Mayor Masters); William Campbell (Keeno); Bruce Cabot (Jack);
Robert Morley (Uncle Lucius); Ronald Squire (Toynbee); David Horne
(James the Butler); Eynon Evans (Mason); Sidney James (The Drunk);
Donald Stewart (The Drummer); Reed de Rouen (Clayborne); Clancy
Cooper (A Barber); Gordon Tanner (Wilkins); Tucker McGuire (Luke's
Wife); Nick Brady (Slim); Larry Taylor (The Gun Guard); Jack
Lester (The Coach Driver); Sheldon Lawrence (Johnny); Susan Denny
(Cora); Charles Farrell (Bartender); Chief Joe Buffalo (Red Wolf).

For this variation of Ruggles of Red Gap, veteran director

Kenneth More and Henry Hull in The Sheriff of Fractured Jaw (1959).

Raoul Walsh journeyed to England to film a satire on the Old West.
To bolster this CinemaScope, color entry, buxom Jayne Mansfield
was used as the femme fatale.
     Jonathan Tibbs (More) is a British inventor who has no suc-
cess in his homeland. He heads to the American West hoping to
sell his company's product to those most in need of firearms. He
arrives in the lawless community of Fractured Jaw. After a few
innocent encounters which make him look fearless he becomes
sheriff of the rough and tumble town. He actually manages to tame
the town with the help of a friendly Indian. Along the way he succumbs to the charms of Kate (Mansfield), the saloon girl. Our hero
is eventually responsible for stopping the local range war.
     Time, no friend to most movies, approved of this effort:
"What comes across is the wistful and delightfully absurd idea that
a good many apparently tame Englishmen secretly like to fancy
themselves racketing around the Wild West like pure cussedness in
cowpants." When curvacious Miss Mansfield was not wiggling about
or singing up a storm (her songs were dubbed by Connie Francis),
there was Henry Hull as a drunken mayor and Robert Morley as a
gout-ridden Englishman to add bounce to the storyline.

SHOOTIN' MAD   (Sherry, 1918)   1,632'

Producer, L. Lawrence Weber; director, Jesse L. Robbins.
Broncho Billy Anderson (Broncho Billy); Joy Lewis (Mary);
Dave Hartford (John Cowan); Fred Church (Bull Martin); Harry Todd
(Mary's Father).

Framed within the format of an old prospector telling the
story of the Old West, this vintage two-reeler finds the town of
Bear Gulch under the control of John Cowan (Hartford) who owns
the local saloon, with Bull Martin (Church) his prime henchman.
Anxious to win the love of Mary (Lewis), Cowan suggests to her
and her dad (Todd) that they settle on Broncho Billy's vacated ranch
spread.   Later, when Broncho Billy attempts to evict the squatters,
he finds that he adores Mary and promptly signs on as a worker
instead.   When Cowan has Mary's dad murdered, the blame is thrust
on Broncho Billy, and he is put in jail.   Later he escapes and prevents Cowan from seducing Mary.   In the showdown, both Cowan and
Bull Martin are implicated in the killing of Mary's dad.   Billy is
made the new sheriff, and as tranquility comes to the frontier town,
Broncho Billy and Mary prepare to wed.
Shootin' Mad was part of a series of two-reelers made by
Broncho Billy Anderson in his comeback bid.   Jon Tuska, in a
Views and Reviews (Fall, 1972) essay on the film, observes, "The
bitter absence of glamor is painfully noticeable in contrast to the
1918 product of Tom Mix or William S. Hart.   Yet even with the
needlessly old-fashioned look, it is Billy at his most poetic that we
see--a crude, unsophisticated statement, not without its own charm."

SHOOTING HIGH   see   MELODY RANCH

THE SIGN OF ZORRO   see   MARK OF ZORRO

SILVER RIVER   (Warner Bros., 1948)   110 min.

Producer, Owen Crump; director, Raoul Walsh; based on the
unpublished novel by Stephen Longstreet; screenplay, Longstreet,
Harriet Frank, Jr.; music, Max Steiner; orchestrator, Murray Cutter; wardrobe, Marjorie Best; makeup, Perc Westmore; assistant
director, Russell Saunders; technical adviser, Colonel J. G. Taylor,
U.S. Army, Retired; art director, Ted Smith; set decorator, William G. Wallace; sound, Francis J. Scheid; montages, James Leicester; special effects, William McGann, Edwin DuPar; camera, Sid
Hickox; editor, Alan Crosland, Jr.
Errol Flynn (Mike McComb); Ann Sheridan (Georgia Moore);
Thomas Mitchell (John Plato Beck); Bruce Bennett (Stanley Moore);

Tom D'Andrea (Pistol Porter); Barton MacLane (Banjo Sweeney);
Monte Blue (Buck Chevigee); Jonathan Hale (Major Spencer); Alan
Bridge (Sam Slade); Arthur Space (Major Ross); Art Baker (Major
Wilson); Joseph Crehan (President U. S. Grant).

Director Raoul Walsh and star Errol Flynn worked together
for the last time on Silver River, a rather tedious effort with a
mundane script and rather limpid performances. It was a sad comedown for Flynn and Ann Sheridan, who had sparkled, a decade
earlier in Dodge City (1939).

After the Civil War, Mike McComb (Flynn) leaves the Union
army and heads Westward. There he becomes involved in the silver
mining business and rises to become a powerful, ruthless figure.
Later he sends one of his men (Bennett) to his death so he can
marry the man's widow (Sheridan). Eventually she becomes disen-
chanted with him. Her departure leads to his reformation.

Utilizing scenes from The Birth of a Nation, Silver River
was most intriguing in its Civil War sequences. But from there
on it was downhill. Above all, Errol Flynn fans were aghast to
see their favorite playing such an unsympathetic role.

Location work on the feature was accomplished in Bronson
Canyon (near Hollywood), the Sierra Mountains (beyond Bishop), and
at the Calabasas ranch.

Reporting on this disappointing feature, Thomas M. Pryor
(New York Times) wrote, '[Walsh] handicapped himself unmercifully
in filming Silver River by cramming all the excitement into the first
ten minutes or so. As a consequence the new picture ... runs
downhill for most of its remaining length. "

SITTING BULL   (United Artists, 1954)   C   105 min.

Producer, W. R. Frank; director, Sidney Salkow; screenplay,
Jack DeWitt, Salkow; assistant director, Richard Dixon; camera,
Charles Van Enger, Victor Herrera.

Dale Robertson (Parrish); Mary Murphy (Kathy); J. Carrol
Naish (Sitting Bull); Iron Eyes Cody (Crazy Horse); John Litel
(General Howell); Bill Hopper (Wentworth); Douglas Kennedy (Colonel
Custer); Bill Tannen (O'Connor); Joel Fluellen (Sam); John Hamilton
(President U. S. Grant); Tom Browne Henry (Webber); Felix Gon-
zalez (Young Buffalo); Al Wyatt (Swain).

J. Carrol Naish* offered a sterling performance in the title
role as the Hunkpapa Sioux chief in this spin-off of the early fifties'
fad for screen biographies of Indian leaders. This presentation,
though, had poor production values and was decidedly inaccurate
from a historical point of view.

Sitting Bull supposedly detailed the events leading up to the
Battle of the Little Big Horn River, with General George Custer

---

*Naish also played Sitting Bull--with a comic touch--in Annie Get
Your Gun (1950) [q. v.].

(Kennedy) presented as an Indian hater who was used by higher
political forces to destroy the redmen. Sitting Bull was presented
as a man with no choice other than war. Unfortunately, this overly
pro-Indian piece did not touch upon the very interesting events in
the chief's life either before or after the famous battle.
    Dale Robertson was the nominal star of the picture in a role
of a pro-Indian soldier accused of aiding the enemy. Proving his
innocence provides the thin plotline. According to this film President Ulysses S. Grant (Hamilton) meets with Sitting Bull after the
battle to set up peaceful coexistence (sic) between the two races.
In actuality, Sitting Bull went to Canada after the confrontation and
the American Army nearly wiped out the Indian people, finally cor-
raling the remaining few Indians on various reservations.

SOLDIER BLUE   (Avco-Embassy, 1970)   C   114 min.

    Executive producer, Joseph E. Levine; producers, Gabriel
Katzka, Harold Loeb; associate producer, William S. Gilmore, Jr.;
director, Ralph Nelson based on the novel Arrow in the Sun by
Theodore V. Olsen; screenplay, John Gay; art director, Frank Ar-
rigo; set decorator, Carlos Grandjean; music-music director, Roy
Budd; songs, Buffy Sainte-Marie; special effects, Herman Townsley;
technical adviser, Eddy Little Sky; camera, Robert Hauser; editor,
Alex Beaton.
    Candice Bergen (Cresta Marybelle Lee); Peter Strauss (Pri-
vate Honus Gant); Donald Pleasence (Issac Q. Cumber); Bob Carra-
way (Lieutenant John McNair); Jorge Rivero (Spotted Wolf); Dana
Elcar (Captain Battles); John Anderson (Colonel Iverson); Martin
West (Lieutenant Spingarn); Jorge Russek (Running Fox); Marco An-
tonio Arzate (Kowa Brave); Ron Fletcher (Lieutenant Mitchell);
Barbara Turner (Mrs. Long); Aurora Clavell (Indian Woman).

    In the annals of Western films there are particular entries
which are noteworthy for their excessive violence and gore. The
front-runner in that category is, of course, The Wild Bunch (1969)
[q.v.]. But there are other contenders: The Hunting Party (1971),
which starred Candice Bergen and Gene Hackman; Duel at Diablo
(1966), with Sidney Poitier, James Garner, Dennis Weaver; and
Soldier Blue. Ralph Nelson, who helmed the bizarrely cast Duel
at Diablo, also directed this entry which attempted to demonstrate
just how cruel and bloodthirsty the U.S. Cavalry could be in contrast to the supposedly vicious savagery of the redskins. The incredible massacre which climaxes the film is substantiated with the
statement, "the greatest horror of all is that it is true."
    Cheyenne Indians attack a paymaster's detachment from the
U.S. Cavalry. The only survivors are Honus Gant (Strauss) and
Cresta Lee (Bergen), the latter engaged to Lieutenant McNair (Car-
raway). Private Gant is amazed at Cresta's friendly attitude toward
the Indians. Previously she had been captured by the Cheyenne and
made a wife to Spotted Wolf (Rivero). The Indian leader had freed
her when he realized she could never be truly happy there. Cresta
now insists that the whites are far more beastly than the Indians!

It is Cresta who points the way for their return to camp,
where she intends to wed McNair just for his money. When Honus
is injured, Cresta nurses him and they fall in love. She goes for
help and encounters McNair and his convoy getting ready to attack
the Cheyenne. Cresta leaves to warn the Indians and when Honus
limps back to camp he wants to follow her in her attempt to make
peace between the forces. But he is refused permission. When
Honus later protests the rape, torture, and killing of the Indians
(who had attempted to show a flag of truce) he is put under arrest.
Cresta, who has survived along with a few Cheyenne, affirms her
attachment for Honus.

The undisguised cruelty of the whites as depicted here is
spoiled a good deal by the abundant clichés in a film already over-
loaded with pious truisms. Bergen, as always, offers a winning
portrayal, but she cannot save the film, lost as it is in its noble
attempt at a message. There were even some cynical souls who
insisted the movie was only made to cash in on the public's love
for violent films.

SON OF PALEFACE see THE PALEFACE

SON OF ZORRO (Republic, 1947) thirteen chapters

Associate producer, Ronald Davidson; directors, Spencer
Bennet, Fred C. Brannon; screenplay, Franklyn Adreon, Basil
Dickey, Jesse Duffy, Sol Show; music, Mort Glickman; special ef-
fects, Howard and Theodore Lydecker; camera, Bud Thackery.

George Turner (Jeff Stewart); Peggy Stewart (Kate Wells);
Roy Barcroft (Boyd); Edward Cassidy (Sheriff Moody); Ernie Adams
(Judge Hyde); Stanley Price (Pancho); Edmund Cobb (Stockton); Ken
Terrell (Thomas); Wheaton Chambers (Baldwin); Fred Graham
(Quirt); Eddie Parker (Melton); Si Jenks (Fred); Jack O'Shea (Hood);
Jack Kirk (Charlie); Tom Steele (Leach); Dale Van Sickel (Murray).

Chapters: 1) Outlaw County; 2) The Deadly Millstone; 3)
Fugitive from Injustice; 4) Buried Alive; 5) Water Trap; 6) Volley
of Death; 7) The Fatal Records; 8) Third Degree; 9) Shoot to Kill;
10) Den of the Beast; 11) The Devil's Trap; 12) Blazing Walls; 13)
Checkmate.

See: Mark of Zorro.

THE SONS OF KATIE ELDER (Paramount, 1965) C 122 min.

Producer, Hal B. Wallis; associate producer, Paul Nathan;
director, Henry Hathaway; story, Talbot Jennings; screenplay,
William H. Wright, Allan Weiss, Harry Essex; music, Elmer Bernstein; costumes, Edith Head; assistant director, D. Michael Moore;
art directors, Hal Pereira, Walter Tyler; camera, Lucien Ballard;
editor, Warren Low.

John Wayne (John Elder); Dean Martin (Tom Elder); Martha
Hyer (Mary Gordon); Michael Anderson, Jr. (Bud Elder); Earl

Holliman (Matt Elder); James Gregory (Hastings); Jeremy Slate (Deputy Sheriff Latta); George Kennedy (Curley); Dennis Hopper (Dave Hastings); Sheldon Allman (Judge Harry Evers); John Litel (Minister); John Doucette (Undertaker Hyselman); James Westerfield (Banker Vannar); Rhys Williams (Charlie Bob Striker); John Qualen (Charlie Biller); Rodolfo Acosta (Bondie Adams); Strother Martin (Jeb Ross); Percy Helton (Storekeeper Peevey); Karl Swenson (Doc Isdell).

Following his successful battle against cancer, genre super-star John Wayne returned to film work with director Henry Hathaway in The Sons of Katie Elder, a rugged actioner which was a good box-office champ.

The story concerns the four adult sons of Katie Elder who return home after their mother's burial. John (Wayne) is a gun-fighter, Tom (Martin) is a gambler, Matt (Holliman) is a quiet but tough man, and Bud (Anderson, Jr.) the youngest son, wants to be respectable. The men are reflective about having left their mother alone and they learn she died impoverished, the homestead having been lost in a card game by their late father, who was killed the same night.

The culprits, Hastings (Gregory) and his son Dave (Hopper) kill the sheriff and place the blame on the Elders, hoping to cover up their own crimes. Thereafter the Elders surrender to the law and are taken by a posse to Laredo where Hastings' men, disguised as deputies, attempt to ambush and kill the brothers. In the

John Wayne and Dean Martin in The Sons of Katie Elder (1965).

skirmish Matt and a deputy (Slate) are murdered. The surviving
Elders rush to town to find a doctor to aid wounded Bud. Still
later the remaining Elders agree to surrender to a U.S. marshal
and, while waiting for his arrival, Tom escapes and kidnaps Dave
Hastings. When Hastings attempts to rescue his son he shoots him
by mistake. Dying Dave reveals the truth about the murder and
the judge overhears the confession. Wounded Tom dies and John
Elder kills Hastings in a gun fight. Thus John and Bud are the
only remaining Elders at the end of this bitter land warfare.
     With its breezy, uncomplicated ambience, The Sons of Katie
Elder remains one of Wayne's most popular vehicles.

THE SOUL OF NIGGER CHARLEY   see   THE LEGEND OF NIGGER
CHARLEY

THE SPOILERS (Selig-Poliscope, 1914) nine reels

     Director, Colin Campbell; based on the novel by Rex Beach;
and the play by Beach and James MacArthur; screenplay, Campbell.
     William Farnum (Glennister); Kathlyn Williams (Cherry Ma-
lotte); Bessie Eyton (Helen Chester); Frank Clark (Dextry); Jack
McDonald (Slap-Jack); Tom Santschi (McNamara); Wheeler Oakman
(Broncho Kid); Norvel MacGregory (Judge Stillman); William H.
Ryno (Struve).

THE SPOILERS (Goldwyn, 1923) 8,020'

     Director, Lambert Hillyer; based on the novel by Rex Beach
and the play by Beach and James MacArthur; adaptors, Fred Ken-
nedy Myton, Elliott Clawson, Hope Loring; camera, John S. Stumar,
Dwight Warren.
     Milton Sills (Roy Glennister); Anna Q. Nilsson (Cherry Ma-
lotte); Barbara Bedford (Helen Chester); Robert Edeson (Joe Dextry);
Ford Sterling (Slapjack Simms); Wallace MacDonald (Broncho Kid);
Noah Beery (Alex McNamara); Mitchell Lewis (Marshall Voorhees);
John Elliott (Bill Wheaton); Robert McKim (Struve); Tom McGuire
(Captain Stevens); Kate Price (Landlady); Rockliffe Fellowes (Mat-
thews); Gordon Russell (Burke); Louise Fazenda (Tilly Nelson); Sam
De Grasse (Judge Stillman); Albert Roscoe (Mexico Mullins); Jack
Curtis (Bill Nolan).

THE SPOILERS (Paramount, 1930) 8,128'

     Director, Edwin Carewe; based on the novel by Rex Beach
and the play by Beach and James MacArthur; adaptor, Bartlett
Cormack; screenplay, Agnes Brand Leahy; sound, Harry M. Lindgren; camera, Harry Fischbeck; editor, William Shea.
     Gary Cooper (Roy Glennister); Kay Johnson (Helen Chester);

Betty Compson (Cherry Malotte); William "Stage" Boyd (Alec Mc-
Namara); Harry Green (Herman); James Kirkwood (Joe Dextry);
Slim Summerville (Slapjack Simms); Lloyd Ingraham (Judge Stillman);
Oscar Apfel (Struve); Edward Coxen (Lawyer); Jack Trent (Bronco
Kid); Edward Hearn (Lieutenant); Hal David (Bill Wheaton); Knute
Erickson (Captain Stevens); John Beck (Hansen); Jack N. Holmes
(Voorhees).

THE SPOILERS (Universal, 1942) 87 min.

    Producer, Frank Lloyd; associate producer, Lee Marcus;
director, Ray Enright; based on the novel by Rex Beach and the
play by Beach and James MacArthur; screenplay, Lawrence Hazard,
Tom Reed; art directors, Jack Otterson, John R. Goodman; music,
Hans J. Salter; music director, Charles Previn; costumes, Vera
West; camera, Milton Krasner; editor, Clarence Kolster.
    Marlene Dietrich (Cherry Malotte); Randolph Scott (Alex Mc-
Namara); John Wayne (Roy Glennister); Margaret Lindsay (Helen
Chester); Harry Carey (Dextry); Richard Barthelmess (Bronco Kid);
George Cleveland (Banty); Samuel S. Hinds (Judge Stillman); Russell
Simpson (Flapjack); William Farnum (Wheaton); Marietta Canty (Ida-
belle); Jack Norton (Mr. Skinner); Ray Bennett (Clark); Forrest
Taylor (Bennett); Charles Halton (Struve); Bud Osborne (Marshall);
Drew Demarest (Galloway); Robert W. Service (Poet); Charles Mc-
Murphy, Art Miles, William Haade (Deputies); Robert Homans (Sea
Captain).

THE SPOILERS (Universal, 1955) C 84 min.

    Producer, Ross Hunter; director, Jesse Hibbs; based on the
novel by Rex Beach and the play by Beach and James MacArthur;
screenplay, Oscar Brodney, Charles Hoffman; art directors, Alex-
ander Golitzen, Alfred Sweeney; assistant directors, Tom Shaw,
George Lollier; music director, Joseph Gershenson; camera, Maury
Gertsman; editor, Paul Weatherwax.
    Anne Baxter (Cherry Malotte); Jeff Chandler (Roy Glennister);
Rory Calhoun (Alex McNamara); Ray Danton (Blackie); Barbara
Britton (Helen Chester); John McIntire (Dextry); Wallace Ford (Flap-
jack Simms); Carl Benton Reid (Judge Stillman); Raymond Walburn
(Mr. Skinner); Ruth Donnelly (Duchess); Willis Bouchey (Jonathan
Struve); Forrest Lewis (Banty Jones); Roy Barcroft (The Marshal);
Dayton Lummis (Wheaton); John Harmon (Kelly); Paul McGuire
(Thompson); Frank Sully and Bob Steele (Miners); Byron Foulger
(Montrose); Arthur Space (Bank Manager); Lane Bradford (Sourdough);
Terry Frost (Deputy).

    When cinema scholars discuss The Spoilers, it is the 1914
production that first comes to mind, despite the fact that four
versions have followed it, three of them being talkies. The 1914
edition is still remembered for its raw, realistic atmosphere and its

The Spoilers, twenty years apart. In the 1923 version (top), Barbara Bedford and Wallace MacDonald. Below, in the 1942 release, Marlene Dietrich, John Wayne and Randolph Scott.

Anne Bancroft, Jeff Chandler and Barbara Britton in yet another
version of The Spoilers (1955).

lengthy brawl between William Farnum and Tom Santschi, which
comprises the climax of the nine-reel film. (These two re-created
this fight in 1930 in Ten Nights in a Bar Room [Road Show Pro-
ductions] and it was almost as lengthy as the original scrap.)
        Made by Selig from Rex Beach's 1906 novel and the Beach-
MacArthur play of the same year, the film dealt with the adventures
of participants in the gold rush in Alaska and the events that occur
in one particular brawling mining town. William Farnum starred
as Roy Glennister who tries to stop lawlessness and claimjumping
in the vicinity and who has the final showdown fight with the evil
McNamara (Santschi). Serial queen Kathlyn Williams portrayed
dancehall girl Cherry Malotte and Wheeler Oakman was her comrade,
Broncho. Colin Campbell directed this lusty melodrama which was
re-issued in 1921.
        Joe Franklin wrote, in Classics of the Silent Screen (1959),
"... The Spoilers was certainly the best picture the generally un-
imaginative Selig company ever put out--and perhaps the only one
that made a real contribution to screen history, eclipsing even
[Cecil B.] DeMille's famous The Squaw Man [1913, q.v.]...."
        In 1923 Samuel Goldwyn issued a second silent version of the
Beach story, directed by Lambert Hillyer who had helmed many of
William S. Hart's early features. Here Milton Sills was Glennister
and Noah Beery was ideal as the corrupt, villainous McNamara.
Anna Q. Nilsson played Cherry, with Barbara Bedford as the

contrasting good girl Helen Chester, and Robert Edeson as Glennister's partner, Joe Dextry.   Photoplay called this remake "as thrilling as ever. "
        The first of three talkies of Beach's book was produced by
Paramount in 1930 as a vehicle for Cinema's all-American hero
Gary Cooper.   William "Stage" Boyd was cast as the villain.   The
remarkably talented and subtle Kay Johnson was Helen Chester, with
Betty Compson this time as the saloon queen Cherry Malotte and
silent film idol James Kirkwood as Joe Destry.   Cooper had been a
last-minute replacement for George Bancroft in the role of Glennister.   William Farnum and Tom Santschi were the technical advisors
on the set for the climactic fight scene between Cooper and Boyd.
The film proved popular with audiences.
        Following her big success in Destry Rides Again (1939) [q. v.],
reactivated superstar Marlene Dietrich was ideal for the rousing
role of exuberant Cherry Malotte.   The part was enlarged for her
and she received top-billing over Randolph Scott, as McNamara, and
John Wayne, as Glennister.   This fourth version of Beach's novel
was issued in 1942 by Universal.   Among the project's other assets
were strong direction by Ray Enright and excellent photography by
Milton Krasner.   This version was Oscar-nominated for its art and
set direction.
        The revamped plot had Klondike saloon owner Cherry (Die-
trich) loving Glennister (Wayne), the part-owner of a gold mine.
He in turn loves the niece (Lindsay) of a corrupt judge (Hinds) who
turns Glennister's mine over to claim grabbers.   When the marshal
is killed, the new gold commissioner, McNamara (Scott), has Glennister jailed.   Cherry then tells Helen Chester (Lindsay) that the
judge and McNamara are in collusion to cheat miners.   Glennister
escapes from jail and with his partner (Carey) reopens their mine,
which McNamara's men guard.   Glennister returns to town and in
the scuffle the judge is killed.   McNamara is also beaten in a fist
fight* and Glennister wins Cherry.
        Although the fight scene--still the big moment of each The
Spoilers--was impressively staged between Wayne and Scott, it was
too slick and obviously assembled with the use of breakaway furni-
ture, tight editing, helpful stuntmen/doubles, and camera tricks.
Interestingly, William Farnum had the supporting role of the lawyer
who works for Glennister and Dextry (Carey).   The film's top performance came from Richard Barthelmess as Broncho, Cherry's
partner and the man who really loves the slippery creature.
        Of this 1942 release, the New York Times wrote, "... the
author and producer have kept their tongue firmly in their cheeks,
even when stout Mr. Wayne and Mr. Scott begin tearing up the set.
It's a lovely brawl. "

_____

*In Pittsburgh Universal allowed Randolph Scott to win out over
John Wayne in maintaining Miss Dietrich's oncamera affections.
Both these projects, plus Seven Sinners (1940) with Dietrich and
Wayne, had been considered for Mae West after the success of her
My Little Chickadee (1940) [q. v.].

The final version to date occurred in 1955 when Jesse Hibbs
directed the first color edition of The Spoilers, a modestly-budgeted
feature (compared to past efforts).   Anne Baxter, in her post-
Twentieth Century-Fox starring days, was Cherry; Jeff Chandler
the resolute Glennister, Rory Calhoun was McNamara and sweet
Barbara Britton played Helen.   This property in no way matched
its predecessors.

THE SQUAW MAN   (Paramount, 1914)   six reels

Directors, Cecil B. DeMille, Oscar Apfel; based on the play
by Edwin Milton Royle; screenplay, DeMille, Apfel.
Dustin Farnum (Corporal James Wynnegate); Wilfred Kingston
(Diana, Countess of Kerhill); Redwing (Nat-U-Rich), Dick La Strange
(Grouchy); Foster Knox (Sir John); Monroe Salisbury (Henry, Earl
of Kerhill); Joe Singleton (Tabywana); Billy Elmer (Cash Hawkins);
Fred Montague (Mr. Petrie); Baby De Rue (Hal); Dick La Reno (Big
Bill); Mrs. A. W. Filson (Dowager Lady Kerhill); Haidee Fuller
(Lady Mabel Wynnegate).

THE SQUAW MAN   (Paramount, 1918)   six reels

Producer-director, Cecil B. DeMille; based on the play by
Edwin Milton Royle; screenplay, Beulah Marie Dix.
Elliott Dexter (Jim Wynnegate); Thurston Hall (Henry, Jim's
Cousin); Katherine McDonald (Diana, Henry's Wife); Helen Dunbar
(Dowager Countess); Winter Hall (Fletcher); Herbert Standing (Dean
of Trentham); Julia Faye (Lady Faye); Theodore Roberts (Bib Bill);
Noah Beery (Tabywana); Ann Little (Naturich); Tully Marshall (Sir
John Applegate); James Mason (Grouchy); Monte Blue (Happy); Jack
Holt (Cash Hawkins); Edwin Stevens (Bud Hardy); Charles Ogle (Bull
Cowan); Guy Oliver (Kid Clarke); Jack Herbert (Nick); M. Hallward
(Lord Tommy); Clarence Geldart (Solicitor); Pat Moore (Little Hal).

THE SQUAW MAN   (MGM, 1931)   twelve reels

Producer-director, Cecil B. DeMille; based on the play by
Edwin Milton Royle; screenplay, Lucien Hubbard, Lenore Coffee;
dialogue, Elsie Janis; sound, Douglas Shearer; camera, Harold Ros-
son; editor, Anne Bauchens.
Warner Baxter (Jim Wynn); Lupe Velez (Naturich); Eleanor
Boardman (Diana); Paul Cavanagh (Lord Henry Kerhill); Lawrence
Grant (General Stafford); Roland Young (Sir John Applegate); Charles
Bickford (Cash Hawkins); Desmond Roberts (Hardwick); Mitchell
Lewis (Tabywanna); Luke Cosgrove (Shanks); J. Farrell MacDonald
(Bill); DeWitt Jennings (Sheriff); Frank Rice (Grouchy); Raymond
Hatton (Shorty); Frank Hagney (Clerk); Victor Potel (Andy); Dickie
Moore (Hal); Harry Northrup (Butler); Julia Faye (Mrs. Jones); Eva
Dennison (Henry's Mother); Ed Brady (McSorley); Lillian Bond (Babs).

Producer-director Cecil B. DeMille must have been greatly enamored with Edwin Milton Royle's 1905 play, for he chose the vehicle as his directorial debut in 1914 and he remade it twice thereafter, in 1918 and as a talkie in 1931. Basically all three renditions followed the same storyline, although the plot tended to creak more with age upon each revamping.

The six-reel 1914 Paramount version opens in England where a captain (Farnum) takes the blame for his cousin's (Salisbury) embezzlement of charity funds. Wynnegate (Farnum) departs for America, hoping to forget his love for Diana (Kingston), the wife of the Earl of Kerhill (Salisbury). She knows full well of her husband's illegal activities. Once in the U.S. Wynnegate heads for Wyoming where he becomes the enemy of a cattle rustler (Elmer) and rescues an Indian girl, Nat-U-Rich (Redwing), from the outlaw. She in turn saves Wynnegate from being killed in a later skirmish. He weds the maiden, who is already pregnant with his child, and, in a later encounter, kills her husband's enemy, Cash Hawkins (Elmer). Later on, Diana comes to Wyoming to inform Wynnegate that her husband has died after confessing his thievery and that Wynnegate has now inherited the title of Earl of Kerhill. When the local sheriff learns that Nat-U-Rich is the killer of Hawkins, she commits suicide. This leaves Wynnegate free to return to England with Diana and his half-breed son.

Of this vehicle, which was DeMille's first feature shot in California, the New York Dramatic Mirror wrote, "... [It is] among the few really satisfactory film adaptation of plays."

In 1917 Lasky-Paramount produced a sequel, The Squaw Man's Son, directed by Edward J. Le Saint, in which Wallace Reid played the son of an Indian who leaves his English wife and returns to his tribe where he weds an Indian maiden after his white wife dies of morphine addiction.

Elliott Dexter and Katherine MacDonald had the leads in De- Mille's 1918 remake of The Squaw Man, of which Variety said, "Technically the picture leaves little to be desired," while Photoplay reported, "this marks Cecil B. DeMille at his best."

When the great producer-director made the story for the third time in 1931 he expanded it from six reels to twelve reels. The result was an overextended, dull film in which Lupe Velez made a very attractive and impressive Mexican-accented heroine. The picture was produced as part of DeMille's short-term pact with MGM.

Mordaunt Hall (New York Times) observed, "It makes an interesting entertainment--one that is too somber in its story to be called amusing and too neatly carpentered in its plot to be called genuine tragedy. The seams of age shine through; it is agreeable and expert melodrama." Photoplay, on the other hand, printed, "There's everything in this version that has been in former ones, only it is more plausibly [!] done."

The 1931 version was issued in Britain as The White Man.

THE SQUAW MAN'S SON   see   THE SQUAW MAN

STAGE TO THUNDER ROCK   (Paramount, 1964)   C   82 min.

Producer, A. C. Lyles; director, William F. Claxton;
screenplay, Charles Wallace; art directors, Hal Pereira, Bob Smith;
set decorators, Sam Comer, James Roach; music, Paul Dunlap; assistant director, Russ Haverick; makeup, Wally Westmore; sound,
Harold Lewis; camera, W. Wallace Kelly; editor, Jodie Copelan.

Barry Sullivan (Sheriff Horne); Marilyn Maxwell (Leah Parker);
Scott Brady (Sam Swope); Lon Chaney (Henry Parker); Jon Agar
(Dan Carrouthers); Wanda Hendrix (Mrs. Swope); Anne Seymour
(Myra Parker); Keenan Wynn (Ross Sawyer); Allan Jones (Mayor Ted
Dollar); Ralph Taeger (Reese Sawyer); Laurel Goodwin (Julie Parker);
Robert Strauss (Judge Bates); Robert Lowery (Seth Barrington); Ar-
gentina Brunetti (Sarita); Suzanne Cupito (Sandy Swope); Wayne Peters
(Toby Sawyer); Rex Bell, Jr. (Shotgun).

This film was one of the best of the budget Westerns produced by A. C. Lyles for Paramount in the mid-sixties. According
to Variety, "... Lyles has developed what appears to be a successful pattern of mixing action and outdoor drama within a framework
of simple psychology to provide acceptable screenfare in the low
budget field."

Sheriff Horne (Sullivan) is about to retire, but he is forced
to hunt down two brothers who have robbed a bank. He kills one
and takes the other (Taeger) prisoner. The defendant's vicious father
(Wynn) vows revenge, so the sheriff takes Reese Sawyer (Taeger) to
an isolated way station to await the next stage back to town. At the
station he finds heavy drinking Henry Parker (Chaney)--the
owner of the place, who will shortly lose the business due to a lack
of funds--his nagging wife (Seymour) and their lonely younger daughter
(Goodwin).

A stage arrives, bringing special deputy Sam Swope (Brady)
who wants Reese's reward money for his wife and small daughter.
Others on the incoming vehicle are Leah Parker (Maxwell), Henry's
older daughter, who is a prostitute, and driver Dan Carrouthers
(Agar) who loves Julie Parker (Goodwin). After a night of unrest
over Reese and the reward money, Ross Sawyer (Wynn) arrives on
the scene and the sheriff is forced to kill the troublemaker. At the
finale, the reward money is used to save the station, Henry swears
to remain sober, and Dan and Julie announce their love for one another.

No matter how impoverished a scenario or production budget,
it is always good to see such familiar faces as those in Stage to
Thunder Rock, many of them once name players now fallen on
leaner times.

STAGECOACH   (United Artists, 1939)   96 min.

Producer, Walter Wanger; director, John Ford; based on the
story Stage to Lordsburg by Ernest Haycox; screenplay, Dudley
Nichols; music director, Boris Morros; music adaptors, Richard

Hageman, Franke Harling; art director, Alexander Toluboff; set
decorator, Wiard B. Ihnen; costumes, Walter Plunkett; assistant
director, Wingate Smith; second unit director, Yakima Canutt;
special effects, Ray Binger; camera, Bert Glennon; editors, Otho
Lovering, Dorothy Spencer, Walter Reynolds.
        John Wayne (The Ringo Kid); Claire Trevor (Dallas); John
Carradine (Hatfield); Thomas Mitchell (Dr. Josiah Boone); Andy
Devine (Buck); Donald Meek (Samuel Peacock); Louise Platt (Lucy
Mallory); Tim Holt (Lieutenant Blanchard); George Bancroft (Sheriff
Curly Wilcox); Berton Churchill (Henry Gatewood); Tom Tyler (Luke
Plummer); Chris-Pin Martin (Chris); Elvira Rios (Yakima); Francis
Ford (Billy Pickett, Jr.); Yakima Canutt (White Scout); Chief Big
Tree (Indian Scout); Harry Tenbrook (Telegraph Operator); Jack
Pennick (Jerry the Bartender); Paul McVey (Wells Fargo Agent);
Walter McGrail (Captain Sickels); Brenda Fowler (Mrs. Gatewood);
Florence Lake (Mrs. Nancy Whitney); Cornelius Keefe (Captain
Whitney); Vester Pegg (Hank Plummer); Bryant Washburn (Captain
Simmons); Nora Cecil (Dr. Boone's Housekeeper); Bill Cody, Buddy
Roosevelt (Ranchers); Chief White Horse (Indian Chief); Duke Lee
(Sheriff of Lorsburg); Mary Kathleen Walker (Lucy's Baby); Helen
Gibson, Dorothy Appleby (Saloon Girls); Joe Rickson (Ike Plummer).

STAGECOACH   (Twentieth Century-Fox, 1966)   C   114 min.

        Producer, Martin Rackin; director, Gordon Douglas; based on
the story Stage to Lordsburg by Ernest Haycox and the screenplay
by Dudley Nichols; screenplay, Joseph Landon; music, Jerry Gold-
smith; song, Lee Pockriss and Paul Vance; art directors, Jack
Martin Smith, Herman A. Blumenthal; set decorators, Walter M.
Scott, Stuart A. Reiss; makeup, Ben Nye; assistant director, Joseph
E. Rickards; sound, Bernard Freericks, Elmer Raguse; special
camera effects, L. B. Abbott, Emil Kosa, Jr.; camera, William H.
Clothier; editor, Hugh S. Fowler.
        Ann-Margret (Dallas); Red Buttons (Mr. Peacock); Michael
Connors (Hatfield); Alex Cord (Ringo); Bing Crosby (Doc Boone); Bob
Cummings (Mr. Gatewood); Van Heflin (Curly); Slim Pickens (Buck);
Stefanie Powers (Mrs. Lucy Mallory); Keenan Wynn (Luke Plummer);
Brad Weston (Matt Plummer); Joseph Hoover (Lieutenant Blanchard);
Oliver McGowan (Mr. Haines); David Humphreys Millers (Billy
Picket); Bruce Mars (Trooper); Edwin Mills (Sergeant Major); Hal
Lynch (Bartender); Norman Rockwell (Townsman); Muriel Davidson
(Woman); Brett Pearson (Sergeant).

        Few Western films have ever had such an overall effect on
the species as John Ford's 1939 version of Stagecoach.   Almost

Opposite: Stagecoach in its classic 1939 version (top), with George
Bancroft, Donald Meek (bald), Andy Devine, Claire Trevor, John
Carradine and John Wayne. In the poor, 1966, remake (below):
Slim Pickens, Van Heflin, Bing Crosby, Alex Cord, Red Buttons,
Ann-Margret, Keenan Wynn, Bob Cummings, Stefanie Powers and
Mike Connors.

singlehandedly this epic Western renewed the genre's popularity outside the B series field.   Unfortunately the classic was badly remade in 1966, causing new generations to wonder what the fuss had
been about concerning the earlier edition.   The new version, in
color and widescreen, was bright but vapid.   It had the detrimental
effect of forcing the original off television and out of the general
limelight.
        The Ford version took place on the stagecoach to Lordsburg,
New Mexico and it zeroed in on the passengers: Lucy Mallory
(Platt), the pregnant woman is on her way to join her Army officer
spouse; Dallas (Trevor), a cafe dancer who has been thrown out of
the town of Tonto; timid liquor salesman Samuel Peacock (Meek); a
drunken physician, Dr. Josiah Boone (Mitchell); Hatfield (Carradine),
a well-mannered gambler; stage driver Buck (Devine); and Sheriff
Curly Wilcox (Bancroft), a U.S. marshal who rides shotgun guard.
Along the dusty, bumpy way, the coach picks up outlaw Ringo Kid
(Wayne) who surrenders to Wilcox until they reach Lordsburg, where
he must settle a feud.   At a way station the group learn that Geronimo is again on the warpath.   Lucy collapses and then goes into
childbirth.   With the aid of Dr. Boone and Dallas she has her baby.
Back aboard the stage, the passengers make a run for freedom (one
of the cinema's most marvelous chase sequences) from the warring
Apaches.   Peacock is injured in the skirmish and Hatfield, who has
fallen in love with Lucy, is killed.   In the nick of time, the cavalry
arrives on the scene to save the group.   Once in Lordsburg, the
Ringo Kid has a shootout with Hank Plummer (Tyler).   Ringo kills
Hank, but is himself injured.   Dallas comes to the Kid's aid and
compassionate Sheriff Wilcox allows the Kid and Dallas to escape to
Mexico to find a new life.
        Stagecoach was produced for $500,000 and grossed $1.3
million in its original and 1944 releases in the U.S. and Canada.
Critical reaction was mixed at the time of issuance, and today, in
reevaluating the film, such historians as J. A. Place (The Western
Films of John Ford, 1973) insist that "when placed within the context of Ford's body of work and judged by that high standard, the
film does not measure up....   The dramatic contrivance characteristic of Stagecoach is rigidly based on the A-B structural scheme--
scenes of action alternating with scenes of character interaction until
four scenes of each have been played out....   Everything we know
about each character we know for a reason, and the reason exists
only for the purpose of the whole script.   There is little that is
mysterious, ambiguous, complex, or intriguing about any of the
characters--each exists primarily as a foil for the others."
        Stagecoach marked John Ford's first use of Monument Valley
which would play a strong part in location work on future films he
made.   It marked the first teaming of Wayne (whose career was
greatly boosted by this release) and Claire Trevor, both of whom
would be seen together later that year in RKO's Allegheny Uprising
[q.v.].
        It is one of the unsolvable mysteries of show business why
film producers always think they can improve upon a classic in a
remake.   Seldom does it ever occur, and it certainly did not in the

CinemaScope, DeLuxe color version of Twentieth Century-Fox. As
Time assessed the revamped edition, "The rebuilt Stagecoach has a
passenger list roughly equivalent to the original's but the trip is dull
going. Mostly, the air of mounting crisis is indicated by having the
actors glare at one another." Judith Crist succinctly spoke the ma-
jority view on this entry on the NBC-TV "Today Show": "This remake of Stagecoach embodies all that has gone wrong with movies in
the past 30 years--unspectacular spectacle, violence for its own
DeLuxe Color-bloody sake, dialogue riddled by maudlin sociology
and five-cent psychiatry, and inept performances by actors catapulting
to star roles by virtue of press agentry rather than talent."
       While action fans had to settle for diminished thrills in the
1966 version, there was the diverting presence of sultry Ann-Margret in Claire Trevor's old role, and the surprising presence of an
unshaven Bing Crosby as Doc Boone, the role that had been so well-
conceived by Thomas Mitchell.

STAMPEDE (Allied Artists, 1949) 78 min. (Filmed in Sepiatone)

       Producers, John C. Champion, Blake Edwards; director,
Lesley Selander; based on the novel by Edward Beverly Mann;
screenplay, Champion, Edwards; art director, Ernest Hickson;
camera, Harry Neumann; editor, Richard Heermance.
       Rod Cameron (Mike); Gale Storm (Connie); Don Castle (Tim);
Johnny Mack Brown (Sheriff Ball); Don Curtis (Stanton); John Elredge
(Onx); John Miljan (Furman); Jonathan Hale (Varick); and: James
Harrison, Ted Elliott, Jack Parker, Chuck Roberson, Tim Ryan,
Kenne Duncan, Carol Henry, Adrian Wood, I. Stanford Jolley, Mar-
shall Reed, Philo McCullough, Charlie King, Duke York, Wes
Christensen.

       Say "Stampede" and most people will immediately associate
with a rush of oncoming cattle. It is strange that Hollywood did not
use the word more frequently for the title of a Western. (As it
was, it had supplied the tag for a 1921 Texas Guinan feature, a
British silent dealing with the life of Sudanese Arabs, and a 1936
Columbia Western.)
       In 1949 ex-Republic player Rod Cameron starred in this ro-
bust range thriller directed deftly by veteran Lesley Selander from
E. B. Mann's book. Cameron as Mike and Don Castle as Tim were
the feuding cattle baron brothers involved with settlers who are being
cheated out of their water rights by crooks. Long-time cowboy star
Johnny Mack Brown--now on leaner days--was cast as the sheriff
forced to deal with these touchy situations, while Gale Storm (the
future "My Little Margie") was pert as the heroine.
       The lofty Bosley Crowther (New York Times) was quite an-
noyed at having to sit through this "Grade C Western" and insisted,
"We'll bet you no cow would be so foolish as to sit all the way
through this film."

STRANGE INCIDENT   see   THE OX-BOW INCIDENT

STRANGER ON THE RUN   (NBC-TV, 1967)   C   97 min.

Producer, Richard Lyons; director, Don Siegel; story, Reginald Rose; teleplay, Dean Riesner; music, Stanley Wilson; art director, W. D. Decives; camera, Bud Thackery; editors, Richard
Belding, Richard Wray.

Henry Fonda (Ben Chamberlin); Michael Parks (Vincent Mc-
Kay); Dan Duryea (O. W. Hotchkiss); Lloyd Bochner (Gorman); Tom
Reese (Weed); Sal Mineo (Blaylock); Anne Baxter (Valvera Johnson);
Bernie Hamilton (Dickory).

Henry Fonda in his many years of filmmaking has made some
remarkable Westerns (many detailed in this volume).   He has also
had some misfires, ranging from Welcome to Hard Times (1967) to
My Name Is Nobody (1974), and including Firecreek (1968), and The
Cheyenne Social Club (1970), the latter two co-starring his pal
Jimmy Stewart.

One of Fonda's better cowboy films is the telefeature Stranger
on the Run, which was carefully helmed by director Don Siegel.

Borrowing the ploy from The Most Dangerous Game (1932),
the story tells of an old drunk Ben Chamberlin (Fonda) who is
bounced off a train at Banner, a God-forsaken town in a parched
valley.   He soon discovers that the local law enforcers are bored
hired killers who want some action now that they have subdued the
ranchers.   When the local prostitute is murdered, deputy Vincent
McKay (Parks) gathers together his fellow deputies--all hired killers
(Duryea, Mineo and Reese) to track down Ben, who insists he is
innocent.   After capturing him, Hotchkiss (Duryea) helps him to escape.   Ben is later recaptured but makes his exit once more, this
time taking refuge at Valvera Johnson's (Baxter) farm.   The chase
is by no means over, and before the finale there is a confrontation
between Ben and McKay.

Those who saw Welcome to Hard Times will recognize the
same town set used here.   One reason why this made-for-TV movie
came out so well was that director Siegel, according to Stuart
Kaminsky in Don Siegel: Director (1974), "treated it [the project]
as he would any other film, with no evidence of compromise with
medium. "

THE STRANGER WORE A GUN   see   THE SHEEPMAN

SUPPORT YOUR LOCAL GUNFIGHTER   see   SUPPORT YOUR
LOCAL SHERIFF

SUPPORT YOUR LOCAL SHERIFF   (United Artists, 1969)   C
93 min.

Producer, William Bowers; associate producer, Bill Finne-
gan; director, Burt Kennedy; screenplay, Bowers; art director,

Gene Evans, Walter Brennan and Dick Peabody in Support Your
Local Sheriff (1969).

Leroy Coleman; set decorator, Hugh Hunt; makeup, Stan Smith;
costumes, Norman Burza; assistant director, Ray De Camp; sound,
Bruce Wright; special effects, Marcel Vercoutere; camera, Harry
Stradling, Jr.; editor, George Brooks.
    James Garner (Jason McCullough); Joan Hackett (Prudy
Perkins); Walter Brennan (Pa Danby); Henry "Harry" Morgan (Mayor
Olly Perkins); Jack Elam (Jake); Bruce Dern (Joe Danby); Henry
Jones (Preacher Henry Jackson); Walter Burke (Fred Johnson); Dick
Peabody (Luke Danby); Gene Evans (Tom Danby); Willis Bouchey
(Thomas Devery); Kathleen Freeman (Mrs. Dancers); Gayle Rogers
(Bar Girl); Richard Hoyt (Gunfighter); Marilyn Jones (Bordello Girl).

    Unlike Paramount's Waterhole #3 (1967) with James Coburn,
which went astray with its satiric, almost slapstick comedy, this
jaunty effort was well appreciated by the public. It garnered over
$5 million in distribution from both U.S. and Canadian rentals. As
the Los Angeles Times perceived, "There is just enough perforating
of bodies, as it were, to keep the franchise but in its heart and
soul Support Your Local Sheriff is a nonviolent, antiviolent western.
And a very funny one, at that. With Sam Whiskey [1969, with Burt
Reynolds, Clint Walker], this makes two funny and pacific westerns
in less time than it takes to oil a Buntline Special."
    While a grave is being dug for the latest gunslinger victim

in the town of Calendar, the mayor's (Morgan) daughter (Hackett)
spies gold in the soil. Overnight the town becomes a gold rush
arena. Local hellion Pa Danby (Brennan) and his clan soon discover they own the only road leading into town and they impose a
twenty per cent tariff on all gold carted out through their territory.
Finally the townfolk decide to hire a strong sheriff to stop this lawlessness. Soldier-of-fortune Jason McCullough (Garner), on his
way to Australia, is hired. He soon sets out to defeat Pa and his
bunch of rowdies. He not only cleans up the town, but he wins the
affection of Prudy Perkins (Hackett).
    In 1971 director Burt Kennedy made a follow-up, called
Support Your Local Gunfighter, but it was tepid compared to the
original and "only" earned $2 million in distributors' domestic
grosses. The new edition had James Garner running away from
his wedding and being mistaken for a gunfighter and forced to take
up that dangerous trade to stay alive.

SUTTER'S GOLD   (Universal, 1936) 94 min.

    Producer, Edmund Grainger; director, James Cruze; based
on the biography by Blaise Cendrars and story by Bruno Frank;
screenplay, Jack Kirkland, Walter Woods, George O'Neil; camera,
George Robinson, John P. Fulton.
    Edward Arnold (John Sutter); Lee Tracy (Peter Perkin);
Binnie Barnes (Countess Elizabeth Bartoffski); Katherine Alexander
(Mrs. Anna Sutter); Addison Richards (James Marshall); Montagu
Love (Captain Kettleson); John Miljan (General Juan Batista Alvardo);
Robert Warwick (General Rotscheff); Harry Carey (Kit Carson); Mit-
chell Lewis (King Kamehanehe); William Janney (John Sutter, Jr.);
Ronald Cosbey (John Sutter, Jr. at Age Eight); Nan Grey (Ann
Eliza Sutter); Joanne Smith (Ann Eliza Sutter at Age Three); Billy
Gilbert (General Ramos); Aura Da Silva (Senora Alvarado); Allen
Vincent (Alvarado, Jr.); Harry Cording (Lars); Sidney Bracy
(Smythe); Bryant Washburn (Captain Petroff); Gaston Glass (Lieu-
tenant Bacalenakoff).

    Thankfully, Universal had Show Boat with Irene Dunne,
to pull it out of the financial hassle surrounding this costly and
ignored spectacle.
    Originally the project was to be helmed by Russian director
Sergei M. Eisenstein. Eventually it was director James Cruze who
handled the project and tried to make it the talking replica of his
hugely-successful silent feature, The Covered Wagon (1923) [q.v.].
To its credit the picture was a splashy, well-mounted biography
with a grand performance by Edward Arnold as Sutter. But it was
far too episodic and wandered too far afield dramatically to capture
mass appeal.
    Taken from Blaise Cendrars' biography and a story by Bruno
Frank, the film tells of how poor Swiss immigrant Johann August
Sutter (Arnold) conceives and builds an empire with Mexican and
California land grants, only to lose everything when gold is discovered in his mill race in 1848. Graphically depicted are scenes

of his workers deserting him, gold seekers taking claim of his lands, marauders burning his crops and destroying his orchards, vandals tearing down his buildings and killing his son. As a result of this catastrophe he is left poverty-stricken and half-mad, engaging in fruitless litigation (right up to the U.S. Congress) in an attempt to retrieve his vast holdings.

Frank S. Nugent (New York Times) nailed the coffin over the film's financial future when he wrote that it was "... one of the major disappointments of the season.... [It has] a spurious glitter." (One can only wonder how the project would have developed and been received had Michael Curtiz directed the film for Warner Bros., and had Paul Muni or Edward G. Robinson starred in Arnold's role.)

Footage from Sutter's Gold would often turn up later on in other Universal films, including the Richard Arlen-Andy Devine starrer, Mutiny on the Blackhawk (1939).

While one can laud the performance of Binnie Barnes as the regal Russian adventuress beloved by the avaricious Sutter, the inclusion of this episode in the feature only served to rob the story of credibility and its dramatic focus.

TAKE A HARD RIDE   (Twentieth Century-Fox, 1975) C 103 min.

Producer, Harry Bernsen; associate producer, Maria-Luise Alcarez; director, Anthony M. Dawson [Antonio Margheriti]; screenplay, Eric Bercovici, Jerry Ludwig; music, Jerry Goldsmith; assistant directors, Scott Maitland, Pepe Lopez Rodero; second unit director, Hal Needham; art director, Julio Molina; dialogue supervisor, Paul Costello; makeup, Carmen Martin; stunt coordinators, Needham, Juan Majon; special effects, Luciano D'Achille, Antonio Molina; camera, Riccardo Pallotina; editor, Stanford C. Allen.

Jim Brown (Pike); Lee Van Cleef (Kiefer); Fred Williamson (Tyree); Catherine Spaak (Catherine); Dana Andrews (Morgan); Jim Kelly (Kashtok); Barry Sullivan (Sheriff Kane); Harry Carey, Jr. (Dumper); Robert Donner (Skave); Charles McGregor (Cloyd); Leonard Smith (Cangey); Ronald Howard (Halsey); Ricardo Palacios (Calvera); Robin Levitt (Chico); Buddy Joe Hooker (Angel).

By the mid-seventies, the number of big screen Westerns began to decrease dramatically. Genre stars like John Wayne, Robert Mitchum, and Charles Bronson were working in melodramas, while perennial Western stalwarts like James Stewart and Henry Fonda were generally not working in films. Even the number of foreign-made oaters were on the decline. Thus this Spanish-produced Western, shot in the Canary Islands, came on the scene like a breath of fresh air. Despite its somewhat mediocre quality, this film may fan some new life into the field.

When trail boss Morgan (Andrews) from Texas is found to be dying, his foreman Pike (Brown) promises to take the $86,000 from the herd's sale back to the fine folk in Sonora. No sooner is he on his way than he is attacked by a gang of marauders, but he is saved by gambler Tyree (Williamson) who is also after the loot. The two black men head for the border with a posse led by Sheriff Kane

(Sullivan) hot in pursuit. The two men are also being stalked by
vicious bounty hunter Kiefer (Van Cleef). Along the tough way, the
duo save Catherine (Spaak) and Indian youth Kashtok (Kelly) from outlaws. No sooner have they cleared up this danger than they are
under attack by Kiefer and his men. Catherine is gunned down when
she tries to escape with the money. Kiefer later kills the sheriff
when the latter refuses to join the chase. By the wrap-up, which
ends on an inconclusive note, Pike and Tyree blow up a mine killing
Mexican cutthroats and then head for Sonora with Kiefer still on their
trail.

The acting honors here go to Van Cleef with his characterization of the evil, ghost-like Kiefer, a fast-draw killer who hunts men
for their bounty. At the finish he is injured but still on the track of
the money carriers. Obviously, the end of the film hints at a possible sequel.

THE TALL T (Columbia, 1957) C 77 min.

Producer, Harry Joe Brown; director, Budd Boetticher; based
on a story by Elmore Leonard; screenplay, Burt Kennedy; art director, George Brooks; music director, Mischa Bakaleinikoff; sound,
Ferol Redd; camera, Charles Lawton, Jr.; editor, Al Clark.

Randolph Scott (Pat Brennan); Richard Boone (Usher); Maureen
O'Sullivan (Doretta Mims); Arthur Hunnicutt (Ed Rintoon); Skip Ho-
meier (Billy Jack); Henry Silva (Chink); John Hubbard (Willard Mims);
Robert Burton (Tenvoorde).

This was the second in the series of well-made adult Westerns
Randolph Scott turned out with director Budd Boetticher. Here the
script was by future genre director, Burt Kennedy. Scott and Harry
Joe Brown's producing company created the project, which was filmed
in Technicolor.

Pat Brennan (Scott) loses his horse in a bet he made that he
could ride a bull. (He can't!) He then wangles a ride on a stagecoach drive by an old friend, Ed Rintoon (Hunnicutt). Aboard the
stage are a honeymooning couple (O'Sullivan and Hubbard). Three
outlaws (Boone, Silva, Homeier) mistakenly hold up the stage and
take Pat and Doretta Mims (O'Sullivan), an heiress, in hopes of
getting some ransom money from the woman's father. While being
held captives, Pat and Doretta work together in turning the outlaws
against one another, which results in the eventual death of the three
bandits.

The Tall T is a compact little feature which interpolates beautifully the characters' interplay with fetching Western backgrounds
(especially the contrast between lush settings and the arid desert
arena). An interesting aspect of this feature is the character of
timid, plain Doretta, whose husband has married her for her money.
As she works with Pat, she blossoms into an individual, a sexually
attractive female very much worth having. (At one point in the narrative, she successfully seduces outlaw Billy Jack [Homeier].) At
the finale, it is no surprise that Pat and Doretta have fallen in love.

TELL THEM WILLIE BOY IS HERE   (Universal, 1969) C   98 min.

Producer, Philip A. Waxman; director, Abraham Polonsky;
based on the book Willie Boy by Harry Lawton; screenplay, Polonsky;
assistant director, Joseph Kenny; art directors, Alexander Golitzen,
Henry Bumstead; set decorators, John McCarthy, Ruby Levitt; music,
Dave Grusin; music supervisor, Stanley Wilson; sound, Waldron O.
Watson, David H. Moriarty; camera, Conrad Hall; editor, Melvin
Shapiro.

Robert Redford (Christopher Cooper); Katharine Ross (Lola
Boniface); Robert Blake (Willie Boy); Susan Clark (Elizabeth Arnold);
Barry Sullivan (Ray Calvert); Charles McGraw (Frank Wilson);
Charles Aidman (Benby); John Vernon (Hacker); Shelly Novack (Fin-
ney); Ned Romero (Tom); John Day (Sam Wood); Lee De Broux (Meat-
head); George Tyne (Le Marie); Robert Lipton (Charlie Newcomb);
Steve Shemayne (Johnny Hyde); Lloyd Gough (Dexter); John Hudkins
(Man); Jerry Velasco (Chino); Gary Walberg (Dr. Mills); Jerome
Raphel (Salesman); Johnny Coons (Clerk); Stanley Torres (Committee-
man); Kenneth Holzman, Joseph Mandel (Reporters); Spencer Lyons
(Cody); Everett Creach (Fake Indian).

It is a well-regarded fact that an intelligent, offbeat slant to
a well-trod subject does not automatically make the project a commercial success. Such was the case with Tell Them Willie Boy Is
Here, which, despite the presence of rising superstar Robert Redford, did not make a sufficient impact upon the filmgoing public to
be labeled even a marginal success.

In 1909, Paiute Indian Willie Boy (Blake) returns to Banning,
California for the yearly tribal feast. He also intends to court Lola
Boniface (Ross) whose father refuses to consent to their marriage.
When the old man finds the young lovers together a scuffle ensues,
and the older man is killed. While the tribe does not condemn this
accidental homicide, the whites feel this is the start of a new uprising. Assistant sheriff Christopher Cooper (Redford) is ordered
to chase the fleeing couple. In actuality, pleasure-loving Cooper
would rather court and seduce Dr. Elizabeth Arnold (Clark), the
Reservation superintendent. Willie manages to elude Cooper and
eventually Cooper must abandon the hunt to serve as a bodyguard
for the visiting President Taft. But the posse continues to search
for Willie and in an attempt to shoot their horses Willie accidentally
kills one of the men. Now Cooper has no choice but to hunt down
Willie. When Lola realizes she is slowing down Willie's escape,
she takes the alternative taught her by Indian tradition--she commits
suicide. The stalking continues and finally Cooper confronts Willie
whom he shoots reluctantly. As the facts prove, the whole killing
episode was fruitless.

It is no accident that this anti-discrimination, pro-individual
and anti-society project was directed by Polonsky. He was one of
the victims of the Senator Joseph McCarthy Red witch hunt, and this
vehicle offered him an excellent opportunity to portray his own plight
by analogy with that of early twentieth century Willie Boy. As Jack
Spears in Hollywood: The Golden Years (1971) rightly noted, this is

"A complex, often brilliant film; it uses hostility toward the Indians to mirror the primitivism and inequities of the American culture."
       The question is why the film did not have a bigger cult following, once the main stream of moviegoers passed over the production as a misfire. Perhaps the British Monthly Film Bulletin perceived the problem, "For a film dealing with human fallibility, Willie Boy is just a fraction too infallible, just a touch too smooth, just a mite too comfortable. Everybody says the right things, and in the right way, and it's the very rightness that turns out wrong. In the last resort, the eradication of Willie is so anaesthetised that its emotional impact is negligible, just as the death of Lola is insulated so carefully ... that the traumas it should set up are almost wholly avoided."

THE TERROR OF THE RANGE   (Pathé, 1919)   seven chapters

       Director, Stuart Paton; based on the book The Wolf-Faced Man by W. A. S. Douglas, Lucien Hubbard.
       With: Betty Compson, George Larkin (John Hardwick), H. B. Carpenter, Fred M. Malatesta, Ora Carew.
       Chapters: 1) Prowlers of the Night; 2) The Hidden Chart; 3) The Chasm of Fear; 4) The Midnight Raid; 5) A Threat from the Past; 6) Tangled Tales; 7) Run to Earth.

       One of the shortest theatrical serials (seven chapters) ever made, this heavy melodrama was adapted from W. A. S. Douglas and Lucien Hubbard's book, The Wolf-Faced Man.
       A government agent (Larkin) is sent West to investigate a series of robberies and murders by a gang led by the title character, a man who wears a wolf's head during the raids. Eventually the law man concentrates on a ranch where the bandits have their headquarters, and he rounds up the lawbreakers including their leader. He also wins the love of Betty Compson, the film's romantic interest.

THE TEXANS   (Paramount, 1938)   92 min.

       Producer, Lucien Hubbard; director, James Hogan; story, Emerson Hough; screenplay, Bertram Millhauser, Paul Sloane, William W. Haines; camera, Theodor Sparkuhl; editor, LeRoy Stone.
       Joan Bennett (Ivy Preston); Randolph Scott (Kirk Jordan); May Robson (Granny); Walter Brennan (Chuckawalla); Robert Cummings (Alan Sanford); Raymond Hatton (Cal Tuttle); Robert Barratt (Isaiah Middlebrack); Harvey Stephens (Lieutenant David Nichols); Francis Ford (Uncle Dud); Chris-Pin Martin (Juan Rodriguez); Anna Demetrio (Rosita Rodriguez); Clarence Wilson (Sam Ross); Jack Moore (Slim); Richard Tucker (General Corbett); Edward Gargan (Sergeant Crady); Otis Harlan (Henry); Spencer Charters (Chairman); Archie Twitchell (Corporal Thompson); William Haade (Sergeant Cahill); Irving Bacon (Private Chilina); William B. Davidson (Mr. Jessup); Bill Roberts

(Mustang); Richard Denning (Corporal Parker); Frank Cordell, John
Eckert, Slim Hightower, Scoop Martin, Whitey Sovern, Slim Talbot
(Cowboys); Jimmie Kilgannon, Edwin John Brady, Carl Harbaugh,
Dutch Hendrian (Union Soldiers); Oscar Smith (Black Soldier); Jack
Perrin (Private Soldier); Ernie Adams, Edward J. LeSaint, James
Quinn (Confederate Soldiers); Harry Woods (Cavalry Officer); Wheeler
Oakman (U.S. Captain); Everett Brown (Man with Watches); Margaret
McWade (Middle-Aged Lady); Vera Steadman, Virginia Jennings
(Women on Street); James Kelso (Snorer); J. Manley Head (Fanatic);
Philip Morris (Fen); James Burtis (Swenson); Esther Howard (Ma-
dame); James T. Mack, Lon Poff (Moody Citizens); John Qualen
(Swede); Kay Whitehead (Stella); Ralph Remley (Town Lawyer); Pat
West (Real Estate Man); Laurie Lane, Helaine Moler (Girls).

Taken from Emerson Hough's work, this film was a remake
of North of '36, which Paramount had made in 1924 with Jack Holt.
Using much stock footage, the new edition "was big, but disjointed,
clumsily put together and lacking in any kind of style" (William K.
Everson, A Pictorial History of the Western Film, 1969). But at
the time of release, it was booked along with other higher class
Paramount products and got good distribution.
    Filmed on location, the production is set in the years follow-
ing the Civil War. Kirk Jordan (Scott) drives a herd of 10,000 cattle belonging to Granny (Robson) and Ivy Preston (Bennett) from
Texas to Kansas, thus opening the Chisholm Trail. Along the 1,500-
mile trek through Indian territory they have trouble with the Indians
as well as carpetbaggers who are on their scent. Mixed into the
conglomerate plot is the formation of the Ku Klux Klan and the
emergence of the trans-continental railroad.
    To satisfy action customers, the picture contains a blizzard,
various dust storms, as well as Indian and cavalry raids. In addition, it benefits especially from the presence of Western character
actor Walter Brennan.

TEXAS (Columbia, 1941) 94 min. (Filmed in sepia)

    Producer, Sam Bischoff; director, George Marshall; story,
Lewis Meltzer, Michael Blankfort; screenplay, Horace McCoy,
Meltzer, Blankfort; art director, Lionel Banks; music, Morris
Sroloff; assistant director, Norman Deming; camera, George Mee-
han; editor, William Lyon.
    William Holden (Dan Thomas); Glenn Ford (Tod Ramsey);
Claire Trevor ("Mike" King); George Bancroft (Windy Miller); Edgar
Buchanan (Doc Thorpe); Don Beddoe (Sheriff); Andrew Tombes (Ten-
nessee); Addison Richards (Matt Laskan); Edmund MacDonald (Com-
stock); Joseph Crehan (Dusty King); Willard Robertson (Wilson);
Patrick Moriarity (Matthews); Edmund Cobb (Blout); Lyle Latell
(Boxer).

    As a follow-up to its costly but lethargic Arizona (1941) [q.v.]
Columbia made Texas. Although produced on a small budget, it was

Claire Trevor and Glenn Ford in Texas (1941).

actionful and amusing. It used stock footage to good advantage and
had a nice score as well as good camerawork. It was originally
issued in blue-tinted sepia print. The only unfortunate aspect of the
project was that it wasted Claire Trevor in a too-small female lead
role.

The story concerned two drifters, Dan Thomas (Holden) and
Tom Ramsey (Ford), who are reprieved from jail (on a vagrancy
charge) when Dan agrees to tackle the local boxing champ (Latell).
The fight results in a riot and the two men manage to escape, only
to be mistaken by a sheriff (Beddoe) and his posse for stage robbers.
Before they can be hanged, the duo manage to escape yet again.
This time around they go their separate ways and end up at odds
when Tod joins ranchers and Dan gets into an outlaw gang led by
dentist Doc Thorpe (Buchanan).

Critics and the public alike were pleasantly surprised by the
offhand quality of Texas. "Something very rare in a Western movie
seems to have crept into [the film's] making ... and the result is a
surprisingly attractive picture. The something rare is nothing less
than a sense of humor, humor about the principal characters, humor
concerning the customarily fair heroine, humor even about the dastardly deeds of the villains ... it's all light and carefree and happy-
go-lucky, and even if the plot is a routine business, the approach to
same helps out enormously."

TEXAS DESPERADOS   see   DRIFT FENCE

THE TEXAS RANGERS   (Paramount, 1936)   95 min.

Director-story, King Vidor; screenplay, Louis Stevens; art
directors, Hans Dreier, Bernard Herzbrun; camera, Edward Cron-
jager.
Fred MacMurray (Jim Hawkins); Jack Oakie (Wahoo); Jean
Parker (Amanda); Lloyd Nolan (Sam McGee); Edward Ellis (Major
Balley); Bennie Bartlett (David); Elena Martinez (Maria); Frank
Shannon (Captain Stafford).

Paramount and director King Vidor joined forces to make
The Texas Rangers in association with that state's centennial year
celebration. What emerged, though, was "pretty maudlin stuff"
(New York Times). Less austere sources found it a rather entertaining, undemanding venture.
Jim Hawkins (MacMurray), Wahoo (Oakie) and Sam McGee
(Nolan) are three train robbers who become separated. In the
decades-old Hollywood convention two of them join the right side of
law (The Texas Rangers) while the third, McGee, becomes an infamous bandit. Wahoo enjoys the life of a Ranger, where there is
always sufficient food and shelter, but Jim continues to consort with
McGee. In fact Jim refuses a command to capture his pal. As a
result he is put in jail and Wahoo is given the assignment. To
achieve his goal, Wahoo joins McGee's gang, but the leader learns
of Wahoo's ploy and kills him, sending his body back to the rangers.
Wanting revenge, Jim then takes over the job and eventually does
get McGee. He then returns to the life of the ranger and the love
of the major's pretty daughter (Parker).
To appease the action fans, the film contained a fair ration
of stage holdups, cattle rustling, Indian attacks, and cabin ambushes.
A mediocre sequel, The Texas Rangers Ride Again, was issued in 1941 with John Howard and Ellen Drew. The 1936 original
was remade as Streets of Laredo in 1949, with William Holden,
Macdonald Carey, and William Bendix starring.

THEY DIED WITH THEIR BOOTS ON   (Warner Bros., 1941)   140
min.

Executive producer, Hal B. Wallis; associate producer,
Robert Fellows; director, Raoul Walsh; screenplay, Wally Klein,
Aeneas MacKenzie; music, Max Steiner; art director, John Hughes;
gowns, Milo Anderson; makeup, Perc Westmore; dialogue director,
Edward A. Blatt; technical advisor, Lieutenant Colonel J. G. Taylor,
U.S. Army, Retired; assistant director, Russell Saunders; sound,
Dolph Thomas; camera, Bert Glennon; editor, William Holmes.
Errol Flynn (George Armstrong Custer); Olivia de Havilland
(Elizabeth Bacon Custer); Arthur Kennedy (Ned Sharp, Jr.); Charles
Grapewin (California Joe); Gene Lockhart (Samuel Bacon); Anthony

Jack Oakie and Fred MacMurray in The Texas Rangers (1936).

Quinn (Crazy Horse); Stanley Ridges (Major Romulus Taipe); John
Litel (General Philip Sheridan); Walter Hampden (Senator Sharp);
Sydney Greenstreet (General Winfield Scott); Regis Toomey (Fitz-
hugh Lee); Hattie McDaniel (Callie); W. G. P. Huntley, Jr. (Lieu-
tenant Butler); Frank Wilcox (Captain Webb); Joseph Sawyer (Ser-
geant Doolittle); Minor Watson (Senator Smith); Gig Young (Lieuten-
ant Roberts); John Ridgley (Second Lieutenant Davis); Joseph Crehan
(President Grant); Aileen Pringle (Mrs. Sharp); Anna Q. Nilsson
(Mrs. Taipe); Harry Lewis (Youth); Tod Andrews (Cadet Brown);
Walter Brooke (Rosser); Selmer Jackson (Captain McCook); William
Hopper (Frazier); Eddie Acuff (Corporal Smith); Sam McDaniel
(Waiter); George Reed (Charles); Pat McVey (Jones); James Seay
(Lieutenant Walsh); Minerva Urecal, Virginia Sale, Edna Holland,
Renie Riano (Nurses); Vera Lewis (Head Nurse); Frank Ferguson
(Grant's Secretary); Hobart Bosworth (Clergyman).

Granted that this biographical account of George Armstrong
Custer is largely fancy, Raoul Walsh (who had replaced Michael
Curtiz as Errol Flynn's main action director) must be credited with
turning out a rousing bit of entertainment. Conceived on a grand
scale and produced in the lush manner so typical of this type of
adventure film, it combined romance, adventure, and picturesque
scenery in one large entertainment package.

Since Flynn and Olivia de Havilland had already become a
well-regarded screen love team, Warner Bros. paired them once
again in this hard-riding drama of the old West. She gave balance
to the flamboyant portrayal provided by Flynn, showing that even in
the mid-nineteenth century there were women who could be intelli-
gently outspoken against injustice and not just springboards for their
husband's philosophies.

Everything in this lengthy feature is a prelude to the climactic showdown between Custer (Flynn) and his small force of troops
and the determined Chief Crazy Horse (Quinn) at Little Big Horn.

The viewer is cautioned not to accept the portrayal of Custer
as pro-Indian to be the actual case, but to regard this horse opera
as diverting entertainment from a time when moviemakers and the
public could more readily convince themselves that fact was what
they wanted it to be, and right and wrong came in unshaded white
and black.

This would be the final co-starring vehicle for Flynn and de
Havilland, although they are both guest players in the studio's all-
star Thank Your Lucky Stars (1943).

THEY PASSED THIS WAY   see   FOUR FACES WEST

THE THREE GODFATHERS (Universal, 1916)   six reels

Director, Edward J. Le Saint; based on the story by Peter
B. Kyne; screenplay, Le Saint, Harvey Gates.
Harry Carey (Bob Sangster); Stella Razeto (Ruby Merrill);
George Berrell (Tim Gibbons); Frank Lanning (Bill Kearney); Hart
(Jack) Hoxie (Rusty Connors); Joe Ricksen (Pete Cushing).

THE THREE GODFATHERS   (MGM, 1936)   82 min.

        Producer, Joseph L. Mankiewicz; director, Richard Boles-
lawski; based on the story by Peter B. Kyne; screenplay, Edward
E. Paramore, Jr., Manuel Seff; music, Dr. William Axt; camera,
Joseph Ruttenberg; editor, Frank Sullivan.
        Chester Morris (Bob); Lewis Stone (Doc); Walter Brennan
(Gus); Irene Hervey (Molly); Dorothy Tree (Blackie); Robert Living-
ston (Frank); Joseph Marievsky (Pedro); Jean Kirchner (Baby).
        TV title: Miracle in the Sand.

THE THREE GODFATHERS   (MGM, 1948)   C   106 min.

        Producers, John Ford, Merian C. Cooper; director, Ford;
based on the story by Peter B. Kyne; screenplay, Laurence Stal-
lings, Frank S. Nugent; art director, James Basevi; set decorator,
Joe Kish; music, Richard Hageman; assistant directors, Wingate
Smith, Edward O'Fearna; camera, Winton C. Hoch, Charles P.
Boyle; editor, Jack Murray.
        John Wayne (Robert Marmaduke Sangster Hightower); Pedro
Armendariz (Pedro Roca Fuerte); Harry Carey, Jr. [William
Kearney (The Abilene Kid)]; Ward Bond (Perley "Buck" Sweet);
Mildred Natwick (Mother); Charles Halton (Mr. Latham); Jane Dar-
well (Miss Florie); Mae Marsh (Mrs. Perley Sweet); Guy Kibbee
(Judge); Dorothy Ford (Ruby Latham); Ben Johnson, Michael Dugan,
Don Summers (Patrolmen); Fred Libby, Hank Worden (Deputy
Sheriffs); Jack Pennick (Luke the Train Conductor); Francis Ford
(Drunk).

        Peter B. Kyne's short story has had a long and profitable
history.   Originally conceived as a Saturday Evening Post filler, it
was first brought to the screen as a short subject for the popular
Western screen star, Broncho Billy Anderson.   The film, shot in
one day, was entitled Broncho Billy and the Baby [q.v.] and dealt
with a bad guy who turns virtuous to save a floundering child.
        So successful was the first film version that Kyne rewrote
his story, published anew in 1910 as "The Three Godfathers."   In
1916 Edward J. Le Saint filmed it with Harry Carey in the lead.
This time it concerned three outlaws, being chased by a posse, who

---

Opposite: Six versions of the story, "The Three Godfathers":
Broncho Billy Anderson in Broncho Billy and the Baby (1909); Harry
Carey and Winifred Westover in Marked Men (1919); Charles Bick-
ford, Raymond Hatton and Fred Kohler in Hell's Heroes (1929);
bottom row: Chester Morris, Walter Brennan and Lewis Stone in
The Three Godfathers (1936); John Wayne, Harry Carey, Jr. and
Pedro Armendariz in The Three Godfathers (1948); and Jack Palance
and Keith Carradine in The Godchild (1974).

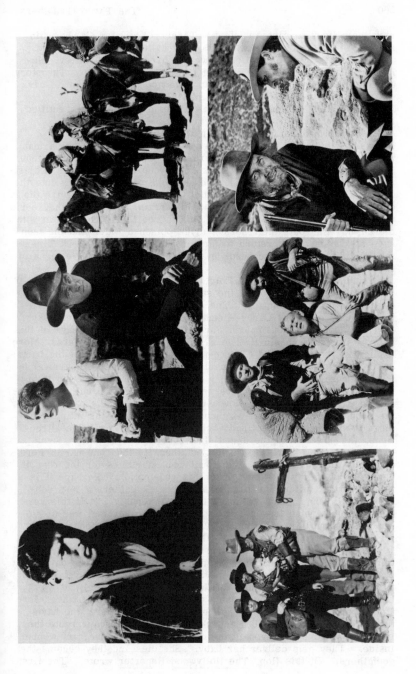

risk their lives to save an infant. Three years later Carey again
starred in the second version, this time called Marked Men [q.v.].
The setting is the Mojave Desert where three outlaws (Carey, Mc-
Donald, Harris) come upon a dying mother and her baby. The story,
as before, is played out as the trio renounce their freedom to save
the child. Only one of the adults survives the ordeal.

The first talking version was made in 1930 and was entitled
Hell's Heroes [q.v.].

MGM next filmed the tale in 1936 under the direction of
Richard Boleslawski. Here Chester Morris starred as Bob, a man
who returns to the town of New Jerusalem with three buddies (Stone,
Brennan, Marievsky) to rob a bank of his one-time neighbors' Christmas savings. They pull the job and elude a posse by riding into the
desert where they expect to gain their freedom, if they survive the
one hundred-mile ride through the arid terrain. However, they come
upon an infant and its dying mother and agree to return to town with
the child. En route their horses drink poisoned water and the men
have no choice but to return to face justice. The New York Times
felt that this version "succeeds in catching the spirit of Westerns of
two decades back."

In 1948 director John Ford, at the peak of his career, directed his second version of the story, this time at MGM for his
own co-production company. The color feature was dedicated "To
the memory of Harry Carey--bright star of the early western sky."
In The Western Films of John Ford (1973), J. A. Place says of this
film: "There are basically two parables in Three Godfathers. More
explicit of the two is the Christmas story with the birth of the baby
on Christmas day, the following of the star, and the safe arrival in
(New) Jerusalem. By becoming his godfathers and dedicating their
lives to him, all three men are redeemed through the child.... The
second parable ... closely woven with the first, is the parable of
the prodigal son.... It is as though redemption means infinitely
more to someone who has had a choice, who has known the attrac-
tions, the power, and the dissatisfaction of a life of crime, cyni-
cism, or immorality.... Three Godfathers is thus unusual in Ford's
oeuvre in that it is not the individual who sacrifices for the rest of
society, but they who sacrifice for his redemption. Perhaps it is
this important difference that makes Three Godfathers a less sub-
stantial film than many of Ford's other Westerns...." If this version can be termed lesser Ford, this is not to say that was an inferior Western by any means. "There is humor and honest tear-
jerking in this visually beautiful film" (New York Times). In this
1948 version, it is Wayne's outlaw who survives among the criminal
trio. The film was shot in Monument Valley in thirty-one days.

Sad to say, when the Kyne story was utilized for yet a sixth
time, as an ABC-TV feature entitled The Godchild (1974), it was
badly diluted, much to everyone's disadvantage. Jack Palance, Jose
Perez, and Ed Lauter are the three Civil War soldiers who have
turned deserters and robbed a bank. Along their escape route they
encounter a covered wagon in the desert and find a pregnant woman
inside. They help deliver her baby. She dies and they become the
godfathers. Of this flop, The Hollywood Reporter wrote, "The first

part is so confusing it is impossible to figure out what is going on.
The script by Ron Bishop is full of clichés and idiotic lines, and
not even John Badham's direction can save this turkey." The telefeature was shot on location in Tucson and the Red Rock Canyon
area of California's Mojave Desert.

THREE SWORDS OF ZORRO   see   MARK OF ZORRO

3:10 TO YUMA   (Columbia, 1957)   92 min.

     Producer, David Heilweil; director, Delmer Daves; story,
Elmore Leonard; screenplay, Halsted Welles; music, George Dun-
ing; song, Ned Washington and Duning; title song sung by Frankie
Laine; gowns, Jean Louis; assistant director, Sam Nelson; art di-
rector, Frank Hotaling; camera, Charles Lawton, Jr.; editor, Al
Clark.
     Glenn Ford (Ben Wade); Van Heflin (Dan Evans); Felicia Farr
(Emmy); Leora Dana (Alice Evans); Henry Jones (Alex Potter);
Richard Jaeckel (Charlie Prince); Robert Emhardt (Mr. Butterfield);
Sheridan Comerate (Bob Moons); George Mitchell (Bartender); Robert
Ellenstein (Ernie Collins); Ford Rainey (Marshal); Barry Curtis
(Mathew); Jerry Hartleben (Mark).

     Much like the more famous High Noon (1952) [q. v.], this solid
entry is well-handled by Delmer Daves. Within the story it is the
pressure of a tight situation that leads peace-loving cowpoke Dan
Evans (Heflin) to confront outlaw Ben Wade (Ford) and his henchmen,
among whom is Charlie Prince (Jaeckel). Among the supporting cast
who supply diverting atmosphere are Felicia Farr as a saloon lady,
Robert Emhardt as the owner of the stagecoach line, Leora Dana as
Heflin's wife, and Henry Jones as a courageous drunkard.
     Of this unheralded film, the New York Times' Bosley Crowther,
reported, "[It] is a good Western film, loaded with suspenseful situations and dusty atmosphere. The opening scene of a stagecoach hold-
up is crisply and ruggedly staged and all the incidents of lawmen
versus bandits are developed nicely from there."

THE THUNDERING HERD   (Paramount, 1925)   7,187'

     Presenters, Adolph Zukor, Jesse L. Lasky; director, William
K. Howard; based on the novel by Zane Grey; screenplay, Lucien
Hubbard; camera, Lucien Andriot.
     Jack Holt (Tom Doan); Lois Wilson (Milly Fayre); Noah Beery
(Randall Jett); Raymond Hatton (Jude Pilchuk); Charles Ogle (Clark
Hudnall); Colonel Tim McCoy (Burn Hudnall); Lillian Leighton (Mrs.
Clark Hudnall); Eulalie Jensen (Mrs. Randall Jett); Stephen Carr (Ory
Tacks); Maxine Elliott Hicks (Sally Hudnall); Edwin J. Brady (Pruitt);
Pat Hartigan (Catlett); Fred Kohler (Follansbee); Robert Perry (Joe
Dunn); Gary Cooper (Bit).

THE THUNDERING HERD   (Paramount, 1933)   62 min.

   Director, Henry Hathaway; based on the novel by Zane Grey;
screenplay, Jack Cunningham, Mary Flannery; art director, Earl
Hedrick; camera, Ben Reynolds.
   Randolph Scott (Tom Doan); Judith Allen (Milly Fayre); Larry
"Buster" Crabbe (Bill Hatch); Noah Beery (Randall Jett); Raymond
Hatton (Jude Pilchuck); Blanche Frederici (Mrs. Jett); Harry Carey
(Clark Sprague); Monte Blue (Joe); Barton MacLane (Pruitt); Al
Bridge (Catlee); Dick Rush (Middlewest); Frank Rice (Blacksmith);
Buck Connors (Buffalo Hunter); Charles McMurphy (Andrews).
   Reissue title: Buffalo Stampede.

   Paramount seemed to have filmed most of Zane Grey's
properties more than once, and frequently many times.   However,
The Thundering Herd went through their production mill only twice.
   In 1925 William K. Howard directed a silent edition in which
two future genre stars appeared: Tim McCoy in a supporting part
and lanky Gary Cooper as an extra.   Photoplay reported, "Equally
as good as The Covered Wagon.   Plenty of action, good cast and
beautiful photography."   What more could one ask?
   Jack Holt starred as Tom Doan, a Kansas farmer who joins
a band of buffalo hunters in 1876.   He meets and falls in love with
Milly Fayre (Wilson) the stepdaughter of an outlaw (Beery) who has
been robbing the buffalo hunters.   Due to the buffalo slaughter the

Harry Carey, Randolph Scott and Raymond Hatton in The Thundering
Herd (1925).

Indians declare war and Tom and Milly are separated.   Later Jett's
own men kill him.   It is Tom who saves Milly when she is nearly
trampled in a buffalo stampede.   Meanwhile the hunters defeat the
Indians.
        In 1933, Henry Hathaway, who would make a specialty of out-
door action films, helmed the talkie remake, in this case a quickie
with Randolph Scott as buffalo hunter Tom Doan and Judith Allen as
the heroine.   Noah Beery recreated his role as the villain.   The
flavorful cast included Harry Carey and Monte Blue, with newcomer
Larry "Buster" Crabbe thrown into the foray.   Much stock footage
from the original was incorporated into this double-bill item.

THE TOLL GATE   (Paramount, 1920)   six reels

        Director, Lambert Hillyer; story, William S. Hart, Hillyer;
screenplay, Hillyer.
        William S. Hart (Black Deering); Anna O. Nilsson (Mary
Brown); Jack Richardson (The Sheriff); Joseph Singleton (Jordan);
Richard Headrick (The Little Fellow).

        This Paramount-Artcraft release was William S. Hart's first
independent production and financially his most successful feature.
        It is the moving tale of outlaw Black Deering (Hart), who is
reformed by the love of a good woman (Nilsson) and her small son
(Headrick).   Earlier in the film Black Deering is seen robbing a
train, but after his redemption he is offered amnesty by the law.
Unfortunately, along the way he has been forced to kill Mary's
(Nilsson) husband, a blackguard who had deserted his family.   At
the finale Mary begs Black Deering to marry her.   He refuses, insisting it would not be in her best interest to marry an outcast.
He then returns to the life of an outlaw, knowing full well that he
is destined to die a violent death.
        The film sported good scenery, a neat posse chase and very
fine dramatics in the interplay between Hart and Nilsson.   However,
not all the critics liked the moralistic-formula story.   The New
York Times criticized, "It is too stereotyped and artificial in its
narrative and too much given to heroics to be plausible."   But as
is still the case, there is a wide gap between popular taste and the
standards set by the mercurial fourth estate.

TONIGHT'S THE NIGHT   see   WAY OUT WEST

TOPEKA   (Allied Artists, 1953)   69 min.

        Producer, Vincent M. Fennelly; director, Thomas Carr;
story-screenplay, Milton M. Raison; music, Raoul Kraushaar;
camera, Ernest Miller; editor, Sam Fields.
        "Wild Bill" Elliott (Jim Levering); Phyllis Coates (Marian
Harrison); Rick Vallin (Ray Hammond); John James (Marv Ransom);

Denver Pyle (Jonas Bailey); Dick Crockett (Will Peters);
Harry Lauter (Mack Wilson); Dale Van Sickel (Jake Manning);
Ted Mapes (Cully); Fuzzy Knight (Pop Harrison); I. Stanford
Jolley (Doctor); and: Michael Colgan, Michael Vallon, Edward
Clark, Henry Rowland.

After his class A productions at Republic, William Elliott
switched to Allied Artists in the early fifties for his final Western
series. Unfortunately the double-bill cowboy film format was coming
to a close. Despite the fact that this batch of Elliott films was
several notches above the average genre budget films of the period,
it could not prevent the ebb tide of the theatrical B Western
film.
Cast as an outlaw who comes to a small town and is hired as
its sheriff in order to rid the area of varmints, the lawbreaker sees
a chance to make some easy money. To accomplish his scheme,
Elliott's anti-hero gathers together his old gang who in turn get rid
of the villains. Later, Elliott is redeemed by the love of a nice
girl (Coates) and he turns on his comrades. From now on the
straight and narrow path is his! As a reward for his seeing the
light he wins a pardon, the hand of the heroine in matrimony, as
well as the money he had earned from his past nefarious deeds.
Thus in many ways this plotline has a different twist from the usual
run of Western programmers.

TRAIL OF THE VIGILANTES (Universal, 1940) 75 min.

Director, Allan Dwan; screenplay, Harold Schumate; art di-
rector, Jack Otterson; costumes, Vera West; camera, Joseph Valen-
tine; editor, Edward Curtiss.
Franchot Tone (Tim "Kansas" Mason); Broderick Crawford
(Swanee); Peggy Moran (Barbara Thornton); Andy Devine (Meadows);
Warren William (Mark Dawson); Mischa Auer (Dimitri Bolo); Porter
Hall (Sheriff Korley); Samuel S. Hinds (George Preston); Charles
Trowbridge (John Thornton); Paul Fix (Lefty); Harry Cording (Phil);
Max Wagner (Joe).

A very respectable cast instilled this potentially mediocre
Western with class and sensibility. Tim "Kansas" Mason (Tone)
has come from the East, an undercover agent out to stop rustler
Mark Dawson (William) and his nefarious activities. Tim becomes
the victim of a by-the-heels hanging. Escaping from this situation
he then gets involved in a saloon brawl in which he is aided by
sidekicks Swanee (Crawford) and Meadows (Devine). Later he falls
in love with underage Barbara Thornston (Moran). After Tim,
Swanee, Meadows, and Dimitri Bolo (Auer, a transplanted Russian
Cossack), along with Barbara, retrieve a calf from a mudhole--in
a very funny sequence--Tim finally puts an end to Dawson's lawless
ways.
Recalling the making of this production-line film, director
Dwan told Peter Bogdanovich in Allan Dwan: The Last Pioneer

(1971), "I hadn't made three scenes before it struck me that this
was not a good drama and that if it were made into a drama, it
would be a miserable thing.... So I got hold of a writer and in a
few hours [back at the studio] we adjusted the script into the same
story done with a tongue-in-cheek approach as a comedy. The
characters who were supposed to be rough, tough, murderous, kind
of people were for the most part just clowns."

THE TREASURE OF SIERRA MADRE   (Warner Bros., 1948)   126
min.

        Producer, Henry Blanke; director, John Huston; based on the
novel by B. Traven; screenplay, Huston; assistant director, Dick
Mayberry; art director, John Hughes; set decorator, Fred M. Mac-
Lean; music, Max Steiner; orchestrator, Murray Cutter; makeup,
Perc Westmore; sound, Robert B. Lee; special effects, William
McGann, H. F. Koenekamp; camera, Ted McCord; editor, Owen
Marks.
        Humphrey Bogart (Dobbs); Walter Huston (Howard); Tim Holt
(Curtin); Bruce Bennett (Cody); Barton MacLane (McCormick); Al-
fonso Bedoya (Gold Hat); A. Soto Rangel (Presidente); Manuel Donde
(El Jefe); Jose Torvay (Pablo); Margarito Luna (Pancho); Jacqueline
Dalya (Flashy Girl); Bobby Blake (Mexican Boy); John Huston (White
Suit); Jack Holt (Flophouse Bum); Ann Sheridan (Streetwalker).

        B. Traven was one of the most mysterious figures in the
literary world, but his novels and short stories have been acclaimed.
This film version of his best-known book is a genre classic. Walter
Clapham wrote in Western Movies (1974), "the real significance of
The Treasure of Sierra Madre in the context of the Western film is
its seminal influence on the genre. Echoes of it constantly sound
in Westerns firmly sited in the traditional period."
        Filmed in the Tampico area of Mexico, this $2.8 million
production starred Humphrey Bogart as the derelict Dobbs, who,
with oldtimer Howard (Walter Huston) and a young man (Tim Holt--
replacing John Garfield in the role), drums up a grubstake and heads
for the Sierra Madres to pan for elusive gold. They do find a rich
vein, but jealousies develop among them. They nearly kill a
stranger (Bennett) who stumbles into their camp; they fight Mexican
bandits who kill Cody (Bennett); and eventually the survivors split
up, with Dobbs being killed by outlaws. Howard finds peace as a
medicine man for Indians, while Curtin (Tim Holt) returns to civilization to explain Cody's death to his widow. Ironically the much-
sought-after gold is lost by the Mexican bandits who do not realize
the contents of sacks they break out. The precious dust blows away
in the wind, back to its mother mountain.
        John Huston won two Academy Awards for this feature, for
direction and script, while his father, Walter Huston, won the Best
Supporting Actor Oscar. The New York Film Critics voted this
sardonic study of greed the Best Film of the Year and gave the
Best Director Award to Huston. Time acknowledged it as "one of

the best things Hollywood has done since movies learned to talk. "
Noted movie critic James Agee reported, "This is one of the most
visually alive and beautiful movies I have ever seen...."
        Treasure abounds with fine performances, from its leads
through its supporting cast. (Actress Ann Sheridan always claimed
that as a lark she dressed up in the costume of a Mexican peasant
and can be spotted walking along the street in one of the film's
earlier sequences.) Barton MacLane was excellent as the work
gang boss who cheats Dobbs and Curtin, and Alfonso Bedoya gave
an outstanding performance as the leader of the Mexican bandits,
Gold Hat, a psychotic who smiles one minute and kills the next.
        Bogart and Walter Huston would repeat their roles on "Lux
Radio Theatre" in 1948. That broadcast is now available on an LP
record from Mark 56 Records.

TRUE GRIT   (Paramount, 1969) C 128 min.

        Producer, Hal B. Wallis; associate producer, Paul Nathan;
director, Henry Hathaway; based on the novel by Charles Portis;
screenplay, Marguerite Roberts; music, Elmer Bernstein; song,
Bernstein and Don Black; production designer, Walter Tyler; set
decorators, Roy Meadows, Elder Ruberg; costumes, Dorothy Jea-
kins; makeup, Jack Wilson; assistant director, William W. Gray;
camera, Lucien Ballard; editor, Warren Low.
        John Wayne (Rooster Cogburn); Glen Campbell (La Boeuf);
Kim Darby (Mattie Ross); Jeremy Slate (Emmett Quincy); Robert
Duvall (Ned Pepper); Dennis Hopper (Moon); Alfred Ryder (Goudy);
Strother Martin (Colonel G. Stonehill); Jeff Corey (Tom Chaney);
Ron Soble (Captain Boots Finch); John Fiedler (Lawyer Daggett);
James Westerfield (Judge Parker); John Doucette (Sheriff); Donald
Woods (Barlow); Edith Atwater (Mrs. Floyd); Carlos Rivas (Dirty
Bob); Isabel Boniface (Mrs. Bagby); H. W. Gim (Chen Lee); John
Pickard (Frank Ross); Elizabeth Harrower (Mrs. Ross); Ken Renard
(Yarnell); Jay Ripley (Harold Parmalee); Kenneth Becker (Farrell
Parmalee).

        One of the most popular Westerns of all time (it earned
nearly $12 million just in U.S. and Canadian rentals), True Grit
won John Wayne his first, and long overdue, Academy Award.
        Highlighted by excellent photography by Lucien Ballard and
a faithful recreation of the period, even to the use of language, the
feature tells of young Mattie Ross (Darby) whose father is murdered
by a renegade farmhand (Corey). She outwits a horse trader (Martin)
to obtain sufficient money to hire drunken U.S. marshal Rooster Cogburn (Wayne) to hunt Tom Chaney (Corey). A Texas Ranger named
La Bouef (Campbell) also wants Chaney for a crime committed in
Texas. Arkansas lawman Cogburn, the one-eyed grizzled veteran,
and the younger La Bouef are at odds as to whether to bring Chaney
to justice in Arkansas or return him to Texas.
        Meanwhile Chaney joins Ned Pepper's (Duvall) gang. Rooster
tracks him to Pepper's hideout and there he is forced to kill a

John Wayne, Kim Darby and Glen Campbell in True Grit (1969).

member of the band.   Later, in the Indian territory, Mattie locates
Chaney and wings him with a gunshot, but she is taken prisoner by
Pepper.   Rooster and La Bouef agree to leave the territory in exchange for the girl's safe release, but the Ranger later rescues her
while Cogburn diverts the outlaws, managing to kill many of them
from his horseback position.   Mattie is now freed but in the escape
the Ranger is fatally injured and only a doctor's care repairs Mattie's wounds from snake bites.   When Mattie and Cogburn return to
her ranch, she asks him to stay but he refuses.   He tells her to
"come see a fat old man sometime."   As he rides off into the distance, his horse jumps a fence, and soon man and steed are no
longer to be seen.
        William Wolf reported in Cue, "Wayne steals the film in the
role of tough, colorful Rooster Cogburn."   Films in Review noted,
"True Grit is filled with colorful colloquialisms, colorful characters,
believable situations and beautiful color photography.   It's an unusual western; an expertly blended combination of humor, tenderness,
and excitement; an altogether enjoyable movie."   The Los Angeles
Times summed up the venture, "True Grit is not the western to end
all westerns.   But it's sure as straight-shootin' a western as ever
was to celebrate all westerns and the West that was and the American dreams of self-reliance, resourcefulness, gumption, git-up-and-
go--and grit.   It's a josh and a joy, irreverent but never disrespect-
ful, a fairy tale which, like all fairy tales, we can believe or not,
and would rather."

Although the critics and public alike lauded Wayne's vivid
portrayal, the film's producers fortunately pared Glen Campbell's
dialogue to the bone. Unfortunately the folk singer was miscast as
the Texas Ranger and nearly spoiled the movie with his inept work.
In 1974 Wayne would journey to the Oregon country to join
with Katharine Hepburn in a sequel to True Grit, entitled Rooster
Cogburn (... and the Lady) (1975) [q.v.].

TUMBLEWEEDS (United Artists, 1925) 7,254'

Producer, William S. Hart; director, King Bagott; story, Hal
G. Evarts; adaptor, C. Gardner Sullivan; camera, Joseph August.
William S. Hart (Don Carver); Barbara Bedford (Molly Las-
siter); Lucien Littlefield (Kentucky Rose); J. Gordon Russell (Noll
Lassiter); Richard R. Neill (Bill Freel); Jack Murphy (Bart Lassi-
ter); Lillian Leighton (Mrs. Riley); Gertrude Claire (Old Woman);
George F. Marion (Old Man); Captain T. E. Duncan (Cavalry Major);
James Gordon (Hinman of the Box K Ranch); Fred Gamble (Hotel
Proprietor); Turner Savage (Riley Boy); Monte Collins (Hicks).

This is the only film William S. Hart made and starred in
after leaving Paramount Pictures in 1924. That studio insisted he
start turning out slick Westerns such as those of Tom Mix and Buck
Jones. Rather than compromise his feelings toward the Old West,
Hart went into independent production with this epic which cost over
$300,000 to make. The film was based on Hal G. Evarts' Saturday
Evening Post story, with Hart producing and one-time matinee idol
King Bagott as the director. (There are some sources which indicate that Hart co-directed the feature.)
This motion picture is Hart's picturization of "the last of the
West," the end of the cattle drives and the opening of the last frontier, the Cherokee Strip in Oklahoma. Rather episodic in construction, the film cast Hart as loner Don Carver, a cattle drover who
has no occupation after the end of the drives. He meets Molly Lassiter (Bedford) and falls in love with her. The couple decide to find
a permanent home on the land made newly available within the
Cherokee Strip. A subplot has Don imprisoned by the villain but
escaping from confinement with the aid of his loyal horse Fritz.
Thus Don is able to participate in the landrush, defeat claim jump-
ers, win land, and consolidate his romance with Molly. The highlight of the film, of course, is the finest landrush sequence ever
filmed (even better than the famous one in Cimarron, 1931, q.v.).
United Artists was not pleased with the resultant film and
the studio wanted to cut it from seven to five reels. Hart refused,
and the company retaliated by delaying release. Hart sued and won,
but the postponement in release cost him some $500,000 in antici-
pated profits. Bitter from this experience, the aging star retired
from the cinema.
In 1939 Astor Pictures re-issued Tumbleweeds with sound effects and a music score added. In addition, they filmed an eight-
minute prologue in which Hart discusses the picture and his career

in movies. Hart's talk to the audience was poignant and proved he
would have been a "natural" as a character lead in talkies had he
chosen such a move. Despite its antiquity, Tumbleweeds was successful in its re-issue.

Perhaps the most fitting tribute to the film has been offered
by Jon Tuska in his Views and Reviews magazine, in which he
labeled this film "one of the greatest Westerns ever made. It is
a work of art in the highest sense...."

TWENTY MULE TEAM (MGM, 1940) 84 min.

Producer, J. Walter Rubin; director, Richard Thorpe; story,
Robert C. Dusoe, Owen Atkinson; screenplay, Cyril Hume, E. E.
Paramore, Richard Maibaum; camera, Clyde DeVinna; editor, Frank
Sullivan.

Wallace Beery (Bill Bragg); Leo Carrillo (Piute Pete); Mar-
jorie Rambeau (Josie Johnson); Anne Baxter (Jean Johnson); Douglas
Fowley (Stag Roper); Noah Beery, Jr. (Mitch); Berton Churchill
(Jackass Brown); Arthur Hohl (Salters); Clem Bevans (Chuckawalla);
Charles Halton (Adams); Minor Watson (Marshall); Oscar O'Shea
(Conductor); Ivan Miller (Alden); Lew Kelly (Man); Lloyd Ingraham
(Stockholder); Sam Appel (Proprietor).

In the last decade of his lengthy screen career, gruff, rough,
crude Wallace Beery moved more and more into the Western genre
for his cinema vehicles. The public seemingly never grew tired of
his unending variations of the desert rat role.

After the demise of Marie Dressler in 1934, Beery had been
in search of a fitting female counterpart oncamera. This feature
was to be the first of a series he was to do with rambunctious,
energetic Marjorie Rambeau. However, the actress was injured
badly in an automobile accident not long after it was filmed and
further pairings did not occur. (Thereafter Wallace would be
matched on film with Marjorie Main.)

This rather complicated melodrama has Bill Bragg (Beery)
and Piute Pete (Carrillo) as miners working in the terrible heat of
Furnace Flat in Death Valley, digging for borax. Crooked Stag
Roper (Fowley) arrives in town and promptly romances the daughter
(Baxter) of a tavern owner (Rambeau). Stag also tries to blackmail
Bragg about his shady past, in order to get from him the location
of the valuable borax vein. For his underhanded schemes, Stag is
later shot by Bragg. The latter high-tails it into the desert where
he nearly dies of thirst before being rescued and vindicated by a
posse.

Undemanding filmgoers thrived on the unmitigated hamming of
Beery and Carrillo, but such staid sources as the New York Times
found this entry "desultory." For the record, this film was the
feature picture debut of Anne Baxter.

TWO GUNS AND A BADGE (Allied Artists, 1954) 69 min.

Producer, Vincent Fennelly; director, Lewis D. Collins;

screenplay, Dan Ullman; music, Raoul Kraushaar; assistant director, Melville Shyer; camera, Joseph Novac; editor, Sam Field.

Wayne Morris (Jim Blake); Morris Ankrum (Sheriff Jackson); Beverly Garland (Gail Sterling); Roy Barcroft (Bill Sterling); William Phipps (Dick Grant); Damian O'Flynn (Wilson); Stanford Jolley (Allen); Robert Wilke (Moore); Chuck Courtney (Val Moore); Henry Rowland (Jim Larkin).

The blossoming of television into mass popularity in the late forties spelled the doom of the theatrical series B Western, although it would be another six years before such Saturday matinee fare finally "bit the dust." The last recognized Western series was made by Allied Artists with Wayne Morris, and the last film he made in it was Two Guns and a Badge. William K. Everson and George Fenin note in The Western (1973), "It was no spectacular swan song for the B, but it was an appropriate and respectable close."

Its rather simple storyline has ex-convict Jim Blake (Morris) being mistaken for a deputy sheriff when he enters a small town. He is soon pitted against a rancher (Barcroft) who actually heads a rustling operation. To complicate matters, Jim falls in love with the lawbreaker's daughter, Gail (Garland).

Two Guns and a Badge was an austere minor effort, uncomplicated by extreme situations with justice triumphing once more in the old West.

TWO WAGONS--BOTH COVERED   see   THE COVERED WAGON

EL ULTIMO DE LOS VARGAS   see   LAST OF THE DUANES (1930)

UNDER THE TONTO RIM   (Paramount, 1928)   5,947'

Presenters, Adolph Zukor, Jesse L. Lasky; associate producer, B. P. Schulberg; director, Herman C. Raymaker; based on the novel by Zane Grey; screenplay, J. Walter Ruben; titles, Alfred Hustwick; camera, C. Edgar Schoenbaum; editor, William Shea.

Richard Arlen (Edd Denmeade); Alfred Allen (Dad Denmeade); Mary Brian (Lucy Watson); Jack Luden (Bud Watson); Harry T. Morey (Sam Spralls); William Franey (One Punch); Harry Todd (Bert); Bruce Gordon (Killer Higgins); Jack Byron (Middleton).

UNDER THE TONTO RIM   (Paramount, 1933)   63 min.

Director, Henry Hathaway; based on the novel by Zane Grey; screenplay, Jack Cunningham, Gerald Geraghty; art director, Earl Hedrick; camera, Archie Stout.

Stuart Erwin (Tonto Duley); Fred Kohler (Murther); Fuzzy

Knight (Porky); Verna Hillie (Nina Weston); John Lodge (Joe Gilbert); and George Barbier, Patricia Farley, Edwin J. Brady, Marion Burdell, Allan Garcia.

UNDER THE TONTO RIM   (RKO, 1947)   61 min.

        Producer, Herman Schlom; director, Lew Landers; based on the novel by Zane Grey; screenplay, Norman Houston; art directors, Albert S. D'Agostino, Charles F. Pyke; set decorators, Darrell Silvera, John Sturtevant; music, Paul Sawtell; music director, C. Bakaleinikoff; assistant director, John Pommer; sound, Jack Grubb, Terry Kellum; camera, J. Roy Hunt; editor, Lyle Boyer.
        Tim Holt (Brad); Nan Leslie (Lucy); Richard Martin (Chito); Richard Powers [Tom Keene] (Dennison); Carol Forman (Juanita); Tony Barrett (Patton); Harry Harvey (Sheriff); Jason Robards, Sr. (Captain McLean); Robert Clarke (Hooker); Jay Norris (Andy); Lex Barker (Deputy Joe); Steve Savage (Curly).

        Three film versions have been made of this 1926 Zane Grey work, the first two by Paramount.
        Herman C. Raymaker directed the silent edition in 1928. Goldminer Edd Benmeade (Arlen) loves Lucy Watson (Brian), the sister of a mining claims recorder (Luden). Edd suspects the latter as the killer of his father. The real killer, Sam Spralls (Morey), convinces Bud Watson (Luden) that he really did the dastardly deed and threatens to expose him unless he signs over to Spralls all the gold claims in the area. Spralls then puts together a gang to take possession of the gold veins. However, by this point Edd learns that Spralls was the killer of his dad. He forms a vigilante group and soundly defeats the villains.
        Handsome, exuberant Arlen, who was one of Paramount's mainstays in the twenties and early thirties, made quite a few Westerns at this point in his career. (In his twilight screen years he would return to the genre for producer A. C. Lyles.) The combination of Arlen and the lovely Mary Brian gave this rendering of the Zane Grey story extra zest. Photoplay judged the picture "fairly exciting."
        The talking remake was accomplished in 1933 by Henry Hathaway, who directed eight Zane Grey stories for Paramount within a two-year period. Most of them starred Randolph Scott, but this entry featured rube comedian Stuart Erwin as Tonto, a slow-thinking cowpoke who finds manhood and wins the love of the boss' daughter (Hillie) through his exploits on the range.
        In 1947, as part of its Western output, RKO made a third version of the novel. But, like most of that studio's adaptations of Grey's work, about the only thing this presentation had in common with the author's original was its title. Lew Landers directed the studio's top cowboy star, Tim Holt, in this effort, with Nan White and Richard Martin support. It told of the attempts of a young westerner (Holt) to hunt down and trap a mysterious band of outlaws.

THE UNFORGIVEN   (United Artists, 1960)   C   120 min.

Producer, James Hill; director, John Huston; based on the
novel by Alan LeMay; screenplay, Ben Maddow; assistant director,
Thomas F. Shaw; music/music director, Dimitri Tiomkin; makeup,
Frank McCoy, Frank Larue; wardrobe, Dorothy Jeakins; art direc-
tor, Stephen Grimes; sound, Basil Fenton Smith; camera, Franz
Planer; editor, Hugh Russell Lloyd.

Burt Lancaster (Ben Zachary); Audrey Hepburn (Rachel Zach-
ary); Audie Murphy (Cash Zachary); John Saxon (Johnny Portugal);
Charles Bickford (Zeb Rawlins); Lillian Gish (Mattilda Zachary);
Albert Salmi (Charlie Rawlins); Joseph Wiseman (Abe Kelsey); June
Walker (Hagar Rawlins); Kipp Hamilton (Georgia Rawlins); Arnold
Merritt (Jude Rawlins); Carlos Rivas (Lost Bird); Doug McClure
(Andy Zachary).

James Hill, who had once been in the film production busi-
ness with star Burt Lancaster, obtained the services of director
John Huston for this elaborate Western.   The film proved to be a
costly venture from the start.   Both Lancaster and co-lead Audrey
Hepburn demanded and received $300,000 each for their services.
Then the production--on location in Durango, Mexico--was delayed

Audrey Hepburn and Audie Murphy in The Unforgiven (1960).

when Miss Hepburn fell off a horse and broke her back.   By the
time the feature was in release, it had cost over $5 million.   Its
domestic distributor grosses provided little or no profit for this
United Artists release.

Racial prejudice and underlying sexuality are the primary
themes of this intricate story.   The scene is the Texas Panhandle
of the late 1800s where the settlers and Kiowa Indians are in constant conflict.   Rumors spread that Rachel Zachary (Hepburn) is
actually a full-blooded Kiowa, and soon the local citizens are
blazing with hatred of this alleged outcast.   Then the Kiowas demand her return, insisting she is the sister of the chief.   Rachel's
foster brother Ben (Lancaster) denies all these charges, repeating
that she is the child of white pioneers killed by the Indians.   Later
it is revealed that Rachel is really a Kiowa, a child stolen from the
Indians to substitute for the infant daughter lost by Mrs. Zachary
(Gish) after childbirth.   Now the settlers insist that Rachel return
to the Indians, so that the trouble will stop.   The Zacharys decline,
except for Cash (Murphy), who is a bigot and leaves his homestead.
When the Kiowas attack the Zachary stronghold, Mrs. Zachary is
killed and Rachel must kill her Indian brother.   Fortunately, Cash
has a change of heart and returns to help the family stave off the
redskins.   Finally peace returns to the area and Ben and Rachel
decide to marry and to remain on the land and combat the prejudice
of their neighbors.

Before release the picture was heavily edited, which caused
the scenario to seem muddled.   Fortunately there are several good
performances in the picture, in both leading and supporting roles.

Because Aldrich and the scripter were anxious to make a
message picture, many critics insisted upon attacking the production
on intellectual grounds (hardly a fair stance for any Western).
Saturday Review complained, "What seems likely is that the [film-
makers] failed to think through the implications of their themes.
They had ideas but lacked a point of view....   Nor does John Huston's direction do anything to strengthen the point of view.   The
reasons for the Texas settlers' unremitting hatred for the Indians
are muffled; and Joseph Wiseman, the vengeful saddle-tramp who
reveals the secret of the girl's shameful origins, remains a man of
mystery throughout."   Even Films in Review's offhanded praise reads
more like an insult, "The Unforgiven isn't an important picture, but
it's the best Huston has directed in some time."

UNION PACIFIC (Paramount, 1939) 133 min.

Producer-director, Cecil B. DeMille; story, Ernest Haycox;
screenplay, Walter DeLeon, C. Gardner Sullivan, Jesse Lasky, Jr.;
adaptor, Jack Cunningham; art directors, Hans Dreir, Roland Anderson; music, George Antheil; camera, Victor Milner, Dewey Wrigley;
editor, Anne Bauchens.

Barbara Stanwyck (Mollie Monahan); Joel McCrea (Jeff Butler);
Akim Tamiroff (Fiesta); Robert Preston (Dick Allen); Lynne Overman
(Leach Overmile); Brian Donlevy (Sid Campeau); Robert Barrat (Duke

Joel McCrea and Robert Barrat in Union Pacific (1939).

Ring); Anthony Quinn (Cordray); Stanley Ridges (Casement); Henry
Kolker (Asa M. Barrows); Francis McDonald (Grenville M. Dodge);
Willard Robertson (Oakes Ames); Harold Goodwin (Calvin); Evelyn
Keyes (Mrs. Calvin); Richard Lane (Sam Reed); William Haade
(Dusky Clayton); Regis Toomey (Paddy O'Rourke); Fuzzy Knight
(Cookie); Lon Chaney, (Dollarhide); Joseph Crehan (General U.
S. Grant); Sheila Darcy (Rose); Julia Faye (Mame); Joseph Sawyer
(Shamus); John Marston (Dr. Durant); Morgan Wallace (Senator
Smith); Byron Fulger (Whipple); Selmer Jackson (Jerome); May
Beatty (Mrs. Hogan); Ernie Adams (General Sheridan); Stanley An-
drews (Dr. Harkness); Jack Pennick (Harmonica Player).

After devoting much of the Thirties to historical spectacle,
producer-director Cecil B. DeMille returned to the West with The
Plainsman (1936) [q.v.] and then Union Pacific. The latter is an
epic saga of the building of the first transcontinental railroad, a
story related in the silent era by John Ford's The Iron Horse (1925)
[q.v.]. Actually the Ford photoplay is a superior work, far more
engrossing than this million dollar production which was shot on location at Iron Springs, Utah and Canoga Park, California. But this
opinion does not diminish the worth of this sweeping melodrama.
Overseer Jeff Butler (McCrea) works for the Union Pacific
Railroad and in the course of events falls in love with an engineer's

daughter, Mollie Monahan (Stanwyck). Jeff's pal Dick Allen (Preston) works for Sid Campeau (Donlevy) who hires saboteurs to stop
the railroad's construction. Later Dick robs the company pay train,
but is defended by Mollie, who persuades him to return the ill-got-
ten funds. When the Indians attack the worktrain, Mollie, Jeff, and
Dick must battle it out with the savages. The Army arrives in time
to save the train worker but Dick is killed by unrepentent Sid Campeau, who in turn meets his fate. Eventually the railroad is finished
at Promontory Point--the point where the two railroad companies join
their tracks. Mollie and Jeff remain together.
       In the course of the 133-minute spectacle, DeMille spares no
expense to give the viewer all the standard form of Western entertainment, but, in this case decked out in elaborate form, whether it
be an Indian attack, the building of the railroad tracks, or a scene
in a gambling saloon. And of course there are colorful performances
by marvelous character players such as Lynne Overman and Akim
Tamiroff as the pals of rugged Joel McCrea, or slick Anthony Quinn
as the assistant of slimy gambler, Brian Donlevy. Refusing to be
limited by her heroine's role, Stanwyck offers a vital performance
as J. M. Kerrigan's daughter, the mature tomboy postmistress who
can handle six-shooters, an Indian attack, or a courtship with equal
dispatch and a lilting Irish charm.

UTVANDRARNA see THE NEW LAND

VADO, L'AMMAZZO E TORNO (ANY GUN CAN PLAY) (Italian-
Spanish, 1967) C 103 min.

       Director, Enzo G. Castellari; screenplay, Romolo Guerrieri,
George Simonelli, Castellari; music, Francesco De Masi.
       Edd Byrnes (Clayton); Gilbert Roland (Monetero); George Hilton
(The Bounty Hunter); Kareen O'Hara (Wapa); Pedro Sanchez (Pajondo);
Gerard Herter (Backman).

       The chief joy of this spaghetti Western is to witness silent
screen personality Gilbert Roland, looking fitter than his co-stars,
romping through the silly storyline with appropriate masculinity and
zest.
       The Bounty Hunter (Hilton), having collected a slew of reward
money on wanted bandits, decides his next hit will be the infamous
bandito Monetero (Roland). The Bounty Hunter catches up with Monetero just before he is to be executed by army officers. The Hunter's
aim is to persuade Monetero to reveal the whereabouts of a hidden
cache of gold from a previous robbery. Involved in the search is
Clayton (Byrnes), a young bank official who had a hand in the robbery. Eventually The Hunter, Monetero, and Clayton team up to
split the gold between them.
       As Variety analyzed, "[It] is a routine programmer, no worse
nor better than most of the Italian oaters and, considering the remarkable absence of blood, okay for general audiences (although crime
does pay eventually)."

VALLEY OF THE SUN (RKO, 1942) 79 min.

    Producer, Graham Baker; director, George Marshall; based
on the story by Clarence Budington Kelland; screenplay, Horace Mc-
Coy; music, Paul Sawtell; camera, Harry Wild; editor, Desmond
Marquette.
    Lucille Ball (Christine); James Craig (Jonathan); Sir Cedric
Hardwicke (Warrick); Dean Jagger (Jim Sawyer); Peter Whitney
(Willie); Billy Gilbert (Justice of the Peace); Tom Tyler (Geronimo);
Antonio Moreno (Chief Cochise); George Cleveland (Bill Yard); Hank
Bell (Shotgun); Richard Fiske, Don Terry (Lieutenants); Chris Willow
Bill (Apache Indian); Fern Emmett (Spinster); Al St. John, Harry La-
mont, Al Ferguson, Chester Conklin, Ed Brady, Lloyd Ingraham,
Frank Coleman (Men on Street); Francis McDonald (Interpreter); Har-
ry Hayden (Governor); Bud Osborne (Rose); Steve Clemento (Knife
Thrower).

    RKO advertised this George Marshall-directed Western as its
biggest outdoor epic since <u>Cimarron</u> (1930) [q.v.]. Actually it was
a much smaller-budgeted actioner which cast Dean Jagger as Jim
Sawyer, a corrupt Indian agent in the Arizona Territory. While
cheating the Indians and romancing restaurant owner Christine (Ball),
he becomes a rich, powerful man. It is government agent Jonathan
(Craig), who doubles as a renegade Indian scout to gain Sawyer's
confidence, who is the hero of the piece. Along the way, naturally,
Jonathan and Christine become romantically attracted to one another.

Billy Gilbert, Dean Jagger and Lucille Ball in <u>Valley of the Sun</u>
(1942).

Despite its somewhat pedestrian nature (at least by Forties' standards--today it would be most welcome), Valley of the Sun did showcase quite a few good performances. There is Billy Gilbert's funny cameo as a justice of the peace, along with Tom Tyler's appearance as the vicious Geronimo, as well as bits by former silent screen comics Al St. John and Chester Conklin.

THE VANISHING AMERICAN (Paramount, 1926) 9,916'

Presenters, Adolph Zukor, Jesse L. Lasky; director, George B. Seitz; based on the novel by Zane Grey; screenplay, Ethel Doherty; adaptor, Lucien Hubbard; technical advisor, Louisa Wetherill; camera, C. Edgar Schoenbaum, Harry Perry.

Richard Dix (Nophaie); Lois Wilson (Marion Warner); Noah Beery (Booker); Malcolm McGregor (Earl Ramsdale); Nocki (Indian Boy); Shannon Day (Gekin Yashi); Charles Crockett (Amos Halliday); Bert Woodruff (Bart Wilson); Bernard Siegel (Do Etin); Guy Oliver (Kit Carson); Joe Ryan (Jay Lord); Charles Stevens (Shoie); Bruce Gordon (Rhur); Richard Howard (Glendon); John Webb Dillon (Naylor).

THE VANISHING AMERICAN (Republic, 1955) 90 min.

Producer, Herbert J. Yates; director, Joseph Kane; based on the novel by Zane Grey; screenplay, Alan LeMay; art director, Walter Keller; music, R. Dale Butts; camera, John L. Russell, Jr.; editor, Richard L. Van Enger.

Scott Brady (Blandy); Audrey Totter (Marian Warner); Forrest Tucker (Morgan); Gene Lockhart (Blucher); Jim Davis (Glendon); John Dierkes (Friel); Gloria Castillo (Yashi); Julian Rivero (Etenia); Lee Van Cleef (Jay Lord); George Keymas (Coshonta); Charles Stevens (Quah-tain); Jay Silverheels (Beeteia); James Millcan (Walker); Glenn Strange (Beleanth).

Relying on the Zane Grey novel for source material, the first one-third of this feature detailed the history of the American Indian nation, from the overthrow of the cliff dwellers to the coming of the Spanish. The story then jumped ahead to World War I to show how the Indians fought with the troops only to return after the Armistice to barren land with their crops despoiled and their tribes under the yoke of corrupt government officials. (This theme would be paralleled in The Outsider [1961], in which Tony Curtis as American Indian Ira Hayes was a World War II hero. After the war, however, he could not cope with the discrimination practiced against his folk and himself by the white man.) The modern story in The Vanishing American is related as the background of the life of one brave, Nophaie (Dix), and his downhill fight to rectify the situation.

With a good deal of location shooting, the picture provided Richard Dix with his finest screen role and in it he gave his best performance. Harrison's Reports said it "is a picture that will live in one's memory after hundreds of them have faded away." In Hollywood: The Golden Era (1971), Jack Spears wrote in his essay on

"The Indian on the Screen," that The Vanishing American "is perhaps the best motion picture about Indians ever made."
        In 1955 Republic chose to remake the film under contract
director Joseph Kane. It was shot largely in Utah. Journeyman
producer-director Kane had wanted to shoot it in color but had to
settle for black-and-white. Nor did he obtain the services of the
desired leading lady, Barbara Stanwyck, whose fee was too expensive for the project. Instead, Audrey Totter was cast as Marian
Warner, with Scott Brady in the Dix role of the young Navajo Indian
who tries to stop landgrabbers from taking his people's land.
Geronimo's real-life grandson, Charles Stevens, was also in the
cast, appearing as Quah-tain.
        Unfortunately the 1955 remake was snubbed by the critics
and was played off on the action circuits and quickly forgotten,
particularly as it came near the close of Republic's production of
theatrical films.

THE VANISHING LEGION   see   LAST OF THE MOHICANS

VERA CRUZ   (United Artists, 1954)   C   94 min.

        Producer, James Hill; co-producers, Harold Hecht, Burt
Lancaster; director, Robert Aldrich; based on the story by Borden
Chase; screenplay, Roland Kibbee, James R. Webb; music, Hugo
Friedhofer; orchestrator-music director, Raul Lavista; song, Fried-
hofer and Sammy Cahn; sound, Manuel Topete, Galdino Samperio;
camera, Ernest Laszlo; editor, Alan Crosland, Jr.
        Gary Cooper (Benjamin Trane); Burt Lancaster (Joe Erin);
Denise Darcel (Countess Marie Duvarre); Cesar Romero (Marquis
de Labordere); Sarita Montiel (Nina); George Macready (Emperor
Maximilian); Ernest Borgnine (Donnegan); Henry Brandon (Danette);
Charles Bronson (Pittsburgh); Morris Ankrum (General Aguilar);
James McCallion (Little-Bit); Jack Lambert (Charlie); Jack Elam
(Tex); James Seay (Abilene); Archie Savage (Ballard); Charles Hor-
vath (Reno); Juan Garcia (Pedro).

        The production team of Harold Hecht and Burt Lancaster
signed Gary Cooper to co-star with Lancaster in this slam-bang
actioner which was directed by Robert Aldrich. Previously, Aldrich had directed Lancaster in Apache (1954) [q.v.].
        Set in the period of the 1866 Mexican Revolution, two U.S.
soldiers of fortune, Benjamin Trane (Cooper) and Joe Erin (Lancaster), become mercenaries, willing to fight for whichever side
has the most to offer them. At a fancy ball, the duo encounter
Countess Marie Duvarre (Darcel) who persuades them to escort her
on the trip to Vera Cruz. It will be a difficult journey, she advises them, because she is carrying a gold shipment destined for
the Emperor's forces. Later, she suggests they steal the gold and
split it among themselves. However, the Marquis (Romero) flees
with the gold and the mercenaries have to ride after him to retrieve

Gary Cooper, Burt Lancaster and Cesar Romero in <u>Vera Cruz</u>
(1954).

it. Nina (Montiel), the revolutionary girl who loves Trane, convinces him that the funds ought to go to the people. In the climactic showdown, Erin refuses to release the gold and Trane reluctantly
shoots him.

    <u>Vera Cruz</u>* was a strikingly beautiful film which compensated
for its thin plot. It was mainly the performances of its leads which
held the piece together and made the film so popular (it grossed $5
million domestically). Ironically the <u>New York Times</u>, more mind-
ful of art than commerciality, insisted, "there is nothing to redeem
this film...."

VIRGINIA CITY (Warner Bros., 1940) 121 min.

      Executive producer, Hal B. Wallis; associate producer,
Robert Fellows; director, Michael Curtiz; screenplay, Robert

---

*Tony Martin's singing of the title theme was deleted from the film
before its national release, although the song was issued on RCA
Victor records.

Buckner; music, Max Steiner; orchestrator, Hugo Friedhofer; assistant director, Sherry Shourds; dialogue director, Jo Graham; art director, Ted Smith; makeup, Perc Westmore; sound, Oliver S. Garretson, Francis J. Scheids; special effects, Byron Haskin, H. F. Koenekamp; camera, Sol Polito; editor, George Amy.

Errol Flynn (Kerry Bradford); Miriam Hopkins (Julia Hayne); Randolph Scott (Vance Irby); Humphrey Bogart (John Murrell); Frank McHugh (Mr. Upjohn); Alan Hale (Moose); Guinn "Big Boy" Williams (Marblehead); John Litel (Marshal); Douglass Dumbrille (Major Drewery); Moroni Olsen (Dr. Cameron); Russell Hicks (Armistead); Dickie Jones (Cobby); Frank Wilcox (Union Soldier); Russell Simpson (Gaylord); Victor Kilian (Abraham Lincoln); Charles Middleton (Jefferson Davis); Monte Montague (Stage Driver); George Regas, Paul Fix (Murrell's Henchmen); Thurston Hall (General Meade); Charles Trowbridge (Seddon); Howard Hickman (General Page); Charles Halton (Ralston); Ward Bond (Sergeant); Sam McDaniel (Sam); Harry Cording (Scarecrow); Trevor Bardette (Fanatic); Tom Dugan (Spieler); Spencer Charters (Bartender); George Reeves (Telegrapher).

A follow-up to the very successful Dodge City (1939) [q.v.], this film used several economy measures. Filmed in black-and-white, it re-used several still standing sets from the earlier picture. It did have location shooting in Monument Valley and the Painted Desert region of Northern Arizona. While it was a rather tame Western by comparison to other Errol Flynn entries, the motion picture did offer good action moments and fine performances by Flynn and Randolph Scott.

The film was based on an actual incident, and had Flynn playing Kerry Bradford, a Union soldier who escapes from a Confederate prison and is sent West to stop the shipment of $5 million in gold from Virginia City to the South. Vance Irby (Scott) is the Reb who is in charge of the shipment and Julia Hayne (Hopkins) is the southern saloon girl working as an undercover agent for her homeland. As part of this ruse to stop the transaction, Kerry is forced to join Vance and Julie in opposing a Mexican bandit (Bogart) who is also after the loot. When Vance is killed defeating John Murrell (Bogart), Kerry buries the gold, hoping to use it at the war's end to rebuild the South.

Perhaps the most interesting aspects of this film took place behind the cameras. Temperamental director Michael Curtiz did not get along at all with either Flynn or Hopkins, while Bogart had no love for either Flynn or Scott. Curtiz did succeed in obtaining decent performances from Flynn and Scott, but he was run ragged trying to turn out convincing characterizations from either Bogart or Hopkins.

For the record, Virginia City is not a sequel to Dodge City, although at the end of the latter film, Colonel Dodge (Henry O'Neill) requests Flynn and his pals to head to Virginia City to bring law and order there.

Opposite: Alan Hale, Errol Flynn and Guinn "Big Boy" Williams in Virginia City (1940).

THE VIRGINIAN (Paramount, 1914) five reels

Producer-director, Cecil B. DeMille; based on the novel by
Owen Wister; screenplay, DeMille; camera, Alvin Wyckoff; editors,
Mamie Wagner, DeMille.

Dustin Farnum (The Virginian); Winifred Kingston (Molly
Wood); Billy Elmer (Trampas); Monroe Salisbury (Mr. Ogden); Anita
King (Mrs. Ogden); Tex Driscoll (Shorty); Jack W. Johnston (Steve);
Sydney Deane (Uncle Hughey); Hosea Steelman (Lincoln McLean);
James Griswold (Stage Driver); Horace B. Carpenter (Spanish Kid);
Dick La Reno (Ballam); Mrs. Lewis McCord (Mrs. Balaam).

THE VIRGINIAN (Preferred Pictures, 1923) 8,010'

Presenter, B. P. Schulberg; director, Tom Forman; based
on the play by Owen Wister and Kirk La Shelle and the novel by
Wister; screenplay, Hope Loring, Louis D. Lighton; camera, Harry
Perry.

Kenneth Harlan (The Virginian); Florence Vidor (Molly Woods);
Russell Simpson (Trampas); Pat O'Malley (Steve); Raymond Hatton
(Shorty); Milton Ross (Judge Henry); Sam Allen (Uncle Hughey); Bert
Hadley (Spanish Ed); Fred Gambold (Fat Drummer).

THE VIRGINIAN (Paramount, 1929) 90 min.

Producer, Louis D. Lighton; director, Victor Fleming; based
on the play by Owen Wister and Kirk La Shelle and the novel by
Wister; screenplay, Edward E. Paramore, Jr.; adaptor, Howard
Estabrook; assistant director, Henry Hathaway; titler, Joseph L.
Mankiewicz; sound, M. M. Paggio; camera, J. Roy Hunt; editor,
William Shea.

Gary Cooper (The Virginian); Walter Huston (Trampas);
Richard Arlen (Steve); Mary Brian (Molly Wood); Chester Conklin
(Uncle Hughey); Eugene Pallette (Honey Wiggin); E. H. Calvert
(Judge Henry); Helen Ware (Ma Taylor); Victor Potel (Nebraskey);
Tex Young (Shorty); Charles Stevens (Pedro); Jack Pennick (Slim);
George Chandler (Ranch Hand); Ernie Adams (Saloon Singer); Fred
Burns (Ranch Hand); Randolph Scott (Rider).

THE VIRGINIAN (Paramount, 1946) C 90 min.

Producer, Paul Jones; director, Stuart Gilmore; based on the
play by Owen Wister and Kirk La Shelle and the novel by Wister;
adaptor, Howard Estabrook; screenplay, Frances Goodrich, Albert
Hackett; Technicolor consultants, Natalie Kalmus, Robert Brower;
art directors, Hans Dreier, John Meehan; set decorator, John Mc-
Neil; assistant director, John Murphy; music, Daniele Amfitheatrof;
sound, Roy Meadows, John Cope; special camera effects, Gordon
Jennings; process camera, Farciot Edouart; camera, Harry Hallen-
berger; editor, Everett Douglass.

Fay Bainter and Barbara Britton in <u>The Virginian</u> (1946).

Joel McCrea (The Virginian); Brian Donlevy (Trampas); Sonny
Tufts (Steve); Barbara Britton (Molly); Fay Bainter (Mrs. Taylor);
Tom Tully (Nebraska); Henry O'Neill (Mr. Taylor); Bill Edwards
(Sam Bennett); William Frawley (Honey Wiggen); Paul Guilfoyle
(Shorty); Marc Lawrence (Pete); Vince Barnett (Baldy).

Producer-director Cecil B. DeMille first brought Owen Wister's 1902 classic novel to the screen in 1914 as a five-reeler for
Paramount.   Dustin Farnum played the title role of the easy-going
happy cowpoke who falls for a pretty schoolmarm (Kingston).   However, he is forced to take part in the hanging of a buddy (Johnston)
who was involved with cattle thieves.   The leader of the outlaws,
Trampas (Elmer) calls The Virginian (Farnum) a bad name, to
which the hero replies, "When you call me that--smile!"   (Yes,
this film is the origin of that famous line.)   After the outlaws are
rounded up, The Virginian and Trampas have a showdown; the latter
is killed.   At the close-out The Virginian has cemented his romantic
relationship with Molly Wood (Kingston).

Of this landmark photoplay, The New York Dramatic-Mirror
reported, "Drama, comedy and photographic spectacle are the triple
alliances met in the picturization of Owen Wister's story."   The Los
Angeles Daily Times printed, "Some splendid horsemanship is shown
and the rugged mountain scenery amid which the action of the story
is laid adds greatly to the charm of the picture."

In 1923 Owen Wister and Kirk La Shelle wrote the stage version of Wister's perennially popular novel.   That same year Preferred
Pictures offered the second screen version of the story.   Photoplay
magazine termed it "an exceptionally good western."   Expanded to
eight reels, this version had Kenneth Harlan as The Virginian and
Florence Vidor as the Wyoming school teacher he adores.   He alien-
ates her, however, when he helps hang his friend Steve (O'Malley).
Later The Virginian is wounded in a fight with evil Trampas (Simpson) and Molly (Vidor) nurses him back to health prior to the final
showdown.

The best-known screen version was released by Paramount in
1929.   It was the first talkie edition of the Wister work.   Victor
Fleming directed and was assisted by Henry Hathaway.   Once again
the story finds The Virginian (Cooper) and Steve (Arlen) in friendly
competition for the attention of schoolmarm Molly Wood (Brian), although The Virginian also fights with Trampas (Huston) over a saloon
girl.   The Virginian then catches Steve rustling cattle for Trampas
and warns him to desist.   But later Steve and two others are caught
and hanged.   Knowing Trampas is the major culprit, The Virginian
hunts him.   On the day that The Virginian and Molly are to wed,
there is the final showdown, with The Virginian the victor.

This ninety-minute film was shot on location near Sonora in
the High Sierras and Randolph Scott served as Cooper's special
dialogue coach.   The film was a big box-office hit and was re-issued
in 1935.

Ever anxious to duplicate a past success, Paramount made yet
another version of the novel, this time adding Technicolor as a bonus
attraction.   Joel McCrea was The Virginian, with Brian Donlevy as

Trampas, Sonny Tufts as Steve, and Barbara Britton as Molly. By
this point in time, however, the storyline was wearing thin and
failed to intrigue many viewers, even with the addition of color and
the adult orientation of the script.

In 1962 "The Virginian" TV series debuted over NBC-TV and
ran until 1970. This ninety-minute weekly color show starred James
Drury in the title role and offered Doug McClure as Trampas, who
is no longer a villain. In 1970 the series was retitled "Men from
Shiloh" and starred Stewart Granger, with Drury continuing as The
Virginian for the one-season run.

Episodes from the TV series were issued abroad theatrically
in the mid-sixties, including The Devil's Children (1963), The Final
Hour (1963) and The Brazen Bell (1966).

WAGONMASTER (RKO, 1950) 86 min.

Producers, John Ford, Merian C. Cooper; associate producer, Lowell Farrell; director, Ford; story, Ford; screenplay,
Frank S. Nugent, Patrick Ford; music, Richard Hageman; songs,
Stan Jones; art director, James Basevi; set director, Joe Kish;
costumes, Wes Jeffries, Adele Parmenter; assistant director, Wingate Smith; second unit director, Cliff Lyons; camera, Bert Glennon; editor, Jack Murray.

Ben Johnson, Harry Carey, Jr. and Ward Bond in Wagonmaster
(1950).

        Ben Johnson (Travis Blue); Harry Carey, Jr. (Sandy Owens);
Joanne Dru (Denver); Ward Bond (Elder Wiggs); Charles Kemper
(Uncle Shiloh Clegg); Alan Mowbray (Doctor A. Locksley Hall); Jane
Darwell (Sister Ledyard); Ruth Clifford (Fleuretty "Florie" Phyffe);
Russell Simpson (Adam Perkins); Kathleen O'Malley (Prudence Per-
kins); James Arness (Floyd Clegg); Fred Libby (Reese Clegg); Hank
Worden (Luke Clegg); Mickey Simpson (Jesse Clegg); Francis Ford
(Mr. Peachtree); Cliff Lyons (Sheriff of Crystal City); Don Summers
(Sam Jenkins); Movita Castenada (Young Navajo Girl); Jim Thorpe
(Navajo Chief).

        A latter-day The Covered Wagon (1923) [q. v.], this John Ford
production featured Ward Bond as Elder Wiggs, the wagonmaster
disciple of Brigham Young. He hires two drifters, Travis Blue
(Johnson) and Sandy Owens (Carey), to lead a congregation of Mormons
from Crystal City to beyond the San Juan River into Utah. Along
the way they pick up a wagon medicine show and a group of outlaws
running from a posse. Included in the action is trouble with Navajo
Indians, and such events as one of the train members being whipped
for molesting an Indian maiden, the bandits being killed trying to rob
the train, the fording of a river, and the final emergence of romantic alliances for both Travis and Sandy.
        In The Western Films of John Ford (1973), J. A. Place writes,
"The emotional quality of Wagonmaster is like that of Rio Grande
[1950, q. v.] and She Wore a Yellow Ribbon [1949, q. v.]--very rich in
gentle, nostalgic emotion, underscored by comedy, and not disturbed
by a disruption in the eventual integration of all emotional elements
into the whole. This deceptively unpretentious film is in many ways
the high point of Ford's Westerns. Ford's optimism and pessimism
are in perfect balance. The darker side of his vision gives an emotional depth lacking in earlier films like Stagecoach [1939, q. v.] and
Drums Along the Mohawk [1939, q. v.], but the optimism prevails and
renders this film essentially undisturbing and only gentle in its nostalgia, not bitter like the later films."
        It was shot on location in Utah. John Ford wrote the original
story and the film remained one of his special favorites. "Along
with The Fugitive [1947] and The Sun Shines Bright [1953], I think
Wagonmaster came closest to being what I had wanted to achieve,"
he later said. The New York Times evaluated this picture as "under
Ford's leadership ... a trip well worth the taking."
        It is interesting to note, in passing, that Ward Bond would
achieve great fame later in the decade as the star of the long-running
teleseries, "Wagon Train," which was based on this film. Ford himself would direct an occasional episode of this Western video
program.

THE WALKING HILLS (Columbia, 1949) 78 min.

        Producer, Harry Joe Brown; associate producer, John Hag-
gott; director, John Sturges; screenplay, Alan LeMay; additional
dialogue, Virginia Roddick; art director, Robert Peterson; set

decorator, James Crowe; music, Arthur Morton; music director,
Morris Stoloff; costumes, Jean Louis; makeup, Dave Grayson; as-
sistant director, Sam Nelson; sound, Lodge Cunningham; camera,
Charles Lawton; editor, William Lyon.
    Randolph Scott (Jim Carey); Ella Raines (Chris Jackson);
William Bishop (Shep); Edgar Buchanan (Old Willy); Arthur Kennedy
(Chalk); John Ireland (Frazee); Jerome Courtland (Johnny); Josh
White (Josh); Russell Collins (Bibbs); Charles Stevens (Cleve);
Houseley Stevenson (King); Reed Howes (Young King).

    One of the more entertaining and unjustly neglected Westerns
of the Forties was this John Sturges-directed picture. A very compact story (seventy-eight minutes), it contained excellent performances, superb direction, and highly-atmospheric photography. Unfortunately, the film had a theme too similar to that of Warner
Bros.' The Treasure of Sierra Madre (1949) [q.v.] and was released
at about the same time as this Humphrey Bogart vehicle. Only years
later, when shown on TV, would the Sturges picture get just attention from viewers.
    The rather simple, but highly intriguing storyline has several
men (Scott, Bishop, Buchanan, Kennedy, Ireland, Courtland) and a
girl (Raines) searching for a wagon train full of gold buried years
before in the desert of Death Valley. Along with the search is interpolated the psychological backgrounds of the characters: Jim
Carey (Scott) as an escaped killer, Chalk (Kennedy) as a gold-hungry
man, and young Johnny (Courtland) who also has a criminal record.
Beautiful Chris Jackson (Raines) provides the passion necessary to
keep the plotline interesting while Edgar Buchanan as Old Willy offers the comedy relief. Only the inept acting of Courtland marred
this superior effort.

WANDERER OF THE WASTELAND (Paramount, 1924) C 5,775'

    Presenters, Adolph Zukor, Jesse L. Lasky; supervisor,
Lucien Hubbard; director, Irvin Willat; based on the novel by Zane
Grey; screenplay, George C. Hull, Victor Irvin; titles, Oscar C.
Buchheister; camera, Arthur Ball.
    Jack Holt (Adam Larey); Noah Beery (Dismukes); George
Irving (Mr. Virey); Kathlyn Williams (Magdalene Virey); Billie Dove
(Ruth Virey); James Mason (Guerd Larey); Richard R. Neill (Colli-
shaw); James Gordon (Alex MacKay); William Carroll (Merryvale);
Willard Cooley (Camp Doctor).

WANDERER OF THE WASTELAND (Paramount, 1935) 62 min.

    Producer, Harold Hurley; director, Otho Lovering; based on
the Zane Grey novel; screenplay, Stuart Anthony; camera, Ben
Reynolds; editor, Everett Douglass.
    Dean Jagger (Adam Larey); Gail Patrick (Ruth Virey); Ed-
ward Ellis (Dismukes); Benny Baker (Piano Player); Larry "Buster"

Crabbe (Big Ben); Trixie Friganza (Big Jo); Monte Blue (Guerd
Larey); Raymond Hatton (Merryval); Fuzzy Knight (Deputy Scott);
Charles Waldon, Sr. (Mr. Virey); Anna Q. Nilsson (Mrs. Virey);
Stanley Andrews (Sheriff Collinshaw); Pat O'Malley (Jed); Glenn
(Leif) Erickson (Lawrence); Jim Thorpe (Charlie Jim).

WANDERER OF THE WASTELAND[•] (RKO, 1945) 67 min.

Producer, Herman Scholm; directors, Edward Killy, Wallace
Grissell; based on the novel by Zane Grey; screenplay, Norman
Houston; art directors, Albert S. D'Agostino, Lucius Croxton; music
director, C. Bakaleinikoff; music, Paul Sawtell; camera, Harry J.
Wild; editor, J. B. Whittredge.

James Warren (Adam Larey); Audrey Long (Jean Collinshaw);
Richard Martin (Chito); Robert Barrat (Uncle Collinshaw); Robert
Clarke (Jay Collinshaw); Harry Woods (Guerd Eliott); Minerva Urecal
(Mama Rafferty); Henry D. Brown (Papa Rafferty); Tommy Cook
(Chito as a Boy); Harry McKim (Adam as a Boy); Jason Robards,
Sr. (Dealer).

The major importance of this Western, derived from Zane
Grey's 1923 novel, is that it was the first feature-length film to be
lensed entirely in the two-color Technicolor process.   Shot in six
weeks, the picture was a commercial hit.   Photoplay noted, "The
picture wins by sheer beauty, acting and directing."
The story concerns an old prospector (Beery) who saves a
young mining engineer (Holt).   The latter has shot his brother in an
argument and then was wounded by a sheriff while escaping.   Later,
Adam Larey (Holt) goes to his sweetheart (Dove) but her father (Irving) thinks his wife (Williams) has been unfaithful.   In his fury he
causes an avalanche that kills both him and his wife, leaving Magdalene (Williams) an orphan.   Adam later confesses to Magdalene what
he has done.   She urges him to submit to the law.   Thankfully,
Adam discovers that his brother was only injured in the scrape and
that he is now free to wed Magdalene.
After the coming of talkies, two rather mundane versions of
the novel were filmed.   A decade after the first release, Paramount
re-made the story as a black-and-white B Western under the direction of Otho Lovering.   Here Dean Jagger was the mining engineer
with Gail Patrick as the object of his affections.   Edward Ellis,
Benny Baker, and Buster Crabbe were co-starred.
In 1945, as part of its Zane Grey series, RKO made the third
picture version of the novel.   Starring James Warren and Audrey
Long it was an almost complete rewrite of the Grey story.

THE WAR WAGON (Universal, 1967) C 101 min.

Producer, Marvin Schwartz; director, Burt Kennedy; based on
the novel Badman by Clair Huffaker; screenplay, Huffaker; music,
Dimitri Tiomkin; song, Tiomkin and Ned Washington; art director,

John Wayne and Kirk Douglas in The War Wagon (1967).

Alfred Sweeney; assistant directors, Al Jennings, H. A. Silverman;
wardrobe, Robert Chiniquy, Donald Wolz; sound, Waldon O. Watson;
camera, William H. Clothier; editor, Harry Gerstad.

John Wayne (Taw Jackson); Kirk Douglas (Lomax); Howard
Keel (Levi Walking Bear); Robert Walker (Billy Hyatt); Keenan Wynn
(Wes Catlin); Bruce Cabot (Frank Pierce); Valora Noland (Kate);
Gene Evans (Hoag); Joanna Barnes (Lola); Bruce Dern (Hammond);
Terry Wilson (Strike); Don Collier (Shack); Sheb Wooley (Snyder);
Ann McCrea (Felicia); Emilio Fernandez (Calita); Frank McGrath
(Bartender); Chuck Roberson (Brown); Red Morgan (Early); Hal Need-
ham (Hite); Marco Antonio Arzate (Wild Horse); Perla Walter (Rosita).

"The War Wagon is a bit like the Western of old, with action
all the way. But there is a difference. Bruce Cabot is as unmitigated a villain as ever railroaded an innocent man to jail in order
to steal a goldmine, but he is a smiling villain, a friendly rattle-
snake. Indeed, the real villain of the piece is the menacing 'war
wagon' of the title, an early version of the armored car, complete
with revolving turret and Gatling gun" (Arthur Knight, Saturday Review).

Taw Jackson (Wayne) is released from jail on parole, having
been framed in the first place by Frank Pierce (Cabot), who stole
his gold-filled land. Taw seeks revenge on Pierce, planning to steal

Pierce's armor-plated war wagon which is due to carry a load of
gold dust worth a half million dollars. To help carry out this plan,
Taw gets the assistance of Lomax (Douglas), who used to work for
Pierce; Billy Hyatt (Walker), a drunken demolition specialist; Levi
Walking Bear (Keel), a renegade Indian; and Wes Catlin (Wynn), a
wagon driver. Pierce offers Lomax $12,000 to kill Taw, but the
gunman realizes he can make more profit from robbing the war
wagon. With the aid of the Kiowa Indians, Taw sets his plan in
motion. In the execution of the robbery, Pierce is shot dead by
Lomax and the gold dust is put into flour barrels in Catlin's wagon.
      Suddenly everything goes afoul; the Kiowas attack their co-
horts, kill Catlin and try to steal the gold. Even though the warring Indians are killed in a nitro explosion, others arrive on the
scene to collect the spillage from the wagon, thinking the contents
are much-needed flour. But Taw is not discouraged. He knows
that Lomax has hidden some gold dust and Taw intends to be on the
spot when Lomax claims it.
      "The good old-fashioned Western? The War Wagon is just
that. They're still making that kind of movie. What's new about
this one is, of course, that Burt Kennedy, who is a master of the
old West, has directed it with a certain amount of humor and some
old pros to back it" (Judith Crist, NBC-TV "Today Show").
      The War Wagon grossed some $6 million in U.S. and Cana-
dian distributors' rentals.

WARLOCK   (Twentieth Century-Fox, 1959) C 122 min.

      Producer-director, Edward Dmytryk; based on the novel by
Oakley Hall; screenplay, Robert Alan Arthur; music, Leigh Harline;
music director, Lionel Newman; orchestrator, Edward B. Powell;
color consultant, Leonard Doss; art directors, Lyle Wheeler, Herman
Blumenthal; set decorators, Walter M. Scott, Stuart A. Reiss; wardrobe designer, Charles LeMaire; makeup, Ben Nye; fire arms technical adviser, Rodd Redwing; assistant director, Stanley Hough; sound,
Alfred Bruzlin, Harry Leonard; special camera effects, L. B. Ab-
bott; camera, Joe MacDonald; editor, Jack W. Holmes.
      Richard Widmark (Johnny Gannon); Henry Fonda (Clay Blais-
dell); Anthony Quinn (Tom Morgan); Dorothy Malone (Lilly Dollar);
Dolores Michaels (Jessie Marlow); Wallace Ford (Judge Holloway);
Tom Drake (Abe McQuown); Richard Arlen (Bacon); DeForest Kelley
(Curley Burne); Regis Toomey (Skinner); Vaughn Taylor (Richardson);
Don Beddoe (Dr. Wagner); Whit Bissell (Mr. Petrix); J. Anthony
Hughes (Shaw); Donald "Red" Barry (Calhoun); Frank Gorshin (Billy
Cannon); Ian MacDonald (MacDonald); Robert Osterloh (Professor);
Mickey Simpson (Fitzsimmons); James Philbrook (Cade); Robert Adler
(Foss); Saul Gross (Bob Nicholson); Ann Doran (Mrs. Richardson);
Bartlett Robinson (Slavin).

      "Colorful and noisy Western.... It is beginning to look as if
a Western can't amount to very much these days unless it's in CinemaScope and color, runs for at least two hours, mixes three or four

Dorothy Malone, Anthony Quinn and Henry Fonda in Warlock (1959).

plots and subplots and has as many stars. That's how it is with
Warlock.... What's more, it's pretty exciting, once it gets all the
plots staked out and its several important characters distributed to
their proper sides" (New York Times).
        Marshal Clay Blaisdel (Fonda) is hired by the town of
Warlock in 1880 to bring order to the community and to prevent the
San Pablo cowboys from being so raucous when they hit down. Clay
is joined by club-footed gambler Tom Morgan (Quinn). After the
San Pablo group have been taken care of, one of their number,
Johnny Gannon (Widmark), volunteers to become Blaisdell's deputy.
Meanwhile Clay romances Jessie Marlow (Michaels), while Gannon
sees a good deal of Lilly Dollar (Malone), who is Morgan's previous mistress and who detests both Clay and Morgan for having
shot the man whom she intended to marry.
        When the big showdown comes with the San Pablo group,
angered Morgan prevents Blaisdell from dealing with them, which
means Gannon must confront them alone. Fortunately the male
citizens of Warlock support Johnny in this meeting. Later, in a
gunfight, Clay must kill Morgan, and then he is drawn into a duel
with Johnny. Clay refuses to shoot, throwing his weapons in the
street and riding off to his own destiny.
        As in The Rounders (1965) and Stranger on the Run (1967)
[q.v.], Henry Fonda demonstrates admirably how well suited he is

392   Waterhole

to the Western format. With his all-American demeanor, he is
capable of projecting any variation of the typical American person,
especially the frontiersman.

WATERHOLE #3   see SUPPORT YOUR LOCAL SHERIFF

WAY OUT WEST   (MGM, 1936)   65 min.

        Producer, Stan Laurel; director, James W. Horne; story,
Jack Jevne, Charles Rogers; screenplay, Rogers, Felix Adler,
James Parrott; music director, Marvin Hatley; camera, Art Lloyd,
Walter Lundin; editor, Bert Jordan.
        Stan Laurel (Himself); Oliver Hardy (Himself); James Finlay-
son (Mickey Finn); Sharon Lynne (Lola Marcel); Stanley Fields (The
Sheriff); Rosina Lawrence (Mary Roberts); James Mason (Anxious
Patron); James C. Morton, Frank Mills, Dave Pepper (Bartenders);
Vivien Oakland (Stagecoach Passenger/Molly the Sheriff's Wife);
Harry Bernard (Man Eating at Bar); Mary Gordon, May Wallace
(Cooks); Avalon Boys Quartet [Chill Wills, Art Green, Walter Trask,
Don Brookins] (Themselves); Jack Hill (Worker at Mickey Finn's
Palace); Sam Lufkin (Stagecoach Baggage Man); Tex Driscoll (Bearded
Miner); Flora Finch ("Maw"--a Miner's Wife); Fred "Snowflake"
Toones (Janitor); Bobby Dunn, John Ince, Fritzi Brunette, Frank
Montgomery, Fred Cady, Eddie Borden, Helen Holmes (Audience at
Saloon); Lester Dorr (Cowboy); Dinah (The Mule).

        Few Western spoofs have ever been as funny or as enduring
as Stan Laurel and Oliver Hardy's Way Out West. It was the
comedy champs' sole foray into the genre and it was far more successful than other movie lampoons by Buster Keaton, the Marx
Brothers, Abbott and Costello and others. William K. Everson
writes in The Films of Laurel and Hardy (1967), ''With the possible exception of Sons of the Desert, Way Out West must rank as
the best of all the Laurel & Hardy features ... [it] is 100-proof
undiluted Laurel & Hardy, and one of their best showcase vehicles.''
        Laurel and Hardy--playing themselves as only they could--
arrive in the frontier town of Brushwood Gulch, planning to hand
over the deed to a gold mine to their recently-deceased partner's
daughter (Lawrence). Crooked saloon proprietor Mickey Finn (Finlayson) soon finds out about the deed and has his comely partner Lola
Marcel (Lynne) pose as the inheritor. After giving the siren the
deed, the boys discover the real owner, who works as a maid for
Finn. Now the Easterners are determined to obtain the deed back
for the rightful owner. They fail and are booted out of town, but
the determined duo return at night, rummage through Finn's saloon
until the deed is discovered and they pass it on to the rightful
owner.
        Full of fine and well-developed comedy sequences (all within
a brief sixty-five minutes), the picture is a delight from start to

finish. Among the best scenes are those where Hardy falls into a
pot hole while he and Stan lead a mule across a river; when Hardy
attempts to instigate small talk with a woman stage passenger only
to discover she is the sheriff's wife when they reach town; and when
a free-for-all fight erupts between Finlayson and Lynne on one side
and Laurel and Hardy on the other. Laurel and Hardy also under-
take a brief tap-dance sequence in the picture and later they offer
a straightforward rendition of "In the Blue Ridge Mountains of Virginia," which highlights Oliver's fine baritone voice (and has Chill
Wills dubbing in the vocal tones of Stan).

Working titles for this joyous feature were Tonight's the Night
and In the Money. Marvin Hatley received an Academy Aware nomi-
nation for his music score to the picture.

THE WAY WEST (United Artists, 1967) C 122 min.

Producer, Harold Hecht; director, Andrew V. McLaglen;
based on the novel by A. B. Guthrie, Jr.; screenplay, Ben Maddow,
Mitch Lindemann; music, Bronislau Kaper; music director, Andre
Previn; song, Kaper and Mac David; art director, Ted Haworth; set
decorator, Robert Priestley; costumes, Norma Koch; makeup, Frank
McCoy; assistant directors, Terry Morse, Newt Arnold, Tim Znne-
mann; sound, Jack Solomon; special effects, Danny Hays; camera,
William H. Clothier; editor, Otho Lovering.

Kirk Douglas (Senator William J. Tadlock); Robert Mitchum
(Dick Summers); Richard Widmark (Life Evans); Lola Albright (Re-
becca Evans); Michael Witney (Johnnie Mack); Sally Field (Mercy
McBee); Katherine Justice (Amanda Mack); Stubby Kaye (Sam Fair-
man); William Lundigan (Michael Moynihan); Paul Lukather (Turley);
Roy Barcroft (Masters); Jack Elam (Weatherby); Patric Knowles
(Colonel Grant); Ken Murray (Hank); John Mitchum (Little Henry);
Nick Cravat (Calvelli); Harry Carey, Jr. (Mr. McBee); Roy Glenn
(Saunders); Michael McGreevey (Brownie Evans); Connie Sawyer
(Mrs. McBee); Anne Barton (Mrs. Moynihan); Eve McVeah (Mrs.
Masters); Peggy Stewart (Mrs. Turley); Stefan Arngrim (Tadlock,
Jr.); Hal Lynch (Big Henry); Timothy Scott (Middle Henry); Gary
Morris (Paw-Kee-Man); Eddie Little Sky, Michael Keep (Sioux
Braves); Clarke Gordon (Caleb Greenwood); Mitchell Schollars (In-
dian Boy); Jack Coffer, Everett Creach, Jim Burk, Gary McLarty
(Drovers); Paul Wexler (Barber).

With such a trio of masculine stars, this picture should have
been a big moneymaker. But Variety summed up the problem in
one word: "Dull." The film grossed only $1.67 million domesti-
cally.

Widowed Senator William J. Tadlock (Douglas) in the 1840s
plans a wagon trek to the northwest frontier. Among the pioneers
in his convoy are Dick Summers (Mitchum), an aging trail scout
who suffers from failing eyesight, Lije Evans (Widmark), a spirited
farmer, his spouse Rebecca (Albright) and their sixteen-year-old

Stubby Kaye, William Lundigan, Kirk Douglas and Harry Carey, Jr.
in The Way West (1967).

son (McGreevey). Also along for the ride are newlywed Johnnie and
Amanda Mack (Witney and Justice) and the sloppy McBee family.
En route, Johnnie shoots a Sioux chieftain's son, thinking the shad-
owy figure is a wolf. The Indians demand revenge and Tadlock
eventually must hang Johnnie. During a dangerous river crossing
Tadlock's son (Arngrim) is drowned. As misery piles up upon
misery the settlers contemplate changing course from Oregon to
California. But Tadlock maneuvers them northward. At the final
gorge before reaching their destination Tadlock is killed when the
crazed Amanda Mack cuts the rope to the leader's pulley contrap-
tion. After the funerals, the remaining wagon train folk embark
down the Columbia River. Dick Summers, his task complete,
watches them disappear into the distance.

     "It is hard to believe that anybody could have made such a
hackneyed hash of that fine A. B. Guthrie, Jr. novel.... Working
with history and folklore that should have inspired a great film--it
did in one called The Covered Wagon back in 1923--they have hacked
out a DeLuxe-colored fiction of a wagon-train trip to Oregon, which
is so stagy and unrealistic that it makes an old Western fan want to
scream. Not only are the incidents of conflict fashioned to the concepts and the patterns of television western serials, but they are
directed by Mr. McLaglen and played by his brightly costumed cast
in a style that almost brings into the picture the lights and cameras
and all the stuff of artifice" (New York Times).

WELCOME TO HARD TIMES   see   STRANGER ON THE RUN

WEST OF THE BADLANDS   see   THE BORDER LEGION (1940)

THE WESTERNER   (United Artists, 1940)   100 min.

   Producer, Samuel Goldwyn; director, William Wyler; story,
Stuart N. Lake; screenplay, Jo Swerling, Niven Busch; music, Dimi-
tri Tiomkin; assistant director, Walter Mayo; costumes, Irene Sal-
tern; art director, James Basevi; set decorator, Julia Heron; sound,
Fred Lau; camera, Gregg Toland, Archie Stout; editor, Daniel Man-
dell.
   Gary Cooper (Cole Hardin); Walter Brennan (Judge Roy Bean);
Doris Davenport (Jane-Ellen Mathews); Fred Stone (Caliphet Mathews);
Paul Hurst (Chickenfoot); Chill Wills (Southeast); Charles Halton (Mort
Borrow); Forrest Tucker (Wade Harper); Tom Tyler (King Evans);
Arthur Aylesworth (Mr. Dixton); Lupita Tovar (Teresita); Julian
Rivero (Juan Gomez); Lillian Bond (Lily Langtry); Dana Andrews
(Bart Cobble); Roger Gray (Eph Stringer); Jack Pennick (Bantry);
Trevor Bardette (Shad Wilkins); Bill Steele (Tex Cole); Blackjack
Ward (Buck Harrigan); James "Jim" Corey (Lee Webb); Buck Moulton
(Charles Evans); Ted Wells (Joe Lawrence); Joe De La Cruz (Mex);
Frank Cordell (Man); Captain C. E. Anderson (Hezekiah Willever);
Arthur "Art" Mix (Seth Tucker); Dan Borzage (Joe Yates); Helen
Foster (Janice); Charles Coleman (Langtry's Manager); Heinie Conklin

Gary Cooper, Doris Davenport and Walter Brennan in The Westerner
(1940).

(Man at Window); Lucien Littlefield (A Stranger); Stanley Andrews
(Sheriff); Hank Bell (Deputy).

The succeeding years have been good to this Samuel Goldwyn
production. It is still regarded as a genre classic, despite its dated
and mundane aspects. The pivotal presence of Gary Cooper's traditional strong, silent hero and Walter Brennan's amusingly vicious
performance as Judge Roy Bean (for which Brennan won his third
Academy Award) make this movie a joy to watch. Wyler might have
used to advantage more exteriors for outdoor scenes, rather than the
conventional soundstage artificial settings, but such criticism is
basically carping against a custom of that time.

Cole Hardin (Cooper), a drifter, is charged with horse stealing and is brought to the saloon court of Judge Roy Bean (Brennan),
the man who claims to be the only law "west of the Pecos." When
Cole learns that Bean is a staunch admirer of performer Lily Langtry (Bond), Hardin concocts a story and convinces the Judge that he
knows the actress quite well. The pleased judge has Cole freed so
that he will obtain a lock of her hair for Bean. Later Cole steals
the judge's gun and makes off in the night, continuing on to California. But he stops at the farm of Caliphet Mathews (Stone) and
the farmer's daughter Jane-Ellen (Davenport) convinces him to stay
there. Thereafter Cole and the judge maintain an uneasy truce;
later Bean's men are ravaging the countryside and in the scuffle
Mr. Mathews is killed. Cole tracks Bean to Fort Davis where the
judge has purchased all seats in the theatre that night in order to
enjoy a performance by Miss Lily. In one of the cinema's best-
remembered scenes, the curtain goes up that night to reveal Cole
onstage with both guns in firing position. In the shootout Bean is
fatally wounded. Before he dies, Cole leads the man to finally meet
Miss Lily.

When this film is compared to The Life and Times of Judge
Roy Bean (1972) [q.v.] with Paul Newman in the Brennan role, the
virtues of the earlier romantic and atmospheric product become obvious. This swank sagebrush tale was deliberately conceived as
more of a character study than just another action adventure.

Stuart N. Lake, for his original story, and James Basevi, for
his art direction, were both Oscar-nominated. This film also served
to introduce Forrest Tucker and Dana Andrews to films, both rather
impressive as hot-headed farm youths.

WESTWARD THE WOMEN (MGM, 1952) 118 min.

Producer, Dore Schary; director, William A. Wellman; story,
Frank Capra; screenplay, Charles Schnee; music, Jeff Alexander;
art directors, Cedric Gibbons, Daniel B. Cathcart; camera, William
Mellor; editor, James E. Newcom.

Robert Taylor (Buck); Denise Darcel (Danon); Henry Nakamura
(Ito); Lenore Lonergan (Maggie); Marilyn Erskine (Jean); Hope Emer-
son (Patience); Julie Bishop (Laurie); John McIntire (Roy Whitman);
Renata Vanni (Mrs. Maroni); Beverly Dennis (Rose).

Because of the paucity of plot director William A. Wellman
was forced to instill this "different" Western with plenty of action
and offbeat situations to hold audience interest. As a whole he did
not succeed, although he did turn out an interesting hybrid of the
genre which was "blithely uneven, part western, part weeper and
part burlesque" (New York Times).

Robert Taylor starred as Buck the wagonmaster who leads a
convoy of females to nineteenth-century California to meet their mail-
order husbands. Along the rugged way they fight Indians, skin wagon
horses, have babies, and rile Buck. On the whole, the women prove
admirably that they can do whatever men have accomplished in the
field of pioneering. Of the distaff supporting cast, Denise Darcel
(Danon) was excellent as the fiery French girl, while Amazon-like
Hope Emerson (who would later be featured in The Guns of Fort Petticoat (1957) in which Audie Murphy and a group of women protect
their lives against marauding Indians), Lenore Lonergan, and Henry
Nakamura (as the Japanese cook) supplied the laughs.   •

Of special note is the fact that the scenario is based on a
story by veteran director Frank Capra.

Television picked up on the Westward the Women concept some
two decades later when, in 1970, ABC-TV offered the video feature,
Wild Women. This time, though, the girls in question were jail in-
mates used as "brides" for men mapping out trails in Texas in the
1840s.

WHILE SATAN SLEEPS (Paramount, 1922) 6,089'

Presenter, Jesse L. Lasky; director, Joseph Henabery; based
on the story "The Parson of Panamint" by Peter B. Kyne; screenplay, Albert S. Le Vino; camera, Faxon M. Dean.

Jack Holt (Phil); Wade Boteler (Red Barton); Mabel Van Buren
(Sunflower Sadie); Fritzi Brunette (Salome Deming); Will R. Walling
(Bud Dening); J. P. Lockney (Chuckkawalla Bill); Fred Huntley (Ab-
solum Randall); Bobby Mack (Bones); Sylvia Ashton (Mrs. Bones);
Herbert Standing (Bishop).

See THE PARSON OF PANAMINT

WHITE EAGLE see THE RED RIDER

WHITE GOLD (Producers Distributing Corp., 1927) 6,108'

Supervisor, C. Gardner Sullivan; director, William K. Howard;
based on the play by J. Palmer Parsons; adaptors, Garrett Fort,
Marion Orth, Tay Garnett; art director, Anton Grot; camera, Lucien
Andriot; editor, Jack Dennis.

Jetta Goudal (Dolores Carson); Kenneth Thomson (Alec Carson);
George Bancroft (Sam Randall); George Nichols (Carson--Abe's
Father); Robert Perry (Bucky O'Neill); Clyde Cook (Homer).

One of the so-called lost classics of the cinema (only a few

prints remain and no negative supposedly survives), this film is no
longer in public circulation.   Based on J. Palmer Parsons' 1925
play, the feature was made for Cecil B. DeMille's production unit.
Despite some fine reviews (Harrison's Reports stated, "Deeper psychology is revealed in this film than in in any other ever produced
in America"), the film was a commercial failure.
        The picture's title refers to wool, and its plot concerns a
Mexican dancer Dolores Carson (Goudal) who marries a sheep
rancher named Alec Carson (Thomas) and goes to live on his remote ranch.   Alec's father (Nichols) distrusts the girl and tries to
draw his son away from her.   When a ranch hand named Sam Randall (Bancroft) is hired the situation becomes more tense.   The girl
and her spouse quarrel.   One night while the angered Alec is sleeping in the bunkhouse, Sam comes to see Dolores, and the next
morning Carson claims that he caught them together.   In a scuffle,
Sam is killed.   Dolores refuses to dignify the situation with an ex-
planation of•her activities and she throws away the gun with which
Sam was killed.   Because her husband fails to believe in her, she
leaves the ranch.
        When he died in 1954 director Howard already had made a
revised script of White Gold, hoping to cast Charles Laughton in the
lead.   Sadly the project never materialized.   Despite the financial
failure of the silent film, it proved to have a great artistic influence
on several subsequent entries, including The Wind (1928) [q.v.] and
the recent Zandy's Bride (1974).

THE WHITE MAN   see   THE SQUAW MAN (1931)

WILD BILL HICKOK   (Paramount, 1923)   6,8923'

        Presenter, Adolph Zukor; producer, William S. Hart; di-
rector, Clifford S. Smith; story, Hart; screenplay, J. G. Hawk;
camera, Dwight Warren, Arthur Reeves.
        William S. Hart (Wild Bill Hickok); Ethel Grey Terry (Ca-
lamity Jane); Kathleen O'Connor (Elaine Hamilton); James Farley
(Jack McQueen); Jack Gardner (Bat Masterson); Carl Gerard (Clayton Hamilton); William Dyer (Colonel Horatio Higginbotham); Bert
Sprotte (Bob Wright); Leo Willis (Joe McCord); Naida Carle (Fanny
Kate); Herschel Mayall (Gambler).

        In the preface to this silent feature, star and story writer
William S. Hart apologized to the audience for not looking more
like the real Hickok.   Despite the physical disparity, the film turned
out to be a rather faithful biography of the well-known lawman/Indian
fighter/Wild West Show star.
        Set after the Civil War, the film has gunfighter Hickok (Hart)
heading for Dodge City where he becomes a gambler but does agree
to fight lawlessness in the community.   An outlaw leader, Jack Mc-
Queen (Farley), escapes from jail and Hickok must hunt him down.
In the showdown McQueen is killed.   Later, when Bill finds himself

falling in love with a married woman, he leaves town rather than cause a scandal. In the supporting cast were Ethel Grey Terry as Calamity Jane and Jack Gardner as Bat Masterson.

Photoplay noted of this film that it was "a picture filled with gunplay and other stunts his [Hart] admirers like."

Over the years, the role of Wild Bill Hickok would be played oncamera by such actors as Gary Cooper (The Plainsman, 1937), Gordon Elliott (The Great Adventures of Wild Bill Hickok, 1938), Richard Dix (Badlands of Dakota, 1941), Howard Keel (Calamity Jane, 1953), Don Murray (The Plainsman, 1966) and on the fifties' teleseries by Guy Madison.

THE WILD BUNCH (Warner Bros.-Seven Arts, 1969) C 140 min.

Producer, Phil Feldman; associate producer, Roy N. Sickner; director, Sam Peckinpah; story, Walon Green, Sickner; screenplay, Green, Peckinpah; art director, Edward Carrere; assistant directors, Cliff Coleman, Fred Gammon; music, Jerry Fielding; music supervisor, Johnny Burke; wardrobe, Gordon Dawson; makeup, Al Greenway; sound, Robert J. Miller; special effects, Bud Hulburd; camera, Lucien Ballard; editor, Louis Lombardo.

William Holden (Pike Bishop); Ernest Borgnine (Dutch Engstrom); Robert Ryan (Deke Thornton); Edmond O'Brien (Sykes); Warren Oates (Lyle Gorch); Jaime Sanchez (Angel); Ben Johnson (Tector Gorch); Emilio Fernandez (Mapache); Strother Martin (Coffer); L. Q. Jones (I. C.); Albert Dekker (Pat Harrigan); Bo Hopkins (Crazy Lee); Dub Taylor (Mayor Wainscoat); Jorge Russek (Lieutenant Zamorra); Alfonso Arau (Herrera); Aurora Clavel (Aurora); Elsa Cardenas (Elsa); Fernando Wagner (German Army Officer); Paul Harper, Constance White, Lilia Richards (Bits).

Not since Bonnie and Clyde (1967) had there been such tumultuous dissension among the critics about a motion picture. Once again the argument was the same: was the abundant violence in this film gratuitous or integral to the storyline. Also, just as director Sam Peckinpah had such difficulties with his earlier Major Dundee (1965) [q.v.], so here his film (originally some 190 minutes) was chopped down more and more after each press showing.

By 1913 the old style outlaw gangs are becoming a thing of the past. However, aging Pike Bishop (Holden) and his band of desperadoes ride into the Texas border town of San Rafael to rob the railway office. Although they have dressed like U.S. Cavalry men, Deke Thornton's (Ryan) mercenaries are waiting for Bishop's crew. A group of temperance workers are caught in the crossfire leading to a massacre. Bishop's gang escapes into Mexico while the bounty hunters drop their pursuit in order to pilfer loot from the corpses. Only when he stops to meet an old confederate, Sykes (O'Brien), does Bishop realize that the money bag does not contain gold, but iron washers. Later on Bishop encounters Pancho Villa's vicious opponent, General Mapache (Fernandez), and is forced to agree to have his wild bunch rob an army gun supply train and sell

its contents to the bandits for a mere $10,000. Fearing a double-
cross, Bishop has each of his men arrive in town with only part of
the rifle supply, each in turn accepting a portion of the fee in exchange for the delivery. Angel (Sanchez), the last to make the
delivery is held captive by Mapache's men.

Because Bishop's men have nothing left but their pride and
loyalty, they decide to fight for Angel's release. But Mapache slits
the boy's throat. Bishop then kills the bandit leader and in the ensuing melee some 200 Mexicans are slaughtered as well as Bishop
and his men. Thornton and his crew arrive to collect the corpses
for the bounty, but Sykes and the people of Angel's village ambush
them. At the finale, Sykes and Thornton, who now have the gold,
decide to join forces. Thornton sighs, "It ain't like it used to be,
but it's better 'n nothin'."

There was no dispute over Joseph Gelmis's (Newsday) words
when he wrote, "The Wild Bunch is the bloodiest movie I've ever
seen, maybe the bloodiest ever made." For one reason or another,
the film appealed to the public and the film grossed some $5.25
million domestically.

Arthur Knight tried to arbitrate the controversy over this
blood and gore entry. He wrote in the Saturday Review, "There
are, at the very least, two ways of looking at violence. On the one
hand, there is shock. Someone does something horrible to some-
body else--stabs, mutilates, shoots in cold blood--and the immediate
instinct is to protest, especially if it happens in a movie.... The
other approach is to recognize that violence lies all about us and go
to such extremes in depicting it that the viewer is ultimately re-
volted and turns against it in any manifestation.... I would prefer
to believe that Sam Peckinpah was sincere when he stated that he
wanted to make a picture so strong, so stomach-churning, so detailed in its catalogue of horrors that all the glamour, all the attraction of violence for its own sake would promptly disappear. I think
he is wrong, but I very much doubt that anyone who was not totally
honest in his wrongheadness could ever come up with a picture as
wholly revolting as this.... Every member of The Wild Bunch is
so thoroughly hateful and corrupt as to richly deserve the fate that
Peckinpah has in store for him--but I suspect that Peckinpah feels
that so does all mankind."

Then there were critics like Andrew Sarris (Village Voice)
who thrust the main controversy aside to peck at the structure of
Peckinpah's project. "Even in its currently mutilated version ...
[it] is too long, the plot too lumpy, the acting wildly uneven, and
the continuity too often suspended for effects of pretty pictorialism.
The director is apparently unable to do more than one thing at a
time within a single shot. Hence, the film lurches wastefully back
and forth between brutal realism and sentimental liberalism. The
editing, crudely old-fashioned much of the time, seldom misses an
opportunity to cop out on a cynical action shot of one character with
a remorseful reaction shot of another." Then Sarris adds a bouquet
of praise, "Still and all, The Wild Bunch is one of the few American
films of recent memory that doesn't seem to have been concocted by
a market research computer."

Director Peckinpah would continue to make violence a paying proposition, as in the British-shot Straw Dogs (1971) or the Hollywood venture The Getaway (1972) with Steve McQueen. Each of these was a tremendous moneymaker. Far less successful were his subsequent Westerns, including The Ballad of Cable Hogue (1970), Junior Bonner (1972) [q.v.], Pat Garrett and Billy the Kid (1973) [q.v.], or the contemporary Western-bloodshed tale, Bring Me the Head of Alfredo Garcia (1974). Star Holden would find a new box-office trend to follow after The Wild Bunch, appearing in the carbon copy, but financial turkey, The Revengers (1972), and the present day bloodshed-masochism/sadism tale, Open Season (1974).

Regardless of the bloodshed there were definite champions of The Wild Bunch among the fourth estate. Time listed it "one of the year's best," and the New York Times acknowledged it was "a fascinating movie." The Los Angeles Herald-Examiner declared it "an extraordinary accomplishment ... a highly personal vision of what man is and how he relates to his world."

WILD WOMEN see WESTWARD THE WOMEN

DER WILDTOTER see LAST OF THE MOHICANS

WILL PENNY (Paramount, 1968) C 108 min.

Producers, Fred Engel, Walter Seltzer; director-screenplay, Tom Gries; music, David Raksin; song, Raksin and Robert Wells; art directors, Hal Pereira, Roland Anderson; set decorators, Robert Benton, Ray Moyer; costumes, John Anderson, Ruth Stella; makeup, Wally Westmore; assistant director, Daniel J. McCauley; sound, John Carter, John Wilkinson; special camera effects, Paul K. Lerpae; camera, Lucien Ballard; editor, Warren Low.

Charlton Heston (Will Penny); Joan Hackett (Catherine Allen); Donald Pleasence (Preacher Quint); Lee Majors (Blue); Bruce Dern (Rafe Quint); Ben Johnson (Alex); Slim Pickens (Ike Wallerstein); Clifton James (Catron); Anthony Zerbe (Dutchy); Jon Francis (Horace Greeley Allen); Roy Jenson (Boetius Sullivan); G. D. Spradlin (Anse Howard); Quentin Dean (Jennie); William Schallert (Dr. Fraker); Dal Jenkins (Sambo); Luke Askew (Foxy); Anthony Costello (Bigfoot); Chanin Hale (Girl); Gene Rutherford (Rufus Quint).

It is discouraging for both the makers and the industry as a whole when a well-tooled project such as Will Penny fails to capture the public's fancy. Such a failure convinces other producers to abandon uncompromising projects and stick to tried-and-true commercial ventures.

The reviewers felt this entry was praiseworthy. "... [It] has all the potentials of being a really good and different Western because for once we see the life of the cowboy as I suspect it was lived, in the cold and solitude and dreariness of it, in the simple-minded

boringness of driving a herd or of riding the line in the winter to
keep the cattle on the range.   And it has another unusual feature,
an unhappy and valid ending, true to the character and to life rather
than to the myth of the West.   Unfortunately plot mechanics turn the
film into a very run-of-the-mill Western for a long stretch of the
story, with once again the emphasis on coincidence and, alas, on
sadism....   A pity this, because there is so very much of quality
(in scene and atmosphere and Charlton Heston's excellent characterization) that is vitiated thereby--albeit not, fortunately, in its en-
tirety" (Judity Crist, NBC-TV "Today Show").

At the end of an arduous cattle drive in 1880s Montana middle-
aged cowpuncher Will Penny (Heston) joins with Blue (Major) and
Dutchy (Zerbe) in seeking winter employment.   While out hunting,
the trio are attacked by the crazy Preacher Quint (Pleasence) and his
three sons.   In the encounter Will kills one of the men.   Quint and
his other sons, Rufe (Dern) and Rufus (Rutherford), swear revenge.
Penny later gets a job and goes to the mountain cabin which he is to
make his headquarters for the winter.   There he meets Catherine
Allen (Hackett) and her son Horace (Francis) who are joining her
husband in California.   Will is later ambushed by Quint and it is
Catherine who nurses him back to health.   During the coming days
a bond grows between the two adults.   But Quint and his sons attack
and capture Will; they threaten to assault Catherine sexually.   Will
escapes and with Blue and Dutchy kills Quint and wounds his sons.

By this point Catherine would like to settle down and farm
with Will, but he tells her, "I don't have them years no more ...
as for farmin', I'm a cowboy.   I been one all my life."   He rides
off with Blue and Dutchy looking for a new job.

Will Penny, one of Tom Gries' finest screen efforts, only
grossed $1.3 million domestically, barely enough to pay back pro-
duction costs.

WINCHESTER '73 (Universal, 1950) C 92 min.

Producer, Aaron Rosenberg; director, Anthony Mann; based
on the story by Stuart N. Lake; screenplay, Robert L. Richards,
Borden Chase; art directors, Bernard Herzbrun, Nathan Juran; music
director, Joseph Gershenson; camera, William Daniels; editor, Edward Curtiss.

James Stewart (Lin McAdam); Shelley Winters (Lola Manners);
Dan Duryea (Waco Johnny Dean); Stephen McNally (Dutch Henry
Brown); Millard Mitchell (High Spade); Charles Drake (Steve Miller);
John McIntire (Joe Lamont); Will Geer (Wyatt Earp); Jay C. Flippen
(Sergeant Wilkes); Rock Hudson (Young Bull); John Alexander (Jack
Riker); Steve Brodie (Wesley); James Millican (Wheeler); Abner Biber-
man (Latigo Means); Tony Curtis (Doan); James Best (Crater); Gregg
Martell (Mossman); Frank Chase (Cavalryman); Chuck Roberson (Long
Tom); Carol Henry (Dudeen); Ray Teal (Marshal Noonan); John Dou-
cette (Roan Daley); Chief Yowlachie (Indian); Edmund Cobb (Target
Watcher); Ethan Laidlaw (Station Master); Jennings Miles (Stagecoach
Driver).

WINCHESTER '73   (NBC-TV, 1967)   C   97 min.

Producer, Richard E. Lyons; director, Herschel Daugherty; based on the story by Stuart N. Lake; teleplay, Stephen Kandel, Richard L. Adams; based on the screenplay by Borden Chase, Robert L. Richards; music, Sol Kaplan; art director, Frank Arrigo; camera, Bud Thackery; editor, Richard G. Wray.

Tom Tryon (Lin McAdam); John Saxon (Dakin McAdam); Dan Duryea (Bart McAdam); John Drew Barrymore (The Preacher); Joan Blondell (Larouge); John Dehner (High-Spade); Barbara Luna (Meriden); and: John Doucette, David Pritchard, Paul Fix, John Hoyt, Jack Lambert, Jan Arvan, Robert Bice, Ned Romero, George Keymas.

In this intriguing, if episodic, outdoors tale James Stewart joined forces with director Anthony Mann and worked for a percentage basis salary rather than taking the customary flat fee. It was a practice that would become commonplace in another two decades. The film also launched Stewart's Western career, picking up where he had left off with Destry Rides Again (1939) [q.v.].

Lin McAdam (Stewart) and High Spade (Mitchell) ride into Dodge City in 1873 looking for the killer of McAdam's father. In a marksmanship contest, Lin wins a Winchester '73 repeating rifle and in doing so defeats Dutch Henry Brown (McNally), the actual killer of his father. Dutch later steals the unique gun and leaves Dodge

Dan Duryea and James Stewart in Winchester '73 (1950).

City, but he loses the weapon to an Indian trader (McIntire) in a
card game.   The trader in turn is killed by Indians who take the
gun, but they lose it in an attack on a cavalry detachment.   A
coward, Steve Miller (Drake), then obtains the firearm but is killed
by a notorious highwayman, Waco Johnny Dean (Duryea), who gives
the gun back to Dutch.   McAdam and High Spade are still on the
trail of the killer and the gun thief.   Eventually Lin corners Dutch
on a mountain top and kills him in a gun fight.   Having avenged his
father's murder, he retrieves the gun, and can make peace with the
world.
        Using a gimmick already worked in such films as Tales of
Manhattan (1942)--tracing the history of change of ownership of some
physical item--Winchester '73 proved to be a rousing adventure
story, never focusing too long on any one set of characters or situations.   In her pre-dramatic, blowsy period, Shelley Winters made a
fetching Lola Manners.
        On March 14, 1967, NBC-TV presented a jumbled re-make
of the property as the final telefeature of their 1966-67 video season.
A mediocre production (especially in comparison to the original), it
told of a hateful prisoner (Saxon) who returns home and steals the
rifle from his sheriff brother (Tryon), and of the latter's struggle
to regain the valued weapon.   Of passing interest was the casting of
Dan Duryea, from the 1950 version, as a friend of the hero, and
Joan Blondell as a boisterous saloon keeper.   Judith Crist summed
up this entry in TV Guide: "It's run-of-the-mill."

THE WIND   (MGM, 1928)   6,721'

        Director, Victor Seastrom; based on the book by Dorothy
Scarborough; screenplay, Frances Marion; titles, John Colton; set
designers, Cedric Gibbons, Edward Withers; theme song, Herman
Ruby, William Axt, Dave Dreyer, and David Mendoza; assistant di-
rector, Harold S. Bucquet; costumes, Andre-ani; camera, John
Arnold; editor, Conrad Nervig.
        Lillian Gish (Letty); Lars Hanson (Lige); Montagu Love
(Roddy); Dorothy Cumming (Cora); Edward Earle (Beverly); William
Orlamond (Sourdough); Laon Ramon [Leon Janney], Carmencita John-
son, Billy Kent Schaefer (Cora's Children).

        Although 1927's White Gold [q.v.] was not a successful film
it did greatly influence the genre.   Because of it star Lillian Gish
insisted that Dorothy Scarborough's book The Wind be bought as a
vehicle for her.   In this project, Miss Gish worked with two of the
top artists from Sweden, director Victor Seastrom and co-star Lars
Hanson.
        The film detailed the story of a well-bred Southern girl
(Gish) who travels to Texas.   In the course of her journey she is
molested by a man she later murders.   Then she marries Lige
(Hanson), a cowboy, and moves with him to the lonely desert.   The
pressure of the ambience, especially the incessant, blowing wind,
slowly drives her mad.

With very realistic photography, the film was shot on location in the Mojave Desert. Exhibitors were distressed by the film's
downbeat ending--the girl being lost in a sandstorm--and insisted
that the ending be junked. The studio shot a new finale in which
Letty (Gish) and Lige are reconciled. As added inducement to the
public, sound effects and talking sequences were employed. Photoplay rated this low-keyed offering "a fine and impressive drama."

WINDS OF THE WASTELAND (Republic, 1936) 53 min.

Producer, Nat Levine; supervisor, Paul Malvern; director,
Mack V. Wright; story/screenplay, Joseph Poland; music super-
visor, Harry Grey; camera, William Nobles; editors, Murray Sel-
deen, Robert Jahne.
John Wayne (John Blair); Phyllis Fraser (Barbara); Yakima
Canutt (Smoky); Douglas Cosgrove (Drake); Lane Chandler (Larry);
Sam Flint (Dr. Forsythe); Lew Kelly (Rocky); Bob Kortman (Chero-
kee); Ed Cassidy (Dodge); W. Merrill McCormick (Pete); Bud Mc-
Clure, Jack Ingram (Guards); Charles Locher [Jon Hall] (Pete); Joe
Yrigoyen (Pike); Chris Franke (Grahame).

In the late thirties, Republic Pictures began to earn its reputation for turning out the best over-all action films in Hollywood.
This little gem from that studio helped to consolidate that reputation
as well as advance the career of John Wayne.
The storyline concerns the transitional period in America in
which mail delivery was moving away from the pony express to
stagecoaches. It features Wayne and his buddy (Chandler) purchasing
a broken down stagecoach and repairing it to enter in a race with a
rival stageline. The prize was a $25,000 government mail contract.
Despite the villains trying to stop them, the duo win the contest to
Sacramento and now can establish their business on a solid footing.
Winds of the Wasteland is one of the best of Wayne's earlier
Westerns, what with its sense of the flavor of the Old West and the
engaging stagecoach race which should please any action fan.

WINNERS OF THE WEST (Universal, 1921) eighteen chapters

Director, Edward Laemmle; screenplay, Ford Beebe, Robert
Dillon.
Art Acord (Arthur Standish); Percy Pembroke (Louis Blair);
Jim Corey (Squire Blair); Burt Wilson (Dr. Edwards); Myrtle Lind
(Elizabeth Edwards); Burton C. Law (Captain John C. Fremont).
Chapters: 1) Power of Gold; 2) Blazing Arrow; 3) Perils of
the Plains; 4) The Flame of Hate; 5) The Fight for a Fortune; 6)
Buried Alive; 7) Fires of Fury; 8) Pit of Doom; 9) Chasm of Peril;
10) Sands of Fear; 11) Poisoned Pool; 12) Duel in the Night; 13)
Web of Fate; 14) Trail of Mystery; 15) Unmasked; 16) Hidden Gold;
17) Cave of Terror; 18) The End of the Trail.

Screen lead Art Acord died under mysterious circumstances

in 1931. But during the Twenties he was a top serial star and one
of Universal's most popular players. This eighteen-chapter cliffhanger, written by Ford Beebe and Robert Dillon, presents Acord
as a hunter and trapper who is part of Captain John C. Fremont's
(Law) attempt to take California for the U.S. from Mexico. Afterward Acord takes part in the huge 1849 gold rush and comes across
an old map detailing a lost case of gold belonging to Sir Frances
Drake. Villains pilfer the map from Acord and, in trying to relo-
cate it, he finds love with heroine Myrtle Lind. Eventually he retrieves the map and obtains the treasure.

This film was one of a number of historical adventures
translated into the serial format and issued by Universal during the
Roaring Twenties. Winners of the West covered the period from the
mid-1840s to San Francisco in the pre-Civil War era. One theatre
owner, however, complained that the chapterplay had "too much
history and not enough thrills."

On the other hand, Jessie Robb in Moving Picture World reported, "Great care has been taken to make the picture historically
accurate in costumes, sets, manners and the smallest details.
There is plenty of action extremely well directed. The cast has
been selected not only to look but to act the strenuous life of the
hardy pioneers. Excellent photography."

WINNERS OF THE WILDERNESS (MGM, 1927) 68 min.

Executive producer, Irving Thalberg; director, W. S. Van
Dyke II; story, John Thomas Neville; continuity, Josephine Chippo;
titles, Marion Ainslee; settings, David Townsend; wardrobe, Lucia
Coulter; camera, Clyde De Vinna; editor, Conrad A. Nervig.

Colonel Tim McCoy (Colonel Sir Dennis O'Hara); Joan Craw-
ford (Renee Contracouer); Edward Connelly (General Contrecoeur);
Roy D'Arcy (Captain Dumas); Louise Lorraine (Mimi); Edward Hearn
(George Washington); Tom O'Brien (Timothy); Will R. Walling
(General Edward Braddock); Frank Currier (Governor de Vaudreuil);
Lionel Belmore (Governor Dinwiddie); Chief Big Tree (Pontiac); Jean
Arthur (Woman).

Among the best historical Westerns ever made was the celluloid series turned out by MGM in the late Twenties with Colonel Tim
McCoy. These features had excellent historical flavor as well as
possessing literate scripts, sensible performers, tight direction, and
decent production budgets. With the coming of talkies, the studio
was forced to cut back on some types of features, and these McCoy
Westerns were dropped. Sadly, no other studio would ever capture
the same fine standards in the sound era.

Winners of the Wilderness was the second of sixteen Westerns
in which McCoy performed for Metro between 1926 and 1929, and it
is set in the pre-Revolutionary period with McCoy cast as Sir Dennis
O'Hara, an Irish officer in the British army who sets out for the
Ohio Valley to spy on the French. Dressed in a mask and cape he
steals a treaty that the French and the Indian Chief Pontiac (repre-
senting his six nations of braves) are about to sign. Upon being

chased, O'Hara ends up in the bedroom of Renee Contrecouer (Crawford) whose father (Connelly) is a turncoat.   Later O'Hara fights
Pontiac (Chief Big Tree) in the forest and wins the encounter.   At
a ball given by the French the gallant officer wins the affection of
Renee.   However, trouble seems to plague O'Hara and he soon finds
himself challenged to a duel by Gallic officer Captain Dumas (D'Arcy),
an event which never occurs.

    Next in the chronicle occurs the defeat of General Braddock's
forces by the French and Indians, with Dumas turning the captured
O'Hara over to the Indians despite Renee's entreaties.   O'Hara is
sentenced to die, but Chief Pontiac spares his life because O'Hara
had shown his courage in the encounter with the Indian leader.   In
a subsequent sword fight, O'Hara vanquishes Dumas and carries off
Renee to the British camp where they are wed.   All this action is
encompassed within a brief sixty-eight minutes!

    In retrospect, Jon Tuska in Views & Reviews (Vol. 3 No. 2,
1971) calls the film '[McCoy's] finest silent film, and, in fact, perhaps the finest film he ever made ... a powerful, compelling drama,
with brilliant direction, and superb dramatic interplay between Tim
McCoy and Joan Crawford.'' It would be another seventeen years
before Miss Crawford would really shine in the genre, as the exotic
star of Johnny Guitar (1954) [q.v.].

THE WINNING OF BARBARA WORTH (United Artists, 1926) 8,757'

    Presenter, Samuel Goldwyn; director, Henry King; based on
the novel by Harold Bell Wright; adaptor, Frances Marion; art director, Karl Oscar Borg; camera, George Barnes.
    Ronald Colman (Willard Holmes); Vilma Banky (Barbara
Worth); Charles Lane (Jefferson Worth); Paul McAllister (The Seer);

Clyde Cook, Ronald Colman and Gary Cooper in The Winning of
Barbara Worth (1926).

E. J. Ratcliffe (James Greenfield); Gary Cooper (Abe Lee); Clyde
Cook (Tex); Erwin Connelly (Pat); Sam Blum (Blanton).

This offering is probably best remembered today for the fact
that it gave Gary Cooper his first memorable cinema role. Actually
the picture has some other memorable credits as well. As a Samuel
Goldwyn production, directed by Henry King, it was written for the
screen by the inestimable Frances Marion and adapted from Harold
Bell Wright's enduringly popular 1911 novel. (The film did not follow the book plot very closely--nothing new for Hollywood.)
Ronald Colman stars as an engineer who is in charge of a
Southwest project in which arid wasteland will be made fertile
through an enormous irrigation plan. One of his underlings, Abe
Lee (Cooper), finds a fault in the dam but no one believes him.
Local financier, James Greenfield (Ratcliffe) tries to break up Willard Holmes' (Colman) romance with Barbara Worth (Banky), who
is the daughter of the owner (Lane) of the land under reconstruction.
Lee manages to warn Holmes before the dam bursts, but he is killed
in the process. Quick-witted Holmes saves the situation and eventually wins Barbara's hand in marriage.
The New York Herald-Tribune noted of this prestigious production, "At times annoying, but at other times it has moments of
real beauty," while Picture Play decided, "There is too little as it
is to have enlisted the fine skill of Henry King and the talents of
Vilma Banky and Ronald Colman. They are all out of their element." Nevertheless the public--thanks greatly to Goldwyn's typically saturation publicity campaign--was eager to see another entry
in the Colman-Banky love team performances and flocked to this
venture. The film's success proved that the sagebrush tale could
be adapted to the mass market love story motif, given the right
circumstances, director, star and producer.

WYOMING OUTLAW (Republic, 1939) 62 min.

Producer, William Berke; director, George Sherman; based
on characters created by William Colt MacDonald; story, Jack Nat-
teford; screenplay, Betty Burbridge, Natteford; music, William Lava;
camera, Reggie Lanning; editor, Tony Martinelli.
John Wayne (Stony Brooke); Ray Corrigan (Tucson Smith);
Raymond Hatton (Rusty Joslin); Donald "Red" Barry (Will Parker);
Adele Pearce [Pamela Blake] (Irene Parker); LeRoy Mason (Balsin-
ger); Charles Middleton (Luke Parker); Katherine Kenworthy (Mrs.
Parker); Elmo Lincoln (U.S. Marshal); Jack Ingram (Sheriff); Dave
Sharpe (Newt); Jack Kenney (Amos); Yakima Canutt (Ed Sims).

This entry in The Three Mesquiteers series was based on
an actual incident about a small town waiter who kills a bandit who
had been terrorizing the territory. This version has the Mesquiteers (Wayne, Corrigan, Hatton) fighting against a dishonest politician who has been selling work jobs to poor ranchers. A subplot
has Will Parker (Barry) as a young man drawn into crime for

self-protection. As a hounded criminal he meets his demise in the
mountains, a scene similar to the classic one employed later in
High Sierra (1941).
     Wyoming Outlaw was one of the most austere of the Mesqui-
teer series. Above all, it launched the career of Donald Barry.
Soon Republic would have him playing the lead in the serial Adven-
tures of Red Ryder (1939) [q.v.], and from there he became a top
Western and dramatic star for the studio. The leading lady of this
film, Adele Pearce, later adopted the professional name of Pamęla
Blake and became a leading serial heroine. Playing a supporting
role in this feature was Elmo Lincoln, the screen's first Tarzan.
Also on hand in Wyoming Outlaw were Yakima Canutt and David
Sharpe, two of the studio's top stunt men.

YELLOW SKY   (Twentieth Century-Fox, 1948) 98 min.

     Producer, Lamar Trotti; director, William A. Wellman;
based on the novel by W. R. Burnett; screenplay, Trotti; art directors, Lyle Wheeler, Albert Hogsett; set decorators, Thomas
Little, Ernest Lansing; music, Alfred Newman; orchestrator, Ed-
ward Powell; assistant director, William Eckhardt; makeup, Ben
Nye; sound, Bernard Fredricks, Harry M. Leonard; special effects,
Fred Sersen; camera, Joe MacDonald; editor, Harmon Jones.
     Gregory Peck (Stretch); Anne Baxter (Mike); Richard Wid-
mark (Dude); Robert Arthur (Bull Run); John Russell (Lengthy);
Henry "Harry" Morgan (Half Pint); James Barton (Grandpa); Charles
Kemper (Walrus); Robert Adler (Jed); Victor Kilian (Bartender);
Paul Hurst (Drunk); William Gould (Banker); Norman Leavitt (Bank
Teller); Chief Yowlachie (Colorado); Eula Guy (Woman).

     This W. R. Burnett novel seemed to be a combination of the
author's High Sierra (1941) remade into the Western Colorado Territory, (1949, q.v.) and Peter B. Kyne's The Three Godfathers
[q.v.]. As directed by William A. Wellman, Yellow Sky was full
of passion, violence and excitement, set against the arid desert atmosphere, much like The Petrified Forest (1936).
     The story told of seven bandits who rob an Arizona bank.
One of their number is killed and the others (Peck, Widmark, Morgan, Russell, Arthur, Kemper) head for the badlands. They wind
up in the salt flats of a ghost town run by an old man (Barton) and
his granddaughter (Baxter). Tempers flare when the old man hides
their precious, stolen gold.
     In reviewing this Western in Hollywood in the Forties (1968)
Charles Higham and Joel Greenberg wrote, "Joe MacDonald's brilliant high-key camerawork--especially in the salt flat scenes, hard
and white and clear--made something visually compelling out of trite
situations, poor scripting and worse acting."
     A little-known remake of Yellow Sky was produced in South
Africa in 1967. The Jackals, with Vincent Price and Dana Ivarson
starring. This Twentieth Century-Fox release was produced and
directed by Robert D. Webb. This time the setting was 1883 South

Africa with five fugitive bank robbers flocking to the Transvaal,
hoping to make a quick fortune by stealing the gold stakes of an
aging prospector (Price) and his granddaughter (Ivarson).

YOJIMBO   see   PER UN PUGNO DI DOLLARI

ZORRO   see   MARK OF ZORRO

ZORRO CONTRE MACISTE   see   MARK OF ZORRO

ZORRO E I TRE MOSCHETTIEREI   see   MARK OF ZORRO

ZORRO LE RENARD   see   MARK OF ZORRO

ZORRO RIDES AGAIN   (Republic, 1937)   twelve chapters

        Associate producer, Sol C. Siegel; directors, William Witney,

John Carroll (masked) in Zorro Rides Again (1937).

John English; based on a character created by Johnston McCulley;
screenplay, Morgan Cox, Ronald Davidson, John Rathmell, Barry
Shipman, Franklyn Adreon; music, Alberto Columbo; camera, William Nobles.

John Carroll (James Vega/Zorro); Helen Christian (Joyce
Andrews); Reed Howes (Philip Andrews); Duncan Renaldo (Renaldo);
Richard Alexander [Brad Dace (El Lobo)]; Nigel de Brulier (Manuel
Vega); Robert Kortman (Trelliger); Jack Ingram (Carter); Roger
Williams (Manning); Tony Martelli (Captain of Rurales); Edmund
Cobb (Larkin); Mona Rico (Carmelita); Tom London (O'Shea); Harry
Strang (O'Brien); Jerry Frank (Duncan).

Chapters: 1) Death from the Sky; 2) The Fatal Minute; 3)
Juggernaut; 4) Unmasked; 5) Sky Pirates; 6) The Fatal Shot; 7)
Burning Embers; 8) Plunge of Peril; 9) Tunnel of Terror; 10) Trap-
ped; 11) Right of Way; 12) Retribution.

See Mark of Zorro.

ZORRO THE AVENGER   see   MARK OF ZORRO

ZORRO'S BLACK WHIP   (Republic, 1944) twelve chapters

Associate producer, Ronald Davidson; directors, Spencer
Bennet, Wallace Grissell; based on the character created by Johns-
ton McCulley; screenplay, Basil Dickey, Jesse Duffy, Grant Nelson,
Joseph Poland; second unit director, Yakima Canutt; music director,
Richard Cherwin; special effects, Theodore Lydecker; camera, Bud
Thackery.

George J. Lewis (Vic Gordon); Linda Stirling (Barbara Mere-
dith); Lucien Littlefield (Tenpoint); Francis McDonald (Hammond);
Hal Taliaferro (Baxter); John Merton (Harris); John Hamilton (The
Banker); Tom London (The Commissioner); Tom Chatterton (The
Merchant); Jack Kirk (The Marshal); Jay Kirby (Randolph Meredith);
Si Jenks (Zeke Hayden); Stanley Price (Hodges); Tom Steele (Hull);
Duke Green (Evans); Dale Van Sickel (Daley).

Chapters: 1) The Masked Avenger; 2) Tomb of Terror; 3)
Mob Murder; 4) Detour to Death; 5) Take Off That Mask!; 6) Fatal
Gold; 7) Wolf Pack; 8) The Invisible Victim; 9) Avalanche; 10) Fangs
of Doom; 11) Flaming Juggernaut; 12) Trail of Tyranny.

See Mark of Zorro.

ZORRO'S FIGHTING LEGION   (Republic, 1939)   twelve chapters

Associate producer, Hiram S. Brown, Jr.; directors, William Witney, John English; based on the character created by
Johnston McCulley; screenplay, Ronald Davidson, Franklyn Adreon,
Morgan Cox, Sol Shor, Barney Sarecky; music, William Lava;
camera, Reggie Lanning.

Reed Hadley (Diego/Zorro); Sheila Darcy (Volita); William
Corson (Ramon); Leander de Cordova (Felipe); Edmund Cobb

(Gonzales); C. Montague Shaw (Pablo); John Merton (Manuel); Budd
Buster (Juan); Carleton Young (Juarez); Guy D'Ennery (Francisco);
Paul Marlan (Kala); Joe Molina (Tarmac); Jim Pierce (Moreno);
Helen Mitchel (Donna Maria); Curley Dresden (Tomas); Charles King
(Valdez); Al Taylor (Rico); Charles B. Murphy (Pepito).
        Chapters: 1) The Golden God; 2) The Flaming 'Z'; 3) Des-
cending Doom; 4) The Bridge of Peril; 5) The Decoy; 6) Zorro to
the Rescue; 7) The Fugitive; 8) Flowing Death; 9) The Golden Arrow;
10) Mystery Wagon; 11) Face to Face; 12) Unmasked.
        See Mark of Zorro.

WESTERN SHOWS ON RADIO

Compiled by Vincent Terrace

ALL-STAR WESTERN THEATRE
with: Foy Willing, The Riders of the Purple Sage
(Syndicated, 1946)

THE ANDREWS SISTERS EIGHT-TO-THE BAR RANCH
with: The Andrews Sisters, William Elliott, George "Gabby"
Hayes
(Blue Network, 1944; ABC, 1945)

BOBBY BENSON AND HIS B-BAR-B RIDERS (a.k.a. B-BAR-B
RANCH, and BOBBY BENSON'S ADVENTURES)
with: Tex Ritter, Ivan Curry, Craig McDonnell, Don Knotts
(CBS, 1932; Mutual, 1949)

THE BUCK JONES SHOW (a.k.a. HOOFBEATS)
with: Buck Jones
(Syndicated, 1937)

CALIFORNIA CARAVAN
with: Virginia Gregg, Michael Hayes, Herb Vigran
(Mutual, 1949)

CIMARRON TAVERN
with: Paul Conrad, Chester Stratton, Ethel Everett,
Stephen Courtleigh
(CBS, 1945)

THE CISCO KID
with: Jackson Beck, Louis Sorin
(Mutual, 1943)

CURLEY BRADLEY--THE SINGING MARSHAL   (Also known as THE
CURLEY BRADLEY SHOW)
with: Curley Bradley, Don Gordon
(Mutual, 1949)

DANIEL BOONE, INDIAN SCOUT
(Syndicated, 1948)

DEATH VALLEY DAYS
    with: Tim Daniel Frawley, Edwin Bruce
    (Blue Network, 1930)

DEATH VALLEY SHERIFF
    with: Robert Hoag, Alyn Landick
    (CBS, 1944)

DESTINY'S TRAILS
    with: Stacy Harris, Kay Loring, Lesley Woods
    (Syndicated, 1945)

DOCTOR SIX GUN
    with: Karl Weber, Bill Griffis
    (NBC, 1952)

FORT LARAMIE
    with: Raymond Burr, Vic Perrin
    (Syndicated, 1954)

FRIENDSHIP RANCH
    with: Don Parker, Billy Daniels, Tex Antoine
    (NBC, 1944)

FRONTIER FIGHTERS
    (Syndicated, c. 1935)

FRONTIER GENTLEMAN
    with: John Dehner
    (Syndicated, 1955)

FRONTIER TOWN
    with: Jeff Chandler
    (Syndicated, 1953)

GENE AUTRY'S MELODY RANCH
    with: Gene Autry, Pat Buttram, Jim Boles
    (CBS, 1940)

GOLD RUSH DAYS
    (Syndicated, 1948)

GUNSMOKE
    with: William Conrad, Parley Baer, Georgia Ellis, Howard
    McNear
    (CBS, 1955)

HASHKNIFE HARTLEY
    with: Frank Morton, Barton Yarborough
    (Mutual, 1950)

HAVE GUN--WILL TRAVEL
    with: John Dehner
    (CBS, 1957)

HAWK DURANGO
      with: Elliott Lewis, Frank Lovejoy, Lucien Littlefield
      (CBS, 1945)

HAWK LARABEE
      with: Barton Yarborough, Tony Barrett
      (CBS, 1946)

HOPALONG CASSIDY
      with: William Boyd, Andy Clyde
      (Mutual, 1949)

THE JOHNNY MACK BROWN SHOW
      with: Johnny Mack Brown, Isleta Gayle
      (CBS, 1939)

THE LONE RANGER
      with: Brace Beemer, John Todd, James Lipton, Hay Michaels
      (Mutual, 1933)

MARK TRAIL
      with: Matt Crowley
      (Mutual, 1950)

MELODY ROUNDUP
      with: Bob Nolan and The Sons of the Pioneers
      (NBC, 1944)

THE PHANTOM RIDER
      with: Tex Ritter
      (Syndicated, c. 1935)

PLANTATION PARTY
      with: Whitey Ford, Dolly and Milly Good, The Range Riders
      (NBC, 1938)

PRAIRIE FOLKS
      with: Erik Rolf, Helen Warren, Kingsley Colton, Joe Hel-
      hesen, Tony Kraber
      (NBC, 1940)

RED RYDER
      with: Reed Hadley, Carlton KaDell, Tommy Cook, Henry
      Blair
      (Mutual, 1942)

REVEILLE ROUNDUP
      with: Tom Wallace, Louise Massey, The Westerners
      (NBC, 1941)

RIDERS OF THE PURPLE SAGE
      with: The Riders of the Purple Sage
      (Syndicated, 1937)

RIN-TIN-TIN
        with: Francis X. Bushman, (later) Lee Duncan
        (Syndicated, 1930s; 1950s)

THE ROY ROGERS SHOW
        with: Roy Rogers, Dale Evans, Gabby Hayes, Pat Brady,
        The Sons of the Pioneers
        (Mutual, 1944)

THE SHERIFF
        with: Bob Warren, Donald Briggs, Olyn Landick
        (ABC, 1945)

SILVER EAGLE (a.k.a. SILVER EAGLE MOUNTIE)
        with: Jim Ameche
        (ABC, 1951)

THE SIX SHOOTER
        with: James Stewart
        (NBC, 1952)

SKY KING
        with: Earl Nightingale, Jack Lester
        (ABC, 1947)

THE SMILEY BURNETTE SHOW
        with: Smiley Burnette
        (Syndicated, 1950s)

THE SONS OF THE PIONEERS
        with: Bob Nolan and The Sons of the Pioneers (Pat Brady,
        Hugh Farr, Karl Farr, and Lloyd Perryman)
        (Syndicated, 1940s)

STRAIGHT ARROW
        with: Howard Culver
        (Mutual, 1949)

TALES FROM THE DIAMOND K
        with: Ken Maynard
        (Syndicated, 1930s)

TALES OF THE TEXAS RANGERS
        with: Joel McCrea
        (NBC, 1951)

TENNESSEE JED
        with: Johnny Thomas, Don MacLaughlin
        (ABC, 1945)

THE TOM MIX RALSTON STRAIGHTSHOOTERS
        with: Curley Bradley, Russell Thorson
        (NBC, 1933)

WESTERN CARAVAN
      (NBC, 1950)

WILD BILL ELLIOTT   .
      with: William Elliott
      (Syndicated, 1951)

WILD BILL HICKOK
      with: Guy Madison, Andy Devine
      (Mutual, 1952)

WESTERN SHOWS ON TELEVISION

Compiled by Vincent Terrace

ACTION IN THE AFTERNOON
    with: Jack Valentine, Mary Elaine Watts, Blake Ritter,
    Phil Sheridan
    (CBS, 1953-54)

THE ADVENTURES OF CHAMPION
    with: Barry Curtis, Jim Bannon
    (CBS, 1955-56)

THE ADVENTURES OF JIM BOWIE
    with: Scott Forbes
    (ABC, 1956-58)

THE ADVENTURES OF KIT CARSON
    with: Bill Williams, Don Diamond
    (Syndicated, 1956)

THE ADVENTURES OF RIN-TIN-TIN
    with: Lee Aaker, James Brown, Joe Sawyer
    (ABC, CBS, 1954-64)

ALIAS SMITH AND JONES
    with: Ben Murphy, Peter Duel, Roger Davis
    (ABC, 1971-73)

ALIBI'S TENT SHOW
    with: Max Terhune
    (Syndicated, 1951)

ANNIE OAKLEY
    with: Gail Davis, Brad Johnson, Jimmy Hawkins
    (ABC, 1953-58)

BARBARY COAST
    with: William Shatner, Doug McClure
    (ABC, 1975-76)

BAT MASTERSON
    with: Gene Barry
    (NBC, 1957-61)

THE BIG VALLEY
    with: Barbara Stanwyck, Richard Long, Peter Breck, Linda
    Evans, Lee Majors
    (ABC, 1965-69)

BLACK SADDLE
    with: Peter Breck, Russell Johnson, Anna-Lisa
    (NBC, 1959-60)

BONANZA
    with: Lorne Greene, Dan Blocker, Pernell Roberts, Michael
    Landon
    (NBC, 1959-73)

BOOTS AND SADDLES
    with: Jack Pickard, Michael Hinn, Patrick McVey
    (Syndicated, 1957-58)

BRANDED
    with: Chuck Connors, John Carradine
    (NBC, 1965-66)

BRAVE EAGLE
    with: Keith Larsen, Keena Nomleena, Kim Winona
    (CBS, 1955-56)

BROKEN ARROW
    with John Lupton, Michael Ansara
    (ABC, 1956-58)

BRONCO
    with: Ty Hardin
    (ABC, 1959-60)

BUCKSKIN
    with: Sallie Brophy, Tommy Nolan
    (NBC, 1958)

BUFFALO BILL, JR.
    with: Dick Jones, Nancy Gilbert, Harry Cheshire
    (Syndicated, 1955)

THE BUFFALO BILLY SHOW
    with: (voices of): Bob Clampett, Joan Gardiner, Don Messick
    (CBS, 1950)

BUTCH & BILLY & THEIR BANG BANG WESTERN MOVIES
    with: (voices of): Steve Krieger, Danny Krieger
    (Syndicated, 1961)

THE CALIFORNIANS
    with: Adam Kennedy, Sean McClory, Nan Leslie, Richard
    Coogan
    (NBC, 1957-59)

CALL OF THE WEST (retelecasts of DEATH VALLEY
    DAYS)
        with: host John Payne
        (Syndicated, 1969-70)

CHEYENNE
        with: Clint Walker
        (ABC, 1957-63 - originally telecast as part of WARNER
        BROS. PRESENTS, 1955)

CIMARRON CITY
        with: George Montgomery, Audrey Totter, John Smith
        (NBC, 1958-59)

CIMARRON STRIP
        with: Stuart Whitman, Jill Townsend, Randy Boone
        (CBS, 1967-68)

THE CISCO KID
        with: Duncan Renaldo, Leo Carillo
        (Syndicated, 1951-55)

COLT .45
        with: Wayde Preston, Donald May
        (ABC, 1957-61)

COWBOY G-MEN
        with: Russell Hayden, Jackie Coogan
        (Syndicated, 1952-53)

THE COWBOYS
        with: Moses Gunn, Diana Douglas, Jim Davis
        (ABC, 1974)

THE DAKOTAS
        with: Larry Ward, Chad Everett, Jack Elam
        (ABC, 1963)

DANIEL BOONE
        with: Fess Parker, Patricia Blair, Ed Ames
        (NBC, 1964-70)

DAVY CROCKETT
        with: Fess Parker, Buddy Ebsen
        (ABC, 1954-55)

DEATH VALLEY DAYS
        with: hosts: Stanley Andrews (the Old Ranger), Ronald
        Reagan, Robert Taylor, Dale Robertson
        (Syndicated 1952-72)

THE DEPUTY
        with: Henry Fonda, Allen Case, Betty Lou Keim
        (NBC, 1959-61)

DESTRY
        with: John Gavin
        (ABC, 1964)

DICK POWELL'S ZANE GREY THEATRE
        with: host: Dick Powell
        (CBS, 1956-62)

DIRTY SALLY
        with: Jeanette Nolan, Dack Rambo
        (CBS, 1974)

DUNDEE AND THE CULHANE
        with: John Mills, Sean Garrison
        (CBS, 1967-68)

DUSTY'S TRAIL
        with: Forrest Tucker, Bob Denver, Jeannine Riley, Lori
        Saunders
        (Syndicated, 1973)

EMPIRE
        with: Richard Egan, Terry Moore, Anne Seymour, Ryan
        O'Neal
        (NBC, 1962 - retitled REDIGO, with Richard Egan, 1963-64)

F TROOP
        with: Forrest Tucker, Larry Storch, Melody Patterson, Ken
        Berry, Bob Steele, Frank DeKova
        (ABC, 1965-67)

FRONTIER
        with: host: Walter Coy
        (NBC, 1955-56)

FRONTIER CIRCUS
        with: Chill Wills, John Derek, Richard Jaeckel
        (CBS, 1961-62)

FRONTIER DOCTOR (a.k.a. MAN OF THE WEST/UNARMED)
        with: Rex Allen
        (Syndicated, 1958-59)

FRONTIER JUSTICE (re-telecasts of DICK POWELL'S ZANE GREY
    THEATRE)
        with: hosts: Lew Ayres, Melvyn Douglas
        (CBS, 1958-59)

FURY (a.k.a. BRAVE STALLION)
       with: Peter Graves, Bobby Diamond, William Fawcett
       (NBC, 1955-66)

THE GABBY HAYES SHOW
       with: Gabby Hayes, Clifford Sales
       (NBC, 1950-51)

THE GENE AUTRY SHOW
       with: Gene Autry, Pat Buttram
       (ABC, 1950-55)

THE GUNS OF WILL SONNETT
       with: Walter Brennan, Dack Rambo
       (ABC, 1967-69)

GUNSLINGER
       with: Tony Young, Preston Foster
       (CBS, 1961)

GUNSMOKE
       with: James Arness, Amanda Blake, Milburn Stone, Dennis
       Weaver, Ken Curtis
       (CBS, 1955-75)

HAVE GUN--WILL TRAVEL
       with: Richard Boone, Kam Tong, Lisa Lu
       (CBS, 1957-63)

HAWKEYE AND THE LAST OF THE MOHICANS
       with: John Hart, Lon Chaney
       (Syndicated, 1957-58)

THE HIGH CHAPARRAL
       with: Leif Erickson, Cameron Mitchell, Linda Cristal
       (NBC, 1967-71)

HONDO
       with: Ralph Taeger, Noah Beery, Jr.
       (ABC, 1967-68)

HOPALONG CASSIDY
       with: William Boyd, Edgar Buchanan
       (NBC, 1948-52)

HOTEL DE PAREE
       with: Earl Holliman, Jeanette Nolan, Judi Meredith
       (CBS, 1959-60)

IRON HORSE
       with: Dale Robertson, Gary Collins
       (ABC, 1966-68)

JEFFERSON DRUM
    with: Jeff Richards, Eugene Martin, Cyril Delevanti
    (NBC, 1958-59)

JOHNNY RINGO
    with: Don Durant, Mark Goddard, Karen Sharpe
    (CBS, 1959-60)

JUDGE ROY BEAN
    with: Edgar Buchanan, Jack Beutel, Jackie Loughery
    (Syndicated, 1956-57)

LANCER
    with: Andrew Duggan, Wayne Maunder, James Stacy,
    Elizabeth Baur
    (CBS, 1968-70)

LARAMIE
    with: John Smith, Robert Fuller, Hoagy Carmichael, Spring
    Byington
    (NBC, 1959-63)

LAREDO
    with: Neville Brand, Peter Brown, William Smith
    (NBC, 1965-67)

LAW OF THE PLAINSMAN
    with: Michael Ansara, Robert Harland
    (NBC, 1959-62)

LAWMAN
    with: John Russell, Peter Brown, Peggie Castle
    (ABC, 1958-62)

THE LEGEND OF CUSTER
    with: Wayne Maunder, Slim Pickens
    (ABC, 1967)

THE LEGEND OF JESSE JAMES
    with: Chris Jones, Allen Case
    (ABC, 1965-66)

THE LIFE AND LEGEND OF WYATT EARP
    with: Hugh O'Brian, Damian O'Flynn, Alan Dinehart III,
    Lash LaRue
    (ABC, 1955-61)

THE LONE RANGER
    with: Clayton Moore, Jay Silverheels, John Hart
    (ABC, CBS, 1948-61)

THE LONER
    with: Lloyd Bridges
    (CBS, 1965-66)

Western Shows on TV

MacKENZIE'S RAIDERS
    with: Richard Carlson, Louis Jean Heydt, Brett King,
    Morris Ankrum
    (Syndicated, 1958-59)

A MAN CALLED SHENANDOAH (a.k.a. SHENANDOAH)
    with: Robert Horton
    (ABC, 1965-66)

THE MAN FROM BLACKHAWK
    with: Robert Rockwell
    (ABC, 1959-60)

THE MAN WITHOUT A GUN
    with: Rex Reason, Mort Mills
    (Syndicated, 1958-59)

MAVERICK
    with: James Garner, Jack Kelly, Roger Moore, Diane
    Brewster
    (ABC, 1957-62)

THE MEN FROM SHILOH
    with: James Drury, Stewart Granger, Doug McClure, Lee
    Majors
    (NBC, 1970-71)

MY FRIEND FLICKA
    with: Gene Evans, Anita Louise, Johnny Washbrook
    (ABC, CBS, NBC, 1957-66)

NBC SUNDAY MYSTERY MOVIE: HEC RAMSEY
    with: Richard Boone, Henry "Harry" Morgan, Rick Lenz
    (NBC, 1972-74)

NICHOLS
    with: James Garner, Stuart Margolin, Neva Patterson,
    Margot Kidder
    (NBC, 1971-72)

THE NINE LIVES OF ELFEGO BACA
    with Robert Loggia
    (ABC, 1958-59)

THE OUTCASTS
    with: Don Murray, Otis Young
    (ABC, 1968-69)

THE OUTLAWS
    with: Barton MacLane, Don Collier, Judy Lewis, Jack
    Gaynor
    (NBC, 1960-62)

Western Shows on TV

425

OVERLAND TRAIL
with: William Bendix, Doug McClure
(Syndicated, 1960-61)

THE PIONEERS (retelecasts of DEATH VALLEY DAYS)
host: Will Rogers, Jr.
(Syndicated, 1963)

PISTOLS 'N PETTICOATS
with: Ann Sheridan, Douglas Fowley, Carole Wells, Ruth McDevitt, Lon Chaney, Robert Lowery
(CBS, 1966-67)

PONY EXPRESS
with: Grant Sullivan, Bill Cord
(Syndicated, 1960-61)

QUICK DRAW McGRAW
with: (voices of) Daws Butler, Doug Young
(Syndicated, 1958-59)

THE RANGE RIDER
with: Jock Mahoney, Dick Jones
(Syndicated, 1951-53)

RANGO
with: Tim Conway, Guy Marks, Norman Alden
(ABC, 1967)

RAWHIDE
with: Eric Fleming, Clint Eastwood, Sheb Wooley, Paul Brinegar
(CBS, 1958-66)

THE REBEL
with: Nick Adams
(ABC, 1959-62)

RED RYDER
with: Ricky Lane, Louis Letteur, Elizabeth Slifer
(Syndicated, 1956-57)

THE RESTLESS GUN
with: John Payne
(NBC, 1957-59)

THE RIFLEMAN
with: Chuck Connors, Johnny Crawford, Paul Fix
(ABC, 1958-62)

THE ROAD WEST
with: Barry Sullivan, Kathryn Hays, Andrew Prine, Brenda Scott
(NBC, 1966-67)

THE ROY ROGERS SHOW
> with: Roy Rogers, Dale Evans, Pat Brady
> (NBC, CBS, 1951-64)

SHANE
> with: David Carradine, Jill Ireland, Tom Tully, Christopher Shea
> (ABC, 1966-67)

SHERIFF OF COCHISE (a.k.a. U.S. MARSHAL)
> with: John Bromfield, Stan Jones
> (Syndicated, 1956-59)

SHOTGUN SLADE
> with: Scott Brady, Monica Lewis
> (Syndicated, 1959-60)

STAGECOACH WEST
> with: Wayne Maunder, Robert Bray, Richard Eyer
> (ABC, 1960-61)

STEVE DONOVAN, WESTERN MARSHAL
> with: Douglas Kennedy, Eddy Waller
> (Syndicated, 1955-56)

STONEY BURKE
> with: Jack Lord
> (ABC, 1962)

STORIES OF THE CENTURY (a.k.a. FAST GUNS)
> with: Jim Davis, Mary Castle, Kristine Miller
> (Syndicated, 1956-58)

SUGARFOOT
> with: Will Hutchins
> (ABC, 1957-60)

TALES OF FAMOUS OUTLAWS (a.k.a. LASH OF THE WEST)
> with: Lash LaRue
> (Syndicated, 1951)

TALES OF THE TEXAS RANGERS
> with: Willard Parker, Harry Lauter
> (ABC, 1955-59)

TALES OF WELLS FARGO
> with: Dale Robertson
> (NBC, 1957-62)

THE TALL MAN
> with: Barry Sullivan, Clu Gulager
> (NBC, 1960-61)

TATE
>with: David McLean
>(NBC, 1960)

TEMPLE HOUSTON
>with: Jeffrey Hunter, Jack Elam
>(NBC, 1963-64)

THE TEXAN
>with: Rory Calhoun
>(CBS, 1958-59)

TEXAS JOHN SLAUGHTER
>with: Tom Tryon, Harry Carey, Jr., Betty Lynn
>(ABC, 1958-59)

THEY WENT THAT'A WAY
>Documentary series depicting the history of the Western
>film; hosts: Ruane Hull, Jon Tuska
>(Public Broadcasting Service, 1971)

THE TIM McCOY SHOW
>with: Tim McCoy
>(Syndicated, 1951)

TOMAHAWK
>with: Jacques Godin, Rene Caron
>(Syndicated, 1957-58)

TOMBSTONE TERRITORY
>with: Richard Eastham, Pat Conway
>(ABC, 1957-59)

TRACKDOWN
>with: Robert Culp
>(CBS, 1957-59)

TRAILS WEST (re-telecasts of DEATH VALLEY DAYS)
>with: host: Ray Milland
>(Syndicated, 1958-61)

THE TRAVELS OF JAIMIE McPHEETERS
>with: Dan O'Herlihy, Kurt Russell
>(ABC, 1963-64)

26 MEN
>with: Tris Coffin, Kelo Henderson
>(ABC, 1958-59)

TWO FACES WEST
>with: Charles Bateman (dual role)
>(Syndicated, 1961-62)

UNION PACIFIC
       with: Jeff Morrow, Judd Pratt, Susan Cummings
       (Syndicated, 1958-59)

THE VIRGINIAN
       with: James Drury, Doug McClure, Lee J. Cobb, Pippa
       Scott
       (NBC, 1962-70)

WAGON TRAIN
       with: Ward Bond, John McIntire, Robert Horton, Terry
       Wilson, Frank McGrath
       (NBC, ABC, 1957-65)

WANTED: DEAD OR ALIVE
       with: Steve McQueen, Wright King
       (CBS, 1958-61)

WESTERN HOUR (re-telecasts of THE RIFLEMAN and DICK
    POWELL'S ZANE GREY THEATRE)
       with: host: Chuck Connors
       (Syndicated, 1963)

WESTERN STAR THEATRE (re-telecasts of DEATH VALLEY DAYS)
       with: host: Rory Calhoun
       (Syndicated, 1963)

WESTERN THEATRE (re-telecasts of DICK POWELL'S ZANE GREY
    THEATRE)
       with: Barbara Stanwyck, Phyllis Kirk, James Whitmore
       (NBC, 1959)

THE WESTERNER
       with: Brian Keith, John Dehner
       (NBC, 1960)

THE WESTERNERS (re-telecasts of DICK POWELL'S ZANE GREY
    THEATRE, JOHNNY RINGO, THE LAW OF THE PLAINSMAN)
       with: host: Keenan Wynn
       (Syndicated, 1966-67)

WHIPLASH
       with: Peter Graves
       (Syndicated, 1961-62)

WHISPERING SMITH
       with: Audie Murphy, Guy Mitchell, Sam Buffington
       (NBC, 1961-62)

WICHITA TOWN
       with: Joel McCrea, Jody McCrea
       (NBC, 1959-60)

THE WIDE COUNTRY
     with: Earl Holliman, Andrew Prine
     (NBC, 1962-63)

WILD BILL HICKOK
     with: Guy Madison, Andy Devine
     (Syndicated, 1952-54; CBS, 1954-57; ABC, 1957-58)

THE WILD WILD WEST
     with: Robert Conrad, Ross Martin
     (CBS, 1965-69)

WRANGLER
     with: Jason Evers
     (NBC, 1960)

YANCY DERRINGER
     with: Jock Mahoney, X Brands
     (CBS, 1958-59)

WESTERN BIBLIOGRAPHY

by Edward Connor

Introduction

The thousand western novels listed in this bibliography are mainly the product of the twentieth century. The nineteenth is represented by the five "Leatherstocking" novels of James Fenimore Cooper and Henry Inman's Tales of the Trail.

A. B. Guthrie's The Way West (1949) and Robert Lewis Taylor's Travels of Jaimie McPheeters (1958) won Pulitzer Prizes.

The New York Times Book Review Index, 1896-1970 was most helpful in drawing up this Bibliography, as were Filmed Books and Plays, 1928-1969 by A. G. S. Enser; The Fiction Catalog, 8th edition; and Books in Print, 1975.

BIBLIOGRAPHY

ABBOTT, Keene. Wine o' the Winds. 1920.

ADAMS, Andy. Log of a Cowboy. 1903.
Ranch on the Beaver. 1927.

ADAMS, Frank R. Gunsight Ranch. 1939.

ADAMS, Ramon Frederick. Burrs Under the Saddle. 1964.
Rampaging Herd. 1959.
Six Guns and Saddle Leather. 1954.

AMES, Joseph B. Flame of the Desert. 1928.
London from Laramie. 1925.
Lone Hand. 1926.
Man from Painted Post. 1923.
Shoe-Bar Stratton. 1922.

ARNOLD, Elliot. Blood Brother. 1947.
Time of the Gringo. 1953.

430

ATSHELER, Joseph A.   Great Sioux Trail.   1918.

AUSTIN, Frank.   King of the Range.   1935.
                 Return of the Ranchers.   1933.
                 Sheriff Rides, The.   1934.

AYDELOTTE, Dora.   Run of the Stars.   1940.
                   Trumpets Calling.   1938.

BAKER, Karle.   Star of the Wilderness.   1942.

BALLEW, Charles.   Bandit of Paloduro, The.   1934.
                   Cowpuncher, The.   1934.
                   Treasure of Aspen Canyon.   1935.

BARRETT, Monte.   Tempered Blade, The.   1946.

BARRY, Jane.   Maximilian's Gold.   1966.
               Shadow of Eagles, A.   1964.
               Time in the Sun, A.   1962.

BAXTER, George Owen.   Free Range Lanning.   1922.
                       Red Devil of the Range.   1934.
                       Shadow of Silver Tip.   1925.

BEACH, Rex E.   Barrier, The.   1908.
                Beyond Control.   1932.
                Call of the Blood.   1934.
                Don Careless and Birds of Prey.   1928.
                Flowing Gold.   1922.
                Heart of the Sunset.   1915.
                Iron Trail.   1913.
                Mating Call.   1927.
                Pardners.   1905.
                Rainbow's End.   1916.
                Silver Horde.   1909.
                Spoilers, The.   1906.
                Valley of Thunder.   1939.
                Wild Pastures.   1935.

BEAN, Amelia.   The Feud.   1960.

BENNET, Robert Ames.   Brand Blotters.   1939.
                       Crossed Trails.   1937.
                       Death Rides the Range.   1935.
                       Hot Lead.   1937.
                       Out of the Depths.   1913.
                       Sheepman's Gold.   1939
                       Texas Man.   1934.
                       White Buffalo.   1935.

BENNETT, Dwight.   Cherokee Outlet.   1961.

BERGER, Thomas. Little Big Man. 1964.

BERRY, Don. Moontrap. 1962.

BERRY, Raymond A. Smoky Waters. 1935.

BILLINGS, Buck. Six-Gun Vengeance. 1933.

BINDLOSS, Harold. Ghost of Hemlock Canyon. 1927.
                   Pine Creek Ranch. 1926.

BIRNEY, Hoffman. Dead Man's Trail. 1937.
                  Eagle in the Sun. 1935.

BLAKE, Forrester. Johnny Christmas. 1948.

BODDY, E. Manchester. Yellow Trail. 1923.

BOSWORTH, Allan B. Long Way North. 1959.

BOWER, B. M.   Bellehelen Mine. 1924.
                  Black Thunder. 1926.
                  Cow-Country. 1921.
                  Dry Ridge Gang. 1935.
                  Eagle's Wing. 1924.
                  Family Failing. 1941.
                  Flying U. Ranch. 1914.
                  Flying U. Strikes. 1934.
                  Haunted Hills. 1934.
                  Heritage of the Sioux. 1916.
                  Man on Horseback. 1940.
                  Open Land. 1933.
                  Pirates of the Range. 1937.
                  Points West. 1928.
                  Ranch at the Wolverine. 1914.
                  Rim o' the World. 1920.
                  Rodeo. 1929.
                  Shadow Mountain. 1936.
                  Singing Hill. 1939.
                  Spirit of the Range. 1940.
                  Starr of the Desert. 1917.
                  Starry Knight. 1939.
                  Swallowfork Bulls. 1929.
                  Tiger Eye. 1930.
                  Trail of the White Mule. 1922.
                  Voice at Johnnywater. 1923.
                  White Wolves. 1927.
                  Whoop-Up Trail. 1933.
                  Wind Blows West. 1938.

BOWMAN, Earl W. Ramblin' Kid. 1920.

BOYD, James. Bitter Creek. 1939.

BRALEY, Berton.   Sheriff of Silver Bow.   1921.

BRAND, Max (Frederick Faust).   Alcatraz.   1923
                                            Bandit's Honor.   1927
                                            Blackie and Red.   1926.
                                            Blue Jay.   1927.
                                            Brothers on the Trail.   1934.
                                            Bronze Collar.   1925.
                                            Brute, The.   1925.
                                            Bull Hunter.   1924.
                                            Dan Barry's Daughter.   1924.
                                            Destry Rides Again.   1930.
                                            Donnegan.   1923.
                                            Fightin' Fool.   1939.
                                            Fire-Brain.   1926.
                                            Free Range Lanning.   1921.
                                            Golden Lightning.   1959.
                                            Gunman's Gold.   1939.
                                            Hair Trigger Kid.   1951.
                                            Happy Jack.   1936.
                                            Happy Valley.   1931.
                                            Hunted Riders.   1935.
                                            Iron Trail.   1938.
                                            King Bird Rides.   1936.
                                            Long Chance.   1941.
                                            Long, Long Trail.   1923.
                                            Longhorn Feud.   1933.
                                            Marbleface.   1939.
                                            Mistral.   1930.
                                            Mystery Ranch.   1930.
                                            Night Horseman.   1952.
                                            Outlaw, The.   1933.
                                            Pillar Mountain.   1928.
                                            Pleasant Jim.   1928.
                                            Rancher's Revenge.   1934.
                                            Rustlers of Beacon Creek.   1935.
                                            Seven of Diamonds.   1935.
                                            Seven Trails.   1949.
                                            Seventh Man.   1921.
                                            Silvertip's Round-Up.   1949.
                                            Silvertip's Strike.   1942.
                                            Silvertip's Trap.   1943.
                                            Six Golden Angels.   1937.
                                            Slow Joe.   1933.
                                            Smiling Charlie.   1931.
                                            South of Rio Grande.   1936.
                                            Stranger, The.   1957.
                                            Streak, The.   1937.
                                            Thunderer, The.   1933.
                                            Timbal Gulch Trail.   1934.
                                            Tragedy Trail.   1951.
                                            Trailin'.   1920.
                                            Trouble Trail.   1938.

BRAND, Max (continued)   Untamed, The. 1919.
                                Valley Vultures. 1932.
                                White Wolf. 1926.

BRAUTIGAN, Richard.   The Hawkline Monster. 1974.

BRECK, John.   When Hell Came Thru. 1929.

BROWN, Dee.   Bold Cavaliers. 1959.
                 Bury My Heart at Wounded Knee. 1971.
                 Fort Phil Kearny. 1962.
                 Gentle Tamers, The. 1958.
                 Girl from Fort Wicked. 1964.
                 Grierson's Raid. 1954.
                 Settler's West (with Martin F. Schmitt). 1955.
                 They Went Thataway. 1960.
                 Trail Driving Days. 1952.
                 Wave High the Banner. 1942.

BURNETT, William Riley.   Adobe Wells. 1953.
                           Mi, Amigo. 1959.
                           Saint Johnston. 1930.

BURT, Katherine Newlin.   Tall Ladder, The. 1932.
                           This Woman and This Man. 1934.

BUSCH, Niven.   Duel in the Sun. 1944.
                 Furies, The. 1948.

CAMERON, Caddo.   Due for a Hangin'. 1939.

CAMPBELL, Walter S.   Dobe Walls. 1929.

CARDER, Leigh (Eugene Cunningham).   Border Guns. 1935.
                                      Bravo Trail. 1935.

CASE, Robert Ormand.   Yukon Drive, The. 1930.

CATHER, Willa.   Death Comes for the Archbishop. 1927.

CHAPMAN, Arthur.   Mystery Ranch. 1921.

CHISHOLM, A. W.   Boss of Wind River. 1911.
                   Precious Waters. 1913.
                   Yellow Horse. 1926.

CLAGETT, John.   Buckskin Cavalier. 1954.

CLARK, W. V.   Ox-Bow Incident, The. 1940.
                Track of the Cat. 1949.

COLTER, Eli.   Outcast of Lazy S. 1933.

COMFORT, Will. Apache. 1931.

CONNOR, Glenn A. Thunderbolt. 1928.

CONSTANT, Alberta. Oklahoma Run. 1955.

COOK, David C. Port of Honor. 1958.

COOK, Will. Elizabeth by Name. 1958.

COOLIDGE, Dane.   Bear Paw. 1941.
                    Bloody Head. 1940.
                    Comanche Chaser. 1938.
                    Gunsmoke. 1928.
                    Hell's Hip Pocket. 1938.
                    Horse-Ketchum. 1930.
                    Long Rope. 1935.
                    Lost Wagons. 1923.
                    Ranger Two-Rifles. 1937.
                    Scalp-Lock. 1924.
                    Shadow Mountain. 1919.
                    Silver and Gold. 1919.
                    Texican, The. 1911.
                    Trail of Gold. 1937.
                    Wally Laughs-Easy. 1939.
                    War Paint. 1929.
                    Wolf's Candle. 1935.
                    Wunpost. 1920.
                    Yaqui Drums. 1940.

COOPER, Courtney R.   Oklahoma. 1926.
                      White Desert. 1922.

COOPER, James Fenimore.   Deerslayer, The. 1854.
                          Last of the Mohicans. 1854.
                          Pathfinder, The. 1853.
                          Pioneers, The. 1853.
                          Prairie, The. 1854.

CORCORAN, William. Blow, Desert Winds! 1935.

CORLE, Edwin. Billy the Kid. 1953.

CRANE, Robert. Thunder in the West. 1934.

CULLUM, Ridgwell. Wolf Pack. 1927.

CULP, John H.   Born of the Sun. 1959.
                Men of Gonzales. 1960.

CUNNINGHAM, Eugene.   Gun Bulldozer. 1939.
                      Pistol Passport. 1936.

CUNNINGHAM, Eugene (continued).   Quick Triggers. 1935.
                                   Ranger Way. 1937.
                                   Red Range. 1939.
                                   Spiderweb Trail. 1940.
                                   Texas Sheriff. 1934.
                                   Texas Triggers. 1938.
                                   Whistling Lead. 1936.

CURWOOD, James Oliver.   Alaskan, The. 1923.
                          Ancient Highway. 1925.
                          Back to God's Country. 1920.
                          Country Beyond, The. 1922.
                          Danger Trail. 1910.
                          Flaming Forest. 1921.
                          Gentleman of Courage. 1924.
                          God's Country and the Woman. 1915.
                          Gold Hunters. 1909.
                          Golden Snare. 1921.
                          Green Timber. 1930.
                          Grizzly King. 1918.
                          Honor of the Big Snows. 1911.
                          River's End. 1919.
                          Son of the Forests. 1930.
                          Swift Lightning. 1919.
                          Wolf Hunters. 1908.

DAVIS, Don.   Death on Treasure Trail. 1941.
               Return of the Rio Kid. 1940.

DAVIS, James F.   Road to San Jacinto. 1936.

DODGE, Louis.   American, The. 1934.
                 Bonnie May. 1916.
                 Children of the Desert. 1917.

DORRANCE, Ethel and James.   Glory Rides the Range. 1920.
                               Lonesome Town. 1922.

DORRANCE, James.   Forbidden Range. 1930.
                    Rio Rustlers. 1928.

DOWDEY, Clifford.   Tidewater. 1943.

DRAGO, Harry Sinclair.   Desert Water. (1933).
                          Smoke of the .45. 1923.

DRESSER, Dave.   Boss of the Lazy 9. 1936.
                  Coyote Gulch. 1936.
                  Doctor Two-Guns. 1939.
                  Fight for Powder Valley. 1942.
                  Gringo Guns. 1935.
                  Gunsmoke on the Mesa. 1941.

DRESSER, Dave (continued) Law Man of Powder Valley. 1942.
                           Lynch-Rope Law. 1941.
                           Mustang Mesa. 1937.
                           Powder Valley Vengeance. 1943.
                           Tenderfoot Kid. 1939.

DUFFUS, Robert L. Jornada. 1935.

DUNN, J. Allan. Girl of Ghost Mountain. 1921.
                 Rimrock Trail. 1922.

EMERSON, L. W. Cimarron Bend. 1936.
                Rawhide. 1936.

ERDMAN, Loula. Edge of Time. 1950.
                Far Journey. 1955.

ERMINE, Will. Plundered Range. 1936.
               Rider of the Midnight Range. 1940.

ERSKINE, Laurie York. Laughing Rider. 1924.
                       Valor of the Range. 1926.

EVARTS, Hal G. Settling of the Sage. 1922.
                Tomahawk Rights. 1929.
                Tumbleweeds. 1923.

FELTON, Harold W. Pecos Bill, Texas Cowpuncher. 1950.

FERBER, Edna. Cimarron. 1930.

FERGUSSON, Harvey. Conquest of Don Pedro. 1954.
                    In Those Days. 1929.

FIELD, Peter. Feud at Silvermine. 1965.

FISHER, Vardis. Children of God. 1939.
                 Mothers, The. 1943.
                 Mountain Man. 1965.

FOREMAN, L. L. Don Desperado. 1944.
                Mustang Trail. 1965.
                Rogue's Legacy. 1968.

FORREST, William. Trail of Tears. 1958.

FOSTER, Bennett. Badlands. 1938.
                  Cow Thief Trail. 1937.
                  Man Tracks. 1943.
                  Pay-Off at Ladron. 1937.
                  Rider of the Rifle Rock. 1939.
                  Seven Slash Revenge. 1936.
                  Winter Quarters. 1942.

438   Western Bibliography

FOUST, Joanna. Prairie Chronicle. 1932.

FRIEL, Arthur O. Cat-o'-Mountain. 1924.

FRIEND, Oscar J. Round-Up, The. 1924.

FULLER, Alice Cook. Gold for the Grahams. 1949.

GANN, Walter. Lawless Guns. 1937.
               Trail Boss. 1937.

GARFIELD, Brian. Lawbringers, The. 1962.
                  Valley of the Shadow. 1970.
                  Vanquished, The. 1964.

GATES, Eleanore. Plow-Woman, The. 1906.

GATES, H. L. Riders to the Dust. 1935.

GILL, Tom. Firebrand. 1939.
            Red Earth. 1937.

GLIDDEN, Frederick D. Coroner Creek. 1946.
                       Crimson Horseshoe. 1941.
                       Dead Freight for Piute. 1941.
                       Play a Lone Hand. 1951.
                       Radiser of the Rimrock. 1939.
                       Ride the Man Down. 1943.
                       Stagline Feud. 1941.
                       Station West. 1947.
                       Vengeance Valley. 1951.
                       War on the Cimarron. 1940.

GORDON, Charles A. To Him that Hath Shall Be Given. 1921.

GORDON, Homer King. Code of Men. 1926.

GRAHAM, Carroll. Border Town. 1934.

GRANT, Douglas. Two-Gun Sue. 1922.

GRAY, Westmoreland. Hell's Stamping Ground. 1935.

GREGORY, Jackson. Ace in the Hole. 1941.
                   Captain Cavalier. 1928.
                   Dark Valley. 1937.
                   Desert Thoroughbred. 1926.
                   Emerald Trails. 1928.
                   Far Call. 1940.
                   Girl at the Crossroads. 1940.
                   High Courage. 1934.
                   I Must Ride Alone. 1940.

GREGORY, Jackson (continued). Lonely Trail. 1943.
Mad O'Hara of Wild River. 1939.
Man from Texas. 1942.
Mountain Men. 1936.
Red Law. 1941.
Riders Across the Border. 1932.
Rocky Bend. 1938.
Secret Valley. 1939.
Showdown on the Mesa. 1933.
Sudden Bill Dorn. 1937.
Trail to Paradise. 1930.
Valley of Adventure. 1935.

GREW, David. Two Coyotes. 1924.

GREY, Zane. Arizona Ames. 1932.
Arizona Clan. 1958.
Betty Zame. 1915.
Black Mesa. 1955.
Blue Feather. 1961.
Border Legion. 1916.
Call of the Canyon. 1924.
Code of the West. 1934.
Deer Stalker. 1925.
Desert Gold. 1913.
Desert of Wheat. 1919.
Drift Fence. 1932.
Fighting Caravans. 1929.
Forlorn River. 1927.
Hash Knife Outfit. 1933.
Heritage of the Desert. 1910.
Horse Heaven Hill. 1959.
Knights of the Range. 1936.
Last of the Plainsmen. 1908.
Last Trail. 1909.
Light of Western Stars. 1914.
Lone Star Ranger. 1915.
Lost Wagon Train. 1937.
Man of the Forest. 1920.
Mysterious Rider. 1921.
Nevada. 1928.
Raiders of Spanish Peaks. 1938.
Rainbow Trail. 1915.
Riders of the Purple Sage. 1912.
Robbers' Roost. 1932.
Shepherd of Guadaloupe. 1930.
Spirit of the Border. 1906.
Stairs of Sand. 1943.
Stranger from the Tonto. 1956.
Sunset Pass. 1931.
Tappo's Burro and Other Stories. 1923.
30,000 on the Hoof. 1940.

GREY, Zane (continued).   Thunder Mountain. 1935.
                          Thundering Herd. 1925.
                          To the Last Man. 1921.
                          Trail Driver. 1936.
                          Twin Sombreros. 1940.
                          U. P. Trail. 1918.
                          Under the Tonto Rim. 1926.
                          Valley of Wild Horses. 1947.
                          Vanishing Indian. 1936.
                          Wanderer of the Wasteland. 1923.
                          West of the Pecos. 1937.
                          Western Union. 1939.
                          Wildfire. 1917.
                          Wild Horse Mesa. 1928.
                          Wilderness Trek. 1944.
                          Wyoming. 1953.
                          Young Lion Hunters. 1911.

GRINSTEAD, J. E.   Great Red Border. 1940.
                   Hell's Acres. 1941.
                   Hot Lead. 1941.
                   Killers of Green's Cove. 1942.
                   King of Hualpi Valley. 1940.
                   Phantom Rustlers. 1940.
                   Texas Ranger Justice. 1941.
                   War Above the Timberline. 1939.
                   War on the Range. 1941.

GRUBER, Frank.   Bitter Sage. 1954.
                 Buffalo Grass. 1956.
                 Bugles West. 1954.
                 Bushwackers, The. 1959.
                 Highwayman, The. 1955.
                 Lonesome River. 1957.
                 Quantrill's Raiders. 1954.
                 Smoky Road. 1949.
                 Town Tamer. 1958.

GULLICK, Bill.   Hallelujah Trail, The. 1965.
                 Liveliest Town in the West. 1970.
                 Snake River Country. 1971.
                 They Came to a Valley. 1967.

GUNN, Tom.   Painted Post Law. 1936.
             Painted Post Roundup. 1939.
             Sheriff of Painted Post. 1936.

GUTHRIE, Alfred Bertram.   Arfive. 1970.
                           Big It, The. 1960.
                           Big Sky, The. 1947.
                           These Thousand Hills. 1956.
                           Way West, The. 1949.
                           Wild Pitch. 1973.

HALL, Jarvis. Up the Rito. 1926.

HALL, Marshall R. Valley of Strife. 1925.

HANKINS, A. M. Lonesome River Justice. 1943.

HARDY, Stuart. Montana Bound. 1936.

HART, William S. Hoofbeats. 1933.

HAWTHORNE, Hildegarde. Wheels Toward the West. 1932.

HAYCOX, Ernest. Bugles in the Afternoon. 1944.
                 Trail Smoke. 1936.

HENDRYX, James B. Hard Rock Man. 1940.
                   New Rivers Calling. 1943.
                   Outlaws of Halfaday Creek. 1935.
                   Promise, The. 1915.
                   Texan, The. 1918.
                   Yukon Kid, The. 1934.

HILL, Francis. Outlaws of Horseshow Hole. 1901.

HILL, Grace L. Girl from Montana. 1922.

HILLES, Helen Train. Cowboy Holiday. 1933.

HILTON, Francis W. Gray Sage. 1938.
                    Manaha Kid. 1940.
                    Phantom Rustlers. 1934.
                    Pioneer Herd. 1937.

HOFFMAN, W. D. Knights of the Desert. 1927.

HOLMES, Thomas K. Heart of Canyon Pass. 1921.

HOLT, Tex. Lawless Trail. 1940.
            Texas Terror. 1941.

HOOD, Robert Allison. Quest of Alistair. 1921.

HOOKER, Forrestine C. Long Dim Trail, The. 1920.
                       When Geronimo Rode. 1924.

HOUGH, Emerson. Covered Wagon, The. 1922.
                 Mother of Gold. 1923.

INMAN, Henry. Tales of the Trail. 1898.

IRWIN, Will. Columbine Time. 1922.
              Youth Rides West. 1925.

JACKSON, Frederick. Risky Rustling. 1933.

JAMES, Will.   All in the Day's Riding.   1933.
               Cow Country.   1927.
               Paradise Range.   1934.
               Sand.   1929.
               Three Mustangeers, The.   1933.

JANIS, Elsie.   Counter Currents.   1926.

JENKINS, Will.   Outlaw Sheriff.   1934.

JESSUP, Richard.   Comanche Vengeance.   1957.

JOHNSON, George M.   Gun Magic.   1934.
                     Gun-Slinger, The.   1927.
                     Texas Range Rider.   1933.

JOSCELYN, Archie.   Guns of Lost Valley.   1940.

KEATING, Lawrence A.   Deputy of San Riano.   1933.
                       Fleming's Folly.   1934.
                       Sunset Range.   1933.

KEENE, James.   McCracken in Command.   1959.
                Sixgun Wild.   1961.

KELLAND, Clarence B.   West of the Law.   1958.

KELTON, Elmer.   Barbed Wire.   1958.
                 Buffalo Wagons.   1957.

KENT, W. H. B.   Range Rider.   1943.

KETCHUM, Philip.   Apache Dawn.   1961.
                   Buzzard Guns.   1960.
                   Gun Code.   1959.
                   Gunslingers, The.   1956.
                   Night of the Coyotes.   1956.
                   Rider from Texas.   1955.
                   Six-Gun Maverick.   1957.

KJELGAARD, Jim.   Lost Wagon.   1955.

KNIBBS, Henry H.   Wild Horses.   1924.

KNIGHT, Kim.   Dangerous Dust.   1941.

KREPPS, Robert W.   Gamble My Last Game.   1958.

KYNE, Peter Bernard.   Dude Woman.   1940.
                       Enchanted Hill.   1924.

KYNE, Peter Bernard (continued).   Lord of Lonely Valley. 1932.
                                     Parson of Panamint. 1929.
                                     Three Godfathers. 1924.
                                     Tide of Empire. 1928.
                                     Valley of the Giants. 1918.

L'AMOUR, Louis.   Broken Gun, The. 1971.
                   Burning Hills. 1972.
                   Callaghen. 1972.
                   Conagher. 1969.
                   Day Breakers. 1967.
                   Desert Road. 1972.
                   Down the Long Hills.   1968.
                   Empty Land. 1969.
                   Ferguson Rifle, The. 1973.
                   First Fast Draw. 1970.
                   Flint. 1971.
                   Gallaway. 1974.
                   Guns of the Timberland. 1968.
                   Hanging Woman Creek. 1973.
                   Heller with a Gun. 1971.
                   High Graders. 1970.
                   Hondo. 1971.
                   Key Lock Man. 1970.
                   Kid Rodelo. 1969.
                   Kilkenny. 1971.
                   Killoe. 1970.
                   Kilrone. 1970.
                   Kiowa Trail. 1968.
                   Last Stand at Papago Wells.   1971.
                   Lonely Men. 1969.
                   Man Called Noon, The. 1973.
                   Man from Skibbereen. 1973.
                   Matagorda. 1967.
                   Mojave Crossing. 1968.
                   Mustang Man. 1969.
                   North to the Rails. 1971.
                   Quick and the Dead, The.   1973.
                   Radigan. 1972.
                   Reilly's Luck. 1970.
                   Shalako. 1968.
                   Showdown at Yellow Butte.   1971.
                   Silver Canyon. 1972.
                   Sitka. 1967.
                   Taggart. 1967.
                   Tall Stranger, The.   1970.
                   Treasure Mountain. 1972.
                   Under the Sweetwater Rim.   1971.
                   Utah Blaine. 1971.

LANGDALE, H. R.   Andy of Pirate Gorge. 1952.
                   Treasure Beyond Red Mesa.   1953.

444   Western Bibliography

LEMAY, Alan. Cattle Kingdom. 1933.
              Gunsight Trail. 1931.
              Painted Ponies. 1927.
              Searchers, The. 1954.
              Smoky Years. 1935.
              Thunder in the Dust. 1934.
              Unforgiven, The. 1957.
              Useless Cowboy. 1943.

LEWIS, Alfred Henry. Sunset Trail. 1905.

LILLIBRIDGE, Will. Where the Trail Divides. 1907.

LINFORD, Dee. Man Without a Star. 1952.

LOGAN, Ford. Fire in the Desert. 1954.

LOMAX, Bliss. Gringo Gunfire. 1941.
               Last Call for a Gunfighter. 1958.
               Pardners of the Badlands. 1942.
               Riders of the Buffalo Grass. 1952.

LOOMIS, Noel M. Buscadero. 1953.
                 Hang the Men High. 1957.
                 Holsters and Heroes. 1955.
                 Johnny Concho. 1956.
                 Maricopa Trail. 1957.
                 North to Texas. 1956.
                 Short Cut to Red River. 1958.
                 Twilighters, The. 1955.
                 West to the Sun. 1955.
                 Wild Country. 1956.

McCULLEY, Johnston. Iron Horse Town. 1952.
                     Range Cavalier. 1933.
                     Rangers' Code. 1924.

MacDONALD, William Colt. Action at Arcanum. 1958.
                          Bad Man's Return. 1947.
                          Blind Cartridges. 1951.
                          Bullets for Buckaroos. 1936.
                          California Caballero. 1936.
                          Comanche Scalp. 1955.
                          Crimson Quirt. 1943.
                          Destination Danger. 1955.
                          Devil's Drum. 1956.
                          Flaming Lead. 1957.
                          Lightning Swift. 1953.
                          Powdersmoke Range. 1934.
                          Ranger Man. 1951.
                          Rebel Ranger. 1943.
                          Riders of the Whistling Skull. 1934.

MacDONALD, William Colt (continued). Roarin' Lead. 1935.
Six-Shooter Showdown. 1939.
Sleepy Horse Range. 1938.
Spanish Pesos. 1937.
Three-Notch Cameron. 1952.
Trigger Trail. 1937.

McNEIL, Everett. With Kit Carson in the Rockies. 1909.

MANN, E. B. Blue-Eyed Kid. 1932.
Comanche Kid. 1936.
Gun Feud. 1939.
Gunsmoke Trail. 1942.
Shooting Melody. 1952.
Thirsty Range. 1935.
With Spurs. 1937.

MANNING, David (Frederick Faust). Ronicky Doone's Treasure.
(1926).

MANNING, Marie. Judith of the Plains. 1903.

MARKSON, David. Ballad of Dingus Magee. 1966.

MARSHALL, Gary. Raiders of the Tonto Rim. 1935.

MARTIN, Charles M. Deuce of Diamonds. 1937.

MILLER, David. Ghost Dance. 1959.

MILLER, Warner H. Medicine Gold. 1924.

MOORE, Amos. Ranger Rides Alone, The. 1936.
Ranger's Round-Up. 1940.
Sandy of Skyline. 1935.
Six-Gun Cyclone. 1937.

MORROW, Honore W. Devonshers, The. 1924.
Exile of the Lariat. 1923.

MORSE, Harriet C. Cowboy Cavalier. 1908.

MORTON, Guy. Rangy Pete. 1922.

MULFORD, Clarence Edward. Bar 20. 1921.
Bar 20 Days. 1911.
Bar 20 Rides Again. 1927.
Black Buttes. 1923.
Buck Peters. 1912.
Coming of Cassidy. 1913.
Corson of the JC. 1927.
Cottonwood Gulch. 1925.

MULFORD, Clarence (continued).   Deputy Sheriff. 1930.
                                  Hopalong Cassidy. 1910.
                                  Hopalong Cassidy Returns. 1925.
                                  Hopalong Cassidy's Protege. 1926.
                                  Johnny Nelson. 1920.
                                  Man from the Bar 20. 1918.
                                  Mesquite Jenkins, Tumbleweed.
                                     1932.
                                  Orphan, The. 1908.
                                  Round-Up, The. 1933.
                                  Rustlers' Valley. 1924.
                                  Trail Dust. 1934.

NELSON, A. P.   Cowpuncher of Badwater. 1936.

NEWCOMB, Covelle.   Silver Saddles. 1944.

NEWTON, D. B.   Six-Gun Gamble. 1951.

NICHOLSON, Meredith.   Main Chance, The. 1903.

NIEHARDT, John G.   Lonesome Trail. 1907.

NIVEN, Frederick.   Wolfer, The. 1923.

NYE, Nelson.   Come A-Smokin'. 1953.
               Desert of the Damned. 1932.
               Hired Hand. 1954.
               Maverick Marshall. 1958.
               Not Grass Alone. 1961.
               Parson of Gunbarrel Basin. 1955.
               Pistols for Hire. 1941.
               Texas Tornado. 1955.
               Wide Loop. 1952.

O'CONNOR, Jack.   Boom Town. 1938.

OGDEN, George W.   Cherokee Trails. 1928.
                    Cow Jerry. 1925.
                    Duke of Chimney Butte. 1920.
                    Man from the Bad Lands. 1933.
                    Stockyards Cowboy. 1937.
                    Trail's End. 1921.
                    West of Dodge. 1926.
                    Whiskey Trail. 1936.
                    White Roads. 1932.

O'MARA, Jim.   Death at War Dance. 1952.
               Free Grass. 1951.
               Rustler of the Owlhorns. 1952.

O'ROURKE, Frank. Bandoleer Crossing. 1961.
Bravados, The. 1957.
Concannon. 1953.
Diamond Hitch. 1956.
Gun Hand. 1953.
Gunlaw Hill. 1961.
Hard Men. 1956.
Last Ride, The. 1958.
Legend in the Dust. 1957.
Man Who Found His Way. 1957.
Mule for the Marquesa, A. 1964.
Ride West. 1954.
Segundo. 1956.
Texan Came Riding, A. 1958.

OVERHOLSER, Wayne D. Bitter Night. 1961.
Cast a Long Shadow. 1955.
Desperate Man. 1957.
Gunflame. 1953.
Gunlock. 1956.
Law Man. 1954.
Lone Deputy. 1957.
Nester, The. 1953.
Smoke of the Gun. 1958.
Standoff at the River. 1961.
Tomahawk. 1958.
Tough Hand. 1954.
Valley of Guns. 1953.
Violent Land. 1954.

PAPIER, Anson. Black Creek Buckaroo. 1941.

PARKER, Frances. Winding Waters. 1909.

PARKHILL, Forbes. Troopers West. 1945.

PARRISH, Randall. Beth Norvell. 1907.

PATTEN, Lewis B. Five Rode West. 1958.

PAYNE, Stephen. Riders of the Rocker K. 1935.

PEARCE, Dick. Impudent Rifle. 1951.
Rustless Border. 1953.

PEEPLES, Samuel Anthony. Barron of Boot Hill. 1954.
Canyon Country. 1951.
Frontier Street. 1958.
Hanging Hills. 1952.
Johnny Sundance. 1953.
Lobo Horseman, The. 1955.
Marshal of Medicine Bend. 1953.

448   Western Bibliography

PEEPLES, Samuel Anthony (continued).   Six Gun Heritage. 1955.
                                        Spell of the Desert. 1951.
                                        Trouble at Tall Pine. 1954.

PENDEXTER, Hugh.   Bird of Freedom. 1928.
                   Gate Through the Mountain. 1929.
                   Old Misery. 1924.

POOLE, Richard.   Desert Passage. 1953.
                  Peacemaker, The. 1954.
                  West of Devil's Canyon. 1958.

PORTER, William.   Lawbringers, The. 1954.

PRESCOTT, John.   Journey by the River. 1954.

PRESTON, Arthur.   Saddle Tramp. 1928.

RAINE, William MacLeod.   Bandit Trail. 1949.
                          Big Town Round-Up. 1921.
                          Black Tolts. 1932.
                          Border Breed. 1935.
                          Broad Arrow. 1933.
                          Bucky Follows a Cold Trail. 1937.
                          Clattering Hoofs. 1946.
                          Colorado. 1928.
                          Desert's Price. 1924.
                          Glory Hole. 1953.
                          Gunsight Pass. 1921.
                          Hell and High Water. 1943.
                          High Grass Valley. 1955.
                          Justice Comes to Tomahawk. 1952.
                          Mansize. 1922.
                          Oh, You Tex! 1920.
                          On the Dodge. 1938.
                          Reluctant Gunman. 1954.
                          Riders of Buck River. 1940.
                          River Bend Feud. 1939.
                          Roaring River. 1934.
                          Run of the Brush. 1936.
                          Sons of the Saddle. 1938.
                          Square Shooter. 1935.
                          Tangled Trails. 1921.
                          They Called Him Blue Blazes. 1941.
                          To Ride the River With. 1936.
                          Trail of Danger. 1934.
                          Trail's End. 1940.

REARDON, Joseph.   Cerro Lobo. 1942.

REESE, John.   High Passes, The. 1955.
               Singalee. 1969.
               Sure Shot Shapiro. 1968.

RENO, Zola Helen.   Reno Crescent.   1951.

RHODES, Eugene M.   Copper Streak Trail.   1922.
                    Stepsons of Light.   1921.
                    Sunset Land.   1957.

RICHMOND, Roe.   Death Rides the Dondrino.   1954.
                 Maverick Heritage.   1951.
                 Montana Bad Man.   1957.
                 Wild Breed, The.   1961.

RIGSBY, Howard.   Rage in Texas.   1954.
                  Reluctant Gun, The.   1957.

RISTER, Claude.   Red River Gunman.   1941.

ROAN, Tom.   Gamblers in Gunsmoke.   1952.
             Outlaw in the Saddle.   1954.

ROBERTS, Morley.   Painted Rock.   1907.

ROBERTSON, Frank Chester.   Fall of Buffalo Horn.   1928.
                            Firebrand from Burnt Creek.   1941.
                            Grizzly Meadows.   1943.
                            Larruping Leather.   1933.
                            Lawman's Pay.   1957.
                            Lost Range.   1946.
                            Man Branders.   1928.
                            Rip Roarin' Rincon.   1930.
                            Round Up in the River.   1945.
                            Saddle on a Cloud.   1953.
                            Silver Cow.   1929.
                            We Want That Range.   1931.
                            Wild Riding Runt.   1934.

RODNEY, George Brydges.   Canyon Trail.   1933.
                          Glory Hole, The.   1934.
                          Mormon Trail, The.   1933.
                          Raiders of the Cherokee Strip.   1940.
                          Riders of the Chaparral.   1935.
                          Sidewinder Trail, The.   1937.
                          Tenderfoot.   1933.
                          Vanishing Frontier, The.   1936.

ROE, Vingie.   Black Belle Rides the Uplands.   1935.
               Sons to Fortune.   1934.
               Val of Paradise.   1921.

ROSS, Zola Helen.   Land to Tame, A.   1956.

ROUNDS, Glen.   Montana Outlaw.   1934.
                Whitey and the Blizzard.   1952.

Whitey and the Rustlers. 1951.

RUSSELL, Charles M. Trails Plowed Under. 1927.

SABIN, Edwin. Desert Dust. 1922.

SANDERS, Charles Wesley. Crimson Trail. 1927.
                        Killer's Code. 1934.
                        Riders of the Oregon. 1932.

SANTEE, Ross. Bubbling Spring. 1949.
              Hardrock and Silver Sage. 1951.

SAVAGE, Les Jr. Doniphan's Ride. 1959.
                Land of the Lawless. 1951.
                Outlaw Thickets. 1952.
                Shadow Riders of the Yellowstone. 1951.

SCHAEFER, Jack. Canyon, The. 1953.
                Monte Walsh. 1963.
                Out West. 1955.
                Pioneers, The. 1954.
                Shane. 1949.

SCHULTZ, James W. Sun Woman. 1925.

SCOTT, B. B. Two-Gun Trail. 1940.

SCOTT, Bradford. Guns of Silver Valley. 1937.

SELTZER, Charles Alden. Arizona Jim. 1939.
                        "Beau" Rand. 1921.
                        Boss of the Lazy Y. 1915.
                        Brass Commandments. 1923.
                        Clear the Trail. 1933.
                        Coming of the Law. 1912.
                        Kingdom of the Cactus. 1936.
                        Land of the Free. 1927.
                        Raider, The. 1929.
                        Ranchman, The. 1919.
                        Square Deal Sanderson. 1922.
                        Triangle Cupid. 1912.
                        Two-Gun Man. 1911.
                        Vengeance of Jefferson Gawne. 1917.
                        West! 1922.
                        West of Apache Pass. 1934.

SHAPPIRO, Herbert. Valley of Death. 1941.

SHEDD, Harry Graves. Over Grass-Grown Trails. 1900.

SHERMAN, L. R. Law of the Six-Gun. 1941.

SMALL, Sidney Herschel.   Splendid Californians.   1928.

SNOW, Charles H.   Argonaut Gold.   1936.
                    Outlaws of Red Canyon.   1940.
                    Riders of the Range.   1939.
                    Rider of San Felipe.   1930.
                    Sheriff of Yavisa.   1941.
                    Six-Guns of Sandoval.   1935.
                    Smugglers' Ranch.   1934.
                    Snow-Rebel of Ronde Valley.   1943.
                    Wolf of the Mesas.   1941.

SPEARMAN, Frank H.   Gunlock Ranch.   1935.
                     Laramie Holds the Range.   1921.

STAFFORD, J. R.   When Cattle Kingdom Fell.   1911.

STANLEY, Chuck.   Apache Thunder.   1953.
                  Marshall San Clay.   1952.
                  Mountain Men.   1951.

STARR, Clay.   Bring Me Wild Horses.   1951.

STEELE, Bob.   Raid on the Broken Bow.   1959.

STEVENS, James.   Homer in the Sagebrush.   1928.

STEWART, Logan.   Warbonnet Pass.   1953.

STRANGE, Oliver.   Outlaw Breed.   1934.
                   Outlawed.   1936.
                   Sudden Takes Charge.   1940.

STRONG, Zachary.   Mesa Gang.   1940.

STRYKER, Fran.   Lone Ranger's New Deputy.   1951.

STUART, Matt.   Deep Hills.   1954.
                Lonely Law.   1957.
                Smoky Trail.   1951.
                Wild Summit.   1958.
                Wire in the Wind.   1952.

SUMMERS, Richard.   Vigilante.   1949.

SUMNER, Nick.   Boss of the Broken Spur.   1954.

TASSIN, Ray.   Steele Trails of Vengeance.   1961.

TAYLOR, Grant.   Caravan into Canaan.   1934.
                 Gunsmoke Hacienda.   1936.
                 Whip Ryder's Way.   1935.

452 Western Bibliography

TELFAIR, Richard. Secret of Apache Canyon. 1960.
Sundance. 1960.

TERRELL, Upton. Adam Cargo. 1935.
Little Dark Man, The. 1934.

THOMAS, Lee. Broken Creek. 1953.
Wolf Dog Town. 1953.

THOMPSON, C. Hall. Under the Badge. 1957.

THOMPSON, Jim. Wild Town. 1958.

THOMPSON, Thomas. Bitter Water. 1960.
Born to Gunsmoke. 1956.
Brand of a Man. 1958.
Gunman Brand. 1951.
Monument of Glory. 1961.
Rawhide Traveler. 1957.
Steel Web. 1953.
They Brought Their Guns. 1954.
Trouble Rider. 1954.

THORNE, Hart. Saddle Men of the C Bit. 1937.

THORP, Raymond W. Crow Killer. 1959.

THORMON, Steve. Gun Lightning. 1955.

TITUS, Harold. Last Straw. 1920.

TODD, Lucas. Showdown Creek. 1955.

TOLBERT, Frank X. Bigamy Jones. 1954.
Staked Plain, The. 1958.

TOMPKINS, Walter A. Border Bonanza. 1943.
Deadhorse Express. 1940.
Gold on the Hoof. 1953.

TOUSEY, Sanford. Twin Calves. 1940.

TOWNSEND, Ray. Sundown Basin. 1955.

TRACE, John. Range of Golden Hoofs. 1941.
Rough Mesa. 1940.
Trigger Vengeance. 1940.

TRACY, Richard. Thunder River Ranch. 1935.

TREYNOR, Albert M. Hands Up. 1928.

TURNER, William O.   Long Rope. 1959.
                     Proud Diggers, The. 1954.
                     Treasure of Fan Tan Flat. 1961.
                     War Country. 1957.

TUTTLE, Wilbur C.   Deadline, The. 1941.
                    Ghost Trails. 1940.
                    Hashknife of the Double Bar 8. 1938.
                    Hashknife of Stormy River. 1935.
                    Henry the Sheriff. 1936.
                    Hidden Blood. 1943.
                    Keeper of the Red Horse Pass. 1937.
                    Morgan Trail. 1928.
                    Mystery at the JHC Ranch. 1932.
                    Outlaw Empire. 1960.
                    Redhead from Sun Dog. 1930.
                    Rifled Gold. 1934.
                    Salt for the Tiger. 1952.
                    Santa Dolores Stage. 1934.
                    Shotgun Gold. 1940.
                    Silver Bar Mystery. 1930.
                    Singing River. 1939.
                    Tumbling River Range. 1935.
                    Valley of Twisted Trails. 1931.
                    Wandering Dogies. 1938.

VAIL, Robert W. G.   Voice of the Old Frontier. 1949.

VENABLE, Clark.   All the Brave Rifles. 1929.

WALKER, Turnley.   Day after the Fourth. 1958.

WARD, Don.   Branded West. 1956.
             Gunsmoke. 1957.
             Hoof Trails and Wagon Tracks. 1957.

WARD, Jonas.   Name's Buchanan. 1956.
               One-Man Massacre. 1958.

WARD, Nanda.   Black Sombrero. 1952.

WARE, Clyde.   Innocents, The. 1969.

WARE, Edmund.   Rider in the Sun. 1935.

WATERS, Frank.   Wild Earth's Nobility. 1935.

WAYNE, Joseph.   Johnny Pistol. 1960.
                 Long Wind. 1953.
                 Return of the Kid. 1955.
                 Showdown at Stony Crest. 1957.
                 Snake Stomper, The. 1951.

WELD, John. Don't You Cry For Me. 1940.

WELLMAN, Paul I. Broncho Apache. 1950.
                 Comancheros, The. 1952.
                 Jubal Troop. 1939.

WELLS, Lee. Day of the Outlaw. 1955.
             Gun for Sale. 1959.

WEST, Kingsley. Time for Vengeance, A. 1961.

WEST, Tom. Ghost Gun. 1952.
            Outlaw Brand. 1957.

WEST, Ward. Halfway to Timberline. 1935.

WHITAKER, Herman. Settler, The. 1908.

WHITE, Dale. Vigilantes, Ride! 1956.
              Young Deputy Smith. 1961.

WHITE, Henry. Snake Gold. 1926.

WHITE, Stewart Edward. Killer, The. 1920.
                        Long Rifle, The. 1932.

WHITE, William Patterson. Cloudy in the West. 1928.
                           Heart of the Range. 1921.
                           Hidden Trails. 1920.
                           Sweetwater Range. 1927.

WHITMAN, S. E. Scout Commander. 1955.

WHITSON, John H. Justin Wingate, Ranchman. 1905.
                  Rainbow Chasers. 1904.

WHITTINGTON, Harry. Desert Stake Out. 1961.
                     Trap for Sam Dodge, A. 1961.
                     Trouble Rides Tall. 1958.
                     Vengeance Is the Spur. 1960.

WILSON, Charles G. Guns in the Wilderness. 1952.

WILSON, Mrs. Woodrow. New Missioner, The. 1907.

WINTER, William West. Boss of Eagle's Nest. 1925.

WIRE, Harold Channing. Indian Beef. 1941.
                        North to the Promised Land. 1948.

WISTER, Owen. When West Was West. 1928.

WOODS, Clee. Riders of the Sierra Madre. 1935.

WORMSER, Richard. Gone to Texas. 1970.
Slattery's Range. 1957.

YORDAN, Philip. Man of the West. 1955.

YORE, Clem. Hard Riding Slim Magee. 1929.
Mississippi Jimmy. 1933.
Trigger Slim. 1934.

YOUNG, Carter Travis. Shadow of a Gun. 1961.
Wild Breed, The. 1960.

YOUNG, Gordon. Days of '49. 1925.
Red Clark for Luck. 1940.
Red Clark of the Arrowhead. 1935.
Red Clark on the Border. 1937.
Red Clark Rides Alone. 1933.
Red Clark, Two-Gun Man. 1939.
Tall in the Saddle. 1943.

ABOUT THE STAFF

JAMES ROBERT PARISH, Los Angeles-based biographer, was born near Boston. He attended the University of Pennsylvania and graduated as a Phi Beta Kappa with a degree in English. A graduate of the University of Pennsylvania Law School, he later headed Entertainment Copyright Research Co., Inc. Thereafter he was a film interviewer-reviewer for Motion Picture Daily and Variety. He is the author of such books as The Fox Girls, The Paramount Pretties, The RKO Gals, Actors TV Credits (1950-72), Hollywood's Great Love Teams, The Elvis Presley Scrapbook, and The Jeannette MacDonald Story. He is co-author of The Cinema of Edward G. Robinson, The MGM Stock Company, The Great Spy Pictures, Film Directors Guide: The U.S., Film Directors Guide: Western Europe, Vincent Price Unmasked, and others. Mr. Parish also frequently writes film criticism for national magazines.

MICHAEL R. PITTS is a journalist and free-lance writer who resides in Anderson, Indiana, where he is public relations director of the Madison County Council of Governments, a planning organization; editor of Anderson Newspapers' weekly television magazine, Televisit; and film reviewer for Anderson's Channel 7 television. A graduate of Ball State University in Muncie, Indiana, with an M.A. in journalism, he formerly worked in public education and as a newspaper entertainment editor and staff writer. Mr. Pitts has been published in cinema journals both here and abroad and with Mr. Parish he has co-authored The Great Spy Pictures, Film Directors: The U.S., and The Great Gangster Pictures.

T. ALLAN TAYLOR, godson of the late Margaret Mitchell, has long been active in book publishing and is presently production manager of one of the largest abstracting and technical indexing services in the United States. He has served as editor of such volumes as The Fox Girls, The MGM Stock Company, The George Raft File, Hollywood's Great Love Teams, and The Great Spy Pictures.

Brooklynite JOHN ROBERT COCCHI has been viewing and collecting data on motion pictures since childhood and is now regarded as one of the most thorough film researchers in the world. He is the New York editor of Boxoffice magazine. He was research associate on

The American Movies Reference Book, The Fox Girls, The Paramount Pretties, and many other volumes, and has written cinema-
history articles for such journals as Film Fan Monthly and Screen
Facts. He is also the author of a pictorial quiz book on The
Westerns. He is the co-founder of one of Manhattan's leading film
societies.

EDWARD MICHAEL CONNOR was born in Willimansett, Massa-
chusetts. Later he moved to New York and joined the staff of the
Pius Xth School of Liturgical Music. Thereafter, he trained choirs
in New York and New Jersey. He joined the National Board of Review in 1954 and the National Catholic Office for Motion Pictures
in 1959. He has contributed many articles on motion pictures to
Films in Review, Screen Facts, and Screen Careers, and for
several years was musical editor of Films in Review. He has
supplied introductions for The Great Gangster Pictures and The
Swashbucklers and has had two books published, Prophecy for Today
and Recent Apparitions of Our Lady. An avid cinema goer, Mr.
Connor resides in Manhattan.

RICHARD G. PICCHIARINI is a free-lance theatre and film researcher ensconced on New York's Upper West Side. He has contributed to Playbill and is the author of A History of the Tony
Awards: 1947-76. Recently absent from the stage, he has a long
array of regional acting credits as well as appearing in an off-off
Broadway production of Hamlet in 1974.

New York-born FLORENCE SOLOMON attended Hunter College and
joined Ligon Johnson's copyright research office. Later she was
director of research at Entertainment Copyright Research Co., Inc.,
and she is presently a reference supervisor at ASCAP's Index
Division. Ms. Solomon has collaborated on such works as The
American Movies Reference Book, TV Movies, The Elvis Presley
Scrapbook, and Liza! She is the niece of noted sculptor, the late
Sir Jacob Epstein.

VINCENT TERRACE, born May 14, 1948 in New York, is a graduate of the New York Institute of Technology, possessing a Bacca-
laureate Degree in Fine Arts Communications. He is the author of
The Complete Encyclopaedia of Television Programs: 1947-1974,
Charlie Chan: A Definitive Study, and The Complete Encyclopaedia
of Radio Programs: 1920-1960.